DAVID II, 1329–71

heir of its traditional incumbents, Murdoch of Menteith, who had betrayed the Balliol-Soules conspirators.[21]

Robert's other grants in central Scotland were limited to many confirmations of monastic and secular church lands – in particular, rewarding the help he had received from the Abbeys of Scone, Dunfermline and Cambuskenneth and William Lamberton, bishop of St Andrews. The king also looked to a number of robust, ambitious knights, including: William Lindsay (Chancellor 1316–9); John Menteith of Arran and Knapdale, who had betrayed Wallace in 1305 (and whom Robert granted the large western lordship of Strathgartney); John Inchmartin, sheriff of Perth; once again, Alexander Fraser, who served as sheriff of Stirling; the Menzies brothers, Alexander and Thomas (given Glendochart and Fortingall baronies in north-west Perthshire); the king's bastard son, Robert; Walter Steward, Robert's son-in-law (given Methven barony near Perth and lands in Fife); and Malcolm, earl of Lennox, and Sir Henry Annan who served as sheriffs of Clackmannan. These and the many other smaller grants made by Robert in the 1320s must have been reinforced by the royal household's frequent presence in central Scotland for councils, parliaments and other formal occasions.[22]

The king's household was most often to be found, however, between Bannockburn and the late 1320s, at Edinburgh in the royal heartlands of Lothian and the south-east Lowlands. It was here that Robert's resettlement was at its most intense. The king must have spent a fair sum rebuilding Edinburgh Castle and adding a royal park at its northern foot after 1320.[23] But in terms of available resources, royal thanages and forest lands were thinner on the ground for redistribution south of Forth and much land was owned by monastic houses. However, a number of forfeitures had given Robert a large reservoir of land to redistribute in this quarter. Some of these southern lands had been granted out before their formal seizure in the Cambuskenneth parliament of November 1314, a necessary ploy to encourage men to fight for their recovery from English occupation. Yet it soon became apparent that Robert was again intent on favouring particular men as his agents in this region often as a counter to others. Sir Robert Lauder of the Bass was elevated to the justiciarship of Lothian and would briefly serve as Chamberlain in 1333; Walter Steward received a wedding gift of the valuable Lothian baronies of Bathgate and Ratho in 1315; Thomas Randolph as 'Warden south of Forth' received Berwickshire lands; Robert Keith,

---

21 A. Ross, 'Men for all Seasons? The Strathbogie Earls of Atholl and the Wars of Independence. Part 1 – Earl John (1266x1270–1306) and Earl David III (c. 1290–1326)', *Northern Scotland*, 20 (2000), 1–30; Penman, 'Soules conspiracy', 25.
22 For Robert I's itinerary 1306–29 see *Atlas of Scottish History to 1707*, 166–70.
23 *Chron. Fordun*, i, 370n.

the Marischal, was sheriff of Edinburgh for part of the 1320s; Sir John fitz Walter became sheriff of Berwick by 1328. There were also small grants for many of the men and kindreds who remained loyal to the Bruces after 1329: the Douglases of Lothian (or Kingscavil); the Frasers; the Grahams of Abercorn; the Sinclairs; Murdoch of Menteith; the Murrays; the Stewarts of Bonkle; and Reginald More, Chamberlain (1329–33 and 1334–41) and Precentor of the lands of the Knights Hospitaller in Scotland, based at Torphichen, West Lothian.[24]

However, the chief beneficiaries of Bruce patronage in the south-east were two lords. Sir Alexander Seton – who may have passed David Strathbogie in the night by defecting to the Scots at Bannockburn – received many grants of Lothian baronies and smaller land pockets after 1319; Seton would serve as a household steward for David II and as Precentor of the Knights Hospitaller about 1345–8.[25] The 'Good' Sir James Douglas also received Lothian baronies as well as his regality lordships of Lauderdale and Selkirk forest. These lords and their followings must have been in part designed to check the activities of Patrick Dunbar, earl of March, another magnate with English interests who – like the earls of Fife and Strathearn – only entered Robert's peace after 24 June 1314, Patrick, indeed, only after he had put Edward II safely on a boat home after his flight from defeat at Bannockburn. Although pardoned, Patrick also received little or no favour from his new Bruce lord *c.* 1315–29, while others were promoted in the south-east.[26]

The south-west of Scotland, however, was a far more difficult and potentially explosive proposition. Home to the Bruce family lands in Scotland, but also a heartland of Balliol and Comyn power, the civil war had raged longest here after 1306. The Bruce brothers had found cause to launch several herschips of Galloway, the last in 1313. But even after Bannockburn and the final forfeiture of the Balliols, Comyns and their south-western allies like the MacDowells and McCans, the new regime struggled to install lasting royal agents able to harness the clannish tenantry of this region. The death of Edward Bruce, lord of Galloway and earl of Carrick, in October 1318 deprived Robert of the one lord who might have become a dedicated lieutenant for the crown in this quarter. In the first half of Robert's reign few other magnates were favoured by the crown in Ayrshire, Dumfriesshire and Galloway. But it was not until 1318–20 that Robert turned to alter-

---

24 For these sheriffs and More, see *ER*, i, 106, 279 and ii, cxxiii-iv; I.B. Cowan, P.H.R. Mackay and A. Macquarrie eds., *The Knights of St John of Jerusalem in Scotland* (SHS, Edinburgh 1983), 193–4.

25 *ER*, i, 139–287; *The Knights of St John of Jerusalem in Scotland*, 49–52.

26 For March's actions, see *Chron. Lanercost*, 227–8; *Chron. Scalacronica*, 143–4; Duncan ed., *The Bruce*, 512–3 [xiii, 610–20], where the poet describes Dunbar of March as an 'Inglisman'.

native agents for the south-west in his big three, James Douglas, Thomas Randolph and Walter Steward. At that time, Douglas was given the barony of Staplegordon east of Annandale, other Dumfriesshire lands and the toun, castle and forest of Jedburgh; Randolph received Annandale itself along with the hotly disputed isle of Man; the Steward received the Ayrshire lordship of Cunningham.[27]

This royalist shift within the south-west must have provoked some of the plotting of William Soules of Liddesdale and other former Balliol men from that region. Despite his recovery in 1318 of his family's traditional office of Butler from a seemingly magnanimous king, Soules must have felt threatenened within his local sphere of influence.[28] But Soules' removal in 1320 allowed Robert to step up his intrusion of crown men. Douglas received some of Soules' lands as well as the Balliol lands of Buittle (1321, 1325); Holyrood Abbey received a teind of projected justice pleas taken between the rivers Cree and Nith (1323); Robert's favourite Abbey, Melrose, was assigned the crown's casualties from Roxburghshire (1325) to be collected by Douglas. Robert's grandson, Robert Steward, received the extensive Soules' baronies in the same shire (1327). There was also lesser royal favour in the south-west for the likes of the Carruthers and other traditional Bruce affinity men from Annandale: Sir John Lindsay; the Carricks; the Crawfords; the Boyds of Noddsdale; the Stewarts of Darnley and Dalswinton; the Wallaces; the Mores (sheriffs of Ayr); the Kirkpatricks (sheriffs of Dumfries); and the Flemings. The head of the latter house, Malcolm Fleming of Cumbernauld, was also serving as keeper of Dumbarton Castle by 1327 (taking over from the earl of Lennox), as a steward of David Bruce's household and, it seems, the child prince's 'foster-father': it was Fleming who would attempt to fill the vacuum left by the deaths of Edward Bruce, lord of Galloway and earl of Carrick (1318), and his bastard son, Alexander Bruce (1333).[29]

After March 1324, Robert had the son he needed so badly to take up the family lands, bringing some hope of controlling the south-west: the award of Liddesdale to the king's bastard son, Robert, and the presence of Alexander Bruce (who would become earl of Carrick upon David II's accession) must have increased this dynastic presence. However, that in practical terms Robert I clearly found it difficult to get a grip on the south-west is suggested

27 R.D. Oram, 'Bruce, Balliol and the Lordship of Galloway: the South-West of Scotland and the Wars of Independence', *TDGNHAS*, 4th series, lxvii (1992), 29–47.

28 Penman, 'Soules Conspiracy', 54–7; Grant, *Independence and Nationhood*, 15–6.

29 For these sheriffs and Fleming, see: *RMS*, i, nos. 80–1 and App. ii, no. 325; *ER*, i, 123, 151, 180, 249, 144–269 *passim*. My thanks to Richard Oram for a copy of his recent conference paper emphasising the regional importance of Fleming of Cumbernauld before 1346.

by the absence of a separate justiciar of Galloway, a sheriff of Wigtown and crown income from such offices throughout the final decade of the reign: in 1324 Robert even had to formally recognise the traditional right of the men of Galloway to exemption from the summary justice and billeting of royal officers.[30]

A similar lack of hands-on crown control (and income) affected Robert's dealings with the west coast and isles of Scotland. As a child, an exile and a warrior king, Robert amassed considerable experience of the Irish sea world and Gael. He could also call upon the loyal support of such ambitious west-coast lords and in-laws as the Steward and Campbells of Lochawe. Yet in a region which was even more separatist than the south-west, Bruce had more typically to play upon local rivalries and animosities and make speculative, *de facto* land grants in order to win support. Thus the vital backing of the MacDonalds was heavily bought against their rivals, the Comyns' in-laws the Macdougalls of Lorn, in return for Robert granting John MacDonald and his son, Angus Og, extensive islands and coastal lands, including much of the mainland Comyn lordship of Lochaber in the north-west, along with Ardnamurchan and Morvern. Similarly, until their forfeiture for unspecified crimes in 1325, Bruce bought the anti-Macdougall support of the MacRuaridhs of Garmoran. Otherwise Robert, continuing the work of Alexander III and – at least on paper – of John I before him, had to be content to build up a buffer of support and strongholds between central Scotland and the western approaches. Malcolm, earl of Lennox, was made sheriff of Dumbarton; Tarbert Castle was reinforced; Sir John Menteith of Arran and Knapdale was given further Argyll lands (Glenbreakerie) in return for the service of a twenty-six-oar galley; a number of men received Lanarkshire baronies including Sir Walter fitz Gilbert and Sir James Douglas; and Abbot Bernard of Arbroath, Bruce's trusted Chancellor, was made bishop of the Isles in 1326.[31]

But as if that was never enough, and as if Robert himself recognised the danger posed by uncertain, traditionally autonomous forces in that quarter, after 1326 the king – ailing from whatever 'grosse maladie' later generations were to label as leprosy – set up home in a purpose-built manor house at Cardross near Dumbarton, complete with fishery, falcon aviary, gardens and nearby moorings for the 'King's Great ship'. This site had Arthurian associations similar to those of Dumbarton's castle rock. Fittingly in

---

30 *RMS*, i, App. i, no. 59; Oram, 'Bruce, Balliol and the Lordship of Galloway', 41–2.
31 Barrow, *Bruce*, 289–92; A. Grant, 'Scotland's 'Celtic Fringe' in the Late Middle Ages: the MacDonald Lords of the Isles and the Kingdom of Scotland', in R.R. Davies ed., *The British Isles, 1100–1500* (Edinburgh 1988), 118–41; R. Andrew McDonald, *The Kingdom of the Isles: Scotland's Western Seaboard, c. 1100–c.1336* (East Linton 1997), ch. 6.

Robert's twilight days, it looked west to the region where he and his brothers had been fostered as children and which had given him succour in his hour of need in 1306–7. But it was from here that Robert set out in February 1329 on an ayre which reveals that despite all he had achieved the king recognised the threat that a lack of control over the western approaches and Galloway posed to his dynasty.

Robert's purpose was to make a pilgrimage to the shrine of St Ninian at Whithorn before his death. But his itinerary took his household through Ayrshire, Carrick and by April into the heart of the Comyns' former Galloway lands. Moreover, he used the journey to stop off and grant at least thirty charters to potential crown supporters in the western isles, Argyll and south-west of Scotland: in this way he secured the further services of two oared-galleys, four armed men, four archers and a spearman to add to the over forty extra knights, thirty archers and ten galleys (at least) which his patronage had raised since 1306. In the same way, after death Robert surely planned the presence of his heart at Melrose Abbey as a counter to the heart of John Balliol's father, interred at Sweetheart Abbey, as well as a deterrent to any English army crossing the border in the future.[32]

Robert's fears would again prove justified. They were not simply based on his struggle to leave a strong and able lieutenant to police these outlying zones. Rather his concerns went to the heart of the peace settlement with England concluded the previous summer. His gravest worry must have been about the thorny issue which recent research has suggested Robert may have in fact fudged and found too hot to handle in his treaty with Isabella and Mortimer. For it now seems clear that there was some agreement between the English and Scottish negotiators for the restoration of some or all of the 'Disinherited' and a return to cross-border landholding by aristocratic families and church in both England and Scotland.[33]

The immediate problem was that the chief interests among the English Disinherited claiming lands in Scotland, either through legal inheritance or grants by Edward I, represented powerful lobbies to which Isabella and Mortimer had to pander. These included individual chiefs like Henry Beaumont (claiming his Comyn in-laws' earldom of Buchan), Henry Percy (Urr in Galloway and Redcastle in Angus), Thomas Wake (Kirkandrews and Liddesdale), Henry Ferrers (Galloway and Lothian lands), Richard Talbot

---

32 *ER*, i, 56, 118, 124–5, 127; *RRS*, v, nos. 362 to 374(A); *RMS*, i, App ii nos. 607–10, 612–5, 622–4; D. Brooke, *Wild Men and Holy Places: St Ninian, Whithorn and the Medieval Realm of Galloway* (Edinburgh 1994), 142–5; G.G. Simpson, 'The Heart of King Robert I: Pious Crusade or Marketing Gambit?', in B.E. Crawford ed., *Church, Chronicle and Learning in Medieval and Early Renaissance Scotland* (Edinburgh 2000), 173–86.

33 S. Cameron and A. Ross, 'The Treaty of Edinburgh and the Disinherited (1328–1332)', *History*, 1999, 237–56.

(some of his father-in-law's lands of Lochaber) and Gilbert Umfraville of Proudhue (the Angus earldom). But influential churches in northern England, like the bishopric of Durham and the Abbey of Holm Cultram, also sought the recovery of their lost Scottish holdings. Their disappointment at their frustration in the armistice talks must have threatened the stability of both the peace deal and the party of Edward III's keepers. To add to their number, there remained a handful of Scottish magnates and their heirs in exile desperate to recover their lands, men who had long served English interests headed by Beaumont's son-in-law, David Strathbogie (Atholl, Strathbogie and half of Lochaber), Walter Comyn (Kilbride), the Macdougalls (Lorn) and the MacDowells, McCans, Mowbrays and other lesser folk.[34]

Beaumont, Percy and others of the Disinherited attended the Anglo-Scottish peace talks of 1327–28. They were also present with Queen Isabella at the wedding of David and Joan at Berwick on 12 July 1328. A fortnight later, at Glasgow, shortly before he set out to help install his wife's nephew as earl of Ulster, Robert I confirmed to Henry Percy his father's Scottish lands. In theory this gave Percy the go-ahead to recover this territory through the Scottish courts. When set alongside Edward III's later complaints of 1330–33 that the Scots had failed to restore lands in Scotland to English lords and churches 'in accordance with the treaty', this suggests that – either during the original peace talks, or by proxy at the wedding itself – Robert had been forced to recognise that the Disinherited had to be included: some mutual restoration of territory and subjects must follow.[35]

Robert may indeed have found a desire for this in Scotland where only a generation before the majority of significant magnate kindreds – and several monastic houses – had long held English lands. Repossession of the Bruce family lands in Yorkshire and Huntingdon moreover might have provided another binding tie to secure the peace. It might also have further strengethened the vested interest of lordship attached to the Bruce regime by further rewarding Robert's key domestic supporters. This may explain why by May 1329 it was the 'Good' but tremendously ambitious Sir James Douglas who was the first Scot restored to his family's lost English lands: within a year a lesser Scots knight, Sir Henry Prendergast, had also recovered his Northumberland lands.[36]

However, it is likely that within weeks of David Bruce's marriage, Robert had decided he could not feasibly honour any such clause about the Disinherited. Logically he must have found himself in much the same

34 Nicholson, *Edward III and the Scots*, ch. v, 'The Disinherited'.
35 *RRS*, v, no. 353; *CDS*, iii, nos. 1013, 1022–4, 1029, 1033.
36 *Foedera*, ii, 762; *CDS*, iii, nos. 675, 1036.

catch-22 of lordship which had undermined Edward I's attempts to win submission and support from predominantly Scottish-based lords while retaining the loyalty of those Englishmen who had helped him initially conquer the northern kingdom. It was a dilemma which went right to the heart of all regime-building: neither king could reward his closest supporters without alienating others and there was not enough to satisfy all.[37]

Robert must have realised very quickly that the return of even just the most select and influential of the Dishnerited from Westminster – enough to ease Isabella's fears – would have badly disrupted his resettlement of Scotland. Even the first concession he had made – the restoration to Percy of Urr in Galloway and Redcastle in Angus would have snubbed Thomas Randolph and his own bastard, Robert Bruce. These lieutenants might be compensated elsewhere in Scotland (or England). But many of the other Disinherited claims aimed at entire provincial earldoms and lordships, many of them in the difficult hotbed of the south-west. Men like John MacDonald of the Isles would besides not tolerate the return of their local feud rivals (the Macdougalls). Moreover, many of the families who had made it good under Bruce had been almost purely 'Scottish' families before 1306 with few or no English holdings. Such houses as would not naturally welcome a return to cross-border politics and the dilution of their new hard-fought pre-eminence in Scotland included the Stewarts, Campbells, Randolphs and others.

It would be under Randolph as Guardian after Bruce's death in June 1329 that the Scottish royal government would continue to refuse point-blank to restore English landowners in Scotland. This suggests divisions in Scottish attitudes to restoring cross-border landholding. Most pro-Bruce Scots, headed by Randolph and the Stewarts, opposed a return to the status of smaller fish in a big aristocratic pond, while others, perhaps including James Douglas, hoped to expand their interests further. If this was so, Robert I's abandonment of plans to restore the Disinherited may have been a result of his own quickly-formed conviction that he should retrace his steps. Certainly, in 1364, in opposition to David II's plans to restore the descendants of the Disinherited as part of a deal with Edward III and his sons, many Scots were of the view in parliament that '[King] Robert, such a wise, vigorous and able man, did not agree' to any restoration of the Disinherited and insisted that Scotland's subjects should be loyal to only one king.[38] Yet in reality, in the last of his annual parliaments or councils, Robert may have been obliged to bow to considerable pressure from a majority of his own counsellors – those who had benefited most from his patronage between 1314 and 1328 –

---

37 For Edward I's patronage dilemma, see Watson, *Under the Hammer*, 30–57; M. Prestwich, *Edward I* (London 1988), 469–516.
38 Duncan, 'A Question about the Succession, 1364', clause 39.

and to abort his deal with Percy and others. This may explain why it was not apparently until *c.* 1328–29 – and perhaps even then not until *after* Robert's death – that the earldoms of Atholl and Angus were finally granted out to new owners in the pro-Bruce families of the Campbells of Lochawe and Stewarts of Bonkle. This may also explain a small part of the later chronicle gossip about James Douglas, like Edward Bruce before him, becoming too big for his boots: perceived as a potentially 'molestful' threat to David Bruce and Randolph, Robert's greatest knight, Douglas, was thus bound to a promise to take his king's heart to the Holy land after death so as to keep him out of trouble.[39]

But these underlying tensions also hint at the poised man-trap of political consequences Robert I may have perceived as inevitable fallout from his landholding policies, no matter which line he took. For there were other categories of men to be satisfied in addition to the Disinherited. Above all, there was the painfully grey area of those Scottish magnates of note and their families and regional followings who had entered Bruce's peace after Bannockburn but found themselves excluded from royal favour, government office and regional influence. The earls of Fife, Strathearn and March headed this group and would quickly join Edward Balliol for a time when he invaded Scotland after 1332. But there were also contemporaries and close supporters of Bruce whose ambitions may have been close to outstripping their new king's political and material largesse since 1314.

In provincial lords like John MacDonald of the Isles, the 'Good' Sir James Douglas, Walter Steward, Thomas Randolph and Hugh, earl of Ross, there is surely more than a hint of the potentially restless, over-mighty subject. Among their number and their heirs were men who expected continued reward and increasing autonomy in return for their continued service to Bruce. There was also internecine rivalry between them and fewer neutral, kingdom-minded figures to mediate such conflict after the deaths of Robert Wishart, bishop of Glasgow (d. 1316), and Lamberton of St Andrews (d. 1328).

Douglas and Walter Steward (d. 1327), in particular, might have expected an earldom, equating their status with that of Randolph. By 1325 Douglas

---

39 Bishop John Leslie (?1527–96), *The Historie of Scotland*, eds. E.G. Cody and W. Murison (2 vols., Edinburgh 1895), ii, 13. This motive for sending Douglas on crusade has been strongly challenged, however, with the suggestion of pure 'sentiment' as just cause for this choice of knight – see S. Cameron, 'Sir James Douglas, Spain and the Holy Land', in T. Brotherstone and D. Ditchburn eds., *Freedom and Authority: Scotland, c. 1050–c. 1650: Historical and Historiographical Essays Presented to Grant G. Simpson* (East Linton 2000), 108–17. For Edward Bruce as an over-ambitious lord, see Duncan ed., *The Bruce*, 344–54; *Chron. Fordun*, i, 347–8; J. Sinclair, *The Life and Times of Edward Bruce* (unpublished BA dissertation, University of Stirling, 2002), *passim.*

was giving some signs of being prepared to defy crown jurisdiction over small matters in the borders, moves which could only serve to encourage his highly militarised regional affinity. His expert use of border warfare, intimidation, protection and sentiment to sustain his own empire may also have threatened to provoke renewed national warfare without Robert's input: Abbot Bower relates the tale of how a 'Twynham Lourison' seized a royal official at Ayr only to be driven into exile by Douglas's wrath and was encouraged to approach Edward Balliol, then in France, with the advice that many Scottish families would support a Balliol coup against Bruce and his allies.[40] Similarly, after David Bruce's birth in 1324, Walter Steward might have been logically rewarded by a promise from the king that his son, Robert Stewart – Bruce's grandson and the heir presumptive to the kingship – would be the crown's 'assignee' to the earldom of Fife. This would have secured a key role for this blood royal in any future royal inauguration ceremony – in which the Fife earl led the king from the Scone altar to enthronement stone – just as Bruce's agreement with Earl Duncan of Fife in 1315 had envisaged. Yet although Robert Stewart was recognised as second in line to the throne by a third parliamentary act of succession in November 1326, no official tailzie of Fife to the Stewarts, if there was one, has survived: as we shall see, Robert as Steward would pursue possession of the earldom of Fife in defiance of the Bruce crown for the rest of his aristocratic life.[41] Elsewhere, MacDonald of Islay – perhaps angered that the Stewarts and Ross had received Bruce marriages while he had not – would switch sides from Bruce to Balliol and England in the 1330s and 1350s, playing one off the other while he set himself up as 'lord of the Isles'. The former pro-Balliol earls of Ross would similarly act as laws unto themselves in the north in the 1330s. Generally after 1332, Ross, MacDonald, Robert Steward and the descendants of Douglas, the earl of March and the Stewart earl of Angus, would repeatedly challenge David II's authority.[42]

In this sense it can be said, with hindsight, that one of the greatest legacies of Robert I to his son was a highly expectant nobility which the Scottish crown would struggle to always satisfy and contain. Robert had enjoyed the honeymoon period of this relationship. His magnates had been content with their initial rewards and found an outlet for their energies in war against England and in consolidating their own territorial and political influence.

40 *Chron. Bower*, vii, 65–6; Brown, *Black Douglases*, 26–8.
41 *APS*, i, 465–8; *RRS*, v, no. 301. For the role of the earl of Fife in royal inaugurations, see J.W.M. Bannerman, 'The King's Poet and the Inauguration of Alexander III', *SHR*, lxviii (1989), 120–49, 132–3; Duncan, *Kingship of the Scots*, 70–1, 116, 136–46.
42 *Acts of the Lords of the Isles, 1336–1493*, eds. J. Munro and R.W. Munro (SHS, Edinburgh 1986), lxxiv–v.

But in dying when he did Robert would be spared the difficulties of policing his great subjects through a period of peace followed by the chaos of renewed war, when his subjects' energies would be directed to affairs within Scotland and their position *vis à vis* the crown and their neighbours: this would have come, too, at a time when the king's landed demesne was sorely depleted.

In the last few years of his reign Robert was forced, too, to set the crown on the slippery slope of securing magnates' loyalties with large pensions: for example, his own bastard, Robert, received 500 merks a year; the new Constable, Hay, took £200 p.a.; 128 merks p.a. went to Robert Steward; and Sir Henry Sinclair, the king's keeper of forests north of Forth and bailie of Caithness, was granted an annual of 40 merks in 1328 'until he has been given forty merks of land or four hundred merks of money'.[43] Such favour was a symptom of the necessary alienation of crown resources since 1314, and as early as November 1326 (seemingly before the earldoms of Atholl and Angus had been regranted) Robert had had to admit to parliament that he was without fiscal means to sustain a household and government 'becoming his station without the intolerable burdening and grievance of his commons'. In response he received a lifetime grant of a tenth of all rents from an apparently grateful political community. Then in 1329, parliament granted an additional three-year tenth to help pay off the promised war reparations to England.[44] Yet it is very hard to tell what might have happened had Robert needed further cash for his expanding government or sought to retrieve some of the territory and resources he had alienated. As well as the problems of trying to 'live of his own', had Robert lived longer than his fifty-five years he would have found himself king of a community awash with competing Bruce, Randolph, Douglas and Stewart brothers and cousins and many other magnate scions. David II would be spared quite such an overcrowded arena by the deaths of many Scottish lords in the terrible war losses of 1332 and 1333. But as an adult Robert I's son would still have to juggle many such conflicting noble interests alongside his own royal prerogative.

Robert must have given some thought to such future contingencies after David's birth. An awareness of his own mortality and the perennial Anglo-Balliol threat undeniably drove him to seek as much closure and control of events as possible in the war with England before his demise. Yet in doing so Robert must have known that vital components of what he had achieved by early 1329 were a compromise. His strongest achievements indeed could be said to have been to guard against the expected return of a circling storm: a

43 *ER*, i, lxxvi; *RRS*, v, no. 360.
44 *APS*, i, 12–7, 475–6.

well-motivated and, thus far, well-rewarded, loyal nobility committed to investing their future in Bruce lordship of an independent Scotland; a potent martial tradition with a limited but winning formula for anti-English warfare led by able lieutenants who, if aging, all had maturing sons to take up their batons; a potentially strong, if largely untested, deterrent alliance with France (1326); and, finally, papal recognition of Bruce kingship and Scottish sovereignty culminating in posthumous receipt in 1329 of a bull awarding future kings of Scots the rite of coronation and unction enjoyed by the Plantagenets, a favour secured through the offices of nationally-minded Scottish churchmen for the most part chosen by the king.[45]

In all but the last of these pillars, Bruce's Scotland was being geared up to face unfinished business in the likely event that the peace of 1328 would not hold. Perhaps most telling and ironic of all – besides his pilgrimage and recruitment ayre in the south-west in spring 1329 – the legend prevails that in his final hours Bruce, above all, warned his son and subjects not to fight pitched battles.[46]

Yet that this death-bed speech – like so much of the Scottish chroniclers' tableaux of Robert's end – is filtered through the calamitous events which befell the kingdom after 1332 (and in particular in 1346) is suggested by the plain fact that David Bruce was probably born too late to have been heavily influenced by his father in person. Born at Dunfermline, David was thereafter nursed for a while on the bishop of St Andrews' manor of Inchmurdoch in Fife where he would be married for a second time in 1363. But as a babe-in-arms he was soon established in his own household as earl of Carrick in the Bruces' Turnberry castle (where he may have had a pet lion). His contact with the royal household in this period was presumably limited. He may have been present at two-and-a-half years old in the 1326 parliament at Scone which issued the third act of succession. But David's first formal state occasion other than his own christening was surely his wedding at Berwick aged four to Joan of the Tower. The royal couple seem to have visited King Robert at Cardross on their return from their betrothal. David may have spent Christmas with the royal court at Glenkill on Arran in 1328 and received a visit from his ailing father at Turnberry in February 1329.[47]

No other details of David's upbringing before 1329 have survived. Unlike Robert I and his father and, more especially, his grandfather, David must have received his knowledge of his family's traditions and of his father's actions at second-hand. In some ways this may have spared him an overdose

45 *Chron. Bower*, vii, 5–9; *Vetera*, 244–5.
46 Duncan ed., *The Bruce*, 749–55.
47 *ER*, i, 109, 118, 213.

of any popular image of Robert I as the hero-king. The son would arguably have much less veneration than subsequent generations for the person and policies of the more famous father. Nevertheless, David entered a regal office with established ways of doing things and with expected, if not demanded, patterns of behaviour for a Bruce king of Scots.

Most obviously, in 1324 Bernard of Arbroath had celebrated the joyous news of David's birth with verse which asserted that he would grow to:

> play at combat in the gardens of the English, or else may God make a lasting peace between the kingdoms.

It is extremely difficult to gauge the comparative mood of the political community upon Robert's death. It was surely not as doom-laden as Walter Bower portrayed it to have been from the viewpoint of the 1440s. Some Scotsmen may indeed have banged their fists and torn their clothes like madmen at Robert's passing but Scotland was not as rudderless a ship as it had been in 1286: this time there was a designated *male* heir and a single Guardian.[48] Yet by early 1329 it may have seemed to many Scots only a matter of time before the first of the options expressed by Abbot Bernard – leadership in war against the auld enemy – would be required of David. The uncertainty of the Anglo-Scottish peace and David's immaturity go a long way to explaining why on 7 June 1329 there was no immediate removal of David from Turnberry to Scone Abbey and the ancient moot hill for inauguration or coronation, no resounding 'The King is Dead! Long Live the King!' for the Bruce dynasty. In fact it would be two-and-a-half years before David was crowned and anointed as king. By then most Scots would know that the realm was on the brink of renewed war against that predicted foe.

---

48 *Chron. Bower*, vii, 47–53; Duncan ed., *The Bruce*, 755–7.

TWO

Kings' Row: National and Civil War Anew, 1329–41

'It wes to Scotland a gud chance
That thai made thaim to werrey in France.
Andrew Wyntoun,
Orygynale Cronikil, c. 1400–20[1]

The Guardianship of Thomas Randolph

The minority of Alexander III, who came to the throne aged just nine years in 1249, had been a tense decade, punctuated by squabbles between Scottish magnate factions for possession of the boy king and by fatherly(-in-law) interference from Henry III of England. The Scottish Guardianships appointed in the name of the Maid of Norway (1286–90), and between Wallace's defeat at Falkirk in 1298 and English reconquest of Scotland in 1304, had also been marked by internal power struggles ultimately overshadowed by the dogged incursions of Edward I. The minorities of the Stewart kings of the fifteenth-century would precipitate further Scottish power struggles.[2]

Scotland without an adult king after June 1329, however, did not spiral swiftly into turmoil. At first glance the kingdom appears to have enjoyed a three-year interregnum of flat calm. This had much to do with the fact that Edward III remained under the influence of his French mother and her lover until October 1330 and would only enter his twenty-first year in 1332. Until then the peace would hold. But this seeming tranquillity was also anchored in the relatively strong domestic continuity and stability which Robert I had ensured his government would retain beyond his life, despite doubts about the 1328 treaty. In Thomas Randolph, earl of Moray, the Scots had a respected senior statesman and fearsome general – a past envoy to the papal Curia, Paris and London and a campaign victor from Bannockburn to Old Bylands – a man earmarked for the post of Guardian since 1315. For later chroniclers Randolph could be pedestalled in this office as a shining example

1 *Chron. Wyntoun*, vi, 90–1.
2 A. Young, 'Noble Families and Political Factions in the Reign of Alexander III', in N. Reid ed., *Scotland in the Age of Alexander III, 1249–1286* (Edinburgh 1988), 1–30; Nicholson, *Scotland – the Later Middle Ages*, 27–68; M.H. Brown, 'Scotland Tamed? Kings and Magnates in Late Medieval Scotland – a review of recent work', *IR*, xlv (1994), 120–46.

to any Scottish king in the maintenance of order: Fordun's contemporary source for the period wrote that 'he ruled the kingdom and executed justice so devotedly and even-handedly that we do not read of anyone surpassing him in this direction from the first establishment of the law'. As we have seen, according to Barbour, writing about 1371–5, Robert I's death provoked crazed grief and dread of the future in even the bravest Scottish knights. Yet according to chroniclers closer in time it would be Thomas Randolph's death which was bemoaned as the moment disaster really befell Scotland for a second time.[3]

The endurance of Bruce government in the years immediately after Robert's passing did not depend solely on Randolph's attention to new laws such as those which protected the property of travellers and farmers from brigands and thieves. The royal government of 1329–32 remained largely King Robert's. Adam Murray, bishop of Brechin (an illegitimate son of the Ramsays, a kindred who would be prominent in David II's service), continued as Chancellor until 1335. This cleric had helped Randolph conclude the treaty of Corbeil with France in 1326 as well as serving as an envoy to the pope in Avignon for the then excommunicated Robert I who had ensured his nomination to his diocese in 1328. Another churchman, Robert of Peebles, served as Chamberlain from 1327 until his death in November 1329: he was succeeded by a deputy, layman Reginald More. But as before 1329 it was to be Scotland's churchmen who provided much of the administrative and diplomatic backbone for the survival of the independent kingdom over the next twenty years.[4]

The few extant records of the Scottish estates and exchequer from this period suggest the existence of an efficient working bureaucracy. Councils or parliaments and fiscal audits were held annually. Large monetary contributions from the sheriffs (with incumbents remaining unchanged) as well as the bishoprics and royal burghs were collected promptly by midsummer 1331. This allowed for the complete payment, on time, of the £20,000 damages owed to England as a condition of the 1328 peace. Only eleven acts issued either in the name of David 'Rex Scottorum' or of Randolph as Guardian survive until the latter's death, in his mid-fifties, in July 1332. But they confirm the strong continuity in government personnel. Among their witnesses were Sir Alexander Fraser, King Robert's uncle by marriage and a former Chamberlain; Robert Lauder of the Bass, justiciar of Lothian; Hay the Constable; Keith the Marischal, who had also helped secure the French alliance; John Campbell, earl of Atholl; Murdoch, earl of Menteith; Patrick

---

3 *Chron. Fordun*, i, 353–4; *Chron. Wyntoun*, vi, 382–92; *Chron. Bower*, vii, 57–9; Duncan ed., *The Bruce*, 755–7 (xx, 265–70).
4 *RRS*, vi, pp. 10–11 and nos. 5–8, 10; Watt, *Scottish Graduates*, 405–7, 443–5.

Dunbar, earl of March; Donald, earl of Mar, King Robert's nephew and former ward; Sir Alexander Seton, steward to David Bruce; and such household knights as James Fraser and William Muschet (whom Robert I had given the Perthshire thanage of Auchterarder).[5]

Alexander Seton was aided in his royal household duties by similar men – David Barclay of Brechin, Robert Bruce of Liddesdale and Malcolm Fleming of Cumbernauld. It is unclear whether David travelled the country, in the company of the Guardian, or whether he remained at Turnberry Castle or within a particular royal residence in the east or west. About 1330, the saddles, hat and spurs bought for the child king – and the transfer of his stud of horses from 'the north' to Berwick – suggest that David often followed Randolph. David was also to be found briefly at Cardross just after his father's death: in 1330 he spent his sixth birthday (5 March) at his half-cousin's holding of Clackmannan on Forth. But it is Fleming, the keeper of Dumbarton Castle, who seems to have played the key role as surrogate parent to the child king in the 1330s, being described by later writers as David's 'foster-father'. It is likely that Robert Bruce had continued his family's tradition of fostering offspring to allied west-coast families: this may have given David, like his father, some facility in Gaelic. Nonetheless, David may also have spent much of his early childhood and schooling in the company of his two sisters, Mary and Margaret, as well as various magnate children like Robert Steward (who was, though, eight years older), the Guardian's sons, Thomas and John Randolph, several Douglas children, Edward Bruce's bastards, Alexander and Thomas, and perhaps also Thomas Stewart, son of the new earl of Angus.[6]

The next generation, then, clearly received a firm hand to guide their upbringing. David's household before 1334 is also known to have included Dominican friars and a number of books purchased for him, as well as time for learning how to hunt and fight.[7] But any training in life, arms and kingship which David may have received up to the increasingly impressionable age of ten must have imbued him with an awareness of the need for an equally firm hand in ruling his kingdom.

There is some evidence of tension within the Scottish political community in the first few years after Robert I's death. Randolph may have had to act to check the autonomy of some of the first Bruce king's regional allies. In

5 *RRS*, vi, nos. 1 to 10 with one unnumbered act; *APS*, i, 73, 293 (*RPS*, 1330/1, 1331/ 1–2); *ER*, i, 137–243; *CDS*, iii, nos. 1017–8; *CPR*, ii, 345.
6 *ER*, i, 137, 141–2, 249–50, 256–8, 287, 324, 340, 364, 380–1; *Chron. Bower*, vii, 83; Barrow, *Robert Bruce*, 26, 321. An act issued in David's name at Brechin on 6 February 1331 recorded the resignation by the Chancellor, Sir Thomas Charteris, of some former Comyn lands to the king while at Clackmannan (*RRS*, vi, no. 5).
7 *ER*, i, 297, 431.

Galloway the Guardian had to head off a band allegedly set on his own assassination: Randolph may have looked to his own sons and Alexander Bruce, now earl of Carrick, to pacify this region in the future. Continuing his role as justiciar north of Forth, Randolph also had to undertake summary justice assizes in Inverness-shire where he is reported to have hanged some fifty wrongdoers from the walls of Eilean Donan castle in Wester Ross. This may have had some bearing upon an escalating feud there between Hugh, earl of Ross – heavily rewarded by King Robert in Cromarty, Ross and Buchan – and John Mackenzie of Kintail, who had led Highland forces at Bannockburn. The heirs of Randolph and Ross would clash over control of land and the law in the north later in the decade.[8]

But there were not merely teething problems with the crown's outlying provinces. Randolph may also have faced troubled relations with Robert I's other lieutenants. Friction between Randolph's second son, John, and the slightly senior royal heir presumptive, Robert Steward – by 1331 a youth of fifteen – would certainly break out after 1334. This may have stemmed not only from the natural rivalry between the young sons of great magnates and from their competition at that time for control of men and resources in the wake of Edward Balliol's and England's invasion of Scotland in 1332–3; it may also have sprung from Thomas Randolph senior's attitude to the Stewart succession. Randolph may have been reluctant to concede to the Stewarts any additional land or influence at a time when Duncan, earl of Fife, had probably resumed relations with his English wife, Maria de Monthermer, a granddaughter of Edward I. Male children from this match would have negated any chance that Robert Steward would be assigned the earldom of Fife by the crown under the terms of King Robert's 1315 pardon of earl Duncan: a daughter, Isabella of Fife, may have been born (at the latest) about 1329–32.[9]

In addition, any favour Randolph showed towards Alexander Bruce, earl of Carrick, despite his illegitimacy as an heir of Edward Bruce, may also have given the Stewarts cause for concern about their right of succession to the throne. Intriguingly, both Fordun's source and Bower later reported that in 1344, a man claiming to be Alexander – who would actually perish in battle against Anglo-Balliol forces in 1333 – appeared in Scotland to retrieve his lands. This pretender so upset David II and the Steward that he was executed, without fair hearing according to some. But it was the Steward who had more to fear from a Bruce alternative heir or even gossip about such a figure. Through Scottish chronicles assembled after the Steward's

8 *Chron. Fordun*, i, 353–4; *Chron. Wyntoun*, vi, 383–7; *Chron. Bower*, vii, 57–61; A. Mackenzie, *A History of the Mackenzies* (Inverness 1894), 49–50.

9 Maria de Monthermer was given permssion (*CDS*, iii, no. 8) to travel to Scotland in 1321 so Isabella may have been born sometime during the 1322–7 truces.

accession as king in 1371, there seems to have been a campaign to blacken Alexander Bruce's name. Wyntoun's anonymous source for the reign asserts that Alexander and the men of Carrick joined Balliol and the Strathbogie claimant to Atholl (Alexander Bruce's uncle) in 1332, only to be re-captured by Randolph's second son, John, third earl of Moray; Bower would later add that Alexander received a regrant of the lordship of Galloway from Balliol; a later sixteenth-century continuator would further insist that Alexander was in fact captured and executed by John Randolph.[10] This smear campaign may have reflected Robert Steward's fears about the consequences of his own actions in the 1330s and doubts about his family's right of inheritance of the throne.

These tensions may only have been beginning to bubble away in the background before 1334. But as Guardian, Thomas Randloph may also have narrowly avoided open disagreement with that other pillar of the Bruce party, the 'Good' Sir James Douglas, because that flower of chivalry was obliged to leave the country. King Robert's dying wishes were carried out to the letter. While his body was interred at Dunfermline Abbey where an ornately decorated tomb of French marble had been begun, his heart was removed, embalmed and placed in a silver casket. In September 1329 Douglas secured a seven-year safe-conduct from Edward III's government to allow him to take Robert's heart through England and across to the continent en route for the Holy Land. Douglas was well received by the royal court in London on his way south in late 1329, cementing the good relations with England which had been re-opened when he recovered his family's English lands in May of that year.[11]

That Douglas was prepared to leave Scotland at this time and spend vast sums on projecting his image as guardian of the blood-red Bruce heart speaks not only to his sense of duty but also to considerable confidence on his part about the peace, the Bruce kingship and agreements about mutual restoration of the Disinherited. Landing at Bruges, Douglas entertained some of the cream of European chivalry aboard his ship in royal style before becoming embroiled in the Spanish crown's own crusade against the Saracens. Foiled in his ultimate goal, Douglas nonetheless met a glorious if premature death in battle on 25 August 1330 alongside his companions Sir

---

10 *Chron. Wyntoun*, v, 426; *Chron. Bower*, vii, 83–5, 93; *Liber Pluscardensis*, ed. F.J.H. Skene (Edinburgh 1877–80), 200. With Scotland now free from papal interdict, Thomas Randolph, who visited Rome in 1324 and received a crusader's plenary indulgence, might have been able to have Alexander Bruce legitimised. In much the same way, Archibald Douglas, although a bastard of the 'Good' Sir James, could be given a place in the Douglas succession, eventually succeeding as third earl (Brown, *The Black Douglases*, 53–75; *RRS*, vi, no. 51).

11 *Foedera*, ii, 771; Cameron, 'Sir James Douglas, Spain and the Holy Land', 111.

Robert Menzies, William Sinclair, two Logan esquires and Sir Simon Lockhart of the Lee. Only Sir William Keith, brother of the Marischal, seems to have survived from this armed Scottish pilgrimage, returning home with Douglas's corpse: Bruce's heart was graciously returned by the Saracens and interred at Melrose, presumably within Randolph's lifetime.[12]

So it was not until December 1330, four months after Douglas's death, that Edward III began to complain openly by letter that David II's regency regime had failed to restore the lands of any of the Disinherited in England other than Henry Percy 'in accordance with the terms of the treaty' of Edinburgh-Northampton. Thus it is likely that Randolph – whose new regality was made up predominantly of forfeited Comyn lands – was proving even more unco-operative than Robert I, more so after the demise of Douglas who had had his lands in England restored before his departure. In August 1331, indeed, English watchers on the border complained that Randolph and his ally, William Douglas of Lothian (a distant cousin of the 'Good' Sir James), 'do as they please in regard of the redress of offences' in breach of the peace. The Northumberland abbey of Holm Cultram – confirmed in its Scottish lands in Lothian and the borders by Robert I as early as 1321 – likewise complained in January 1331 of 'forays' against their northern lands by the Scots, despite the presence there of the tomb of King Robert's own father.[13]

Such activity suggests that at least a small section of the Scottish community hankered for a return to the profitable days of open border warfare. Douglas of Lothian would certainly make his fame and fortune in war against England in the later 1330s: he clearly coveted the border lands and potent military lordship of his famous cousin. On 21 March 1331 while at Berwick, the Guardian seemed to countenance William Douglas's actions with a royal grant of Peeblesshire lands.[14] For Randolph, though, it was perhaps more a case of being prepared to stand behind indignant claims of breaches of the peace on the borders and infringements of jurisdiction as a way of avoiding the really thorny issue of restoring Disinherited magnate and church lands out of his own and other lords' new patrimony. March days were named for spring 1331 at Berwick for discussion of the cases of individual Disinherited lords in this matter. But nothing came of such talks and in September 1331 Randolph, in support of Patrick Dunbar, earl of

---

12 *Oeuvres de Froissart*, ii, 207–11; Brown, *Black Douglases*, 27. On 18 October 1331 Randolph arranged for perpetual masses to be said for his own and the king's soul at Elgin cathedral (*Registrum Episcopatus Moraviensis*, 291–3; Barrow, *Bruce*, 324).

13 *CDS*, iii, nos. 1013, 1022, 1029, 1033–4, 1036; *CPR*, ii, 510; F. Grainger and W.G. Collingwood eds., *The Register and Records of Holm Cultram* (Kendal 1929), 55–6, 121, 143; *RRS*, v, no. 170.

14 *RRS*, vi, no. 7.

March, even went as far as to dispatch Robert Lauder as justiciar of Lothian to summon the bishop of Durham to a Scottish parliament at Scone to hear his claim to the Berwickshire lands of Upsetlington.[15]

However, despite these crisp exchanges – and behind such continued pleasantries as Edward III allowing his brother-in-law's court to buy four hundred quarters of wheat and malt at Lincoln market in April 1331 to make up for another harsh Scottish winter – the young English king may have had a much wider agenda from the beginning. On 16 October 1330, three days before his arrest of Roger Mortimer, Edward III issued a safe-conduct to cross the Channel to England for Edward Balliol and his retinue. Much of the vengeful English king's thinking was directed by the inter-mediary offices and wealth of Sir Henry Beaumont. As well as aiding the young king's assertion of his independence from his mother's party, it was Beaumont and David (II) Strathbogie, the forfeited earl of Atholl (whose aunt Edward Bruce had wronged in siring Alexander Bruce) who travelled to Balliol in Picardy in the summer of 1331 and finally persuaded him to commit to their enterprise.[16] This activity behind the scenes makes it likely that Edward III's continued letters – right up until August 1332 – to King David, Randolph and such other Scots as James Ben, the new bishop of St Andrews, and the bishops of Glasgow and Dunkeld, Donald, earl of Mar, Malise, earl of Strathearn, Duncan, earl of Fife and Patrick, earl of March, demanding the restoration of the lands in Scotland of Beaumont and Strathbogie and others, was merely legalistic posturing. From the first, Edward III was in search of an excuse and opportunity to smash the shameful peace of 1328 and reconquer Scotland.

Yet in sending his appeals – and perhaps other more secret communications – to some of these substantial Scots, King Edward was pitching to a receptive audience. The earls of Fife, March and Strathearn all had English or Comyn connections and could claim to have been pardoned but not favoured by Robert I after the events of 1314 forced them, like many other Scottish nobles and prelates, to comply with Bruce policy on many public occasions while their regional influence was eroded by crown men: all three would indeed defect to Balliol in Scotland in 1332–3.[17] Moreover, on 15 October 1331, Donald, earl of Mar, who had been loyal to Edward II after living in England until 1327, was granted passage south with a dozen unnamed followers, giving him a chance to visit both the English king and Balliol, who by winter of that year was installed on Beaumont's Yorkshire lands. A contemporary English chronicle claimed that in 1331:

15 *CDS*, iii, nos. 1024, 1034; PRO C47/22/10, no. 49; printed in Duncan, 'Early Parliaments of Scotland', 55–6. See also *RRS*, vi, nos. 480–1.
16 *CDS*, iii, no. 1010; Nicholson, *Edward III and the Scots*, 62–3.
17 Young, *The Comyns*, x–xi (genealogical table); Penman, 'Soules conspiracy', 43–4.

[Mar] herde telle how that Sir Edward [Balliol] was comen into Engeland, and come to him, and made with him grete joye of his commyng agayne, and saide to him, and bihight that alle grete lordes of Scotland shulde bene to him entendant, and holde for him as Kyng, as right heir of Scotland, and so miche thai wolde done, that he shulde be crounede Kyng of that lands, and to him ded feaute and Homage . . .[18]

This could be later propaganda justification for English military aggression. But Mar – like these other earls of ancient stock and many lesser Scots – may have looked to Balliol as a likely source of renewed lordship now able to legally claim the right to displace the partisan Bruce dynasty which besides would be unable to make many fresh land grants until David reached adulthood. More immediately, if Mar did approach Balliol in 1331 with an offer of the crown, he may have been encouraged to do so by early signs of terminal illness in Randolph and by one other glaring fact: David had not yet been crowned as king.

There may be a reasonable explanation for this long delay. The Scots may simply have been waiting for details from the papacy of just how a king should be crowned and anointed: it was a far more formal ceremony than the traditional inaugural placing of Scotland's new kings on the Stone of Scone followed by a blessing and recitation of oaths and genealogy. Or the Scots may have been waiting until David was of a reasonable age (seven years old) as well as secure in health so as to repeat the required oaths of the ceremony in person: English chroniclers would make much of David's infancy by claiming he soiled the inaugural altar.[19] Or the Scots may have been awaiting the results of tricky horse-trading for the delayed return of the Stone of Destiny of Scone from Westminster: the restoration of the stone – refused by angry parishioners of Westminster in 1328 – may have been expected after the Scots' payment of the last of the reparations instalments in mid-summer 1331. Randolph certainly expected receipt of England's final documentary acknowledgement of full peace and Scottish independence after the Scots' final payment. Indeed, the Scottish political community may have viewed the fulfilment of its treaty obligations – agreed in parliament at Holyrood in March 1328 – as so important as to warrant the postponement of the new king's installation and then to insist this

---

18 *CDS*, iii, no. 1040; *The Brut, or the Chronicles of England*, ed. F.W.D. Brie (2 vols., Early English Text Society, London 1906–8), ii, 274.

19 *Chronica Monasterii de Melsa*, ed. E.A. Bond (3 vols., London 1868), ii, 361–2; J. Barnie, *War in Medieval Society: Social Values and the Hundred Years War, 1337–99* (London 1974), 51.

ceremony take place in another full parliament.[20] Besides, in theory at least, the delay was not unique: the Maid of Norway would have been inaugurated some four years after the death of her grandfather had she survived the journey to Scotland in 1290.

However, 'David's presence in Scotland and his father's hurriedly improvised inauguration in 1306 – taking the crown without the stone or the attendance of the earl of Fife – make rational excuses for such a long delay after 1329 seem questionable. It is surely possible that there was sufficient doubt and dissent in Scotland, even among strong Bruce supporters from the 1320s in the royal government, as to the desirability of another infant monarch. It is likely that the earls of Fife and Strathearn had refused to participate in any coronation. Better then, in the light of painful experience within living memory, to avoid further civil or national war by holding off from crowning the infant David and leaving the door open to invite the adult Edward Balliol back as king on good terms – perhaps even setting the condition of Balliol's confirmation of much of the Bruce land resettlement? Thus only when it became apparent – either through Mar's embassy in late 1331 or through earlier intelligence – that Balliol was hand-in-glove with the Disinherited and Edward III, intent on smashing that landed resettlement and the 1328 peace, did a majority of Scots finally decide to commit themselves to the present regime and to crown David.

A full parliament was called by Randolph for November 1331 to be held at Scone: indeed Mar's trip to test the waters with Balliol may have been prompted by summonses issued in late September.[21] But on Sunday 24th November – a week before the feast of St Andrew and Advent but, really, two years and five months late – James Ben, bishop of St Andrews, another of the negotiators of the 1326 alliance with France, placed new child-sized coronets and holy oil on the heads of David and his queen, Joan, as they both sat enrobed in cloth of gold. According to Bower, the previous day David had been knighted – presumably by the Guardian – alongside Thomas Randolph (junior), Thomas Stewart, the minor earl of Angus, and 'many other' nobles. Duncan of Fife and Malise of Strathearn do not seem to have fulfilled their traditional ceremonial roles. Presumably, though, these men did perform homage and fealty to their lord alongside all other freeholders and tenants-in-chief. Festivities were then uncorked with minstrels and feasting.[22]

---

20 Duncan, 'Early Parliaments of Scotland', 55–7; M. Penman, 'Parliament Lost – Parliament Regained? The Bruce Regime and the Estates, *c.* 1329–71', in Brown and Tanner eds., *Parliament and Politics in Scotland: 1286–1567*; N. Aitchison, *Scotland's Stone of Destiny* (Stroud 2000), 120.

21 *APS*, i, 73 (*RPS*, 1331/2).

22 *Chron. Bower*, vii, 71; *ER*, i, 389, 403.

It was undoubtedly a majestic affair. But it may not have done enough to alleviate widespread doubts in Scotland about the stability of the Bruce succession. When combined with Stewart fears about the legitimacy of their guarantees of inheritance from the Bruces, this may explain why Archdeacon John Barbour later felt the need to obliterate the memory of this long delay in crowning the new king: in fact, the author of *The Bruce* asserts that this ceremony took place in 1326 at the same time as the issue of the last parliamentary Act of Succession and the ratification of the Franco-Scottish alliance, shortly *after* David's wedding to Joan of the Tower as part of the peace (which actually occurred in 1328), all within King Robert's lifetime.[23]

But in late 1331, it is unlikely that Randolph – even though he was now surely aware of Edward Balliol's presence – used this coronation parliament to raise funds and issue summons for hosting against expected invasion from England. Indeed, the occasion seems to have been used instead to make a public declaration of the crown's fulfilment of its English reparations debts: the costs of a lavish coronation could now be met. But the contemporary English knight and author of the *Scalacronica*, Sir Thomas Gray – who would be captured by the Scots in 1355 – relates with some charm Edward III's presentation to the Scots of the demands of the Disinherited in the first half of summer 1332 whilst he was fully aware that Balliol and Beaumont were poised to take their assembled private army into Scotland. Randolph, similarly aware of the threat, is said to have brushed aside the matter and urged King Edward to 'allow them to take their measures and let the ball roll'.[24] Some weeks before this surely over-dramatised exchange was said to have taken place, Randolph had mobilised southern Scotland and taken up residence at Musselburgh just to the east of Edinburgh. Thus far the Scots had been led by a steady hand. As a general, justiciar, feudal lord and dynast, the Guardian would have had enormous formative influence upon David Bruce as he entered adolescence. But by 20 July 1332, before battle could be joined, Randolph was dead, probably from a cancer.

Crucially, neither he nor parliament seems to have been able or willing to name a contingency successor in the two years since James Douglas's death, an oversight perhaps further suggestive of grave doubts within the regime. Rumours that Randolph had been poisoned by a monk in English pay were understandable in the sudden removal of such an inspiring Bruce captain.[25]

---

23 Duncan ed., *The Bruce*, 14–7, 30, 744–9 (xx, 65–150). This version of events may have been designed to make David's enkinging fit with the French practice up to *c.* 1120 of consecrating heirs to the throne during the reign of their predecessor (*idem*, *Kingship of the Scots*, 66–8).

24 *ER*, i, 403; *Chron. Scalacronica*, 88. The Scots must also have paid off the 12,000 florin (£1,200) cost of the coronation papal bull.

25 *Chron. Wyntoun*, vi, 400; *Chron. Bower*, vii, 66, 73 where the editors have diagnosed Randolph's illness as cancer of the liver.

Balliol's Revenge – David's Exile, 1332–4

Randolph's untimely death threw the Bruce Scots into internal disarray. They were left without any of the natural leaders who had fought and ruled alongside King Robert – men designated to serve as successive Guardians by acts of carefully controlled parliaments before 1329; and now, differences of opinion over the Balliol and Bruce causes broke to the surface once more in Scotland. An emergency council was hastily assembled at Perth about 2 August 1332. It met with the certain knowledge that Edward Balliol and the Disinherited were about to land somewhere in Scotland and that many magnates present at Perth might prefer to join them. In view of the Bruce Scots' swift collapse in the following weeks the Scottish chroniclers' attempts to put a positive spin on this assembly are highly revealing:

> All the magnates, both churchmen and laymen . . . after a great deal of wrangling and sundry disputes, they, with one voice, chose Donald, Earl of Mar, as guardian of the kingdom.

Wyntoun's source, too, noted the 'gret huge discencioun' which hindered the Scots' choice of their next Guardian.[26] In the end, though, Mar was a prudent rather than an aggressive choice. He had experience of the English and might be able to make an approach to Balliol and Edward III: he may even have had an illegitimate child, Thomas, by a Balliol woman. But Donald of Mar was also third-in-line to the throne after the children King David and Robert Stewart. Despite Mar's ambivalent behaviour of 1331, Balliol's status as an 'absolute creature of England' and uncertainty about the landed disruption his party might cause if restored to Scotland seems to have driven the new King's Lieutenant or Guardian to commit himself to lead resistance to the invaders.

The odds favoured Donald's men overwhelmingly. Balliol and Beaumont landed from several ships at the royal manor of Kinghorn in Fife on 6 August with a force of only 2–3,000 men, mostly paid troops on foot: Edward III had given them no official help. But Balliol's landfall, route and tactics (and presumably propaganda sent out in advance) quickly exposed the cracks in the Bruce Scots' resolve. It seems likely that Balliol faced little opposition and found some initial support as he moved through Fife to Dunfermline (just as an English invasion of 1317 had attempted) and then pushed inland towards Scone; Balliol was able to draw monies from the monastic houses of Fife. Mar besides had had little time to prepare his numerically much larger force and his generalship seems to have been uninspiring, perhaps divisive. When the two armies met on 11 August at Dupplin Moor, a few miles south-west of Perth, the

26 *Chron. Fordun*, i, 354; *Chron. Wyntoun*, v, 402; *Chron. Lanercost*, 268.

Scottish host was betrayed by William Murray of Tullibardine (a past follower of the Strathbogie earls of Atholl) and folded under superior English archery and armed infantry deployment. Among the dead were Mar; Thomas Randolph (the younger), the new second earl of Moray; Murdoch, earl of Menteith; Sir Alexander Fraser the Chamberlain; and the king's half-brother Robert Bruce of Liddesdale (who may have accused Mar of incompetence and treachery). The earls of Fife and Strathearn and much of their following – admittedly after some losses – preferred to submit to Balliol.[27]

This victory, and the failure of Bruce ships to cut out the Disinherited vessels in the Tay, precipitated defections to Balliol on a large scale. Sir Eustace Maxwell of Caerlaverock Castle in Dumfriesshire – acquitted of complicity in the Balliol-Soules plot of 1320 – brought an army north-east to aid the invasion force at Perth. His approach persuaded Patrick Dunbar, earl of March (whom Bower describes as then 'Guardian south of Forth'), with a southern pro-Bruce host, to turn back from as close as Auchterarder and to decline battle against Balliol. Between mid-1333 and 1335 Dunbar would be in Edward III's pay. But Bower reports that long before then the clergy of the earldoms of Fife and Strathearn and the deaneries of Gowrie (from Perth through Angus to Dundee) and Fothrif (west Fife and Kinross), and much of the former Balliol-Comyn following of the south-west, all went over to the resurgent Balliol camp.[28]

After his murder of the Red Comyn in 1306, Robert Bruce had taken six weeks to have himself inaugurated as king attended by the bishops of St Andrews and Glasgow, three earls (Lennox, Mar and Atholl) and a handful of lesser lords, but without the Stone of Destiny. On 24 September 1332 at Scone, just seven weeks after his return, Balliol was crowned and anointed king of Scots using his father's former muniments. His coronation attendance was arguably as impressive as Robert's, if not more so. For although James, bishop of St Andrews, had fled to Flanders (where he would die in 1333), Balliol could call upon the earl of Fife and William Sinclair, King Robert's famous 'fighting' bishop of Dunkeld (another former Atholl man whose loyalty to Bruce before 1315 is questionable), to perform the

27 For the military events of 1332–3 in this and the following paragraphs, see *Chron. Fordun*, i, 354–7; *Chron. Wyntoun*, v, 402–3 and vi, 4–12; *Chron. Bower*, vii, 73–93; *Chron. Scalacronica*, 88–98; Nicholson, *Edward III and the Scots*, chs vi–ix; C.J. Rogers, *War Cruel and Sharp: English Strategy under Edward III, 1327–60* (Woodbridge 2000); chs 3–4; K. DeVries, *Infantry Warfare in the Early Fourteenth-century: Discipline, Tactics and Technology* (Woodbridge 1996), ch. ix.

28 For Maxwell, see *CDS*, iii, nos. 1129, 1149, p. 317 and *Chron. Lanercost*, 269. For March see *CDS*, iii, nos. 1115, 1121, 1126 and *Chron. Bower*, vii, 77–9; *CDS*, iii no. 1119 for Malise, earl of Strathearn. For Balliol's coronation, see *APS*, i, 539–42 and R.C. Reid, 'Edward Balliol', *TDGNHAS*, xxxv (1956–7), 38–64.

necessary offices.[29] In addition, Earls Malise of Strathearn and Patrick of Dunbar, as well as a sizeable body of lesser knights and clerics of central Scotland, may have been present. Much of this submission was obviously given under duress as Balliol began to make ayres to collect homage and fealty. But a significant proportion of it must have been sincere or at least the equivocal actions of men prepared to see what unfolded, not altogether surprised by another wild swing of fortune and the armed return of a dynasty which had been expelled in similar fashion only a generation before by a now endangered house.

Yet for many others the lightning success of Balliol and the Disinherited – and some high profile defections – made the task ahead clearer. The Bruce Scots remained in the majority and it was now that the descendants of those families best rewarded by King Robert mustered themselves to defend their recently-won patrimony and lord. David's supporters by no means saw their situation as irretrievable. The young king remained in the realm, probably moved along with his wife and sisters shortly after Dupplin to Fleming's keeping on Dumbarton rock. Another 'King's Lieutenant' was quickly appointed in Sir Andrew Murray of Bothwell and Garioch, David's uncle and son of Wallace's partner. The grandson and namesake of another Wallace compatriot, Sir Simon Fraser, boosted the Scots' morale by retaking Perth burgh and capturing Duncan, earl of Fife, who it seems had accepted office as Balliol's warden in the north alongside his newly-returned cousin, David Strathbogie, earl of Atholl.

The administration of Guardianship appeared to be working as well as ever in the circumstances. It survived the capture of Andrew Murray by Balliol's men near Bothwell sometime in October 1332. The 'Good' Sir James's brother, Archibald, filled the vacancy and scored a telling victory with the help of John Randolph, the new earl of Moray, at Annan in Dumfriesshire on 16–7 December. The Disinherited's small force was routed and expelled from Scotland, exposing the tenuous grip, even in southern Scotland, of their initial success; Edward Balliol fled half-dressed to Carlisle in the night leaving his brother, Henry, to die. The forty-nine-year-old Balliol's lacklustre leadership might indeed have amounted to nothing had it not now been for the bellicosity of Edward III. Surprised by the victory at Dupplin, Edward had moved his administration to York for the ostensible purpose of safeguarding his northern border. But he did not have long to wait for an excuse to begin raising cash and troops to intervene personally in Scotland. At Roxburgh on 23 November 1332, Balliol had acknowledged the English king as his feudal superior and, in return for the Plantagenet maintainence of the Balliol line in Scotland, promised to both serve England

---

29 *CDS*, iii, no. 301; *Chron. Fordun*, i, 355; Barrow, *Bruce*, 149–52.

against all enemies at home and abroad and to cede to the English crown much of southern Scotland consisting of the shires of Edinburgh (with its constabularies of Linlithgow and Haddington), Berwick, Roxburgh, Selkirk, Dumfries and Wigtown: these were shrival jursidictions valued in total at £2,000. To cement this tie of vassaldom Balliol proposed to wed Edward's sister, Joan, breaking her under-age and unconsummated betrothal to David (and Balliol's recent marriage to an Italian noblewoman): the usurped Bruce would be offered safe passage away.[30]

But Douglas's victory at Annan and Balliol's embarrassing escape at the year's close made it highly unlikely that David and his queen would fall into Anglo-Balliol hands without English military commitment. Had Edward III learned that John Randolph had set out for France to invoke the 1326 alliance, his pretext that Scotland posed a threat to England's security would have been justified. Yet Edward's true motivation had already been revealed earlier in December 1332 at a parliament at York where the 1328 peace was denounced as illegal and unbinding over him as Scotland's true overlord.

In the end the Bruce Scots had almost six months to prepare for Edward III's expedition. The defences they added to the premier trade burgh and castle of Berwick – under the command of Alexander Seton, Robert Keith and earl Patrick of Dunbar (back briefly in Bruce service) – were substantial. By the time Edward III's army arrived in late May to help a Balliol force reduce the town, the siege had already lasted two months. It was still pressing by 19 July when a Scottish host of probably 8–10,000 men in three divisions – similar to the army at Bannockburn – approached to relieve the defenders in advance of a deadline set by the invaders. But, despite being outnumbered 2:1, the deadly dismounted archery and expertly deployed men-at-arms of Edward's contract army – and, probably, divided Scottish generalship – claimed the day again. Listed among the Scottish dead on this field were King's Lieutenant Archibald Douglas and his nephew William, son and heir of the 'Good' Sir James; Alexander Bruce, earl of Carrick; John Campbell, earl of Atholl; the earls of Lennox, Ross and Sutherland; as well as (perhaps) several Stewarts, Frasers and other kindred siblings and cousins: the total Scottish death toll may have run into thousands with an unmerciful Edward III determined to execute lesser Scottish prisoners. Edward Balliol may have thought

---

30   CDS, iii, no. 728; Nicholson, *Edward III and the Scots*, 100–1, 160–2 for what
     follows; M.A.E. Green, *Lives of the Princesses of England* (6 vols., London 1849–
     55), iii, 114. Balliol also offered to increase Joan's dower in Scotland by £500. For
     Balliol's marriage, see *Giovanni Boccaccio – The Decameron*, ed. G.H. McWil-
     liam (London 1972), 812: sometime about 1329–31 Balliol may have wed
     Margherita of Taranto, niece of Robert, king of Naples, an ally of Edward III,
     but quickly divorced her (A. Beam, 'One Funeral and a Wedding: The Neglected
     History of Scotland's Forgotten Kings', *History Scotland*, Vol. 3 no. 1 Jan/Feb
     2003, 16–23).

ill of this method of winning over his would-be subjects' hearts and minds.[31]

This rout on Halidon Hill proved to be a far more telling blow because it was also backed up with a sizeable English occupation force. More Bruce Scots were now obliged (if, in some cases, only briefly) to recognise the reality of a vassal Balliol return and English overlordship. A parliament held by Balliol in Perth in October 1333 – overseen by the English king – and a second at Edinburgh in February 1334 were attended by prelates such as the bishops of Brechin, Dunkeld, Glasgow and Aberdeen, several abbots, and magnates like Patrick of March (who now received an English pension of 600 merks), a recovered Duncan of Fife (whose daughter, Isabella, Edward III's cousin, was taken south at this time), Malise of Strathearn, Malcolm Fleming, Alexander Seton, Robert Keith, Simon Fraser, Robert Lauder, John Graham and, perhaps, Thomas, the child earl of Mar.[32] By early 1334, indeed, the Bruce Scots could only claim to have a handful of mainland castles left in their possession: Dumbarton (back under Fleming), Loch Leven in Fife (under Alan de Vipont), Kildrummy in Mar (under David's aunt, Christian Bruce) and Urquhart in Moray (under Robert Lauder). There was undoubtedly little or no co-ordinated Bruce administration or revenue collection at this time. Meanwhile an English regime built around sheriffs and based at Berwick began to take hold of southern Scotland, and English garrisons backed up Balliol's tentative presence in central Scotland and north of Forth. On 12 June 1334, Balliol would confirm his alienation of the southern shires to his English lord and master: a week later he renewed his homage to Edward III at Newcastle in person.[33]

For the Bruce Scots, the situation was undoubtedly grim and it was understandable that a decision should now be taken to evacuate David II and the rump of his government. This would leave behind only a fragmented guerilla operation.[34] The embassy to Paris of John Randolph, earl of Moray,

31 R. Nicholson, 'The Siege of Berwick, 1333', *SHR*, xl (1961), 19–42; Rogers, *War Cruel and Sharp*, ch. 4; DeVries, *Infantry Warfare*, ch. ix. For a discussion of the 'quiet revolution' in English tactics away from the preferred semi-contract/semi-feudal armies of mounted cavalry and infantry with a small number of archers (seen at Bannockburn) to the dismounted paid contract armies of roughly half-knights/men-at-arms and half-archers, deployed from 1333 on, see A. Ayton, 'English Armies in the Fourteenth-Century', in A. Curry and M. Hughes eds., *Arms, Armies and Fortifications in the Hundred Years War* (Woodbridge 1994), 21–36.

32 *Chron. Lanercost*, 283–4; *Rot. Scot.*, i, 208, 255, 271–3; *CDS*, iii, no. 1108. Mar would be presented to Edward III at Newcastle later in 1334 and placed in the care of William of Carswell about 1347–8.

33 *Ibid*, no. 1127; *Chron. Wyntoun*, vi, 18; Nicholson, *Edward III and the Scots*, ch. x; B. Webster, 'The English Occupations of Dumfriesshire in the Fourteenth-century', *TDGNHAS*, xxxv (1956–7), 64–80. For Robert Lauder's vacillation between the Scots and English, see *Rot. Scot.*, i, 264–5, 271, 385–6.

34 Fifteenth-century English propagandists would claim that after Halidon Hill David actually did homage to Edward III with forged submissions dated at Edinburgh and Holyrood on 1 November 1333 (PRO E39/96/4; *CDS*, iv, nos. 1842–3).

had already borne fruit. Philip VI – though slow to act – felt he could not escape his treaty obligations to Scotland even if Pope John XXII (d. September 1334) viewed Scotland as a trivial irritant which should not halt preparation for a pan-European crusade. Philip despatched a flotilla of ten supply ships to Scotland in the winter of 1332–3 only to see them blown off course by storms: there may have been others. But in the spring of 1334, £1,000 did arrive from France for David's keepers to distribute among his supporters together with an offer of sanctuary. In May 1334 David, Queen Joan, Margaret and Mary Bruce and the late Guardian's sons and nephew William, John and Archibald Douglas boarded a ship from Dumbarton, presumably taking prevailing winds south and west into the English Channel.[35]

In favourable weather, such a trip might take only three or four days. Chronicler Jean Froissart would later embellish this journey, relating how David's party almost sailed into Southampton in thick fog but were saved by the guidance of William Douglas of Lothian.[36] But in fact the royal party's passage was straightforward enough. They landed, about 22 May, in Normandy and travelled south-east to be met by King Philip, perhaps at the Abbey of St Dénis outside Paris. Here a number of expatriate Scots served in orders. One of them, Richard Lescot (the Scot), wrote treatises advising Philip on Franco- and Anglo-Scottish affairs and penned a chronicle which was highly favourable to the Bruce cause. A Scottish knight well known to the French, Sir Humphrey Kirkpatrick (who had been granted the lands of Torthorwald in Dumfriesshire by Robert I and was the son of David's sheriff of Ayr, Roger Kirkpatrick), may have introduced the royal party to the French king.[37] From this brief audience, David's sorry party was

---

35 *ER*, i, 449, 464; *Chronique de Richard Lescot, Religieux de Saint Dénis, 1328–44, avec continuation à 1349*, ed. J. Lemoine (Paris 1896), 33; *Les Grandes Chroniques de France*, ed. J. Viard (10 vols., Paris 1953), ix, 137–8. After listening to the Douglas's family lore in 1365, Froissart (*Oeuvres de Froissart*, ii, 528–3) would assert that David hid with William Douglas of Lothian in Jedburgh forest before going into exile.

36 For Froissart's later embellishment of William Douglas of Lothian's role in David's escape in the 1330s, see below, ch. 10.

37 *Chronique de Richard Lescot*, 34–5. In another version of this work Lescot stated that David came to France with his brother, perhaps confusing John Bruce with John Douglas (BN Nouv. Acq fr. 6214 f. 59r-60). For Humphrey Kirkpatrick, see *RRS*, v, no. 189. According to Lescot, 'Aufrey Kyrepatric' went on to become Abbot of St Dénis – Humphrey can certainly be associated with that house's lands by 1341 (AN JJ 74/4757). Kirkpatrick's and Malcolm Fleming's roles in helping David and his party escape were mentioned in: *Les Grandes Chroniques*, ix, 141; *L'Istoire et Croniques de Flandres*, ed. Kervyn de Lettenhove (2 vols., Brussels 1879), i, 354; and *Chronographia Regum Francorum, 1270–1405*, ed. H. Moranville (3 vols., Paris 1897), ii, 31. *The Chronique Parisiene Anonyme de 1316 à 1339*, ed. A. Hellot (Paris 1885), also written by a resident of St Dénis, contains much material about the Bruce-Balliol rivalry of the 1290s and Robert I's reign.

transferred north to a suite of chambers in Château Gaillard in Normandy, a magnificent rock-bound fortress, built in the twelfth-century by the crusading Richard I of England, overlooking the Seine and pilgrim trails east; by the fourteenth-century, however, it had become a more functional, greyer administration post and royal prison.[38]

It is hard to imagine just how much a ten-year-old boy king would have understood of his plight in being torn from his birthright by his father's sworn enemies. It would only be while he grew to adolescence in France and encountered many strong influences, as well as learning about the events and personalities of the past and present, that David began to form his own opinions as to the future. But it would also be during his exile that the conflicting interests amongst the Bruce Scots which would most shape David's adult rule, began to emerge.

The Triumph of Guardianship, 1334–8?

With David in France were a handful of men well equipped to perpetuate the Bruce cause and appeal to their hosts. This group was dominated – predictably – by churchmen. Adam Murray, bishop of Brechin, had helped secure the French alliance in 1326, as had Walter Twynham, abbot of Kilwinning – they were both former Chancellors; William Dalgarnock, abbot of Kelso, would serve as David's tutor in the arts. A number of other clerics – John Lindsay, bishop of Glasgow, John Pilmor, bishop of Moray, John, abbot of Coupar-Angus, the king's Dominican confessor Walter Blantyre, Thomas Fingask, an Aberdeen canon, and clerks Adam Buttergask and Walter Moffat – would all serve as envoys to and from Scotland before 1341. These men must have played a large part in deciding and implementing policy for the crown during David's youth, roles for which they were well rewarded after 1341: David would help Fingask to become bishop of Caithness, raise Moffat as Archdeacon of Lothian and make Buttergask a clerk of the wardrobe. Similar rewards would be extended to a number of Scottish churchmen studying and teaching in the 'English Nations' at the universities of Paris and Orléans in the 1330s: such clerics as David de Mar (archdeacon of Brechin by 1342), Walter de Coventre (bishop of Dunblane by 1361), Walter Greenlaw (a papal collector, dean of Glasgow by 1349 and archdeacon of Brechin by 1352) and William Landellis (bishop of St Andrews by 1342), would certainly go on to serve David and his government. Several laymen would also base themselves at David's French court. Robert Keith, the Marischal, would teach the king skills of arms, as perhaps did Reginald More, the Chamberlain, Sir Alex-

---

38 S. Sonchon, *Château Gaillard* (Condé sur Noireau 1985), 17, 29, 77; J. Gillingham, *Richard I* (Norfolk 1999), 301–6.

ander Seton and Fleming. Both More and Seton were involved with the lands of the Scottish Knights Hospitaller: their roles must have appealed at that time to Philip VI.[39]

For since 1329 the French king had been planning a grand crusade to recover the Holy Land for western Christendom. By 1334 Philip had finance from the papacy based at Avignon in south-western France and had begun to assemble vast armies and fleets supplied by the various crowns and aristocratic houses of Europe, as well as the knightly orders including the Hospitallers of St John.[40] Philip's determination to preserve this climate of European peace and collective action may have contributed to his commitment to upholding his alliance with Scotland. But as Philip's relations with a proud and aggressive Edward III deteriorated after 1331 – over the perennial question of English homage for Aquitaine and control of Channel shipping and ports – Anglo-French war seemed far more likely than a joint crusade under the French king's command: in turn, Philip increasingly needed an allied Scotland as an active northern check on England. It was probably a mixture of such calculation – and the arrival of David's party – which saw Philip insist at the eleventh hour that the Scots be included in Anglo-French peace talks held in May 1334, a demand which provoked Edward to break off contact with Paris. But growing French anticipation of war undoubtedly gave Philip cause to help and increase his influence over the Bruce Scots: at the same time, the Scots were better able to persuade the French of the need to redirect crusade resources to the war in Scotland in addition to the supplies which they would regularly send and the pension of 2,000 livres which David's court received annually while in exile.[41]

Many older Scots at that time – or those with knowledge of the period 1286–1306 – could recall bitterly how events in and between England and France could overwhelm the military and political balance in Scotland (as in 1302 when a French defeat by the Flemish left the Balliol Scots without an ally against England). But while European high politics would play its part in the minds of the Bruce Scots fighting on the ground in Scotland, in that

39 *ER*, i, clvii–ix; Watt, *Scottish Graduates*, 54, 72, 114–5, 139–40, 187–9, 243–6, 328, 351–3, 383–2, 400–1 450–1, 549–50; *The Knights of St John of Jerusalem in Scotland*, 49–52, 193–4.

40 C.J. Tyerman, 'Philip VI and the Recovery of the Holy Land', *EHR*, 100 (1985), 25–52; N. Housley, *The Later Crusades: From Lyons to Alcazar, 1274–1580* (Oxford 1992), 30–59.

41 BN MSS Clairambault 212 no. 64; *RRS*, vi, no. 24; J. Viard ed., *Journaux du Trésor de Phillipe VI de Valois* (Paris 1899); *Les Grandes Chroniques*, ix, 142–4; J. Sumption, *The Hundred Years War: Vol. I – Trial by Battle* (London 1990), 135. French chronicles record that Philip VI offered Edward III land concessions in Gascony if he would join the crusade, but that after this had been agreed Philip insisted David II should be included in the peace, something to which the English envoys were not empowered to speak.

realm in 1334 a more basic, desperate battle had to be fought by individual pockets of men anxious above all to secure their family lands. Their contact with David's court in France and with others throughout Scotland must have been badly disrupted, a lack of direction which aggravated the command tensions which soon emerged.

After the heavy losses of 1332–3 it was not too surprising that the magnate who led the recovery of Bruce resistance as 'King's Lieutenant' in that year should be such as the seventeen-year-old Robert the Steward, David's nephew and heir presumptive. After Halidon Hill – where Robert had led a division – Balliol and Edward III had seized the Stewart lands in Lothian, Roxburghshire, Clydesdale, Ayrshire and Renfrewshire, including the castles of Rothesay and Bute: most of these had then been granted by Balliol to David Strathbogie, the disinherited earl of Atholl who also recovered that earldom and the lordships of Strathbogie, Badenoch and Lochaber. But after fleeing as a refugee from Rothesay with his charters to join the king at Dumbarton, the Steward remained behind voluntarily to recover his patrimony. He may indeed have been knighted by the king before his departure for France and granted the border lordship of Liddesdale. Steward's rapid recovery of Cowal, Bute and Dunoon in mid-1334, with the help of the Campbells of Lochawe and other local men, may even have cleared the seaways for the royal party's escape.[42]

But the Steward's actions and events thereafter would contribute to a strong sense on his part that he was essentially a self-made man and one not well-liked or trusted by those closest to the young king. According to Prior Wyntoun's contemporary source – and, later, to Abbot Bower – the Steward began to use Dumbarton rock as a base to launch counter-attacks which recovered much of Clydesdale, Renfrew, Carrick, Kyle and Cunningham 'to David's faith'. When in July 1334 John Randolph, earl of Moray, returned from his embassy to France, the same sources assert that he was 'welcomed' by the Steward and the two men were elected joint guardians by the 'magnates and communities' of the kingdom: this echoed the apparent north/south lieutenancies of Mar and March in 1332. The chroniclers further concur that in 1334 the new partners worked together to recover Stewart lands from Balliol's Lieutenant, David Strathbogie. They were aided

---

42 *Chron. Wyntoun*, vi, 4, 26; *Chron. Bower*, vii, 93–7; G.W.S. Barrow, 'The ferry at Inverennok', *IR*, 52 (Spring 2001), 101–4. I would like to thank Stephen Boardman for this point about the royal party's escape route in 1334. At Bute on 25 May 1334 the Steward gave a Eygen Campbell the lands of Rosneth (J.R.N. Macphail ed., *Highland Papers* (4 vols., Edinburgh 1914), iv, 11). In council in February 1341 the Steward would claim he had been knighted and granted Liddesdale by the king at the same time – logically this can only have occurred between the death in July 1333 of Archibald Douglas (who had claimed Liddesdale for himself) and David's departure in May 1334 (*RRS*, vi, no. 44).

by Edward III's reluctance to over-commit to Scotland and heated squabbling about the division of lands amongst the Disinherited. By the end of the year Edward Balliol had been pushed out once again to sorry refuge in Berwick.[43]

However, there is little or no actual evidence, beyond chronicle hints, of the Steward and Randolph co-operating in command. Randolph – who was just younger than the Steward – might understandably have been concerned, both for his own and David's sake, at the apparent popularity, autonomy and geography of the Steward's leadership. Bower, inflating the Steward's image retrospectively as 'a young man of attractive appearance above the sons of men, broad and tall in physique, kind to everyone, and modest, generous, cheerful and honest . . . ', also notes how he: 'began to attract certain brave men to his side, and to draw Scots of good sense towards him, to enlarge his army every day, and to attach their hearts to himself in mutual affection and firm loyalty'. The building of an armed affinity was necessary and understandable but Randolph may have felt threatened by the Steward's appeal to such men as 'William Carruthers with his brothers . . . Thomas Bruce [of Clackmannan, another bastard of Edward Bruce] . . . with good men from Kyle'. These were traditionally Annandale followers and Bruce and Randolph men.[44]

Randolph may also have been suspicious of the Steward's plans to advance his designs on the earldom of Fife now that Earl Duncan (who had been warded in Kildrummy Castle in 1332 by Guardian Andrew Murray) might be accused of treason and his daughter (also held briefly in Kildrummy) was in ward in England. On 16 April 1335, at Arbroath, the Steward did issue an act alone as 'King's Lieutenant', in which he ordered the bailies of the royal Fife manor of Kinghorn to pay a rental of four merks to the Abbey of Arbroath, seat of Robert I's chancery. Then, according to the earliest available Scottish chronicle source[45] – in the section of annals collected by Fordun but written probably by Thomas Bisset, prior of St

43 *Chron. Wyntoun*, vi. 40–3; *Chron. Bower*, vii, 103–9.

44 *Ibid*, vii, 105, 218 n.42; S. Boardman, 'Chronicle Propaganda in Fourteenth-century Scotland: Robert the Steward, John of Fordun and the 'Anonymous Chronicle'', *SHR*, lxxvi (1997), 23–43, 23–35. William Carruthers was granted lands by David II acting as Lord of Annandale in 1344 when a John Carruthers was David's Chancellor in Annandale (*RRS*, vi, no. 81).

45 *Chron. Bower*, iii, 423–5 (biography of Bisset); *Liber Carta Prioratus Sanctii Andree in Scotia* (Bannatyne Club, Edinburgh 1841), 397; D. Broun, 'A New Look at *Gesta Annalia* attributed to John of Fordun', in B.E. Crawford ed., *Church, Chronicle and Learning in Medieval and Early Renaissance Scotland* (Edinburgh 1999), 9–30; Boardman, 'Chronicle propaganda in Fourteenth-century Scotland', 24. Dr Boardman intends to go into print with detailed arguments concerning Bisset's likely authorship of this missing chronicle extract used by Fordun in his *Gesta*.

Andrews (d. 1363) – a 'parliament' was held by the Bruce Scots in April 1335 at Dairsie, a manor of the bishops of St Andrews in Fife. At that time, the Steward's forces were engaged nearby in a siege of Earl Duncan's castle at Cupar and the recovery of its hinterland close to the earldom's caput at Falkland. In doing so, the Steward may have been acting alone while Randolph fought in the north. For in the previous autumn (and by February 1335 at the latest) Randolph had forced or persuaded David Strathbogie to submit to the Bruce faith in Lochaber and appointed him his lieutenant in the north: this seems to have been achieved by agreeing to restore the Strathbogie heir to his titles of Atholl, Lochaber and Badenoch and the hereditary office of Constable, but may also have involved a promise by Randolph to back Strathbogie's own familial claim for Fife.[46]

Such land concessions – displacing Robert I's favour north of Tay to the Gordons, the Hays, the (swithering) MacDonalds and the Stewart allies, the Campbells of Lochawe – was clearly a measure of the difficulties the Bruce party found itself facing in Scotland in 1334–5. But it is unclear whether or not this amounted to a challenge to the position and ambitions of Robert Steward who would secure the earldom of Atholl for himself by 1342. Undeniably, Strathbogie – head of a kin experienced in changing sides for its own benefit – seems to have been able to play on emerging divisions in the Bruce guardianship. For according to Fordun's Fife source, Strathbogie arrived at the Dairsie parliament – really a war council – in April 1335 with:

> A great force . . . [and] . . . by reason of the latter's insolence nothing was there done worthy of aught but scorn. This man [Strathbogie] cleaved to Stewart, who was then not governed by much wisdom, and, looking down upon the earl of Moray, became very troublesome to all who were there.[47]

---

46 *RRS*, vi, no. 11; *Chron. Fordun*, i, 358; *Chron. Bower*, vii, 107. A. Ross, 'Men for all Seasons? The Strathbogie Earls of Atholl and the Wars of Independence. Part 2 – Earl David IV (1307–35)', *Northern Scotland*, 21 (2001), 1–15, at 6–7, notes that in August 1335, Strathbogie issued a charter styled as earl of Atholl and constable of Scotland witnessed by the Steward, Randolph, Patrick earl of March and Andrew Murray (NAS GD 50/130/6) and that in 1376 Robert II (Robert Steward) restored Strathbogie to the Gordon family in a charter which recorded Guardian Andrew Murray's grant of these lands to David Strathbogie [*RMS*, i, no. 566]: however, this restoration of Strathbogie's lands may have been promised by John Randolph prior to Andrew Murray's release from England in summer 1334 and Randolph's own capture in August 1335. Strathbogie was forfeited of his English lands by Edward III in February 1335 (*CPR 1334–38*, 61, 81, 84, 89).

47 *Chron. Fordun*, i, 358–9. This is very reminiscent of the fractious meeting of the Guardians at Peebles in 1299 when the parties of Robert Bruce and John Comyn came to blows over dynastic loyalty (Barrow, *Bruce*, 107; M. Penman, *The Scottish Civil War* (Stroud 2002), 11–2, 52–4).

Such late fourteenth-century chronicle criticism of the Steward's role in the 1330s was undoubtedly coloured by his later conflict with the Bruce crown. But it is possible that Strathbogie had already offered the as yet unwed and childless Robert Steward a deal guaranteeing his family lands if he submitted to Balliol and Edward III. Strathbogie was descended from a third son of a mid-thirteenth-century earl of Fife and had a claim to that earldom in the event of the main line's extinction: thus his close association or 'cleaving' with the Steward at the 1335 gathering, held in Fife, may have involved promises over that earldom and earl Duncan's unwed heiress, Isabella, then in English ward, perhaps even in Strathbogie's control.[48] If, as Alisdair Ross has suggested, Strathbogie (who was eldest male heir to both the Comyns and the Balliols after 1333) could table offers to the Steward in 1335 which extended to some deal about the Scottish kingship itself, the resulting tension may have been even greater. Thus Atholl may have been able to exploit the Steward's concerns about the presence of a Bruce royal army in Fife as well as his growing fear that David's closest advisers wanted both the Steward's replacement in the short-term in favour of a Lieutenant more directly answerable to the court in Château Gaillard, and in the long-term the Stewarts as a whole removed from the royal succession.[49]

This aim of ousting Robert Steward as Lieutenant is certainly suggested by an exchequer audit report intromitted to David's government sometime in 1337 in Aberdeen by the then deputy Chamberlain, Andrew Buttergask, whose brother Adam, a cleric, on occasion served as an envoy to and from Gaillard. Andrew, who was also deputy justiciar to Randolph as justiciar north of Forth, asserted that in 1334–5 he could not collect the few burgh customs of Aberdeen, accessible to the Bruce party and assigned to the exiled royal household, because of a dispute between the Steward and the earl of Moray. The Steward had sent in his own collector, his cousin, Sir Robert

---

48 According to Sir Thomas Gray, Isabella of Fife would marry for love Sir William de Felton, a Northumberland knight (*Chron. Scalacronica*, 126). Felton undoubtedly served in Edward III's armies in Scotland after 1333, doing a stint as keeper of Roxburgh and as justiciar of occupied Scotland about 1347 (*Rot. Scot.*, i, 696–7; J.S. Roskell, L. Clark & C. Rawcliffe, *The History of Parliament: the House of Commons, 1386–1421* (4 vols., London 1993), ii, 289). The Strathbogies had lands in Northumberland and elsewhere in England. As late as 1360 these included the manor of Felton (which had also once belonged to the Balliols), for in that year – the same year Isabella of Fife wed Robert Steward's second son, Walter Stewart, as her second husband – the lands of Felton were given to Aymer of Atholl, brother of David (II) Strathbogie, IV earl of Atholl (d. 1335): Aymer had two daughters, Isabella and Maria, emphasising the family's closeness to Maria de Monthermer and the Fife line (NRO 76 ZSW Swinburne Mss (Part 1) 3/11–3 and 5/54–58; NRO Newcastle 358/ 1–46 Riddell Mss/7; J.C. Hodgson, *A History of Northumberland* (15 vols., Newcastle 1893–1940), vii, 85, 113–6, 232–40; *Scots Peerage*, i, 420–30).
49 Ross, 'Men for all Seasons? Part 2', 9.

Menzies, an Atholl knight (who would fight in Strathbogie's force at Culblean in late 1335). Buttergask had also been unable to collect income from the royal thanage of Aboyne in Aberdeenshire (which Robert I had given to Sir Alexander Fraser) because the Steward had given these lands to Menzies after forfeiting them from Reginald More, the royal Chamberlain, who had returned from France to be accused by the Steward of submitting to Balliol in 1332.[50]

To make these messy, bitter matters worse, the Steward had illegally collected £40 from the custumars of Aberdeen at a time when David's court in exile was stepping up moves to ensure that revenue from the north-east – as well as supplies like saleable wool, flour, wine, salmon and furnishings – had a direct line through that region of Scotland and across the sea to Gaillard via trusted crown agents. Also in April 1335, Adam, bishop of Brechin, stepped down as Chancellor in favour of layman Thomas Charteris, a former clerk of the audit for King Robert and the grandson of a Chancellor for Alexander III and the early Guardians (d. 1302). As a Perthshire and Berwickshire knight with such connections Charteris would have been better placed to enforce the duties and the collection of revenues for this key office: that he would serve John Randolph as the chief representative of the crown at this juncture is suggested by Guardian Thomas Randolph's grant of Perthshire lands to Charteris in 1331 and the latter's family origins in Annandale.[51] Charteris would clearly be expected to oversee the port of Aberdeen which was to fulfil the same vital lifeline role as it had done for King Robert's war effort after 1308. Over the course of the four years after 1337 an Alexander Cragbarry and Robert Keith, the Marischal, served as successive sheriffs of Aberdeen and as envoys to Gaillard. In 1336–7 the income of the neighbouring regality of Moray was collected by Maurice Grant, a Randolph man but also sheriff of Inverness; in 1339 Randolph's deputies, Andrew Buttergask and William Meldrum, held justice ayres in Elgin and Aberdeen.[52]

50 *ER*, i, cl–cli, 435–6; D.P. Menzies, *The Red and White Book of Menzies* (Glasgow 1894), 69–71. About 1333–5 David II's seals had been used to confirm Robert Menzies' lands of Cranach (near Loch Tay) given to him originally by David Strathbogie, earl of Atholl.

51 *ER*, i, 35–49, 113–4, 149–50, 207–8, 213–4, 235, 462; *RRS*, vi, nos. 5, 6, 18; Watt, *Scottish Graduates*, 85–6. A Patrick Charteris had also witnessed a Thomas Randolph grant to John Stewart, earl of Angus, in 1331 (W. Fraser ed., *The Douglas Book* (4 vols., Edinburgh 1885), iii, x).

52 *ER*, i, 436, 439, 440–7, 450, 465 (account by Reginald More for David in France certified by those with the king in Gaillard); *RMS*, i, App. ii no. 761. A justice ayre had been held in Lothian in 1333. At Halidon Hill in 1333, the division of Thomas (II) Randolph, earl of Moray, had contained several members of the Grants on Spey; about 1333 John Randolph made John le Grant keeper of Darnaway castle near Forres; Robert I had granted the Grants the lands of Iverallan in Strathspey (W. Fraser ed., *The Chiefs of Grant* (3 vols., Edinburgh 1883), i, 22–37).

By the Dairsie parliament of April 1335, then, Robert Steward was at odds with the man who was probably co-guardian, John Randolph, and presumably with other members of David's government; they were fighting over control of the direction of the war and crown resources. Allied to this, the north-east had become the battlefield for dispute between local rivals, with David Strathbogie laying claim not only to his own former lands but to neighbouring southern Moray and the northern Perthshire holdings of the Fife earls at Strathord, Strathtay and Strath Braan, while the Steward surely sniffed around the earldom he would eventually secure by 1342, Atholl. Mar, too, with the minor Earl Thomas in England along with the captive Andrew Murray of Bothwell and Garioch (until the second half of 1334), had been up for grabs (and had even proved a source of friction between Strathbogie and Edward Balliol).[53] The vacant role of adult king to lead the Scottish war effort may also have been thrown into the mix. As a result, numerous points of conflict and other personal animosities must have erupted at the Dairsie war 'parliament'. Wyntoun's source asserts that Strathbogie was the real trouble-maker there and that he aimed to slay Sir William Douglas of Lothian, an adherent of Randolph, who accused Strathbogie of keeping him (Douglas) in captivity too long before release. But this chronicle statement itself may have been designed to deflect historical attention from the fact that David's close counsellors desired the removal of the Steward as Lieutenant and heir presumptive.

The intention had probably been to replace Robert with Sir Andrew Murray of Bothwell and Garioch, David II's uncle, who had been Guardian briefly before his capture in 1333 and whose wife held Kildrummy castle in Mar. According to Fordun's source, open conflict between the Steward and Randolph at the 1335 assembly was only avoided by the mediation of Douglas of Lothian, Alexander Mowbray (a conspirator against King Robert in 1320 who had now defected away from Balliol) and Andrew Murray, who had been released about July 1334. Sometime in the period 1334–7 the Scottish exchequer had certainly been authorised to hand over £1,000, originally intended for King Robert's marble tomb at Dunfermline, as ransom for Murray.[54]

As events transpired, however, the Steward – rather like Robert Bruce himself who quit as co-Guardian alongside his enemy John Comyn of Badenoch about 1300 – jumped before he was pushed and acted to protect his own interests.[55] By 24 August 1335, David Strathbogie had defected

---

53 *Chron. Fordun*, i, 357; Ross, 'Men for all Seasons? Part 2', 6.
54 *ER*, i, 450–1. Interestingly, Fordun's source states that this parliament was attended by 'Robert Steward, and the Earl of Moray, then guardian [n.b. singular] of Scotland'. This may, though, be a retrospective pro-David II attempt to further blacken the Steward's name (*Chron. Fordun*, i, 358).
55 Sayles, 'The Guardians of Scotland and a Parliament at Rutherglen in 1300', 245–50.

back to Edward III and Balliol. These royal partners had brought a joint army to Perth: by September Strathbogie was restored as Balliol's warden in the north and charged with receiving Scots defectors into his peace. But at the same time as his own switch Strathbogie had brokered a submission deal for Robert Steward which secured his western family lands. However, later evidence hints that this transfer might also have involved a deal whereby the Steward would marry Isabella, heiress to Fife, then in the ward of her grandfather, Ralph de Monthermer, earl of Gloucester, a man from whom Strathbogie's father had had to recover his own earldom of Atholl in 1307 (after it had been forfeited by Edward I). The formidable presence of Edward III at Perth and a simultaneous sea-borne attack on the Clyde by Anglo-Balliol supporters from Ireland may have further induced the Steward to surrender on such good terms.[56]

But Robert Steward may have quickly regretted his pragmatic actions. Initially, the tide did seem to be turning strongly against the Bruce Scots. Sometime in May, June or July 1335, John Randolph was obliged to visit Tarbert Castle in an attempt to secure an alliance with John MacDonald of the Isles whom Abbot Bower would rightly describe as 'too well disposed to the English': MacDonald would ally himself with Balliol and England by September 1335 in return for promises over lands including Skye, many other isles and the ward of Lochaber. However, Randolph's unlucky capture by English forces in early August 1335 would have left the field clearer for the Steward as sole Lieutenant. Yet now it only paved the way for the re-election, by a council at Dunfermline, of the elder Guardian whom David's administration surely really wanted and badly needed, Andrew Murray of Garioch and Bothwell.

As Lieutenant, Murray was able to score a quick and famous victory over David Strathbogie's forces at Culblean in Aberdeenshire on 30 November

---

56 CDS, iii, no. 1174; *Chron. Scalacronica*, 99, 100–1; *Adae Murimuth (1275–1347) Continuato Chronicum Robertus de Avesbury de Gestis Mirabilibus Edwardii Tertii*, ed. E.M. Thompson (London 1889), 299–301. There is further proof to suggest that the Steward did defect at this time: his Chancellor, one Nigel Carruthers, a canon of Glasgow, was given a safe-conduct to England on 10 October 1335 (*Rot. Scot.*, i, 382). Sometime that year the Steward granted a charter at Restenneth Abbey in Angus witnessed by the knights Godfrey de Ros, Robert Lauder, John Rattray, Hugh Gourlay and Thomas Fauside: Ros had been Balliol's sheriff of Ayr until his capture by Stewart forces in 1334 but by January 1336 Ros had joined Eustace Maxwell of Caerlaverock as a conservator of the truce for Edward III (*Registrum Honoris de Morton* (2 vols., Edinburgh 1853), ii, 33–4; W. Fraser ed., *The Book of Caerlaverock: the Memoirs of the Maxwells, Earls of Nithsdale, Lords Maxwell and Herries* (2 vols., Edinburgh 1873), i, 102–3). Ros and Gourlay were forfeited by David II in 1341–2 for serving England (*RMS*, i, App. ii nos. 854, 904); Rattray was the son of Eustace, one of the Soules conspiracy suspects of 1320; the aged Lauder dotted back and forth between camps c. 1334–5 (*Rot. Scot.*, i, 271, 385–6).

1335. The twenty-six-year-old Atholl earl may now have been viewed by Edward III as the most likely candidate for a future vassal Scottish kingship but Strathbogie was intent first of all on prosecuting a vicious local war. However, once trapped by Murray's host in the forest lands controlling the passes from Mar and Garioch through to Banffshire and Moray, Strathbogie was slain and the north-east overrun by David II's party.[57] Some of the Steward's associates who had elected to follow Strathbogie in what was essentially a local war – for example, Sir Robert Menzies – were now captured but freed to rejoin the Bruce cause along with other prominent waverers like Patrick Dunbar, earl of March (who was embittered after an English attack on his person and his Northumberland lands in 1334). But after Culblean – with his deal with Strathbogie a dead letter – the Steward could only lie low as *persona non grata* with both camps. Evidence of Robert Steward's whereabouts over the next three years only surfaces once, placing him at Seton in Lothian in September 1337 acting merely as a quiet witness to an act by knights closer to David's court, like Alexander Seton.[58]

Culblean was a morale-boosting triumph for the Bruce cause. But what really tipped the scales in favour of David's supporters in Scotland was the drift towards actual rather than phoney war between Edward III and Philip VI and their armed kingdoms. The 1330s have long been underestimated as a period when in fact the auld alliance operated at its most stubborn and sustained level. French cash and supplies arrived in Scotland fairly regularly, and after 1335 there was at least the believable threat of joint Franco-Scottish military action. Sometime in 1334–5 a number of French and Flemish knights may have made reconnaissance in Scotland, among them Arnoul d'Audrehen, sire d'Aubigny, a future Maréchal for the French crown, and Eugene de Garancières. The latter may have welcomed David and his party to France in 1334 in the company of Charles de Montmorency, who would act as Philip VI's Maréchal at the battle of Créci in 1346: both these French knights would lead an expedition of over 1,000 French troops to Scotland in 1355.[59] What contact these knights may have had with David's court after 1334 is uncertain. But while moves were afoot in mid-

---

57 *CDS*, iii, pp. 322, 374–5, nos. 1171–2 [Randolph], 1182 (MacDonald); *Chron. Fordun*, i, 358–9 (' . . . the great tyranny and cruelty this Earl of Atholl practised among the people words cannot bring within the mind's grasp; some he disinherited, others he murdered; and, in the end, he cast in his mind how he might wipe all the freeholders from off the face of the earth'); *Chron. Bower*, vii, 111; Ross, 'Men for all Seasons? Part 2', 6–13. Murray must have been elected Guardian at a council shortly before or after the battle of Culblean.

58 BL Harley MSS 4693/f. 8, 13b (charter to Alexander Seton, 8 September 1337).

59 *Rot. Scot.*, i, 323, 327; *Chronique de Jean le Bel*, i, 274; *Oeuvres de Froissart*, ii, 528–37; *ER*, i, 450–4 – Garancières stayed at Aberdeen in 1335 where he had to pay for fire damage to a house.

1335 to change the Lieutenancy in Scotland, the Scots in exile secured vocal support for their cause from the hugely influential local prelate of Château Gaillard, Pierre Roger, the archbishop of Rouen, president of Philip VI's Chambre des Comptes (Treasury) and soon to be Pope Clement VI (1342–53): in July 1335, Roger announced to the French court that some 6,000 French troops, including 1,000 men-at-arms, were to be sent to aid the Scots.[60]

Without a final break with Edward III, however, the French were reluctant to make good this bold promise straight away. Some joint Franco-Scottish privateering was conducted in the English Channel in 1335 but Philip preferred to help broker Anglo-Scottish truces. In the second half of 1335 the Scots had been able to secure ceasefires for days or weeks at a time for themselves through clear co-operation between their Scottish and French leaders.[61] But it required intervention by the French crown and two Cardinal envoys from the Pope in the winter of 1335–6 to secure a long Anglo-Scottish truce between 26 January and 30 December 1336. Andrew Murray was obliged to halt his sieges of Lochindorb (Moray) and Cupar (Fife) castles and relay to David's court details of a strange peace package. This was an offer tabled by Pope Boniface's Cardinals in an attempt to save the Crusade – it involved a full Anglo-Scottish peace with Edward Balliol elevated as King of Scots to be wed to Joan of the Tower with David Bruce as his heir, divorced but compensated with English lands. Even though there would have been a fair chance of David succeeding to the Scottish throne thereafter as Balliol was fifty-three, he would be an English vassal: this plan was instantly rejected by the Gaillard court.[62]

But the momentum of Culblean threw up some equally remarkable non-peace plans. Philip VI's crusade was officially cancelled on 13 March 1336.

60 Sumption, *Hundred Years War*, i, 145–6; J. Campbell, 'England, Scotland and the Hundred Years War in the Fourteenth-century', in J. Hale, R. Highfield and B. Smalley eds, *Europe in the Late Middle Ages* (London 1965), 184–216, 190. John de Pilmor, whom David II would make bishop of Moray, became a clerk of the archbishop of Rouen in the 1330s (Watt, *Scottish Graduates*, 450–1).

61 Sumption, *Hundred Years War*, i, 146–7. On 22 February 1335, French ambassadors received a safe-conduct from Edward III to enter Scotland; thirty Scots were granted passage to talks with English and French ambassadors at Newark on 22 March. In late October 1335, Andrew Murray and Robert Lauder attended talks at Bathgate in West Lothian. In November they were joined, first, at Berwick by Thomas Charteris, Andrew Douglas and the cleric John Craig; and second, at Newcastle by William Keith and William Douglas of Lothian. In December forty Scots were to meet French and Papal envoys at Berwick, including Murray, John Wishart bishop of Glasgow, John abbot of Coupar Angus, Thomas Fingask, John Monypenny, Lauder, Robert Keith, John Craig and William Douglas (*Rot. Scot.*, i, 323, 327, 385–6, 388, 390–1; *Foedera*, iv, 676–7.)

62 PRO E39/11; *Rot. Scot.*, i, 395, 397–8, 410, 417, 431; *Foedera*, i, 930; Sumption, *Hundred Years War*, i, 154.

Sometime in late 1335 or early 1336, though, plans were prepared for a huge French expeditionary force to Scotland. Rauol de Brienne, Comte d'Eu to the north of Rouen and Gaillard, was to lead 1,200 men-at-arms, 5,000 archers and 20,000 infantry, transported by almost 300 ships already victualled for the Crusade, to land on the Scottish east coast. All of the officials whom Philip VI appointed to organise this armada – Barthélemy du Drac, Jean de Cangé, Gilbert Poulin and the bailies of Rouen, Caen and Caux – hailed from Normandy. This must have given David's resident court scope for considerable input to this armada.[63]

Yet these plans do seem incredible. The cost to the French treasury was projected at a minimum of 180,000 livres, two-thirds of Philip's annual income. This surely underestimated grossly the cost of resupplying and transferring ships from southern ports even though many vessels had already been moved to face the mounting English threat: new war galleys would also have to be built. Although many French knights and esquires may have sought a chance for glory, there must have been tremendous opposition in France to such costly aid for a weaker ally which would provoke Edward III.[64]

Nonetheless, after Scottish envoys at Lyon in late March 1336 had reminded Philip VI of his promises to Scotland, this invasion plan does seem to have been put in motion – or steps taken to give that illusion as disinformation. By late May to early June there were strong fears in Westminster of a descent from Scotland on the northern English counties. According to Edward III's intelligence, the Scots were to be led by two of David's council at Gaillard, Alexander Seton and Walter Twynham, while the French were to make a simultaneous diversionary raid on Portsmouth: it was reported that seamen and their 300 transports and thirty galleys had assembled at Harfleur and arms were being made and stockpiled all along the French coast.[65]

63 AN P. 14/73–74 (the full inventory of men, arms and supplies of the plan) and JJ 74/
    4892. Philip VI gave the Comte d'Eu some 4,000 livres in 1343 as compensation for
    the lands he held in Ireland and England of Edward III which he had felt sure he
    would lose because of the planned expedition to Scotland, for which Eu states he left
    – probably to reconnoitre – in December 1335 (BN Nouv. Acq. fr. 9236).
64 Sumption, *Hundred Years War*, i, 156–61. A similar French invasion plan to invade
    England with over 200 ships would be rumoured in 1340 [C. de la Roncière,
    Histoire de la Marine Française (2 vols., Paris 1899–1900), i, 421–44].
65 BL Cotton Vesp. F VIII f. 11; PRO SC 37/137 [5 May 1336] and SC 1/39/32 [19
    July 1336]; *Rot. Scot.*, i, 420–1, 446 [June 1336]; Sumption, *Hundred Years War*, i,
    159. *Les Grandes Chroniques*, ix, 153, asserts that Philip VI held a *parlement* at
    Avignon in 1336 at which it was decided to help the Scots against England;
    however, no taxation was levied by that assembly. Alexander Seton did return
    to Scotland sometime before September 1337 [see n 58 above]: in December that
    year he issued a charter at Seton in Lothian witnessed by Patrick, earl of March,
    Alexander Ramsay of Dalhousie and Henry Preston, 'sheriff of Lothian' [G. Seton,
    A History of the Family of Seton (2 vols., Edinburgh 1896), ii, 844].

Such a military threat must have seemed all the more real in the light of the progress made since Culblean by Andrew Murray and other young, aggressive Scottish commanders. They had cleared most of Scotland north of Tay of Anglo-Balliol occupation and attempted sieges of the garrisons of Perth and Edinburgh. In response, Edward III decided to cut off the likely landing zone of any French army, the north-east. This was a decisive display of force. By 23 July 1336, the English army had reached the cathedral burgh of Elgin and relieved Strathbogie's widow from siege in Lochindorb Castle. Edward then wasted the earldom of Moray and much of Aberdeenshire and burned the burgh of Aberdeen: south-west Scotland was also devastated by English troops.[66] Yet despite these herschips the English king could not re-occupy these regions on a permanent basis, and as late as 24 August 1336 his government was still fearful of a French expedition. But French plans, if any, had already had to be aborted as Philip looked to his own defences.[67]

Nonetheless, the French alliance had not been – as one historian has suggested – a 'total failure' for Scotland.[68] With Edward's withdrawal and, after April 1337, his open declaration of war against France, the Bruce Scots were left to push back a sorely reduced Anglo-Balliol presence in Scotland. As Fordun's source had it: 'happily for the kingdom of Scotland [there] was begun a very fearful war between the Kings of England and France'. Many of the Disinherited English knights followed their Plantagenet lord to the continent, leaving Balliol a sad, aging frontier commander without title or wife. In pursuit of Gascony and the French crown Edward III was forced to fall back on contingencies for containing his northern border such as an alliance with MacDonald of the Isles or more general truce and peace talks: the latter were initiated without result in September 1336, July and October 1337 and April 1338.[69] In the meantime, there was little King Edward could do to block continued French aid to David's men. In mid-1337 two ships from Flanders were captured en route to Scotland. On board were the wives and children of Scottish magnates, John, bishop of Glasgow and David's clerks, Walter Moffat

---

66 *Rot. Scot.*, i, 446; *Chron. Fordun*, i, 360–1; *Chron. Wyntoun*, vi, 76–8; *Chron. Bower*, vii, 119–25; G.W.S. Barrow, 'The Wood of Stronkalter: a Note on the Relief of Lochindorb Castle by Edward III in 1336', *SHR*, xlvi (1967), 77–9.

67 R. M. Haines, *Calendar of the Register of Simon de Montacute, Bishop of Worcester, 1334–7* (Worcester 1996), no. 1027. *CCR*, ii, 702 states that at this time Edward had agreed to 'treat with David de Brus concerning truces and final peace . . . and now the king of France and the Scots refused to consent to the affairs begun by the said envoys, and the king of France publicly asserts that he wishes to favour the Scots as much as he can, and causes galleys and ships to be sent against the king and his realm'.

68 B. Webster, 'Scotland without a King, 1329–41', in Grant and Stringer, eds., *Medieval Scotland*, 223–38, at 232.

69 *Rot. Scot.*, i, 449, 455, 463, 518–9; *Acts of the Lords of the Isles*, 1–4; McDonald, *The Kingdom of the Isles*, ch. 9.

and Thomas Fingask. The bishop apparently died defending his reported cargo of £30,000 of silver and 'charters, conventions and indentures which had been concluded between the king of France and the Scots'.[70]

But the Scots were by now more than holding their own without active French intervention. Late 1336 had seen Murray's forces devastate much of Scotland just north of Forth, compounding a war of attrition in which 'through the ceaseless marauding of both sides, the whole land of Gowrie, Angus and Mearns was, for the most part, reduced to a hopeless wilderness, and to utter want'. By March 1337 Murray had penetrated into Fife 'where he levelled with the ground [earl Duncan's] tower of Falkland, plundered the land everywhere around, took the inhabitants prisoners, and put them up for ransom': the garrisons of nearby Leuchars and St Andrews were also overrun, followed swiftly by Murray's own stout castle at Bothwell in Lanarkshire. Into the summer, as Edward III struggled to prepare a Channel invasion fleet and to buy allies against Philip on the continent, William Douglas besieged Berwick-upon-Tweed briefly. The English burgh garrisons of Perth and Stirling were also harried while their hinterlands renewed their loyalty to Bruce. Between January and June 1338, 'Black Agnes' Randolph, wife of Earl Patrick of March, resisted stoically the English siege of Dunbar Castle, the southern-most Bruce stronghold: 'thereupon followed, on the part of both English and Scots, the wholesale destruction of Lothian'. Annual parliaments or councils, partial exchequer audits and patchy justice ayres would also resume in Bruce Scotland at this time. After the failure of Anglo-Scottish peace talks in April 1338 the Scots would entertain no further offers for two years: according to Fordun's source, only Cupar and Perth remained to be recovered north of the river Forth.[71]

However, in April 1338 there was a significant change in the Scottish Guardianship and a loss of the single-mindedness displayed in the Bruce cause since 1335. Andrew Murray died of a sudden illness or wounds received after a herschip of the Lothians and a siege of Edinburgh castle. He would later be interred in Dunfermline Abbey close to his Bruce kin.[72] But Murray's office was to be filled for a second time by Robert Steward.

---

70 *Chron. Lanercost*, 287, 305, which also claimed that David had done homage to
     Philip VI about this time; Watt, *Scottish Graduates*, 400–1. Such was the Scottish
     momentum by 1337 that Froissart later dated the 20,000-man expedition planned
     in 1335 to the 1337 campaign season (P. Contamine, 'Froissart and Scotland', in
     G.G. Simpson, ed., *Scotland and the Low Countries, 1124–1994* (East Linton
     1997), 43–58).
71 *Chronique de Quatre Premiers Valois, 1327–93*, ed. S. Lucé (Paris 1862), 31–2;
     quotes from *Chron. Fordun*, i, 361–3; *Chron. Wyntoun*, vi, 100–154; *Chron.
     Bower*, vii, 137–51. Loch Leven Castle in Fife may also have fallen to the Scots
     about this time – William Douglas of Lothian's brother, John, was keeper there by
     October 1339 (*RRS*, vi, no. 17).
72 *Chron. Fordun*, i, 363.

'An old man in his deeds': Steward Guardianship, 1338–41

By summer of 1338, the Steward's position had altered drastically. He was now twenty-two – still very young – and the father of at least two sons. He had not married his partner, Elizabeth More – and was perhaps holding out in hope of marrying the heiress to Fife: but more offspring by More would follow. Most of the Stewart family lands had also been recovered. David Strathbogie of Atholl was dead and John Randolph, earl of Moray, had been an English captive for three years. The wasting of the Scottish nobility in battle since 1332 meant that Andrew Murray's death left the Steward as really the only clear provincial magnate of royal blood who could lead the cause, at least in central and south-western Scotland. The Steward thus had a unique opportunity to advance his own fortunes in the king's absence. His interference in crown finances in 1334–5 had been scrutinised in 1337 but these resources were once more open to him.

Nonetheless, it is likely that the Steward's election as Lieutenant in a Council of autumn 1338 – or his brazen assumption of that role – did not meet with the approval of David's close counsel in France. It probably also met with minimal respect from many of the young Scottish knights with their own local followings who had begun to make a name for themselves in Bruce service. Abbot Bower – earnestly trying to salvage the Steward's career in retrospect from criticism levelled by David and his supporters – described the Steward as a man of mature wisdom and his second lieutenancy as a time when:

> he travelled through each province, accepting everyone who had adhered to the English to be loyal to King David and scrutinised everywhere the customs and deeds of his compatriots; and to prevent the poor from suffering malicious prosecution by the powerful, he diligently made enquiries to curb them. Then the kingdom began to prosper, the farmers to cultivate the fields, the church of God to be respected, monks to resume His service and be restored to their former state . . .[73]

In reality, however, the Steward's influence may have been limited to nominal oversight of prolonged but in the end successful sieges of Perth and Stirling and the occasional parliament with uncertain agendas, whilst local men prosecuted their private frontier wars against their Scottish neighbours and English troops unhindered.

However, although he enjoyed little national success the Steward was not slow to plant his own flag in central Scotland's ancient earldoms. Just as

---

73 *Chron. Bower*, vii, 145. Edward Balliol seems to have led an abortive attempt to relieve Perth sometime in 1338–9 (PRO SC 1/42 nos. 94–5).

Guardian Archibald Douglas had done, the Steward may also have tried to take control of the vacant lordship of Liddesdale in the marches. But closer to his Clydeside heartlands, in October 1339 – two months after the fall of Perth – the Steward oversaw a parliamentary assize which found Malise, eighth earl of Strathearn, innocent of both treason and the 'surrender of his earldom to Edward Balliol'.[74] By overseeing this decision in parliament the Steward may have hoped to establish a legal precedent which would protect his own holdings from royal forfeiture as punishment for his brief defection to Edward III and Balliol in 1335 as well as the lands of other waverers such as Duncan, earl of Fife. The Steward clearly had designs on the valuable lands of Strathearn – a title we shall see he would finally secure by 1357: but he may already have come to an understanding with earl Malise and his co-heiresses in 1339.

Malise's pardon, however, was clearly not the result desired by David's government. As a young adult reinstalled in his kingdom, David II would find cause to reopen the trial of Strathearn in 1344. In 1341–2, as we shall see, David would also try, unsuccessfully, to block the Steward's claim to the vacant earldom of Atholl, the northern Perthshire province bordering on Strathearn (and lordships owned by the earls of Fife) which the Steward must have moved in on decisively between 1335 (Culblean) and 1341, forging close associations with *Clann Donnchaid* (the Robertsons) and other mili-tarised Atholl *cateran* kindreds. Furthermore, after 1341 David would also try – with greater success – to poach the loyalty of Maurice Murray of Drumsargard, a cousin and Lanarkshire adherent of the Steward in the later 1330s: in 1339 the Steward may have helped Maurice secure marriage to Joanna, sister of Sir John Menteith of Arran, Knapdale and Strathgartney (the large lordship between Menteith and Strathearn). John Menteith was a Stewart cadet and descendant of the earls of Menteith (through which earldom he might also lay claim to the earldom of Fife by a tailzie of 1309): in addition, Joanna of Menteith was already widow successively of Malise, seventh earl of Strathearn, and John Campbell, earl of Atholl (d. 1333), son of Neil of Lochawe and Mary Bruce. Yet after 1341 David would recognise Maurice Murray as earl of Strathearn and Sir John Graham of Abercorn as earl of Menteith: this was royal favour which clearly snubbed Steward designs hatched in the previous decade. It is also logical to assume that after 1338 the Steward advanced his interest in the earldom of Fife – as he had tried to do in 1335 – and on the sad, lonely and aging Earl Duncan of Fife's Perthshire baronies of Strathtay, Strath Braan and Strathord. The

---

74 J.M. Thomson, ed., 'A Roll of the Scottish Parliament, 1344', *SHR*, ix (1912), 235–40; *RRS*, vi, no. 17 (*RPS*, 1339/1). Malise had surrendered Strathearn to Edward III so that it could be granted to John de Warenne, earl of Surrey (*CDS*, iii, no. 1119).

Steward would be bailie of these lands for Duncan by 1345–6, in theory creating a massive Stewart regality of influence across central Scotland.[75]

But as well as stoking up trouble in a complex chess game against the crown for the future, the Steward's territorial plans brought him into conflict with other ambitious magnates before 1341. Wyntoun's source reports that at the siege of Perth in 1339 the Steward led one division while others were led by Maurice Murray, William Douglas and William, the new earl of Ross:

> Bot of Rose the Erl Williame,
> With his court fra hym passit hayme,
> Thai, that at the asseigis hay,
> Fast wer bikkerande ilka day . . .

The Steward's quarrel with Ross may have stemmed from the earl's assumption of Randolph's vacant office of justiciar north of Forth. In 1339 Ross held justice ayres at Cupar in Fife and, perhaps, at Perth. The Steward and Ross were surely also embroiled in an escalating feud for control of Kintyre on the Argyll coast, a dispute which would not be settled until a Steward-Ross marriage was made in 1355. But the most likely source of trouble between the two lords was the fate of Strathearn: as we shall see, by 1344, Ross would have been named as guardian of Malise of Strathearn's second daughter and sought to advance her claim to her father's lands. Steward-Ross antipathy in central Scotland may, though, have begun in the late 1330s. According to local traditions, about 1341, the large Perthshire barony of Strathardle – bordering on north-western Atholl – was wasted by the Munros, adherents of the Ross earls. Strathardle had been granted by King Robert to his sheriff of Perth, John, a native of the lands of Inchmartin in the same shire (d. *c.* 1332), a descendant of a bastard son of Earl David of Huntingdon and thus a cousin of the Bruces: Inchmartin was also a follower of Duncan of Fife and had submitted to Balliol alongside that earl in 1332.[76]

In the wake of intense recent fighting such land competition was perhaps

75 Boardman, *Early Stewart Kings*, 1–15; *RRS*, v, no. 72 with detailed discussion of the 1309 tailzie and some of the Atholl, Menteith and Fife links.

76 *Chron. Wyntoun*, 134–5; *Registrum de Dunfermlyn* (Edinburgh 1842), 259, for Ross as justiciar; for John Randolph's man, Andrew Buttergask, as deputy justiciar at Elgin on 10 October 1337, see W. Cramond, ed., *The Records of Elgin, 1284–1800* (2 vols., Aberdeen 1903), i, 12; *ER*, i, 102 and *Chron. Lanercost*, 102 for Inchmartin; for Strathardle see Grant, 'Thanes and Thanages', 78. For the earl of Ross in Norway and the Kintyre feud, see J.R. Ross, *The Great Clan of Ross* (Toronto 1972), 55–6, and Mackenzie, *A History of the Mackenzies*, 49–59. For the Munros, see BL Add MSS 19,797 f.3, Papers of the Duke of Argyll in 1756 and A. Mackenzie, *A History of the Munros of Foulis* (Inverness 1898). A share of the Munros' spoils was demanded by the Mackintoshes who were also rivals of the Camerons who had been in the Steward's division at Halidon Hill in 1333 (A. M. Mackintosh, *The Mackintoshes and Clan Chattan* (Edinburgh 1903), 4–39; A. Mackenzie, *A History of the Camerons* (Inverness 1884), 13).

inevitable. According to Fordun's source, Murray's guardianship had seen 'all the country he marched through . . . reduced to such desolation and distress, that more perished afterwards through starvation and want, than the sword devoured in time of war'.[77] The dwindling tenantry and slump in rents must also have heightened conflict over vacant land. But Robert Steward and William of Ross were not the only magnates to take advantage of this wartime power vacuum. John MacDonald continued to eat into the island and mainland interests of the Macdougalls, MacRuaridhs and Randolphs, from Islay to Lochaber, after Balliol's confirmation to the self-styled 'Lord of the Isles' of many of these lands.[78] But in the south, lesser men, far more warlike and personally energetic than the Steward with his vast network of tenants, exploited an attractive and thrusting style of 'military lordship' to carve out their own territorial jursidictions and military followings.

These 'flowers of chivalry' were headed by William Douglas of Lothian, the former Randolph adherent and cousin of the 'Good' Sir James, and Alexander Ramsay of Dalhousie, also in Lothian. Both men had fought for Andrew Murray at Culblean. Thereafter Douglas battled to fill the void on the marches left by the deaths of Sir James (d. 1330) and his brother, Archibald Douglas (d. 1333) – and the infancy in France of his 'nephew', William, Archibald's son and heir to the Black Douglas regality. This 'knight of Lothian' recovered many of the lands of that shire, Lauderdale and Selkirk, Douglasdale, Liddesdale and Teviotdale and his ascendancy in Scotland was recognised by grants of land in Lothian and Fife from the Steward and Earl Duncan respectively in 1339–40.[79] Alexander Ramsay on the other hand would be celebrated by subsequent generations as a model knight, champion of a 'school' of chivalry to which all the Scottish nobility of the day sent their sons: his Lothian following exploited the vacillation of Patrick, earl of March, to establish Ramsay's control of much of the south-east by 1341 in David's name. A number of lesser Scottish knights and esquires – often in Douglas's and Ramsay's retinues – would be celebrated for their triumphs and defeats in the several violent Anglo-Scottish tournaments which punctuated the short border truces of 1338–41.[80]

The activities of these charismatic men of blood suggest that, by 1340 at

77 *Chron. Fordun*, i, 361–2.
78 *Acts of the Lords of the Isles*, lxi, lxxiv-v.
79 Brown, 'The Development of Scottish Border Lordship, 1332–58', 3–22. In 1339–40, the Steward gave William Douglas the lands of Bondington in Dalkeith, and about 1340 earl Duncan gave Douglas 'Dechmete' in Fife barony (*Registrum Honoris de Morton*, ii, nos. 46, 50). On 21 August 1339, Duncan gave Douglas lands in the Perthshire barony of Kinnoul (NAS GD 150/6).
80 *Chron. Fordun*, i, 365; *Chron. Wyntoun*, vi, 166–8; *Chron. Bower*, vii, 141–3, 153–5; C. Edington, 'The Tournament in Medieval Scotland', in M. Strickland, ed., *Armies, Chivalry and Warfare in Medieval Britain and France* (Stamford 1998), 46–52; J. Barker, *The Tournament in England, 1100–1400* (Woodbridge 1986), 31–40.

least, the battle to recover all Scottish territory from Anglo-Balliol occupation could be won, even though there remained a number of royal residence garrisons – Stirling, Edinburgh, Roxburgh and Berwick – to seize or starve out. There must have been a growing expectation in Scotland that King David, now entering his sixteenth year, would return. As much was inferred by Douglas of Lothian's passage (or passages) to Château Gaillard sometime in 1339–40. According to French chronicler Jean le Bel, Douglas and (sic) John Randolph returned from France in the second half of 1340 with Arnoul d'Audrehen, sire d'Aubigny, and some 200 French troops; the Scottish chroniclers, too, assert that Douglas returned in June 1339 with French knights and ships which aided in the capture of Perth. Certainly, on 8 May 1340 a royal act was issued in King David's name – from Dumbarton Castle – confirming another lesser Scottish lord's grant to Douglas.[81]

This is the first surviving act issued by David apparently acting in his own capacity as king and thus bypassing the Steward as Lieutenant: the Steward witnessed this act along with Patrick, earl of March, Alexander Seton, Malcolm Fleming, William Livingston and Maurice Murray. A second royal act was issued on 24 May from Arbroath, perhaps protecting the abbey and royal chancery there from the Steward's interference in its revenues. Douglas had clearly found a young monarch keen to begin flexing his muscles.[82]

David had grown into his teens in comfortable wardship in a region of France peppered with tombs and shrines dedicated to that scourge of the English crown, the martyr archbishop of Canterbury, Thomas à Beckett (to whom Arbroath Abbey had been dedicated by William I of Scotland in 1175). Anti-English feeling had surely quickly impressed itself upon David as far more relevant than Philip's planned crusade, even though in 1336 the French king may have hinted to the Pope that his Scottish guests had taken the cross and had at least promised to participate.[83] But the periodic mobilisation of the forces and resources of Normandy – on at least one occasion for an expedition to Scotland – must have formed the backdrop to David's own training for manhood and war with England. By late autumn of 1339 he was deemed to be of age and took to the field at Buirenfosse near La Capelle on the northern French marches with Flanders. Flying his own newly-commissioned banners, David and, presumably, a small Scottish contingent joined Philip VI, the kings of Bohemia and Navarre, and – according to Jean Froissart – 'knights without number' in a stand-off against Edward III's army.[84]

81 *Chron. Le Bel*, i, 274–5; *RRS*, vi, 18.
82 *Ibid.*, no. 19.
83 M. Leve, 'Thomas Beckett à Gisors et son culte l'Eure', *Connaissance d'Eure*, nos. 89–90 (1993), 24–5; Tyerman, 'Philip VI and the Recovery of the Holy Land', 48–52.
84 *Oeuvres de Froissart*, iii, 430–5; BN MSS Nouv. Acq. Fr. 9238–9 (Buirenfosse accounts); *ER*, i, 297 banners made for David in France; Sumption, *Hundred Years War*, i, 286–8.

Since he had landed in Flanders in July 1338, the English king – now in his majority at twenty-six years old – had been anxious to bring his French counterpart to battle: crippling debts and the loss of several English garrison towns in Gascony in 1338–9 made this an even greater imperative. The colour, power and majesty of such royal hosts of chivalry arrayed for war cannot have failed to have had a strong effect on the young king of Scots. But when Edward's men dismounted and dug in on high ground at Buirenfosse bounded by archers and trees, the French force declined to fight. Edward III was denied a decisive engagement before his money and allies ran out.

David would thus have to wait until he returned to Scotland to be blooded in battle, although it is likely he took part in some of the tournaments held in France at this time. His occasional presence in Philip's retinue throughout 1339–41 – magnified by his later passion for knight errantry – may even have been enough to win David a place in the chivalric court literature of France.[85] But in 1338–9 David and his courtiers may have had practical influence in procuring French naval raids on southern England as well as French ships and reputable knights to aid the Scots' siege of Perth. It is also known that sometime in 1340 David sent money for masses to be said for his soul at the Dominican Chapter General in Milan, perhaps as a precaution in preparing to put his own life at risk by returning to Scotland.[86] There were several reasons for doing so of which David must have been personally aware by late 1340–early 1341, not merely the Scots' cumulative success in clearing out the enemy.

Most obviously, David and his close counsellors must have had mounting paranoia about the freedom of action of the Steward and other Scottish patriots. The Steward's territorial designs must have been apparent. His interference in royal resources – first investigated under Murray in 1337 –

85 J. Viard, ed., *Itinéraire de Philippe VI de Valois* (Paris 1913), 41–3. *L'Histoire de Trois Nobles Fils de Rois*, a French epic poem – translated into English and known in Scotland by the early fifteenth-century – may have based its character of 'David, prince of Scotland' in part upon the second Bruce king (and the crusading Earl David of Huntingdon, d. 1219), in a tale about the heirs of the Kings of England, Scotland and France who took part in a joint crusade and tournaments against the Turks, marrying each others' sisters at the triumphant close. This fictional David was accompanied by an unnamed '*earl* of Douglas'. William, lord of Douglas (the future first earl of that ilk), also spent his childhood at Gaillard in France until *c.* 1348 and like David would later express an interest in the Crusades – he would also fight at Poitiers in 1356 for the French crown – see below, ch. 6 (*The Three King's Sons*, ed. F.J. Turnivall (2 vols., London 1895); R.L.Graeme-Ritchie, ed., *The Buik of Alexander* (3 vols., Edinburgh 1925), i, xlii-xliii).

86 *CCR 1339–41*, 6, 550–1; Nicholson, *Scotland – the Later Middle Ages*, 138; W. Moir-Bryce, 'The Black Friars of Edinburgh', *BOEC*, iii (1910), 13–104, 40 (Milan).

was confirmed by the exchequer audit of 1340 when it was reported that further monies from Aberdeen's custumars had again been 'wrongfully received by Robert Lauder for the Guardian'. The Steward's personal Chamberlain, David Carruthers, was also at Aberdeen as a customs collector that year alongside David's confessor, Walter Blantyre – now returned from France – with Reginald More, the Chamberlain, and Robert Keith, sheriff of Aberdeen. Clearly David's men and the Steward were again openly competing for control of resources. Separate mandates for fiscal audits issued by both David and the Steward in 1340–1 suggest an awkward division of authority.[87]

Such tensions must have infected Scottish councils or parliaments held at Scone in October 1340 and Dundee in May 1341 – presumably with royal approval – both of which granted small tax contributions, probably of 3d in the £ on all rents. These levies would yield just £1,205 by 1342. Many of Scotland's farm, church and burgh lands were, of course, lying waste. But, as the Bruce Scots' territorial recovery gathered pace, this tax income included monies from Dundee, Linlithgow and Haddington. Extra cash may have been needed to fund the transfer of David and his household from France or for military campaigns to be launched upon his return: David certainly had to borrow petty cash from merchants at Calais in 1341. That his return had been fully expected since May 1341 at the latest is suggested by David's royal letters issued in that month from Château Gaillard – acknowledging receipt of household supplies of wood and pension payments from the French crown; and from Dundee, further protecting the regality of the chancery abbey of Arbroath. The issue of letters from Dundee, moreover, points to David's counsellors in Scotland preparing for his disembarkation on the east coast just north of the mouth of the river Tay.[88]

However, by May 1341, David, now seventeen, had even greater reason to return. In March of that year William Douglas and his men forced Cupar garrison in Fife to surrender and then in April overran Edinburgh Castle using the Robin Hood-like trick of hiding men in supply carts: Douglas's half-brother, another William, became this stronghold's new keeper. Stirling Castle was also by then surrounded by three Scottish divisions and weakening. According to Wyntoun's source and Bower, both writing post-1371, the Steward as Guardian now sent word for the King to return.[89]

87 *ER*, i, 458, 460, 463.

88 *Ibid*, i, clxv, 501, 513–4; *RRS*, vi, nos. 22–5; *APS*, i, 73. Sir William Livingston was sheriff of Haddington by 1340.

89 *Chron. Fordun*, i, 363–4; *Chron. Wyntoun*, vi, 124–44; *Chron. Bower*, vii, 141–9. *Chron. Le Bel*, ii, 280 asserts that the English had given David two months to return to Scotland or else his subjects must do homage to Edward III: this – and the later fifteenth-century assertion that David had done homage to the French for Scotland – surely reflects English propaganda (*Chron. de Melsa*, ii, 373).

But in reality, the Steward must have dreaded David's home-coming, anticipating the crown's likely reversal of his fortunes since 1338. Calls for the king's passage home probably came from friendlier loyalist quarters, from those hopeful of reward or of royal confirmation of their newly-won possessions and status; perhaps Fleming, Douglas of Lothian, Maurice Murray or Ramsay, and perhaps others hoping for John Randolph's recovery (a task the Steward neglected) and respite from the predation of lords like Ross and the Guardian.[90] Yet if David left it any later, he might have no strongholds of note left to recover as an emphatic means of signalling his arrival and reassertion of his personal lordship over Scotland's host. The teenage monarch's presence would be over-shadowed by more experienced warrior knights and the established influence of provincial magnate leaders.

The French, though, must also have been applying pressure for David's return. In January 1340 – egged on by Count Robert of Artois – Edward III had declared himself king of France, and in the summer he launched a fresh invasion of the Low Countries through Boulogne. Philip VI's armies were able to thwart the English siege of Tournai and force Edward to agree to a nine-month truce embracing Flanders, Scotland, Gascony and the seas in September 1340. But the toll on French finance, soldiers, galleys and seamen had been enormous: Philip had also lost much credibility after declining to engage Edward's army for a second time. In even deeper debt and with his European allies deserting, Edward had, though, been forced to return to Westminster in November of that year to again – as in 1339 – try to redress the mounting grievances of the English Commons in parliament and to justify the costs of a many-front war facing stalemate in France and reversal north of the Tweed. Immediate Scottish assaults on northern England might have been able to exploit this English military and political crisis, just as King Robert had harried a troubled Edward II at key moments throughout his reign. But by April 1341 Edward III would cease the unpopular and ruthless purges of his government he had at first felt necessary and would instead defuse his problems with timely concessions to his subjects. Thereafter he began to plan a fresh continental campaign. It was surely as a distraction from, or blow to, this expected English onslaught that Philip VI felt a restored Scottish king should contribute: David's French ship would get him home just three weeks before the truce was to expire on 24 June 1341. He surely left with a strict understanding that the Scots should now

90 According to Froissart, Sir Robert Erskine and Simon Fraser went to fetch David (*Oeuvres de Froissart*, iii, 432–5). Erskine was then a Steward follower but would become a crown man after 1357. Erskine can be found witnessing a charter of John Maxwell at Dryburgh Abbey in 1340 along with the Steward, the earl of March, Maurice Murray of Drumsargard and William Livingston (Fraser, ed., *The Book of Caerlaverock*, ii, 410).

take the war across the border to Edward and conclude truces with England only with Philip's say-so.[91]

If they had not already been aware of the English crown's problems, Philip and David could have been briefed as to the state of English affairs by John Randolph, earl of Moray. The French indeed – with input from Gaillard – had started talks for Randolph's freedom in June 1340. He seems to have been paroled after almost six years of captivity around 6 February 1341– just as Edward III began mustering his next invasion force: Patrick, earl of March, Alexander Seton, William Livingston and several south-eastern knights of the following of Alexander Ramsay had been entered as hostages for his brief release. Randolph made straight for David, and although he had to re-enter captivity for a short time, he may have periodically acted as an envoy to France until his definite return to Scotland in early 1342.[92]

Many factors, then, played their part in the timing of David's return. It must have been a highly emotional journey to contemplate and undertake. He had been absent for seven years; Scotland had not had an adult Bruce king for over a decade. David was the same age Edward III had been when he asserted his personal majority, seventeen: nonetheless, he was still an adolescent, inexperienced ruler. Yet David must have been increasingly aware that he would be returning to his father's kingdom charged with the tasks of supporting his French patron in war, of recovering Scottish territory still under English sway, and of settling obvious internal scores. Scotland's political landscape had become dominated in his absence by slightly older, aggressive and ambitious warrior lords and knights who had little or no personal experience of strong personal monarchy, only their own sense of what they had earned and deserved on the back of the territorial settlement before 1329: that balance of power had to be redressed.

The burden of expectation upon the Scottish King was thus perhaps impossibly heavy. As David and his queen, sisters and counsel boarded ship at Boulogne sometime in the last week of May 1341 – in the company of some of Philip VI's knights, including Arnoul d'Audrehen – they might all have been wondering, had he in fact missed the boat?

---

91 Sumption, *Hundred Years War*, i, 292–383; W. Ormrod, 'Edward III and the Recovery of Royal Authority in England, 1340–60', *History*, lxxii (1987), 4–19.
92 *Rot. Scot.*, i, 592, 599; *Foedera*, ii, 1130, 1132, 1147, 1160, 1166, 1169, 1188. This contradicts the assertion that Randolph was released by autumn 1340, in Nicholson, *Scotland – the Later Middles Ages*, 138; *CCR 1339–41*, 540.

THREE

The Young Lions:
David's First Kingship, 1341–6

'The young king [David] despaired when he saw the people of his kingdom . . . he turned to his wife and wept . . . when he had heard the complaints of these and others, he comforted them the best he could and said that he would avenge them or lose all that remained to him or die in the attempt . . . '

Chronique de Jean le Bel, c. 1350[1]

The King's Return, 1341

Jean Froissart visited Scotland in 1365 at the recommendation of his countrywoman, Edward III's queen, Philippa of Hainault. As a result, towards the close of the fourteenth century, Froissart would pen several versions of his heroic *Chroniques* of war and chivalry in England, France and elsewhere in Europe including men and deeds worthy of note in Scotland: for many of the events of the Scottish wars before 1357 he would rely upon the eye-witness accounts of French chronicler Jean le Bel, a guest of the Plantagenets in 1327. Froissart himself stayed for 'quarter of a year' in the company of David II and a number of his great magnates and more famous knights, in particular the various Douglas scions. The king and his close counsellors would grasp that opportunity to impress upon their guest a view of events since 1332 prejudiced by family outlooks and the later politics of the reign, a bias which glorified the actions and image of the Bruce monarchy and sought to hide its problems from history. Fordun's source for the same period – probably written by Thomas Bisset, prior of St Andrews (d. 1363) – was similarly crafted in the second half of the fourteenth-century to favour the king and his inner circle.[2]

Thus Froissart's record makes no mention of the Steward's significant contribution to the Scottish war effort on David's behalf in the 1330s. Instead it is William Douglas of Lothian and other champion knights who are credited in the chronicler's narrative with the Bruce recovery, laying the ground for David's return to Scotland in 1341 as a moment of 'grande joie'. Froissart asserts that David landed at Edinburgh (or, in another version,

---

1 *Chron. Le Bel,* ii, 281–2.
2 *Oeuvres de Froissart,* iii, 432–6; Contamine, 'Froissart and Scotland', 54–6. For Bisset, see ch. 2 n45.

somewhere in Moray) to be met and carried into residence shoulder-high by Douglas, Sir Robert Erskine (David's right-hand man in the 1360s), Simon Fraser, Alexander Ramsay and the rest of the barons and knights of Scotland. The king's subjects then marked his return with festivity and feasting, celebrations also alleged by Fordun's source and his continuator, Bower, who asserted that 'all Scots were delighted beyond belief at his arrival, and held feasts with joy and dancing'. Froissart, following le Bel, added that in return David vowed publicly to avenge the attacks of the English 'else he would lose his kingdom, and his life into the bargain'; that said, Froissart's king summoned a parliament to prepare an immediate invasion, a step David would only really take in 1346.[3]

The only downside to this restoration admitted by Froissart was that when David took the several French knights he named as accompanying the king home across the sea on a tour of the realm, these visitors are said to have seen only 'a country full of woods and mist' and joked that 'no wealthy man can be Lord of a country like this'. Froissart would also later report the shock of an expedition of over one thousand French knights to Scotland in 1385 when the poverty of the realm (and the Scots' preference for evasive guerilla tactics) led to a falling-out and scuffles between hosts and hungry guests.[4] But Scotland in 1341, too, can only have given the appearance of a sorely wasted kingdom. Most of the realm's castles and burghs had been razed or burned at least once during the previous decade. The land was scarred and in many places barren and unworked after four decades of conflict with only a few years' respite after 1323 and between 1328 and 1332; harsh winters had also taken their toll during a European-wide climatic cooling.[5] By the time David set foot back in his native land the eastern Lowlands in particular must only just have been beginning to show signs of firm repopulation and a revival of economic activity outwith the north-east, Angus, Fife and isolated pockets further south. This harsh reality was echoed in truth by the low-key, hesitant return of the king.

For in fact David's party – not with the 'fleet' reported by Fordun's source, but probably only two modest French barges – was obliged to land about Saturday 2 June at the small town of Inverbervie on the Angus coast; not at a royal burgh like Dundee or Aberdeen, certainly not at the port of Leith for

3 *Oeuvres de Froissart*, iii, 432–6; *Chron. Fordun*, i, 365–6; *Chron. Bower*, vii, 151.
4 *Oeuvres de Froissart*, iii, 435, and x, 336; H. Brown, *Early Travellers in Scotland* (Edinburgh 1891, reprint 1978), 8–15. Froissart also lamented the eternal lack of iron and leather for good war-horse equipment in Scotland and the frugal diet.
5 I.D. Whyte, *Scotland Before the Industrial Revolution: An Economic and Social History c. 1050–c. 1750* (Harlow 1995), 39, 42; P. Yeoman, *Medieval Scotland* (London 1995), 110–1. As we have seen, the chroniclers highlighted especially the damage caused during the lieutenancy of Andrew Murray (*Chron. Fordun*, i, 358–61; *Chron. Wyntoun*, vi, 76–98).

Edinburgh. A later tradition, that David's ship was blown off course and narrowly escaped shipwreck, causing him to found a Carmelite chapel at Inverbervie in thanks, may contain a seed of truth.[6] But it is probably rather the case that David and his close counsellors had no choice but to land as quickly as possible at a quiet, safe venue, free from both Anglo-Balliol forces and from the influence of the Lieutenant and royal heir-presumptive, Robert Steward.

Some trouble between David and his elder nephew and heir was clearly anticipated in the light of clashes since 1335 over control of royal policy and resources. This may have been enough to cause the Steward to avoid David's presence and court for the first six months of his active rule in Scotland (or at least to be excluded from the king's inner circle). David himself began by touring much of the region which had sustained his court in exile and where his authority was most secure. Five acts protecting the lands and income of the former chancery abbey of Arbroath were issued from Arbroath and Dundee on 17–18 June before David moved on by the 20th to Kildrummy Castle, held by his aunt Christian Bruce, widow of Guardian Andrew Murray. Two days later David was at Aberdeen, probably to reward the burgh's sustenance of his court in France and to replenish his funds, whilst there he may also have granted Inverbervie the status of a free burgh. The king may then have moved further north, perhaps to Elgin or to the caput of the Moray lordship of Badenoch, Lochindorb Castle, hotly contested in 1335–6. But by 18 July he had moved south to Stirling to visit the ongoing siege of its English castle garrison. A month later – on 11 August – David can be found at Dumbarton Castle, the Steward's base since 1334 and where French supplies would continue to enter the country for some time to come.[7]

The Steward was not present as a witness to any of the surviving acts issued during this circuit. Instead, David's fledgling court was attended at least by a number of prelates and magnates: the bishops of Aberdeen, Brechin, Ross and Moray, the abbots of Dunfermline, Coupar Angus and Lindores; Duncan, earl of Fife, William, earl of Ross, Robert Keith the Marischal, David Hay the constable and the knights Malcolm Fleming, William Douglas, Philip Meldrum, Alexander Seton, John Graham of Abercorn (and Dalkeith), John Bonville, John of Cambron, and Roger Mortimer of Inverbervie; two men still named as esquires, Maurice Murray and Alexander Ramsay; and Thomas Charteris the Chancellor. It is likely that Adam, bishop of Brechin, Keith, Seton, Fleming, and, now, Douglas and Ramsay, formed the core of David's close counsel and guided his actions.

6 D.E. Easson, *Medieval Religious Houses: Scotland* (London 1957), 114.
7 *RRS*, vi, nos. 25–37, 483.

But the Steward's absences from Stirling and Dumbarton are especially curious. According to Wyntoun's source and Bower, the Steward oversaw the fall of Stirling (which these writers date correctly to April 1342), granted its keeping to Maurice Murray of Drumsargard and then withdrew to the Stewart family lands in the west.[8] But the Steward would appear at the king's court throughout spring 1342. This makes it more likely that Robert Steward withdrew west from the royal reach in mid-1341 and that it was David himself who would appoint Maurice, a knight and local war-leader who was attending court as the king's 'cousin' by winter of that year. David may even have made Maurice Stirling Castle's keeper when he visited there in July 1341 as a means of spurring on the siege. In the same fashion, in summer 1341 David may have re-installed Malcolm Fleming as keeper of Dumbarton – that 'very strong castle on the border of wild Scotland' – reducing the influence of the Steward.[9]

The king thus entered early on a process of undermining the Steward's amassed and intended territorial and political influence and with good cause. David's nephew, his senior by eight years, must have seemed a fearful figure to the inexperienced, teenage monarch, a magnate who had already served a testing apprenticeship in power and sired at least three sons. David presumably learned more upon his return of the Steward's collection of homages, landgrabbing, embezzlement and wavering dynastic loyalties since 1332 – a stark contrast to the sacrifices of Andrew Murray and John Randolph. However, David also seems to have been well advised and to have realised quite quickly that if he was to be able to both reduce his heir-presumptive's autonomy and, more generally, re-assert the Bruce writ kingdom-wide after a prolonged absence, he would have to harness to the crown the service of the many other regional magnates and knights whose leadership and armed retinues had recovered Bruce Scotland before 1341. David's charter witness lists in the first four months of his reign in Scotland underline his awareness of the importance of such men.

Patronage would be the key to this process of reviving support for his person and crown, of winning for David his expected royal role as leader of his subjects in war. He began rebuilding from the moment he returned, confirming the rights (often enshrined in charters by Robert I) of key institutions like the abbeys of Arbroath and Scone in his first few weeks home. Yet, naturally, any calculated restructuring of the Bruce settlement of Scotland would also involve favour which confirmed many men in the

---

8 *Chron. Fordun*, i, 363–4; *Chron. Wyntoun*, vi, 136; *Chron. Bower*, vii, 141, 145; CDS, iii, no. 1383.
9 According to Patrick Abercromby *c.* 1700, the Steward had installed his own keeper in Dumbarton Castle about 1340 (*The Martial Achievements of the Scottish Nation* (2 vols., Edinburgh 1711–5), ii, 81).

positions of local influence which they had carved out of the disruption of war since 1332 as well as elevating others as new royal locality agents.

Thus in the beginning David seems to have worked with those men he knew best as well as making some attempts to divide and rule other subjects. In this David did not shirk controversy and the flexing of the royal will. Starting with a bang, while at Stirling in July 1341 he made a crucial grant to the warrior who had visited him in France, Douglas of Lothian, of the vacant Perthshire earldom of Atholl. Douglas's uncle, Andrew, was already sheriff of Perth but this was also an act which must have been designed to deny the sulking Steward the key lands of the Strathbogies.[10] David also sought to make use of Douglas's military prowess after the general truce embracing England, Scotland and France had expired on 24 June. In late August of 1341 the young king took part in his first raid into northern England in the knight of Lothian's company. This brief, unremarkable foray penetrated as far south as Heddon Laws near the River Tyne in Northumberland a few miles west of Newcastle. It did little to advance the recovery from occupation of the few remaining border strongpoints, principally Roxburgh and Berwick. But it did signal David's commitment to the French alliance at a time when Philip and Edward had nonetheless agreed to extend their truce. The Steward did not take part.[11]

Instead, Robert Steward seems only to have appeared unavoidably in David's presence at a full parliament summoned to Scone for mid-September that year.[12] Expectations must have been running extremely high as to the intended agenda of the crown at this assembly. Unfortunately, few of the official recorded acts of this gathering of the estates have survived. Nonetheless, it is evident that David and his advisers sought to further re-assert royal authority, sanction the rebuilding of government and begin, generally, to put the king's house in order by scrutinising some of his subjects' behaviour over the past ten years.

David's commitment to restore the machinery of everyday administration was confirmed by the appointment of Sir Alexander Seton and Adam, bishop of Brechin – two of the king's closest counsellors in France – as lords auditors of causes and complaints, probably in response to pressure from the estates for a start to be made on the backlog of territorial and jurisdictional cases. At the same time an inquest must also have been appointed under Robert Keith, Marischal and sheriff of Aberdeen – another Gaillard exile – to ascertain the right of the bishop of Aberdeen, Alexander Kinnimound (a

10 *RRS*, vi, no. 31; *RMS*, i, no. 196 (Andrew); Brown, 'The Development of Scottish Border Lordship, 1332–58', 9–13.
11 *Chron. Bower*, vii, 151–3, 243n. David had granted Douglas charters on 18 July and 11 August 1341.
12 *APS*, i, 293–4, 512–3 (*RPS*, 1341/1–6); *RRS*, vi, nos. 33–7.

possible author of the Declaration of Arbroath in 1320), to the second teinds of his diocese. This commission – and David's inspection of the land rights of monastic houses like Scone – underlines the crown's determination to secure revenues from predation by magnates like the Steward, William, earl of Ross (the self-appointed justiciar north of Forth) and others. It is possible that David and his advisers may have attempted a partial revocation of grants made during his minority even though that would not technically end until his twenty-fifth year (in 1349).[13]

These tasks, though, were surely secondary during David's first parliament to the more fundamental need simply to present himself to his subjects and take renewed oaths of homage and fealty, a process the king may have begun during his summer ayre. But for some key men this must have involved publicly seeking royal pardon for breaking their coronation oaths of loyalty of 1331.

David may have relished the opportunity to make this a central issue of any dealings he now had with the Steward. There does survive a note of a general confirmation from about this period – issued by David either in this 1341 parliament or in a council which would be held in Aberdeen in February 1342 – of all the Steward's lands, with the exception of the Lothian baronies of Bathgate and Ratho which had been given by King Robert to his new son-in-law, Walter Steward, in 1315. It is likely that this amounted to a grudging pardon from the crown for Robert Steward's submission to Edward III and Balliol in 1335 and perhaps for his interference in royal revenue: the retention of the two valuable baronies would have strengthened the king's position in Lothian where he would now have to find shoulder room alongside Douglas and his adherents.[14]

The only other lord for whom such a general confirmation of lands is extant – granted sometime *c.* 1341–4 – is Patrick Dunbar, earl of March. He had perhaps served as a Guardian south of Forth briefly in 1332–3 but defected to Anglo-Balliol service between the battles of Halidon Hill and Culblean.[15] These paper remissions were really the only freely given crown favour these two great regional lords would receive from David over the next five years. Similar pardons might also reasonably have been required by

13 *RRS*, vi, nos. 33–4, 484; *Registrum Episcopatus Aberdonensis*, i, 69, 73; *ER*, i, clxiv, 501, 511–4. On 29 March 1342 David ordered the Chancellor, Thomas Charteris, to annul all grants made by past abbots of Lindores in Fife which had already been revoked in parliament by Robert I and Thomas Randolph as Guardian, as per a decision made in the parliament of September 1341 (*Chartulary of Lindores Abbey, 1195–1479*, ed. J. Dowden (SHS 1903), 173).

14 *RMS*, i, App. ii, no. 823. Alexander III had bought Bathgate and Ratho from the de Bohun family about 1282 for £989 (A.A.M. Duncan, *Scotland – the Making of the Kingdom* (Edinburgh 1975), 587).

15 *RMS*, i, App. ii, no. 947.

the earls of Fife and Strathearn, temporary defectors to Balliol after 1332, both with Comyn connections: they would also receive as little from the second Bruce king as they had from the first. If so, the Steward was now being lumped in by David with magnates cold-shouldered by Robert I before 1329 for their Balliol leanings after Bannockburn. Arguably, the Steward would receive even less favour than the Murrays of Tullibardine whom David would forgive in 1341 for their father's betrayal at Dupplin.[16]

Thus although he now became the regular first lay witness to David's royal acts, it must have been obvious to the Steward by late 1341 that his access to crown resources had been cut off. According to sixteenth-century Scottish chroniclers, David promised at this parliament to reward those who had fought and fallen for the Bruce cause since 1332, even commanding a list of the dead and deserving to be collated.[17] David's patronage thereafter would certainly be generous and widespread. Yet while the Steward would be denied any advancement in Atholl, Strathearn and Fife, other men continued to profit.

In particular – whether through naïve trust of a former adherent of John Randolph and a man who had flattered David on a visit to Gaillard, or out of an anxious need to secure an instant armed following and credibilty in the ongoing war against England – the king continued to favour William Douglas. During the Scone parliament David confirmed the knight's phy-sical domination of the Middle March regions of Eskdale and Ewesdale: this extended William's control of Selkirk forest and the Black Douglas sphere of influence from Lauderdale to Dumfriesshire during the childhood in France of his nephew and namesake William, lord of Douglas. The king must also have sanctioned Douglas of Lothian's control of Edinburgh Castle and accepted the knight's wily clerical ally, William Bullock, a former Cham-berlain to Edward Balliol, as a replacement for the suspect Reginald More, the Bruces' Chamberlain since 1329.[18]

But David also began to elevate other potential regional lieutenants. Malcolm Fleming, the king's 'foster-father', had received a grant in free warren of his Lanarkshire lands of Lenzie, Kilmarnock and Dalziel on 20 June 1341. Then, shortly after the Scone parliament, on 9 November – while David was at the west-coast burgh of Ayr – Fleming was granted the hereditary earldom of Wigtown, with regality rights over these western Galloway lands policed in the thirteenth century by the Comyns as sheriffs.[19] The new

16 *RRS*, vi, nos. 14, 54; NAS GD 38 1/62/8.
17 *Chron. Boece*, 323.
18 *RRS*, vi, no. 36; *ER*, i, 499–515 *et passim* (includes payment of £53 to William Douglas for bringing arms from France to the siege of Perth in 1339 and £33 as his brother's fee as keeper of Edinburgh castle); Brown, *Black Douglases*, 37–40.
19 *RRS*, vi, nos. 30, 39.

Wigtown title was, admittedly, made up of a limited pocket of these sensitive regional lands but the five knights' service Fleming was to owe for this sasine underlined his potential value as a Gaelic-speaking lord thought capable of recovering and controlling for the crown this highly volatile region of Balliol-Comyn sympathies. Taming the south-west had been a task for which King Robert had arguably been unable to find any single lord fit to succeed: by 1341 there was the added threat of Edward Balliol's presence on his Galloway coastal island fortress of Hestan, stirring to arms periodically kindreds like the MacDowells and Maxwells of Caerlaverock.[20] Moreover, as Wigtown lay amidst the Steward's holdings of Kyle-Stewart and Cunningham, the Bruce earldom of Carrick, the Randolph lordships of Annandale and Nithsdale and the Douglas Dumfriesshire lands, a strengthened Malcolm Fleming might have been earmarked as a counter–balance to Robert Steward's ambitions in the absence of active adult Bruce, Randolph and Douglas incumbents in that quarter. Fleming's keepership of Dumbarton Castle also served to check the Steward in Clydeside and the pretensions to the lands of Menteith of the Stewart kinsman, Sir John Menteith of Arran and Knapdale. David's regular relays between Edinburgh and Dumbarton over the next few years may, though, have been necessary to reinforce Fleming's writ and keep Malcolm detatched from the Steward. It is also just possible that Fleming's daughter, 'Margory', was an early mistress of the king.[21]

These were obviously carefully calculated acts of patronage. But in addition to such direct royal favour, in late 1341 David also confirmed grants to the adherents and kin of several key magnates: a grant by Robert Keith to Sir John Maitland of Covington barony in Lanarkshire, a grant of Fife lands (Carnock, close by Dunfermline) by William Ramsay of Colluthie to his brother Alexander Ramsay of Dalhousie, and a grant by John Randolph – not yet fully free from custody in England – to one of his Moray tenants.[22] In all of these acts there were early signs of David's hastening commitment to attracting the support for the crown of men of chivalry with proven war records and substantial followings. His intent may have been underlined once again sometime in November or December 1341 when he participated in another short, low-key raid into Northumberland

---

20 Oram, 'Bruce, Balliol and the Lordship of Galloway', 42–7; Reid, 'Edward Balliol', 42–6.

21 R.D. Oram, 'Devorguila, the Balliols and Buittle', *TDGNHAS*, lxxiii (1999), 179–80. *ER*, i, 509, 511 for 'Margory Fleming'. David would visit Dumbarton about: 11 August 1341; 4 July and 10 December 1342; 17 October 1344; 25 May, 10 July, 28 September, 18 October and 28 December 1345; 5 May and 27 August 1346 (see *RRS*, vi). David and the Steward and their followers would squabble over control of Dumbarton after 1357 – see below, ch. 7.

22 *RRS*, vi, nos. 35, 37, 40–1; *RMS*, i, App. ii. nos. 111–3.

then agreed to a short truce (during which Anglo-Scottish jousts were held on the border).[23]

David was clearly energised, keen to settle old scores and make his mark. Yet only a few minor figures – particularly from the south-west – seem to have suffered full forfeiture for their Anglo-Balliol sympathies at his hands at this time: these were condemnations which largely confirmed their earlier expulsion by local rivals.[24] David had shown himself prepared to begin to marginalise powerful figures like the Steward and March for their equivocal loyalties. However, he was prepared to forgive others, a clear measure of his pressing need for reliable support. Also while at Ayr in November 1341 David seems to have confirmed to John MacDonald of Islay and his bastard son, Angus Og, much of the isles and mainland holdings offered to this kindred by Edward III and Balliol in 1336.[25] Significantly, this included both Kintyre and the Isle of Skye, lands originally granted by Robert I to the Stewarts and the earls of Ross respectively. Sometime in 1341–2, David also seems to have pardoned the MacRuaridhs of Garmoran of their forfeiture by Robert I in 1325.[26] With pressing concerns elsewhere, David could have little real input into the strained politics of the western isles and Argyll after the expulsion of the Macdougalls. It was really a quarter of his realm with which he would never come to grips. Nevertheless, he hoped clearly to entice MacDonald and MacRuaridh ambition, perhaps, as Abbot Bower later put it, 'persuading and inducing one chieftain to kill or capture another', or, more ideally, to act as a further check on the Steward in the west and on Ross in the north-west. So grateful was John MacDonald for David's initial sanction of his growing lordship of the Isles that he would send the king a pair of hawks in 1342. Ranald MacRuaridh would be so loyal as to bring a force to serve in the royal host in 1346.[27]

Baronial Backlash, 1342

At first glance at the few available sources, by winter of 1341–2 David had made a promising start to his adult majority, despite his humble home-

23 *Chron. Bower*, vii, 151–3; *Oeuvres de Froissart*, iii, 465.
24 For David II's forfeitures *c*. 1341–6, see *RRS*, vi, nos. 14, 36, 54, 77, 80–1, 93, 99, 102–3, 491; *RMS*, i, App. ii, nos. 732, 756, 777, 779, 799, 806, 808, 830, 833, 835, 846, 854, 870, 875, 891, 895, 900–2, 904, 907, 911, 921, 924, 952, 1021, 1024, 1041, 1053, 1058, 1097, 1098, 1103, 1108, 1112–3, 1119, 1122, 1125, 1127. Of those forfeited, the biggest first-time victims post-1329 were probably Sir Lawrence Preston and Malise, earl of Strathearn – for the latter see below. However, an equal number of lands resigned by minor nobility in the presence of the king *c*. 1341–6 may have been imposed punishments for temporary defection.
25 *Ibid*, no. 114; *RRS*, vi, no. 72; *Acts of the Lords of the Isles*, 1 and Appendix no. 1; *Rot. Scot.*, i, 463, 524–5; *CDS*, iii, no. 1382.
26 *RRS*, vi, no. 73; Barrow, *Bruce*, 290–2.
27 *Chron. Bower*, vii, 361; *ER*, i, 511.

coming. Counselled shrewdly by senior figures like Adam, bishop of Brechin, Robert Keith and others, the young king had marked his return through a resumption of royal patronage and a high-profile itinerary, if one limited to royal heartlands and residences. The wartime freedom exploited by certain magnates in David's absence had seemingly been quickly curtailed. Most Scotsmen had welcomed and begun to look once again to their king as a source of rebuilding and self-advancement. David himself had adopted the mantle of authority in a moderately confident, convincing manner. His court had from the first become a difficult, intimidating arena for those magnates, the Steward especially, whose ambitions could be seen to represent a challenge to the crown's dominance.

On the wider front, David's initial blooding in the art of war against England – two quick raids – had been unspectacular. But these incursions and, surely, the continued siege of Stirling Castle, had been enough to keep the French cash and supplies coming and even provoked Edward III to make a show of force by spending the winter of 1341–2 at Melrose Abbey in the Scottish East March.[28] Melrose was shrine to Robert Bruce's heart but Edward's presence there achieved no repair of his occupation administration south of Forth, serving really only to betray his 'melancholic' disenchantment with his Scottish war efforts: he showed no interest in revitalising the fortunes of Edward Balliol who at almost sixty and still childless cut an increasingly sad, forgotten figure marooned in the Solway Firth. David did not dare offer any sort of battle to the English king at this time. But Edward III had been distracted by Scotland, if only for a short time, from his preparations for intervention in Brittany against Philip VI's allies, an assault he intended to make the moment the extended Anglo-French truce ended on 24 June 1342.[29]

David's royal performance intensified as the year drew to a close. His household most likely spent Christmas in and around Edinburgh, probably at the Augustinian Abbey of Holyrood, from where on 6 and 19 January 1342 he resumed his attempts to encourage royalists in the south-east. He granted the Edinburgh barony of Gorton to Sir John Preston, and the barony of Dalkeith (resigned by Sir John Graham) and the Lothian lands of traitor John Mowbray to Sir William Douglas. It is likely that these two strong household knights immediately accompanied David with their Lothian retinues on a third raid into northern England sometime in the first two weeks of February 1342.[30]

---

28 *ER*, i, 490, 521, 529, records payment for carts transporting (French?) goods from Dumbarton to Ayr, Kilwinning, Haddington, Linlithgow and Stirling, as well receipt of goods in kind – flour, barley etc. For the £500 from France, see BN MS Clairambault 212.64; for Edward III at Melrose, see *Chron. Knighton*, 39.
29 Sumption, *Hundred Years War*, i, 408–9.
30 *RRS*, vi, nos. 41–3; *Chron. Bower*, vii, 153.

Like his two previous assaults in 1341, this harassment of Northumberland came at a time of uneasy Anglo-French truce which included the Scots
as Philip VI's ally: indeed, Scottish ambassadors for peace talks with
England were appointed in February 1342 and included William Douglas.
However, at that time it may have been deemed necessary for David and
his experienced Lothian knights to break the truce and raid to supplement
the crown's meagre winter victuals and revenues.[31] Significantly, on this
occasion David seems to have flown his own banners, although Abbot
Bower would later assert that at this time the king fought under the
colours of John Randolph, earl of Moray and lord of Annandale. Yet it
was only now – by 19 January 1342 at least – that Randolph was fully
liberated through the offices of the French king, exchanged for the Scots'
captive the earl of Salisbury by the bishop of St Andrews and Alexander
Ramsay and returned finally to take up his role as David's closest adviser.
Indeed, over the course of the next four years it would at times be as if
each man – both still short of twenty in 1341–2 – became subsumed
within the other. David would certainly issue acts before 1346 as 'lord of
Annandale' and together they would pursue a domestic agenda which
aimed at restoring the Bruce-Randolph partnership in government of the
previous generation.[32]

Both David and John – in the full flush of knightly youth – must have
taken part in the royal tournament held at Aberdeen in early February, a
festive occasion of feasting and relatively lavish pageantry which was to
coincide with a council (14–21 February) of king, prelates and nobles.[33] But
it was in the course of this assembly that the actual fragility of control over
his lay subjects of a young king only nine months into his active reign
became dramatically apparent.

David must have been extremely relieved to have Randolph's commanding presence back as a further counter to the Steward and to contain
headstrong characters like Douglas of Lothian, now earl of Atholl. Yet,
remembering the extreme tensions of the 1335 parliament at Dairsie, the
return of Randolph may have prompted both these lords to look to their
own lands. Douglas had also presumably enjoyed the king's tournament,
just as he and other Scots had impressed in jousts held with the English that

---

31 *ER*, i, 535; *Rot. Scot.*, i, 621. The designated peace talks embassy also included
    Adam, the bishop of Brechin, Patrick earl of March, Thomas Charteris the
    Chancellor and William Bullock, but whether these talks went ahead or not is
    uncertain.
32 *Oeuvres de Froissart*, iii, 464–5; *Chron. Bower*, vii, 153; *Rot. Scot.*, i, 628; *RRS*, vi,
    no. 43.
33 *Ibid*, no. 46, letter patent from David confirming David Hay the Constable's land
    rights despite the grant of the 'palace' used in the tournament at Aberdeen to a John
    Simrell.

winter on the borders.[34] But behind the scenes Douglas must have entered into an agreement with Robert Steward which threatened to unravel key features of David's territorial resettlement begun the previous year. The young king had clearly sought to limit or harness the regional hegemony of these individual magnates. But at the Aberdeen council he was forced – when confronted by a legal suit brought by the Steward – to recognise the council's award of his heir-presumptive's claim to the former Soules, Bruce and Douglas border lordship of Liddesdale. The Steward claimed this land had been granted to him by the king *c*. 1333–4 but what he really wanted was the former Strathbogie title of Atholl and he used this council decision to exchange Liddesdale for this Perthshire earldom with William Douglas. Both men were now enormously strengthened and enriched in their established spheres of interest.[35]

It may also have been on this occasion that the Steward secured his royal confirmation of all his lands except Bathgate and Ratho: these were Lothian baronies he may now have been prepared to sacrifice in exchange for Atholl and a pardon for his submission in 1335. David may thus have been partly compensated although, in truth, no evidence survives that the crown was able to take revenues from these two Lothian baronies or to re-alienate them: the Steward may have remained defiantly in possession. But in February 1342 David was already surely surprised and enraged, especially with Douglas whom he had so lavishly rewarded since June 1341. For it must now have been painfully apparent – if not long before – that the king's physical, moral and political influence over the freedom fighters of the past decade was severely limited, despite his ability to oversee conveyancing on paper and not least by their occupation before David's return from France of such vast tracts of territory, several key royal offices and their military lordship over extended networks of middling Scots in the localities. The Steward and Douglas may have been genuinely able to influence many of the magnates present at the Aberdeen council: they could trade upon the war effort and sacrifices they had made in David's absence. They may have found support from such figures as the earls of Fife and March, or even William, earl of Ross, who was probably anxious to retain the justiciarship north of Forth despite Randolph's return. David's recent promotions can have helped little: Malcolm Fleming, in particular, was not yet able to use his title of Wigtown. The sudden defiance and reversal of David's patronage plans must thus have rendered especially sinister Douglas's influence over the principal residence of Edinburgh (where his brother, also William Douglas, was keeper), the sheriffship of Perth, the

---

34　*Chron. Knighton*, 39–40.
35　*RRS*, vi, nos. 44–5 (*RPS*, 1342/2/1). The fact that the Steward was able to defend his sasine to Liddesdale suggests that the crown did not in fact attempt a full revocation of minority grants in late 1341.

crown's purse strings (through Bullock as Chamberlain), border warfare and ongoing truce talks with England.[36]

Faced with such a setback and restriction of movement, David and his court seem to have withdrawn inwardly during the weeks after the February council. David spent his eighteenth birthday (5 March) quietly at Dunfermline, where his father's body and many of the royal MacMalcolm line were buried. Then he headed north-east once again in late March, when he seems to have made a short pilgrimage to Elgin and Kinloss in Moray, probably accompanied by Randolph. By 14 April David was at his aunt's Kildrummy Castle in Mar once more where he issued letters patent ordering the Chamberlain, sheriffs and justiciar north of Forth (the earl of Ross) to pay second teinds to the bishop of Aberdeen, an order which would have to be repeated several times over the next few years.[37]

When the king did return to more public circles, he seems still to have been under pressure to comply with the concerns of his greatest subjects. For at Dundee on 29 May David confirmed an entail which saw William Douglas of Liddesdale recognised as heir-presumptive to the vast family lands of his teenage 'nephew' and ward William, lord of Douglas, who was still in France and now inherited his title after the resignation of the spiritually troubled Hugh, Lord Douglas. Liddesdale was thus recognised ahead of a bastard of the 'Good' Sir James, Archibald, the future 'Grim' lord of Galloway and a man who would be heavily favoured after 1357 by David II whom he had grown up alongside at Château Gaillard. The witnesses to this surely reluctant royal act in spring 1342 included the bishops of Aberdeen and Brechin and the Steward followed by Duncan of Fife and Patrick of March; of David's lesser household knights only Robert Keith, the Marischal, sealed this grant – John Randolph was absent.[38]

However, by then a shift in the balance of baronial power had also taken place in the borders which would soon allow David scope to reduce Douglas autonomy and reassert himself at court. On 30 March 1342, their scaling ladders undetected, Alexander Ramsay of Dalhousie and his men recovered Roxburgh Castle, in much the same way as Sir James Douglas had surprised the English garrison there in 1315.[39] But Roxburgh was a caput of much of

36 For John Douglas, see: *ER*, i, 508; *RRS*, vi, no. 17 (as keeper of Loch Leven, 1339). *Rot. Scot.*, i, 621 for William as march Warden.

37 *RRS*, vi, nos. 48–50, 484.

38 *Ibid.*, no. 51. For Archibald, see Brown, *Black Douglases*, ch. 3. William Douglas also received the barony of Aberdour in Fife from John Randolph, earl of Moray, in February 1342; on 22 May 1342 Hugh, Lord Douglas, granted another charter to Sir William at Edinburgh witnessed by David Barclay, William Livingston, Andrew Douglas, William Bullock, Richard Small dean of Glasgow, William Fairley and James Sandilands (*HMC, xi, Duke of Hamilton*, 207).

39 *Chron. Fordun*, i, 365; *Chron. Wyntoun*, vi, 160; *Chron. Bower*, vii, 153–5.

the lands of Teviotdale which had been recovered to the Scottish faith since 1335 by Douglas of Liddesdale. David must have been aware of this when he summoned another council to meet at the Augustinian priory of Restenneth in Angus in mid-June 1342. This small monastic house had a close family connection for the king. His brother, John Bruce, perhaps a twin born in 1324, buried there: on 10 June 1344, possibly around the anniversary of John's death, David would grant a £20 pension from the customs of Dundee to pay for masses for his lost sibling's soul at Restenneth.[40] Yet in 1342 David also seems to have used this select venue as the stage for a revival of his patronage to men he could trust.

Grants survive from the Restenneth council to Malcolm Fleming and his neighbour, the Bruce stalwart, Malcolm, earl of Lennox. David's confidence may also have been boosted by the final fall of Stirling Castle in mid-April 1342 and the entry of Maurice Murray of Drumsargard as keeper. But according to the main Scottish chroniclers, about this time David also appointed Alexander Ramsay as sheriff of Teviotdale: Ramsay may already have been warden of the East March and have received a royal gift of the barony of Hawthorndean in Roxburghshire, forfeited by Sir Lawrence Preston. David may also already have been involved in a raid into England which saw him act as the patron of Ramsay's sizeable and experienced military affinity. Douglas's jealous response to this favour was swift and shocking. Probably in late June, he interrupted a court being conducted by Ramsay at Hawick (the caput of a barony given by Robert I to James Douglas) and seized the new sheriff, imprisoning him to the west in the formidable castle of Hermitage; here, after seventeen days, this flower of chivalry starved to death.[41]

In the short term, David may have hoped that these two fiery Lothian rivals would balance each other out: in 1341 he had already granted Douglas the barony of Dalkeith which bordered directly on Dalhousie. Moreover, according to Bower:

> many indeed think that Alexander's death was caused among other reasons by the king's inadvertence and negligence, not to say vacillating behaviour. He had carelessly conferred the sheriffdom of Teviotdale first on the foresaid William, and then on the renowned Alexander . . .

Fordun's earlier source, in contrast, makes no mention of an original grant of the office to Douglas and asserts that 'shortly before, all misunderstand-

40 *RRS*, vi, nos. 52–3; *RPS*, 1342/6/1; *RMS*, i, App. ii, no. 118. BL Harley MSS. No. 115, ff. 6–7) (cited in Green, *Lives of the Princesses of England*, iii, 157 n3) is surely mistaken in asserting that David Bruce had a son who died young.
41 *Chron. Fordun*, i, 365–6; *Chron. Wyntoun*, vi, 160; *Chron. Bower*, vii, 153–5.

ing had been settled, and friendships renewed afresh' between the two Lothian knights.[42] But the loss of so valuable a warlord as Ramsay cannot have been desirable for the king. David's miscalculated attempt to divide and rule may indeed have cost him a personal friend and worsened a long-running feud. But it undoubtedly gave him the moral high ground from which to break Douglas for the murder of a king's officer.

However, although the timing of the events of 1342 is somewhat unclear, it is possible that David had further provoked Douglas. It is the pro-Bruce contemporary source of Fordun which places the tale of David's arrest, on charges of treason, of William Bullock, Douglas's close ally and royal Chamberlain since 1341, *before* news of Ramsay's murder. This chronology is possible: Bullock intromitted his last account as Chamberlain at Dundee on 11 June 1342 and his confinement may have followed at the nearby Restenneth council. He was replaced as Chamberlain by a cleric, John de Roxburgh, possibly a Ramsay man. The chroniclers concur that Bullock – a figure held in high regard by both the Scots and the English for his administrative skill and wise counsel – was imprisoned on the king's orders by Sir David Barclay of Brechin, a former royal household steward for David as a child and a past sheriff of Fife but also an associate of many of the Lothian cadre of knights for whose loyalty David, Ramsay and Douglas were in competition. Warded in the castle of Lochindorb in the former Randolph of Moray lordship of Badenoch, Bullock too was starved to death, by 8 August at the latest.[43]

Bullock was thus not dead before Douglas was last a royal charter witness at Restenneth on 18 June, shortly before he moved against Ramsay. But in Bullock's demise there must be read clear evidence that David's character contained a vindictive streak, trading murder for murder with his rebellious subject. It is probably the case that David ordered Bullock killed out of sheer frustration at not being able to inflict the full penalty of the law upon Douglas for Ramsay's death. The royal wrath was considerable:

> The King Davy
> Tuke in till hert rycht hevely
> Ramsais dede, at slane wes sa;
> Forthy he pressit him to sla
> This ilk William of Douglas
> That warely him withdrawn has . . .[44]

---

42 *Chron. Wyntoun*, ii, 357; *Chron. Bower*, vii, 153.

43 *ER*, i, 499, 515, 535 *et ad indecim*; *HMC*, xi, 207. As Alisdair Ross suggests, following John Randolph's attempt in 1334–5 to tempt David Strathbogie of Atholl, heir to the Comyns of Badenoch, to enter Bruce service, the lordship of Badenoch may have been held by the crown and thus detached from the Moray regality granted by Robert I to Thomas Randolph (Ross, 'Men for all Seasons? Part 2', 6–7).

44 *Chron. Wyntoun*, vi, 166–8.

David must have assembled a small host to pursue Douglas. However, Wyntoun's source and Bower also relate – not unconvincingly – that Robert Steward intervened, on Douglas's request, to calm or thwart David's full revenge. The Steward could have sheltered Douglas in Perthshire and surely mediated not just because he was powerful enough to do so but to protect his recent exchange (or 'excambion') of Atholl for Liddesdale with the Douglas knight: the latter's forfeiture by the king could have undone the deal which these nobles had forced their king to accept in council at Aberdeen in February. Some accommodation may thus have been reached at Dumbarton on 4 July when David also entailed the Argyll lands of the late Dugall Campbell to his brother, Gillespie Campbell, a follower of the Steward, but noticably still denied him his father's lands of Lochawe.[45]

David's personal authority and the fear and respect he warranted were, then, clearly still painfully limited by the influence of his heir-presumptive and former Lieutenant. But Douglas's disgrace did shift the status quo in the Lothians and East and Middle Marches distinctly in favour of the king. Douglas himself would only re-appear at court as a charter witness in May 1345, giving the impression of a man generally cowed into submission.[46] He did serve as a march warden alongside John Randolph during Anglo-Scottish peace talks at Lochmaben in August 1343 which cemented a three-year general truce agreed the previous January by the English and French and finalised in June. Yet, remarkably, about the same time (spring-summer 1343) Douglas seems to have found his status in Scotland sufficiently threatened by the king to consider entering the liege service of Edward III – through the mediation of Edward Balliol and Henry Percy – so as to safeguard his border lands.[47] By then Douglas's influence elsewhere had certainly declined. David may have appointed a John Barclay as keeper of Roxburgh Castle in 1342: the Aberdeenshire knight, Philip Meldrum, a regular daily councillor for David before 1346, was paid in this office in 1343.[48] By 26 November 1344 at the latest, probably much earlier, Alexander Ramsay's brother, William Ramsay of Colluthie (near Cupar) in Fife, a renowned jouster and sometime crusader whom David would make earl of Fife in 1358, had been appointed sheriff of Edinburgh, thus displacing William Douglas's brother as castle-keeper. This also allowed the crown to increase its revenue from that key burgh from just £112 intromitted by Bullock in June 1342 – admittedly at a time when

45 *Chron. Bower*, vii, 155–7; *RRS*, vi, no. 54.
46 *Ibid*, no. 91. David Hume of Godscoft, *A General History of Scotland Together with a Particular History of the Houses of Douglas and Angus* (Edinburgh 1644) described Liddesdale as a 'banished man' from court until just before the battle of Neville's Cross.
47 *Rot. Scot.*, i, 637, 640; *Foedera*, ii, 1239–40. Many thanks to Michael Brown for stressing this point.
48 *Chron. Bower*, 157; *ER*, i, 535.

Edinburgh was described as 'totally waste' – to £545 in August 1343.[49] A similar displacement would later befall Douglas's uncle, Andrew, as sheriff of Perth. More generally, David may have been able to improve his revenue: only £2,529 19d had been intromitted by Bullock in total in his last annual account (including some £1,205 from the two small contributions granted by councils in 1340–1).[50]

However, much of this reported damage to Edinburgh may have been inflicted in the course of an ongoing Lothian feud aggravated by Ramsay's death. After his murder, according to Fordun's source:

> Feuds and misunderstandings, undying, as it were, and endless arose in the kingdom, not only among the lords, but even among the common people; so that, thenceforth, they murdered each other with mutual slaughter, and slew each other with the sword.[51]

There is ample evidence of open conflict between the followings of Douglas and Ramsay in the south-east after 1342. But the role of King David in assuming the active lordship of Ramsay's adherents – thus providing himself with the personal affinity of skilled warriors he had lacked in 1341 – deserves emphasis. According to Wyntoun's source and Bower, David took part in further raids into northern England about this time, probably to harry Edward III while he intervened in Brittany after October 1342 and before the aforementioned three-year general truce was agreed in June 1343. During one such assault David had cause to redeem from English captivity 'with a great weight of gold . . . five of his squires whom he knighted there, namely Stewart, Eglintoun, Cragy, Boyd and Fullarton'. These men were among a larger group named earlier by the chroniclers as members of Ramsay's affinity: 'Haliburton, Herries, Patrik of Dunbar and Dischington, Stewart, Eglintoun, Cragy, Boyd, Foularton'. All were experienced graduates of Ramsay's school of arms which enjoyed such fame (as John Mair insisted in his *History of Greater Britain* in 1521) that all the Scottish nobles of the day sought to 'enroll' their sons.[52]

---

49 *Ibid*, 492, 500, 502–3, 523; NAS RH1/2/911 – a charter by the Steward of 26 November 1344 confirming a grant by Alan Stewart to a burgess of Edinburgh witnessed by the bishop of St Andrews, Maurice (Murray, by then) earl of Strathearn, John Roxburgh and William Ramsay sheriff of Edinburgh. Ramsay had been injured in the head winning a truce-time joust against English knights with unrebated lances and raised visors *c*. 1340–1 (*Chron. Wyntoun*, vi, 102–4).

50 *ER*, i, clxv, 477–542. In 1331 the Chamberlain's income had been £9,415: £1,474 from the sheriffs, £499 from the burgh provosts and £1,799 from the burgh custumars; Bullock took £500 from the sheriffs, £318 from the burghs and £379 from the customs in 1342.

51 *Chron. Fordun*, i, 365–6.

52 *Chron. Wyntoun*, vi, 160–5; *Chron. Bower*, vii, 151; Sumption, *Hundred Years War*, i, 400–2; J. Maior, *A History of Greater Britain*, ed. A. Constable (SHS 1892), 284–5.

Almost all of these Ramsay men – and many of their kin – would be well rewarded by David either before October 1346 or after October 1357: most would be captured fighting for their king at Neville's Cross. Walter Haliburton would hold Dirleton Castle of the crown by 1360, having served as an ambassador to Rome for David in 1349 and as sheriff of Berwick, as well as receiving the Berwickshire lands of Lamberton before 1345.[53] William Dischington of Ardross would serve David as a sheriff of Fife, a justiciar, march warden and master of royal building works; John Herries would be given the free barony of Terregles in Dumfriesshire in 1359 and serve as an ambassador to England and keeper of Stirling Castle.[54] Sir Patrick Dunbar – half-brother of Patrick, earl of March – was the father of David's future mistress, Agnes Dunbar, and her brothers, George, future tenth earl of March, and John, future lord of Fife, both key placemen of the king in the 1360s; Sir Patrick would visit David in captivity in England;[55] Alexander Stewart received grain fermes and the Lanarkshire barony of Cambusnethan from David in 1343–5 and would be bailie of Annandale and lord of Darnley by 1345, making a name for himself fighting the English after 1346; Thomas Boyd of Kilmarnock – son of King Robert's ally Robert of Noddsdale (also killed in 1333) – can be found for the first time as a knight witnessing a crown charter at Dumbarton in July 1342, about which time the king gave him forfeited lands in the south-west.[56] John Craigie married a sister of Douglas of Liddesdale but would serve David as an envoy to England after 1363 and receive a confirmation of his Edinburgh lands; Sir Adam Fullarton, a knight by April 1344, would visit David in captivity and offer his son as a hostage for the king's release, as would Alexander Stewart, Livingston and John Barclay, in 1354–7.[57] Only Sir Hugh Eglintoun, a noted vernacular poet, would become a solid adherent (and in-law) of Robert Steward after 1346: but in 1342–3 David granted him the lands of Bondington and Norton in Edinburgh.[58]

53 *RRS*, vi, nos. 126, 175, 319; *RMS*, i, App. ii. nos. 809, 921, 1042; *CDS*, iii, nos. 1481, 1496, 1548; *ibid.*, iv, no. 154.

54 For Dischington, see *RRS*, vi, no. 361; *RMS*, i, nos. 217, 293, 327; *ER*, i, 591; *ibid*, ii, 112, 114, 358, *et ad indecim*. For Herries, see *RRS*, vi, nos. 210, 373; *RMS*, i, no. 192, 282, 346; Fraser, ed., *The Book of Caerlaverock*, ii, 412–5; *ER*, i, 583; *ER*, ii, 129, 333; *Rot. Scot.*, i, 891, 897.

55 *Scots Peerage*, iii, 254–61; *Rot. Scot.*, i, 709, 797; and below, ch. 11.

56 For Stewart, see *RRS*, vi, nos. 100, 376; *RMS*, i, App. ii. no. 152. For Boyd, see *RRS*, vi, no. 54.

57 For Craigie, see *RMS*, i, no. 267. For Fullartoun see *CDS*, iii, no. 1576; *Rot. Scot.*, i, 768 (hostages).

58 *RMS*, i, App. ii. no. 922; *CDS*, iv, no. 27; W. Fraser, ed., *The Memorials of the Montgomeries* (2 vols, Edinburgh 1859), i, 16–7; M.P. McDiarmid and J.A.C. Stevenson, eds, *Barbour's Bruce* (Scottish Text Society, Edinburgh 1985), i, 15–6 n11.

Building a Bruce Following, 1342–3

This Lothian chivalric cadre – with lands throughout south-east Scotland and Fife – formed the most readily identifiable component of a much wider policy of continuing crown patronage to church institutions, lesser knights and esquires which David intensified from 1342 onwards. This amounted to over two hundred grants at least in the course of the next two years: only an outline of this ongoing resettlement can be given here.[59] But the king's confidence had clearly grown after Douglas's slip. David's subsequent largesse improved his influence over regions of his kingdom other than the south-east with varying degrees of success; but it generally saw him able increasingly to appoint men of his own choosing as royal officers in several localities and to reduce the control of some of the greater magnates.

A number of other men and institutions received royal favour in the south-east. From Dumbarton and Dunfermline on 10 and 30 December 1342 respectively, David granted Holyrood Abbey an extension of its ecclesiastical regality and the right to provide chaplains for the royal household; the abbeys of Newbattle and Kelso also had their lands confirmed and increased in 1342–3. Among lay grantees, Sir James Tweedie received the lands of Drumelzier in Peeblesshire; the king also made a number of smaller grants of Roxburghshire lands now that he controlled that shire. Sir William More, son of the former Chamberlain and precentor of the valuable (and chiefly Lothian) lands of the Scottish Knights of St John, was given Abercorn barony on the Forth just west of Edinburgh, resigned by Sir John Graham, in 1342. David also made many smaller grants of land in and around Edinburgh to lesser men.[60] He may already have decided upon the burgh as his regular residence, graced as it was with a castle repaired and extended by the English garrison of the 1330s, complete with stables and tilting ground added to the park built by King Robert.[61]

In contrast, in the south-west in 1342–3, David's extant grants suggest that his intervention was not so decisive. The king himself skirted Galloway on annual ayres, staying at Middlebie (6 December 1343) and Mouswald (10 September 1344) in Annandale, lands he gave to the Bruces' traditional servants, the Carruthers family.[62] Sometime in early 1342, Malcolm Flem-

---

59 For fuller details, see Penman, 'The Kingship of David II', ch. 4 and Appendix 1. As with Robert I's *acta*, *RRS*, vi can be supplemented by William Roberston's seventeenth-century index of rolls of lost acts of David II (*RMS*, i, App. ii), most of which can be roughly dated by roll to a particular year.

60 *RRS*, vi, nos. 59, 60, 71, 89–90, 101; *RMS*, i, App. i, no. 116 and App. ii, nos. 770, 772, 807, 815, 847, 856–7, 916.

61 C. Malcolm, 'The Gardens of the Castle', *BOEC*, xiv (1925), 101–20; *ER*, i, 238, 487, 506–8; I. MacIvor, *Edinburgh Castle* (London 1993), 35–7.

62 *RRS*, vi, nos. 78, 81; *RMS*, i, nos. 92–3. Curiously, *Atlas of Scottish History to 1707*, 171, discounts David's visits to Annandale, although he was attended there by the Annandale men, John Carruthers, Chancellor of Annandale and John Stewart of Dalswinton.

ing was also granted the Dumfriesshire barony of Mochrum, originally held by Alexander Bruce, earl of Carrick, but since his death (1333) claimed by Patrick Dunbar, earl of March: on 18 June 1342 David exchanged Mochrum with Patrick for the Rhinns in Galloway. In the same year, the neighbouring lands of Enoch were confirmed to the Atholl knight (and a fiscal officer for the Steward in 1334–5), Sir Robert Menzies, who had been to Spain in 1330 with King Robert's heart. Andrew Buttergask, Randolph's deputy before 1341, received the lands of Sannak in the same shire.[63] But Fleming was still not yet able to use his Wigtown title and no royal revenues were collected from this quarter: David seems neither to have visited Carrick nor to have appointed a justiciar for Galloway.

The king was able to do more in Ayrshire and Lanarkshire. By July 1342 Robert Wallace of Auchincruvie – a deputy keeper of Dumbarton for Fleming before 1341 – was sheriff of Ayr with new lands in Kyle and Carrick; his cousin, John Wallace of Riccarton, would be sergeant of Carrick by 1344–5.[64] A Gilbert Carrick was made life coroner of Ayr in 1342. Maurice Murray of Drumsargard in Lanarkshire, keeper of Stirling, received the barony of Stanehouse in the same shire as well as the Roxburghshire barony of Sprouston (originally given by King Robert to his own bastard son). Maurice probably served also as sheriff of Lanark while his son, William, was given Strathaven barony in that shire. Thanks to David, by 1346 the Murrays' new neighbours were William Livingston (granted half of Wiston barony), William Jardine (Roberton barony), John Maitland (Covington barony) and James Sandilands (the other half of Wiston) as well as Alexander Stewart of Darnley.[65] The heavy concentration of these knights in Lanarkshire must have served as a further check on the Steward in his western heartlands.

In the far north and former Comyn stronghold of the north-east most of David's initial significant patronage would be distributed in 1345–6. But in 1342–3 he gave signs of a will to increase his control of these regions. By November 1342, Thomas of Fingask, one of David's envoys around Europe before 1341, had been made bishop of Caithness.[66] Sometime that year, the

---

63 *RRS*, vi, no. 2; *RMS*, i, App. ii, nos. 869, 927. In 1369, David would regrant Mochrum to the earl of March's successor, George, tenth earl, a man much more in favour with the king.

64 *RRS*, vi, nos. 74, 79; *RMS*, i, App. ii, nos. 727, 750, 788, 792, 836–7, 840, 845, 928, 1032, 1039; C. Rogers ed., *The Book of Wallace* (2 vols., Grampian Club 1889), i, 8–15. About 1343, the Steward granted lands in Kyle Stewart to Robert Wallace (NAS RH1/2/112); the loyalty of Robert's son, Duncan, may have been contested by David and the earl of Douglas after 1357 – see below, ch. 11.

65 *RMS*, i, App. ii, nos. 775, 822, 904, 1015, 1097 (Maurice Murray); 738 (Fleming); 824 (Maitland); 967 (Sandilands); 1010 (Stewart); 1013 (Jardine). *RRS*, vi, nos. 38 (Maitland), 94 (Sandilands), 100 (Stewart); *Atlas of Scottish History to 1707*, 205.

66 Watt, *Scottish Graduates*, 187–9.

aforementioned royal servant, Andrew Buttergask, received extensive lands and forestry in Banffshire including the baronies of Westford and Troup, the latter forfeited by Hamelin de Troup, sheriff of Banff and an Edward Balliol supporter acquitted of a part in the conspiracy of 1320. Sir Philip Meldrum, the new sheriff of Banff, received similar grants in Aberdeenshire, as did his brother, William, a deputy justiciar alongside Buttergask.[67] There may also have been early favour from David for the son of a Robert I loyalist who was sheriff of Aberdeen by 1345–6, Sir Alexander Fraser, as well as for the 1342 incumbent, Robert Keith, the Marischal, and his brother, Edward. In 1342–3 David may also have rewarded his future brothers-in-law William, earl of Sutherland, and a Robert Glen, men he would really reward with lands in 1345–6.[68]

In Scotland just north of Tay in 1342–3, as well as further favouring the religious houses at Arbroath and Restenneth, David was also able to begin attracting and rewarding the service of the natural regional affinities of the earls of Mar and Angus.[69] Both lords were then minors, Thomas of Mar in ward in England (where he had been taken in 1334) and Thomas Stewart of Angus (of the Bonkle Berwickshire Stewarts elevated by Robert I), possibly a member of the household of his kinsman Robert Steward, raised alongside the former Lieutenant's four sons, or resident in France alongside William, Lord of Douglas.[70] In the absence of these two young earls David offered service and lands not just to the Keiths and Hays (whose main lands lay in this region) but to the likes of Sir Roger Mortimer of Inverbervie, who had waited upon his king at his return in June 1341; Lawrence Gilliebrand and Walter Moigne, who would serve David in Mar and the north-east after 1357, with Moigne receiving Drum forest in Kincardineshire about 1343; members of the Ramsay kindred, who probably filled the hereditary office of sheriff of Forfar after receiving lands in that shire and Kincardineshire; Sir David Chalmers – rewarded by

---

67 *RRS*, vi, nos. 25, 87, 213 (Meldrums); *RMS*, i, App. ii, nos. 729, 769, 779, 782, 791, 842, 892 (Buttergask); 851, 890 (Philip Meldrum); *ER*, i, 535 and ii, 1. William Meldrum may have been a Hospitaller, receiving a grant from the Precentor of the Order on 28 March 1345 in Aberdeen at the same time as David II was in that burgh (*Knights of St John of Jerusalem in Scotland*, 49–50).

68 *ER*, i, 34, 107, 542; *RRS*, vi, no. 96; *RMS*, i, App. ii, nos. 761, 939, 960, 975, 977, 990, 999, 1020, 1071, 1090, 1103; Fraser, ed., *The Sutherland Book*, i, 29–31 and iii, 14–5. David's half-sister, Maud Bruce, was married to a Thomas Isaac to whom David paid £6 in 1342 for an unspecified office (*ER*, i, 510).

69 *RRS*, vi, nos. 22, 25 to 29, 70, 52, 53; *RMS*, i, App. ii, no. 118 and App. ii, nos. 923, 925, 958.

70 For Mar, see: *Chron. Lanercost*, 283–4; *Rot. Scot.*, i, 208, 255, 271–3; *CDS*, iii, no. 1108. For Angus, see *Scots Peerage*, i, 169–71. David made some grants before 1346 to Margaret Abernethy, Countess of Angus, mother of Thomas Stewart (*RRS*, vi, no. 76; *RMS*, i, App. ii, no. 1030).

Robert I – who received Breirtoun in that shire too from King David. In addition, Reginald Cheyne, whose family had held the sheriffship of Kincardine before 1306, was given the royal thanage of Newdoskis in that shire presumably in return for knight service; William Fraser of Cowie, an esquire named by Wyntoun's source and Bower for his part in aiding Douglas's capture of Edinburgh Castle in 1341, received Durris thanage and other lands in Kincardineshire.[71]

These Lowland laymen formed the beginnings of a solid royalist following for David and they were presumably not simply attracted by his generous resumption of royal patronage after more than a decade. David's personal energy and vigour must have been impressive, especially if he coupled this with a professed interest in wider chivalric pursuits. David may have continued to hold lists between 1342 and 1346, especially after raiding across the Anglo-Scottish border had to cease with the three-year truce of June 1343. But it is also striking that a number of the knights and esquires he would favour before the Battle of Neville's Cross in October 1346 were men involved in crusading expeditions in the 1350s and 1360s either to join the Teutonic knights of Prussia or pan-European attempts to recover the Holy Land. David would make his sponsorship of such endeavours very public after 1357. But the predominantly Angus, Mar and Lothian men like William Ramsay of Colluthie, David Barclay of Brechin, Walter Moigne, Walter and Norman Leslie, Lawrence Gilliebrand, Thomas Bisset of Upsetlington (in Berwickshire), Sir Patrick Dunbar and others deeply involved in such crusading campaigns – indeed, Dunbar (d. 1357) and Norman Leslie (d. 1365) would perish on crusades – may have been drawn to the young Bruce king's early leanings towards their lifestyle, especially after his abortive commitment to Philip VI's crusade.[72] These men would have brought their own considerable military experience and professional armed followings to serve this exciting new prospect as monarch. Wyntoun's contemporary source paints just such a picture of David both at this time and after 1357:

71 *RMS*, i, App. ii, nos. 841 (Buttergask), 874 (Moigne), 876 (Wallace), 879 and 1118 (Chalmers), 955 (Malcolm Ramsay), 957 (William Chalmers), 959 (Gilliebrand) 963 (Patrick Ramsay), 979 (William Menzies), 1023 (Cheyne), 1027 (Keith), 1050 (Fraser), 884 (Mortimer); *RRS*, vi, nos. 28, 62 (Mortimer); *Chron. Wyntoun*, vi, 144 (Fraser); A. Grant, 'Thanes and Thanages', 66, 74–5. Lawrence Gilliebrand also received lands in Little Morphy, Aberdeenshire, from Margaret Bruce, David's sister (NAS GD 42/1).

72 M. Penman, 'Christian Days and Knights: the religious devotions and court of David II of Scotland, 1329–71', *Historical Research*, lxxv (2002), 249–72; S. Boardman, 'David II: Scotland's Crusader King?' (occasional seminar paper, Department of Scottish History, University of Edinburgh 1996), 1–13; A. Mac-Quarrie, *Scotland and the Crusades*, 80–3.

> Often Justyng, dansing and playing . . .
> He raid with faire court throu all his lands . . .
> . . . chevalrous and worthy
> Forthy he schupe him halely
> On Goddis fais to travale,
> And for that way he can him traill,
> Had he nocht been preventyt with died.[73]

However, David's growing chivalric image did not appeal to all Scots. There remained regions of Scotland where his personal lordship and intervention continued to provoke controversy and magnate reaction, areas where he and his court were not welcome.

In the late fourteenth century the English chronicler, Henry Knighton, asserted that about 1342–3:

> A dispute arose in Scotland between King David, who had made himself king, and John [MacDonald] of Islay and others there. But King David bowed to their will, for if he had not he would have lost the kingdom . . .[74]

Undeniably this annal contains much exaggeration. No such major crisis is revealed by the available Scottish government sources for 1342–3. After his clash with Douglas, David seems to have stuck steadfastly to his core royal stomping grounds. A fairly light royal itinerary saw him move from Restenneth in June 1342 to Dumbarton in early July (perhaps stopping off at Dunfermline or Stirling on 23–4 June to commemorate the battle of Bannockburn), back into Fife to Lindores Abbey by 20 August, and up to his aunt Christian Bruce at Kildrummy again by 27 August.[75] David may then have spent autumn raiding across the border with Ramsay's affinity and the earl of Moray. The king's next extant royal act was issued on 28 November, again at Kildrummy. But by December David was back at Dumbarton. Christmas – with David sporting a new oufit made at Aberdeen – was spent at Dunfermline with a full court containing Queen Joan, William Landellis the new bishop of St Andrews, Robert Steward, Duncan, earl of Fife, Moray, Patrick, earl of March, Maurice Murray, Malcolm Fleming and Thomas Charteris the Chancellor.[76] By early January 1343 David was back at Lindores once more, seemingly astride a new 'charger' perhaps purchased in France. By 4 March he was still in – or had returned to

---

73 *Chron. Wyntoun*, vi, 168, 244. The loss of the *Exchequer Rolls* for mid-1343 to autumn 1346 makes it impossible to verify payments for tournaments and other such pursuits.
74 *Chron. Knighton*, 41.
75 *RRS*, vi, nos. 53 to 57.
76 *Ibid*, nos. 58–62; *ER*, i, 521; *Chron. Bower*, vii, 153–5.

– Fife at St Andrews. A day later, the king's nineteenth birthday, he was at Earl Duncan of Fife's chief residence, Falkland: birthday celebrations may also have been held at Dunfermline. Then in late April-early May the king and a full court seem to have spent at least two weeks in Aberdeen. By 18 May he was headed south again via Perth.[77]

Nevertheless, between 6 and 12 June 1343 David was at Ayr where (during what may have been a full council) he did issue a number of charters affecting landholding in the western isles and Argyll. Most notably, 'after diligent discussion and bearing the peace of our realm in mind', David granted anew John MacDonald's possession of all the lands granted to him by Edward Balliol (although this lord was, of course, not named) but now with the exception of Kintyre and Skye.[78]

David may have been obliged to reduce the MacDonald domination of the west coast and inner Hebrides, which he had confirmed on paper in autumn 1341, because of general fears of widespread feuding in this quarter. But it is far more likely that the crown faced collective pressure on the one hand from the Steward and his allies John Menteith of Arran and Knapdale and the Campbells of Lochawe; and on the other from William, earl of Ross, and his local rival Ranald MacRuaridh. In July 1342 David had confirmed to Archibald Campbell of Lochawe his brother's lands in Argyll, to which he added the barony of Melfort in Argyll in May 1343.[79] But the fact that David seems to have withheld confirmation of Archibald's father's lands of Lochawe suggests he was trying to punish or detach the Campbells as allies of the Steward, to whom David had denied neighbouring Kintyre. In autumn 1341 David had also tried to overturn King Robert's concession of Skye to the earls of Ross. But at Ayr on 12 June 1343 David's fresh grants on paper presumably released this island from MacDonald to Ross control. David does seem, though, to have tried to counterbalance this concession by simultaneously confirming a charter by William, earl of Ross (dated 4 July 1342 at Urquhart castle) to Reginald MacRuaridh of lands in Kintail, in North Argyll, and by confirming his own royal restoration of the coastal lordship of Garmoran to the MacRuaridhs: these were grants which must have contributed to the murderous reaction from Ross three years later. At the same time in Ayr in June 1343, David also seems to have granted lands to three of Ross's other northern feud opponents: Torquil MacLeod of Harris

---

77 *RRS*, vi, nos. 63–70; *ER*, i, 483, 511. The several acts involving abbeys issued at Aberdeen, as well as a land grant to the Campbells of Lochawe, suggest that David may have held a council at this time.

78 *RRS*, vi, nos. 71–2; *Acts of the Lords of the Isles*, Appendix, nos. A2 and B24. David also chose this occasion to extend the abbey of Holyrood's regality and grant this house the right to provide royal chaplains.

79 *RRS*, vi, nos. 54, 69.

(the barony of Assynt in Sutherland in return for the service of a twenty–oar galley) and his kinsman, Malcolm; the MacNaughtons (lands in Islay for a twenty-oar galley); and the Mackenzies.[80]

Yet the overriding tone of the conveyancing David was obliged to undertake in June 1343 was one of royal climbdown. Ground had been lost to the Steward and Ross, and in re-confirming MacDonald's control of the vast lordship of Lochaber, David and John Randolph, earl of Moray, were surely recognising the extension of the Isles lord's power within the Bruce-created regality of Moray during their prolonged absences from 1334–5 to 1341–2. MacDonald was now to hold Lochaber 'free from action and dispute', challenges surely contemplated and perhaps begun by the crown since 1341. David's ability to intervene in the politics of the coastal Gael and north-west mainland would always remain remote and unconvincing: it was never a region he, unlike his father, felt strong enough to visit in person. The king was besides far more concerned to take the initiative in central Scotland, in Perthshire and the kingdom of Fife.

By 29 June 1344 at least – probably sometime in 1342 – William Douglas of Liddesdale's disgrace had allowed David to replace Andrew Douglas as sheriff of the vast shire of Perth with Andrew Buttergask, Randolph's deputy justiciar and chamberlain, a man well rewarded by the crown in 1342–3. The royal income from Perth increased from £94 in 1342 to £142 in 1343.[81] Limited as these sums were, the Steward in Atholl and Methven must have begun to feel pressure from David's increasing involvement with Perthshire men and lands. In addition, on 13 November 1342, Pope Clement VI had agreed to David's choice of candidate for the vacant church of Rait in Perthshire: the king's man, Robert Semple, had presented himself at the Curia in fear of his life from the Steward's candidate 'to whom the rights did not belong'.[82] By January 1343, David had also confirmed Sir Robert Menzies in the north-western Perthshire barony of Fortingall and lands around the *Abnethia* of Dull – north of Atholl – which had been gifted to that knight by King Robert's

80 *Ibid*, nos. 72–3, 485–8; D. MacNaughton, *The Clan MacNaughton* (Edinburgh 1977), 18–21; Mackenzie, *History of the Mackenzies*, 50–58; A. Mackenzie, *History of the MacLeods* (Inverness 1889), 9, 287. In 1342, the earl of Ross and the MacDonalds had concluded a marriage alliance which may have paved the way for some collusion between them against the crown in 1343 (NAS RH2/6/4). The earl of Ross was a charter witness at Aberdeen on 1 May 1343 but was perhaps not at Ayr in June where there were no witnesses recorded to the Isles acts: there was, however, a witness list to David's Holyrood grant – the bishop of St Andrews, the Steward, the earl of March, the earl of Moray, Maurice Murray, Malcolm Fleming and Thomas Charteris the Chancellor.
81 *ER*, i, 499–542 *passim*; *RMS*, i, no. 196.
82 *CPR*, ii, *Papal Letters 1342–63*, 67; *ER*, i, 521. For David II and the Steward's dispute over the lands of Rait in the 1360s, see below, ch. 10.

natural son, Robert Bruce of Liddesdale, and Duncan, earl of Fife, respectively.[83] These were small but significant royal gains.

On a much larger scale, that the king fully intended to deny the Steward's hopes of inheriting the earldom of Fife via the terms of the tailzie-pardon concluded by King Robert and Earl Duncan in 1315 must also have become clear by this juncture. David's frequent presence in Fife throughout 1342–3 is striking, especially at the ancient Fife earls' spiritual home of Lindores (where its founder, Earl David of Huntingdon (d. 1219), was buried) and their caput of Falkland where David spent his birthday in 1343. Earl Duncan was regularly present at court at this time – interestingly witnessing charters immediately after the Steward – and may have been pressurised by the crown into resigning and alienating lands. On 22 August 1342, at Lindores, David inspected letters by Duncan confirming disputed boundaries of a John Ireland's Perthshire barony of Murthly (near Dunkeld); on 31 December 1342 at Dunfermline David confirmed Duncan's grant of the lands of Thomaston in Fife (near Cupar and Colluthie) to Sir Roger Mortimer of Inverbervie. Mortimer is likely to have been the father of the woman named as King David's mistress by at least 1359–60 (or perhaps much earlier), a Katherine Mortimer. But Roger Mortimer had also been amongst Earl Duncan's Fife retinue when he had submitted to Balliol in 1332: David was clearly stealing him away from the Fife earl.[84]

Between 1342–3 and 1346 David would confirm and grant new lands in Fife and Kinross to many other Fife knights and esquires and some royalist outsiders – Sir William Ramsay of Colluthie and his kin, Sir Walter Haliburton, Sir David Annan, John Monypenny, Sir David Weymss of Weymss (sheriff of Fife), Simon Gourlay (appointed coroner of Fife in 1342) and David Chalmers – as well as to his relations Christian Bruce and Robert Glen (his half-brother-in-law by 1345): again, several of these holdings had

---

83 *RRS*, vi, nos. 63–4; *RMS*, i, App. ii. nos. 1045 (lands in Kinross to Thomas Menzies), 979 (Aylth forest in Kincardine to William Menzies). Sometime between 1342 and 1346 the Steward as 'Lord of Atholl' confirmed Alexander Menzies' grant of lands in Atholl to his son, Robert (NAS GD 1/408). At this time the Steward was forging links with the *Clann Donnchaidh* in Atholl (Boardman, *Early Stewart Kings*, 7; NAS GD 45 Dalhousie Muniments IV Sec. 27, 74).

84 *RRS*, vi, nos. 55–6, 61–6; K.J. Stringer, *Earl David of Huntingdon: A Study in Anglo-Scottish History* (Edinburgh 1985), 53 *et ad indecim*; *Chron. Lanercost*, 272. My thanks to Simon Taylor of the University of St Andrews for help in identifying Thomaston, between Dairsie and Cupar, as lands which made Roger Mortimer a near neighbour in Fife of Sir William Ramsay of Colluthie who would wed Katherine Mortimer; see below, chs 7 and 8 and M. Penman, 'The Earl, the King, his Lover and the Ransom', *History Scotland*, Vol. 2, no. 1, Jan/Feb 2002, 26–31.

been resigned by Earl Duncan.[85] Moreover, by late 1342 David had already written in conjunction with Philip VI to the former Archbishop of Rouen and now Pope Clement VI to secure William Landellis, an experienced continental and papal lawyer of Fife baronial stock, as bishop of St Andrews after a nine-year vacancy in that See: this may conceivably have either ended or enhanced the king's access to the diocese's income.[86]

David must have pursued many of these ends in direct competition with the Steward who seems to have stuck close by Duncan of Fife during the 1340s, perhaps having reached an understanding with the aging and apparently ailing earl (born *c.* 1285) as to his succession and only child, Isabella. This perhaps explains why although the Steward as earl of Atholl became guardian of Duncan's three large east-Perthshire baronies of Strathtay, Strath Braan and Strathord by 1345, or perhaps earlier, he still held back from formal marriage with the mother of his several children, Elizabeth More.[87] Earl Duncan would eventually die in 1353. But according to Northumbrian knight Sir Thomas Gray, captured by the Scots in 1355 after a long career in border warfare:

> [David] declared [the earldom of Fife] was in his right to bestow owing to the forfeiture as he said of Duncan earl of Fife in the time of Robert de Brus, his father, for the slaying of an esquire named Michael Beaton, whom he had cause to be slain in anger at a hawking party, wherefore the said King David alleged that the said Earl, in order to obtain from the king remission of the forfeiture, had by indenture devised the reversion of the earldom to the said king his father, in the event of his [Duncan's] dying without heir-male, which he did. But the said earl had a daughter by his wife, the king of England [Edward I]'s [grand] daughter, the Countess of Gloucester. This daughter [Isabella] was in England, and it was intended that she should be sold to Robert the Steward of Scotland [for a wife], but she married for love William de Felton, a knight of Northumberland, who was her guardian at that time . . .[88]

85 *RMS*, i, App. ii, nos. 760, 765 (Alexander Ramsay), 766 (Monypenny), 780, 889 (Christian Bruce, of lands resigned by earl Duncan), 971 and 976 (Weymss, of lands resigned by Duncan), 964 (Henry Ramsay), 994 (Nesome Ramsay), 1021 (John Ramsay), 1029 (Glen), 1118 (Chalmers), 1119 (Annan), 1132 (Bisset). David also gave Nesome Ramsay and William Ramsay robes in 1343 (*ER*, i, 523, 533, 540).
86 *CPR*, iii, 5; *Foedera*, i, 1224; Watt, *Scottish Graduates*, 36–8, 328. The vacancy income of St Andrews had been assigned briefly to David's Carrick household *c.* 1328–9 (*ER*, i, 109).
87 *HMC*, vii, 305; NAS Murthly Castle Muniments GD 121/box 4/bundle 10/no. 3; Penman, 'The Scots at the Battle of Neville's Cross', 169–70.
88 *Chron. Scalacronica*, 126; *RRS*, v, no. 72.

Gray is clearly well informed about Robert I's pardon and re-tailzie of Fife in 1315, but just when Isabella married William Felton is not exactly known. They were certainly married before 5 April 1345 when the Northumbrian lands of Edlingham (which had belonged to Patrick Dunbar, earl of March, until his defection back to the Scots in 1335) and Newton were confirmed to Felton and 'his wife, Isabella'. But if Isabella had been born after Maria de Monthermer, daughter of Ralph Monthermer, earl of Gloucester, was allowed to return to Duncan in Scotland in 1320–1, then she could have wed Felton 'for love' sometime in the late 1330s. A grant to Felton from Queen Philippa of England on 30 June 1338 of the manor of Wark-on-Tyne (for the duration of the childhood of its righful owner, David Strathbogie, the disinherited earl of Atholl, son of the man slain at Culblean in 1335) may actually have been a wedding gift carved out of lands held by thirteenth-century kings of Scots. The most likely year for their match seems to be as Isabella and Felton had a son, significantly christened Duncan, most likely born about 1339: in 1351, Edward III and his queen would seek papal provision for this Duncan to a Northumbrian benefice because Sir William Felton 'on his wife's side is kindred to the king'.[89] But if Isabella was not born until the peace of *c.* 1329–32, her marriage to Felton may have occurred as late as the period 1341–5. Either way, before Robert Steward finally gave in and had his marriage to, and offspring by, Elizabeth More legitimised by papal dispensation in 1347, he may still have hoped to make Isabella his wife, thus gaining title to Fife.[90]

Robert's military efforts when he became Lieutenant for David for a second time in 1338, as well as the Steward's deal with Douglas in 1342 over possession of the former Strathbogie earldom of Atholl, may have been designed to boost his claim to Fife. As we have seen, the Strathbogies were Fife descendants and, in August 1335, after a tense parliament at Dairsie in Fife, David Strathbogie had defected from the Bruce party back to Balliol, taking the Steward with him. In 1307 Strathbogie's father had had to recover his title of Atholl for £10,000 from Ralph de Monthermer, earl of Gloucester, father of earl Duncan's wife and the man whom Edward III had granted title to the forfeited lands of Atholl in 1334–5. The deal the Steward may have cut with Strathbogie in 1335 could thus have involved an agreement with Gloucester (brokered by Strathbogie) as to Isabella's mar-

89 NRO 76 ZSW Swinburne Mss (Part 1) 3/11–3 and 5/54–58; NRO 358/1–46 Riddell Mss/7; *CDS*, iii, no. 8; Hodgson, *A History of Northumberland*, vii, 85, 113–6, 232–40. For Duncan Felton, see, *CDS*, v, no. 812; Roskell, Clark and Rawcliffe, eds, *The History of Parliament: the House of Commons, 1386–1421*, ii, 289; *CPR*, iii, 69, 428. On 10 June 1339, Edward III increased Maria, Countess of Fife's weekly allowance to an annuity perhaps to mark the birth of an English-controlled heir to Fife (*CDS*, iii, no. 1312).
90 *CPP*, i, 124; *RRS*, vi, p. 45; see below, ch. 5.

riage, presumably in Earl Ralph's (or perhaps Strathbogie's) ward. This deal collapsed with David Strathbogie's death at Culblean in November 1335.[91] Thereafter, Isabella was free to wed William Felton, a key royal border officer with important tenurial and personal connections. In fact, Felton served Edward III variously as escheator and sheriff of Northumberland (c. 1341–5) and keeper of Roxburgh Castle (alongside John de Coupland, King David's captor of 1346); Felton was also justiciar (or escheator) for English-occupied Scotland and had dealings with several Fife men briefly in English allegiance (including William Ramsay of Colluthie and Thomas Bisset of Upsetlington, the knights whom David II would make successive earls of Fife after 1357). Finally, Felton may have been a Strathbogie tenant on lands in Northumberland.[92]

Isabella of Fife's wardship in England, then, makes it likely that David made it plain in public before the Battle of Neville's Cross – sometime c. 1341–6 – that he regarded Earl Duncan's house as certain to fail in the male line, a denial of female succession which might conceivably be applied, too, to the kingship itself, further denying Robert Steward, son of Marjorie Bruce. David must also have made it plain by his actions that he would never recognise the Steward as the crown's assignee to Fife. Some slim indication of the resulting friction between David and the Steward over Fife is hinted at in the royal exchequer records for 1342–3 which note that the Steward burned timber at Crail intended for burgh mills which were either assigned to the household of David's sisters or attached to the moor there that the king seems to have invested some effort in cultivating.[93]

David's interference in central Scotland, though, became undeniably bolder and more complex after the reverse he suffered in his western isles speculation in June 1343. On 17 September 1343, while at Dunfermline the day before moving on to Scone, David ordered the sheriff of Perth and his bailies to restore Sir John Logie to his father's vast west-Perthshire barony of Strathgartney. This had been given by King Robert to John Menteith of Arran and Knapdale's grandfather after Logie senior's forfeiture for his role in the 1320 Balliol plot.[94] Logie junior, however, was perhaps already the first husband of David II's future mistress, Margaret Drummond, whom the king would wed in 1363. Before 1346, David would extend patronage to Margaret's Drummond kindred in Perthshire. Logie's recovery of Strath-

---

91 Penman, 'The Scots at the Battle of Neville's Cross', 169–70; and above, ch. 2.
92 *Calendar of Inquisitions Miscellaneous*, ii (1307–48), nos. 1547, 1893; *Calendar of Patent Rolls, Edward III 1338–40*, 149, 339; *Rot. Scot.*, i, 696–7, 689 (Felton dealing with a John de Landellis and William Ramsay, Scots in English allegiance c. 1341). For the Felton-Strathbogie link, see *Scots Peerage*, i, 430.
93 *ER*, i, 521.
94 *RRS*, vi, no. 75; *APS*, i, 524; W. Fraser, ed., *The Red Book of Menteith* (2 vols., Edinburgh 1880) ii, 238–9.

gartney may have been blocked by the Steward as Lieutenant and as Menteith's cousin before 1341: the Steward as Lieutenant again would certainly allow John Menteith to reoccupy Strathgartney after David's capture in 1346. But Logie's revival in 1343 also bolstered the position of Sir John Graham whom David seems to have recognised sometime after 1341 as earl of Menteith by right of his marriage, thus once again denying Sir John Menteith's kindred who had been guardians and hopeful claimants to that earldom before 1322 and, probably, since 1333. Many of these rival claims in central Scotland were bound together by a tailzie of 1309 by which the heirs of the earls of Menteith also held a recognised claim to the earldom of Fife in the event of the failure of Duncan's line.[95]

This snub to Sir John Menteith, and David's general obstruction of Steward ambition in central Scotland, must have made gatherings at Scone between 18 September and 31 October 1343 incredibly fraught affairs. The meetings behind the royal acts issued in this period do not seem to have constituted a formal council or parliament – despite the venue.[96] However, David certainly ended these Scone sessions with a bang. While still there on 31 October, David granted the earldom of Strathearn to Sir Maurice Murray of Drumsargard by right of his 1339 marriage to Joanna Menteith, sister of John of Arran and Knapdale and widow successively of John Campbell, earl of Atholl, and Malise, seventh earl of Strathearn. No witness list survives for this act but it may have been very similar to the substantial group named for another royal charter dated that day (inspecting a charter of Margaret, mother Countess of Angus): the bishops of St Andrews, Glasgow, and Brechin, Duncan, earl of Fife, Robert Steward, John Randolph, earl of Moray, Robert Keith (Marischal), David Hay (Constable), Philip Meldrum (sheriff of Banff) and Andrew Buttergask (sheriff of Perth).[97] The fact that the Steward sealed *after* Duncan on this occasion and was not described as usual as 'our beloved nephew' perhaps suggests that David had tightened the screws on his heir-presumptive, surrounding him and the Fife earl with royalist supporters all well rewarded by the crown since 1341. Murray's elevation – in addition to his appointment as keeper of Stirling Castle – undeniably undermined the Steward's dominance of central Scotland and the Clyde valley: Maurice would have been able to call upon not only his own following but the Atholl-Strathearn ties of his new wife.[98]

95 *RRS*, v, no. 72; *RRS*, vi, nos. 104, 212; *Scots Peerage*, vi, 135–41.

96 *APS*, i, 65 does not acknowledge a parliament at this time, but see the uncertainly dated *RRS*, vi, no. 489. The paucity of *ER*, i, for 1343–6 makes this impossible to verify. The *RPS* editors argue against the holding of a Scone parliament at this time.

97 *RRS*, vi, nos. 76–7; *CPR, Papal Letters*, ii, 546.

98 This Murray network of connections would be inherited by Archibald Douglas when he wed Maurice's daughter in 1362 (Brown, *Black Douglases*, 56; see below, ch. 8).

Moreover, David gave Sir Maurice sasine of his new earldom despite the fact that it had been the Steward as Lieutenant, at a parliament in Perth in October 1339, who had overseen the pardon of Malise, eighth earl of Strathearn, for surrendering his earldom to Balliol and England.[99]

Whether the Steward remained in David's company for the rest of the year is unclear. But the king seemed comfortable enough with his position to roam further afield than usual: on 6 November 1343 he applied, perhaps while at Holyrood, to the Pope for the right to choose confessors for himself, his queen, his sisters and Malcolm Fleming. Yet a month later David was at Middlebie in Annandale where he made Sir Alexander Stewart of Darnley his bailie in all cases involving Annandale men between that lordship and Clydesdale. Christmas that year was spent back at Stirling with the castle now repaired.[100]

Partisan Politics, 1344–5

David turned twenty in March 1344. He may have looked back with cautious satisfaction upon his achievements of the previous three years, a sense that he was finally getting somewhere. It had been a period in which he had learned a lot and done much to reassert the domestic authority and initiative of the Bruce dynasty in the Scottish kingship's Lowland heartlands. A recognisable and extensive royal following was by then prominent, actively restoring royal administration in the localities: David had secured his own choice of men in all of the household and most of the locality offices of the crown from Banff in the north-east to Dumbarton in the west and the march-wardenships in the south. However, he must have been conscious that he had as yet not led his troops in person to any significant military success – either in Scotland or over the border – and that he had still not been able to curb decisively the self-interest and influence of great magnates like the twenty-eight-year-old Steward, the earl of Ross, John MacDonald or William Douglas: the royal writ was still diluted even in regions other than the traditional outlying zones of the realm.

Yet 1344, perhaps somewhat falsely due to the paucity of records, gives the impression of a year of unremitting tension building towards a watershed in crown-magnate relations. Unluckily for David, by 13 February 1344 it was apparent that his designs had not gone as smoothly as planned since the previous autumn. On that day at Edinburgh it is known that David was attended (at least) by the Steward, Patrick, earl of March, and the royalist knights Maurice Murray, Thomas Charteris, Malcolm Fleming, William Livingston and Philip Meldrum.[101] But Murray was not then styled

---

99 Thomson, 'A Roll of the Scottish Parliament, 1344', 235–7.
100 *RRS*, vi, no. 78; *CPP*, i, 27.
101 *RRS*, vi, no. 80; *RMS*, i, App. ii, no. 886.

as earl of Strathearn. It is uncertain whether this was due to the quirks of David's chancery clerk (Maurice would never use the title in royal charters); or the Steward's physical occupation of Strathearn, a title he would eventually secure in 1357; or the continued lordship presence there of Malise, eighth earl of Strathearn. But weeks before June 1344 – when a parliament was held once more at Scone – it must have become apparent that David's grant of the title of Strathearn to Murray by right of his marriage, and perhaps also Maurice's influence over his wife's terce lands in Atholl from her first marriage, had in some way been challenged or blocked. The year 1344 may indeed have been marked by signs of what one historian has described as 'intermittent and fitful government', hinting at a crisis in power.[102] Yet what ensued makes it clear that David and his close advisers spent the spring securing vital support to push through the royal will on this and other political matters.

A full record of the June 1344 parliament survives and makes fascinating reading.[103] David and his close advisers evidently sought Malise's full re-indictment and punishment for his contact with Edward Balliol and England before 1339. However, the absent earl was well defended, and despite 'diverse opposing allegations given on the part of the lord king' the matter had to be put to an assize of nineteen men. Before this body, as in 1339, Malise of Strathearn was again tried and found innocent of treason. However, on this occasion the separate distinction was made that Malise was nonetheless guilty of surrendering his earldom to England: his lands were thus deemed to be forfeit to the crown. As such, this assize gives the clear impression of having been a packed bench. Just how the personnel of this jury was selected is unclear but it was headed by the earls of Fife, Wigtown (with Fleming for the first time thus styled) and Menteith (John Graham) and otherwise dominated by knights well rewarded by the king since 1341: John Maxwell, Thomas Boyd, William Livingston, John Crawford, Andrew Douglas, William Ramsay, David Weymss, Hugh Eglintoun, David Barclay, Alan Cathcart, Robert Menzies, Alexander Cragie, Michael Scott and three clerics. The Steward, Campbells of Lochawe and John Menteith of Arran – the men with various claims to Strathearn, Atholl and Fife – were excluded. Moreover, David's tight control of this public assertion of his right to dispose of Strathearn may also have been carefully limited to a repeat of the charge of surrender of lands – and not full treason – because although the Steward (and Duncan of Fife) might easily have been tarred with the same brush for such actions in 1335, several men now favoured by

---

102 Webster, 'David II and the Government of Fourteenth-century Scotland', 56.
103 For what follows, see Thomson, 'A Roll of the Scottish Parliament, 1344', 235–40; *RPS*, 1344/1–7.

the crown – William Ramsay of Colluthie, Thomas Bisset of Upsetlington, John Maxwell of Caerlaverock, John Logie of Strathgartney – might also have been forfeited for temporary defection.[104]

David's parliamentary repossession of Strathearn in June 1344 thus allowed him to confirm Maurice Murray as earl shortly thereafter.[105] It also dented the landed ambitions of William, earl of Ross, who along with Roger, bishop of Ross, acted as attorney in the parliament chamber for the absent Malise (who was possibly in ward). Earl William had a vested interest in doing so for on 28 May 1344, in his full title as earl of Orkney and Caithness as well as Strathearn, Malise had granted Ross, his brother-in-law, control of the marriage of Malise's second daughter and co-heiress, Isabella: this was a deal which would surely have brought Ross part of Caithness, more if he pressed for it.[106]

Ross's obsession with Caithness and Orkney remained really outside David's interests. But another closely allied item of parliamentary business in June 1344 affecting the status quo in the north underlined the close partnership in power which David and John Randolph, earl of Moray, sought to recover at other magnates' expense. No details of the legal debate and surely heated argument which raged in this session have survived, only a note of the decision that

> in presence of the prelates and nobles of the realm . . . Sir John Randolph, earl of Moray . . . confessed that he had no right to the offices of justiciar benorth the Firth of Forth by way of heritage, but for obtaining the said office put himself in our lord the king's will.[107]

This was no less than an enabling act by which David could remove William, earl of Ross, as justiciar, a post he had assumed after the death of Guardian Thomas Randolph in 1332 or John Randolph's capture in 1335. Such

---

104 *Rot. Scot.*, i, 382 (Steward), 584 (Bisset), 689 (Ramsay); *Chron. Lanercost*, 272 (Mortimer and other Fife knights); *CDS*, iii, no. 1081, 1184, 1292 (English payment for services in Edinburgh castle to William Ramsay, Alexander Craigie), 1323 (Scots in garrisons of Edinburgh or Stirling for Edward III); Webster, 'Scotland Without a King, 1329–41', 226, 229, 234.

105 *RMS*, i, App. ii, no. 896.

106 B. Crawford, 'The Earls of Orkney-Caithness and the Relations with Norway and Scotland, 1158–1470' (unpublished Ph.D. thesis, University of St Andrews, 1971), 21–39, 112–34, 163–78, 217–24. Malise, earl of Strathearn/Orkney-Caithness had had five daughters: the eldest by Malise's first wife, had the rightful claim to Caithness, but the earl of Ross would push the claim of the second daughter (by Malise's second wife, Ross's sister), his niece, Isabella, whom he would wed off to William Sinclair of Rosslyn about 1344 (W. Saint-Clair, *The Saint Clairs of the Isles* (New Zealand 1898), 91).

107 Thomson, 'A Roll of the Scottish Parliament, 1344', 39–40; *RPS*, 1344/3.

intervention by David would end Ross's embezzlement of royal income in the north.

There is no clear proof that David did sack Ross and appoint Randolph as justiciar between 1344 and 1346. But besides the pretext of Ross's financial impropriety the crown could also have acted to stop William's feud with the Mackenzies, a long-running sore which tradition maintains saw the earl devastate Kintail about 1342–4 and hang Chief Kenneth Mackenzie about 1346.[108] Sir Maurice Murray, now earl of Strathearn, did receive some form of justiciary post about 1344–6 and the king would definitely dismiss Ross as jusictiar north of Forth for abuse of office in 1359, presumably after Ross had re-monopolised that office after the deaths at Neville's Cross of both Randolph and Murray. David may also have been involved in northern justice ayres himself before 1346, as he would be after 1357. Ayres had been held at Inverbervie in Angus in 1341 and at Inverkeithing and Cupar in Fife in 1342. Moreover, the young king can certainly be found requesting a number of papal marriage dispensations for matches between feuding families brought to peace. According to Andrew Wyntoun's source, David also intervened personally in such disruptive cases, for example arresting an Alan de Wyntoun (a crusader) for his seizure of a daughter of Sir Alexander Seton and obliging the accused to wed the girl (although this was a case within Lothian's jurisdiction).[109]

The rest of the 1344 parliament also seems to have been a public success and expression of confident authority for David. There was an assertion of the rights of the bishop of Aberdeen to the second teinds of the diocese (long disputed by Ross as justiciar), bolstering the finances of the new prelate, William de Deyn, who as abbot of Kilwinning had accompanied David to France.[110] Finally, there was a recorded contract of cautioners drawn up to pacify the feud between the followings of William Douglas of Liddesdale and the late Alexander Ramsay of Dalhousie. The earls of Fife, Sutherland and Strathearn (Maurice Murray) and Sir William Cunningham acted as cautioners for Ramsay's men, and (in a suggestive grouping) the Steward and the earls of March and Wigtown for Douglas's party. The violence which David may have first provoked in 1342 had clearly rumbled on in the Lothians, often – as the chroniclers complained – spilling out of hand: this was quite strong if indirect criticism of the king who had really assumed the lordship of Ramsay's affinity.

108 Mackenzie, *A History of the Mackenzies*, 49–52.
109 *RMS*, i, App. ii, nos. 968, 973; *ER*, i, 483, 499, 501–3, 543, 546, 557, 570; *ibid.*, ii, 82; *Chron. Wyntoun*, vi, 190; MacQueen, *Common Law and Feudal Society in Medieval Scotland*, 153, 156. See also *CPR*, iii, 27 (marriage between William Murray and Duncan Campbell's daughter, to end 'homicides and scandals') and Fraser, ed., *The Sutherland Book*, i, 30–1.
110 Watt, *Scottish Graduates*, 149–50.

But Patrick Dunbar, earl of March, acted here according to the crown's wishes despite being frozen out since June 1341 from royal patronage affecting the south-east. Indeed, the aged Patrick (born *c.* 1283) – like Earl Duncan of Fife – must have felt himself rudely bypassed in favour of future generations more easily controlled by the Bruce regime. Neither earl had received any substantial favour from either Bruce king. When David visted Dunbar Castle sometime in 1343–4 he may have extended favour to Earl Patrick's half-nephews and heirs (the children of Sir Patrick Dunbar, the Ramsay follower), George and John Dunbar and their sister, Agnes, a future mistress of the king.[111] David may also then have shown favour (as he would after 1357) to other men among March's retinue, like Alexander Recklington, keeper of Dunbar Castle: all these Dunbar-based laymen would express a strong interest in the crusades after 1346 and enter royal service. Such was Earl Patrick's sense of exclusion that he may have asked sometime in 1344 for a royal pardon for his defection in the 1330s and confirmation of all his lands. David clearly had a strong grip on the south-east of Scotland by 1344.[112]

As far as the Scottish chroniclers (and Froissart) were concerned, the next two years of David's life and reign – until the campaign which would end at Neville's Cross in autumn 1346 – contained no event or royal deed worthy of note. The few surviving government sources also suggest at first glance a distinct lull in domestic politics. Yet in the wake of the successful June 1344 parliament the king really stepped up his patronage to further strengthen his regional support. Throughout the rest of 1344 and into autumn 1345 David seems to have issued almost two hundred grants to useful locality men and to have safeguarded the rights of crown-founded churches and towns.[113]

No substantial royal grants affected the far north but David may have tried to weaken the hold of William, earl of Ross, over the merchants of the burgh of Inverness when he travelled to Netherdale in Banffshire in December 1344 and issued letters prohibiting anyone but the Chamberlain from interfering in Inverness's weights and measures.[114] But there was much further favour in the north-east for established crown men like Sir Philip Meldrum, the Buttergasks, Cheynes and Chalmers, Alexander Cragie, John Lyle, Robert Glen (husband of David's sister Maud) and Alexander Fraser (now made sheriff of Aberdeen).[115] David's eldest full sister received

---

111 *ER*, i, 518.

112 *RMS*, i, nos. 160, 187 and App. ii, no. 947; *Rot. Scot.*, i, 897.

113 See Penman, 'The Kingship of David II', Appendix 1 for a regional breakdown of *RMS*, i, App. ii, nos. 888–1010, lost acts roughly dateable to 1344–5.

114 *RRS*, vi, no. 85; *ER*, i, 526.

115 *RMS*, i, App. ii, nos. 908, 941, 959, 967, 1016, 1068, 1104, 1127, 1130; *RRS*, vi, nos. 93–5; *ER*, i, 499–542.

Forfarshire and Kincardineshire lands as did the Ramsays, the Chamberlain John Roxburgh, William Menzies, Peter Prendergast (granted the thanage of Tannadice, given by King Robert to Alexander Bruce) and the abbey of Restenneth. David may also have helped his aunt Christian Bruce oversee her sons' – Andrew Murray's heirs – occupation of their father's lands in the north-east and at Bothwell in Lanarkshire, while the large and valuable lordship of Garioch next to the earldom of Mar was reclaimed to the crown.[116] In Fife, David granted Falkland lands to Christian after they had been resigned by Earl Duncan (who may have been compensated with the coquet of the burgh of Cupar): Duncan also resigned lands which went to Sir David Weymss, sheriff of Fife, and the king continued to favour the Ramsays and many lesser men in that shire.[117] Sir William Livingston, a regular daily councillor of the king, was given the forfeited barony of Callendar north of Stirling when David stopped at Dumbarton on 10 July 1345.[118] In Perthshire David's grantees in 1344–5 were very deliberate choices including Andrew Buttergask the sheriff of Perth, Alexander Menzies (confirmed in Fortingall), a John Stewart (perhaps the Steward's brother or the knight of Dalswinton) and Sir Malcolm Drummond (brother of David's future mistress, who was appointed coroner of Perth in mid-1345) and his uncle John (whom David would make earl of Menteith in 1360).[119] By July 1344 David had secured papal approval of his choice of another key Perthshire church post in Richard from Pilmor in Fife (brother of John, bishop of Moray, a Gaillard councillor) as the new bishop of Dunkeld, snubbing both the Steward's choice, a Duncan of Strathearn, and a cleric supported by Edward III.[120]

David continued to distribute more land in the Lothians, Peeblesshire and Berwickshire than anywhere else, including further grants to Sir William Ramsay as sheriff of Edinburgh, Sir Walter Haliburton, Sir Hugh Eglintoun,

---

116 *RMS*, i, App. ii, nos. 984, 1083. Many men from this northern cadre can be found with Christian Bruce at Kildrummy Castle in this period: in August 1345 Christian issued a charter witnessed by the bishop of Aberdeen, the earl of Sutherland, Philip Meldrum, William Abernethy, Alexander Leslie and Andrew Buttergask (*HMC, lx, Mar & Kelly*, 2). Similarly, in 1345 David Lindsay of Crawford issued a charter at Monimail, Fife, witnessed by the earl of Sutherland, Edward Keith and David Barclay (*HMC, xi, Duke of Hamilton*, 210).

117 *RMS*, i, App. ii, nos. 889, 893, 909 (office of keeper of king's moor, Crail), 926, 932, 935, 944, 964, 971, 976, 994, 1016, 1021, 1029, 1042, 1045, 1055, 1059, 1065, 1076, 1080, 1118, 1119, 1132.

118 *RRS*, vi, no. 93 – this barony had first been granted to Henry Douglas, a brother of William of Lothian, *c*. 1341 (*RMS*, i, App. ii, no. 756).

119 *Ibid*, nos. 897, 908, 924, 933, 941, 943, 978, 996, 1017, 1054, 1057, 1058, 1086, 1104, 1120, 1122, 1123, 1125.

120 Watt, *Scottish Graduates*, 451–2; A.D.M. Barrell, *The Papacy, Scotland and northern England, 1342–78* (Cambridge 1996), 197, 202–4.

Simon Gourlay, Sir James Sandilands, Maurice Murray and William Chalmers (who was given the keeping of North Berwick port, the southern terminus of the ferry across the Forth to Earlsferry in Fife).[121] In the southwest David continued to refrain from heavy-handed intervention. In the second half of 1344, not only did he confirm many clan chieftains in their lands and titles but he forgave former enemies like the Maxwells of Caerlaverock and the MacDowells (who would formally submit *c.* 1345); the king also confirmed the concessions of Alexander III and Robert I that crown officers would not have rights of arbitrary justice over the men of Galloway.[122] However, some patronage was awarded in Dumfriesshire with lands for Gilbert Carrick and the Mar man Lawrence Gilliebrand, while John Randolph, earl of Moray, was given a commendatorship of the sheriffdom of Dumfries and a life justiciary over Annandale and Man. David also seems to have confirmed the bounds of Malcolm Fleming's earldom of Wigtown, a title that lord now used regularly in royal charters.[123] As we have seen, in Ayrshire there were grants for the local kin of Wallace and Danielston; and in Lanarkshire, the barony of Wiston was given to Sir James Sandilands (who already held lands in Fife and the south-east) and lesser lands to Maurice Murray's son.[124]

Again, David backed up a good many of these grants in person with an itinerary which took him from Scone in June 1344 to Dumbarton by 17 October, Stirling by 15 November, Netherdale in Banffshire (as mentioned) by 31 December, Dunfermline by 9 March 1345, and Aberdeen by 28 March (where he may have issued the burgh with a pardon for unspecified transgressions). A full council was then held at Edinburgh in mid-April for which no record of decisions survives: the bishops of St Andrews, Glasgow and Brechin, the earls of March and Wigtown, the Chancellor and Sir William Livingston were the only witnesses to a charter issued during its sitting.[125] Between 25 May and 10 July David shuttled between Edinburgh and Dumbarton attended by the Steward, Randolph,

121 *RRS*, vi, nos. 80, 95; *RMS*, i, App. ii, nos. 887, 891, 899, 901, 902, 911, 916, 917, 922, 931, 937, 938, 950, 952, 962, 965, 969, 981, 985, 992, 995, 1003, 1009, 1026, 1034, 1041, 1047, 1048, 1053, 1060, 1061, 1067, 1068, 1070, 1073, 1085, 1092, 1093, 1094, 1096-8, 1121.
122 *Ibid*, nos. 910, 912 (clan of Gillolane, Gilbert McGillolane chief), 913 (Kenelman, Michael McGorth chief), 914 (Kennedy), 982 (McGowan – Donald Edzear chief); 1005-8 (MacDowells as constables of Kirkcudbright), 1081 (Maxwell), 1012; W.R. Kermack, 'Kindred of the Bear', *The Scottish Genealogist*, xix, i, (1972), 14-5; Oram, 'Bruce, Balliol and the Lordship of Galloway', 42-7.
123 *RRS*, vi, nos. 78, 81, 102, 491; *RMS*, i, App. ii, nos. 894, 903, 906, 915, 927, 930, 936, 973, 1064, 1100, 1105-14, 1116.
124 *RRS*, vi, nos. 83, 94, 100; *RMS*, i, App. ii, nos. 895, 904, 928, 929, 1010, 1013, 1014, 1024, 1025, 1040, 1043, 1063, 1066, 1089.
125 *RRS*, vi, nos. 80-90; *RPS*, 1345/1.

March, Wigtown and the Chancellor. His next extant act places him back at Edinburgh on 2 September (granting Wiston to Sandilands) with the same witnesses. Three weeks later the court had returned for a third time that year to Dumbarton where the earls of Strathearn and Sutherland were also in attendance. By 6–10 October 1345 David had moved east only as far as Lanark. Here William Douglas of Liddesdale was recorded for the first time since June 1342 as a royal charter witness. David had now seemingly forgiven the knight and allowed him to take up the office of sheriff of Teviotdale and keeper of Roxburgh Castle, a crown admission that Douglas's participation was absolutely necessary to the renewed prosecution of war against England.[126]

In short, as he had done since his return from France, David clearly worked hard in 1344–5 to promote his lordship and dynasty. Yet despite the coping stone of the June 1344 parliament and the ongoing territorial resettlement, David had arguably still not managed any singular spectacular success which would tip the scales of power – both at the centre and in the localities – decisively in his favour. As king he may indeed have felt that he had still not made his mark as ruler in such a manner as would trumpet the unchallenged authority of his house and political will over Scotland, signalling a convincing recovery of the Bruce position of *c.* 1320–9.

The birth of a Bruce heir at this stage might have changed all that. The provision of an heir by a king now in his twenty-second year was a duty any loyal subject might have fully anticipated. But aside from natural expectation David must have been beginning to feel intense pressure to provide for his succession in the light of his antagonists' fertility. Both the Steward and Edward III had four sons each already emerging from infancy, as well as daughters.[127] David meanwhile was childless and likely to stay that way, for he may already have become estranged from Queen Joan or have shown himself to be incapable of fatherhood, even with mistresses. If this was so, the Steward could in theory afford to bide his time and ride out David's attempts to erode and contain his territorial empire. If he could continue to deprive David of sufficient power – or of an excuse to disinherit the Stewarts – then Robert Steward could remain reasonably safe in the knowledge that, by the terms of his father's marriage to Marjorie Bruce and the parliamentary entails of 1318 and 1326, one of his sons would succeed as king even though Robert himself would probably die shortly before the younger David. The Steward may even have named his first three sons John, Walter

126 *RRS*, vi, nos. 91–96.
127 Boardman, *Early Stewart Kings*, 41; M. Packe, *King Edward III* (London 1983), xii-iii.

and Robert with this in mind, following King Robert's choice of John for his twin son (who had died in infancy) as a way of obliterating the record of any 'John I of Scotland' in John Balliol. Beyond this eventual succession Robert Steward could rely upon his large family to recover, network and control a vastly extended patrimony dominating central Scotland.[128]

However, this relatively comfortable default situation for the Steward soon threatened to change, and grave worries over the succession infiltrated the increasingly tense crown-magnate relations of 1344–5. Both Fordun's contemporary source and, later, Abbot Bower took time to record that in July 1344 – shortly after that controversial Scone parliament – David had cause to hang at Ayr a man claiming to be Alexander Bruce, earl of Carrick, bastard son of Edward Bruce by a Strathbogie woman. The anxious attendance at this execution of David, Robert Steward and Malcolm Fleming of Wigtown was noted as if to emphasise that the pretender had been only too correct to fear that 'he might be put to death by those who occupied his lands' (in Fleming's case through armed force since 1341). It also added weight to Bower's insistence that in executing this claimant:

> . . . some believe proper judicial procedure had not in all points been observed. Because of this many still think that he was the real Alexander and condemned to an unjust death so that his lands could be retained by others.[129]

It may be the case that many observers between 1344 and Bower's writings of the 1440s felt that any heir of Edward Bruce – even if legitimated after the fact – had a reasonable claim to the throne ahead of the Stewarts by the terms of the 1315 parliamentary act of succession. It has already been speculated that this may explain the blackening of Alexander Bruce's name by post-1371 commentators.[130] Such a claimant might also have had an outside chance of inheriting the lands of Atholl, Fife and Buchan/Badenoch through his Strathbogie blood. Yet in fact, by 1344–5, David himself may have had either sufficient concern to react violently towards such talk of an alternative Bruce successor, or to have had sufficient cause at first to encourage this threat to Stewart (and, perhaps, wavering Fleming) interests. For the king may already have laid plans to identify and elevate his own firm choice of legitimate alternative heirs-presumptive to his throne ahead of the Steward and his brood.

According once more to Bower, by the late 1350s at least, David had come to regard John Sutherland, son of William, earl of Sutherland, and the king's

---

128 Boardman, *Early Stewart Kings*, chs 2–3.
129 *Chron. Fordun*, i, 366–7; *Chron. Bower*, vii, 159.
130 See above, ch. 2.

sister, Margaret Bruce, as his heir-presumptive instead of the Steward. Interestingly, Hector Boece, writing in the early sixteenth century, asserted that upon his release from English captivity in 1357 David forced through parliament a formal recognition of an 'Alexander Sutherland' as his heir, surely a confusion of Alexander Bruce and John Sutherland.[131] William, earl of Sutherland (who as a minor had been in King Robert's ward), and Margaret Bruce had been wed sometime after David had secured a papal dispensation for this match in December 1342 (through the offices of Thomas Fingask, the new bishop of Caithness). Initially this dispensation may have been sought by the crown to help pacify the north by extinguishing unspecified feuds in that region: David may have hoped to harness Sutherland as an ally against the earl of Ross's predation in Caithness.[132]

Yet the marriage of Earl William and Margaret may not have taken place until autumn 1345 when David granted them the thanages of Douny in Forfarshire, Fettercairn, Aberluthnott and Kincardine in Kincardineshire (c. 28 September) and a free regality for their earldom (10 October).[133] Alternatively, these grants – which presumably brought a fair return for the crown in knight service – may even have marked news of a pregnancy or birth for Margaret, a *full* sister of David II by King Robert's second wife, Elizabeth de Burgh of Ulster. In David's eyes any nephew or niece from this sister would have been infinitely preferable to his heir-presumptive the Steward, son of Marjorie, a *half-sister* of David, a daughter of King Robert by his first wife, Isabella of Mar. There are other examples in fourteenth-century Scotland where dynastic chiefs or scions may have considered disinheriting the offspring from a first marriage in favour of the children of a second or denying elder heirs their share: for example, the lines of John MacDonald of the Isles and Malise of Strathearn.[134] When Margaret Bruce, who seems to have died in labour, gave birth to a son probably sometime in summer 1346, his christening as 'John' suggested that this was what David intended: as a John, the young Bruce-Sutherland nephew once again promised to eradicate the name of John I (Balliol) of Scotland.

131 *Chron. Bower*, vi, 377; *Liber Pluscardensis*, 240; *Chron. Boece*, ii, 333; Boardman, *Early Stewart Kings*, 8–9, 39.
132 *Vetera*, 278; Fraser, ed., *The Sutherland Book*, i, 30–1; Watt, *Scottish Graduates*, 187–9. Margaret Bruce is also alleged to have had an illegitimate son about 1345–6 by a Mackenzie; David II would help this child become Prior of Beauly in Ross-shire (*Highland Papers*, ii, 13). John Sutherland's descent through Margaret Bruce would be used in the reign of James VI to establish the royalist and regality rights of the family (MacKay, *The Book of MacKay*, 46–7).
133 *RRS*, vi, no. 96; *RMS*, i, App. ii, nos. 120–1; Fraser, ed., *The Sutherland Book*, iii, 12–5; Grant, 'Thanes and Thanages', 66–7, 74–6, 78.
134 H.L. MacQueen, 'The Kin of Kennedy, 'Kenkynnol' and the Common Law', in Grant & Stringer, eds, *Medieval Scotland*, 274–96, 291; Crawford, 'The Earls of Orkney-Caithness', 26–39, 178–83.

With this child to look forward to, in autumn 1345 David may have been filled with hope of an imminent leap of fortune in his favour. At the same time, such thoughts may have been further encouraged by the opportunity to emphatically win his spurs and impress his subjects which David perceived in the re-eruption of the war embracing England, Scotland, France and Flanders.

FOUR

Reversal of Fortune: Disaster at Durham, 1346

'... we with England will not enter parley,
Nor never make fair weather, or take truce,
But burn their neighbour towns, and so persist ...
... till your king
Cry out: 'Enough, spare England now for pity!'
'King David' in *King Edward III*,
attributed to Shakespeare[1]

The Build-up to Invasion, 1345–6

By spring of 1345 Edward III had already decided that he would tear up the three-year truce of Malestroit – agreed in June 1343 – twelve months early and launch a fresh assault on Philip VI in the coming summer. He did so with the resurgent backing of his nobility, parliament and people whose anti-French fervour the English government whipped up with propaganda denouncing the loss of Gascony and Philip's incitement of the Scots. Such English single-mindedness meant that talks for a full peace, earnestly mediated by Cardinals dispatched by Pope Clement VI as a sequel to the truce, had ceased by November of 1344. By the new year (which began in late March in the Middle Ages) the Pope had given up hope of a peace settlement which might revive the universal crusade.[2]

On 14–5 June 1345 Edward's government formally abandoned the truce. He was planning for a three-front campaign across the Channel. However, complex logistics, Flemish politics and ill sea-winds would delay Edward's own armada, destined for Normandy, while the earl of Northampton's advance force failed to make any real impact upon the tortured struggle for Brittany in the autumn. But by the end of August a third army led by the bold diplomat and strategist, Henry de Grosmont, master of Lancaster and earl of

---

1 G. Melchiori, ed., *King Edward III by William Shakespeare* (Cambridge 1998), i, i, 22–34.
2 For the rapidly changing European scene described in this and following sections, see Sumption, *Hundred Years War*, i, 441–550; Campbell, 'England, Scotland and the Hundred Years War in the Fourteenth century'; C. J. Rogers ed., *The Wars of Edward III: Sources and Interpretations* (Woodbridge 1999) which reproduces the Campbell article and others as well as primary sources; M. Prestwich, *The Three Edwards: War and State in England, 1272–1377* (London 1980), 165–88; A.K. McHardy, 'Some Reflections on Edward III's Use of Propaganda', in J.S. Bothwell ed., *The Age of Edward III* (Woodbridge 2001), 171–92.

Derby, had already marched deep into Gascony, stunning the exhausted and disorganised French defenders. Derby captured the town of Bergerac and all the fortresses surrounding Perigeux; then on 21 October he defeated a French relieving army at Auberoche, giving him free rein over most of the Duchy as its nobility returned to Plantagenet allegiance in droves.

It is only at this stage, however, that any clear indication of Scottish military activity in support of France can be pinpointed, perhaps the first such action since an abortive siege of Lochmaben Castle in Annandale by the Scots in September-October 1343. According to the English Chancellor, it was reported as early as June of 1344 that:

> in Scotland they are saying quite openly that they will break the truces as soon as our adversary (Philip) desires, and will march against England doing all the damage in their power . . .

In response, northern England was placed on a war footing with Edward Balliol named among its captains, though he was not styled in this correspondance as 'king of Scots'.[3] This time, however, there was a genuine threat of conflict behind the false alarms. Like the rest of Europe, David II must have been aware that Edward III was merely stalling at the peace talks while he prepared his expedition to France. There must also have been a mounting Scottish thirst for renewed border warfare, not just among professional soldiers like Douglas of Liddesdale and the affinity of Ramsay knights, but within an athletic monarch anxious to win his spurs in an action of note as well as to recover precious Scottish territory, especially Berwick-on-Tweed and the Bruce family castle of Lochmaben. Glory in battle was a natural ambition for a young king and knight who had experienced only three or four unspectacular mounted raids and the restrained honours of tilting at the lists. According to Wyntoun's source, David about 1344–6 cut an impressive but impatient figure – he was:

> Stout, young and joly
> And yarnyt for to se fechting . . .[4]

Froissart too – later regaled in person by the Scots king and his knights with tales of 1346 – insisted that 'Le Rois David fuist volontiers demoures pour attendre les Engles et la bataille, et le adventure de Dieu'.[5] There was, besides, a huge debt to repay to Philip VI for shelter, funds, continued supplies and consistent French diplomatic pressure to ensure Scotland's

3 J. Strachy *et al.* eds, *Rotuli Parliamentorum* (6 vols, London 1767–77) ii, 147; *Chron. Lanercost*, 341; A.A.M. Duncan, 'A Siege of Lochmaben Castle in 1343', *TDGNHAS*, xxxi (1954), 74–7.
4 *Chron. Wyntoun*, vi, 168.
5 *Oeuvres de Froissart*, iii, 452–3.

inclusion in the truces of the past decade. But more recently David may also have been angered by the papal envoys' renewed suggestion in 1344 that peace could be secured if Philip persuaded the Scottish king to resign his realm to Edward III, who would then give up his claim to the French crown and Gascony while David was compensated with lands in Europe (perhaps the aforementioned French duchy). The Scots may only have been spared pressure to discuss or comply with this wild compromise because Edward III's lawyers insisted that Scotland was already his and refused to negotiate further; this was a retort which took no heed of Edward Balliol whose claim to Scotland the Curia, too, had now abandoned.[6]

This phoney truce of the first half of 1345 gave David more than enough time to prepare for war. Yet despite all these motivations and their apparent hunger for a fight, the Scots only acted sometime about 25 October 1345 to distract the English as they descended upon France. Even then, the Scots' first incursion was merely another typical guerrilla raid, lasting only six days. David probably did not take part. Instead, John Randolph, earl of Moray and lord of Annandale, and Douglas of Liddesdale – presumably leading a contingent of men of the West March – penetrated Cumberland, according to the Lanercost chronicler skirting Carlisle only to turn back at Penrith. David may, though, have taken part in another brief raid on the same region a few days later.[7]

These attacks may have been a reconnoitre for the larger Scottish invasion of late 1346 or simply an attempt to cut off the supply lines of the English garrison at Lochmaben. But it is far more likely that as yet David did not feel himself to be sufficiently stable in power at home to summon a full Scottish host for a prolonged absence from his kingdom. This was understandable

6 *CPR, iii, Papal Letters, 1342–62*, 5; *Foedera*, i, 1224. See above, ch. 2 for diplomatic efforts in 1336 to persuade David to resign Scotland and his English royal wife to Balliol. In 1344 Clement VI urged David in a letter of 16 February 1344 to 'acquiesce in the counsels of the prelates of his realm and others who love justice, peace and truth; and . . . send envoys to the pope to meet those of the kings of France and England'. In 1342 the Pope had also favoured candidates backed by Edward III and Edward Balliol to be bishops of Galloway and Argyll (Watt, *Scottish Graduates*, 181, 278; Barrell, *The Papacy, Scotland and northern England*, 197–9).

7 PRO SC 41/19; *Chron. Lanercost*, 324; M. Summerson, *Medieval Carlisle: the City and the Borders from the Late Eleventh to the Mid-Sixteenth-century* (2 vols, London 1993), i, 272–9 with map; *Calendar of Inquisitions Miscellaneous*, ii, no. 2051, which records an inquisition held by the English at Carlisle reviewing how 'William de Douglas and very many other Scots enemies on Monday after Michaelmas 19 Edward III [1345] entered Cumberland and burned and destroyed lands and goods; David de Bruys with his great army, the earl of Murray, William de Douglas, and very many others on Monday after St Luke 19 Edward III entered the said county and for six days ravaged the lands and robbed the inhabitants of their goods; a similar raid was made on Monday before St James 20 Edward III: on Saturday after the octave of Michaelmas 20 Edward III [October 1346] the said David and very many others entered the said county and lay for 4 days at the peel of Lydell and burned and wasted divers lands and robbed the inhabitants of their goods'.

given the Scottish territorial and jurisdictional struggles which seem to have come to the fore at the Scone parliament of June 1344, as well as the heightening tensions which must have surrounded David's interest in the issue from the Sutherland-Bruce marriage and his continued resettlement of lands and offices in 1345; above all, David and Joan were as yet without an heir of their own. The king may have thought it wise to bide his time even though the political confrontations of the last year – over Strathearn, the northern justiciary, Fife and the succession – seemed to be edging his way. More practically, although David could call on the Scottish host for forty days' free service, he may still have been badly short of funds, a lack of resources which he could not guarantee would be offset by French gold or a parliamenatary grant of war tax in anticipation of the free booty of war. The situation in France, besides, could not yet have presented itself as so dire to the Scots as to warrant their immediate over-commitment on Philip's behalf. Instead, David and his close council preferred to continue the processes of winning his subjects' hearts and minds through patronage and of overawing the self-willed great magnates of the realm.

The crown's largesse and the royal court's itinerary of late 1345 and 1346 were just as intense as, and no less calculated than, those of the previous year. From Lanark on 10 October 1345 David had moved to Earl Patrick's castle of Dunbar once more by the 15th where he confirmed Lothian lands to Sir Robert Maitland, a future husband of David's future mistress, Agnes Dunbar, the March earl's half-niece.[8] Three days later David was back in the west at Dumbarton. By 4 November he was in Aberdeen with the Steward and earls of Moray, March, Strathearn and the royal household: these men witnessed a royal grant issued there of the Aberdeenshire barony of Cluny to the rising stars, William, earl of Sutherland, and Margaret Bruce. By 22 November David had advanced to Elgin where William, earl of Ross, and Roger, bishop of Ross, joined the court, surrounded by royalist witnesses to the king's grant in free barony of the forfeited Strathbogie lands of Rothiemay in Banffshire to Sir William Abernethy, another Angus man of chivalry. Christmas that year was spent back at Dumbarton with the Steward and the earls of Moray, Strathearn and Wigtown at least: on 28 December David granted the former Ramsay adherent Sir Alexander Stewart of Darnley – now king's bailie of Annandale – the grain fermes and tenants' service of the Lanarkshire barony of Cambusnethan.

David's whereabouts in the first half of 1346 are less detailed. By 30 March he was at Edinburgh where the coastal lands and seemingly impregnable castle of Dunnottar in Kincardineshire were given to the earl of Sutherland and his royal wife: again the witnesses recorded were the

8 For the following itinerary and grants, see *RRS*, vi, nos. 97 to 108.

Steward, Moray, March and Maurice of Strathearn. By 5 May David was back yet again at Dumbarton with the same men. A prolonged council may have been held at Perth between about 3 and 28 May that year: this could have given some attention (and perhaps funds) to war preparations but no record of proceedings survives. On 28 May David granted the Edinburgh barony of Barnbougle to Bartholomew Leon (David's constable of Kinghorn in Fife) after its resignation by John Graham, earl of Menteith.[9] By 1 July David was back at Edinburgh.

As well as these dateable acts David kept up a steady stream of grants which cannot now be precisely dated or located within this period.[10] This included yet more Fife, Kinross, Perth and Angus lands for the Ramsays, Menzies and other lesser local kindreds; Dumfriesshire lands for the former Balliol supporters, the MacDowells (as well as the office there of commendator); Ayrshire lands for Hugh Danielston, Hugh Blair and other families; Kincardineshire forest lands for Sir David Fleming, son and heir of Malcolm of Wigtown; the Lanarkshire barony of Roberton for the Annandale man, Sir William Jardine; the Roxburghshire barony of Hawick – originally gifted by King Robert to his bastard, Robert (d. 1333) – now given to Maurice, earl of Strathearn; more Perthshire lands for John and Malcolm Drummond, kin of David's future mistress, Margaret Logie; Aberdeenshire forest lands and an unspecified office (perhaps sheriff of Kincardine) for the Marischal's brother, Edward Keith; Clackmannanshire and Edinburgh lands for David's moneyer, Adam de Argento; the former Strathbogie barony of Duns in Forfarshire for knight William Wiseman; Lothian lands for another Alexander Ramsay adherent, Sir Walter Haliburton; Fife lands for David's other brother-in-law, Robert Glen, and his wife, Maud Bruce, who also received the Aberdeenshire thanages of Formartine and Kintore, held in the past of the crown for two knights' service; a cash annuity for Margaret, Countess of Angus; and confirmation of some of the lands of his mother, Christian Bruce (David's aunt), to John Murray of Bothwell. David also made a number of lesser grants of lands 'forfeited' by minor figures, suggesting an increased determination on his part to make loyalty in the localities explicit.[11]

Many of these grantees would be slain or captured in battle alongside the king at Neville's Cross. Indeed, in light of the Scottish casualty lists in war against England which could be compiled by the end of 1346 it does seem as though David spent much of the preceding year-and-a-half rewarding men he hoped or expected would fight in his great host as well as serve his regime

9 *RPS*, 1346/1; Boardman, *Early Stewart Kings*, 16.
10 *RMS*, i, App. ii, nos. 992 to 1087.
11 For example, David seems to have pardoned a former Argyll supporter of Balliol, Gilbert of Glasserie (*RRS*, vi, no. 103).

on an everyday basis. But if the king did intend a major campaign, he continued to build towards it slowly, perhaps even to resist pressure from France for such an effort.

However, by mid-1346 Philip VI was desperate for a diversionary Scottish front. In January of that year he had received badly needed funds from Pope Clement VI who had lost his patience with England. But the aging, unfit and hesitant Philip was really in no state of mind to either organise his defences adequately against Edward III's expected invasion of Normandy that summer, or to effectively lead and rally French overstretched forces in person when battle unavoidably had to be engaged. French losses in Gascony continued to mount as Edward – who had grown tired of his inconstant and expensive continental allies – prepared a new, purely English invasion fleet of over 700 vessels and 10,000 men to disembark from Portsmouth. Terror-struck by news of this muster, Philip wrote to the Scots king (and perhaps some of his individual magnates and bishops) on 20 June 1346. It was probably not his first epistle to David in recent months but now the tone was beseeching:

> I beg you, I implore you with all the force I can, to remember the bonds of blood and friendship between us. Do for me what I would willingly do for you in such a crisis, and do it as quickly and thoroughly as with God's help you are able.[12]

David probably received this letter in early July at the latest, by which time Edward III's armada had sailed for Normandy. The Scots king must already have approved another quick raid by Moray and Douglas of Liddesdale in June, although the chronicler of the northern English priory of Lanercost does assert that David himself joined this party under Randolph's banner of Annandale as the Scots targeted cattle on the Derwent hills near Aldstone in Cumberland: scarcity of victuals may also have guided Scottish tactics. Other near-contemporary English sources suggest that Randolph and Douglas quarrelled about besieging the small border peel of Liddale in Cumberland and were in the end soundly repulsed by a force led by Henry Percy and Ralph Neville.[13] However, it is unlikely that before this foray was made and Philip's letter arrived, David had decided to name a date in late September for the muster of a full Scottish host. Indeed, in late July, the Scots agreed to a short (and, surely contrary to their understanding with King Philip, a separate) truce to end on 29 September.[14]

In the end it would require near French collapse for David to fully commit

---

12 *Chron. Hemingburgh*, ii, 421–2. Philip certainly sent a copy of this letter to Patrick Dunbar, earl of March.
13 *Chron. Lanercost*, 326; PRO SC 42/156a.
14 *Rot. Scot.*, i, 667, 674.

his host. Landing at La Hogue on 12 July, Edward III and his sixteen-year-old heir, the Black Prince of Wales, marched inland past Rouen and Château Gaillard as the French retreated before them along the Seine to within twenty miles of Paris. With his back to the wall and his Gascon forces out of reach, Philip fired off another plea to David. Written on 22 July at the Abbey and royal residence at St Dénis – where a number of expatriate Scots were in orders – this letter must have had a greater impact in Scotland: it may even have been delivered by the Carrick knight with strong ties to St Dénis, Humphrey Kirkpatrick, who was not only patronised by David about this time and may have fought at Neville's Cross but, as we have seen, would later be noted by Froissart for his noble actions in bringing David to France in 1334. This time Philip cannily spoke of the opportunity now afforded David:

> The English king has . . . most of his army with him here, another division in Gascony and yet another in Flanders . . . [meanwhile all of England] is a defenceless void . . .

Philip even made the cynical suggestion that if David were to invade now, not only would Edward be forced to return to England but the French could chase him across the Channel. The Valois king may even have dispatched a small contingent of French knights and esquires to Scotland to persuade David of their bond of amity and the chance for conjoint action.[15]

The Scottish king and his close advisers would never have been so naïve as to believe that this plan would work and that they would soon meet Philip in London. But David clearly still felt a campaign of limited military objectives was worth the risk even so late on in the season and after the massive defeat of Philip's army at Créci on 26 August 1346. There, dismounted English men-at-arms and archers, well protected on their flanks by the natural features of the battlefield, decimated repeated waves of French cavalry. Philip was lucky to escape after losing two horses and sustaining arrow wounds to the face: John, king of Bohemia – present with David and Philip at Buirenfosse in 1339 – and eight French princes of the blood were killed. Edward III's tired troops then laid siege to Calais.[16]

David's actions in autumn 1346 were not, then, prompted by any notion that a Scottish *chevauchée* into northern England would really save the imperilled French. Rather, he seems to have become convinced that, even

---

15 *Chron. Hemingburgh*, ii, 422–3; AN JJ 76/6217 is a remission by Philip VI of December 1346 in which he grants a pardon, at the intercession of the king of Scots (sent sometime before the Battle of Neville's Cross), to Perrinet, son of Adam Lescot, another kindred associated with David's arrival at St Denis Abbey in 1334.

16 Rogers, ed., *The Wars of Edward III*, nos. 75–79; *idem, War Cruel and Sharp*, chs 11–12; K. de Vries, *Infantry Warfare*, 155–75.

though he was too late to help Philip, the decision to muster the Scots host should not be cancelled as a decisive and profitable progress through Cumberland and Northumberland would fulfill David's debts to France. But perhaps more importantly, such a campaign would also be a highly effective statement of his royal authority over his own subjects. Indeed, even though he could have reduced the size and targets of his host if news of Créci reached Scotland in time, David's army may have been organised and led with this singular aim: plunder, ransoms for hostages, gratitude from the French and maybe even victory in a pitched battle would be welcome bonuses.

However, if David and his inner circle sensed a great opportunity for such a unifying, crown-led effort to overcome the otherwise factional state of Scottish politics and the qualified nature of the king's power, their interpretation of the position achieved since 1341 was to be contradicted; this campaign would result, not in resounding popular success for the crown, but would instead expose the partisan feeling and festering divisions within the Scottish establishment. David was about to reap the bitter harvest of the policies and personal antagonisms he had felt it necessary to sow over the last five years.[17]

A Road to London: the Battle of Neville's Cross, 17 October 1346

David probably issued orders for the muster of the Scots host sometime in mid- or late August. Determined to have this campaign confirm his authority, he despatched these summons to all corners of his realm. Details of David's preparations for this campaign have long since been lost with the *Exchequer Rolls* for the period 1343–57. But it does seem that to cope with this hoped-for countrywide response, at least two staging points were organised, one north and one south of the river Forth. David's known movements in late summer suggest that he intended to oversee the forces gathering at Perth. On 27 August, he was at Dumbarton with the Steward, Moray, March, Wigtown and the Chancellor; by 1 September he was at Edinburgh with the same men. But by 8 September the court had moved back up the Forth valley to Stirling where David granted a hereditary office as sheriff of Peeblesshire ('Tweedale') to Sir Patrick Fleming, the earl of Wigtown's brother. About this time, David may also have offered a final olive branch and extra motivation to Sir William Douglas of Liddesdale with a grant of the Lanarkshire barony of Roberton, thus seemingly revoking a grant on which the ink must have been barely dry, that of these same lands to the Annandale knight, William Jardine, given sometime over the last winter.[18]

---

17 Penman, 'The Scots at the Battle of Neville's Cross'.
18 *RRS*, vi, nos. 106–08, 490–1; Grant, 'Disaster at Neville's Cross', 15–35.

If David did agree to the reshuffle of these lands at this time, it must reflect his concern to secure the experienced men he wanted as his host's division commanders. According to Prior Wyntoun's contemporary (and largely pro-Stewart) Scottish source, when the Scots crossed the border in October 1346, David himself had command of one division, the earl of Moray and Douglas of Liddesdale (co-captains in the raids of 1345–6) the second, and Robert Steward the third; Bower would add that Patrick, earl of March, was co-commander of the third division.[19] The outcome of the campaign does suggest that this was how the Scottish host was deployed. Such an arrangement besides reflected the factional – and perhaps even the cultural – divisions within the Scottish community. For the first two divisions were surely mostly made up of the best of the mounted chivalry and well-armed infantry of the realm, at their heart the Lowland chivalric cadre David had worked so hard to cultivate since 1341: the affinities of Annandale and Carrick, Liddesdale, Lothian and Fife (whose sixty-year-old earl David seems to have kept by his side), as well as the men of Moray, the shires of Banff and Aberdeen, and Mar, Angus and eastern Perthshire. The key individual captains of these troops would have included Randolph (whose earldom of Moray owed eight knights to the crown), Maurice, earl of Strathearn, Malcolm, earl of Wigtown, William, earl of Sutherland (now the lord of several north-eastern baronies and former thanages owing further knights' service), John Graham, earl of Menteith, Douglas of Liddesdale, Keith the Marischal, Hay the Constable and the Ramsay affinity of Lothian. These crack divisions may also have been joined by the few French knights and esquires present in Scotland. In all, Bower claimed, there were about 2,000 such warriors and 'well-armed men'. They would have been garbed in full armour, bearing the bright and bold surcoats of arms from which so many of their bodies would later be identified on the field. It is fair to assume that David and some of his lieutenants might also have invested in new banners and equipment: according to Froissart, the late Sir Alexander Ramsay of Dalhousie's grandson and namesake bore the king's standard.[20]

In stark contrast, the third division under the Steward and March may have included their regional followings – men from Atholl, Renfrew, Clydesdale and those not tagged by the crown from the south-east. But this force must generally have been dominated by the less experienced common tenantry of the king's realm and the lightly-armed footmen of the western Gael.[21] This may have been a deliberate slight by David and his favoured circle: they would have the martial glory while the Steward

19 *Chron. Wyntoun*, vi, 170–8; *Chron. Bower*, vii, 249–53.
20 *Oeuvres de Froissart*, v, 126–45.
21 Grant, 'Disaster at Neville's Cross', 32–3.

watched the horses at the back. Yet despite its limited prestige the Steward's division was the largest of the Scottish battle divisions, perhaps totalling more than five or six thousand men – 'a great army of those that were lightly armed'. In all the Scottish host totalled surely no more than 10–12,000 men.

But even before the northern companies set out to meet up with their southern counterparts, the third division may have been sorely depleted, perhaps even losing a first-choice commander, because of what one noble perceived as David's unfair lordship of late. The royal summons had met with a favourable response from some kindreds in the north-west, though not it seems from John MacDonald of the Isles. But all the Scottish chroniclers record that at the nunnery of Elcho near the Perth muster, William, earl of Ross, and his men stole in during the night to slay Ranald MacRuaridh and his attendants, Ross's bitter feud enemies over Garmoran and Skye since David had restored the MacRuaridhs in 1341–3. Like Alexander Ramsay, slain three years earlier by Douglas of Liddesdale:

> This Randal missed was greatly
> He was a good man, and worthy.
> And from, they saw, this misfortune,
> And said it was right evil taking,
> That at the first of their stirring
> That worthy man should be slain so,
> And so great crowds desert them now . . .

Ross and his following certainly withdrew from the host, most likely in fear of their lives but perhaps through some arrangement with a king who, despite such an omen and the flight of men, was determined to push south. Ironically, the late fifteenth-century scribe of the priory of Pluscarden later asserted that in doing so the young king ignored the advice of Douglas of Liddesdale, the killer of Alexander Ramsay in similar circumstances in 1342, to call off the attack and punish Ross for murder.[22] Douglas, though, had his own motives for stalling the Scottish campaign. On 27 September 1346, the English king's council heard from a watcher in the north that two days earlier Douglas had been at the peel of Liddale and seized all the lands there of Thomas, Lord Wake, one of Balliol's Disinherited allies. It had been over the siege of Liddale – the nearest Cumberland strongpoint which bordered on Douglas's new march lordship – that the knight and John Randolph had apparently argued three months earlier.[23] Douglas may

22 *Chron. Wyntoun*, vi, 174; *Highland Papers*, i, 17; *Liber Pluscardensis*, 222–3.
23 *CDS*, v, no. 803.

have been understandably reluctant to see his king assert his own influence over this region.

But it was at Liddale about 7 October that Wyntoun's source asserts that the Scottish host converged and 'assemblit haill'. David's and the Steward's divisions had probably made passage south through Annandale and Liddesdale while Moray and Douglas had followed a similar route after first mustering somewhere like Peebles. It took the Scots a few days to reduce Liddale, a delay most likely due not to the Scots' perennial shortage of sappers and siege equipment but to the leisurely pace of progress which David seemed keen to make. For it must have been instantly clear that although the English government had tried to rouse what little northern resources they could in general defense against the Scots throughout 1346, the Scottish invasion now launched after the end of the July-September truce had not been anticipated.[24]

Without danger of challenge David clearly intended to make a far more relaxed, almost hunt-like royal progress through the accessible countryside. This was not to be a textbook copy of the swift mounted guerrilla raids or forestalling pincer attacks perfected by King Robert, Thomas Randolph and James Douglas after 1311.[25] For sure, there would be plunder and the extraction of 'tribute' for truces from individual English settlements. But David was just as concerned to raise his profile. There was to be little element of surprise: David may even have taken the trouble to write to northern English lords on an individual basis warning them to stay out of his path if they valued their lands.[26] Moreover, according to Thomas Sampson, a Yorkshire cleric who would write a letter based on eye-witness reports recounting the Scots' defeat within days of the battle, David camped throughout his expedition in 'tents and pavilions of the richest and noblest sort, the likes of which had not been seen in these parts for a long time'. Finally, the chronicler of the priory of Lanercost – a traditional wealthy target for the Scots which may have been hit again in 1346 – reported David's desire to spare the church and market towns of Hexham, Corbridge, Darlington and Durham from burning 'because he intended to obtain his victual from them'. Such plans bespoke a large, steadily moving Scottish force not dependent upon the miserly rations of oat cake and raw stolen meat which chronicler Jean le Bel reported Scottish raiders favoured in King Robert's time. Wine, decent meats, fresh bread and a possibly lavish baggage train must have denied David's host rapid mobility but allowed the young

24 *Rot. Scot.*, i, 668–74; Y.N. Harari, 'Inter-Frontal Cooperation in the Fourteenth-century and Edward III's 1346 Campaign', *War in History*, vi (1999), 379–95.
25 MacNamee, *Wars of the Bruces*; Grant, 'Disaster at Neville's Cross', 33–4.
26 *Historia Roffensis* 93v f.; C.J. Rogers & M.C. Buck, 'The Scottish Invasion of 1346', *Northern History*, (1998), 51–82, 57–8.

king to entertain his captains and French guests in the field, in many ways emulating Philip VI.[27]

This display, and the version of events which David and his supporters had embellished by the time of Jean Froissart's visit to Scotland in 1365, must have influenced that chronicler's later presentation of the 1346 campaign as a chivalric adventure. In Froissart's account David declares his vow of 'doing some gallant deeds of renown before their return to Scotland' to a force of 40,000 men, including 3,000 knights, many of them invited by the Bruce king from 'Sweden, Norway and Denmark' either for love, honour or pay.[28]

David may indeed have been able to call upon the European connections of his own court of 1334–41 and the men of chivalry in his and Moray's divisions. In addition to his field household he certainly deployed nationalist icons and ritual designed to attract men of chivalry. In much the same manner as his father may have carried St Columba's relics into battle in 1314, so David sanctified his own cause in 1346 by bearing a relic once possessed by Queen Margaret of Scotland, a piece of Christ's Holy Cross, a cult increasingly popular in the late Middle Ages. This was not the original 'Black Rood' of St Margaret which Edward I had removed from Scotland in 1296 and which had not been returned north in 1328: that cross may indeed have been transferred to the English royal household from the treasury as late as January 1346. However, another cross had probably been removed from keeping and veneration in the royal residence at Edinburgh or David's favoured Abbey of Holyrood (the house which now provided royal household chaplains) for the purposes of the campaign.[29] It must have appealed to those several Scots knights who had participated in, and in the 1350s and 1360s would return to, both the

---

27 Sampson's letter is reproduced in *Oeuvres de Froissart*, v, 488–92 and translated in Rollason and Prestwich eds, *Battle of Neville's Cross*, 134–7 and Rogers ed., *The Wars of Edward III*, no. 81; *Chron. Lanercost*, 346. There are some obvious exaggerations and errors in Sampson's letter, e.g. stating the Scottish army to be 40,000 men and the Scottish divisions to be the Steward, Strathearn and Wigtown in the vanguard, David, Douglas and March in the middle, and Moray at the back. Further contemporary descriptions of the battle are reproduced in Rogers, 'The Scottish Invasion of 1346' with an appendix by the author and M.C. Buck; J. Raine ed., *Historical Papers and Letters from the Northern Registers* (Rolls Series 1857), 374, 384–95.

28 *Oeuvres de Froissart*, v, 126–45, which also states that just before the invasion jousts were held with the English at which William Douglas and a Simon Fraser – whom Froissart had both named as visiting David in France and who would both be captured at Neville's Cross – took part.

29 G. Watson, 'The Black Rood of Scotland', *Transactions of the Scottish Ecclesiological Society*, ii (1909), 28–47; L. Rollason, 'Spoils of War? Durham Cathedral and the Black Rood of Scotland', in Rollason and Prestwich eds., *Battle of Neville's Cross*, 57–65.

Reisen crusades of the Teutonic knights in Prussia and attempts to recover the Holy Land: this body of men included the Leslies, Ramsays, Bissets, Sir Patrick Dunbar, David Barclay, Walter Moigne, Lawrence Gilliebrand and others like John Randolph and William Douglas (whose ancestors had also shown an interest in crusading). Use of a talisman cross may also have reflected preaching which David's churchmen took up in 1346 in echo of the clergy of King Robert, proclaiming war against England to be as important as a crusade against the infidel. Predictably, this was matched by military faith on the English side: Sampson reported that the English army which emerged to fight David in 1346 carried a banner of the cross urging battle for the salvation of their realm; it also fought to protect St Cuthbert, patron of Durham.[30]

It was such an impassioned force which Froissart went on to describe fancifully as sacking Durham and taking by siege Wark Castle in the Middle March, both considerable feats of arms for any Scottish host. But in fact Froissart's narrative betrays David's retrospective attempt to widen and glorify the record of a campaign which never really ignited and which ended disastrously. English medieval chroniclers sought to achieve the opposite, vilifying the campaign by claiming that at Liddale David had the English captain, Sir Walter Selby, and his men massacred unshriven (two decades earlier, Selby had surrendered nearby Mitford Castle to the English while in King Robert's peace). But even worse, one English poet related that, enraged by protests from his subjects against his boast to press on to London, a hot-headed and too-proud David II slew his own page boy for voicing criticism, only then to turn around and create 'five score' new Scottish knights.[31] Like Le Bel and Froissart, some English commentators also claimed that David had an army of 40,000 men. But it was only in the late sixteenth century, in *King Edward III* – a play now attributed to Shakespeare – that the Scottish army's actions were wildly over-exaggerated so as to glorify the English victory. In this drama:

30 *Chron. Knighton*, 68–73 for English troops; Penman, 'Christian Days and Knights', 254–5; W. Paravicini, *Die Preussenreisen des Europaischen Adels* (3 vols, Simaringen 1989), i, 135–8; Macquarrie, *Scotland and the Crusades*, 85–8; M. Prestwich, 'The English at the Battle of Neville's Cross', in Rollason and Prestwich eds., Battle of Neville's Cross, 1–14.

31 *Chron. Lanercost*, 337; F.J. Child, *The English and Scottish Popular Ballads* (5 vols., London 1888), iii, 282–7 'Durham Field'. See also R.H. Robbins ed., *Historical Poems of the XIVth and XVth Centuries* (New York 1959), no. 10 'The Battle of Neville's Cross' by Lawrence Minot; and *Rerum Britannicarum Medii Aevi Scriptores: Political Poems and Songs* (2 vols, London 1857), i, 40–53, 83–7, 141–3, 188. *Chron. Le Bel*, i, 284, asserts that David had 60,000 men and was on his way to Wales when he was routed by an army led by Queen Philippa (who was then in France).

The treacherous king [David] no sooner was informed
Of your [Edward] withdrawing of your army back,
But straight, forgetting of his former oath.
He made invasion of the bordering towns:
Berwick is won, Newcastle spoiled and lost,
And now the tyrant hath begirt with siege
The castle of Roxborough, where enclosed
The Countess of Salisbury is like to perish.[32]

Shakepeare's Edward III had to rescue this maiden (as in Froissart's narrative) and humiliate the bellicose and greedy Scottish king who had planned to share the countess and her jewels with another villain of the play, 'Douglas'. Shakespeare also invoked the memory of David's defeat and capture (conflated with James I's fate of 1406–24) in his later great English historical play, *Henry V*.[33]

In reality, however, the Scots' progress in 1346 was inglorious and uneventful. They most likely sacked Lanercost Priory and the small peels of Redpath and Newforth and burned the villages around Carlisle, obliging that walled town to pay 300 merks for a short truce. Then, about 10 or 12 October, the Scots pushed east into Northumberland, running parallel with Hadrian's wall along the river Tyne towards Newcastle, probably stripping the town and priory of Hexham – where the host may have lingered for three days – and then Corbridge market with its nearby tower at Aydon. Thereafter the Scots turned south, crossing first the Tyne at Ryton and then the River Derwent after which they may have split briefly into two flanking forces. On 15 October word was despatched to Westminster that Scottish troops had ridden over Sir Robert Herle's quite widely scattered lands of Styford, Newbigging, Broomhaugh, Ryding, Shotley and Slaley, rustling some 70 oxen, 83 cows, 142 bulls, 32 calves, 316 sheep and other goods. David seemed to be cutting a wide swathe south-east and counting on a long (well-fed) sojourn.[34] He was now approaching the rich farm and manor lands of the cathedral chapter of Durham. The sum of 1,000 merks suggested by one English source as the truce tribute which David now

---

32 Melchiori ed., *King Edward III*, i, i, 124–31.

33 For you shall read that my great-grandfather/ Never went with his forces into France/ But that the Scot on his unfurnish'd kingdom/ Came pouring, like the tide into a breach,/ With ample and brim fullness of his force;/ Galling the gleaned land with hot essays,/ Girding with grievous siege castles and towns;/ That England, being empty of defence,/ Hath shook and trembled at the ill neighbourhood./ She hath herself not only well defended,/ But taken, and impounded as a stray,/ the king of Scots; whom she did send to France,/To fill King Edward's fame with prisoner kings . . . (Act i, ii, 146–63).

34 *CDS*, iii, no. 1501; J.W. Dickenson, *The Battle of Neville's Cross* (Durham 1991), 8–15.

demanded in negotiations with Durham points to plans for a stay of a few weeks or the intention of returning some months later at the ceasefire's end to press for more or to burn the lands under ransom. The Scots must have opened these talks with the clergy of Durham on 16 October from their camp on the bishop's manor in the Bearpark to the west of the town: here they settled in by destroying all the grain stores, driving off the livestock and felling trees. Clearly, David intended to attack the town around Durham cathedral and castle in the next few days if the money was not forthcoming.[35]

But as the cause of what followed, David's generalship was to be criticised not just by English commentators. Both Wyntoun's source and Bower – writing during the reigns of Stewart kings – assert that David had ignored Douglas of Liddesdale's wise advice to turn back after the capture of Liddale. Douglas was an experienced guerrilla but any such opinion must have seemed transparently self-interested to David. However, Bower the cleric also makes great play of David's arrogant dismissal on the eve of battle of a warning vision of St Cuthbert. In Bower's book, just as English pirates deserved to drown for plundering St Columba's shrines along the Forth in the 1350s, so David deserved his fate for his destruction the next day of Cuthbert's lands and for following the advice of 'bold and impetuous young men . . . and flatterers'.[36] Yet it is likely that Bower penned this homilitic aside in response to the local English tradition that grew up around the battle. This legend holds that in 1346 Prior William Fossour of Durham – head cleric in the absence of the bishop of Durham with Edward III in France – also had a warning dream message from St Cuthbert on the eve of the fighting. As a result, the next day he mounted the corporax of St Cuthbert – the cloth used to cover the high altar chalice – on a spear and carried it and a cross as banners to a hillock known as Maiden's Bower to the north-west of the Bearpark and the battlefield; here, the monks of Durham prayed and sang throughout the action.

However, many more practical reasons can be given for David's defeat and capture. The Scots may have simply underestimated the northern English capacity for mustering their defence, despite the absence on the continent of their king along with many great magnates and the heavy war burdens in tax and supply requisition of the past few years. Scottish scouts'

---

35 *Chron. Lanercost*, 330–2; *The Anonimalle Chronicle*, ed. V.H. Galbraith (Manchester 1927), 24; *Chron. Knighton*, 69–71.

36 *Chron. Bower*, vii, 109–11, 257; J.R.E. Bliese, 'Saint Cuthbert and War', *Journal of Medieval History*, xxiv (1998), 215–41, 237–8; Dickenson, *Neville's Cross*, 10. Ironically, on 6 May 1346, David had granted lands in Carrick in return for the annual payment of a penny on the feast of St Cuthbert (*Calendar of the Laing Charters, 854–1837*, ed. J. Anderson (Edinburgh 1899), 11–2).

intelligence had certainly not informed David that William Thursby, Archbishop of York, and such northern barons as Henry Percy, Ralph Neville, Thomas Rokeby, Gilbert d'Umfraville (pretender earl of Angus), John Mowbray and the sheriffs of Northumberland and Yorkshire had been able to raise a significant militia, mustering thirty miles south at Richmond. This army – which would eventually be paid out of the English crown's total expenditure on the North's defences in 1345–7 of over £14,000 – moved north via Barnard Castle where it was joined by Edward Balliol with over a hundred mounted men. This probably brought the English strength to some 1,000 men-at-arms, some 1,700 archers and 4–5,000 infantry from Yorkshire, Lancashire and other shires around the Trent.[37]

The English had advanced to the park of Auckland Castle ten miles south of Durham by the evening of 16 October. It was the vanguard of this force advancing at dawn on the 17th which surprised Douglas's force of 500 Scottish foragers at Ferryhill and pursued them full-tilt north across the Sunderland bridge over the River Wear, back towards the Scots host. As we have seen, Douglas lost many men near the bridge (at a site thus known as Low Butcher's Race) and burst in upon an unprepared Scottish camp. But David and his captains were able to mobilise their men in good order. By roughly nine o'clock that morning the two armies were drawing up about a quarter of a mile apart along the ridge running east-west then known as Red Hills, a mile from Durham and a mile east of the Bearpark.[38] By noon battle lines were firmly drawn. Here they faced each other with banners arrayed until two o'clock that afternoon ('the hour of terce'), according to Sampson. The Scots had not been able to occupy the higher ground but had deployed their three divisions – from west to east, Moray/Douglas, then David, then Steward/March from the English viewpoint – drawn up level and dismounted behind a low hedge. But in the end there was no formidable natural boundary to prevent the Lancastrian archers from advancing to prey upon the Scots, so as to force them to engage with the four English divisions or to retreat.

Of course, David did not have to give battle. But his superior numbers, confidence and domestic agenda may have caused him to welcome the chance and ignore the warning advice allegedly given him by his father on his deathbed. David may indeed have been preparing to attack when a few

37 Prestwich, 'The English at Neville's Cross', 3–10; Reid, 'Edward Balliol', 43–5. Balliol was paid a total of £417 for 90 days' service with 50 men-at-arms, one banneret, 8 knights, 40 esquires and 50 mounted archers (*Rot. Scot.*, i, 691–2).

38 R.A. Lomas, 'The Durham Landscape and the Battle of Neville's Cross', in Rollason and Prestwich eds., *Battle of Neville's Cross*, 66–77; A.H. Burne, 'The Battle of Neville's Cross', *Durham University Journal*, xli (1949), 100–6; F. Graham, *Famous Northern Battles* (Newcastle 1977), 12–6.

hundred English archers – probably on their left flank – moved within range and began to shower the Scots. As recent studies of the battle have shown, it is uncertain whether or not the ferocity of this bombardment provoked a Scottish charge: there is Wyntoun's source's famous tale that John Graham, earl of Menteith, asked for a hundred horsemen to scatter these bowmen and, being refused – whether through David's fear or guile is not stated – charged ineffectually on his own, narrowly escaping with his life only to be captured later. But it may be that the relatively thin ranks and inaccuracy of the English archers inspired the Scots chivalry to advance shields high.[39]

Yet as they did so the Scots found that the topography of their defensive position constrained their freedom of movement and co-operation badly. Moray's and Douglas's division formed the vanguard: but their schiltrom was hindered in its advance, probably towards the English left flank, by rough broken ground and was quickly discomfited. After heavy losses, the rump of this division – with or without Moray and Douglas is unclear – then fell back to join the king's presumably advancing middle schiltrom. But just as Edward II's forces at Bannockburn had been crippled by the 'straitness of the place', jammed between a wall of enemy spears and boggy streams and unable to fan out, so David and his closest earls and lords in 1346 now found themselves in 'a rycht anoyous place'. Badly reduced and anxious for 'rowme to stand and fycht', these two chivalry divisions eventually began to withdraw – presumably fighting rearguard as they went – towards the Steward's and March's third division now in the rear. This sporadic fighting may have taken as long as three hours and included periods of mutually agreed rest for the front-line troops: Sampson and others note that the Scots' defeat was certain by five o'clock vespers. It is likely that neither of the first two retreating Scottish divisions reached the third and that it was during this confused stage of close-range archery and desperate close-quarters fighting that David sustained his head wounds:

> For of arowis sic shot thare was
> That feill were woundit in that place.[40]

The two arrows presumably pierced either David's raised shield or the 'parapilio' of his helmet, the barbs embedding themselves in his face and leaving the king or his attendants to break off the shafts. It was an honourable wound, which Froissart took pains to note, almost identical to that sustained by Philip VI at Créci weeks earlier.

---

39 *Chron. Wyntoun*, vi, 180–2. The manoeuvres of the battle described here follow the interpretation offered by Grant and Prestwich in Rollason and Prestwich eds., *Battle of Neville's Cross*.
40 *Chron. Lanercost*, 225–7; *Chron. Wyntoun*, vi, 182–5; Barrow, *Bruce*, ch. 12 for 1314.

Seeing the waves of premier fighting men of the first two Scottish divisions overwhelmed, first by bowplay and then advancing English men-at-arms, it is unlikely that the Steward and Earl Patrick of March remained to fight much longer after the first arrows and enemy infantry reserves began to reach their own ranks, perhaps led by no less a figure than Edward Balliol. It is indeed logical to assume that Steward and March had charge of the host's horses and used that opportunity to withdraw, abandoning the other divisions and the royal baggage train. Some English sources suggest that these two Scottish lords lost many men in shaking off their pursuers: but escape they did.

According to both Wyntoun's source and Bower – the pro-Stewart chroniclers – Steward and March were wise to do so. But for Fordun's anonymous scribe, writing before 1363, these two were cowards who 'took to flight, and got away unhurt'. This impression is echoed in contemporary English chronicle accounts, which may have been informed by the bitter words of David himself in captivity. According to Lanercost priory's scribe:

> If one (March) was worth little, the other [the Steward] was worth nothing . . . Overcome by cowardice . . . these two turning their backs, fought with great success, for with their battalion, without any hurt, they returned to Scotland and thus led off the dance, leaving David to caper as he wished.[41]

This is surely closer to the truth. Earl Patrick, now in his sixties, had received nothing from the Bruce dynasty since 1314 but his life and pardons for his support of both John and Edward Balliol, whilst his status, lands and following had been whittled away: the Scotsmen slain that day at Neville's Cross might now benefit Patrick's East Lothian lordship. Robert Steward must have been even more privately overjoyed to see his Scottish rivals fall. He had already survived (and escaped) one costly Scottish defeat at Halidon Hill in 1333, living to exploit the resulting vacuum in Scottish leadership and territorial lordship over the next eight years. In 1346 it must have looked like an even greater massacre. John Randolph, Maurice Murray and Keith the Marischal, Hay the Constable and Charteris the Chancellor were all dead; Duncan of Fife, Malcolm of Wigtown, John Graham of Menteith and many other knights were listed either dead or captured; William, earl of Sutherland, David's favourite brother-in-law, might not yet escape or survive. David had besides given the Steward absolutely no reason to

---

41 *Chron. Fordun*, i, 367; *Chron. Bower*, vii, 259–61; *Chron. Wyntoun*, vi, 185; *Chron. Lanercost*, 338–9; *Chron. Pipewell*, cited in C.J. Rogers & M.C. Buck, 'The Scottish Invasion of 1346', 81; *Chron. Scalacronica* (Stevenson/Leland), 301 – the Steward and March 'fled'. The Lanercost chronicle also asserts that March had refused David's offer of command of the first Scottish division.

remain and fight. He could instead return safely to a realm where the Bruce settlement had been blown wide open. The earldoms of Fife, Strathearn and Menteith were there for the taking by his family, as were some of the lands of the Moray regality, especially Badenoch adjacent to Atholl; Earl Patrick of March would claim the Moray earldom itself by marriage. The royal purse strings would also again be vulnerable to plunder. All of that and more would be guaranteed legitimately to Steward at the still young age of thirty if David too fell in the savage hand-to-hand combat which must have concluded the battle: Robert Steward would be king. It will never be known just how close to Scone the Steward rode before he heard word of David's survival. He must have taken close adherents like the embittered Sir John Menteith of Arran/Knapdale and perhaps the ambitious Thomas Stewart, earl of Angus (whom the Steward would soon make Chamberlain), with him as he fled.

Despite his ugly wounds, David may also have had the chance to flee. Some English accounts assert that he escaped a few miles south as far as Merrington before capitulating. One local tradition has it that he hid under a bridge at Aldin Grange, just at the southern edge of the Bearpark, only for his reflection in the water to give him away to his pursuers. But it is more likely that David, still boxed in by the terrain, held his ground on the battlefield, surrounded by pockets of his loyal household officers, knights and esquires, as one English source had it, '[standing] together like a round tower, protecting the king in the middle, until there were barely forty left surviving, of whom not one could flee away': according to Prior Fossour, David made his last stand on an area known as Findon Hill with about eighty of his men. In Sir Thomas Gray's and Froissart's narratives David fought bravely, his mailed fist punching out the two front teeth of his eventual captor, Northumberland esquire and border reiver, John de Coupland.[42] David's surviving men then seem to have struggled to find English nobles to preserve them in submission.

However, the available names of those Scots killed or captured on that day confirm graphically the partisan loyalties of the Scottish host. The available casualty list of almost one hundred names reads like a who's-who of those men best rewarded by David since 1341 and many knights the king would favour after his release in 1357. It includes almost all of David's household government and daily council as well as the chivalric cadre of skilled lesser Lowland knights and esquires from the north-east, Angus, Fife and the Lothians he had built up since 1341. This very nearly justifies

---

42 Prestwich, 'The English at Neville's Cross', 12; *Chron. de Melsa*, iii, 61–2; *Chron. Scalacronica*, 117–8; *Oeuvres de Froissart*, v, 144–5; *Chronicon Galfridi le Baker de Swynebroke*, ed. E.M. Thompson (Oxford 1889), reproduced in Rollason and Prestwich eds, *Battle of Neville's Cross*, 149–51.

Bower's later boast that going into battle the king had been ' . . . fully reassured and supported by the knightly young men of military age'.[43] In total, about two to three thousand Scots, probably almost all from the first two divisions, had been killed or captured; only a few score of minor Englishmen of note were recorded as lost.

Table 1. Scottish Casualties, 17 October 1346 [44]

Scots named as killed at Neville's Cross and patronised by David II, 1341–6 (those whose patronage has been discussed above and in Ch. 3 are italicised):

John Randolph, earl of Moray; *Maurice Murray*, earl of Strathearn; *Robert Keith*, Marischal; *Edward Keith?*; *Gilbert Hay*, Constable; *Thomas Charteris*, Chancellor; *John Roxburgh*, Chamberlain; *Philip Meldrum*; *John Bonville*; *Thomas Boyd*; *Andrew Buttergask*; *John Crawford*; *William Fraser of Cowie*; *Humphrey Kirkpatrick* 'and his brother' [*Reginald?*]; *Henry Ramsay*; Humphrey de Bois; Roger Cameron; David fitz Robert; William Haliburton; William Hay; Gilbert Inchmartin; David Lindsay; Edmund Keith; John Lindsay; John More; Adam Moygrave; William Mowbray; William Ramsay[?]; Michael Scott; John Sinclair; Alexander Strachan and his son/namesake ['the most valiant knights of the land of Scotland'[45]]; Adam Nixon; Patrick Heryng; Robert Maitland; John Stewart of Dreghorn; Alan Stewart; Adam Whitson; John Maitland.

Scots named as captured at Neville's Cross (and patronised by David II, 1341–6):

David II; *William Douglas* of Liddesdale; *Malcolm Fleming*, earl of Wigtown; *John Graham*, earl of Menteith; *Duncan*, earl of Fife; *Walter Haliburton*; *William Ramsay* of Colluthie; *William More* of Abercorn; *Gilbert Carrick*; *David Annan*; *Alexander Stewart* of Darnley; *Patrick Dunbar*; *William Jardine*; *William Livingston*; William Murray; *John Preston*; *Walter Moigne*; Thomas Lypp [*RRS*, vi, no. 94Ad]; *Adam Fullarton*; *Robert Wallace*; *Bartholomew de Leon*; *John Herries*; John Stewart of Dalswinton [warden of the West March by 1344?]; Nicholas Knockdalian [*RMS*, i, App. ii, no. 1063]; John Douglas [*ibid*, no. 1068]; Neso Ramsay [*ibid*, nos. 964, 994, 998, 1072]; John Maxwell [*RRS*, vi, nos. 89, 129];

43 *Chron. Bower*, vii, 151.
44 Sourced from *Rot. Scot.*, i, 678–9; *Oeuvres de Froissart*, v, 144–5 and 489–93; letter of Thomas Sampson and Chronicles of Lanercost, Meaux Abbey, Annonimalle, and le Baker reproduced in Rollason and Prestwich eds., *Battle of Neville's Cross*. The fact that some names seem to appear in both the lists of the dead and the captured points to the confusion of the battle and the presence of large numbers of one kindred in the Scottish divisions, e.g. Haliburton, Kirkpatrick, Ramsay.
45 *Chron. Anonimalle*, 23–4.

Fergus Crawford; Alexander Steel; William de Vaus [*RMS*, i, nos. 103, 121, sheriffship of Elgin, 1363]; William Mowbray; John Sinclair; David Fitz-walter [*RRS*, vi, nos. 271, 418]; Andrew Campbell [*ibid*, nos. 232, 393]; George Abernethy [*ibid*, nos. 99, 417, justiciarship 1368], *Lawrence Gilliebrand* [*RMS*, i, App. ii, nos. 903, 959, 1354; *ER*, i, 618, steward of the queen's house; *ibid*, ii, 52, envoy to London, 1360]; *Alexander Ramsay*; Alexander Haliburton; William Baillie [*RRS*, vi, no. 166(A); *RMS*, i, App. ii, no. 1011] John Giffard; Roger Crawford [*ibid* nos. 843, 1005]; John Stewart, bastard; Patrick Polwarth [*ER*, i, 414 sheriff of Fife, 1332]; David Murray; Robert Chisholm [*ibid*, 569, account as sheriff of Inverness, 1359; *ibid*, ii, 143, as keeper of Urquhart castle, 1362]; David Graham; Patrick Herries; John Haliburton; Roger Kirkpatrick?; *James Sandilands* [*RRS*, vi, nos. 94, 114, 115, 127, 131, 163]; Henry Douglas [*ibid*, nos. 411, 452, 455]; *Henry Kerr* [*ibid*, no, 332; *ER*, ii, 38]; Hector MacBeth [*Rot. Scot.*, i, 703].

Overall, this was a resounding English triumph. The Scots had suffered the worst defeat in their history, a ghastly blow which modern Scottish memory inevitably blocks out by focusing on Bannockburn or the more romantically tragic toll of Flodden Field in 1513 with the deaths of James IV and most of his nobility. But in its day, Neville's Cross – together with Dupplin and Halidon Hill – must have wiped away the humiliation of 1314 for many Englishmen. Within a few years there was to be an outpouring of English song and verse, celebrating the humiliation of the arrogant Scots and their pro-French king:

> Than Sir dauid the Bruse makes his mone,
> The faire coroun of scotland haues he forgone:
> He luked furth into france, help had he none,
> Of sir philip the valais ne yit of sir John.[46]

In 1346, news reached London within three days to rekindle the public enthusiasm which had been sparked by Edward III's victory at Créci only weeks earlier. For the English king it must have come as a great relief that a very real Scottish threat could be neutralised at so little expense; he now had David captive as a bargaining chip to boot.

In late October 1346, Edward ordered that all Scots taken in battle were to be held for the crown and not released for private ransom. But it was not

---

46 Extract from 'The Battle of Neville's Cross' by Lawrence Minot, in Robbins ed., *Historical Poems of the XIVth and XVth Centuries* 31–7, 50–60; see also 'Durham Field' and 'The Knight of Liddesdale', in Child ed., *The English and Scottish Popular Ballads*, iii, 282–8. For reporting of the battle in Italian, German and Spanish sources, see Ditchburn, *Scotland and Europe*, 276 n65.

immediately clear what Edward – who would remain at the siege of Calais until late November – intended to do about his most important prisoner or about the kingdom of Scotland itself. Edward did remember some of those whom he had to thank. The captured Rood of St Margaret was eventually to be gifted to the chapter of Durham. The clergy of the town would return the corporax of St Cuthbert to a specially decorated place of veneration behind the high altar of the cathedral where it hung alongside the captured banner of the Scottish king, as well as that of Sir Ralph Neville, until it was destroyed during the English Reformation. The Durham clergy would also commemorate the date of the battle (St Luke's Eve) with procession and song until the early nineteenth century.[47]

Neville himself would pay to have an elaborate new monument erected at the battlefield site – the Neville's Cross which replaced the original simple cathedral sanctuary marker – adorned with the figures of Christ crucified, the Virgin and St John the Evangelist; Neville also reaped many royal rewards for his generalship, becoming Edward III's household steward and Warden of the west and middle English marches, as well as securing a place for his own marble tomb in Durham Cathedral itself (a mausoleum decorated with images of the battle which Scottish prisoners of Cromwell defaced in 1650). The other English noble captors of Scottish knights and esquires were similarly compensated and rewarded. According to Froissart, John de Coupland refused to surrender David to anyone but Edward and blackmailed the English king into redeeming his royal brother-in-law for a high price; yet in truth, Edward must have been quite happy to knight Coupland, grant him a pension of £500 and seal a full pardon absolving him and his fellows (men like Robert Bertram who had captured William Douglas in the battle) of their crimes of border banditry as payment for David.[48]

Just what physical and mental state the Scottish king was in, however, remains uncertain. David may have been whisked from the field and installed in nearby Ogle Castle before battle closed. But he was certainly soon taken to Wark-on-Tweed by Coupland, then to Bamburgh Castle on the east coast of Northumberland, perhaps for passage south by sea. Two barber surgeons from York were quickly brought in and well paid to treat him as he 'lay there having been wounded with an arrow . . . and to extract the arrow and heal him with despatch'. David's life may have been endangered, certainly he would receive treatment for unspecified ills at

47 Dickenson, *Neville's Cross*, 26–8.
48 M.C. Dixon, 'John de Coupland – Hero to Villain', in Rollason and Prestwich eds., *Battle of Neville's Cross*, 36–49; J. Linda Drury, 'The Monument at Neville's Cross', in *ibid*, 78–96. See also C. Given-Wilson and F. Bériac, 'Edward III's Prisoners of War: the Battle of Poitiers and its Context', *EHR*, Sept. 2001, 802–33, at 809–14 for a discussion of English treatment of Scots captives in 1346–7.

irregular moments throughout the rest of his life: his wounds may have left him chronically or degeneratively afflicted. Froissart would, of course, note that an arrow barb remained embedded in the king's head, causing painful headaches at each full moon.[49]

But it is also Froissart's account which unintentionally hints at David's humiliation and rueful regret at the dilemma in which he now found himself. The chronicler asserts that as he lay wounded while his captors argued over his head-money David warned them that if he died of his injuries, then the Scots would 'make themselves a new king tomorrow', perhaps a sly reference to the Steward. Similarly, the local (and fictional) tradition that while David was imprisoned in Nottingham Castle (sic) awaiting transfer, he scratched images from the story of Christ's passion into the dungeon wall, lends itself to the understandable notion of a king who had lost everything now trusting in God to restore his fortunes and grant him revenge upon those of his subjects who had abandoned him.[50] It is unlikely that David had grown to be the kind of man who would dwell long upon his poor choice of battle ground and tactics, or even the loss of his many close friends and councillors before his very eyes. It is far easier to imagine that his own fate and the betrayal of Ross, the Steward and March must have been far more hurtful to consider.

Some such thoughts must have begun to impress themselves upon David when, on 16 December 1346, Edward ordered his uncle, Thomas Rokeby (who had fought in Edward Balliol's affinity at Neville's Cross), to transfer 'David de Brus' from York to the Tower of London. Sometime, then, about 2 January 1347 David, mounted on a black courser, and probably with his hands and feet shackled to his horse (just like William I of Scotland after his capture by the English in 1174) was led through the streets of London past crowds of cheering and jeering townspeople, and then taken by barge across the Thames to the Tower: Edward III and his queen were then in France and if David was interviewed at Westminster, he was most likely received by the eight-year-old Lionel of Clarence and his guardians.[51] Yet no matter how grave his situation seemed, David cannot have imagined it would take more than ten years to secure his release – longer than both the period of his life spent in Scotland before May 1334 and his childhood exile in France.

49 C.H. Talbot & E.A. Hammond, *The Medical Practitioners in Medieval England: A Biographical Register* (London 1965), 94, 387; *Chron. Bower*, vii, 261, 462–4n. For David's later ills, see *ER*, ii, 6, 29, 149, 178, 357 and NAS RH 2/4/562/15/3/57 (Transcripts of English Issue Rolls, 1310–65).

50 *Oeuvres de Froissart*, v, 144–5; Abercromby, *The Martial Achievements of the Scottish Nation*, ii, 141. Green, *Lives of the Princesses of England*, iii, 146, maintains that David was sent to Nottingham Castle *c*. 1353, at the behest of Queen Joan, to distance him from his mistress.

51 *Rot. Scot.*, i, 679–85; Green, *Lives of the Princesses of England*, iii, 135–6.

FIVE

In a Lonely Place:
the Captivity of 'David de Brus', 1346–52

'In the mean whyle that King Davy was prisoner, the lordes of
Scotland, by a litle and a litle, wan al that they had lost at the bataille
of Duresme; and there was much envy among them who might be
hyest; for every one rulid yn his owne cuntery . . .'

Sir Thomas Gray, *Scalacronica*, c. 1355[1]

The Steward's Lieutenancy, c. 1347–50

Two themes undeniably dominated Scottish affairs over the next decade. On
the one hand, Robert Steward and other regional magnates were free to
reassert and expand their territorial and political spheres of influence
without harassment from the crown. On the other, David II and his few
surviving and committed supporters had to initiate repeated and increasingly frantic attempts to broker his release from England.[2] As a result, for
some modern commentators, the period 1346–57 was marked by a rapid
and almost total collapse in Scottish royal government and law and order in
the absence of an active adult king. Crown administrative records for these
years have certainly almost completely perished (if they were kept): the
available picture of events in Scotland during David's captivity is frustratingly patchy.[3] This can also be viewed as a decade of ongoing but messy, indecisive Anglo-Scottish warfare with limited Scottish government direction.
Thus, according to these writers, after his eventual return in late 1357,
David would have to work intensively to remedy the disruptive effects of all
this chaos.[4]

For contemporary commentators, too, this was a turbulent age. Indeed it
is almost explicit in the churchmen's histories by Fordun's and Wyntoun's
anonymous sources, and especially by Abbot Bower, that the deadly Black

1 *Chron. Scalacronica*, 118.
2 Boardman, *Early Stewart Kings*, 12.
3 There are no *APS* records for this period other than a few charters issued during
councils; there are only some twenty to thirty charters in *RMS*, i, or *RRS*, vi, which
can be dated to between October 1346 and October 1357 with a place of issue (also
recorded as *RPS*, 1347/1–2; 1350/1; 1354/1–3; 1357/1/1–2; 1357/9/1–4); for the
exchequer audits, see below n.9.
4 Nicholson, 'David II, the historians and the chroniclers'; Webster, 'David II and the
Government of Fourteenth-century Scotland'.

Death – the 'pestilence among men' – which reached Scotland from England and Europe in late 1349 was a terrifying punishment merited not just by the universal sinfulness of man but by the magnate violence and greed which they depict as dominating Scotland after Neville's Cross.[5]

Yet at the same time, these Scottish chroniclers, writing under different regimes as crown servants, are divided, and often ambivalent, in their attitudes towards the king and the Steward during David's captivity. Wyntoun's source remains mostly pro-Stewart. Yet in its lament, 'Quhy couth he [David] nocht haif benn in pess/ And reullit his land in richtiusnes/ And haldin him self out of dangere?', there is perhaps as much complaint about the Steward's controversial Regency which was necessitated by David's capture as about the king's own bad generalship in October 1346. Fordun's source lays the blame clearly with the Steward as Lieutenant, or 'Warden', after 1346: 'how he governed the kingdom intrusted unto him, his deeds show forth unto all times'. Yet at the same time, even in this royalist history, there was implicit criticism of David, whose policies and actions had stoked the rivalries which had led to his own sad plight in the Tower of London and the eclipse of royal authority. Both Fordun's and Wyntoun's sources must have known that the domestic and diplomatic clashes between the interests of the absent king and the Steward which dominated the next eleven years were an extension of all that had gone before, the fall-out of tensions really since 1334.[6] These early turf wars set the agenda for the rest of David's reign. In this conflict both parties would be equally aggressive.

Robert Steward, of course, set out with a windfall of advantages in late 1346. David's party had been so completely destroyed in battle – both his household and his locality network – that the surviving rump of his support, headed by William Landallis, bishop of St Andrews, Adam Murray, bishop of Brechin, William, earl of Sutherland, Malcolm Fleming, earl of Wigtown (who escaped from English captivity in late 1346), perhaps the heirs of the late Marischal and Constable, and maybe even Queen Joan, could offer little resistance or alternative to the Steward's assumption of the lieutenancy. This he probably did officially with the approval of a council held at Perth (close to the Steward's lordship and castle of Methven) about 3 May 1347. His earliest extant act as 'King's Lieutenant' dates from 8 October that year: that title, rather than 'Guardian', perhaps hints that his powers were in some

---

5 *Chron. Fordun*, i, 368–9; *Chron. Bower*, vii, 273–5. The historical debate as to the actual method of transmission of this plague epidemic has been re-opened with new evidence arguing against its previously supposed bubonic and pneumonic forms (S.K. Cohn, *The Black Death Transformed: Disease and Culture in Early Renaissance Europe* (London 2002); thanks to Richard Oram for this reference).

6 *Chron. Fordun*, i, 369–77; *Chron. Wyntoun*, vi, 168.

measure limited on paper by the wishes of this council and that the estates by no means failed to act in the absence of the king. Indeed, the highly controversial politics of the next decade would lead to an increase in community influence through parliament.[7]

However, Robert Steward was at first able to appoint his own officers. By at least August 1348 – probably over a year earlier – Sir Robert Erskine, a Lanarkshire tenant of the Steward, was acting as Chamberlain with esquire Norman Leslie as his deputy: Leslie was an Angus man who would continue in this post under Thomas Stewart, earl of Angus, when that lord became the Steward's choice as Chamberlain about 1351–2. William de Caldwell, a cleric from Neilston in Ayrshire, may also have been appointed Chancellor by the Steward about 1347–8.[8]

But although he now controlled the royal coffers and the king's great seal, the Steward does not seem to have tried or been able to begin to assert central control over all the crown's regional resources. The apparent breakdown in the central intromission and auditing of sheriffs' and bailies' income due to the crown suggests that instead the Steward, while protecting some royal revenue he could use, often allowed regional magnates to simply siphon off local monies for their own use.[9] William, earl of Ross, certainly seems to have done this within his own northern sphere of control and beyond, exploiting the demise of his brother-in-law, John Randolph, earl of Moray, by re-assuming the prized office of justiciar north-of-Forth and plundering the revenues of the dioceses of Moray and Aberdeen and the regality of the Abbey of Arbroath.[10] The Steward himself pocketed re-

---

7 *Chron. Fordun*, i, 368; *Chron. Wyntoun*, vi, 188; *Chron. Bower*, vii, 271–3, 466n; *RRS*, vi, no. 112; *Chron. Anonimalle*, 28 and *CFR*, vi, 250 for Fleming; Penman, 'Parliament Lost – Parliament Regained?'.

8 BL Add. MSS. 33, 245 f. 53b-54 for Erskine; NAS GD 79/1/7 for Leslie; Watt, *Scottish Graduates*, 72–3 for Caldwell.

9 There is only a single sheriff's account for 1347 for Aberdeenshire (by William Meldrum) in *ER*, i 542–4; in 1358 a few sheriffs would intromit partial accounts which reached back for a few details sometimes as far as 1353 or 1348 (Kinross, Clackmannan, Aberdeen, Perth).

10 *RRS*, vi, no. 116: on 17 December 1346 letters were issued in David's name at Finavon in Forfar ordering the justiciars and other royal officials not to exact tallages in the lands of the Abbey of Arbroath; at Forfar on 7 July 1348 an act by the earl of Ross as justiciar was issued charging a Dundee burgess with exacting an unlawful toll on the Abbey (*Registrum de Panmure*, ed. H. Maule of Kelly (2 vols., Edinburgh 1874) i, 167–9); in March 1352 David (while on parole in Scotland) would order his justiciars not to interfere in the Abbey's customs (*RRS*, vi, no. 123). On 4 November 1353 letters in David's name issued at Berwick ordered William Keith, the Marischal, to stop aiding his brother, John, to occupy unjustly lands in the Mearns owned by the Abbey (*ibid*, nos. 109, 124). In October 1354 the Steward ordered Thomas, earl of Angus as Chamberlain to maintain the Abbey against the encroachment of John Keith – in March that year David had confirmed two of William Keith's charters (*ibid*, nos. 133–5).

sources throughout central Scotland. He installed one of his close adherents, Sir John Danielston, as sheriff of Perth (and perhaps of Dumbarton). By March 1347, if not before, the Steward also had access to income from the earldom of Fife where he – or Robert Erskine on his behalf – was bailie for Earl Duncan, then captive in England. The Steward may have long given up hope of wedding Duncan's heiress, Isabella, who by April 1345 at the latest had married the Northumbrian knight, William de Felton; but the Steward may have begun to intrude the influence of his second son, Walter Stewart, into Fife and its associated Perthshire lordships.[11]

Where he could, the Steward did allow his allies and kin to enjoy the spoils of David's defeat. Sometime in 1348, Sir John Menteith of Arran and Knapdale was made sheriff of Clackmannanshire (controlling passes from Stirling into Fife), displacing either Robert I's hereditary placemen there, the earls of Lennox, or David's possible choice, Sir Edward Keith. John Menteith must also have been allowed to re-seize the central lordship adjacent to his own lands and Lennox, namely Strathgartney, wresting it back from David's associate, John Logie (restored in 1342). John Menteith was perhaps also able to trespass upon some of the earldom of Menteith.[12] Similarly, Thomas Stewart, earl of Angus, may have been allowed to begin to enjoy the revenues of the burgh of Stirling, the royal lands of Crail and Earl Duncan of Fife's Perthshire barony of Strathord.[13] The fortunes of Patrick Dunbar, earl of March, in the south-east must also have revived due to the absence of both the king and Douglas of Liddesdale as the focus of lordship for the chivalry of Lothian. The Steward may similarly have begun to advance his own influence north of Atholl into the Moray regality's offshoot, the lordship of Badenoch, where his fourth son, Alexander Stewart, would be lord in the late 1360s.[14] The Steward's first son and heir, John Stewart of Kyle, could also have begun to intrude upon the Bruce earldom of Carrick. Then, on 21 November 1348, the Steward requested a papal marriage dispensation (granted on 10 December) for John Murray of Bothwell, the Pantler and son of David II's aunt, Christian Bruce, to wed Margaret Graham, daughter and heiress of John Graham, earl of Menteith. By then, the captured Graham had been brutally executed by Edward III –

---

11 *ER*, i, 553, 574 and *Scots Peerage*, viii, 520–3 for Danielston; *HMC*, vii, 305 (Erskine); *CPR*, iii, 539 (Steward and others witnessing Fife affairs *c.* 1354); NAS GD 121 Murthly Castle Muniments Box 4/Bundle 10/no. 3 (Fife); Boardman, *Early Stewart Kings*, 13–9.
12 *RRS*, vi, nos. 212, 492.
13 *ER*, i, 555, 585–6, 622, 624.
14 A. Grant, 'The Wolf of Badenoch', in W.D.H. Sellar ed., *Moray, Province and People* (SSNS 1992), 143–61; S. Boardman, 'Lordship in the North-East – the Badenoch Stewarts I: Alexander Stewart, Earl of Buchan, Lord of Badenoch', *Northern Scotland*, xv (1996), 1–30.

drawn by horses, no less, for defecting back to the Bruce Scots in the 1330s (a fate which might also have befallen the Steward and March if they had been captured at Neville's Cross). The Steward's third son, Robert, would pursue the earldom of Menteith after he came of age about 1358. But in John Murray between 1347 and his death in 1351 (and in his brother and successor, Thomas Murray) the Steward secured a valuable regional ally who would serve him as a 'lieutenant' until 1357 while assuming control of much of Menteith and perhaps of the valuable lordship of Garioch near Mar.[15] The Steward may also have made John's kinsman, a William Murray, keeper of Edinburgh Castle (and perhaps sheriff there), allowing that knight to pursue his own violent ambitions in the Lothians, acts which were condemned by the chroniclers.[16]

This was essentially *laissez-faire* lordship by the Steward. He allowed men to take what they had coveted before 1346 and could now access. But he also took more direct action to protect his own interests, including the control of Scottish foreign policy. About 12 November 1347, at a council held at Dundee, acts were issued under the great seal in David's name only which banned all Flemings from Scotland and transferred the Scottish staple – the designated port of trade – from Bruges in Flanders to Middelburg in Zeeland.[17] As the townsmen of Flanders had just turned against their count and his controller, the king of France, this council's actions committed Scotland to helping Philip VI while conflict continued in Europe, despite an extended general truce of April 1347. It also suggests that the Steward was not going to seek peace with England and its allies despite the heavy cost of Neville's Cross; nor was he going to use this staple move as a bargaining lever in talks for David's release.

Instead, the Steward continued to use the royal seals to secure contingencies which really assumed – or hoped or planned – that David would not return as king. Just a fortnight later, on 22 November 1347, a papal dispensation was requested in the name of both David II, Philip VI of France and seven bishops of Scotland (including Landellis of St Andrews) which would legitimise the Steward's marriage to Elizabeth More and their offspring – four sons and two daughters by 1346. This request was quickly

---

15 *Vetera*, 290; *CPP*, iii, 303; *RRS*, vi, nos. 135, 139; *Rot. Scot.*, i, 687–8; *ER*, i, 547, 550 (remissions to Murray's men), 576 (Ardchary in Murray's hands), 583 (Crawford-John in his hands).

16 *Chron. Wyntoun*, vi, 188; *Chron. Bower*, vii, 159, 469. According to these sources Murray helped an Alan Wyntoun (who is known to have died in the Holy Land *c.* 1347) seize the daughter of Sir Alexander Seton, causing open feuding in the Lothians.

17 *RRS*, vi, no. 110–1; A. Stevenson, 'The Flemish Dimension of the Auld Alliance', in G.G. Simpson ed., *Scotland and the Low Countries, 1124–1994* (East Linton 1996), 28–42, at 38–40.

granted by Avignon on 10 December 1347, suggesting express delivery by the Steward's messengers.[18] As yet, though, the English had granted no Scots access to their king: thus it is likely that the Steward had made free use of David's name and seal.

Legitimation of the Lieutenant's sons was a sensible, necessary precaution in the event of David's death in captivity. A council of Scotland's surviving political community – dominated by Steward supporters – may have understandably approved that this request be sent to ward off a repeat of the dangers of 1286–92. However, the Steward's actions may have been unauthorised and self-interested, prompted by dynastic doubts raised not only by David's recent favour to his full-nephew, John Sutherland, but also by the re-entry of John's father, William, earl of Sutherland, into the Scottish marriage market in November 1347. For fifteen days before the Steward's papal request, Sutherland had requested a similar dispensation to wed Joanna Menteith, the much-coveted widow in turn of Malise, seventh earl of Strathearn, John Campbell, earl of Atholl, and now Maurice Murray, earl of Strathearn.[19] Like Maurice's marriage in 1339, and his elevation to his title by David in 1343–4, Sutherland's proposed second match – and the terce (lands due to a wife) held by Joanna in both Atholl and Strathearn – must have posed a direct threat to Stewart landed interests in central Scotland: Sutherland may even have thus foiled the second marriage hopes of Robert Steward himself. Moreover, in doing so it is possible that Sutherland may have been acting on words from his king. For Earl William had been captured at Neville's Cross but, for reasons unknown, returned quickly to Scotland.[20]

Sutherland may have been further instructed by other men sent north by the king. No official Scottish embassy received permission to visit David in London from Scotland between early 1347 and January 1348, the first year of his captivity. Letters could of course be sent, and there may have been some early calls in Scottish councils for release talks to be sought which the Steward as Lieutenant resisted. But clearly this did not stop David himself – once he had recovered from his wounds – from initial private attempts to make contact with the rump of his supporters in Scotland and to begin to rebuild his influence. In doing so David naturally turned to the survivors of the chivalric cadre of lesser Scottish laymen he had built up with his patronage since 1341. He must also have expended a vast amount of personal effort in improving his relations with his captors, gaining their trust and increasing his freedom of movement around the Tower and Plantagenet circles in London.

18 *CPP*, i, 124 and iii, 265; *Vetera*, 289, no. 577.
19 *Regesta Vaticana*, vol. 184 f. 116 (cited in *Scots Peerage*, vii, 327–8).
20 Some Scottish prisoners – Fleming, Stewart of Dalswinton – were released by their English noble captors without Edward III's permission (Given-Wilson and Bériac, 'Edward III's Prisoners of War', 812–4).

Thus on 20 November 1347 – about the same time as Sutherland and the Steward despatched their appeals to the Papacy – Edward III's government issued safe-conducts for the captive knights, William Ramsay of Colluthie (David's sheriff of Edinburgh) and Patrick Dunbar (one of many former adherents of Alexander Ramsay of Dalhousie, William's brother) to leave for Scotland on the business of 'David de Brus'. This got the ball rolling. On 7 December 1347, Sir William Livingston, sheriff of Haddington and a close daily counsellor of David before 1346, received a safe-conduct to come south from Scotland to visit his king along with Walter Blantyre, David's Dominican confessor. Then on 30 January 1348, Blantyre, William Ramsay, Patrick Dunbar and another captive knight who favoured by the king both before and after 1346, Sir David Annan, were permitted to leave for Scotland on 'David de Brus's business'.[21]

In despatching and receiving these men David was probably acting optimistically on the basis of hope given him by Edward III's realistic attitude towards the Scottish kingship. Despite the triumph of Neville's Cross and the welcome vengeance the English king had thus scored against the son of the man who had many times humiliated his father, Edward II, some glaring practical truths must now have come into play. David II turned twenty-three on 5 March 1347; he was married to Edward III's sister, Joan. Thus there was at least a possible basis for a long Anglo-Scottish peace, perhaps even alliance. The English king and his council were besides anxious to consolidate their recent victories, especially on the continent, and to maintain truces agreed at Calais in late 1346, and extended throughout 1347, so as to delay renewed full-scale war with France. Edward could not afford simultaneous conflict with Scotland, certainly not an attempt to re-impose a conquest or political settlement on the entirety of that realm. Such a Scottish campaign held none of the attractions of wealth and glory which obsessed Edward and his nobles across the Channel. But most obviously, even if Edward chose to re-install his own vassal king of Scots, Edward Balliol was by now sixty-three years old, unwed and childless: in all likelihood, even if unchallenged in Scotland, the vassal Balliol line would have to be replaced quite soon. Edward III's regime was thus left with no choice but to abandon its sponsorship of Balliol's cause, just as in 1347 it also dropped its exiled claimant to the duchy of Brittany, John de Montfort, in favour of his rival, Charles of Blois, captured by the English shortly after David.[22]

Balliol still worked in Edward III's name, surely in the hope of realising his

21 *Rot. Scot.*, i, 707–15 *passim*; PRO E403/325 to 381 *passim*; Watt, *Scottish Graduates*, 54 (Blantyre).
22 Given-Wilson and Bériac, 'Edward III's Prisoners of War', 822.

sponsored bid for the Scottish kingship. In January 1347 he hired Henry Percy and Ralph Neville and their followings for a year: Wyntoun's source states that during those months this group raided as far as Glasgow and Falkirk and into the Lothians. They did so from Balliol's re-established bases at Caerlaverock and Hestan Island which by the winter of 1347–8 lay within an expanded English frontier zone. In addition, after Neville's Cross, northern English forces retook much of the shires of Roxburgh, Jedburgh, Berwick, Peebles, Selkirk and Dumfries (along with their main castles) as well as the southern zones of the lands of Eskdale, Annandale, Nithsdale, Liddesdale and coastal Galloway.[23] The Steward and other lords took refuge temporarily north of the Forth-Clyde line. About 4 November 1346, Edward III's envoys had also offered a fresh alliance to another of David's problem subjects, John MacDonald of the Isles, at that time still probably at odds with the Steward over Kintyre.[24] But Edward III showed no real appetite for war with Scotland beyond this creation of a buffer zone and maverick allies to protect his northern border, one which the Scots soon began to push back from Selkirk forest. Edward must have believed it was either far better to deny outright individual ransoms for the Bruce king and other Scottish captives so as to keep their countrymen quiet, or for England to hold the Scots off and deal with a pliant David de Brus – fearful of a Stewart succession – to secure a general settlement. Either way, England had to recognise David as king of an independent Scottish kingdom in principle if not in name. In that sense, Neville's Cross was to be more of a turning-point in Anglo-Scottish relations than Bannockburn or the peace of 1328.

By April 1348 the private preliminary exchanges of the previous year had given the English king cause to issue a safe-conduct to an apparently official Scottish embassy, headed by the royalist bishops of St Andrews, Caithness and Brechin and the barons David Lindsay of Crawford, Robert Erskine (the Chamberlain), William Meldrum (well rewarded by David before 1346 and a deputy justiciar north-of Forth for the earl of Ross), James Sandilands and Andrew Ormistoun.[25] This group represents the first signs of the beginnings of a revived royal party in Scotland. By mid-1348, indeed, David and his associates had re-established some clear lines of communication with Scotland. Queen Joan was able to send papal petitions in her own and her husband's names: about October 1348 she may have had indefinite leave to

23 *Chron. Wyntoun*, vi, 188–9; Sumption, *Hundred Years War*, i, 570–85; Webster, 'The English Occupation of Dumfriesshire in the Fourteenth Century', 64–80; Reid, 'Edward Balliol', 43–5; Oram, 'Bruce, Balliol and the Lordship of Galloway', 45–6; C.J. Neville, *Violence, Custom and Law: the Anglo-Scottish Border Lands in the Later Middle Ages* (Edinburgh 1998), 37–41.
24 *Foedera* iii, part i, 93; *Acts of the Lords of the Isles*, xxv-xxvi, lxiv-lxv, lxxiv-lxxvi.
25 *Rot. Scot.*, i, 715.

visit David in London.[26] Moreover, David and his friends seem to have made use of the connections of another English captive, William Douglas of Liddesdale. Both Sandilands and Ormistoun visited Douglas in the Tower in 1347 but by late 1348 David himself would be requesting safe-conducts for these knights as 'his people': the pair would visit the king again in February 1349.[27]

David's ability to work with Douglas – on a release plan for which the first evidence surfaces in late 1349 – was based primarily on their mutual desire for freedom: in March-April 1348, the English parliament had granted Edward III a fresh tax upon the condition that neither of the war 'criminals' David or Liddesdale be released.[28] But David and the knight may also have shared a growing resentment of the Steward's predation on their Scottish interests. For example, in making John Danielston sheriff of Perth after the death of the crown's man, Sir Andrew Buttergask, at Neville's Cross, the Steward may also have snubbed Liddesdale's uncle, Andrew Douglas, Buttergask's predecessor: Andrew Douglas had been included on one of the safe-conducts of August 1348 to come to London on David's behalf. The Douglas knight must besides have been desperate to secure a deal which safeguarded Liddesdale from permanent English annexation by the Wake family or from Stewart or Dunbar intrusion.

Throughout 1348 David seems to have reached out to a number of other regional Scottish magnates, probably in the hope of building up a consensus of opposition to the Steward's partisan lieutenancy. Sometime after 12 August 1348, the king was visited in the Tower by Patrick Dunbar, earl of March; he was followed by the aged Sir Alexander Seton, Robert I's key Lothian man, a former household steward for David and, by 1348, pre-centor of the Scottish Knights Hospitaller.[29] However, as much as David and his supporters may thus have been able to exploit magnate ambitions and fears, the same forces may have disrupted progress towards forcing the Steward into securing David's release. Most obviously, David's dealings with Douglas of Liddesdale must have been spurred on impatiently towards securing a release deal, but also horribly complicated after *c.* 1347–48, by the return from childhood exile at Château Gaillard of the knight's now adult 'nephew', William, Lord of Douglas. The young lord immediately set about regaining control of his Black Douglas regality lands from his god-father's influence. Basing himself at Edinburgh by December 1348 (where he

26 *Ibid*, 727 – the Queen's valet, a Robert Barbour, had leave to enter England throughout this period (*ibid*, 724, 729, 731, 755); *RRS*, vi, pp. 45.
27 *Rot. Scot.*, i, 715, 718.
28 *Rotuli Parliamentorum*, ii, 201; J. Sumption, *The Hundred Years War: Vol. II – Trial by Fire* (London 1999), ii, 144
29 *Rot. Scot.*, i, 721–2.

made his maternal uncle, David Lindsay of Crawford, castle-keeper), Lord William quickly resumed leadership of his family's Douglasdale men. His presence must have contributed to the reflaring of the Lothian feud sparked off by Liddesdale's murder of Alexander Ramsay in 1342. This was a running battle which would see a band led by a John St Michael murder David II's former household steward, Sir David Barclay, in the streets of Aberdeen in 1351 in retaliation for Barclay's slaying not only of William Bullock (at the king's orders in 1342) but of Liddesdale's brother, John, and father, James of Dalkeith, sometime *c.* 1346–50.[30]

However, William Lord Douglas's activities also point to another unpredictable magnate pursuit which may have disrupted David's negotiations with Edward III and the Scots. For, taking to war like a duck to water, Lord William began to launch raids on the English occupation regime from the forests of Selkirk and Jedburgh. The younger William clearly had a vital interest in ensuring that any peace deal with England which the knight of Liddesdale helped make involving his release and unwelcome return to Scotland did not compromise Black Douglas lands south of Forth. The young lord also coveted Liddesdale itself, which his father, Archibald Douglas, had first acquired as Guardian in 1332–3. At the same time, just like Sir James, Archibald and Liddesdale before him, profitable war against England was still a vital form of lordship by which Lord William looked to attract and expand his following. Yet, these complex motives aside, genuine innate hatred of the English must already have formed a hard core to the Lord Douglas's being. Brought up on tales of the 'Good' Sir James, he may also have thirsted for revenge for his father's death in defeat in 1333 at Halidon Hill. Lastly, Lord William must have felt as indebted to France as David himself had done between 1341–6.

French pressure, too, undoubtedly played its part. In 1348, Philip VI sent twenty suits of armour and surely other supplies to Scotland.[31] Correspondence between the French government and Scottish magnates may also have been regular in 1347–8 as it would be throughout 1349–52. In London, David may have been happy to see *some* Scottish military action as a lever to persuade Edward III of the value of a full peace and his release. This may partly explain why in late June 1348 or 1349 the odd couple of Patrick, earl of March, and William, earl of Sutherland, reportedly raided for livestock as far south as Bamburgh, causing much destruction there and around Roxburgh Castle (areas then under the control of David's captor, John de

---

30 *Chron. Fordun*, i, 369; *Chron. Wyntoun*, vi, 192; *Chron. Bower*, 271–3; Fraser ed., *The Douglas Book*, i, 216–221; Brown, *Black Douglases*, 43–6.
31 *Les Journaux du Trésor de Philippe VI de Valois*, no. 1278; Campbell, 'England, Scotland and the Hundred Years War in the Fourteenth Century', 198.

Coupland), and only narrowly avoided capture.[32] But David and his supporters would never have wanted the majority of Scottish magnates to remain too dependent upon alliance with France and committed to war with England, especially when this was an area of policy direction and resources which the Steward could dominate as Lieutenant. By late 1348 this was not just because David had seen at first hand the futility and potential cost for the Scottish crown of alliance with France but because he was clearly getting somewhere in talks with Edward III. Significantly, much of this progress was based on growing respect and friendship between David and his brother-in-law and nephews. Indeed, these were the beginnings of the amicable relations between these royals which Wyntoun's source would see fit to describe as a 'rycht grete specialtie' by the 1360s.[33]

On 23 April 1348 – the feast day of St George, in the same month as passage was granted to the first official Scottish embassy to David – the captive Scottish king took part in the glittering triumphal tournament at Windsor held to celebrate the birth of Edward III's sixth son and to proclaim Plantagenet military prowess throughout Europe. Wearing a surcoat of red velvet bearing a silver-white rose, and mounted on a horse with blue velvet harness, David took to the field with the *incognito* English king and many of his leading nobles, alongside other valuable captives. How well or fully David participated is not recorded and the tournament was won by Raoul, Comte d'Eu, Philip VI's former Constable (the man originally charged with leading the French expedition to Scotland planned for 1335–6). But as a natural sequel to this public gathering, David may also have been present in August 1348 when Edward initiated many of the English knights from this spectacular joust into his new royal Order of the Garter, at the same time endowing a chapel for this Order to St George at Windsor.[34]

The gathering and celebration of such a strong cadre of chivalry around the English monarch – including Edward III's heir and namesake, the future Black Prince, and his most successful continental commander, Henry de Grosmont, earl of Derby and master of Lancaster – must have impressed upon David the political value of such a means of focusing and building support around a king's court and person. It is evident that as well as serving as a pious banner for Edward's military campaigns, the

---

32 PRO SC 1/54/30.
33 *Chron. Wyntoun*, vi, 242.
34 G.F. Beltz, *Memorials of the Order of the Garter* (London 1841), 380; D. Boutlon, *The Knights of the Crown: The Monarchical Orders of Knighthood in Later Medieval Europe, 1325–1520* (Woodbridge 1997), 96–166, 114–6 (for a discussion of the uncertain dating of the Order's foundation); *The Buik of Alexander*, i, cliv, cxcvi; Sumption, *Hundred Years War*, ii, 1–2.

Order of the Garter also reflected political loyalties within the English court and council and was a valuable source of patronage.[35] Some of the political skill, confidence and determination exuded by Edward cannot have failed to rub off on David as a model for asserting royal power over aristocratic ambitions.

Edward was undoubtedly displaying David as a war trophy in 1348. But their contact must also have provided the common ground of a genuine interest in chivalry and Christian piety over which these in-laws could, to some extent, identify. However, dialogue between the two monarchs, and between David and his Scottish supporters, was unavoidably disrupted by the arrival of the plague in London by November 1348, just as Edward left for Calais for talks which further extended the Anglo-French truce.[36]

The abject terror and misery which this epidemic inflicted upon a medieval European populace almost totally ignorant of disease transmission mechanisms is impossible for a modern audience to imagine. The ghastly ravaging of the human body by 'King Death' was ugly and terrifying if mercifully swift. By September of 1348 the plague had already reached the coastal ports of England and carried off Edward III's daughter, Joan, betrothed to the king of Castile. Between then and August 1349 it would claim some 20–30,000 of London's population – well over a third – a casualty rate which would almost be matched nationwide. Townsfolk, the poor and especially the very young, the old and the sick suffered worst, but the disease showed little regard for age, gender or station:

> the plague carried off so vast a multitude of both sexes that nobody could be found who would bear the corpses to the grave. Men and women carried their own children on their shoulders to the church and threw them into a common pit.

Of the spiritual leaders whose task it was to comfort both those afflicted and spared, three archbishops of Canterbury died within a year and almost a fifth of all English bishops were taken along with over a third of the general clergy. The English Chancellor, the king's physician and many government clerks and locality officers also perished. By December Edward III had been forced to halt his preparations to invade France, to cancel a parliament set for January 1349 and retreat to the countryside: normal government would only resume – still

---

35 J. Vale, *Edward III and Chivalry: Chivalric Society and its Context, 1270–1350* (London 1982); C. Given-Wilson, *The Royal Household and the King's Affinity: Service, Politics and Finance in England, 1360–1413* (London 1986), 142–59, 280–1; W.M. Ormrod, 'The Personal Religion of Edward III', *Speculum*, lxvi (1989), 849–77; Boulton, *The Knights of the Crown*, 125–42; Penman, 'Christian Days and Knights', 255–6.

36 Sumption, *Hundred Years War*, ii, 17.

remarkably quickly – in autumn 1349. Thus in sheltering from what medieval folk blamed as a marauding 'miasma' or cloud of disease, David must have spent a fearful year within the confines of the Tower of London. St George, patron saint of the Garter, but also a figure invoked universally against plague throughout Christendom, was surely never more in demand.[37]

When this nightmarish epidemic spread to midland England, the Scottish embassy of the bishops of St Andrews, Brechin and Caithness, again accompanied by Erskine, Lindsay and Meldrum, may not have been able to use the safe-conduct issued to them in February 1349. But the Scots were included in the uneasy European ceasefire agreed upon at Guines in Gascony at that time.[38] This truce, the improving personal relations between the two kings, and David's apparently revived personal energy, may have helped induce Edward to show some sympathy to David's own chivalric cadre. For between May and December 1349, as the plague eased in the south, some of the lesser Scottish knights captured at Neville's Cross – Walter Haliburton, David Annan and William de Vaus – were granted their freedom by Edward after they had sworn, in the presence of David II and 'upon the gospels and upon the faith of chivalry', never to bear arms against the English king again and to pay small ransoms.[39] Clearly, in agreeing to neutralise some of his closest followers as *hors de combat* in any future conflict with England, David was committing his realm to seeking a full peace with Edward III and the abandonment of the French alliance. These prisoner releases, moreover, coincided with Edward and David sending a joint petition – dated 9 June 1349 – to Pope Clement VI seeking benefices for Yorkshire clerics. Significantly, it was in this petition that the English regime styled David for the first time since his capture as 'king of Scots'.[40]

However, although by this time Edward III and his council may have tabled some package of terms for their royal captive's release, David and his supporters were still unable to dictate events in Scotland or to speed up progress there in efforts to negotiate his freedom. In June 1349, northern English intelligence reported to Edward that:

---

37 P. Zeigler, *The Black Death* (1969), 167–9; W.M. Ormrod, 'The English Government and the Black Death of 1348–49', in W.M. Ormrod ed., *England in the Fourteenth Century* (Woodbridge 1986), 175–88; W.M. Ormrod and P. Lindley eds., *The Black Death in England* (Stamford 1996).

38 *Rot. Scot.*, i, 727; Sumption, *Hundred Years War*, ii, 17, 49.

39 *Rot. Scot.*, i, 728–31; *CDS*, iii, nos. 1549, 2008 (December 1349, de Vaux promises to pay 200 merks ransom to Edward III); Given-Wilson and Bériac, 'Edward III's Prisoners of War', 812–3, emphasises that the English king often took less in ransom from his captives than he had to pay in compensation to the Englishmen who had captured them in battle: clearly, Edward hoped for a military or political gain through their cheap release rather than a fiscal reward.

40 *RRS*, vi, pp. 45–6; *CPP*, i, 164.

The Scots are greatly cheered because of the pestilence [in England]; they daily do all the injuries they can by land and sea and capture victuals coming to the town (Berwick) from England. They have made ladders and other engines to come to the town to try if they can take it . . .[41]

Scottish magnates like Patrick the earl of March, Thomas Stewart the earl of Angus, John Stewart of Kyle and William, lord of Douglas, were most likely responsible for this continued aggression in the borders. Their attractive, profitable martial lordship understandably distracted from the king's wishes some of the Lowland chivalric cadre which David himself had led against England: for example, in summer 1349, Alexander Ramsay, junior, and the south-western Kerr kindred led two hundred men on a fierce assault on Roxburgh's burgh walls. This and other Scottish breaches of the truce were nonetheless easily surpassed by continuing French aggression around Gascony. Indeed, in August 1349, Philip VI renounced the new truce and launched an invasion of English-held Saintonge. Edward III would be forced to recross the Channel to attend to his defences in Gascony by January 1350. In the meantime, Anglo-Scottish talks stalled.[42] Clearly, it required some decisive breakthrough in either Franco-Scottish relations or the control of affairs in Scotland, or both, to effect the necessary peaceful and receptive conditions in which to advance plans for David's release.

The First Succession Plan, 1350–2

Probably sometime in late 1349 or early 1350 David II made a very calculated but over-optimistic attempt to kick-start his diplomatic position by writing to Pope Clement VI, his former acquaintance at Rouen. It was to be the first of many such bids by a king who for the rest of his career would invest considerable energy in complicated mechanisms to recover both his diplomatic position and seize the political initiative in Scotland. David's letter – which he entrusted to two Scottish captive knights on parole, Walter Haliburton and Bartholomew de Leon (whom he had made his bailie of Kinghorn in Fife *c.* 1344) – is worth citing in full as transcribed in Clement's response of 9 August 1350:

For four years David king of Scots and some of his barons and knights have been detained in England, while the kingdom has been and is being despoiled by the king of England, so that the captives have neither wealth nor friends to ransom them; he [David] was resisting as

41 *Rot. Scot.*, i, 731–2; *CDS*, v, no. 810; Sumption, *Hundred Years War*, ii, 56.
42 *Ibid*, 57–62, 144–7; PRO SC1/37/80; *CDS*, v, nos. 809–10; *Chron. Bower*, vii, 271–5.

best he could, with the help of the French king, but lost his folk in a war and now lies captive and desolate, and will be freed only with the help of the Pope and the king of France. He therefore implores the Pope to write to the French king to involve him in these affairs, and if a peace or long truce is made between the kings of England and France, the king of Scots may enjoy it and be freed . . .

And the king of England asks the following to permit the king of Scots and his fellow captives to depart. That the king of Scots and the men of his realm should do homage to the king of England now and in the future. And the king of Scotland and his successors, kings for the time, shall always be [ready] with the forces of their realm to help the king of England for the time against the king and kingdom of France. That the king of Scotland of the time shall be held cited to come to the parliaments and great councils of the king of England. That those banished and proscribed from Scotland for their demerits, and their heirs, whose goods were long ago confiscated both by law and by the custom of the realm, and distributed by the king of Scots and his folk among divers persons, should recover their pristine status and their goods. That if it should happen that the king of Scotland of the time should die without a lawful heir born of his body, the king of England, or his son of the time should be king of Scots. And that the present king of England and his folk should have all the castles and fortresses of the kingdom of Scotland under their power, until each and every one of the foregoing is fulfilled.[43]

Edward III and his council might easily have tabled such an opening salvo of demands in 1348–9 for the release of their most valuable captive. The demand for homage of Scotland, military service in English wars, attendance at English assemblies and English possession of Scottish castles, echoed demands made of Scotland's kings not only in the Treaty of Falaise of 1174 – which Henry II had imposed on William the Lion of Scotland after he too had been captured invading England while allied to France – but also by Edward I in the run-up to his judgement in the Scottish succession hearings, now known as the 'Great Cause', of 1291–2. More immediately for David II, diplomatic provision for Edward III to be named as heir to Philip VI of France – displacing the out-of-favour prince, John, duke of Normandy – had briefly been considered by the Valois king after the battle of Créci.[44]

43 *CPP*, i, 203; translation from E.W.M. Balfour-Melville, 'David II's Appeal to the Pope', *SHR*, xli (1962), 86.
44 Duncan, *Kingship of the Scots*, chs 6, 12–3; Watson, *Under the Hammer*, 11–5; Boulton, *Knights of the Crown*, 168–9.

Realistically, however, these harsh English demands can only have been bargaining chips designed to scare the Scots into seeking terms. In the same way, David II surely presented them to Clement VI as the gospel truth and proof of his dreadful plight as a means of securing the Pope's aid in persuading Philip VI to make a final peace and to abide by it, not simply to agree to another phoney truce in which French, Flemish, English and Scottish forces continued to clash on land and sea. If so, David's letter had its initial desired effect and Clement eventually wrote to the new French king, John II (as his father, Philip VI, died on 22 August 1350) advocating an Anglo-French peace. But John was determined to repair the damage done in his father's later years and stepped up French aggression. This would also involve John trying to mobilise the Scots afresh.[45]

Nevertheless, although it cunningly overstates a worst-case scenario for the Bruce dynasty and Scotland, David's letter to the Pope does betray some crucial aspects of the peace-release talks between himself and his supporters and Edward and his council which must have evolved over 1348–9. Plans for the restoration of the Disinherited's descendants to their lost Scottish lands and goods, talk of an Anglo-Scottish military alliance and, most important of all, admission of Edward III or one of his sons to the Scottish succession should David die without an heir, would all form central components of the many deals which David would try to cut over the next decade and a half. Indeed, it was most likely David himself who suggested sometime in 1349–50 that it be a *younger* son of Edward III who should be his heir presumptive in Scotland.[46]

In theory at least, this was an inspired gamble which might have radically boosted both David's diplomatic and domestic circumstances. If accepted by both the Scottish and English political communities, it might have seen David released without payment of a crippling ransom. But more importantly, Robert Steward, David's chief opponent, would be displaced as heir presumptive to the Scottish throne, and much of his political influence broken. The Steward's territorial ambitions might also be undermined if David could find some way to include Duncan, earl of Fife (whose daughter and heiress, Isabella, was a royal cousin of Edward III), in the deal. Interestingly, in 1347, although Duncan had been captured at Neville's Cross, his marriage to a Monthermer had saved him from the same fate of execution for treason against Edward III as had befallen John Graham, earl of Menteith: moreover, it was in February 1350 – just as David seemed to be reaching some sort of agreement with Edward III – that after payment of a

---

45 Campbell, 'England, Scotland and the Hundred Years War in the Fourteenth Century', 199–201.
46 Duncan, 'Honi soit qui mal y pense', 116–31.

£1,000 ransom Earl Duncan was freed to return to Scotland where he would die three years later (although the necessity of raising this sum from Fife's lands must have required the aid of his bailie, the Steward).[47]

Nonetheless, such diplomatic blows to the Steward and royal promises of patronage to other Scottish nobles could aid David in overcoming natural Scottish opposition to his proposal to admit a Plantagenet to the succession so soon after the Scottish sacrifices of the wars since 1296. At least if the new heir-in-waiting was a younger son of Edward III – Prince Lionel (b. 1338) or John, earl of Richmond (b. 1340), say – then there would be less threat of full regnal union between England and Scotland, no swallowing by the greater of the lesser as had been feared by the Scots nobility and church when a marriage was contracted by the uncrowned child queen of Scotland, Margaret, and Edward I's son in 1290. Besides, if David could father his own son after his release, the English prince's succession would not be an issue. David only turned twenty-five years old in March 1349 – attaining his official majority – and he must have been confident of his ability to have children: his relations with Queen Joan may even have improved in step with his friendship with King Edward and his sons.

However, to present and sell any such plan to the Scots, David's support in Scotland and his access to government channels would have to improve drastically. There is some evidence that they did so throughout 1349–50. As well as the return to Scotland of some of his household knights and the continuing dialogue between Edward's council and Scottish embassies – which included key prelates like Landellis and Adam of Brechin as well as the Chamberlain, Robert Erskine – David may also have resumed distribution of patronage at this time. On 20 October 1349, in letters patent issued in David's name and dated at Edinburgh, the Lanarkshire barony of Roberton (which David had granted in 1346 to Sir William Jardine and then to Douglas of Liddesdale, a casualty and a captive of Neville's Cross respectively) was transferred to the Liddesdale follower, Sir James Sandilands of Calder in Lothian, who visited David in London at least twice that year as one of the 'king's people'. This grant was apparently drawn up by Robert Dumbarton, David's clerk of the Rolls since 1341, who also visited David in London in July 1349 and would shuttle regularly between there and Scotland throughout the remainder of the king's captivity. David had clearly regained control of his privy seal from the Steward through this clerk.[48]

The simple reason which had allowed David to do so – a fact previously

47 *CDS*, v, no. 512.
48 *RRS*, vi, nos. 114–5. For a discussion of Robert Dumbarton, Sandilands and a change in the way royal acts were recorded and dated *c*. 1349, see A.A.M. Duncan, 'The Regnal Year of David II', *SHR*, lxviii (1989), 109–15.

unnoticed by modern historians – was that the Steward had been removed as Lieutenant of the realm, a sudden change of office which mirrored events from 1335. Sometime in 1350, a petition was sent from Scotland to the Papacy requesting absolution from the duty of pilgrimage to Rome for 'William Earl of Ross, Thomas Earl of Mar, William de Douglas, lord of the same, guardians of the realm of Scotland . . . they being unable to come to Rome on account of the destruction of the state and the wars'.[49] Admittedly, this might simply have been a general style or title of importance assumed by these magnates. But at least one manuscript version of John of Fordun's *Gesta* of his anonymous source's annals of David's reign contains the assertion that the Steward *was* removed as Lieutenant *c.* 1350 after four years in office: later pro-Stewart Scottish chroniclers chose to ignore this.[50]

The circumstances necessary for such a change of leadership may have been created by the terrifying disruption of the plague as it reached Scotland finally in late summer and autumn 1349. Southern Scotland and the burghs in particular now shared the same fate as Europe, London and middle England. All the Scottish chroniclers bemoan the horror of the experience:

> this evil led to a strange and unwonted kind of death, insomuch that the flesh of the sick was somehow puffed and swollen, and they dragged out their earthly life for barely two days.

Just as Canterbury had been decimated the year before, Abbot Walter Bower later lamented the deaths of over half of the clergy of the chapter of St Andrews in 1349.[51] In the face of a loss of almost a third of all of Scotland's population as a whole within a matter of months, the hasty withdrawal of many Scottish magnates and administration to colder climes north of the Clyde-Forth line might easily have provided the opportunity for the Steward's removal from office, swinging power north to Ross and Mar. The populace besides would have been more concerned with burying the victims in mass pit graves, finding food and avoiding contact with the doomed and the dead.

If this was so, the installation of a triumvirate of Ross, Douglas and Mar reflects the timely ability of David and his few supporters to play upon these magnates' territorial concerns and to seek the co-operation of an alternative regime prepared to work towards the king's release in return for reward. William, earl of Ross, was clearly the leading noble in northern Scotland. By 1349–50, he may have hoped that by coming out in opposition to Robert Steward and working in the king's interests he might secure David's pardon

49 *CPR*, iii, 200.
50 *Chron. Fordun*, i, 368; *Chron. Bower*, vii, 469 n7 for discussion of this manuscript variation.
51 *Chron. Fordun*, i, 368–9; *Chron. Bower*, vii, 273–5.

for his murder of Ranald MacRuaridh in 1346 and his desertion of the host, as well as royal approval of his justiciarship north-of-Forth and free use of the revenues of Moray and Aberdeenshire after the death of John Randolph. More immediately, Ross may have felt threatened by the Steward's designs on Badenoch and the revenues of the justiciarship. Ross and the Steward had quarrelled in 1339 over the latter; they would be at feud over the former and over various lands until the Steward wed Ross's sister, Euphemia (John Randolph, earl of Moray's widow and countess), in 1355. Ross-Stewart tensions must also have been complicated by Earl William's hopes of securing some of the now-vacant earldom of Strathearn through his wardship of a daughter of Malise, late eighth earl of Strathearn.[52] Finally, Ross must have felt threatened by the Steward's improving relations with John MacDonald of the Isles with whom Earl William had clashed in 1343 over Skye. On 18 July 1350, John MacDonald himself wed one of the Steward's daughters, giving the Isles lord (and secret ally of Edward III) control of the similarly disputed lands of Kintyre and greatly increased access to the Great Glen, Lochaber, Garmoran and Skye, where Ross also had ambitions.[53] Thus by 1350, Ross may have hoped for David's support in all these matters if he aided his liberation from the Tower. That Earl William was in contact with the king is suggested by the two embassies to London of 1348–9 which included William Meldrum, Ross's deputy justiciar, and the earl's action of 30 April 1350 in naming his brother, Hugh Ross of Philorth (also a deputy justiciar), as his heir in Ross and other lands in Buchan 'on condition of obtaining the consent of the king'.[54]

Like the earl of Ross, William, lord of Douglas, was a natural provincial leader, dominating Scottish territory south-of-Forth – holding Edinburgh

52 Crawford, 'The Earls of Orkney-Caithness', 175–83; Boardman, 'Lordship in the North-East, I', 1–3.
53 *CPR*, iii, 381 and Boardman, *Early Stewart Kings*, 7, 28 n31, for the Stewart-MacDonald marriage. To secure this match John of the Isles first had to divorce Amy MacRuaridh, daughter of the Garmoran lord murdered by the earl of Ross in 1346. MacDonald would be confirmed in Garmoran (1372) and Kintyre (1376) by his father-in-law, Robert Steward/Robert II (*Acts of the Lords of the Isles*, xxv-xxxv, 209).
54 W. Fraser ed., *The History of the Carnegies, Earls of Southesk* (2 vols., Edinburgh 1867), ii, 486–7 and NLS ch. 14322 for a justice ayre at Dundee in February 1348 overseen by Samuel Wilton and Andrew Douglas as deputies of Sir Hugh Ross and William Meldrum, in turn deputies of the earl of Ross. See NAS GD 297/163 or RH 1/116 for Hugh Ross as his brother's heir replacing the earl's infirm son, William, who was dead by 1364. Hugh was in Scotland as a charter witness on 17 May 1350 (*Calendar of Writs of Munro of Foulis, 1299–1823*, ed. C.T. Innes (Scottish Record Society, Edinburgh 1940), no. 4), on 4 December 1350 (*Ane Account of the Familie of Innes*, ed. D. Forbes (Aberdeen 1698), 61) and on 30 March 1351 (*Illustrations of the Topography and Antiquities of Aberdeen and Banff*, eds J. Roberston and G. Grut (Spalding Club 5 vols, Aberdeen 1859–62), iii, 205).

Castle and the justiciarship – and by 1349 could make a solid claim to be Scotland's new leading hammer of the English. At the same time, however, Lord William, too, may have felt an increasing need for David's return and future royal sanction to consolidate and increase his territorial interests. But the primary reason *c.* 1349–50 for his assumption of a controlling interest in Scottish government and David's release talks must have been his anxiety to monitor and determine the fate of his family rival, Douglas of Liddesdale. In addition, Lord William may also have been tempted into co-operation by David II and his close supporters not only by promises (or threats) about the Black Douglas lands but also by the offer of marriage to Margaret of Mar, sister of Thomas, earl of Mar, and a second cousin of the king. This was a match which had certainly taken place by November 1357 when it was confirmed by David just after his eventual release.[55]

David would have been able to offer Lord William such inducements through Earl Thomas of Mar himself, the last joint Lieutenant of 1349–50. Thomas was a remarkable figure, a one-off given to independent, almost maverick actions at times, who would display a headstrong sense of his own privilege, content to serve the crown so long as it profited him. He had been removed to England as a child by Edward III in 1334 and presumably brought up at the Plantagenet court. Here David must have met Mar after 1346 and surely found him an energetic and impressive knight, a few years younger than himself, but trained in the spirit of chivalry with which the king liked to imbue his court and followers. David must also have found Mar's ready acceptance of co-existence with England sympathetic to his own need for Anglo-Scottish peace and his release from captivity: Thomas would go on to become a liege man of Edward III in his foreign wars after 1359. Between 1307 and 1327, Thomas's father, Earl Donald of Mar (Robert I's nephew through his first wife and thus David II's cousin), had been a man similarly loyal to an English king, Edward II, before he had served as Guardian for David and fallen at Dupplin (1332). Moreover, the Bruce-Mar marital relationship also gave Thomas a reasonable claim to the Scottish kingship, if one not as strong as the Steward's. In terms of his familial inheritance the Bruce-Mar link was even closer. David's aunt, Christian Bruce, widow of Guardian Andrew Murray (d. 1338) and before him Gartnait, earl of Mar, was keeper of Mar's Kildrummy Castle. David could have stressed to Thomas the need for him to return to Scotland to take up his lands as Christian aged and weakened (dying in 1357 and being buried in Dunfermline Abbey, as the Scottish chroniclers note) and the Mar patrimony became vulnerable to intrusion from other magnates, not least

---

55 Fraser ed., *The Douglas Book*, i, 287; *RRS*, vi, no. 153; Brown, *Black Douglases*, 43–8.

from Christian's sons, John and Thomas Murray, now adherents of the Steward.[56] David may also have tempted Mar into service with promises of royal support for a good marriage: sometime *c.* 1352–4, indeed, Mar would wed Margaret, countess and heiress of Menteith (the daughter of Sir John Graham and his widow, Countess Mary of Menteith) who was the widow of John Murray after his death as a hostage in England in 1351.[57]

Sometime in 1349, then, David must have seen Earl Thomas return to Scotland with the royal blessing and perhaps also with very specific instructions. How Ross, Douglas and Mar linked up to effect the Steward's dismissal is unknown: it perhaps took the form of a decision by a favourably packed council (held, say, at Aberdeen to avoid the plague) which used the excuse of the Steward's inability to assert law and order in the north and to defend the border to remove him; perhaps the advent of David's official majority aged twenty-five in March 1349 provided the occasion. If so, this set a vital precedent for the several further changes of government on the pretext of infirm Stewart rule made in later fourteenth-century royal assemblies (1384, 1388, 1399, 1402).[58] But once the deed was done in 1349–50, it is also unclear just how closely the three new Lieutenants co-operated in everyday government. Logically, they could have divided the kingdom in three: Ross in the north, Mar in the mid-east, Douglas in the south. But the Steward and his allies surely maintained considerable dominance in central and western Scotland, and all of these regional magnates would have continued to use royal powers and resources in their own localities as they thought expedient.

Nonetheless, the Steward (again, according to Fordun's source) may have been panicked enough by his loss of influence to undergo a legitimising marriage ceremony with Elizabeth More sometime in 1349, shortly before her death.[59] For the shadowy revolution in Scottish government which displaced the Steward as Lieutenant clearly aided the progress of David's efforts at release. From May 1350 onwards, as 'meaningful negotiations' were conducted on the border, English royal household clerks began to record increased expense payments for the maintenance in the Tower not of 'David de Brus' – who had started on a merk a day (about 66d) – but of 'David, king of Scots'.[60] Further

---

56 *Scots Peerage*, v, 581–5; *CDS*, iii, no. 1108; *Chron. Fordun*, i, 377; *Chron. Bower*, vii, 305.

57 Fraser ed., *Red Book of Menteith*, i, 116–32; *CPR*, iii, 467, 522.

58 For these post-1371 events, see Boardman, *Early Stewart Kings*, 131–2, 148–53.

59 *Chron. Fordun*, i, 317. *Chron. Bower*, vii, 447 ignores this annal and dates the Steward's second marriage to the 1370s after the death of Robert's second wife (discussed *ibid*, 532–3, n. 41–51).

60 *Rot. Scot.*, i, 741; PRO E403/354 onwards; Duncan, 'Honi soit qui mal y pense', 119. David began to receive regular pouches of £13 6/- 8d. But he also received larger one-off payments to help him pay expenses during talks – £40 in October 1350; £20 at York in late 1350; £133 from John Coupland at York in July 1351.

impetus may have come from another Anglo-French truce agreed at Guines on 13 June 1350, to last until August 1351 and to include the Scots.[61] But from late summer 1350, John II's determination to take the war to England in Gascony in defiance of this ceasefire must have hardened the English resolve for a deal with Scotland. In August 1350 (just as the Pope responded to David's letter and wrote to the French king), Anglo-Scottish talks were held at York: such was the level of expectancy that David himself was given leave to travel to York under guard late in the year. In the same month safe-conducts to London were issued to several of David's chivalric cadre, Sir Lawrence Gilliebrand and the cleric John Cromdale (both Mar men), Andrew and William Meldrum (deputies of Ross as justiciar north-of-Forth), William Livingston and William de Vaus (royal Lothian men but Lord Douglas followers at that time), as well as the Chamberlain, Robert Erskine.[62] By this juncture, if not long before, David had been able to tempt Erskine – and, surely, Chancellor Caldwell – away from their original loyalty to the Steward. Erskine (who was also the Douglas lord's stepfather until the death of his second wife by *c.* 1352)[63] would be able to make the journey back to the Steward's service, perhaps on more than one occasion, and to play both men off against each other to his own advantage; but, as we shall see, from spring 1360 Erskine would most definitely become a king's man, David's most vital domestic and diplomatic fixer.

The unrecorded results of the York negotiations of August 1350 may have been modified with David's input by the end of the year when it becomes clear that some form of 'indenture' had been agreed between Edward III and his council and 'certain men of Scotland'. This phrasing really hints at the reality that David's support in Scotland and the embassy dispatched to York was still too factional in its basis. The indenture thrashed out would obviously have to be presented to the wider Scottish political community for approval, not least because it would require taxation to meet its terms: major opposition to some clauses was clearly anticipated. Moreover, the personnel involved in presenting this plan to the Scottish community throughout 1351–2 not only confirm the sudden political changes in Scotland of *c.* 1349–50, but also the painful limits of David's influence despite this coup.

For the man charged with presenting the indenture to the Scots was,

---

61 Sumption, *Hundred Years War*, ii, 72.
62 *Rot. Scot.*, i, 734, 736, 740–1, 743. For David at York, see PRO E403/355 m. 14, 15 (costs for a new bed and horse for the king), /357 m. 16. For Mar's affinity, see: *Miscellany of the Scottish History Society*, v, 12; *Illustrations of the Topography and Antiquities of Aberdeen and Banff*, v, 155–6, 715–8, 752; NAS GD 124 Mar & Kelly charters.
63 *Scots Peerage*, v, 591–6 – Erskine first wed Beatrice Lindsay, widow of Guardian Archibald Douglas.

somewhat surprisingly, William Douglas of Liddesdale, who was given parole to return to Scotland in December 1350.[64] Little clear detail of events in Scotland over the next two years has survived: the picture remains patchy, at times confusing and apparently contradictory. But the terms of the package which Douglas was empowered to offer have been convincingly identified from a truly remarkable document – preserved in the British Library – first prepared about March 1364 for the purpose of briefing Scottish parliamentarians about the pros and cons of a similar Anglo-Scottish ransom/succession peace deal drawn up by Edward III and David II in London in 1363. This reveals (with frustrating brevity) that at a parliament in Dundee about 15 May 1351 the Scots were asked to consider terms set out by Liddesdale involving the payment of a ransom of £40,000 for their king (roughly £10,000 per year of David's captivity). But the Scots were also to accept a younger son of Edward III as heir presumptive to David's throne, to restore the Disinherited lords to their Scottish lands and to commit Scotland to giving England military aid in her wars.[65]

That David sincerely wanted the Scots to give this deal serious consideration in 1351 is not merely underlined by its tabling in a parliament, a full assembly which only a king could summon. The absent monarch also arranged at this time for the distribution of patronage in an attempt to cement his new-found support and win over Scotsmen on the fence. On 15 May 1351, David's great seal was used to inspect and confirm another grant, recently made, by Duncan, earl of Fife (now back in Scotland), of lands in Fife to David's and Douglas of Liddesdale's regular go-between, Sir James Sandilands and, most significantly, Sandilands' new wife, Eleanor Douglas, countess of Carrick, widow of Alexander Bruce (son of Edward Bruce and cousin of the king) and sister of William, Lord Douglas. This was another act recorded by Robert Dumbarton, David's ambassador clerk of the Rolls.[66] Its witness list reveals the Steward – not styled as king's Lieutenant – seemingly surrounded in the Dundee parliament by royalists old and new, namely the bishop of St Andrews, Thomas, earl of Mar, William, earl of Sutherland, Sir David Lindsay, Sir William Livingston, Erskine and Caldwell, all of whom had had contact with David since 1347.

However, it is clear that both David and his close advisers, and Edward III and his council, expected grave difficulties in bringing this proposed deal to a conclusion. Further negotiations were provisionally scheduled. In March 1351, safe-conducts were issued for 'parlas' to be held at Hexham in Northumberland in late spring to early summer, immediately after the

---

64 *Rot. Scot.*, i, 744.
65 Duncan, 'A Question about the Succession, 1364', 27, 43–5.
66 *RRS*, vi, no. 115.

scheduled Dundee parliament; the Scottish embassy was to include the bishops of St Andrews, Brechin, Aberdeen and Dunblane and the knights Livingston, Erskine, Annan, Haliburton and Douglas of Liddesdale.[67] But many weeks before these contingencies were laid, David and Douglas may also have secretly agreed with Edward what to do in the event of major opposition to the proposed indenture in Scotland.

Fascinatingly cryptic and secretly despatched instructions survive from the English king to Sir Ralph Neville, his northern border commissioner, probably drawn up in early 1351.[68] After thanking Neville for his recent efforts in the York talks, and expressing trust in him, Edward mentions the obstruction of the king's business by 'EB' who will not agree to ways of peace reasonable to one party and the other. Edward expressed anger at this, but added that if 'EB' could be brought to agree, then the king would consider his 'previous war . . . half won'. Then Edward mentioned:

> . . . the new offers of DB and the agreement between him and WD and how the said Sir Hugh will be willing to agree to things and live and die with the suffering in order that he may be able to be certified that the earl of R and the others are willing to agree.

Edward added that if 'EB' would not agree, then a truce should be agreed for 'EB's' lifetime, and the affirmation of others should be sought secretly. Edward then stated that 'all these things depend upon whether DB can carry out what he has promised'. Edward quizzed Neville about the 'manner of speaking' and of making promises he had used to 'EB's' councillors. He asked Neville for 'certification' of the business or the causes impeding it. In closing, he stressed the need for haste because 'opinions differ' and how 'DB has sent for the certification'.

'EB' is obviously Edward Balliol. The former vassal king of Scots – his Scottish dream now confined to Hestan Island in the Solway Firth – had become so fearful of what Edward III might be signing away in his talks with David Bruce that he would on several occasions over the next few years ask for letters of assurance from the English crown that these negotiations would not prejudice the Balliol claim to the Scottish kingship: he had earlier insisted unconvincingly to the English king that 'to ransom prisoners is to do nothing other than to prolong the war'. The first of these empty English royal guarantees to Balliol was issued on 4 March 1351, thus surely roughly

---

67 *Rot. Scot.*, i, 740.
68 Duncan, 'Honi soit qui mal y pense', 121–3 for a translation of these instructions which revises C.J. Johnson, 'Negotiations for the Ransom of David Bruce in 1349', *EHR*, xxxvi (1921), 57–8. My interpretation of these secret orders offers a revision of Duncan's in turn.

dating Neville's secret instructions.[69] That Edward III indicated to Neville that he could wait out a truce for 'EB's' lifetime before closing a deal – in the meantime seeking the agreement of the other interested parties (i.e. the Scots) – only underlined Balliol's frailty and lack of offspring by 1351 at age sixty-seven.

The 'DB' in Edward's orders is therefore clearly David Bruce and his 'new offers' surely included his own idea that a younger son of Edward III – not that king or his eldest heir – should become heir presumptive in Scotland. 'DB' is clearly seeking co-operation from WD – William Douglas, probably the knight rather than the new co-Lieutenant, Lord William – and the 'earl of R and others' whose certification 'Sir Hugh' is to sound out. The 'earl of R' surely refers to William, earl of Ross, the most senior of the new Lieutenants, who could be spoken for by his brother, Hugh, who – as we have seen – may have travelled south in 1350–1 to seek David's approval of his tailzie to the Ross lands. If 'the said Sir Hugh' of Edward's orders was, then, Hugh Ross, he could thus speak to the earl of Ross and 'the others': probably the Lord Douglas, the earl of Mar (if David had not already assured himself of the support of this Anglophile) and additional magnates back in Scotland. Hugh could convince them of the need to be resolved to 'live and die with the suffering' which would result from resistance with force by Robert Steward and his supporters to the imposition of such a treaty. The inference to be drawn, therefore, is that civil war between the parties of the crown and Steward might be provoked.

In the event, all this careful preparation by Edward III and David II may have been justified but only partly successful. According to the later 1363–4 source – which recalled points of debate which must have been voiced in the Dundee parliament of May 1351 – when it came to the issue of an English prince's admission to the succession:

> On this article, some of the council [sic] decided that the requests of the king of England should be accepted, bringing forward for the purpose many arguments to support their case, others of the council asserting the contrary, that it was in no way expedient nor should there be agreement to the requests, also bringing forward reasons for their own part . . .[70]

This discussion seems all very polite and orderly. But in fact this Dundee gathering must have been a heated and highly fractious affair, potentially explosive. David was now trying by proxy to set aside those past parliamentary acts from Robert I's reign (1318 and 1326) which had enshrined

---

69 *Rot. Scot.*, i, 739, 754; PRO C49/6/29.
70 Duncan, 'A Question about the Succession, 1364', 27.

the Steward's place in the succession. David might not be serious about a Plantagenet heir, gambling on fathering a Bruce successor to cancel out any chance of regnal union; and it must have been obvious to most Scots that this was largely a pretext for breaking Stewart influence in Scotland. Yet beyond his personal and territorial worries, Robert Steward must have been able to shout loudest and longest in opposition in parliament to exploit the genuine sense of sacrifice in war against the auld enemy since 1332 – really 1296 – which many Scots must have shared and which he could claim, with some justification, that David's deals with Edward III threatened to forget. It seems possible that, although only four years previously David had been committed to an almost crusade-like assault on northern England, after 1346 the king's search for political and personal expediency – and his new-found admiration for the English king and his sons and nobles like Henry de Grosmont of Derby and Lancaster – had blinded him to the nationalist, anglophobe mood of many of his subjects. David thus lost 'patriotic' support.

Some of the other May 1351 terms must also have provoked a mixed response in parliament. The ransom demand may have seemed light to some, onerous to others. It is likely that David and his supporters were responsible for the issue of a new run of Scottish silver coinage about 1350–1 as a means of aiding the ransom payment: the calling of a parliament at Dundee – where the exchequer often met in the fourteenth century – may also have been designed to coincide with an audit (the records of which are now lost) of what little royal revenue could be collected. However, the deliberately devalued silver content of this new currency issue – which should not now be blamed without question upon Robert Steward's leadership – may have angered many.[71] In addition, many Scottish nobles as well as churchmen and burgesses may have feared for the alliance with France and Scotland's trade with other continental powers – especially Flanders, after the Scottish staple had been returned to Bruges about 1349 (another possible sign of a change in regime) – if Scotland agreed to aid Edward III in his European wars. It is unclear whether or not by this peace package the auld alliance would be allowed to stand simultaneously as it had been in 1328.

However, most significant of all, the proposal to restore the descendants of the Disinherited surely amounted to as grave and far more tangible a threat to some Scottish magnate interests in 1351 as it had been in 1328, shortly after Robert I had redistributed forfeited lands and baulked at the issue of the return of these lords to Scotland in his peace treaty with England.

71 H.J. Dakers, 'The First Issue of David II', *British Numismatic Journal*, xxiii (1938–41), 51–8. The 1351 Scottish issue bears a strong resemblance to that of England in the same year.

The Lord of Douglas and the earls of Mar and Ross, and many of David's closest supporters, would lose just as much land under this clause as would the Steward and others of his generation elevated by the first Bruce king: David's letter to Pope Clement in 1349 had hinted as much in stressing the forfeited lands and goods 'distributed by the king of Scots and his folk among divers persons'. Besides, the wars fought to defend these lands by the Bruce Scots in the 1330s – crucially, in David's absence – must have added to many magnates' faith in themselves as self-made men as well as patriots and leading figures in the kingdom. All of these concerns would form the core of arguments raised in parliaments in response to David's several attempts to broker such a deal with England between 1351 and 1367. In turn, this would increase the theoretical political influence of Scotland's parliament in general.[72]

The May 1351 package was thus rejected by the Dundee parliament, although probably with approval from a majority of members for the modification of some terms to be further pursued at the planned Hexham talks. For the king and his supporters it was back to the negotiating table for some hard bargaining. In this they were nonetheless able to make real progress by autumn 1351. The king may have made considerable personal input to the Hexham talks for he was allowed to remain in northern England – probably at York – until July-August that year. His input to a second round of talks required at Newcastle in August-September was still well represented through the largest Scottish embassy to date, which included the royalist bishops of St Andrews, Brechin, Caithness and Dunblane, the earls of March, Sutherland, Mar and Angus, the Lord Douglas and the knights David Lindsay, William Livingston, Robert Esrkine and William Cunningham of Kilmaurs (whom David would make lord of the earldom of Carrick after 1358).[73]

The revised deal painstakingly argued out by these negotiations has also been identified from material collected for the Anglo-Scottish talks of 1363–4. The evidence suggests that David and his supporters, and the more independently minded Scottish envoys, had really fought to address some of the key concerns voiced at the Dundee parliament. The autumn 1351 indenture thus proposed, first, that the English would restore Scottish territory to the extent it had been at the death of Robert I. A truce of a thousand years would also be observed while no ransom at all for David would be sought. Homage was not mentioned and David would hold Scotland 'without [Edward] demanding anything for it in the future'. There

72 Duncan, 'A Question about the Succession, 1364', *passim*; see below, ch. 9; Penman, 'Parliament Lost – Parliament Regained?'.
73 *Rot. Scot.*, i, 741, 744; PRO E39/358 m. 17, 20.

was still to be a mutual military alliance, but with either country making war paying for the other to help. More specifically, a Scottish force – of roughly 1,000 men – would serve England in its foreign wars, though crucially not in Flanders. The Scots were also to restore Scottish lands of specified value to several of the Disinherited, some of whom were now named. These included David Strathbogie, heir to Atholl, but notably omitted were other claimants like the Wakes so as to allow Sir William Douglas to retain the lordship of Liddesdale.[74]

David's most cherished clause then followed: a *younger* son of Edward III was to become his heir presumptive, succeeding in the event of David's failure to produce a (and here the surviving copy of the indenture contains a lacuna, presumably for the word 'male') child. In addition, however, it was now agreed that in the event of 'debate and dissension between any persons' about the succession in Scotland, the king of England was only to assist his son in this matter, leaving the Scots to settle rival claims – undoubtedly anticipated challenges from the Stewarts – 'by the law, usages and statutes of Scotland': this was not to be another Great Cause as in 1291–2. Finally, specific territorial disputes over Annandale were to be settled privately by David and the earl of Hereford, who had occupied half of this Scottish border lordship since 1347; and the churchmen of both realms were to be restored to the benefices they had held before the Battle of Neville's Cross. Collectively, this package was to be offered to a Scottish parliament and a response was to be brought to talks at Berwick in March 1352.

What the Scottish and English ambassadors and their two kings had largely persisted with throughout 1351, then, was a truce which in many ways revived several of the original clauses of the 1328 peace Treaty of Edinburgh-Northampton, before Robert I back-pedalled on the matter of the Disinherited. Although the late 1351 indenture contained no formal English recognition of Scottish independence, David, as 'King of Scots', would owe Edward nothing other than paid military support. There was to be a partial return to cross-border landholding by nobility and church and the Scottish crown would recover key castles and burghs in southern Scotland, including Lochmaben, Hermitage, Roxburgh and, most impressive of all, the vital wool-port of Berwick. But in addition, David and his supporters had managed to persuade Edward III to compromise in key areas. There would be no ransom paid; Scottish military aid would not endanger Scotland's dependent trade with the Low Countries; and it now

---

74 *APS*, i, 497a (PRO E39/2/2) reproduced in Duncan, 'Honi soit qui mal y pense', 139–41 and discussed at 127–8. As Professor Duncan has shown, the internal evidence of this document makes it clear that it dates to late 1351 and not 1363–4 as the original Thomson/Innes *APS* would have it. The proposal for Scottish military aid to England against Flanders reflects the events of 1348–50.

appears that greater selective sensitivity would be shown to Scotsmen who might lose lands to the Disinherited.

On paper this was a much improved offer compared to that of May 1351. But by the following winter the task of presenting and selling this revised package to the Scottish political community had suddenly become a great deal harder. For probably sometime in the second half of that year, Robert Steward may have been able to recover the sole lieutenancy of Scotland, causing the political realignment of the previous year to break down.

In fact, the recorded evidence of parliamentary debate concerning relations with England in 1364 asserted that the May parliament at Dundee in 1351 had debated matters under the Steward's Guardianship.[75] This may, though, have been an error of memory and the result of disrupted government. But it is likely that – if he had not already done so – the Steward quickly regained influence after the controversial proposals for David's release had been tabled. By the autumn of 1351, certainly, his close ally Thomas Stewart, earl of Angus – who would serve the Steward as a sub-lieutenant of Angus and the Mearns and as Chamberlain before 1357 – had worked his way onto the Scottish negotiating team. The presence also of Mar and the Lord Douglas – but not Ross – at Newcastle in September may point to their displacement from the lieutenancy and a need to contact David in person. The fact that parliament and possibly exchequer audits were held in Dundee in 1351–2 may also point to the influence of Angus and, behind him, the Steward (who had overseen a council at Dundee in 1348).[76]

In fact, by late 1351, the triumvirate's resolve to support David may have been sorely weakened. The Steward may have been able to exploit the Douglas lord's understandable worries about Liddesdale's influence as well as his concerns about the Disinherited. January 1351 had seen the knight, while out on parole, order the assassination of Sir David Barclay in Aberdeen, re-igniting the Lothian feud. Fordun's source certainly noted of the 1350s, the 'great many . . . causes of unfriendliness, and many a grudge stirred up between the two Douglases by their thirst for power'. In this context, the revised Anglo-Scottish indenture of autumn 1351 and its favour to the elder Douglas knight may have alienated Lord William from David's cause.[77] In addition, the Steward may have tendered an olive-branch to William, earl of Ross, whose sister the Steward would eventually wed in 1355. Over the next few months marriage interests may also have been used to distract Thomas, earl of Mar. In September 1352 he would

75 Duncan, 'A Question about the Succession, 1364', 27.
76 *Rot. Scot.*, i, 744 .
77 *Chron. Fordun*, i, 365–6; *Rot. Scot.*, i, 748, 752; Brown, *Black Douglases*, 45, 207.

receive a papal dispensation to wed Margaret, daughter of the late John Graham, earl of Menteith, and widow of John Murray of Bothwell who would die while a hostage for David's parole in late 1351–early 1352.[78] Finally, David's cause must have suffered a blow from the death of the elder statesman Adam Murray, bishop of Brechin, by November 1351.[79]

This was a crisis which David felt required decisive, perhaps desperate, action on his part. Temporary coalition amongst a majority of the Scottish political community had enabled David and his close supporters to continue with negotiations in 1349–51. But once this loose faction began to fragment in the pursuit of individual interests, the king could not rely upon proxy representation in Scotland to seal the deal. Thus, surely after using all his powers of persuasion to convince Edward III that this was the case – making many 'new promises' as Edward III's secret instructions had put it – David arranged to go on parole to Scotland in person and to apply the forces of intimidation and patronage which only a king could wield.

David was thus released temporarily from Newcastle perhaps as early as 14 November 1351: on that day he issued letters patent ordering the Scottish Chancellor to give Arbroath Abbey sasine of the customs of the burgh of Arbroath. In return for his parole, seven Scottish magnate hostages were surrendered as security. This group clearly illustrates the shifting and partisan balance of power in Scotland but really adds to the impression that the Steward was back on top. For although this group was to include the sons and heirs of the Steward and John Murray of Bothwell (though John himself seems to have gone south), the other five were to be: George Dunbar, nephew and heir of Patrick, earl of March (and son of Sir Patrick Dunbar, a Neville's Cross captive and crusader); Hugh Ross, brother of Earl William of Ross; and the sons/heirs of the obvious royalists Malcolm Fleming, earl of Wigtown, Sir David Lindsay, and – perhaps most telling of all – William, earl of Sutherland, i.e. John Sutherland, David's favoured nephew and possible alternative successor.[80]

With the exchange made, David was free to cross over into Scotland, but only in the company of up to two hundred armed English horsemen. But just which Scots and how many in total came to greet and escort their king home temporarily after an absence of five years – and just where in the marches David crossed the border – is uncertain. Secure passage north through

---

78 *Vetera*, 300; *CPR*, iii, 286–7, 303, 522, 595. The fact that this permission to wed would have to be confirmed by the papacy in June 1354 suggests the possibility that the marriage may have been blocked, perhaps by John Murray's brother and heir, Thomas, another 'lieutenant' of the Steward, or had gone ahead without receipt of the first dispensation.

79 Watt, *Scottish Graduates*, 405–7.

80 *Rot. Scot.*, i, 744; *RRS*, vi, no. 117.

Liddesdale, Annandale or the Dunbar earldom would seem a logical choice. But nothing is known of David's activities or how much time (and freedom of movement under his English guard) he was allowed in Scotland before the parliament called for Scone in late February 1352. Again, logically, it might be speculated that David would have hoped ideally to spend the weeks and days before this assembly on the move throughout southern and central Scotland casting around for support for the indenture and his release. But the six royal acts which survive from the duration of the parliament (29 February to 6 March at least) – the only government material extant from this period – present an inconclusive picture of just how much backing and power David was able to muster.[81]

Three of these acts concern the market and fair rights of Scottish burghs, suggesting perhaps that the king was appealing to the tax-paying burgesses in parliament. But the three remaining acts are all confirmations by the king of noble grants – probably made within the previous six months – to Sir Robert Erskine, the Chamberlain. That these were lands granted by Robert Steward (lands in Erskine), Duncan, earl of Fife (Cults in Fife) and Thomas Stewart, earl of Angus (Adamton in Ayrshire) might suggest that David was able to oblige these lords to favour Erskine as the king's man and a leading negotiator with England. But it is perhaps more likely that David was actually forced here, out of his own weakness, to confirm grants which had turned Erskine's loyalty back to the Steward and his associates since the summer of 1351. The witnesses to these acts included several bishops, the Steward, the earls of March, Angus, Sutherland, Wigtown and Lennox, Robert Erskine, Livingston, Sir John Preston and clerk Robert Dumbarton; but the Lord of Douglas and the earls of Mar and Ross, Lieutenants for the king *c.* 1349–50(51?), were conspicuous by their absence.[82]

The outcome of the parliament would seem to confirm this Stewart recovery as the proposed terms for David's release were again rejected

---

81 *Ibid*, nos. 117–22.
82 The witnesses to the original magnate grants to Erskine suggest that the Steward and his allies may have been able to win over or intimidate key Scots. The Steward's charter was witnessed by Malcolm, earl of Wigtown, David Lindsay of Crawford, William Cunningham of Kilmaurs, John Stewart (the Steward's brother?), John Lyle of Duchal, William Caldwell the Chancellor and others; another Steward grant to Erskine for his 'homage and service' was witnessed by the abbot of Paisley, David Lindsay, Caldwell, William Semple and Reginald Crawford (NAS GD 124 Mar & Kelly /406–7). The earl of Fife's charter was witnessed by the bishops of St Andrews and Caithness, the provost of St Andrews, Sir David Barclay, Andrew Valence, Douglas of Liddesdale, Andrew Campbell and Andrew and William Meldrum (*ibid*, /1116, 1117). Angus's charter was witnessed by the bishops of St Andrews and Glasgow, the Steward, William Lord Douglas, John Stewart (the Steward's brother?), Cunningham, John Douglas, John Lindsay, Adam Fullarton, Norman Leslie, William Semple and Reginald Crawford (*ibid*, /1119).

emphatically: this time, then, David was turned down in person by the estates. Indeed, such was the threat perceived in some of the clauses that the Steward may have been able to rouse considerable public anger against the king. The coverage of the 1352 talks by the contemporary English chronicler, Henry Knighton, while tainted by anti-Scottish bias, may have reflected some of the accusations of unpatriotic selfishness levelled at David and the terms he presented in 1352 as well as on subsequent occasions:

> David Brus the king of Scots, who had been a prisoner until then, was sent into Scotland, under guard, sworn to recall the Scots into fealty to the king of England as they used to be, and as the same king David had once been the sworn liege man of the king of England, as the Scots were accustomed to be. However, the Scots answered with one assent and one voice, that whilst they wished to ransom their king, they would never submit themselves to the king of England, so King David returned to the Tower . . . the Scots refused to have their king unless he entirely renounced the influence of the English, and similarly refused to submit themselves to them. And they warned him that they would neither ransom him nor allow him to be ransomed unless he pardoned them for all the acts and injuries they had done, and all the offences that they had committed during the time of his captivity, and he should give them security for that, or otherwise they threatened to choose another king to rule them . . .'[83]

Knighton's assertion that several Scots were sufficently worried about their recent behaviour to seek a pardon from their king is very believable. But the closing threat, that another unnamed king – surely the Steward, not John Sutherland who was a hostage in England – could be raised in David's stead may have been an even greater possibility. Wyntoun's source also warns that when the 1352 plan was rejected, 'word wes of his [David's] losing mare'. As Alexander Grant has pointed out, all these threats contain distinct echoes of the Declaration of Arbroath of 1320 which had warned that even King Robert Bruce might be driven out by the political community if he made 'us or our kingdom subject to the king of England . . . we would make some other man who was able to defend us our king'. Robert I's propaganda had come back to haunt his son.[84]

To justify such a move towards royal deposition the Steward could have made much capital of the threats of the Disinherited and a Plantagenet

---

83 *Chron. Knighton*, 121–2.
84 *Chron. Wyntoun*, vi, 224; G. Donaldson, *Scottish Historical Documents* (Edinburgh 1970), 55–9; Duncan, *The Nation of Scots and the Declaration of Arbroath, 1320*, 36; G.G. Simpson, 'The declaration of Arbroath revitalised', *SHR*, lvi (1977), 11–33, 28–32; Grant, *Independence and Nationhood*, 56–7.

succession, in defiance of the existing parliamentary acts of tailzie of the
kingship. He could also act as custodian of the policy of Franco-Scottish
alliance. Moreover, just as the Steward could exaggerate David's apparent
disloyalty, so the impression that the captive Bruce king was conceding far
too much to Edward III would give sufficient grounds for fifteenth-century
English forgeries of letters of homage for the kingdom of Scotland by David
to the English king dated at Coldingham and Greyfriars, London, in March-
April 1352 (to add to those fabricated for 1333).[85]

Moreover, David's selling-out was a current rumour which John II of
France also played upon. In late September-early October 1351, John wrote
at least four letters to 'the Guardian [n.b. singular], prelates, princes, barons
and nobles of Scotland'.[86] In the first he urged the Scots to continue
supporting France against England at a time when continued warfare
was expected in Gascony despite a year-long truce agreed on 11 September.
In the second letter John warned the Scots of the possibility that David II
would invade Scotland with an English force if necesssary to enforce the
terms of his release: to counter this John offered the support of 500 French
men-at-arms and 500 archers. John's third letter informed the Scots of an
amazing development: he felt he had to promise the Scots that he had refused
to restore the French lands of Edward Balliol who had been considering
making peace with France and Scotland;[87] but at the same time John did ask
the Scots to consider Balliol's approach. Lastly, in his fourth message, John
promised the Scots that his fleet would protect Scottish merchant shipping
which had recently been targeted by the English.

These letters surely had a significant effect in Scotland. The Steward may
have despatched letters or envoys in reply to these missives, sending them
south-about from the castle on Dumbarton rock which he probably now
controlled through John Danielston (with the aging Malcolm Fleming, earl
of Wigtown, marginalised). Further letters, perhaps in reply, would be sent
in August 1352 from John II to the bishop of St Andrews and other key
Scots, guaranteeing the maintenance of the French alliance. Tellingly, the

---

85 E.g. BL Stowe MSS. 1083 or BL Add. MSS. 6,113; *CDS*, iv, nos. 1844–5;
    Nicholson, 'David II, the historians and the chroniclers', 61–3. A fake 14-year
    Anglo-Scottish truce was also drawn up in the fifteenth-century dated to 1352.
86 AN JJ 36/620 and 621; *Oeuvres de Froissart*, xviii, 336–8; *APS*, xii, no. 15; W.
    Robertson ed., *The Parliamentary Records of Scotland* (London 1804), 90, 99–
    100. These letters are discussed in Campbell, 'England, Scotland and the Hundred
    Years War in the Fourteenth Century', 198–201, and Duncan, 'Honi soit qui mal y
    pense', 126–7.
87 Edward Balliol's French lands had been forfeited *c.*1330–8; the final lordship of
    Hélicourt would be transferred to French royal control in 1355 (R. de Belleval, *Jean
    de Bailleul roi d'Écosse et sire de Vimeu* (Paris 1886), 11–2; A. Beam, 'The life and
    career of John Balliol *c.* 1210–68' (unpublished M. Phil. thesis, University of
    Stirling, 2003), 63–6).

500 archers and 500 men-at-arms offered by John in 1351–2 were exactly the expeditionary contingent which Robert Steward would seek from the French against David's will in 1359 and again, after his accession as King Robert II, in 1371.[88] In 1351–2, though, the Steward might also have had contact with Edward Balliol: English royal household clerks did quite bluntly score Balliol off their maintenance accounts about July 1351, although he was restored to his £200 pension soon after.[89]

However, the Steward may have had even greater cause to heed John II's warnings about David's planned use of force. On 1 February 1352 Edward III had issued letters giving any Scots within his peace leave to join William Douglas of Liddesdale in putting down 'a certain party who wish to rise up or rebel against David'.[90] Then, sometime between 1 Febuary and 17 July 1352, the Douglas knight did agree to become Edward's liege man against all men except the Scottish king. Henry Knighton's chronicle would later echo this potential threat of joint Anglo-Scottish action, asserting that the English council had ordered that if the Scottish parliament rejected the package offered, then the earl of Northampton was to lead a force from the north of England into Scotland in the company of David. Actual proof of such a plan may lie in Edward's secret instructions to his border conservators of the truce – which can be dated to about March 1352 – in which he wrote of the terms 'negotiated with [David] before he left London . . . [and that] he had sworn before Edward III to do his best to bring them about'.[91]

But by 28 March 1352 Edward and his council were agreed that if David's negotiations in Scotland failed, then upon his return from parole with Douglas of Liddesdale the pair were to be questioned to see if 'progress could be made in another way'. If there was such a way, David could remain at Berwick or Newcastle until 27 May 'to see what progress he could make in the meantime': in general the English envoys were to 'treat and hear what the Scots have to say, without departing from the previous negotiations'.[92] This was surely a cautious admission from the English government that the uncertain extent of David's support and the likelihood of success in a civil war against the Steward would have to be given an up-to-the-minute assessment. In the meantime, it was highly unlikely that David and Douglas – together with the king's small English guard of two hundred men – could muster a sufficient force. This was realistic planning. For long before the Scone parliament sent its strong negative reply to Berwick in late March

88 M. Penman and R. Tanner, 'An Unpublished act of David II, 1359', *SHR* (October 2003); for 1359, see below, ch. 8.
89 PRO E403 /356 m. 9, /357, m. 23, /358, m. 23, /360, m. 14.
90 *Rot. Scot.*, i, 748.
91 *Chron. Knighton*, 123–4; PRO E39/17/10d.
92 *Foedera*, iii, 78; orders identified by Duncan, 'Honi soit qui mal y pense', 133–4.

1352 and a forlorn David recrossed the border into England, it must have
been apparent that there was even more opposition in Scotland to the king's
person and his succession plan than expected.[93]

Edward III – preparing to campaign in France in the summer – was not
prepared to spend any more time and resources on this diplomatic gamble,
never mind intervene in yet another Scottish civil war, this time for the
Bruce.[94] David too must have been disgusted and humiliated by his situation. His defeat in parliament aside, as his father's son, and in his own
character, he may also have had no taste for shadowy political dealing or
war against his own subjects with English backing. David may have liked
King Edward but not necessarily have trusted him not to follow the tradition
of the past three hundred years and later try to exploit the Scottish crown's
problems further.

Indeed, David's last recorded act before leaving Scotland in 1352 might be
interpreted as a petulant stab at a peace-process which he now realised was
too complicated and out-of-synch with most of his subjects' political
concerns and national character to work, at least in the present circumstances. On 30 March 1352, at the Renfrewshire burgh of Rutherglen,
David used his letters patent to order a grant to Sir Alexander Stewart of
Darnley of modest Lanarkshire lands forfeited by the late Balliol supporter,
Herbert Maxwell. The king did so for the surprisingly large return of the
annual service in war of four archers and four men-at-arms.[95] Darnley – a
former Alexander Ramsay man whom the Scottish chroniclers credit *c.*
1346–57 as fighting alongside Sir John Kennedy of Dunure to recover much
of Dumfriesshire and Galloway from Anglo-Balliol control – had served
David as a justiciar in Annandale before 1346. By his 1352 grant David may
thus have been trying to raise from his traditional family retinue the military
support he had promised Edward III he could find in the event of the Scottish
parliament's refusal of the indenture. But in hindsight, this grant reads
almost as if David were letting Darnley off his leash to join in a resumed
border war against England which the king now knew he was powerless to
stop until greater outside forces came into play. At best, he might hope
Scottish aggression would force Edward III to soften his terms of release.[96]

According to Abbot Bower, then, 'on failing to achieve what he wanted,
[David] hurried to England without delay, once the hostages had been sent
back'. By 16 May 1352, he was back in the Tower of London and
apparently ill.[97]

93 *Rot. Scot.*, i, 749.
94 Sumption, *Hundred Years War*, ii, 90–110.
95 *RRS*, vi, no. 123Ad.
96 *Chron. Bower*, vii, 151; for Darnley before 1346, see above, ch. 3.
97 *Chron. Bower*, vii, 297.

SIX

Ransom, 1353–7

'I wholly, simply, and absolutely yield unto thee my cause, and all right I have, or may have, to the throne of Scotland, so that thou avenge me of mine enemies, the Scottish nation, a race most false, who have always cast me aside, that I should not reign over them.'

John Balliol, in John of Fordun's *Chronica Gentis Scotorum, c.* 1380[1]

Sojourn at Odiham, 1353–6

In early 1352 David's attempts to secure his release from English captivity had taken a crushing blow. Throughout the rest of that year and into the next his contact with his supporters and Scotland would be infrequent and unofficial, reduced once again to the exchange of letters now lost and private embassies by relatively minor members of the king's chivalric cadre who had secured their freedom before 1351 by swearing never to wage war against England: men like the knights Thomas Bisset, David Annan, Walter Haliburton and Andrew Campbell. David's exertions in 1351–2 may have taken some toll on his health: on at least two occasions over the next twelve months the king required the attention of his Scottish doctor, the aptly styled Hector Leche (or Makepeth, a captive of 1346). Queen Joan must also have visited him between July and Christmas 1353, although this time her safe-conduct was valid for only five months.[2] It was only now that the queen withdrew from Stewart-dominated Scotland to reside in England, taking up residence at Hertford Castle (then held by the Wakes but passed to John of Gaunt by 1362) to the north-west of London, perhaps with a view to revitalising talks for her husband's release.[3] But in the meantime, Scotland reverted to a state of war against England and not a little internal strife between magnates. According to Abbot Bower, after David's departure:

1 *Chron. Fordun*, i, 373–4.
2 *Rot. Scot.*, i, 678 and 751 (Leche), 753 (Annan, Campbell and Haliburton paroled to Scotland), 754–5 (Leche), 757 (Bisset to London), 759 (Annan, Campbell and Haliburton to London), 760 (Joan), 763 (Bisset to London January 1354); Bannerman, *The Beatons*, 59–62.
3 Green, *Lives of the Princesses of England*, iii, 144–6, 158 (describing jewels and furs gifted to Joan by Edward III); *CDS*, v, no. 828; *CPR, 1358–61,* 578; M. Prestwich, 'Katherine Mortimer's Death at Soutra', in *SHARP, Fourth Report on Researches into the Medieval Hospital at Soutra, Lothian Region, Scotland* (1990), 110–18, 115.

> John Steward, the guardian's son . . . collected an army together and made
> a stay in Annandale for as long as needed until he brought all the people
> of that region to the allegiance and firm peace of our lord the king . . .[4]

Yet from his gilded cage in the Tower of London, David may have viewed this Stewart activity in the Bruce lands – and in central Scotland, boosted by the death of Earl Duncan of Fife sometime in 1353 – as a repeat of Robert Steward's expansion of his own lordship before 1341. The king can only have resented Scottish aggression and Stewart influence as the main obstacle to the resumption and progress of talks for his release.

Following the Scone parliament of 1352 the Steward had a prolonged period uninterrupted by diplomacy in which to consolidate his position as Lieutenant and to further his territorial influence. It was July 1353, well over a year after the king's stinging rejection on parole in Scotland, before talks had got so far once again as to necessitate a grant of passage for David to Newcastle. No details of the abortive talks there have survived. But if the English chronicler, Henry Knighton, is to be believed, it may in fact have been on this occasion that an assembly of Scots, presumably packed by the Steward as Lieutenant, once again refused the succession-release plan – which David must thus have persisted with after spring 1352 – and threatened to dethrone him and leave him to rot. Whether or not David ever got to Newcastle, or to more fruitless talks scheduled at Berwick in November 1353, is unknown.[5]

However, by mid- to late 1353 the king may have been able to help engineer a small revival of support in Scotland for his release campaign. By March 1353 at the latest, Patrick Leuchars, the new bishop of Brechin after the death of his patron, the royalist Adam Murray, had become Chancellor. Together with Robert Dumbarton, clerk of the Rolls, this officer allowed David to resume some control over his seals and patronage.[6] Throughout 1353–4 the king was thus able to authorise a number of grants to knights who had been royal companions at Neville's Cross, crown officers and/or visitors to London since 1347. This included lands to: William Meldrum, deputy justiciar north-of-Forth; John Stewart of Dalswinton, warden of the West March before 1346; William Maitland of Thirlestane; and Walter Haliburton, an envoy to the Pope of 1449.[7] Then in late July 1353 an Anglo-

---

4 *Chron. Bower*, vii, 297–9.
5 *Rot. Scot.*, i, 750; *Chron. Knighton*, 189.
6 Watt, *Scottish Graduates*, 182–3.
7 For all David's grants in 1353–4, see *RRS*, vi, nos. 123–30, 134–6; Duncan, 'The Regnal Year of David II', 117. For a John Stewart in England *c.* 1350–1, see PRO E403/356 m. 10 (with William Douglas of Liddesdale), /357 m. 21. The odd diplomatic form of David's confirmations to Stewart of Dalswinton and Maitland (Edinburgh, 9 December 1353), noted by Bruce Webster, editor of *RRS*, vi, may point to the disturbed, contested nature of administration at this time.

French truce was agreed which would last until December (and before then be extended until April 1354) which included the Scots as allies of France.[8] By the time word of this ceasefire reached Scotland, David may have had a hand in plucking out a growing thorn in the flesh of his plans, William Douglas of Liddesdale.

For about August 1353 this knight's violent past caught up with him when William, Lord Douglas, and his men slew Liddesdale in a well-laid ambush in Ettrick forest. The lord of Douglas seems to have visited Edward III sometime after 16 January 1353 and might easily have used the occasion to speak to David, thus adding to a personal relationship which must have begun between the two as youths at Château Gaillard and been revived during the negotiations of 1349–52, during some of which Lord Douglas was a Lieutenant for the crown. David's favour to Lord William soon after Liddesdale's demise certainly suggests that he may have sanctioned this final assassination in the Lothian feud. Lord William must already have assumed the natural lordship of many of the south-eastern knights and esquires who had followed Alexander Ramsay before 1342 and then David from 1342–6.[9] Even if not directly involved, the king must have quickly recognised that he could turn Liddesdale's bloody demise to his own advantage. Thus on 12 February 1354, in a charter issued through envoy/clerk of the Rolls, Robert Dumbarton, at Edinburgh – where the lord of Douglas held the castle – David confirmed Lord William in possession of all of his father's lands, including Liddesdale, as well as his sheriffship of Peeblesshire and leadership of his men from Roxburghshire to the Clyde valley.[10]

In theory this was a grant which could be used to undermine the Steward's exchange of Liddesdale for the earldom of Atholl – in defiance of David – with the elder Douglas knight in 1342. It also enhanced the Lord Douglas's potential control over much of the conflict with England in the Marches: if he could induce truce, talks might resume. That David hoped Lord William would be a valuable ally against the Steward is underlined by another grant of 28 February 1354 in which the king had his clerk reissue a confirmation he had first made in May 1351 of Earl Duncan of Fife's inspection of the Lord Douglas's grant of West Calder in Lothian to Sir James Sandilands: the latter Fife, Lothian and Lanarkshire knight had now clearly transferred his allegiance from William the knight to the Black Douglas lord. But as bailie of the late earl of Fife's lands, the Steward may have challenged this royal grant, for it had to be repeated for a third time on 1 April 1354 at a Scottish

---

8 *Foedera*, iii, 291–4.
9 *Chron. Fordun*, i, 365–6, 369–70; *Rot. Scot.*, i, 752, 756; Brown, *Black Douglases*, 45–8, 167–70.
10 *RRS*, vi, no. 126.

council held at the royal manor of Inverkeithing on the southern coast of Fife.[11]

By that juncture, the general truce, and the Lord Douglas's relief at his neutralisation of the knight of Liddesdale's dealings with Edward III, had clearly allowed a royalist peace-seeking lobby within Scotland to regain some of the initiative. The Inverkeithing council seems to have been dominated by crown men, as was the embassy this body must have decided to send to talks at Newcastle in June-July 1354. Admittedly, by April that year at the latest the Steward had replaced the swithering Robert Erskine as Chamberlain with his kinsman, Thomas Stewart, earl of Angus. But many other Scots seem to have been persuaded by the European situation of military stalemate and the likely rewards and forgiveness a royal return by David would bring. On 6 April 1354, indeed, a full year's Anglo-French truce was declared at Guines, embracing the Anglo-Scottish border: by 18 June men like Patrick, earl of March – whom David felt deserved to be described as 'our cousin' in his charters at this time – and Robert Erskine were taking part in fresh release talks.[12]

Yet the one overriding factor that may have persuaded many Scots that David's return should be secured must have been that the deal now under discussion – probably since mid-1353 – was one of a remarkably *apolitical* nature. Edward III and David II had now both apparently dropped the idea of a Scottish succession re-tailzie and associated trade-off clauses for the Scots king's release. This had proved altogether too controversial to sell to a majority of Scots in 1351–2 and now the English king and council were prepared to seek out a straightforward ransom deal which would at least pacify the border with Scotland and give them a reasonable regular income to help with the war against France, a conflict to which Edward was really committed despite the earnest peace talks at Guines overseen by papal Cardinals. Thus the provisional indenture concluded by the English and Scottish commissioners at Newcastle on 13 July 1354 stated that the Scots would pay 90,000 merks over nine years for their king's release (thus now 10,000 merks per year of David's captivity), during which a truce would prevail which would include Edward Balliol and other English allies.[13]

Gone was any mention of restoring the Disinherited (the clause the Lord Douglas and many others must have loathed in 1351–2), military alliance

---

11 *Ibid*, nos. 115, 127, 131. David also seems to have given Sandilands the Lanark-shire lordship of Strathaven *c*. 1353–4, lands he had previously granted to Sir Maurice Murray.

12 *Rot. Scot.*, i, 765; *ER*, i, 620; *Foedera*, iii, 277; Campbell, 'England, Scotland and the Hundred Years War in the Fourteenth-Century', 199–200.

13 *CDS*, iii, no. 1576; *Foedera*, iii, 281–5. This indenture was ratified by Edward III's son and heir, Edward, Prince of Wales.

with England or a change in the Scottish succession. But there was a price to pay. As well as the ransom burden, twenty Scottish noble hostages were to be exchanged for David on 25 August 1354. The list of men named in this capacity makes it painfully clear that the 1354 indenture had been agreed to by a royalist party in Scotland and was designed to favour the crown. The initial list was dominated by the sons and heirs of David loyalists like the earls of Sutherland and Wigtown and lesser knights, but it did not include the heirs of the Steward or William, earl of Ross (who were about to become in-laws). However, the indenture's small print stipulated that although after each ransom payment a hostage would be released (starting with the earl of March's heir), if the Scots defaulted then the heirs of the Steward and March – co-deserters at Neville's Cross – were to be surrendered before David or anyone else. Moreover, the first instalment was to be guaranteed for payment in February 1355 by merchants from the main Scottish royal burghs; but if this sum was not paid, then David would either have to re-enter himself as a prisoner or, if he preferred, hand over two earls and two barons from a list made up of the Steward, the Lord Douglas, Thomas Murray the pantler (a lieutenant in the Mearns for the Steward and whose brother, John, had died while a hostage for the king's parole in 1351) and John MacDonald of the Isles (the Steward's son-in-law by 1350).[14]

It is impossible to imagine that the Steward, Ross or MacDonald would have co-operated willingly with these default terms. In addition, although the burghs may have welcomed the opportunity for peacetime regeneration of trade, many Scots nobles and churchmen may have thought the ransom burden too steep: 10,000 merks amounted to more than the crown's income each year. Heavy taxation would obviously be required at a time of disrupted wartime trade, grave devastation of the land and English occupation of southern Scotland, as well as worsening Scottish coinage devaluation; indeed, in March 1355 Edward III would go so far as to order his subjects to reduce the value they attached to Scottish specie.[15]

It may have been over these issues that the talks stalled. Prior Wyntoun's source certainly hints at a bitter turn to the protracted negotiations, asserting that:

14　The full list of hostages included the sons and/or heirs of: the earls of Sutherland, March and Wigtown, William Cunningham, William More of Abercorn, David Graham, William Livingston, Robert Erskine, Thomas Somerville, John Danielston, Thomas Bisset, Andrew de Valence, Andrew Fullarton, John Stewart of Dalswinton, Roger Fitzpatrick, John Barclay, John Kennedy of Dunure, John Gray of Broxmonth, David Weymss, William Hay of Lochorward.

15　*CDS*, iii, no. 1582; R. Nicholson, 'Scottish Monetary Problems in the 14th and 15th Centuries', *British Archaeological Reports*, 45 (1977), 102–11, 103; Grant, *Independence and Nationhood*, 240 (Table III: Currency Changes).

the lordis of Scotland come there,
And prelatis all that wisest ware.
Foure dais or five thare tretit thai;
Bot thai concord couth be na way,
For the Inglis all angry ware,
And spak ay outwart mare and mare,
Till at the last the Scottis party,
That dred the mekle fellony,
All prevely went hame thar way,
And at that tyme na mare did thai.
The king to Lundone agane wes had,
And thare a langtyme eftir baid.[16]

David's release – under the humiliating supervision of Sir John de Coupland, the English sheriff and castle-keeper of Roxburgh since November 1346 – was delayed until 5 October 1354 and then never happened. By 17 October at least – the eighth anniversary of Neville's Cross – the Steward could be found issuing acts at Edinburgh on his own authority as Lieutenant when he ordered Thomas, earl of Angus, his 'lieutenant in Angus and the Mearns', to protect the rights of the Abbey of Arbroath from noble marauding.[17] Yet in the end, the 1354 indenture collapsed not primarily because of Scottish divisions but because, as ever, the conflict between the English and the French, never really quelled by the truces, swept all before it.

By August 1354 John II of France had abandoned the ceasefire agreed in the spring, a truce which had besides excluded the Scots. Edward followed suit by the autumn and began to prepare for new campaigns in Gascony and Brittany.[18] The Steward would thus again have been able to champion the Franco-Scottish alliance, armed with letters and now offers of cash and military aid from the French king for war against England. Once again men like the lord of Douglas must have found the offer of such gainful employment battering the auld enemy inherently more attractive than the prospect of a dull peace, debt and perhaps a stint as a hostage in an English castle or at best the return of an energetic Bruce king with an uncertain agenda. Douglas certainly set about reclaiming vigorously much of the Marches and Gallo-

16 *Chron. Wyntoun*, vi, 230.
17 *Rot. Scot*, i, 761, 781; *RRS*, vi, no. 133. The Abbey of Arbroath may, though, have responded to David's offers of protection – the Abbot of Arbroath was included among the Scottish envoys to talks scheduled for November 1354 along with the bishops of St Andrews, Aberdeen, Caithness and Brechin, the earl of March, the abbot of Dunfermline, Walter Moffat archdeacon of Lothian, William Livingston and Robert Erskine. According to Bower, the new abbot of Dunfermline, a John de Stramiglaw, had been appointed by the papacy over the head of a man approved by the Dunfermline chapter, the bishop of St Andrews and David II (*Chron. Bower*, vii, 277–9).
18 Sumption, *Hundred Years War*, ii, 137–41, 151–3.

way to Scottish allegiance in 1354–5, expelling the English and forcing the inhabitants to renew their allegiance to David II – in fact bringing some Scottish knights before the Steward as Lieutenant to submit – while at the same time extending his own Douglas military lordship. John II may also have been able to dangle the extra inducement to Douglas and other Scots nobles of a place in his fledgling royal knights' Order of Our Lady, or the Star, created to rival Edward III's Garter and badly short of skilled members after a French rout at Mauron in August 1352.[19]

Having come so close to freedom on a second occasion, David now found his contact with his supporters and realm cut off completely. Once again he had to return heavy-hearted from Newcastle to the Tower. No safe-conducts were issued to his 'people' throughout the rest of 1354 and 1355; no royal acts in David's name survive from the latter year. It must have become frustratingly clear upon his return from the border in late 1354 that Edward III now considered David's status a side-issue to the French war and conflict with the Scots a risk worth taking. By 7 March 1355, the English king had even removed David from proximity to the English court. On that day 'David de Bruys' arrived at Odiham Castle in Hampshire some twenty-five miles south-west of London along the Winchester road, on the opposite side of England's capital to Queen Joan. Here, under the watchful eye of Sir William Trussell and his sergeant, Thomas de Fery, and with a daily allowance of 13/ 4d, David occupied reasonably well-furnished rooms – complete with new bed, table and seasonal wardrobe outfits – and was allowed to hawk and hunt and to worship in his private chapel under guard. However, these conditions were in no way as lavish and respectful as those which would be extended by Edward III to John II of France after his capture in September 1356. John – who unlike David was recognised as a king – would be able to turn the original central White Tower of the Tower of London into a veritable private palace complete with French entourage. By contrast, the English king had ordered Trussell that David was:

> to remain at Odiham Castle, and we wish the said Thomas to stay with him at all time, and that he should have an English esquire and chamberlain of your appointing to attend him. No Scot or other person is to approach him at present without our consent.[20]

19 *Chron. Wyntoun*, vi, 222; *RRS*, vi, no. 137 (submission of Tweedie of Drumelzier); *Scots Peerage*, iv, 98–9; Brown, *Black Douglases*, 47–8; Boulton, *Knights of the Crown*, 177–80. Knights of the Order of the Star – defunct by 1357 – were to attend annual meetings near St Denis and to have their arms and adventures recorded.
20 BL Add MSS 24,511–12; E.W.M. Balfour-Melville, 'Papers relating to the Captivity of David II', *Scottish History Society Miscellany IX* (Edinburgh 1966), 9–35; P. MacGregor, *Odiham Castle, 1200–1500: Castle and Community* (London 1983), 104–6; S. Thurley, 'Royal Lodgings at The Tower of London, 1216–1327', *Architectural History*, 38 (1995), 36–57; R. Cazelles, *Catalogue des Comptes Royaux de Phillippe VI et de Jean II, 1318–1364* (Paris 1984), 50–1.

The English council's desire to hide preparations for their campaign in Scotland sometime in the near future may have dictated such quarantine. Edward must have been angered by the Scots' bellicosity on the border and their contact with the French: in February 1355 he had placed northern England on a war footing. But Edward must also have been frustrated with David's failure to deliver on promises made during the last seven years of protracted negotiations.[21]

English distrust of the Scots was well founded. For although neither Edward nor David can have known it, on 5 March 1355 John II had commissioned Sire Eugène de Garnacières – who had first visited Scotland in 1335–6 – to lead an expedition of some fifty to sixty young Frenchmen of chivalry and their retinues (a couple of hundred men in all at most) on an expedition to Scotland. This token force, guided by two unnamed Scots, would reach Scotland in late April. But Garancières would not be able to fulfill his task to, as one French chronicler put it, 'mettre les Escoz en mouvement de faire guerre aux Anglais' (cause the Scots to make war on England) until late summer.[22] The fragmented Scottish government was undeniably slow and disorganised, hamstrung by individual magnate concerns. But by then the Steward had further stabilised his own interests. By 6 May he had concluded a marriage alliance with William, earl of Ross, whereby the Steward himself wed Ross's sister, Euphemia, the widow of John Randolph, earl of Moray, bringing an end to the two families' feud over Badenoch, Strathearn and other lands.[23] Thus with the tacit support of Ross and the war-loving lord of Douglas the Steward was able to distribute some 40,000 gold écus (about 15,000 merks/£10,000) in bribes sent to Scotland by John II about September 1355 through Scottish merchants in place at the Scottish staple at Bruges in Flanders.[24]

The fractious Scots agreed to take this cash and even to break a nine-month truce with England agreed in September 1355. But according to Fordun's source, they did so only 'after sundry interviews and councils held in sundry places', and in their lust for wealth the French funds were shared out among the chief magnates while 'others, of meaner sort, they sent away

21 *Rot. Scot.*, i, 777–81; Sumption, *Hundred Years War*, ii, 162.
22 BN Fr. n.a. 7413 f. 559–560v, 561v; *Chronique Normandie du XIV Siècle*, ed. A. & E. Molinier (Paris 1882), 108; Campbell, 'England, Scotland and the Hundred Years War in the Fourteenth-Century', 200; Roncière, *Histoire de la Marine Française*, i, 505–6.
23 *CPR*, iii, 287, 574; *Vetera*, 307 no. 620.
24 BN MSS. Clairambault 43 no. 143, 60 no. 6 and 109 no. 141. The French also supplied the Scottish factors – John Mercer, the famous super-burgess from Perth, and Roger Hogg of Edinburgh – with sheep and wool (E. Ewan, *Townlife in Fourteenth Century Scotland* (Edinburgh 1990), 121–4).

empty'.[25] Such a denial of lordship to lesser Scottish men of chivalry was something David could well exploit. But the uneven distribution of this mercenary pay must also have contributed to the dismal venture which was the joint Franco-Scottish expedition of 1355, a damp squib which anticipated the similarly unhappy experience of the farcical expedition to Scotland of John de Vienne and 1,500 French troops in 1385 (when money was also offered to Scottish nobles headed by the Stewarts, Douglases and Dunbars), later described by Froissart. Garancières and the Scots, unable to agree on tactics, appear to have secured no objectives of note in 1355. The French had started to drift home by November, while their leader was detained in Aberdeen until December to hand over captured English armaments and to pay some 1,000 écus in debt, an experience which had also befallen him in 1336. Thus it had really been the Scots alone – under Patrick Dunbar, earl of March and Thomas Stewart, earl of Angus – who overran the English town garrison of Berwick on 6 November 1355 after sneaking ladders up to the walls for the third time in forty years.[26]

It was only at this point that the king's Lieutenant, Robert Steward, ventured out briefly from central Scotland to associate his authority with the siege of Berwick Castle and apparently to urge the French home: the Scots may then even have attempted Norham Castle. This was the only time the Steward would ever come near to crossing the border in anger after 1346 (even as king after 1371). But he would have been undoubtedly able to make much political gain out of the brutality of the English response. Edward III, who had ordered extra defences for the north between June and October 1355 before leaving for France, returned from Calais in early December and summoned a muster of Welsh and northern English archers and infantry at Newcastle. By 13 January 1356 this force reached Berwick where the Scottish town garrison besieging the castle quickly surrendered in return for their freedom: according to Fordun's source the Scots company there had been 'hopeless of getting succour from their own nation, owing to the feuds among the chiefs'; these tensions were also noted by Sir Thomas Gray, one of the English knights captured by the Scots in 1355 and who hinted at the 'envy among them [the Scots] who might be hyest; for every one rulid yn his owne cuntery . . .'.[27]

25 *Rot. Scot.*, i, 782–4; *Chron. Fordun*, i, 370–1; Sumption, *Hundred Years War*, ii, 163–4.
26 PRO E101/482/16; *Chron. Fordun*, i, 371–2; *Chron. Wyntoun*, vi, 198–206; *Chron. Bower*, vii, 279–89. For 1385, see: T. de Loray, *Jean de Vienne, Admiral de France, 1341–1396* (Paris 1877), *passim*; Roncière, *Histoire de la Marine Française*, i, 505–7 and ii, 77–84; Brown, *Early Travellers in Scotland*, 7–15.
27 *Rot. Scot.*, i, 777–1; *Chron. Fordun*, i, 371–2; *Chron. Scalacronica*, 119; BN Add Ch. 4162 for Garancières; Sumption, *Hundred Years War*, ii, 187–90 for English preparations. Later French chronicles like *Les Récits d'un Bourgeois de Valenciennes*, ed. K. Lettenhove (Louvain 1877), 275–6, would attempt to glorify Garancières' campaign as a force of 15,000 which fought the Black Prince.

But while the Scots looked to their own local rivalries, Edward III pressed on. At Coupland's castle at Roxburgh on 20 January, moreover, the English king's obvious desire for some measure of revenge as well as northern security received a remarkable personal boost. The aged Edward Balliol, by now a bitter, disappointed, bankrupt and childless hanger-on of seventy-three, poured out his scorn for the English crown's abandonment of his cause since 1346 and resigned his claim to the Scottish throne to Edward III, symbolically trading in a handful of his native soil and his father's crown in return for a £2,000 annuity: his words – not David's – headline this chapter, as reported by Fordun's anonymous source which added the Bruce party line that '[Balliol] himself gave [Edward III] nothing because from the beginning he had no right to anything'.[28]

Sensing Edward III's mood and with word of Balliol's resignation, the lord of Douglas was prepared to take an independent ten-day truce from the English king and agreed to see if the Scottish nobility would accept Plantagenet sovereignty: there was no talk of David II's return. But the inevitable Scottish rejection of this overture from Edward must have come before the ten days were up.[29] For by 26 January 1356 the English king and his army set about wasting the earldom of Dunbar/March and then, about 2 February, burned Haddington and Edinburgh. Only a lack of supplies prevented an extended *herschip* further north but the English devastated the Douglas lands as they withdrew. The Douglas lord – sheltering according to Froissart in Jedburgh forest with the earls of Sutherland and Mar, Robert Esrkine and Archibald 'the Grim' Douglas, a bastard of the 'Good' Sir James and another refugee from Gaillard – could only nip at Edward's heels as he headed for Carlisle.[30]

Back at Odiham, David, denied visits from his subjects since spring 1355, would only have heard of this destruction of the so-called 'Black Candlemas' of Lothian of 1356 – and of events in the north in general – as second- or even third-hand news from Scotland. This singular act of destruction by Edward III may have encouraged some Scots to seek renewed talks for peace and David's release. In May 1356 safe-conducts to England would again be issued to an embassy of mostly crown supporters, the bishops of St Andrews and Brechin, William Livingston, Robert Erskine, Norman Leslie and clerics Robert Dumbarton and Adam de Lanark (who would later become David's Dominican confessor).[31] But ebbing loyalty to the Bruce king may have been even further eroded by Edward III's assault. It was yet another atrocity

---

28 *Chron. Fordun*, i, 373–4; *Chron. Scalacronica*, 119; *CDS*, iii, nos. 1622 and 1626.
29 *Avesbury Edwardi*, 454–6.
30 *Chron. Fordun*, i, 374–5; *Oeuvres de Froissart*, v, 333–5; Brown, *Black Douglases*, 46–8.
31 *Rot. Scot.*, i, 792; Watt, *Scottish Graduates*, 325–6.

committed against Scotland and endured by its subjects during their king's absence, inflicted by an English monarch whose family only four years previously David had seriously considered admitting to his succession: any bluster by the Steward since 1350–2 about England's and David's collusion to destroy the Scottish realm might now easily have seemed justified. Inevitably, the longer David was away, the more his personal and regal authority waned in his kingdom. Thus for most of the tenth year of his captivity there were no serious Anglo-Scottish summits to negotiate his release.

The provocation of the 'Burnt Candlemas' may also have further loosened some of the personal bonds between David and his cadre of Lothian knights. In the spring of 1356, William, Lord Douglas led a number of these veterans in a concerted campaign in the south-west which saw the Scots retake Caerlaverock and Dalswinton Castles and besiege Lochmaben. But on 18 April, Douglas agreed a private truce with the earl of Northampton and on 3 June he and Sir William Ramsay of Colluthie were granted passage to visit David, apparently to discuss his release.[32] It seems unlikely, however, that either man actually entered England. If they did reach Odiham, it is even less likely that David would have been thrilled to hear their future plans. For by sometime in August 1356 Lord Douglas, Ramsay and an elite company of perhaps as many as 300 Lothian and borders knights and men-at-arms had crossed to France ostensibly on pilgrimage to the shrine of St John at Amiens; but in the end they joined John II at Chartres as he prepared to do battle with the Gascon army of Edward III's eldest son and new general, Edward the Black Prince, before it could link up with those of his father and Henry, now Duke of Lancaster.[33] However, after perhaps a few weeks of anxious waiting, David must have viewed the outcome of this confrontation as almost ideal.

The Road to Berwick, 1356–7

The disaster which followed for the French at the Battle of Poitiers on 19 September 1356 was as unexpected and as complete as Neville's Cross had been for the Scots. According to some chroniclers, it was Douglas – gifted lands and some £500 by a French king desperate for men – who advised fighting the English mostly on foot in the style of Bannockburn. But when an initial French charge – including Douglas and his men and a past visitor to Scotland, Constable Arnoul d'Audrehen – failed and the leading French division was engulfed by English bow-play and men-at-arms, two-thirds of the Valois army withdrew. John II was left to be captured after a brave

32 *Rot. Scot.*, i, 793; *Foedera*, iii, 325–7.
33 *Oeuvres de Froissart*, v, 375.

stand; many of his leading nobles and princes of the blood perished as did, really, John's Order of the Star.[34]

Word of the victory reached England by 2 October.[35] Amidst the jubilation it must have been instantly apparent to David that the international situation – and with it his own – had been revolutionised. France would sue for peace or at best fight only a defensive war; Scotland would be without an active ally. A similar course of events had unfolded after the French defeat at Courtrai in 1302, enabling Edward I to overrun Scotland for a second time. But now in 1356 England also held the French king captive. Edward III would only be prepared to release John as part of a general peace which guaranteed his territorial demands in France and yielded a high ransom. Yet David II's value was now completely secondary to the English king and council and they might be tempted to recoup some of their war costs by ransoming the Scottish king and agreeing to a truce. A sizeable proportion of the Scottish political community might also now be induced to abandon war and allow David's close supporters to re-open negotiations not only because their French ally and patron had been defeated but because there were now more Scots in addition to the king to be recovered. The Lord Douglas had managed to escape capture at Poitiers, in some accounts being dragged from the battlefield by his men, but some of his retinue had been seized and the knights and esquires Ramsay of Colluthie, John Herries, Sir Patrick Dunbar (the earl of March's half-brother) and others were soon resident in the Tower of London.[36]

Thus on 13 December 1356, safe-conducts were issued to the bishops of St Andrews, Brechin and Caithness, William Livingston, Robert Erskine and Sir Thomas Fauside (a Steward retainer) to visit London; they would be joined by a number of clerical procurators appointed to act on behalf of the Scottish dioceses and monastic houses in agreeing to David's ransom, a group which included royal servants like David de Mar, now treasurer of Moray and secretary to Queen Joan, and Alexander Bur, archdeacon of Moray, whom David would later employ as troubleshooting bishop in this northern see. These royalists would form the core of the Scots embassies of 1357, but in January that year the same group were granted passage afresh

---

34 Sumption, *Hundred Years War*, ii, ch. 5; *Chron. Bower*, vii, 299–301; *Chron. des Quatre Premiers Valois*, 45, 50. *Chron. Wyntoun*, vi, 231, claims Douglas was knighted by John II – into the Order of the Star? William already seemed to hold St Säens in Normandy by 1348 (Brown, *Black Douglases*, 210–1).

35 H.T. Riley ed., *Memorials of London and London Life in the XIIIth, XIVth and XVth Centuries* (London 1868), 285–8.

36 *Chron. Fordun*, i, 375–6, relates how Archibald Douglas pretended to be a mere foot soldier and thus escaped imprisonment with the help of his friend, Ramsay. See Barrow, *Bruce*, 124–6 for 1302. Interestingly, one of the rules of John II's Order of the Star was that no member knight was to flee from battle, perhaps explaining Douglas's behaviour at Poitiers.

with the addition of William Keith, the Marischal, and Thomas, earl of Angus, the Chamberlain. As a group these men seem to have been commissioned by the Steward at a council at Perth about 17 January and it is possible that the Lieutenant now saw sense in co-operating and making some effort to control the process of David's return. Angus, John Stewart of Kyle and Thomas Murray of Bothwell would also be listed as intending to participate in the release talks of August 1357 at Berwick alongside David's regulars. But it does seem as though these Steward supporters were absent from both these and the final October talks in that border burgh, indicating perhaps that the Lieutenant's influence declined as the king's return loomed. Certainly, the commissions of proctors to attend the negotiations after August 1357 were recorded separately by each of the three estates of Scotland in council at Edinburgh about 26 September – clergy, nobles and burgesses – and merely confirmed by the Steward. The necessity for these separate commissions also underlines the increased importance of the three estates after a decade in which both the king and his heir presumptive had vied to win the support of a majority of the political community.[37]

Throughout 1356, it is uncertain if David had access to any of these Scottish embassies at Odiham Castle. He continued to receive visits from his personal servants, Doctor Hector, Adam de Lanark and Robert Dumbarton.[38] The latter arranged the issue of grants to some Scottish knights in David's name from late 1356 on, namely John Gray of Broxmonth (a future clerk of the Regsiter whose son was named as a hostage for David in both 1354 and 1357), William Sinclair, James Sandilands and Patrick Ramsay of Dalhousie.[39] David may also have had contact with the Anglophile Thomas, earl of Mar, who had permission to speak to Edward III in May on 'certain causes' and perhaps had a hand in arranging the procedures for David II's first ransom instalment at Bruges where Mar and his clerk, a John Cromdale, were on private business matters in August 1357: Cromdale had visited David in 1350 and Mar would be David's new Chamberlain, ousting the Steward's ally the earl of Angus by 1358.[40]

---

37 *Rot. Scot.*, i, 799, 802–3; *Foedera*, iii, 354, 370–2; *RRS*, vi, nos. 140, 147; *RPS*, 1357/1/1 and 1357/9/1–4; Penman, 'Parliament Lost – Parliament Regained?'. See Watt, *Scottish Graduates*, 67–70, 382–4 for Mar and Bur – David and Joan had requested a papal provision for Bur in 1350 (*CPR*, i, 199).

38 *Rot. Scot.*, i, 803, 808.

39 *RRS*, vi, nos. 139 (confirmation to Gray of lands held formerly by Thomas Murray, Pantler), 140 (40 merks pension for Sinclair from Montrose), 144 (Sandilands' lands in Strathaven, Lanarkshire), 145 (Ramsay's grant to Newbattle Abbey). Duncan, 'The Regnal Year of David II', 117, redates acts of David II – placed by *RRS*, vi, in 1355 – to 1356 or 1357.

40 *Rot. Scot.*, i, 807; Duncan, 'The Laws of Malcolm MacKenneth', 201–2; *ER*, i, 553; A. Stevenson, 'Medieval Associations with Bruges', in Brotherstone and Ditchburn, *Freedom and Authority*, 93–107.

However, around March 1357, David seems to have been removed to the Tower of London for a month or so and may have been able to receive Scottish visitors.[41] This activity formed the background to the Anglo-Scottish border truce agreed in May 1357 – with Lord Douglas, the earl of March and John Stewart of Kyle named as Middle, East and West March wardens for Scotland respectively – and to the final ransom-release indenture of 3 October 1357.[42] Under this 'Treaty of Berwick' the Scots were to pay a massive 100,000 merks (£66,666 13s. 4d.) to England over the next ten years. Instalments were to be handed across the border on the feast of St John the Baptist, 24 June, which was also the anniversary of the Scottish victory at Bannockburn, a fact surely not lost on the English. But while this ransom was paid, a truce would prevail and, again, a proportionally declining number of Scottish noble hostages – starting with twenty – would be held in England.[43]

On paper this was not a bad deal. Since 1354 only 10,000 more merks had been addded to the ransom. David's price was still far less in relative terms than such continental captives as Charles of Blois (released for £168,000 in 1356) had been charged by Edward III; it would always be much less than John II (3–4,000,000 gold écus) would have to pay in both cash and French lands and sovereignty.[44] Moreover, by October 1357 it is clear that David himself and his supporters had been able to adjust and supplement some of the clauses of the treaty of Berwick to benefit the king upon his release. Indeed, David seems to have spent considerable energy in 1357 – as he had done in 1349–52 – in trying to win Edward III over and to secure better terms to soften his subjects to the burdens of his release.

On 1 March 1357 Edward III had sent David a pipe of Gascon wine to mark the feast day of his namesake, St David of Wales, four days ahead of the Scottish king's thirty-third birthday. Then sometime about 22 May that year, just seventeen days after the captive French king had entered England in the custody of the Black Prince (and two days before their grand entry into London), David had a 'conversation' from his window back at Odiham with William Edington, the English Chancellor and bishop of Winchester. It was perhaps this key official who was able to arrange leave for the Scottish king to exit the See of Winchester in Hampshire and to make a pilgrimage to Canterbury, a trip which the captive monarch had argued 'would be greatly to his [David's] ease and agreeable to his guardian'.[45]

41 NAS RH2/4/562 'Transcripts of English Issue Rolls, 1310–65'.
42 *Rot. Scot.*, i, 803.
43 *Ibid*, 811; *RRS*, vi, nos. 148–9.
44 Sumption, *Hundred Years War*, ii, 444–6; Given-Wilson and Bériac, 'Edward III's Prisoners of War', 821–3.
45 *CDS*, iii, no. 1610; Ormrod, *The Reign of Edward III*, 86–90 for Edington. David may also have visited Canterbury in January 1357 (BL Add MSS. 24,512 f. 4–6).

With so much time on his hands, David may well have adopted a far more rigorously pious and contemplative lifestyle during his stay at Odiham. Trussell's accounts record the king's veneration of the feast days of St Michael, St Luke, St Matthew and the nativity of the Virgin in the course of his eventual journey home to Scotland in late September 1357. But before then, accompanied by sixteen horsemen, David did make a three-day pilgrimage (Sunday 10 September to Tuesday 12), passing through Dartford, Rochester and Newington then on to the tomb of St Thomas à Beckett, enjoying players and good roast meat along the way, distributing pennies to the poor and gifting a parsimonious 30d in alms at Canterbury itself.[46] This trip and the eight requests for passage to Beckett's shrine which David would make between 1357 and 1370 were, though, surely also designed to win David the sympathy of the English king. The fact that Edward sent his personal physician, Master Jordan, to give David a final check-up just before his release suggests this may not have been in vain.[47] Moreover, David's request in late May – and Edward's desire to extract the greatest possible glory from the victory of Poitiers – may also have helped secure the Scottish king's invitation out of Odiham in June 1357 to attend and, as in 1348, perhaps participate in another lavish tournament, this time at Smithfield, London (the site of William Wallace's execution in 1305), in the company of John II and other French captives, the English king, the Black Prince and his brothers and Henry of Lancaster. However, David's earlier treatment on 15 March 1357, with 'black powder' (perhaps for cauterising wounds), a waxy poultice and other herbal medicines purchased for 52s 9d from John Adam, Apothocary of London, would seem to suggest that the king's battle scars had not completely healed after more than a decade: Master Jordan's later visit may also point to the aggravation of these wounds in the lists at Smithfield or while hunting.[48]

But in addition to an appeal to their shared code of Christian chivalry, David also made far more practical approaches to Edward III. According

46 *Ibid*, MSS. 24,511; Balfour-Melville, 'Papers relating to the Captivity of David II', 21–9; H. Coxton, *Pilgrimage to Canterbury* (Newton Abbot 1978), 118–9, 155–6.

47 For David's later pilgrimage requests, see *Rot. Scot.*, i, 828 (July 1358), 872 (April 1363), 881 (February 1364), 887 (November 1364), 900 (March 1366), 917 (October 1366), 928 (January 1369); *Foedera*, iii, 787 (February 1370); see also below, ch. 8. For his medical treatment, see Balfour-Melville, 'Papers relating to the Captivity of David II', 31 and NAS RH2/4/562.

48 *CCR: X Edward III, 1354–60* (London 1908), 347; Beltz, *Memorials of the Order of the Garter*, 380; Sumption, *Hundred Years War*, ii, 326–7. W.H. Pyne, *The History of the Royal Residences* (3 vols, London 1819), i, 55, asserts that in his day two sets of armour – worn by David and John II – still existed in the Round Tower at Windsor Castle. A sixteenth-century tradition maintains that it was at the urging of David and John that Edward III began an enlargement of Windsor Castle (P. Johnson, *The Life and Times of Edward III* (London 1973), 129–32).

once more to Knighton, while staying in London at the Blackfriars in the company of Queen Joan just prior to his release in autumn 1357, David offered to help Edward III with his wars. There is no official record that David did so at this time but such an offer (or request) had formed a key part of the deal first proposed for his release in 1350–2 and would do so again when David tried to revive the succession-peace plan between 1359 and 1367. It is quite possible that even as his ransom-release was being finalised in 1357 David tried to revive this succession-release alternative. However, Knighton also adds that in 1357 David not only arranged for Scottish merchants to travel in and out of England with the same rights as English tradesmen – 'as though they were one people and one nation' – but he also arranged for Scottish money to circulate with restored parity in England and for Scottish clerics to study at the English universities.[49] On 28 October 1357 – three weeks after David's release – Edward did indeed issue a general licence for Scottish clerics to study at Oxford and Cambridge: two days later he licensed Scottish merchants to trade in England. By mid-1358 he would also have agreed that English and Scottish coinage should once more be of equal value despite the Scottish slump since 1350.[50]

David and his subjects must have appealed to Edward III on these particular matters. In helping secure them the Scottish king had raised his own stock with the key estates of Scotland whose influence in parliament would be so crucial to his liberation and future government. Many of the churchmen involved in his release talks would sponsor clerics to Oxbridge after 1357: some ninety Scottish clerics would have sought leave to study there by 1400.[51] Their steady trickle south would be surpassed by a massive growth in Anglo-Scottish trade between 1357 and 1371. This commerce – and the restoration of the value of Scottish coin – would of course make it easier to raise taxes from the nobles, church and burghs in parliament and thus to pay the ransom. The burghs certainly seem to have been prepared to guarantee payment of the entire first instalment of the ransom.[52] At the same

---

49 *Chron. Knighton*, 163.

50 *Rot. Scot.*, i, 815–6 for merchant and clerical licences and *passim* for their traffic in England; for the coinage, see *ER*, i, i-xi.

51 Some sixty-two different clerics can be identified seeking passage south to study at Oxbridge between 1357 and 1375, of whom at least eight – Grenlaw, Allincrum, Oxe, Walter Bell, Boyle, Tonirgayth, Blantyre and Smalhame – worked for David or his regime (*Rot. Scot.*, i, *ad indecim*; Watt, *Scottish Graduates*, 8–9, 34, 60–1, 54, 243–6, 498, 535–6; A.B. Emden ed., *A Biographical Register of the University of Oxford to A.D. 1500* (3 vols., Oxford 1957), *ad indecim*; Ditchburn, *Scotland and Europe*, 234).

52 *APS*, i, 19 – the seals of the burghs of Aberdeen, Dundee, Inverkeithing, Crail, Cupar, St Andrews, Montrose, Stirling, Linlithgow, Haddington, Dumbarton, Rutherglen, Lanark, Dumfries and Peebles survive on the ambassadors' commission issued at Edinburgh in the council of September 1357, along with the episcopal seals of Glasgow, Dunkeld, Aberdeen, Moray and Ross.

time, agreements must also have been reached for the procedures of 'March days' for the redress of grievances on the Anglo-Scottish border and the conservation of the truce.[53] A return to peacetime activities – trade, pilgrimage and learning – must have seemed an attractive proposition to many in contrast to the war-torn disruption of the Steward's lieutenancy.

Scottish disgruntlement with the Steward may also have helped David and his supporters reshape some of the clauses of the treaty of Berwick to suit the king's political aims. Most obviously, in 1357, David seems to have been able to revise the list of twenty Scottish hostages originally agreed to in 1354. Only two names were changed from that rota but these amendments saw the sons and heirs of Sir Adam Fullarton (the former Alexander Ramsay retainer) and Patrick Dunbar, earl of March (who had helped in talks in 1354 but whose son, John, had died since[54]), replaced with those of Robert Steward and William, earl of Ross, the new in-laws: John Stewart of Kyle and Hugh Ross would thus be surrendered into English custody instead. The default clauses of the ransom schedule also betray David's antipathy towards some of the men who had abandoned him in 1346 and profited from his imprisonment. After the first instalment of 10,000 merks was paid, John Stewart of Kyle was to be released but nonetheless to be replaced with another son of the Steward. Moreover, Robert Steward himself was still named as one of the potential hostages to be surrendered should David fail to make a payment, although admittedly to be chosen along with two others from a list which now included the earls of March, Mar, Ross, Angus and Sutherland, the lord of Douglas and Thomas Murray of Bothwell. However, if the Scots should be late in paying arrears on instalments – that is, payments already delayed – then David was to send to England two men from a list made up of the Steward, Douglas and Thomas Murray within three weeks of any expired deadline: these three surely represented key men who had encouraged the Franco-Scottish campaigns of 1354–6.[55]

Thus although burdened financially by the treaty and obliged at first to give up such valuable hostages as John Sutherland, David had also forged a

53 Neville, *Violence, Custom and Law*, 33–41, 44–61, has shown how after 1346 Edward III elevated his warden-conservators on the border to oversee a system of border dispute hearings which used mixed Scottish and English juries throughout the 1350s. This system would also oversee the Scots' ransom payments and hostage exchanges and expand generally throughout the 1360s thanks to reciprocal English and Scottish efforts.

54 *Scots Peerage*, iii, 264–9; *Rot. Scot.*, i, 812.

55 *Ibid*, 811–2. David and the Steward may have been competing for the loyalty of Fullarton; the Steward gave him lands in Kyle Stewart in 1344 (*Calendar of Laing Charters*, 11) and in 1350 he had witnessed a charter by the earl of Angus with the Steward (NAS GD124 Mar & Kellie, 1119).

political weapon which he might in theory use in the coming reckoning with his subjects to good effect. The 1357 treaty also laid out guarantees for each country's merchant shipping, as well as the ecclesiastical rights of their clergy and their relationship with Avignon regarding Papal letters. In addition, neither king was to harbour rebels against the other. In particular, this meant that John MacDonald of the Isles, Edward Balliol and other allies of Edward III were to be included in the truce thus established. Crucially, John of the Isles was not to be obliged to pay any part of David's ransom, a clear confirmation that in 1356–7 MacDonald – who requested safe-conducts to England for his kin at that time – had reached some form of alliance with England and generally valued his autonomy within the Scottish realm.[56]

So it was perhaps as much through his own shrewd hard work in lobbying the English king on social and economic matters as through the efforts of his close supporters and the unpredictable swings of fate which had brought about the French king's capture, that David II was free to make his way steadily north to Berwick after 14 September. He was accompanied by two chaplains, six esquires, six valets, and six grooms. He may have sported new robes purchased for him in London and Southampton before his departure but he does not seem to have brought all his household possessions of the previous decade with him, gifting his falcons from Odiham to his keeper, Trussell, who escorted him north.[57] The king must have been only too ready to leave them behind as he was released finally to his own realm on Friday 6 October, three days after the treaty of Berwick was signed and sealed by the Scottish and English embassies.

According to Prior Wyntoun's anonymous source, David was careful to re-enter Scotland without what would have been an unpopular English entourage: 'with him of Ingland brocht he nane, bot a chalmer child allane' – the poetic counterpiece to the bairns who had been the only Scots bold enough to whisper his name in the wake of the invasions of 1332–1334. But in fact David was accompanied, presumably to Edinburgh, by a sizeable contingent of Scots (many of whom had surrendered their heirs as hostages), including at least the bishops of St Andrews, Caithness and Brechin and various clerical procurators; the earls of March, Angus and Sutherland; and the knights Thomas Murray, James Lindsay, David Graham, Robert Erskine, William Livingston, David Weymss (sheriff of Fife), Roger Kirkpatrick, Thomas Bisset, William de Vaus and William Ramsay of Colluthie; Thomas, earl of Mar may also have accompanied

---

56 *Rot. Scot.*, i, 811; *RRS*, vi, no. 148; *Acts of the Lords of the Isles*, lxxiv; *CDS*, iii no. 1639. In 1369 David would reverse this term of the Berwick treaty and seek tax contributions from John of the Isles – see below, ch. 11.

57 Balfour-Melville, 'Papers relating to the Captivity of David II', 31–5.

his lord north. But just as in 1341, Robert Steward was conspicuous by his absence, probably taking refuge on his Perthshire or Clydeside lands after the final full council of his lieutenancy at Edinburgh on 26 September 1357 and understandably fearful of his king's intentions. For similar reasons, the Williams, the Lord Douglas and the earl of Ross, were also absent from Berwick.[58]

Well might these men have been apprehensive. David II had been kept away for ten years, eleven months and eleven days. There was much work to do and many old scores to settle.

---

58 *Rot. Scot.*, i, 811–2; *RRS*, vi, nos. 146–7; *Chron. Wyntoun*, vi, 232. The Steward was at Rothesay over Christmas 1356 (*Inventory of Lamont Papers, 1231–1897*, ed. N. Lamont (Edinburgh 1894), 10–1); on 16 May 1357 he was at Methven (W. Fraser ed., *The Lennox* (2 vols., Edinburgh 1874), ii, no. 24); on 19 May 1357 he was at Loudon Hill in Ayrshire (NAS GD 150/12); in June 1357 he was at Perth (*RRS*, vi, no. 143).

SEVEN

The French Connection: a King Restrained, 1357–9

'King David sone after his returnyng in Scotlannd maid grete punicioun of sindry captanis quhilkis left him in the field of Durehaym, because thai gaif occasioun of fleying to utheris . . .'

Hector Boece, *Chronicles of Scotland*, 1531[1]

The First Weeks Home

Scotland's past has only really ever had one celebrated 'king unleashed'. The traditional view of James I (1406–37), the third Stewart monarch, has been that when he finally returned to Scotland, aged thirty, after eighteen years of captivity in England, he inflicted a terrible and almost immediate revenge upon those Scottish nobles whose self-interest had abetted his original seizure and left him at the English crown's pleasure for so long. Recent research has shown, however, perhaps not surprisingly, that in fact James was much more cautious upon his homecoming than his later vengeful image suggests. Nonetheless, whilst James's wrath was sensibly delayed, his justice when it came was characteristically brutal and decisive, the execution of the Albany Stewarts in 1425 re-asserting firmly his personal and political authority in the face of mounting opposition to his ransom taxation. James could not know that over a decade later, some of his subjects harmed by his tyrannical actions in 1425 would conspire to murder him for interfering in their local concerns.[2]

But James I, of course (and his great chronicler and government employee, Abbot Bower), could so easily have had an earlier model to look to as a 'king unleashed'. David II, aged thirty-four, might indeed have been fully expected to return to Scotland in late 1357 to pour down scorn and vengeance upon those over-mighty nobles – headed, as they would be in 1424, by the Stewart Lieutenant and heir presumptive – whom the Bruce monarch must have felt had undermined and sidelined his kingship for over a decade. Hector Boece's chronicle, written during the turbulent childhood of James V in the early sixteenth century and quoted above, certainly telescoped the events of 1357–60 and insisted to its readership that this had been the case: David sought revenge.

1 *Chron. Boece*, 333.
2 Nicholson, *Scotland – the Later Middle Ages*, 317; Brown, *James I*, xii-iii, 40–71.

Yet in reality any 'gret punicioun' inflicted on his great subjects by David would be even more gradual and must, to present-day commentators, seem much more muted than the later retribution of James I. Although it is likely that, even more so than before 1346, David longed to rule with a strong arm and to break Stewart power especially, he knew that he had to bide his time. He returned, after all, to a kingdom where decisive lordship and political power were split between the several often competing regional magnate lords and kindreds – really the Stewarts (including Angus), Ross, Douglas, MacDonald, and to a lesser degree men like March and Mar – who had led the Scots' war effort since 1347, just as they had championed the Scottish cause before 1341. Besides, little of David's chivalric following and government personnel from his mere five years of active rule before Neville's Cross survived: ten years' worth of fresh noble alliances, territorial blocs and agendas had been forged in his absence. The king furthermore had little close allied kin to speak of himself and uncertain prospects of an immediate heir by his English-born queen, Joan. His personal power and reputation had of course taken severe dents not just in 1346 but in his dealings with England in the Scone parliament while released on parole in 1352 and during the failed talks of 1354: these were negotiations at which his Scottish opponents could so obviously cast suspicion. Now, with the need for a huge ransom to be paid off annually over the very decade of David's life when he should have been at the height of his powers – and with the penalty for late payment a possible return to captivity – it might so easily have been the case that Scotland's leading subjects found themselves able to dictate terms of lordship, government and foreign policy to their king in return for their co-operation and finance. As in England during the Hundred Years War, the urgent need for annual extra-ordinary taxation might also lead to an increase in the legislative powers of the estates over the crown in parliament.[3]

However, whilst each of these factors was to some degree a home truth, David was evidently still able to call upon the natural authority of the crown to begin to recover his position. In particular, as one modern historian has insisted, the speed with which the king and his civil service were able to restore royal government and administration after 1357 was remarkable.[4] In doing so, and in beginning to re-establish his own personal authority, David was able to exploit the understandable clamouring of many Scots for a return to relative normality and access to direct royal patronage and justice after a destabilising, at times chaotic, interregnum. This last certainly seemed to be the damning assessment of what had mostly been Robert Steward's

3 Penman, 'Parliament Lost – Parliament Regained?'.
4 Duncan, 'The Laws of Malcolm MacKenneth', 239–73.

period in power (*c.*1347– *c.*1349 and *c.*1351–57), agreed upon at the first formal forum of the 'second reign'.[5]

David was predictably anxious to finalise and guarantee the terms of his release. Thus instead of waiting the usual forty days to summon a parliament, he called for a speedy 'full council' sometime after his re-entry into Scotland at the end of the first week of October 1357. David spent at least some of the intervening four weeks at Edinburgh but nothing otherwise of his activity or his company in this period is known for certain.[6] Nonetheless, it would be logical to assume that he spent much of his time meeting his key nobles, prelates and officers, consulting on what needed to be done when the council met at Scone about 6 November and perhaps filling some vacant posts. There is no official or chronicle evidence to be found of feasting or other celebrations to mark the king's homecoming: it is, indeed, extremely difficult to gauge the various facets of the surely mixed, anticipatory political mood at this time. But to judge from a number of David's acts between early November and the close of this year, in his first few weeks back he may also have been involved (just as in 1341) in careful personal negotiations with some of his greatest magnates over just what of the existing status quo in Scotland he would have to leave alone or could challenge openly.

The key item of business tabled at Scone was, though, ratification of the ransom treaty, yet this time not merely by 'David de Brus' – as at Berwick itself – but by the king of Scots and the realm's 'three estates'. The burgesses had been involved in fiscal and treaty decisions in Robert I's parliament in 1326. However, that late 1357's council was the first officially recorded Scottish assembly involving the townsmen of the royal burghs alongside the clergy and nobility underlined the priority of the ransom and the inevitable dependence the crown would have to place upon Scotland's chief mercantile commodity – wool – controlled by the burghs, in paying off its debt to Edward III.[7]

The first ransom instalment, indeed, was due on 24 June 1358 and had been underwritten by the royal burghs. With this in mind, the first recorded and seemingly unanimous decisions of the council were: firstly, the immediate empowerment of the crown to requisition wool and woolfells at cost price (4 merks or 53s 4d per sack of wool or every 200 woolfells) for resale at great profit; and, secondly, provision for a fresh assessment by crown 'inquisitors' of the true taxable value of all harvest-time lands, rents, goods, sheepherds and craft and labour workforce in anticipation of a contribution to be levied on all subjects regardless of sex or estate – both lax collection

5 *APS*, i, 74, 491–2 (*RPS*, 1357/11/1–23) for what follows of that assembly.
6 *RRS*, vi, no. 149. No witness lists to royal acts survive for October 1357.
7 *Ibid*, no. 150; G.P. Cuttino, *English Medieval Diplomacy* (Indiana 1985), 84–95;
   Rait, *The Parliaments of Scotland*, 22.

and late payment were to be punished. In addition, provisions were made for controlling the timing of the shearing and sale of sheep (export abroad before assessment was banned) and prohibiting the unlicensed removal of coinage from the kingdom by merchants and clerics.[8]

Ordinary customs and extra-ordinary tax contributions were thus clearly the means through which David and his close advisers intended to fund the ransom: the assessors were to report back at Perth on 14 January 1359, a deadline which would necessitate the assembly of three further councils and a parliament to monitor progress in 1358.[9] But to fulfil the urgent necessity of the first ransom payment David and his councillors were also able to ensure early passage of an act enabling the government to 'enquire from each person separately, of whatever estate or sex they be, how much they are willing to give voluntarily towards the ransom of the lord king in each year of the said term, presenting their names in writing and the sums granted by them'. No written evidence survives to show that David's regime did make use of this potentially lucrative if unpopular power. As we shall see, the 1359 ransom instalment would only be half paid, suggesting either a sore shortfall in crown income from such sources, or a reluctance on the king's part to enforce such 'voluntary' contributions even though the temptation to effectively blackmail those at odds with the king's person and plans since 1346 must have been great. The crown would, though, have recourse to such voluntary 'donations' again through the first recorded act of a council in 1366.[10]

In 1357–8, however, some funds may, at first, have come to the king from the coffers of wealthy subjects through a second avenue addressed by David's homecoming council. David had to look to the restoration of other sources of regular crown income to meet the everyday costs of his household and government. In doing so, another seemingly unprecedented Scottish community decision would provide him with an early opportunity to claw back some of the advantage certain magnates had gained since October 1346. For the Scone meeting also approved a royal Revocation – a potentially sweeping recovery presumably of all lands, wards, marriages of noble minors and other feudal dues belonging to the crown but alienated during both David's minority and his captivity.[11] Admittedly, the terms of this process of repossession may have been designed to satisfy vocal pressure

8 *RPS*, 1357/11/1–3, /5, /10; *ER*, ii, xxxviii–xxxix; Nicholson, *Scotland – the Later Middle Ages*, 164–5; Gemmill & Mayhew, *Changing Values in Medieval Scotland*, 283.

9 *RRS*, vi, nos. 164, 176; *RPS*, 1357/12/1, 1358/1/1–4, 1358/3/1, 1358/8/1–2, 1358/10/1.

10 *Ibid*, 1357/11/4 and 1366/7/1.

11 *Ibid*, 1357/11/9 and /11.

from the estates in October 1357 that the king 'live of his own' from the crown's land and customs income; that is, refrain from further taxing subjects already burdened with the ransom and regrant or remit no royal demesne or revenues without the 'mature counsel' of the estates in council or parliament. This would become a regular bromide of Scottish parliaments throughout the late fourteenth and fifteenth centuries.[12] But David's Revocation was, remarkably, the first of two he would initiate during his reign (1357 and 1367) despite the fact that a king was only really entitled to a single such moratorium at his minority's close on his twenty-fifth birthday. For David, of course, this had passed in the Tower of London. But more importantly, David and his clerks could use a Revocation to begin to reclaim immediately the considerable pockets of valuable land and income either alienated, feued (leased) out or simply neglected by the Steward as Lieutenant in favour of his allies. For the Stewarts themselves this might include the loss of the earldom of Fife and its associated Perthshire lordships; the Chamberlain, Thomas Stewart, earl of Angus, might lose his grip on such nice earners as the fermes of Stirling burgh or the earl of Fife's Perthshire barony of Strathord. More generally, any Scotsman hoping to avoid losing control of royal lands and revenues he had acquired during the king's absence would now have to pay a composition fee to the crown.[13]

To similar ends, however, the 1357 council also approved David's right to review the judicial decisions of his 'Lieutenants' (n.b. the use of the plural), ordering that the lands of all Scotsmen slain since the 'battle of Durham' be seized in the king's hands until he could review any remission granted to their killers.[14] Yet as well as being another potential revenue-generating device this statute and others surely reflected the general will of the estates for the reassertion of law and order. Again, these sensible, conventional acts also gifted the crown a legitimate means of strengthening its hand over the localities as well as a potential weapon for criticising and weakening its domestic opponents. For as well as scrutinising criminal pardons, David was empowered to appoint 'good and sufficient' men as sheriffs, coroners and bailies and where necessary to require those appointed to such posts during his absence (or holding office in heredity), but

---

12 Nicholson, *Scotland – the Later Middle Ages*, 164–5, 177, 285, 340, 378–80, 454–5, 541–4; Grant, *Independence and Nationhood*, 87–8, 162–70, 187–90; R. Tanner, *The Late Medieval Scottish Parliament: Politics and the Three Estates, 1424–1488* (East Linton 2001), 87–8, 110–4, 151–4, 213–4; Brown, *James I*, 49–60; C. McGladdery, *James II* (Edinburgh 1990), 95–6; N.A.T. Macdougall, *James III: a Political Study* (Edinburgh 1982), 124–6, and *James IV* (2nd edition, East Linton 1998), 160–5.

13 E.g. *ER*, i, 543 (wards in Aberdeenshire granted to Norman Leslie and John Preston by the Steward); 555, 585–6, 622, 624 (lands held by Angus).

14 *RPS*, 1357/11/12 and /16.

who, for whatever reason, were unable to fulfil their duties, to present a replacement: presumably this would also allow David to simply appoint new men acceptable to the royal will.[15] At the same time, another statute 'ordained and agreed by the three communities that the lord our king shall hold justice ayres throughout the kingdom in his proper person, especially on this occasion, in order that royal justice be more fully executed and to inspire terror in delinquents so that they abstain from their evil-doing'. This act – together with a call for justiciars, sheriffs, assessors and tax collectors to resume their own judicial and revenue-collection circuits – was surely the most direct indictment of a breakdown of attention to law and order and royal finance during the Steward's Lieutenancies and the office of men like William, earl of Ross, as justiciar north-of-Forth.[16] This impression of lawlessness in need of correction by the strong arm of the crown is reinforced not simply by the council's conventional confirmation of all the privileges of the burghs, foreign merchants, travellers and the Church, but by its simultaneous general call for the king's peace to be maintained and that 'no-one henceforth make war against his neighbour': later events suggest that this act may have had in mind feuds running in Menteith, Lothian and the north since the 1340s.[17]

Thus, on paper at least, this council seems to have placed David's regime in a relatively strong starting position from which to recover the political initiative. At face value these acts suggest that the crown intended a vigorous course of action in reclaiming its rights. These acts may also have been enough to satisfy some of the expectations of particular groups among the estates. Yet in reality the official record of this council's decisions may – like that of many of David's later parliaments – gloss over a great deal of dissension, heated debate, recrimination and defensive posturing at Scone. Some hint, indeed, of the highly charged atmosphere at this assembly may lie in the tale of Prior Wyntoun's source of how upon his return David, swamped by clamouring suitors who pressed close 'as they were wont to do', was forced to keep them at bay by wielding violently the ceremonial mace.[18] Who these men were and whether they were lobbying for redress of grievances, arbitration or patronage (on an individual or general basis) is unclear. But it should be no surprise, then, to find David continuing to tread warily at this time and not acting immediately to exploit the council's enabling acts.

Indeed, by the start of the second week of the council at least, some indication had emerged of the genuine weakness of David's position. By 13

15 *Ibid*, 1357/11/8.
16 *Ibid*, 1357/11/6–7.
17 *Ibid*, 1357/11/13–5 and /17.
18 *Chron. Wyntoun*, vi, 232–4.

November, if not before, David seems to have granted – or, really, to have confirmed – both the earldom of Moray to Patrick, earl of March, and the earldom of Strathearn to Robert Steward.[19] Although the aging Patrick had a genuine claim to the northern title through his wife, Agnes, John Randolph's sister, and had co-operated in the king's release talks of 1356–7, this may not have been what David would have desired ideally for so sensitive a quarter previously allied so closely to the crown.[20] But worse still, the king's concession to the Steward was necessitated surely not because the Stewarts had a legitimate familial or marital claim to the wealthy earldom of Strathearn, but rather because the royal heir presumptive had occupied this region through collusion with its former incumbent earl, Malise, and since the death in battle of Maurice Murray in 1346: the king was in no position to dispossess the Steward immediately after his compromised return. David was thus obliged to confirm these entrenched magnate interests – just as he had been after June 1341 with the Steward in Atholl and Douglas of Liddesdale and Ramsay in the south.

True, the alienation of the earldoms of Moray and Strathearn might have been partly outweighed by the potential return in goodwill to David and the general aura of contentment generated by a revived royal court populated by newly titled nobles. But these grants undeniably reduced the crown's power to intervene in central and northern Scotland. In doing so they confirmed a pattern. For now at least David was similarly obliged to allow the earl of Ross to continue as justiciar north-of-Forth, Thomas Stewart, earl of Angus, to serve as Chamberlain, and the earl of March and William, Lord Douglas, to act as border Wardens (alongside William de Landellis, bishop of St Andrews).[21] Douglas indeed had been the other great beneficiary of the king's captivity. After the knight of Liddesdale's death he had re-occupied much of the Lothians and Western and Central Marches. Despite Douglas's seeming inconsistency in assisting David *c.* 1350–4 and his lucky escape at Poitiers in 1356, his was a regional predominance in the south which David could no more avoid accepting as a *fait accompli* in 1357 than he could those noble palatines north of Forth. Hence Lord William was allowed to continue both as keeper of Edinburgh Castle and justiciar south-of-Forth while David also confirmed all his regality lands and his marriage to the sister of Thomas, earl of Mar (in a charter issued during the Scone council in

19 *RRS*, vi, no. 153.
20 The March earl's half-brother, Sir Patrick Dunbar, had also wed Isabella, John Randolph's younger sister (*Scots Peerage*, iii, 260–9).
21 *ER*, i, 543, 595. On 16 March 1358, March, Douglas and the bishop of St Andrews attended an inquisition at Berwick to hear a border dispute case with their English counterparts as per the treaty of October 1357 (*Calendar of Inquisitions Miscellaneous*, iii, no. 343; C.J. Neville, 'Keeping the Peace on the Northern Marches in the Later Middle Ages', *EHR*, cix (1994), 1–25).

November 1357 and witnessed by the bishops of St Andrews, Glasgow and Brechin, the new earls of Strathearn and March/Moray and the knights William Livingston and Robert Esrkine). But more significantly still, by 4 February 1358 at the latest – perhaps through a grant first mooted when David visited Lanark on 13 December the previous year – Lord William had been made the first Black Earl of Douglas.[22]

As discussed below, David may have quite reasonably had high hopes of good working and personal relations with Douglas, and to a lesser extent with the aged March/Moray and his heirs. But the king had thus been obliged to give a great deal away in terms of land and power within the first few weeks of his return, and it surely rankled. Neither Steward, March/Moray nor Douglas seems to have suffered immediate revocation of any of the offices, royal lands and income they had acquired since 1346; all three lords spent Christmas that year with the king at Stirling.[23]

Royal Resurgence, 1358

David did not, then, explode back on to the Scottish political scene. However, from January 1358, having initially gone some way to placate the fears and satisfy the ambitions of these key nobles, he did begin in earnest to rebuild a royalist following, support which he intended clearly should help him redress the balance of political power in the near future. As before 1346, the king looked naturally to forge an extended affinity among middling Lowland nobles, knights and esquires in addition to well-connected civil service clerics. In his earlier kingship he had been able to attract the loyalty of such men through generous patronage and especially as their leader in war against England. But after 1357 – and in the light of David's unresolved succession-ransom plans with Edward III – he could use no such nationalistic banner. Instead, it becomes increasingly clear that between 1358 and 1370 David sought to cultivate a more neutral but no less potent image as a patron of supra-national chivalry, as it were, and of crown service. As a result his court would grow into a powerful focus for a large number of ambitious laymen with a proven interest in chivalry and the crusades, very often 'lifted out' or poached by David's largesse from the natural regional followings of great Scottish magnates. As the decade wore on, David would also look to build up particular, proven, hard-men nobles with strong followings as his alternative agents in sensitive localities. In this volatile dynamic of divide-and-rule lordship, he would also continue to make good use of strong personal or familial ties in his promotion of officers

22 *RRS*, vi, no. 153 (which also included confirmation of Thomas of Mar's wedding gift of the barony of Drumlanrig in Dumfriesshire); *RMS*, i, App. ii, no. 1222; *ER*, i, 508; Brown, *Black Douglases*, 43–52.
23 *RRS*, vi, no. 156.

or loyal networks, in particular the kindreds of his mistresses and wives.[24]

In early 1358 all this had to begin in a low-key fashion. Thus for the first three months after Christmas David remained predominantly at Edinburgh – where Douglas was castle-keeper – travelling only to Perth in mid-January and rewarding a number of loyal crown men: Sir John Preston (Fife, Perth and Dumfries lands 'notwithstanding the revocation'); Maurice, an illegitimate son of the late Maurice Murray, earl of Streathearn; Malcolm Fleming, nephew of David's ailing foster-father, who was given Lenzie barony in Lanarkshire; Sir John Kennedy of Dunure (a feud rival of the Flemings) who was confirmed in all his Carrick lands; the late Beatrice Douglas, mother of the new Douglas earl, and Eleanor Bruce (née Douglas), the king's great aunt, of West Calder barony near Edinburgh given to them in turn by Duncan, earl of Fife, and William, then Lord Douglas; Adam Torrie and James Mulekinn, Edinburgh burgesses appointed in December 1357 as Warden and Master of the royal mint respectively; Sir William Sinclair of Rosslyn of Edinburgh lands; Sir Walter Haliburton, a Neville's Cross veteran, of the mid-Lothian barony of Bolton; Malcolm, master of the earldom of Lennox; John Gray of Broxmonth, a Clerk of the Register; John of Allincrum, another Clerk and an exchequer auditor; and Sir Adam Gordon, confirming Robert I's grant of the massive forfeited barony of Strathbogie in the north, overlooking passages to Moray and Inverness-shire (which had been briefly restored to the Strathbogie family in 1335). David also made grants at this time to a number of religious institutions including the abbeys of Melrose and Arbroath and, perhaps most significant of all, a grant of the regality of the valuable neighbouring north-eastern lordship of Garioch – formerly the possession of the late Sir Andrew Murray of Bothwell and his now dead wife, David's aunt, Christian Bruce – to the king's cousin and fellow-Anglophile from the 1350s, Thomas, earl of Mar.[25]

Although Thomas Murray, the Pantler – Christian Bruce's son and ally of the Steward – may have resented Mar's sasine of Garioch, none of these grants could be considered overly provocative. At the same time, David's court, while attended in this period by more obviously royalist laymen – William, earl of Sutherland, David Annan, Preston and Livingston, for example – remained open to the Steward, March/Moray and Douglas. However, by 20 March at the latest – but not apparently during the short Edinburgh 'councils' held

24 Boardman, *Early Stewart Kings*, 1–25; Penman, 'Christian Days and Knights', 260–4; Boardman and Penman, 'The Scottish Arms in the Armorial of Gèlre' (forthcoming). For a wider discussion of royal grants as a means of establishing a lord-man relationship of retinue in this period and beyond, see A. Grant, 'Service and Tenure in Late Medieval Scotland, 1314–1475', in A. Curry and E. Matthew eds, *Concepts and Patterns of Service in the Later Middle Ages* (Bristol 2000), 145–79.
25 *RRS*, vi, nos. 154–180; *RMS*, i, no. 662 and App. i, nos. 124–7; Stringer, *Earl David*, 31–4.

about 27 January and 6 February 1358, for which no recorded decisions survive[26] – David had made a major patronage decision which must have been the source of tremendous tension within the political community. For on that date, at St Andrews (when Gordon's Strathbogie grant was confirmed), Sir William Ramsay of Colluthie near Cupar was recorded as witnessing in his new capacity as 'Earl of Fife', appending his seal after the Steward, March/ Moray and Mar. About this time Ramsay also received a gift of £200, a pension of £40 and a grant of control over the royal burgh of Cupar: he was present at court as earl of Fife for much of that year.[27]

The king's presence at St Andrews in Fife itself – where he had gone from Perth on 16 March – along with a number of his closest knights (Mar, Ramsay, Annan and Preston at least) may have been required to install Ramsay in possession. If so, this may have involved the king's physical displacement of Robert Steward or his appointee as bailie of these lands, an office he had occupied since 1346–7, with effectively complete control of the premier earldom since Earl Duncan's death in 1353. Certainly, the crown never seems to have paid the Steward for his expenses in Fife incurred since 1346.[28] As we have seen, David may already have denied the Steward recognition as the crown's assignee to Fife in the 1340s; now in early 1358 the king seemed to hammer a final nail in the coffin of the Steward's vague counter-plan to acquire that title through marriage to Duncan's only child, Isabella of Fife, whose inheritance through the female line David now denied outright. Despite this, Steward remained present at court throughout the year, witnessing acts mostly as the king's 'beloved nephew'.

Ramsay was in many ways the obvious placeman to intrude into Fife. His reputation, experience and military following had grown in David's time. The brother of the great Lothian warlord and flower of chivalry, Alexander Ramsay of Dalhousie (whose following David had inherited after 1342), William had been sheriff of Edinburgh *c*. 1342–6, fought loyally at Neville's Cross, been a visitor to David in England, taken safe-conducts to go on crusades with the Leslies and Sir Patrick Dunbar in 1355 and been a prominent captain in the Scottish contingent at Poitiers in 1356 where he was captured: Ramsay's release at the same time as the king's must have been secured, as with many of David's knights, by an oath never to fight England again.[29] But more importantly, by 1358

26 *RRS*, vi, nos. 168, 172.
27 *Ibid*, nos. 173, 178; *RMS*, i, App. ii, nos. 1228 (note of a grant of Fife to Ramsay), 1249 (Cupar); *ER*, i, 114.
28 *ER*, i, 561, a note of intended payment to the Steward by the crown for his expenses in Fife since 1346: but the amount due is left blank, suggesting it was never paid.
29 *RMS*, i, App. ii, nos. 902, 962, 1070; NAS RH 1/2/126; *Rot. Scot.*, i, 678, 707, 710, 877; *CDS*, iii, no. 1659.

Ramsay may also have had a close personal connection to the king. He was surely the husband of Katherine Mortimer, a woman named in a contemporary English source as David's mistress about this time. That this liaison was public knowledge may explain why Queen Joan sought an indefinite safe-conduct to England and left sometime after May 1358 never to return, although whether or not this reflected a complete breakdown in her relationship with David is unknown. As Michael Prestwich has suggested, this may have been the beginning of a process whereby David intended to annul his marriage to Joan. There is some evidence to suggest that Joan entered the Franciscan religious order before her death in August 1362, and divorce/remarriage was certainly a dynastic tactic which David would attempt to employ later in life.[30] However, even if the separation was David's design and he hoped to re-wed, the possibility of a Bruce heir in the immediate future was ruled out and Joan's withdrawal may have been a major blow to the king.

A mistress, then, may have been of some consolation but also of considerable domestic political value in 1358. According to Sir Thomas Gray, the Northumbrian knight, chronicler and colleague of Isabella of Fife's husband, Sir William Felton:

> David de Brus at this time created William de Ramsay Earl of Fife chiefly, as people said, by persuasion of his [Ramsay's] wife, whom he [David] loved paramours.

This unnamed mistress of the king from an annal for 1358 must surely have been Katherine whom Gray did name as the king's lover in his annal for 1360. Gray – a captive of the Scots *c.* 1355–6 – believed Katherine to have been a Londoner David had met while in the Tower (which could have happened had Katherine visited Ramsay after the battle of Poitiers).[31] Writing almost a century later, the Scottish abbot Bower insisted she had been Welsh, perhaps confusing her surname with the Mortimer earls of March (of which house a chief, Roger Mortimer, died in February 1360, the same year as Katherine herself).[32] But the events of 1358–60 make far greater sense if it is accepted that Katherine was more likely to have been the daughter (or sister) of Sir Roger Mortimer of Inverbervie, a descendant of adherents of Earl David of Huntingdon, brother of William I, and who

---

30 *Rot. Scot.*, i, 822–3, 825; Green, *Lives of the Princesses of England*, iii, 154; Prestwich, 'Katherine Mortimer's Death at Soutra', 115–6.

31 *Chron. Scalacronica*, 126, 162. Ramsay can also be associated with Felton, serving in the English garrison in Edinburgh before 1341 when Felton was justiciar there for Edward III (*Rot. Scot.*, i, 689). For Gray's knowledge of Felton, see A. King, 'Englishmen, Scots and Marchers: National and Local Identities in Thomas Gray's *Scalacronica*', *Northern History*, xxxvi, 2, Sept. 2000, 217–31, at 226–7.

32 *Chron. Bower*, vii, 321; *Chron. Scalacronica*, 150, for earl Roger of March's death.

occupied the Angus coastal region where David had landed upon his return from France in 1341.[33]

Sir Roger had already received favour from David, including confirmation in 1341–2 of a grant from John Campbell, earl of Atholl (d. 1333), of his Angus lands as well as a direct grant from the crown in December 1341 of Thomastoun (between Dairsie and Cupar) in Fife: this was a gift which made him a close neighbour of Ramsay of Colluthie. But Mortimer already had close links with Fife, having served as a knight in Earl Duncan's following about 1332–3. David also added to Roger's interests in that region sometime in 1358 by granting him the lands of Dunmore in West Fife, close to the Forth crossing at Kincardine and the road to Stirling: but perhaps significantly David did so only after Robert Steward had resigned Dunmore to the crown, possibly in return for a compensatory annual pension of £40.[34]

Of course, Katherine – if ever there was the slightest chance of her becoming David's consort – may also have been chosen for her fertililty as much as her charms and lordship connections: again about July 1358, David obliged William Ramsay to marry off his daughter, Elizabeth, a child perhaps born of Katherine (or an earlier wife), to a David Barclay, possibly the Prussian crusading associate of Ramsay, the Leslies and Sir Thomas Bisset of Upsetlington in Berwickshire. Like Ramsay, Bisset had also promised to disavow future war with England: on 24 July 1359 Bisset would even enter Edward III's special protection as a means of solving tensions concerning his border lands. Most telling of all, though, it would be Bisset whom David would impose as his second 'assignee' earl of Fife in 1363.[35] In 1358, however, that Ramsay's title would largely be a front for David's control of Fife and the neighbouring eastern seaboard is suggested by crown patronage to other Lowland associates of these knights. For example, whilst the canny William de Landellis continued to serve the king closely as lawyer and bishop of St Andrews, John Crichton – a holder of Edinburgh lands – became keeper of Loch Leven Castle in Fife and sheriff of neighbouring Kinross-shire, Norman Leslie received a pension from Fife lands, and an Adam Dispensa became constable of Kinghorn.[36]

David's initially successful intervention in Fife was not the only sign of growing royal confidence at this time, especially in reducing the following and power-base of Robert Steward. Indeed, the limited evidence can be taken to suggest that Ramsay's elevation in spring 1358 – amidst a large number of

33 Stringer, *Earl David*, 156–70.
34 *RRS*, vi, nos. 28, 62; *RMS*, i, App. ii, nos. 884, 1262, 1266; *Chron. Lanercost*, 272.
35 *CPR*, iii, 595; *Rot. Scot.*, i, 757, 763, 768, 797, 811, 840.
36 *RMS*, i, App. ii, nos. 1132, 1164, 1180, 1199, 1228, 1239, 1249, 1251, 1262, 1274, 1277, 1280, 1281. David may also have attempted to appoint John Crichton to the sherrifship of Lennox (*ibid*, App. ii, no. 1225).

royal grants issued that year (many of which survive only in note form) – marked a turning point in crown-magnate relations.[37] But inevitably there were still regions where the royal writ was painfully weak. Predictably, David was still unable to venture into or re-align decisively the lordships or personnel of the west coast and Argyll: this is underlined by his confirmation on 25 January of the Steward's adherent, Sir John Menteith of Arran and Knapdale, as sheriff of Clackmannan – the 'wee' shire between Fife and Stirling where it might have been expected that David's half-nephew, Robert Bruce of Clackmannan, would hold courts.[38] Nonetheless, David did continue to speculate in the Gael. Most important of all, on 23 January 1358, while at Edinburgh, David granted to John Macdougall all the lands in Lorn of his father, the late Alexander of Lorn, including his castles along the Firth of Lorn which had been in the possession of the MacDonalds of the Isles since the 1320s.[39]

Just like Thomas, earl of Mar, John Macdougall (known in Scotland as 'the foreigner') had been resident in England until the 1350s. Like the MacDowells and many of the Balliols' other former supporters in the Irish Sea world, Macdougall sought clearly to make his peace with the Bruce regime after Neville's Cross, once it became apparent that Edward Balliol's bid for the crown had been abandoned by the English. Macdougall may thus have returned to Scotland about 1353–4 with David II's blessing to resume possession of his lands in opposition to John MacDonald, self-styled 'Lord of the Isles' and by 1356 both an ally of Edward III and Edward Balliol and the new son-in-law of Robert Steward. As such, Macdougall was the obvious lord to fill the power vacuum in the Inner Hebrides and Argyll coast left after the murder by the earl of Ross of MacRuaridh of Garmoran in 1346. That Macdougall's fortunes were raised by the return of the king in 1357 is confirmed not only by his marriage to the daughter of David's full niece, Joanna Bruce, sometime between 1354 and 1358, but by the fact that the royal grant of 1358 overturned an agreement Macdougall had been obliged to make with MacDonald in 1354 which had left the Lord of the Isles in command of disputed castles, lands and churches: the crown had originally been forced to recognise MacDonald possession of these holdings in 1341 and again during a period of crisis in June 1343.[40] David's new nephew-by-marriage brought with

37 *Ibid*, App. ii, *c.* nos. 1210 to 1300 for these acts.
38 *Ibid*, App. i, no. 125.
39 *RRS*, vi, no. 165.
40 *Acts of the Lords of the Isles*, 5; *Chron. Fordun*, i, 369, where the annal mentioning this marriage is placed *c.* 1350–2; S. Boardman, 'The Tale of Leper John and the Campbell Acquisition of Lorn', in E.J. Cowan and R.A. McDonald eds, *Alba: Celtic Scotland in the Medieval Era* (East Linton 2000), 219–47, 232; *RRS*, vi, nos. 72–3. John Macdougall's favour from the crown after 1358 is noticeable, including David's payment of his expenses at Perth (for a council?), a gift of twelve bows and the exchange of messengers (*ER*, ii, 106, 114, 173).

him potentially valuable alliances with a number of other west-coast kindreds, for example Gilbert of Glasserie (another former Balliol man) and Archibald Campbell of Lochawe. Significantly, both these men received favour from David in the first half of 1358, perhaps in an attempt, certainly in Campbell's case (as he was confirmed in his father's lands on 25 January), to turn them as allies in a west-coast power game as much against Robert Steward, John Menteith and the earl of Ross as against MacDonald. About the same time, David also made a number of grants in favour of the Bruce-loyalist earl of Lennox and his kin.[41] In addition, any sons from the Macdougall-Bruce match might also find some unofficial place in the royal succession as children of a full niece of the king (and the first son of this match would be called John).[42]

However, David's failure, refusal or inability – in stark contrast to his father – to visit strongpoints in the west (other than Dumbarton) and thus to back up Macdougall in person throughout the rest of his reign, leaving him alone among the crown's enemies, surely contributed to a falling out for a time with Lorn in the 1360s. But the king's absence was also conspicuous, and his authority uncertain, in that other difficult Gaelic quarter, the south-west. David did have men he could turn to here but he still lacked an extended network of support made up of his own kin and tenants led by a singular lord in what had once been Bruce heartlands. As a result he favoured a number of lesser nobles here about 1358. Some further favour was extended to the Flemings of Cumbernauld and Biggar. But the death of the king's infirm 'foster-father', Malcolm Fleming, liferent earl of Wigtown, sometime *c*. 1357– 62 served to confirm the crown's view that this kindred no longer had a sufficient following to act effectively in this quarter: Sir William Cunningham of Kilmaurs, another Neville's Cross veteran, was thus appointed guardian or 'lord' of the earldom of Carrick sometime in 1358 (a grant confirmed in 1362). The king also rewarded the head of another traditional south-western kindred, Sir Roger Kirkpatrick, whom the Scottish chroniclers record as having recovered much of south-western Scotland from English occupation despite his capture at Neville's Cross in 1346: he received Dumfriesshire lands and was sheriff of Ayrshire by spring 1358.[43]

41 *RRS*, vi, nos. 166, 183–4. For the various bonds which Macdougall, Campbell and Glasserie had with each other and others in the west at this time, see J.W.M. Bannerman, 'The Lordship of the Isles – Historical background' in K.A. Steer and J.W.M. Bannerman eds, *Late Medieval Monumental Sculpture in the West Highlands* (Edinburgh 1977), 204–8, and *Highland Papers*, i, 75–8 and ii, 119, 142–3. David also made a number of minor grants of Argyll lands at this time (*RMS*, i, App. ii, nos. 1136–7, 1139, 1144, 1171–2, 1183, 1216–7). For David's pardon of Glasserie, see *ibid*, App. ii, no. 1095.

42 Boardman, 'The Tale of Leper John and the Campbell Acquisition of Lorn', 232.

43 *RMS*, i, App. ii, nos. 1147–9, 1154, 1176, 1194, 1205, 1208, 1221, 1230, 1240, 1242–3, 1255, 1260, 1272, 1303; *Chron. Bower*, vii, 297, 309.

Yet beyond this, royal authority in Galloway especially remained unconvincing. Until the latter half of the next decade David was unable to raise
revenue or hold justice ayres in this region which remained largely under the
influence of native kindreds beyond the pale, occasionally overseen in the
1350s by John Stewart of Kyle, the Steward's eldest son, or William, earl of
Douglas. The king's influence furthermore suffered an immediate setback.
According to late fourteenth- and fifteenth-century histories, on 24 June
1358 Roger Kirkpatrick was slain by a James Lindsay – either of Kirkpatrick
(brother-in-law of the Steward) or of Crawford (a cousin of the Douglas
earl) – probably in the course of a feud over Ayrshire lands or Caerlaverock
Castle in Dumfriesshire, but perhaps also in connection with the attempts of
crown inquisitors to assess lands and raise tax in the south-west. Both
Wyntoun's source and Bower – as well as being convinced that this murder
fulfilled a legend that the descendants of the Lindsay and Kirkpatrick who
had helped Robert Bruce kill John Comyn in Dumfries in 1306 would in the
end kill each other – also report that David responded by arresting Lindsay
and trying and executing him in Dumfries. No further evidence for these
events can be found. But if true, then David may well have had the feeling
that history was repeating itself. Kirkpatrick had been destroyed just as
Alexander Ramsay had been killed in office by Douglas of Liddesdale.
However, whereas the king had been forced to spare Douglas, he surely had
no desire in 1358 to dispense completely with the potential services of the
rest of the Lindsay kindred. Sometime about October 1358, he would make
a John Lindsay coroner of Ayrshire and grant the late James Lindsay's
Edinburgh barony of the Byres as well as lands near Inverness, Aberdeen and
Forfar to Sir Alexander Lindsay of Glenesk. The latter knight was another
crusading associate (active in 1358) of the Leslies and Ramsays and a
Forfarshire man often found in the retinue of Earl Thomas of Angus (who in
fact had resigned some of the Forfar lands granted to Glenesk).[44]

In fact, through Lindsay of Glenesk and others, David made rather more
progress when it came to intervening in northern affairs after spring 1358.
As before 1346, this royal resurgence rested on patronage of a growing
network of prelates, burghs, and middling nobles and knights. By early
1359, indeed, most of the royal offices north of Forth would be filled by
crown men: Sir Robert Chisholm as sheriff of Inverness-shire, Williams,
Meldrum and Liddale as sheriffs of Aberdeenshire, William Fotheringham
as sheriff of Banffshire, Thomas Fingask as bishop of Caithness, Patrick de
Leuchars as bishop of Brechin (the Chancellor) and Alexander Kinnimound
(II) as bishop of Aberdeen. About summer 1358 David also made many

---

44 *Chron. Wyntoun*, vi, 241; *Chron. Bower*, vii, 309; *RRS*, vi, nos. 196–7; *RMS*, i,
    App. ii, nos. 1272, 1287, 1311–3; *Rot. Scot.*, i, 824, 830.

Plate 1: A hard act for David to follow. A fifteenth-century manuscript of Walter Bower's *Scotichronicon* commemorates Robert I's victory at Bannockburn in 1314. (By permission of the Master and Fellows of Corpus Christi College, Cambridge)

Plate 2: A second Balliol rules 'bot a litill quhile'. A fanciful rendering of the Bruce Scots' surprise attack on Edward Balliol at Annan in December 1332, just a few weeks after his coronation at Scone. (Author's collection)

Plate 3: The great seal of David II, on the left, modelled on that of his father, is markedly different from that of Balliol, modelled on the seal of his patron, Edward III. (Author's collection)

Plate 4: Childhood exile: David II and Queen Joan given refuge from the war in Scotland in 1334 by would-be crusader, Philip VI of France, illustrated in a fifteenth-century manuscript of Jean Froissart's *Chroniques*. (By permission of La Bibliothèque Nationale, Paris)

Plate 5: Childhood home, c.1334-41: Chateau Gaillard in Normandy, built by the crusading Richard I of England and by the 1330s a French royal residence and prison: a possible architectural influence on David's later plans for Edinburgh's castle-rock. (Author's collection)

Plate 6: The defining moment of a long reign. David II's capture by John de Coupland after the destruction and desertion of the Scottish host at Neville's Cross near Durham, 17 October 1346, illustrated in Jean Froissart's *Chroniques*. (By permission of La Bibliothèque Nationale, Paris)

Plate 7: The man who might have been King? John of Gaunt, Edward III's third son and the prince whom David II sought after c. 1349 to make his heir presumptive instead of Robert the Steward. (Author's collection)

Plate 8: A parting of friends? David II and the taller, robed Edward III from a fifteenth-century illumination of the Treaty of Berwick, 1357, which agreed David's release in return for 100,000 merks' ransom and twenty Scottish hostages. Despite the cost, David found in Edward and his sons kindred spirits and potential allies: he would return to England at least three times before 1371. (By permission of the British Library)

Plate 9: 'The David de Brus Ransom Chest'. Decorated with the arms of Neville to commemorate the victory of 1346, this box probably held all the papers pertaining to David's ransom payments and attempts to renegotiate the peace c. 1357-71. John of Gaunt's son, Henry IV, would bring it on his invasion of Scotland in 1400. (By permission of the Public Record Office)

Plate 10: The man who should be King. Although eight years older than his royal half-uncle, Robert the Steward would inherit the crown in February 1371 despite the best efforts of David to redirect the succession or sire male heirs of his own. Robert in turn would pass power on to his sons by his first wife, Elizabeth More (shown here) despite their retrospective legitimisation. (From *The Seton Armorial* (1691) by permission of Sir Francis Ogilvy, Bt., and the Trustees of the National Library of Scotland)

Plate 11: The gold standard of a confident king? Scotland's first gold nobles of c. 1360-71 were based on a similar issue of Edward III from the 1350s: the ship represents the Mother church. (Author's collection)

Plates 12 & 13: The centrepiece of Scotland's royal court of Christian chivalry. David built his chapel to St Monan on the east coast of the disputed region of Fife between 1362 and 1371. Monan shared a feast day with St David (1 March): the arms of the crown, Douglas (Archibald of Galloway?) and Sandilands are just visible on the interior ceiling corbels. (Author's collection)

Plate 14: Royal Scotland's intended capital? Begun c. 1368, David surely planned this new Edinburgh tower-house as his main residence in the Forth valley overlooking the realm's chief burgh now booming through wool trade with England. The remains of 'David's Tower', destroyed by siege in 1573 and overbuilt with the half-moon battery, have recently been excavated. (Author's collection)

Plate 15: King's Men. A selection of the arms of David's best-rewarded kindreds of knights and esquires from the 1360s, later illuminated in the *Armorial of Gelre*: Sir Archibald Douglas; the crusading Sir Walter Leslie; Sir Robert Erskine; Alexander Ramsay of Dalhousie (jnr.); Sir Walter Haliburton; Sir Richard Comyn. (Author's tracing after the *Armorial of Gelre*, the Royal Library of Belgium)

grants to north-eastern institutions and lesser men, for example of Perthshire lands for Sir Robert Ramsay, sheriff of Forfarshire (20 August, while David was in Perth); confirmation of rights to Arbroath Abbey; the homages and services of the free tenants of the barony of Dundee given to Alexander Scrymgeour, royal standard bearer and constable of that burgh (10 August, while David was in Dundee); Forfar lands to Andrew Buttergask, kin of the late deputy Chamberlain and justiciar; to Robert Glen, David's brother-in-law, of Kintore forest land; the keepership of the thanage of Boyne in Banffshire and stewardship of the royal household to Sir William de Vaus, another Neville's Cross veteran; and, as aforementioned, favour for Sir Roger Mortimer of Inverbervie.[45]

But David's most effective gains in northern Scotland came in the re-casting of two key royal offices. Firstly, sometime between 16 March and 8 June 1358 – during which period David can be found mostly in Edinburgh, though once each at Dumbarton (3 May) and Arbroath (14 May) – Thomas Stewart, earl of Angus, was removed as Chamberlain, the office given to him by the Steward. He was replaced with Thomas, earl of Mar, now also lord of Garioch.[46] Furthermore, Angus was ordered on two occasions (20 March and 1 July) to enter himself as a hostage to England, both before and after payment of the first instalment of the ransom on mid-summer, 24 June. Angus was noticeably absent as a charter witness at court between January 1357 and March 1360, by which time he was clashing openly with the king and his mistress from Forfarshire, Katherine Mortimer, and had broken his word of parole as an English captive.[47] David's favour to men from north-of-Tay like the Leslies, Mortimers and Lindsay of Glenesk must have deprived Earl Thomas of key followers.

David's second boost – the removal of William, earl of Ross, as justiciar north-of-Forth – came at a parliament at Scone held about the week of 10–18 November 1358, which, again, no full record of proceedings survives.[48] It is likely, though, that the king and his key advisers laid the groundwork for this major change of office during the late summer and early autumn: the parliament may in fact have merely confirmed a decision already enforced. Week-long justice ayres were held in autumn 1358 in Inverness (29

45 *ER*, i, 545, 548, 551, 569; Watt, *Scottish Graduates*, 187–9, 301–3; *Registrum Episcopatus Moraviensis*, no. 153; *ER*, i, 562 and *Rot. Scot.*, i, 828 (de Vaus); *RRS*, vi, nos. 182, 185, 192, 193, 194; *RMS*, i, App. ii, nos. 1152, 1232, 1245, 1262, 1296. For a curious tale about David's interference in the see of Aberdeen see H. Boece, *Murthlacensium et Aberdonensium Episcoporum Vitae* (New Spalding Club, Aberdeen 1894), 22–4, which relates how David originally wanted to impose a Frenchman named Nicholas as bishop.
46 *ER*, i, 565; *RRS*, vi, nos. 177, 188.
47 *Rot. Scot.*, i, 812, 818, 821, 828, 832, 834, 840, 847; *RRS*, vi, nos. 141, 233.
48 *Ibid*, nos. 198–203; *RMS*, i, no. 189.

September-), Aberdeen (8 October-), Inverbervie (15 October-), and Forfar, Clackmannan and Perth (19 October-). The earl of Ross might have been expected to head up these circuit courts. But the November 1357 Scone council had called for the king to attend ayres in person. There are certainly gaps of sufficient duration in David's extant itinerary – between his issue of acts in Edinburgh (8 to 28 June), Dundee (18 August), Perth (20 August), Edinburgh again (31 August and 1 October) – to allow for his role as judge on these ayres.[49]

David would have undeniably wanted to fulfill this judicial role so as to underline the November parliament's official removal of Ross. However, unlike the vague parliamentary upholding of Ross's tenure in this post in June 1344 (when he had been challenged by John Randolph, earl of Moray), in 1358 several embezzlement charges may have been laid openly against the earl, principally his misuse of justice profits and continued interference, as before 1346, in the second teinds of the bishopric of Aberdeen and other church revenues. In fact, time seems to have been carefully spent by the crown in the 1358 parliament reviewing jurisdictions and revenues in the north-east and far north: David would have been well supported in this process by the presence of the likes of the lawyer-bishops of St Andrews and Brechin, Sir John Preston, Sir Robert Lauder (heir of Robert I's justiciar) and several other royalist knights as well as the Steward and the earls of March/Moray and Douglas. Thus the king was able not only to issue guarantees of rights such as Elgin Cathedral's annual-rent from Banffshire lands; he was also able to further punish Ross by appointing Sir Adam Urquhart as hereditary sheriff of Cromarty, after the resignation of this office – presumably in parliament – by the earl and his deputy. On the same day, the king also issued letters to the sheriff and bailies of Inverness and the coroner of Caithness to prohibit visits to Orkney (except for pilgrimages or commerce). This was surely in response to Norwegian complaints about the interference of the earl of Ross and his men in Orkney's offices and revenues.[50] These royal grants would be followed up on 28 February 1359 by David's grant of the entire castle and barony of Urquhart – commanding passage down the Great Glen or west into Ross and on to Skye, originally gifted to the Ross earls by Robert I – to William, earl of Sutherland, and his son, John, 'the king's nephew'. Also on that day, the king confirmed the Inverness-shire lands of one of Ross's feud enemies, the Mackintoshes.[51] In addition, David may have tried to win the favour of

49 *ER*, i, 570, 573, 583, 587–8, 590. For David's ayres in general, see MacQueen, *Common Law and Feudal Society in Medieval Scotland*, *ad indecim*, and the same author's 'Pleadable Brieves and Jurisdiction in Heritage in Later Medieval Scotland' (unpublished Ph.D. thesis, Edinburgh, 1985), 96–7, 98–104.
50 *RRS*, vi, nos. 199–203; Crawford, 'The Earls of Orkney-Caithness', 129–34.
51 *RRS*, vi, nos. 208–9; Mackenzie, *A History of the Mackenzies*, 58.

Ross's placeman and nephew in Orkney, William Sinclair of Rosslyn.[52] That this concerted royal assault was a severe blow to Ross interests was confirmed when, in April 1359, the justice profits for the autumn 1358 ayres were entered to the exchequer by the deputy of Sir William Meldrum as sheriff of Aberdeen (himself a former deputy of Ross): this audit recorded Earl William's denial that he had tried to block this intromission but also stated as fact Earl William's collection 'without cause' of revenue from the Caithness lands of his niece and ward, Isabella, daughter of Malise, the late forfeited earl of Strathearn, and Sinclair's wife.[53]

The earls of Angus and Ross, then, were the first direct victims of David's tentative revival of royal power within a year of his homecoming. However, these magnates arguably represented the weakest, slightest targets to be done down among the greater nobles who had profited from the king's captivity. Whilst he isolated and marginalised these men, David still had to tolerate the continued regional influence of Robert Steward, Patrick, earl of March/Moray, and William, earl of Douglas, in central and southern Scotland. It is surely the case, however, that David saw the short-term value – really the unavoidable necessity – of leaning upon the support of powerful nobles like March/Moray and Douglas. After all, their affinities among the chivalry of the Lothians, the south-east and the Marches of Scotland overlapped closely with much of the king's own natural following from 1341–6. Just as James I would later build up his own power base in 1424–5 by co-operation with Douglas adherents, so David may have made use of Earl Patrick's and Earl William's presence and strongholds and men like William Ramsay, earl of Fife, William Livingston, Walter Haliburton, William de Vaus and John Preston, knights to whom March and Douglas had given lordship in the king's absence.[54]

David may also have hoped that recently improved relations with Earl Patrick would bring advantages. March had – like Douglas – certainly co-operated in the ransom deal of 1356–7, becoming particularly close to his cousin, Queen Joan, despite the premature death of his son and heir, John, who had been offered as a hostage to England in exchange for the king in 1351. Indeed, it was the earl of March who delivered the first instalment of the ransom at Berwick to Edward III's grateful representatives on time in June 1358.[55] David had also offered patronage to many March and Moray men before 1346, including Patrick's remaining heirs, the sons of crusader Sir Patrick Dunbar (d. 1357). The king must have expected this to bear fruit quite soon when the aged earl (born *c.* 1283) died.

52 *RRS*, vi, no. 173.
53 *ER*, i, 543, 546, 558.
54 Brown, *Black Douglases*, 219–22.
55 *Rot. Scot.*, i, 768, 809, 817, 827.

The earl of Douglas, however – just like the knight of Liddesdale before him – seems to have had a much more active role to play in such a cautious divide-and-rule approach by the king. David may have hoped to rekindle some of the potentially profitable and amicable relations between the crown and Douglas hinted at about 1349–51, when William served as a joint Lieutenant seeking David's release, and in 1354, when the king seemed to acquiesce in the destruction of the knight of Liddesdale. David's grants to Earl William after his return could be viewed as his making good on promises of good lordship made in the course of the tortured pursuit of his release before 1357. The king was certainly in need of a potent great magnate for a partner in government to fill the void left by the death of John Randolph of Moray and Annandale. David and the Douglas earl may have felt naturally bound by the shared history of their great ancestors, Robert I and the 'Good' Sir James (symbolised by the Douglas arms bearing the blood-red Bruce heart), as well as more recently tied by the Mar-Douglas marriage and a mutual interest in chivalric works. Besides, Douglas's occupation of Edinburgh Castle, many other southern castles and lordships, the justiciarship south-of-Forth and March wardenships gave him massive influence over all-important relations with England. Douglas's intimate involvement in politics through these offices is surely reflected in the great amount of time both men spent in each other's company at Edinburgh.

In this context, David's surprising issue of a grant (now lost) to Earl William sometime in 1358 of the Perthshire barony of Strathord – east of Atholl and a former possession of earl Duncan of Fife but plundered by the Steward and earl of Angus since 1346 – might be viewed as an attempt to use Douglas in the same way as Liddesdale had been granted the earldom of Atholl to counter the Steward in 1342. Over the next few years, David's gift to William of exemptions from heavy customs levied on his wool exports must also be taken as a sign of the king trying to keep the earl onside.[56] Douglas – who owned lands in southern Fife – may also have co-operated happily and profited in the transfer of Fife to William Ramsay, a knight in his retinue at Poitiers.

But beyond this conveyancing there was surely more scope for tension than amity between the king and the leading border lord. For Douglas, above all, had profited from his wartime role against England either on the Marches or in the continental service of the French. On a number of occasions throughout 1358–9, David would have cause to issue letters patent ordering the justiciar south-of-Forth, Douglas, to stop interfering in the regality lands and revenues of the key wool-producing Abbey of Melrose, property which bordered on Earl William's own regality: the

---

56 *RMS*, i, App. ii, nos. 1177–8, 1222–3; *ER*, i, 567, 569 and ii, 90, 132.

king also granted several confirmations and extensions of the holdings of this house where his father's heart was buried, expressly because it was necessary at that time for Melrose to be in Edward III's peace. But Douglas's direct aggression towards England had not even ceased with the treaty of Berwick. A number of Douglas retainers were captured in skirmishes with English wardens and their troops throughout 1357–8. Then, about mid-June 1358 – just as the first ransom instalment was delivered – Douglas and his men overran the English garrison in the formidable castle of Hermitage in Roxburghshire, a stronghold of the slain knight of Liddesdale.[57]

Remarkably, this breach of the truce occurred just days after Douglas had been named in English papers as a hostage to enter English captivity in pledge for David's ransom along with the Steward and the earls of March and Ross.[58] Admittedly, the issue of a safe-conduct for this exchange may have been a simple English precaution in case the Scots failed to meet their first payment deadline and the treaty of Berwick's default clauses had to be invoked. But it is highly unlikely that any attempt by David to arrange the exile of such major Scottish hostages to Edward III's custody to suit his political ends worked on this occasion: the 10,000 merks was paid on the dot and none of these four magnates seems to have been absent as a hostage in summer 1358. Instead, David had to content himself with sending Earl Thomas of Angus (on several occasions throughout that year) and Thomas Murray of Bothwell (after 8 May 1358, possibly in exchange for Sir Hugh Ross of Philorth) as his most valuable collateral prisoners. Nevertheless, the king may have been able to do so whilst at the same time recovering up to half of the original twenty lesser noble hostages, many of whom were the sons and heirs of steadfast crown supporters. Only a few fragments of evidence of the captivity of these less significant prisoners in the custody of the English crown or lords can be found after late 1358. Although the 1350–7 peace talks had resolved that one hostage should be exchanged for every ransom instalment, by spring 1359, as we shall see, only ten Scots apparently remained in England in this role. The despatch of four or five far more valuable hostages by David may have secured the release of the lesser sons and heirs of noble lines loyal to the crown. Their early liberty and thus some unofficial modification of the treaty terms might be taken to indicate that David and Edward III were already keen to come to some new under-

57 *RRS*, vi, no. 219; *Rot. Scot.*, i, 817, 819, 826; *CDS*, iv, no. 18. The Melrose regality may not only have involved the Abbey's lands in the Marches and Dumfriesshire but also lands acquired by that house in Kyle Stewart bordering on Douglas itself; many thanks to Richard Oram for this point.
58 *Rot. Scot.*, i, 826.

standing about the ransom and to conclude the period of truce swiftly in favour of a firm peace.[59]

However, David continued to be denied much of his will as regards some key hostages. Again according to English documentation, the Steward was supposed to enter himself as a hostage in exchange for his son and heir, John Stewart of Kyle, after 24 June 1358 but seems instead to have briefly sent his third son, Robert. John Stewart was still awaiting exchange from captivity in June 1360: as the most valuable prisoner he should have been released first and his retention in the ward of the Percies may have allowed David to liberate additional lesser captives. Yet, more importantly, under the terms of the original 1357 treaty, the king was also obliged to enter his favourite nephew (and later-rumoured alternative heir), John Sutherland, as a hostage: although John was replaced as a captive by his own father for a time after June 1358 (and both Sutherlands were helped regularly with their English expenses by David), the youth would in fact die in England sometime in 1361.[60]

Nonetheless, despite these bubbling crown-magnate tensions, the remaining evidence for the events of the winter of 1358–9 suggests that the earls of Douglas and March/Moray were still to be included in David's allied domestic and diplomatic plans. For by late autumn 1358 it was apparent that David was anxious to build on his relative success in determining the fate of Fife and several key offices and to pursue a plan which, at a stroke, might solve his fiscal and foreign policy burden, break a large part of Stewart power and smooth over the absence of Queen Joan: namely, the revival of the younger son succession-peace plan with Edward III, first proposed about 1350–2.

59 *Ibid*, 831, 837, 838, 847, 849; AN J677 nos. 7, 8. In November 1358 Thomas Fleming, Reginald More, Gilbert Kennedy, John Barclay, David Wemyss and John Valence were in the custody of the sheriff of Northumberland and perhaps due for release (*Rot. Scot.*, i, 831). The likelihood that Malcolm Fleming, earl of Wigtown, died sometime *c.*1357–8, in theory elevating his captive heir in England, Thomas, to the rank of earl (although David recovered Wigtown) and thus more valuable, may have allowed more lesser hostages to be released. After 1358 the only hostages mentioned in extant English records (apart from John Stewart of Kyle, Thomas Murray and the earl of Angus) are Thomas Hay (June 1363, *CDS*, iv, no. 81), John Gray (May 1362, *CCR 1360–4*, 330) and perhaps William Bissett (*Rot. Scot.*, i, 877); Thomas Erskine (warded under John de Coupland) was home by 1366, probably much sooner (*Ibid*, 905). *Chron. Wyntoun*, vi, 249 notes that in 1361 only Murray and John Sutherland remained as hostages.
60 *Rot. Scot.*, i, 826, 828, 831, 837, 838, 849; *Chron. Bower*, vii, 323; *ER*, ii, 49, 78, 113, 166; Fraser ed., *The Sutherland Book*, i, 31. David may also have paid the expenses of the sons of David Graham and John Danielston (*ER*, ii, 116–7). Most of the fathers and families of those hostages whose release is completely unaccounted for – Cunningham, Stewart of Darnley, Livingston, Somerville, Danielston, Kirkpatrick, Hay of Locherwood, Gray – had been or would be well favoured by the crown.

Royal Finance, 1358–9

In fact David may have quite quickly given notice that he would revive his pursuit of this diplomatic panacea in person. After successfully paying the first 10,000-merk instalment of the ransom in June 1358, David sought formal talks with England. On 14 July 1358, indeed, he secured a safe-conduct for himself and a large retinue to travel south. He did not leave immediately, however, and may in part have thought to delay his departure until he was sure of the upper hand and sufficient support within the Scottish political community for what he intended. In the meantime a delegation including the bishops of St Andrews and Brechin and, significantly, the earls of Douglas and March, was granted passage south on 26 October 1358 on 'the business of David de Brus'; the outcome of this embassy, if it went, is not recorded, although it may have laid the all-important groundwork for what followed. However, David must also have delayed his own journey to England until about Christmas 1358 – and sought such intermediate talks – until he was sure of the precarious state of his own finances.[61]

It must have been painfully apparent perhaps even long before the last quarter of 1358 that crown income for the next fiscal year was bound to fall massively short of the 10,000 merks required by 24 June 1359 and would never leave any surplus to pay for the king's household and government. A standard test for strong Scottish kingship is how much regular income a king could raise without protest from his subjects. Some historians – Nicholson and Wesbter especially – have emphasised the impressively 'intensive government' of David's second reign: his ability to raise almost annual taxation and attend to justice with the help of an increasingly bureaucratic administration in which civil servants' pay was regularised and written judicial processes and precedents, underpinning annual councils and parliaments involving enlightened committee work, became the norm.[62] Yet if this apparently smooth, well-financed crown machine did have a period of dominance, it lay far off in the late 1360s. In 1358–9, David's regime clearly struggled to take in monies from the obvious sources highlighted at the November 1357 council and was predictably weak in regions of great magnate influence.

That this was so is revealed by an exchequer audit held in Dundee in April 1359 at the same time as a council in the burgh at what we will see must have been a moment of serious crisis and confrontation for the king.[63] This book-keeping exercise shows that the Chamberlain's individual account intro-

61 *Rot. Scot.*, i, 828, 835.
62 Nicholson, *Scotland – the Later Middle Ages*, ch. 7; Webster, 'David II and the Government of Fourteenth-century Scotland', 122–30; Duncan, 'The Laws of Malcolm MacKenneth', 244–53.
63 *ER*, i, 545–625.

mitted just £279 for the preceding twelve months. This was a huge drop from the £2,529 of the last recorded pre-Neville's Cross Chamberlain's account of 1341–2 and even a slip below the only account returned from Thomas, earl of Angus's term of office, a sum of £361 rendered by his deputy, Norman Leslie, for the period September 1357 to March 1358.[64] Only a portion of this fiscal collapse can surely be explained by wartime damage. Far more of the crown's regular income must still have been in the hands of nobles who had occupied royal demesne lands between 1346 and 1357 and whom David had been unable to dislodge using his Revocation statute. The 1359 audit in fact records many lands and revenues 'in the hands of' named laymen by concession of 'the Regent', i.e. Robert Steward: for example, the earl of Ross, the earl of Angus (who still held Strathord barony in Perthshire), Sir John Danielston (keeper of Dumbarton and sheriff of Perth), Robert Erskine and Hugh Eglintoun (the Steward's future brother-in-law).[65] It should be noted, though, that far more royal demesne was still in the hands of obvious royalists 'by permission of the king notwithstanding the Revocation', including men like William, earl of Sutherland, Sir John Preston, the earl of Mar, and his men Walter Moigne and Lawrence Gilliebrand, Robert Bruce of Clackmannan, Sir William Keith the Marischal and now sheriff of Kincardineshire, William Livingston, John Herries, John Gray and even Queen Joan (although there is no evidence in this period that David paid her the 2,000 merks a year she was due as her marriage terce).[66] David was clearly reluctant to revoke a valuable source of lordship to his key supporters, several of whom had provided hostages.

However, greater problems were apparent in the April 1359 sheriff's accounts. Understandably, no accounts were intromitted from those shires still affected by English assault or occupation, namely Wigtown, Dumfries, Selkirk, Roxburgh and Berwick. But the majority of those shires which did submit monies made no attempt to account for revenue between Martinmas 1357 and Easter 1358: only Aberdeen and Clackmannan gave scrappy figures as far back as 1348, Fife to 1353 and Perth and Kinross to 1355.[67] But there were grave problems for Perthshire's accounts for 1357–9. The sheriff of this great shire – embracing much of

---

64 *Ibid*, 499–514, and ii, 1–3.

65 *Ibid*, i, 543, 555, 558, 570–2, 582, 586 (Angus in control of the thanage of Newdosk in Kincardineshire), 588, 618 (John Danielston in control of Perth mills; the Steward in control of Perth fishings).

66 *Ibid*, 543 (Keith – Kelly), 545 (Sutherland – Formartine/Kintore), 551 (Herries – half of the thanage of Aberdeen), 572 (William Livingston – Haddington fermes; Robert Bruce), 574, 585–6 (Gilliebrand – Little Morphie, Kincardineshire; Keith – Ardbaddy; Sutherland – Aberluthnot & Kincardine; David Fleming – Great Morphie), 588–9; see also Grant, 'Thanes and Thanages'.

67 *ER*, i, 542–93.

Atholl, Strathearn and Menteith – was the Steward retainer, John Daniel-ston. In 1358–9 he (and his deputy Henry Fotheringham) had been 'deforced' of money on their Perth ayre on at least three occasions: once by an unnamed Atholl man, once by Hugh Ross, brother of the earl of Ross and another deputy sheriff of Perth by 1361 (who had also 'for-gotten' to pay rent on some lands), and once by Robert Steward himself. To be fair, men of the new Chamberlain, Thomas, earl of Mar, had also plundered Perthshire land to the tune of £22. But it seems reasonable to assume that in reality Danielston's recorded problems were a cover for disbursement of income permitted by the Steward as Lieutenant and earl of Atholl and Strathearn (and thus the dominant force in Perth where he even controlled the fishing rights) to men like his brother-in-law, Ross, and Thomas, earl of Angus. Danielston had also received royal lands at the Steward's concession as Lieutenant, including the mills of Perth burgh, Tillicoultry in Clackmannanshire and the Lanarkshire barony of Cadzow, which last Robert I had given to Walter Fitzgilbert, whose son, David, must thus have been ousted by Danielston: the crown would not re-confirm Fitzwalter in possession there until December 1368. But Daniel-ston had also, of course, replaced the royalist Flemings of Biggar as keepers of Dumbarton and sheriff of Dumbartonshire about 1346–7: Danielston's account for the latter shire was also incomplete in April 1359.[68]

The absence of royal controls in such shires was echoed elsewhere in the April 1359 accounts. Peeblesshire – where the earl of Douglas was sheriff – yielded only £16 while a further £13 went to the earl. An inquiry was ordered as to why the profits of a justice ayre held by Douglas in Peebles burgh sometime in 1358 had not been intromitted: in total, Douglas's ayres at Peebles and Lanark in 1358 had only earned 40/- for the crown. Similarly, no sheriff's account was entered from Edinburgh where Douglas was predominant and the earl controlled the king's meadow near the burgh – presumably with large sheep flocks grazing upon it; admittedly, though, such a delay may have reflected the lasting damage inflicted by Edward III in 1356.[69] Fife, more surprisingly, also failed to enter its justice profits despite at least two ayres at Cupar in 1357 and perhaps others in 1358: this was

---

68 *Ibid*, 508, 535, 558, 572, 574, 582, 592, 618; *RRS*, v, nos. 50–51, 54 and *RRS* vi, no. 418. David did, though, restore Fitzwalter's control of Cadzow church in 1362 and grant him a 53/- annuity from Tannadice thanage (*ibid*, nos. 271, 443; *ER*, ii, 118).

69 *Ibid*, i, 547, 559–, 567, 569, 626–. As Brown, *Black Douglases*, 55–6, points out, in 1360, John Allincrum as a burgess of Edinburgh and deputy sheriff of Peebles founded a mass at St Giles church in Edinburgh in the names of the king and Douglas earl, illustrating the earl's continued influence there and his shared affinity with the crown.

possibly due to unrecorded difficulties for William Ramsay and the crown in throwing off Steward influence in this region.[70] The one justice ayre which does seem to have returned a decent profit was held at Inverbervie in Angus where David might have fully expected to control events, having undermined Earl Thomas of Angus, patronised a number of men from this shire (including the Ramsay sheriff of Forfar) and taken a mistress from its native kindred. David's presence at ayres after the dismissal of the earl of Ross as justiciar north-of-Forth must also have helped yield the respectable sum of £162 from a Perth ayre in October 1358.[71] Yet it could still be argued that greater sums might have been expected from the backlog of cases from 1346–57. Moreover, fiscal problems continued further north. As we have seen, Earl William of Ross persisted in interfering in judicial revenues in 1358–9: the Aberdeen justiciar court returns were 'not intromitted'. The first Aberdeenshire sheriff's account of April 1359 (dating back to 1348) was rejected as being too small and over £370 in the red: a second intromission (of a further £145) overseen by the earl of Mar was accepted.[72] Mar, indeed, seems to have been able to head up a growing royalist party in the north-east.[73]

But what was perhaps most worrying for the crown about such magnate interference in royal income was the blatant denial of David's authority in key royal burghs, the market centres which would always provide the bulk of income for the ransom and serve as counting centres for locality revenues. The April 1359 returns of burgh fermes and customs further betrayed royal vulnerability. They did total some £2,500 and included extra monies after the estates had again raised the general customs rate sometime in 1358. Yet only £700 (over 1,000 merks) could be set aside for the ransom. Moreover, the audit recorded such diversion of monies as the Steward's control of the valuable fermes of Perth (worth £49 in 1362) and the castle wards of Kilbride; or Thomas, earl of Angus's stubborn lease of the fermes of Crail in Fife (worth about £52) and of Stirling (worth £70 in 1364), a great royal seat from which David was conspicuously absent throughout 1357–8 amidst what was a noticeably limited Lowland royal itinerary. According to the auditors, David had even been forced to withhold repayment of a £21 loan extended to him by the Steward through the bailies of Perth.[74]

70 *ER*, i, 501–3.
71 *Ibid*, 559, 587–8.
72 *Ibid*, 545–8 (including £54 used by the Steward for the 'freedom' of Thomas Murray of Bothwell, probably before 1357), 551–3.
73 E.g. in November 1358 David confirmed a charter by Thomas, earl of Mar, to a canon of Aberdeen which had originally been witnessed by the bishop of Aberdeen, Sir William Keith the Marishcal, Walter Moigne, Lawrence Gilliebrand, John Strathachin and William Liddale, the sheriff of Aberdeen (*RMS*, i, App. i, no. 128).
74 *ER*, i, 594–625; 582, 618–9 (Steward); 622–4 (Angus).

As if all this was not bad enough for the king, there was little or no sign as yet of further badly needed income coming from extraordinary sources. By 20 September 1358 at the latest, David had received word that a request he had despatched to Pope Innocent VI to be allowed to collect a tenth of all ecclesiastical revenues for the next three years to help pay the ransom had been declined (in June). His messengers on this errand seem to have been Scottish Augustinian friars (the order he had used for diplomacy in the 1330s), including perhaps Walter Wardlaw, canon of Aberdeen (and a future papal collector) and David de Mar, treasurer of Moray, papal chaplain and a precentor during the king's final ransom talks.[75] The Pope's rejection might in part have been provoked by David putting out feelers about annulling his marriage to Queen Joan. The Curia's refusal came despite the apparent wide backing David had from key Scottish prelates and the approval of the estates in council – presumably in November 1357 or the first three months of 1358 – which would have been necessary for such an approach; it is surely the case that the majority of the Scottish lay political community must have desired this contribution from the wealthiest estate to ease their burden.

However, the great gaps in the estates' records may also mask problems in the assessment of taxable lands, rents, goods and tenants ordered by the first general council after David's return. The deforcement and embezzlement of royal revenues recorded by the April 1359 audit might have easily been combined with non-cooperation by laymen hampering royal inquisitors in the localities (and any clerk seeking voluntary contributions from indivdual magnates). If the full assessment had been completed – and had its record survived – it would have formed a remarkable snapshot of Scottish society, right down to the names of craftsmen throughout the realm (except, of course, in the lordship of the Isles where, according to the treaty of Berwick, no tax was to be levied for the king's ransom). But the low and regionally uneven returns from the taxes and ordinary levies in the end raised in 1358–9 suggest that the original assessment process was itself fragmentary. Enough may have been done in the first year for the November 1358 parliament at Scone to assent to a contribution of between 3d and 6d in the £ (the final statutes, of course, do not survive). But the assessors were not due to report their findings to the king until January 1359 in Perth (suggesting the royal intention to hold a meeting of the estates there or at Scone). It is thus more likely that it was the council which in the end met alongside the exchequer audit at Dundee in April 1359 which finally authorised this

---

75 *Foedera*, iii, 396, 407; *CDS*, iv, no. 17 – a notarial instrument by the Edinburgh Friars Preachers confirming the papal ruling witnessed by Wardlaw, Mar, several other clerics and David II's half-brother-in-law, Thomas Isaac, Sir William Meldrum and Alexander Scrymgeour (*CPR*, iii, 595, 619).

taxation; a second or third levy must then have been ordered at the next full parliament at Scone in October 1359; the next assembly after that was a council at Perth in April 1360.[76] However, it was not until the audit of May 1360 that the first monies from these three levies began to drift erratically into the king's coffers, logically just over a year after the first exaction.

By then it would have become obvious to the political community that David was badly underfunded, intended to stop paying the ransom, seek a deal with England and to keep what income he had received for other purposes. But even in 1358 and into early 1359 such biting taxation – with only the precedent of Robert I's lifetime tenth of 1326–9 and his three-year levy of another tenth to pay reparations to England (1328–31) – must have been deeply unfamiliar and unpopular to many subjects. As much is again suggested by the curious fate of Patrick, earl of March, who had taken the first ransom instalment to Berwick in 1358 and may have served as an assessor or collector for the crown in the marches: sometime in 1358 he was 'captured' but, presumably, soon released by a James Lindsay, possibly the same knight (associated with either the Steward or Douglas) who had recently slain Sir Roger Kirkpatrick, sheriff of Ayr, who would also have been a tax collector; by mid-1362, John Allincrum, the Edinburgh burgess, royal clerk, exchequer auditor and Douglas's deputy-sheriff of Peeblesshire would also have been killed.[77]

However, the natural dislike of his subjects for taxation and taxmen aside, David's fiscal problems – and the tensions noted by the April 1359 audit – must have been intensified by his actions throughout the winter of 1358 and into spring 1359, actions which were themselves prompted in part by his regime's struggle to raise income. Mid-December 1358 saw David still in Edinburgh. The king and Roger Hogg, a leading Edinburgh merchant and frequent trader with England after 1357, gifted lands to the altar of St Katherine of Alexandria, a crusading favourite, in the burgh church of St Giles; the king also confirmed a minor baronial grant of lands in Fife. On both occasions his seal was appended before those of the bishops of St Andrews and Brechin (the Chancellor), Robert Steward, William, earl of Douglas, Sir Robert Erskine, John Preston and David Annan. But sometime thereafter David took the road for London.[78]

---

76 *ER*, ii, 5, 48 (1st contribution), 47, 49 (2nd), 34, 73–5 (3rd).
77 *Ibid*, i, 558 (Lindsay); ii, 73, 108 (Allincrum). March was absent as a crown charter witness between 17 November 1358 and 20 November 1360 (*RRS*, vi, nos. 201, 249).
78 *Ibid*, nos. 204–6; F. McGurk ed., *CPL to Benedict VIII of Avignon, 1394–1419*, ed. F. McGurk (Scottish History Society, Edinburgh 1976), 300; *Rot. Scot.*, i, *ad indecim*; Ewan, *Townlife in Fourteenth-century Scotland*, 121–7, 152–8.

The King's Plans Checked, 1359

Little is recorded of David's return to England's chief city after just over a year of freedom. It is possible he chose to arrive in time for the feast day of St Thomas à Beckett (29 December). He seems to have been accompanied by a select group headed at least by Thomas, earl of Mar – who demitted his Chamberlain's duties to Walter of Biggar, a clerk of the Wardrobe – Sir Robert Erskine, Sir John Preston and Sir Hugh Eglintoun. However, that the royal party spent £666 on what must have been no more than a seven- or eight-week trip (perhaps much less) suggests that David brought south a sizeable retinue for show on what he considered a vital mission. Throughout their stay, the Scots seem to have resided with the Friars Preachers of London.[79]

The ostensible and perhaps primary aim of the visit was to secure permission from Edward III and his council for a delay in the payment of the second instalment of the ransom. David's troubled finances made this inevitable. In doing so he sought the intercession of his exiled queen, Joan, in persuading her brother of the Scots' sincerity: the couple's relations, then, had perhaps not broken down irrevocably. Thus it was that on 12 February 1359 Edward granted David ('his very dear brother') a six-month payment extension until December 1359. It is likely that after these letters were issued, David set out almost immediately on his return journey, leaving the earl of Mar and the aforementioned household knights to ratify the agreement on 21 February.[80] But the king's haste north was not due to his relief at Edward's concession. Rather, it was surely precipitated by David's agenda resulting from secret talks also held in London with Edward and his closest kin and advisers.

If this was so, it is possible that David had intended to act on this private plan, and not the ransom delay, all along. For he may also have rushed back to Scotland to make a deadline he himself had set, a parliament called before his departure. This can be inferred from his stopping first upon his return by 28 February not at Edinburgh but at Scone, the logical venue for such a vital assembly of the estates (and a venue suggested by the 1358 parliament's original decision that tax inquisitors should report their findings at nearby Perth). At Scone David was attended by northerners who were not to be found frequently at court but who might have travelled south for an assembly of the estates. Moreover, the first of the king's extant acts issued on this day was the aforementioned controversial grant of the castle and barony of Urquhart to his former brother-in-law, William, earl of Sutherland, and his son, John. Not only did this act further undermine the

---

79 *Rot. Scot.*, i, 817, 822–3, 828; *ER*, ii, 48.
80 *Rot. Scot.*, i, 835; *CDS*, iv, no. 27; *RRS*, vi, no. 207.

recalcitrant earl of Ross but in the light of the events of the next few weeks it might also be interpreted as a form of compensation to a family which had for a time been prominent in David's plans for the Bruce succession but now served as key hostages.[81]

However, if David had intended a parliament, it never took place: no witness lists for the king's grants at Scone survive, making it difficult to tell who else had gathered. Perhaps some of the great magnates had been made aware of David's intentions even before he left for England and their suspicions had been confirmed in January and early February. The Steward would have felt undeniably angered and provoked and, as we shall see, David's plans when fully revealed may even have been enough to turn the earls of Douglas and March/Moray away from their recent participation in Anglo-Scottish talks. In this context, a planned Scone parliament may have been boycotted or have flown apart in disagreement before it opened session. This meant that David was obliged to withdraw from Scone, perhaps spending his thirty-fifth birthday with Katherine Mortimer in Fife or at Inverbervie and returning to Edinburgh by 15 March. There he granted the barony of Terregles in Dumfriesshire, after its resignation by Thomas, earl of Mar, to John Herries, a former follower of Alexander Ramsay of Dalhousie and then the lord of Douglas at Poitiers, but an esquire who would be well rewarded by the crown after 1360 and accompany David on future embassies to London. Herries' gift was an act witnessed by a fairly full daily council of the bishops of St Andrews and Brechin, the Steward, the earl of Douglas, Erskine, Eglintoun, Preston, Archibald Douglas and William Liddale, sheriff of Aberdeen.[82] But it was not until 5 April 1359 that David was able to confront the wider community at a council at Dundee where that strained exchequer audit, discussed above, was also held (at the scene of the crown's initial humiliation by the Steward in another assembly in 1351).

Such a delay would have allowed both camps to prepare, and in the end the opposition to David's diplomatic plans may have been so great that the king's remarkable opening gambit at Dundee must have been a dead letter within a matter of moments. For it was on the first day of this council that David issued the seemingly bizarre grant of the earldom of Moray to the great English Garter knight, Henry de Grosmont, 'Duke of Lancaster, earl of Derby and Lincoln, lord of Bergerac [in Gascony] and Steward of England', failing whom to his two heiress daughters and their

---

81 *Ibid*, nos. 208–9; Fraser ed., *The Sutherland Book*, iii, 17.
82 *RRS*, vi, nos. 210, 373; *RMS*, i, nos. 192, 282, 346; *Rot. Scot.*, i, 840, 931–3; *Chron. Fordun*, i, 377.

heirs, to be held 'as freely as by Thomas Randolph': this was witnessed by
the bishops of St Andrews and Brechin, the Steward, Douglas, William
Livingston and Robert Erskine.[83]

The logic behind this seeming bolt from the blue was that David knew
surely from his recent talks in London that Edward III's third son, John
of Gaunt, earl of Richmond, was about to wed Lancaster's second
daughter, Blanche. Of course Gaunt, by 1359 aged nineteen, was the
prince whom seven years earlier David had already tried and failed to
persuade the Scottish parliament to accept as heir presumptive to the
throne in the event of his death without a Bruce son. By now Prince John
(again that Christian name!) had grown to be just the kind of vigorous,
chivalrous knight whom David liked to employ: he had distinguished
himself well in his father's French campaign in 1355, just as he would in
the tournament to celebrate his eventual marriage in May 1359 and upon
his return to fight in France in October 1359.[84] As such, Gaunt was
shaping up to be every bit as impressive a knight as his prospective
father-in-law, Henry of Lancaster, England's premier general. David II
would have met Lancaster at Garter tournaments in 1349 and 1357 and
possibly through the duke's loyal servant, William Trussell, who had
been David's keeper at Odiham *c.* 1354–7. David cannot have failed to
be impressed by Lancaster's Europe-wide fame as a committed crusader
to Prussia and Holy Land: David may even have had the opportunity to
read the devotional treatise penned recently by Lancaster himself. Prior
Wyntoun's source – describing the Anglo-Scottish skirmishes and jousts
of the 1330s and 1340s – would certainly eulogise the duke as 'ay worthi,
wycht and wysse,/And mast ranownyt of bownte,/Off gentrice and of
honeste,/That in til Inglande liffand was': this good press perhaps
reflected the Bruce regime's attempts to play up the value of any
Lancastrian link.[85]

From Edward III's point of view the revival of a succession deal
embracing the Lancaster-Gaunt connection and David II would make
potentially profitable and really quite conventional provision for one of
his many sons, deploying him as a provincial leader of a growing
Plantagenet empire and securing a peaceful northern border and more
men (the Scots host) for war service. Edward might also have been

---

83 *RRS*, vi, no. 211; *CDS*, iv, no. 9.
84 Goodman, *John of Gaunt*, 12–43.
85 K. Fowler, *The King's Lieutenant: Henry of Grosmont, first Duke of Lancaster, 1310–61* (London 1969), 46–7, 186; E.J. Arnould ed., *Le Livre de Seyntz Medicines: the unpublished devotional treatise of Henry of Lancaster* (Oxford, Anglo-Norman Texts II, 1940), 157; *Chron. Scalacronica* (Stevenson-Leland), 312–4; *Chron. Wyntoun*, vi, 100–3; Barnie, *War in Medieval Society*, 59–65.

cheered by the apparent split between David and Queen Joan: she remained in London precluding the threat of a future Bruce son to dissolve the deal and let the Scots king off without even a ransom. Joan herself may have been happy to seek some compensation for the fact that her own issue would never rule Scotland but her nephew's might: Sir Thomas Gray certainly insists that in 1359 Joan 'came . . . to Windsor to confer with her brother the king, and to propose by negotiation a larger treaty'. In much the same way, Edward III and David may also have been privy to plans afoot to disinherit Lancaster's eldest daughter, Matilda, and her husband, William, the count of Holland (whom Edward may have felt untrustworthy as an ally in war), thus making way for Gaunt to take up the massive Lancaster regality (granted palatinate status in 1351) through Blanche: indeed, when Matilda died in 1362 there were rumours that she had been poisoned to this end. Similarly, it was murmured that when Gaunt and Blanche wed in May 1359, the tomb of Thomas, earl of Lancaster (d. 1322) – that great rebel against Edward II – had poured blood in anger.[86]

If it is accepted, then, that David's grant of the former Randolph earldom and regality of Moray to Henry of Lancaster was a prelude to the revival of talks about admitting Gaunt to the Scottish succession, it could be argued that getting England's royal family, leading general and council on board for this gamble was relatively easy. But it would be a far harder task to persuade a majority of the Scottish community to accept Gaunt's entry into their ranks, through the backdoor as it were, as heir to Moray, in anticipation of his re-introduction as a potential royal heir presumptive to trade off against the ransom.

To do so first of all required the forfeiture of Patrick Dunbar, earl of March/Moray. Admittedly, Patrick was related within four degrees to the Lancaster line, had co-operated with David and his regime c. 1356–8 over the ransom, and had a long record of joining the English when it suited him (for example c. 1296–1314 or 1332–5). David may also have been responsible for Dunbar's liberation after his 'capture' by James Lindsay sometime c. 1358–9. But David would surely have had to offer the extra inducements of future compensatory patronage in Scotland for Patrick and his heirs – perhaps the defunct title of Buchan – as well as the possibility of the Dunbars recovering

---

86 *Chron. Scalacronica*, 128; Goodman, *John of Gaunt*, 247–8, 356–60; W. Ormrod, 'Edward III and his Family', *Journal of British Studies*, 26 (1987), 407–18. The possibility that David was happy to risk the Count of Holland's succession to the Moray earldom should not be ruled out: David's great-grandfather had contemplated a division of the royal succession with the house of Holland in 1291–2 (Barrow, *Bruce*, 43–9). Besides, on Henry de Grosmont's death his lands would have been divided legally between his daughters and their spouses with Gaunt perhaps thus receiving the Scottish half.

lands in Berwickshire and in northern England. The latter was a distinct possibility. If David was able to push through his plans to their logical conclusion, a full peace with England might be secured which included the terms first mooted between 1350 and 1352, namely a restoration of the Disinherited and their descendants to lands on either side of the border and a military alliance with England.[87]

That the return of the Disinherited was an issue which must have been raised again when David was in London in winter 1358–9 is suggested by the fact that the Lancastrian claim to the earldom of Moray rested tenuously on Henry de Grosmont's marriage to Isabella, daughter of Henry de Beaumont (d. 1340), Edward Balliol's chief campaigner from 1332–7 and the dispossessed heir to the earldoms of Buchan and Moray by virtue of his marriage to Alice Comyn, niece and co-heiress of John Comyn, earl of Buchan (d. 1310): significantly, it had been the Beaumonts' claim to be restored which Edward III had insisted between 1329 and 1332 that Robert I and the Scots had already agreed to facilitate under the terms of the treaty of Anglo-Scottish peace of 1328.[88] At the same time, in 1359 the likelihood that some form of Anglo-Scottish military alliance would be deployed by David to cement any deal seems to be confirmed by the actions of Thomas, earl of Mar. On 24 February 1359, Thomas, David's cousin and heir presumptive after the Steward and his sons (and recently appointed Chamberlain), revived the close Anglophile association of his father, Donald (d. 1332), and of his own youth by becoming a liege man of Edward III and promising to fight for him in France: in return the English king would pay him 600 merks a year until such time as Mar – who had recently annulled his issueless marriage – might find a suitable bride. In this role, Mar – whose affinity overlapped closely with part of David's own – might be the vanguard of a Scottish contingent in English service once the deal was done: again, highly militarised lords like William, earl of Douglas (Mar's brother-in-law), and many of David's chivalric cadre – who had promised not to fight *against* England – might be attracted to such potentially lucrative service. On 1 May 1359 David inspected a charter by Earl Thomas to Thomas Hill, a valet of both David II (who visited him in England *c.* 1350) and Queen Joan (whom Hill visited in 1359) and a future crusader and envoy to England in 1363 and 1369: in August 1359 Mar and a hundred men

---

87 *Scots Peerage*, iii, 259–64; see ch. 5 above for 1350–2.
88 CDS, iii, nos. 1013, 1024 (Edward III's demand that Patrick, earl of March, restore Upsetlington in Berwickshire to the priory of Durham), 1056–7; Young, *The Comyns*, xi; Nicholson, *Edward III and the Scots*, 70–8. Beaumont had styled himself earl of Moray and constable of Scotland in 1334 (*ibid*, 160).

would be granted passage through England to return to Scotland from the continent.[89]

All of this is fine in theory. However, it must rapidly have become apparent that David was not yet strong enough, nor had he altered the political landscape in Scotland sufficiently since 1357, really 1352, to overcome all opposition. The key objections which must have been raised by important Scots in 1351–2 could still provoke many to stand against the crown's ploy at Dundee in April 1359. Above all, the return of the Disinherited from England would badly disrupt the Bruce land settlement and the baronial gains of the 1330s and 1350s, alienating not just the Stewarts but the Douglases, Dunbars, Rosses and many lesser families like the Keiths, Hays, Lindsays, Frasers and Ramsays: for these houses, their potential Scottish losses would surely far outweigh any possible gains from a reciprocal return to cross-border landholding which might be dangled to win their acquiescence. Moreover, national institutions like the church, heavily politicised since 1286, would have been understandably nervous again at the outside chance of any form of English royal superiority over Scotland. Generally, of course, many Scots' increasingly nationalistic outlook and natural preference for war against England and alliance with France must still have prevailed, especially with the destruction of the 'Burnt Candlemas' of 1356 fresh in Scottish memory. Clearly, David sorely underestimated this patriotic sentiment or over-estimated his own ability to persuade his subjects that he was merely trying to trick the English so as to save money and undermine the Stewarts only to father his own son later: the fact that the English royal in question would still be one step removed from both title to Moray and the crown can have cut little ice.

True, David had used patronage to good effect since October 1357 to win much support and to undermine Robert Steward in particular. Trade and ecclesiastical contact with England had been on the increase since 1357 thanks to David's diplomacy giving him the potentially united backing of two of the three estates for peace with England (and even the outside prospect of regnal union); the king could also call upon a growing body of

89 *Rot. Scot.*, i, 836 (Mar's indenture), 837 (Hill), 841 (August 1359), 893 (Hill as pilgrim); *ER*, ii, 129, 144; *RRS*, vi, no. 215. For Mar's career after 1357 see Duncan, 'The Laws of Malcolm MacKenneth', 261–5. For other men in Mar's affinity who served David, see NAS GD 124 Mar & Kellie; *HMC*, lx (2 vols.) Mar & Kellie; *Illustrations of the Topography and Antiquities of Aberdeen and Banff*, v, 155, 715–8, 752. Many of these Mar men had been involved with the earl's running of the exchequer (*RMS*, i, App. i no. 128). About May 1360, Mar man Lawrence Gilliebrand would travel to Newcastle on the king's business (*ER*, ii, 52). Walter Moigne would be given a royal charter of the forest of Drum in the same month (*RRS*, vi, no. 236) – both Moigne and Gilliebrand would take part on later pilgrimages (e.g. *Rot. Scot.*, i, 901).

Scottish knights and their military followings who had either disavowed war with England or enjoyed employment as continental mercenaries. Yet the harsh reality was that the king's personal circumstances in 1359 added vital new reasons for his subjects to oppose him. By contrast with 1352, it was now clear that David was without a co-operative wife and had no chance of a Bruce heir by Joan. If this state of affairs continued and the deal with England was done, then Scotland *would* have an English-born monarch upon David's death, shoving aside the leading Scottish kindred recognised as heirs by parliamentary entails of 1318 and 1326 and which had fought hard for Scotland since 1332: the Stewarts. Only public knowledge that Queen Joan was sick and dying or that David intended a divorce – impossible to verify but perhaps suggested by her withdrawal to a religious life – might have made a difference.

But perhaps far more importantly, by denying Patrick, earl of March, his Moray inheritance through his Randolph wife, David would – as A.A.M. Duncan has stressed – set a further precedent for denying succession through a female.[90] In theory the Moray grant – in addition to David's intervention by 1358 against the claims of Isabella of Fife – would provide a weapon the king could use to justify abandoning the Stewart succession through Marjorie Bruce and, incidentally, the right of the Steward's second wife to Strathearn, and of the earl of Ross to his niece's claim to Caithness and Orkney. This could have thrown the Steward into sympathy with a panicked William, earl of Douglas, who – while he had sons of his own – may also have hoped to inherit his brother-in-law's earldom of Mar; Thomas of Mar himself may have abandoned his wife, Margaret Graham, countess and dowager heiress to Menteith, in anticipation of the legal implications of David's move over Moray. Countless other Scots may have been similarly alarmed at the prospect of losing inheritance claims in the female line. This as much as anything else may have eroded support for David's actions in spring 1359, even though the irony was that he would be favouring John of Gaunt whose landed windfall had to come through his new wife. This opposition would now be added to the voices of those great magnates – the Steward and his sons, Angus and Ross, Sir John Menteith and Murray of Bothwell – who had been denied patronage and suffered at David's hands as dismissed officers and ransom hostages since October 1357.

It was probably, then, a heady mixture of these fears and grievances aroused once more which saw David face a major backlash to his plans on the very same day he granted the earldom of Moray to Henry of Lancaster in the Dundee council. Beginning on 5 April, indeed, the king issued a number of acts over the next few weeks which amount to a striking reversal of his

90 Duncan, 'Honi soit qui mal y pense', 135.

previously distinctly partisan patronage to crown supporters. It is fair to assume that David either felt obliged to favour such men he had previously snubbed in order to pacify or buy off his critics, or he was actually forced by a concerted party of opposition to make these grants.

The evidence suggests that there was a large measure of duress on the king in April-May 1359. Moreover, the paucity of royal acts extant from this period (some sixty-three acts by David survive from 1358 but only thirty-one from 1359) hints at considerable disruption to the normal routine of government.[91] On 5 April David issued letters restoring Sir John Menteith of Arran and Knapdale to the large lordship of Strathgartney, bordering on Menteith and Lennox, despite the fact that the king had ordered Sir John Logie restored to this fief in 1343: this concession really confirmed Menteith's occupation of these lands since 1346 and must have boosted his kin in their feud there with Logie's in-laws, the Drummonds. That the king had been placed under considerable pressure to do so, though, is suggested by Menteith's charter which noted that Logie's restoration had been undertaken by David 'by the suggestion of certain people' but that now he was 'more truly informed by our council' of who should hold these lands. Thereafter, David does seem to have had freedom of movement to issue grants confirming conveyancing by the crown men, William Meldrum (8 April, at Dundee) and Thomas of Mar (1 May, back at Edinburgh). The first of these grants was sealed by the royalist bishops of St Andrews and Brechin, William Ramsay the earl of Fife, Preston and John Lyle of Duchal in Lanarkshire (a household officer for Queen Joan in 1357–8 and a future constable of Edinburgh Castle for the king) as well as by the Steward and Douglas.[92] But back in Edinburgh – where David seems to have remained for the next month – Douglas's office as sheriff and castle-keeper of Edinburgh may have been used to bring further pressure to bear upon the king. On 3 May David may thus have been obliged to inspect and confirm grants by Thomas Murray of Bothwell first of all to the Steward of the barony of Schenbothie in Clackmannanshire in free barony; and secondly to Sir Robert Erskine of the barony of Walton in Lanarkshire. Erskine, as we shall see, was a Stewart tenant well able to play the king and Steward off against each other for his own gain (as he had done c. 1346–52). Overall these grants may have stilled the concerns of Murray who was still a hostage for the ransom in England.[93]

However, these acts look even more suspicious against the background of foreign policy decisions which seem to have been made in April-May 1359.

91 *RRS*, vi, nos. 157–226; *RMS*, i, App. ii, nos. 1131–1349 may, though, add a considerable number of lost acts roughly dated to both 1358 and 1359.
92 *RRS*, vi, nos. 212–5; *RPS*, 1359/4/1; *ER*, ii, 50, 78, 129, 134.
93 *RRS*, vi, nos. 216–7; *Rot. Scot.*, i, 843.

Faced with David's plans, Robert Steward's immediate reaction would have been to ensure the continuation of the ransom payments and the preservation of his succession rights. Hence it may have been his leadership of opposition to the crown's plans in the Dundee council which saw that body grant the first (or perhaps the second) general tax on all the estates to help raise the next 10,000-merks instalment. However, it is not certain that the wider political community at Dundee was consulted over what happened next. For by 10 May at the latest it had been arranged that not only would a fresh embassy be despatched to take another crack at persuading the Pope to grant a special ecclesiastical tax to help with the ransom; it had also been agreed that the same messengers would first call at the court of the Dauphin Charles of France and try to secure a new Franco-Scottish alliance in which the French should be persuaded to help pay off David's remaining ransom, freeing the Scottish host to make war on England. Admittedly, the Dundee council could have approved such a course of action. But the delay of a month and the internal evidence of the documentation involved does suggest that David was confronted with these options in subsequent uncomfortable private councils.[94]

It is surely too much to believe that David – after all the hard work he had put in by going to London in person, the long pedigree of his plan, the political panacea it offered and his 'grete specialtie' with Edward III and his sons – would have willingly done a *volte face* in April-May 1359 and sought such a radical pro-French alternative to his Anglo-Scottish designs. It is true that in 1369–70 David would re-open talks with the French.[95] But that came after ten long years of negotiations with England and his subjects over the succession-ransom deal had failed. Moreover, the circumstances by 1369 were very different to those a decade earlier. By the later date not only were England and France – the latter now ruled by Charles as king – already back at war anyway, but Queen Joan was dead and David was attempting to divorce his second wife, Margaret Logie. In 1359, however, John II of France was still alive and a captive of Edward III. Negotiations for his release in return for a massive cash ransom and the loss of great swathes of French territory had progressed throughout 1357–9 to the point where an Anglo-French treaty was soon expected to be concluded.[96] The thorny details of these talks aside, David may have been well-informed in London that the French under the Dauphin Charles – hit by the crisis of the Jacquerie revolt in spring 1358 – were really without the resources or political unanimity to

94 For what follows, see Penman and Tanner, 'An Unpublished act of David II, 1359'.
95 *ER*, ii, 328, 348, 355–6, 363.
96 Cuttino, *English Medieval Diplomacy*, 90–4; Campbell, 'England, Scotland and the Hundred Years War in the Fourteenth-century', 202–3; Sumption, *The Hundred Years War*, ii, chs vii and ix. For 1369–70, see ch. 11 below.

continue war against England. Indeed, in countenancing Thomas, earl of Mar's employment in Edward's campaigns on the continent, David may have been looking forward himself to war against France, a country which as an ally had cost him so dearly in 1346. On a personal level in 1359, David's relations with Edward III's sister, Queen Joan, were uncertain yet perhaps on the mend: in August that year the couple would make joint applications to the papacy concerning benefices for their servants.[97]

All this being so, it is far more likely that the the idea to seek a secret Franco-Scottish alliance in 1359 was the will of Robert Steward, his several now adult sons, the earls of Angus (who may have been brought up in France) and Douglas (who was raised in France) and others.[98] As much is certainly suggested by the commission, previously unnoticed by historians, which David issued on 10 May 1358 in Edinburgh to the unusual embassy destined to seek out this pact with the Dauphin. Not only does the internal nature of these instructions – preserved in a contemporary French copy of the resulting Franco-Scottish treaty – suggest that the commission was drawn up by a scribe in the Steward's pay (who had also penned the commission to ambassadors to England issued by Robert as Lieutenant in 1357); but the terms which the 1359 Scottish envoys were empowered to seek were to be binding upon 'the aforesaid king of Scotland, or his lieutenant, or any other person or persons who hold sufficient authority for this'. The commission was thus worded in a manner which deviated from normal practice but in such a way as to be politically useful to the Steward working against the wishes of the crown. It is also unclear just which royal seal was used to authenticate this document, a fact which – together with the absence of a witness list to this important commission – suggests that the Steward and others had acted to coerce the king.[99]

The three Scots sent to Paris in late spring were to impress upon the Dauphin that the Scots had never considered their 'aliances et amitéz' with France as having being severed; however, they were to lament that Scotland could not resume war against the English until David's ransom had been paid and ten Scottish hostages recovered (a group, of course, which included at least one of the Steward's sons). With this in view the envoys were then to ask the French to give Scotland the remaining 90,000 merks of the ransom

---

97 *CPP*, i, 346, which included an application for a canonry at Glasgow for Gilbert Armstrong, one of David's key ambassadors to England.

98 *Scots Peerage*, i, 170. The fact that a marriage dispensation secured by Angus in 1353 had been seconded by John II of France may point to a childhood connection.

99 AN J677 nos. 7 and 8; also to be found at NAS RH1/2/3 (photostat of Paris treaty) and BL Add. MSS. no. 30,666 (a Victorian longhand copy); transcription and translation in Penman and Tanner, 'An Unpublished act of David II, 1359'. This treaty is also discussed in Nicholson, *Scotland – the Later Middle Ages*, 167–8 and Délachenal, *Charles V*, ii, 94–105.

together with aid and counsel in time of peace or war as well as help in persuading the Pope to annul the Anglo-Scottish truce of 1357. In return the Scots could promise to make 'bonne et forte' war against England. But most revealing of all, the envoys were also empowered to cite past promises made by the French to supply the Scots with 500 archers and 500 men-at-arms. These were offers which had been made in letters by John II in September 1351 (and perhaps subsequently) in response to appeals to France made by the Steward as Lieutenant as part of his opposition to David's first attempt to push through the succession-ransom plan with England.[100]

It was the Steward who had engineered the only previous French expedition to Scotland in 1355, a force which brought money enough to tempt the earls of Douglas, March and Angus and others into an outburst of aggression against England, thus baulking David's peace talks with Edward III. Roughly the same figures for French troops to be sent to Scotland – and an offer of 100,000 gold nobles to pay off the remainder of David's ransom – would also be included in a secret military concord made between Robert II (the Steward) and Charles V in March 1371. This would be as little as a month after David II's death and concluded at the same time as a more public renewal of the Franco-Scottish mutual defence alliance. Another similar secret pact which would have brought the Scots 'un mil (1,000) hommes d'armes et escuiers' and 40,000 francs would be made by Robert II in August 1383. Ultimately, of course, Jean de Vienne would bring his ill-fated expedition of about 1,200 Frenchmen to Scotland in 1385 together with a spoil of mercenary cash to pay for war against England which the Stewarts, Douglases, Dunbars and other kindreds divided up happily between them. Thus at all these crucial junctures – 1351–1355, 1371, 1383 and 1385 – it was Robert Steward or his sons who oversaw these French connections.[101] The secret treaty sought in 1359 was surely no different and David was forced to go along with it.

As much might also be inferred from the three Scotsmen chosen to approach the Dauphin in 1359. They were not the traditional community-approved body of at least one bishop, one earl, one baron. Instead, two knights and an esquire with some European experience were chosen. Sir Robert Erskine and Norman Leslie may have represented compromise candidates, acceptable to both David and the Steward. Erskine's connections with the Steward would persist until March 1360 when he very definitely became a crown man in receipt of direct royal patronage: until

100 AN JJ 36/620 and 621; *Oeuvres de Froissart*, xviii, 336–8; *APS*, xii, no. 15; Robertson ed., *The Parliamentary Records of Scotland*, 90, 99–100.

101 BN MSS Clairambault 43 no. 143/60/6 and no. 109/141 (1355); AN J677 nos. 9–13 (1371); *APS*, xii, 19 no. 36 (1383); Brown, *Early Travellers in Scotland*, 8–15; T. de Loray, *Jean de Vienne*, ch. ix (1385).

then he continued to serve on the daily councils of both king and Steward.[102] Leslie had been a deputy of the earl of Angus as Chamberlain, although he may have lost this post after spring 1358. He was also a Baltic crusader and skilled mercenary soldier and would, indeed, be captured by the English fighting for the French at Fauvy in 1360 at the same time as the earl of Mar and some of his men were fighting on the opposing side elsewhere for Edward III: Leslie was accompanied on this expedition to France by his younger brother, Walter, who would make his name as a crusader and an early leader of the mercenary Great Company plundering eastern France in 1360–2 before returning to Scotland and emerging as a favourite of the crown.[103] However, the third envoy in 1359 was someone David may not have been unhappy to employ. Sir John le Grant had been a Randolph man as keeper of Darnaway forest in Moray; as a younger man he may have accompanied Randolph to France c. 1334–41. Thereafter he had seemingly become a Mar or Angus adherent but he had followed William, lord of Douglas, to Poitiers in 1356. Yet he must also have felt his patrimony in Moray threatened by David's grant to Lancaster in 1359. If Grant agreed to participate in the embassy to France that year as an act of self-defence, it cost him dearly. For there is no evidence that a pension of £40 gifted to Grant by David in 1358 was paid after 1359; more damaging still, by the late 1360s the king would have replaced Grant as Darnaway's forester with a Richard Comyn – a man of crusading and Anglophile leanings who in turn would be immediately ousted from this office when the Steward, by now King Robert II, restored Grant after David's death in 1371.[104]

In the end only Erskine and Leslie seem to have made it to the Dauphin's court by early June 1359. But they found the French willing to clutch at straws. Indeed their timing could not have been better. On 24 March 1359 English and French representatives had concluded the second of their provisional treaties of London for John II's release. However, having stalled over the first treaty of 1358, the French now found the price for their king's

---

102 *Chron. Bower*, vii, 313. Before 1362, David did not grant Erskine any direct patronage, preferring instead to confirm Erskine's grants from other lords – e.g. a grant by Thomas, earl of Mar, of lands in Garioch, confirmed in parliament in November 1358 (*RRS*, vi, no. 198). For Erskine as a Steward charter witness, see e.g. *Registrum Honoris de Morton*, ii, nos. 49, 78 and Fraser ed., *Memorials of the Montgomeries*, ii, nos. 4, 5.

103 *ER*, i, 549, 555, 562, 590, 618 and ii, 4; *Rot. Scot.*, i, 837; *Chron. Scalacronica* (Stevenson/Leland), 311; K. Fowler, *Medieval Mercenaries: Vol. I – the Great Companies* (Oxford 2001), 73, 324–6.

104 *Registrum Episcopatus Moraviensis*, i, no. 22; *RRS*, vi, nos. 323, 473; *RMS*, i, no. 825 and App. ii, no. 1265; *Rot. Scot.*, i, 821, 837; Boardman and Penman, 'The Scottish Arms in the Armorial of Gèlre' (forthcoming) for Comyn.

release and peace had risen sharply. By this new agreement John would be freed in return only for a ransom of £666,666 (with the first instalment due on 1 August that year), guaranteed by many French noble hostages: yet they also faced the loss of even more French territory – almost all of the western half of the kingdom, now to be held free of homage by Edward III and his heirs. The French had until 9 June 1359 to ratify these terms, a deadline the Scots must have been aware of in sending out their delegation. But on 19 May, just a week or so before the Scots envoys arrived, the Estates General in Paris rejected the tabled treaty as unpalatable and called upon Charles to make 'bonne guerre'. By the end of that month Edward III was aware of the French response and had resumed preparations for his next campaign.[105]

Clearly, the French had been unrealistically encouraged in their defiance by the dramatic overtures of their sometime ally, Waldemar IV, king of Denmark. Remarkably, in early 1359 he had proposed that a mercenary force of 12,000 Germans and Danes should be landed on the eastern coast of Scotland to overrun England, forestall Edward III's campaign planned for August and free John II, a plan not too dissimilar to the French expedition mooted in 1336. Waldemar even claimed to have contacted the Scots and the Welsh and to have assembled the necessary fleet. All the French would have to do was find 600,000 florins to pay for this armada![106] There is no evidence that the Danish king had sounded out Scotland about a joint invasion although it is possible that the Steward, Ross and others had wind of his plans by April 1359. But it is unlikely that the French were so blind as to imagine that this expedition would be affordable or feasible. Nevertheless, it would surely have been worth their while to stir up what trouble they could on England's borders. The same thinking must have infused Charles' and his council's discussions with Erskine and Leslie.

The actual terms agreed with the two Scots by late June 1359 betray the weaknesses and desperate, speculative mood of the French. The secret treaty took on board many possible eventualities, including the chance that the French might make peace with England (in which case they promised not to break off the Scottish alliance); or that they might not have enough money to pay off David's ransom (in which case they would give what aid and counsel they could). But all Charles felt he could offer

105 R. Cazelles, *Société Politique, Noblesse et Couronne sous Jean le Bon et Charles V* (Paris 1982), 229–87, 318–37, 361; Sumption, *Hundred Years War*, ii, 400–4. But see now C.J. Rogers, 'The Anglo-French Peace Negotiations of 1354–60 Reconsidered' in Bothwell ed., *The Age of Edward III*, 193–213.
106 Sumption, *Hundred Years War*, ii, 403–4; A. Germain, 'Projet de déscente en Angleterre concerte entre le gouvernement français et le roi de Danemark Valdemar III pour la délivrance de Jean roi', *Mémoriales Société Archéologique Montpellier*, iv (1855), 409–34; AN P14 no. 373.

specifically at this stage was a payment of 50,000 merks, just over half the remaining ransom. This sum was to be transferred to the Scots on 5 April 1360 at the Augustinian church in Bruges in the same way as payment had been made to the Scottish nobility in 1355. But in return, the treaty stipulated that 'the King, Governor or the Guardian of Scotland and their heirs and successors' were to make war against England as soon as the ten (unidentified) Scottish hostages were released. Significantly, the treaty's recognition that a Guardian might govern Scotland in the near future echoed the envoys' commission from David which had also left scope for leadership by a 'Lieutenant'. Admittedly, this may simply have been a precaution laid down against the chance that David would default on his ransom and have to re-enter captivity (as John II would in 1363–4); but it could also be used to legitimise the Steward's marginalisation of David and his seizure of power as Lieutenant once more in the near future.

On paper this might have seemed a very good deal for Scotland: over half the ransom paid by proxy, hostages recovered and a chance to break off with England and resume a just, potentially lucrative and glorious war against Plantagenet imperialism. But the fact that Charles had not been able to offer more money – and his refusal to promise specified numbers of French troops – should have warned the Scots. As one modern historan has put it, all this talk with Denmark and Scotland was absolutely 'unreal'. The French had their backs to the wall. Edward III and his armies had overrun most of western France to within a few miles of Paris. Mercenary companies were plundering the rich heart of the kingdom. The Dauphin, his nobility and allies were riven with political and personal rivalries, and key French localities, including republican-minded Paris, were more and more concerned simply to save themselves from English attack. During July and August 1359, Charles failed to persuade his loyal subjects in southern France to contribute cash and victual to fund Waldemar's plan and the Scots' ransom. As it turned out, money would only be raised by Charles to sustain the French war effort throughout 1359 by drastically devaluing the coinage. Troops, too, were in painfully short supply. All this surely meant that the secret Franco-Scottish alliance of June 1359 was just as dead a letter as David's grant of the Moray earldom to Lancaster. It must have been a meaningless deal long before Edward III and John of Gaunt disembarked at Calais with a force 10,000 strong in October. There was some English anxiety about a possible Franco-Scottish invasion that autumn: English border defences were strengthened. But in the end all the French could muster was a small landing in Sussex as late as March 1360 in a misguided attempt to rescue John II: this failed miserably. Yet even before this incursion was launched it must have been obvious that the

French would have to return to their ransom treaty with England. Negotiations for a full peace would begin in earnest after 12 April 1360 when John II had declined Edward III's invitation to do battle before Paris.[107]

Stalemate in Scotland, June–December 1359

Back in Scotland, David was perhaps fortunate that these wider European circumstances prevailed. Yet in fact he may have been able to break free of Edinburgh and the bending of his will by the Stewarts, Douglas and others by as early as 10 June 1359, though not in time to prevent Erskine and Leslie drawing up the French alliance on his behalf. On that date he can be found, perhaps unusually, at Glasgow where he issued letters under his privy seal once more ordering the justiciar south-of-Forth, the earl of Douglas, not to interfere in the regality of the Abbey of Melrose. That this may in some measure have represented the king striking back at the earl for his recent intransigence is further suggested by Douglas's securing a safe-conduct to England by 28 July 1359 (probably requested in June), hoping perhaps that a timely pilgrimage to Canterbury would spare him the royal wrath. Douglas was conspicuously absent as a royal charter witness between June 1359 and 31 January 1360. Patrick, earl of March, also received a safe-conduct to go south in August 1359 and was similarly absent from, or cold-shouldered at, court until November of the following year: sometime between then and August 1360 March would be so out of favour as to deforce the crown's contribution collector for Berwickshire.[108]

David's letters of June 1359, however, were followed up by what could be construed as a number of royal acts which sought to loosen the bonds between lesser men in the localities and great lords like the Steward and Douglas; or acts of confirmation designed to allay fears amongst these earls' tenants that the king was about to punish these magnates severely. Thus at Perth on 2 July David confirmed a grant by Douglas to a minor Perthshire layman, an act witnessed by the Chancellor, the Steward and the royalist knights, David Annan, Walter Moigne and William Gledstanes (a Douglas adherent whose services David now seems to have poached to report on sheep movements in the borders). A day later the king confirmed a pardon issued by Douglas along with the Steward when Lieutenant c. 1355 to Sir James Tweedie of Drumelzier. By 31 July 1359 David was at Dundee where he inspected a grant made by Duncan, earl of

107 Sumption, *Hundred Years War*, ii, 351–430, at 404 ('unreal'); Ayton, 'English Armies in the Fourteenth-Century', 21, 28–9.
108 *RRS*, vi, nos. 219, 220–31, 249; *Rot. Scot.*, i, 840–1; *ER*, ii, 44.

Fife, to the Abbey of Lindores also originally issued during the Steward's lieutenancy.[109]

However, if this represents the king and his close advisers re-asserting royal authority, it was done slowly and cautiously, understandably in the light of the recent backlash against David's plans. Robert Steward was by no means running scared: he was present at court throughout the summer. His hope of a French alliance may have been thwarted long before Erskine returned from the continent (by October at the latest) but so had David's Lancaster-Moray-succession plan; the ransom would continue to be paid. But the Steward must also have been buoyed in this period by his great revival of fortune in the earldom of Fife, the scene of David's quiet triumph the year before.

The Steward's opportunity had come when, sometime shortly after completing his will on 8 September 1358, Sir William de Felton died. According to the Northumbrian chronicler, Sir Thomas Gray, Felton's widow – Isabella of Fife – now returned to Scotland to seek her inheritance.[110] Just when she arrived is uncertain, as is whether or not she came north of her own volition or at the urging of the Steward perhaps in the wake of his coercion of David in April-May 1359 (or, perhaps, of John Stewart of Kyle, still a hostage in northern England). It is possible that Isabella's arrival further exacerbated the political confrontation of these months. But by 20 November 1359 at the latest, Isabella can be found in the Steward's castle at Methven near Perth, styling herself as a widow and as heiress of her father, the late earl Duncan of Fife: in the same month she would take the remarkable step of confirming a grant by King David to Sir John Preston of lands in Fife. It was probably shortly thereafter that Isabella wed Robert Steward's second son, Walter, although this marriage cannot be positively confirmed until July 1361. But long before then she had given her new husband an entail of her earldom which meant it might pass on to Walter's Stewart brothers and their heirs in the event that she (born *c.* 1320 × 29?) and Walter (born *c.* 1337–8) would not have issue.[111]

To what degree this marriage and tailzie were accompanied by the Stewarts' physical displacement of William Ramsay of Colluthie, David's placeman, from Fife in late 1359 and 1360 is not clear. Ramsay was at court

109 *RRS*, vi, nos. 220–1; *RMS*, i, App. i, no. 141; *ER*, ii, 51, 78 (Gledstanes).
110 *Chron. Scalacronica*, 126; *Inquisitiones Post Mortem*, 15 no. 41; Hodgson, *A History of Northumberland*, vii, 113–7; Boardman, *Early Stewart Kings*, 13–4. Gray was, though, absent in France with the Black Prince in 1359 (King, 'Englishmen, Scots and Marchers', 230).
111 NAS GD 122 (Little Gilmour of Libberton and Craigmillar)/141; *Registrum de Monasterii de Passelet* (Maitland Club, Glasgow 1832), 67–8; Fraser ed., *Red Book of Menteith*, ii, 251–4; Boardman, *Early Stewart Kings*, 25, 33 n70 and 37 n127.

as earl on 8 April 1359, but he next resurfaces only in May 1361 with the king at Perth, styled simply as a knight.[112] Ramsay's downfall would, of course, be further cemented by the violent death of his wife, Katherine Mortimer, the king's mistress in June 1360. Yet it is surely the case that Ramsay's marginalisation in late 1359 and the Steward's re-intrusion into Fife – in the wake of diplomatic approaches to France – was almost enough to overshadow the other advances a politically battered David was able to make throughout the remainder of that year.

William, earl of Douglas, seems to have continued to bear the brunt of David's thirst for greater royal control of the political stage. The exact timing of events is again unknown but sometime between summer 1359 and May 1360 – perhaps during the period of the earl's absence from court – David was able to displace William as keeper of Edinburgh Castle, employing in his stead Sir John Lyle of Duchal who would also go on to serve as a royal household steward, display an interest in crown-sponsored crusading and accompany the king on future trips to England: Lyle may also have become sheriff of Edinburgh bringing in his own deputy officials.[113] This really was the beginning of David's adoption of Edinburgh as his working capital and favourite residence. But this change must also have sorely undermined Douglas's ability to act as justiciar in the Lothians and elsewhere south-of-Forth; this was an office he had also probably lost by the summer of 1360 following a final royal warning to leave Melrose Abbey alone. He was replaced by a number of lesser royalist knights. In January 1360 David may also have obliged Douglas to resign Cavers church in Roxburghshire to the Abbey by way of compensation.[114] Finally, by 1 May 1360, David had also replaced the Douglas earl as Warden of the West March with an Annandale knight who had been given this role by the crown before 1346, Sir John Stewart of Dalswinton. By reclaiming both the justiciarship and the wardenship David would have been better placed to protect the lands and revenues of the regality of Melrose and to ensure that

112 *RRS*, vi, nos. 213, 258; *RMS*, i, no. 109; *ER*, ii, 176. Further evidence that William Ramsay was closely associated with David II may lie in the son, David, whom William had by another wife, Agnes, of unknown family (*RMS*, i, no. 791). But it is possible that as late as 1362 William Ramsay was still trying to make use of his Fife title and his lowland following (NAS RH4/30/1, a grant by Ramsay of lands in the earldom of March in Lothian to a Margaret Lassell, witnessed by the abbots of Holyrood and Newbattle, Sir Patrick Hepburn, Sir Walter Haliburton, Sir John Edmonstone, Alexander Ramsay, Gilbert Herries, Alexander Cockburn and Alexander Recklington).

113 *ER*, ii, 50, 78, 134–73, 261 (Lyle as envoy to Flanders); *Rot. Scot.*, i, 876, 905; *RMS*, i, no. 147 (a David Libberton as sergeant of the constabulary of Edinburgh).

114 *RRS*, vi, nos. 227, 37, 417; Brown, *Black Douglases*, 189. Douglas was paid his expenses as justiciar for the fiscal year May 1360–June 1361 but was not paid again in this office until 1371–2 (*ER*, ii, 82, 394).

the 1357 truce with England was not broken by independent southern magnate aggression.[115]

These fundamental changes in the balance of political power in the south were cemented by David's general extension of patronage to a number of Douglas retainers at this time. These included the aforementioned Sir William Gledstanes, John Herries of Terregles, John Gordon of Kenmure, William Towers of Dalry (for whom David would confirm a Douglas charter on 10 January 1360) and, most significant of all, Archibald 'the Grim' Douglas. David may have been responsible by July 1359 for funding the release of Archibald, Towers, Gordon and others from captivity in England after their seizure while raiding across the border in breach of the truce, probably in the service of the earl of Douglas in 1358.[116] Archibald, after his first appearance at the king's court about March 1359 (where he had witnessed David's and Mar's grant to Herries), came to represent royal hopes of a renewed Bruce-Douglas partnership. For not only was this knight an illegitimate son of Robert I's lieutenant, the 'Good' Sir James, who by right of the tailzies of 1342 and 1357 might inherit the Black Douglas and Lothian/Liddesdale lands; Archibald was also a close companion of his fellow Poitiers veteran, William Ramsay of Colluthie, and probably the king's fellow from childhood at Château Gaillard. But in addition, by 1359 Archibald was also a formidable warrior who, according to Bower, 'everywhere had in his following a large company of knights and men of courage': indeed, by the time of chronicler Jean Froissart's visit to Scotland in 1365 Archibald was of sufficient repute to be immortalised as the wielder of a sword which two ordinary mortals would struggle to bear. Yet by then, much of this knight's power had come directly from the royal favour he had enjoyed since 1359–60 as David built him up – really as an alternative to William, earl of Douglas – as the next keeper of Edinburgh Castle, Warden of the West March and, by 1369, lord of Galloway. In 1359–60, though, Archibald may also have been encouraged to support David by the beginnings of diplomatic attempts to bring Maria, the daughter and heiress of William Douglas of Liddesdale, back to Scotland from her wardship in England: Maria Douglas was the only person standing in the way of the inheritance – by right of the controversial tailzie of 1342 – of Archibald and his cousin, James Douglas of Lothian, another future favourite of King David.[117]

---

115 *CDS*, iv, no. 47.
116 *RRS*, vi, nos. 220, 228; *CDS*, iv, no. 40; *Rot. Scot.*, i, 826, 838–9, 848; *RMS*, i, App. ii, nos. 1263, 1275, 1349 (confirmation of Douglas grants); Neville, *Violence, Custom and Law*, 48–9.
117 *Chron. Fordun*, i, 377; *Oeuvres de Froissart*, v, 137; *Chron. Bower*, viii, 35; Fraser ed., *Douglas Book*, i, 321–35; Brown, *Black Douglases*, ch. 3; *RRS*, vi, no. 51; *CDS*, iv, no. 45.

In late 1359 David was also able to achieve smaller gains and some measure of retribution in north-east Scotland. Thomas, earl of Angus, was again named as a hostage/military recruit to England, a fate which would make him increasingly rebellious.[118] Further north, while on a visit to Elgin about 13 August, David issued letters to John de Pilmor, bishop of Moray, to proceed by ecclesiastical censures against those interfering with the lands and revenues of the church of Moray. This could have been directed against either Patrick, earl of March/Moray's men or against the Steward's young fourth son, Alexander, who by the later 1360s would have established his unique brand of violent lordship in the former Randolph province of Badenoch (by right of his father's second marriage).[119] But it is clear that even if he could not grant the earldom to Henry of Lancaster, David fully intended to control the strategically vital province of Moray – bordering on Badenoch which had been part of the Randolph regality – through royalists in this quarter, not just Pilmor and his archdeacon and treasurer, Alexander de Bur (who would succeed Pilmor in 1362) and David de Mar respectively, but through such substantial laymen as William Keith, the Marischal. This crown presence in the north-east would also have acted as a continued bulwark to contain the earl of Ross.

If all of these changes had been set in motion before October 1359, David may have gone into the next meeting of the estates at a parliament at Scone on the second day of that month in a relatively upbeat mood. The few known crown acts issued during this assembly suggest as much. On 3 October David issued additional letters ordering officials not to interfere in Arbroath Abbey's regality; on 23 October he inspected a charter of Thomas, earl of Mar (who had a safe-conduct to fight on the continent for England that month), of lands in the regality of Garioch; then on 26 October, still at Scone, David granted lands in Inverness to the Chapel of the Virgin in that burgh and confirmed the privileges of the Chancellor's diocese of Brechin which bordered on Atholl and Angus. The witnesses to these grants spoke to a royalist predominance in this parliament. The Steward and earl of Ross, indeed, must have felt uncomfortably surrounded as they sealed alongside the likes of the bishops of St Andrews, Brechin and Ross, Walter Wardlaw the archdeacon of Lothian, Alexander Bur the archdeacon of Moray, William Keith the Marischal, Robert Erskine (now back from Avignon), Walter Haliburton, John Herries and David Annan and other unrecorded crown knights: the former allies, the earls of Douglas and Angus appear to have been absent.[120] This may in part explain why, although the recorded

118 *Rot. Scot.*, i, 840.
119 *RRS*, vi, nos. 222, 495; *Registrum Episcopatus Moraviensis*, i, 141; Boardman, 'Lordship in the North-East', 1–3.
120 *RRS*, vi, nos. 223–6; *RPS*, 1359/10/1–3; *Rot. Scot.*, i, 842.

proceedings of this session do not survive, parliament must not only have approved a grant of another tax of 3d to 6d in the £ to raise the ransom but also agreed to the continuation of embassies to England: talks would resume early in 1360.[121]

However, it is not difficult to deduce that there must still have been incredible tension within the political community at this time and – reading between the lines – that David surely had a rough ride at this meeting of the estates. This parliament lasted almost four weeks. Some of this time may have been taken up with arguments over the office changes David sought to make about this time or over rival claims to Fife and Moray (and, as we shall see, over feuding in Menteith involving the Stewarts and Drummonds). But it is possible that the secret alliance with France – no matter how unlikely its value – was still put forward for ratification. Certainly, there must have been some heated debate over the fall-out from David's dealings with Lancaster and Edward III and the resulting backlash against royal authority in April-May 1359. Thus, even though David had considerable support within the community for his Anglo-Scottish plans, what in the end emerged from this Scone assembly was a messy compromise and political stalemate. Given both European and Scottish developments, both the French and Lancaster plans were dropped – at least in formal terms – and efforts were renewed to continue raising ransom funds with perhaps vague concurrence that better fiscal terms, or further postponements, might be sought from England. This scrappy, indecisive outcome may also explain why none of the chroniclers of the period – Scots or English – mention any of the news from Scotland of this year. However, such a reading of the events of 1359 surely makes far greater sense of the dramas of the three years that would follow.

David could certainly only have looked back upon the achievements of his first two years of freedom with mixed feelings. He was undeniably much stonger domestically than he had been in October 1357, with his choice of men in most of the key locality offices.[122] But once again when he had used this crown resurgence as a mandate to ask his subjects to reconsider an unusual gamble in a peace treaty with England – one which might have solved all the Bruce king's problems at a stroke – David had suffered a serious blow to his personal and political authority. Wider events and hard work had enabled the king to ride this out but now his chief antagonist and heir presumptive, Robert Steward, had control of most of the valuable territory of central Scotland, a swelling empire for his sons stretching across Clydeside, Fife, Menteith, Strathearn, Atholl and Badenoch. The Steward

---

121 *ER*, ii, 47, 49, 34, 73–5; *Rot. Scot.*, i, 850.
122 For a map showing the sheriffs of Scotland *c.* 1360, see *Atlas of Scottish History to 1707*, 208.

also seemed to occupy the moral, patriotic and historical high ground in the argument over relations with England. In the wake of these tensions, other key regional nobles – Douglas, Angus, March and Ross – were increasingly at loggerheads with David's kingship and foreign policy: even Thomas of Mar now found himself alone fighting for Edward III.

Nor was it as if these sticky problems could simply be ignored. David still had to raise tax and pay his ransom annually for another eight years or find a way to escape this debt. The figures for 1359–60 suggest that the king would still favour the latter solution. By 20 February 1360 the Scots would only have managed to hand over another 5,000 merks, only half of the expected sum and paid, curiously, in two equal halves of 2,500 merks, not at a border deposit at say, Berwick, but through bankers in Bruges.[123] Edward III seems to have invoked some of the default clauses as a result of the Scots' failure to make full payment by the agreed delayed deadline of December 1359. However, the Scots would manage to pay off all of the third lump sum of 10,000 merks, due on 24 June 1360. This would be due not only to the first returns on the three contributions granted by the estates in 1358–9 but also to the fact that David received a lucky windfall from his recent crisis when the Pope agreed to the fresh request of Erskine, Leslie and a number of Scottish clerics for a Scottish ecclesiastical levy to pay the ransom: the crown was thus granted a tenth of clerical income for three years.[124] The English duly recorded their receipt of the ransom instalment of June 1360 as the 'tertiam solutionem'. But it was obvious that the Bruce regime was still going to struggle to raise both ransom and government and household costs for the next seven years. Worse, as we shall see, whenever David tried to renegotiate the ransom terms between 1361 and 1370 the English would maintain that only 20,000 merks had ever been paid in all, clearly disregarding the late 5,000 merks paid in David's crisis year of 1359.

So the still childless David must have been painfully aware that he had little choice but to press on with the diplomatic and fiscal panacea he had first attempted in 1350–2. Nonetheless, such was the level of opposition and sheer fright that he had provoked in his subjects in 1359 – amongst both heartfelt crown opponents and some supporters – that it would be over two years before he was ready to initiate such a move in earnest again. Yet even before then the king's deteriorating relations with some of his great subjects would have precipitated tragic results.

---

123 *Rot. Scot.*, i, 845–6.
124 *Chron. Bower*, vii, 313; Barrell, *The Papacy, Scotland and northern England*, 23–4.

EIGHT

Dark Passage: Plague, Jealousy, Money, Murder and War, 1360–2

'Which countrey of Fyfe along the Scottish sea,
And from saynt Androws, to the Oyghles, they say,
Is xliii myles long of good countrey'
Chronicle of John Hardyng, c. 1420[1]

The Murder of Katherine Mortimer

The frustrations of his first two full years of freedom in Scotland must have been immense for David II. On a purely personal level, his apparent estrangement from the exiled Queen Joan left him unable to father a legitimate heir whilst most of his great noble contemporaries had growing families or room to manouevre in the marriage market. This dilemma added to David's political and diplomatic difficulties. Without the certain prospect of a male heir he could not persuade or manipulate a majority of the Scottish political community into gambling on a succession-peace deal with England to cancel out the ransom, throwing over Robert the Steward's right of inheritance in the process; yet had he had a son David would not have been able to do a deal with Edward. In general throughout 1358–9, just when he seemed to be making headway in one locality or direction, David had suffered a reverse in another.

Conversely, having survived a serious challenge to his control of foreign policy and the loss of control over the earldom of Fife in 1359, the years 1360–62 could be said to represent the beginning of a stormy but significant advance for the king towards some of his key goals. In this, David's own energy, determination and force of will, his ability to win support and to isolate and wear down his opponents, are all readily apparent. But so too is the ultimately limited nature of what he had to offer some of his most influential subjects. David's actions over the next three years would see him win considerable backing throughout Scotland and move to the brink of success in crucial areas. But at the same time he would provoke reactions of far greater violence than before from some of his noble antagonists on at least two occasions, possibly more.

The winter of 1359–60 found the king seemingly content to withdraw

---

1 Brown, *Early Travellers in Scotland*, 18. Hardyng spent over three years in Scotland gathering intelligence for Henry V and Henry VI of England.

into his court for a time and to regroup after the dramatic events of the previous months. After the Scone parliament of October 1359, the available evidence does not relocate David until 12 January 1360 on friendly ground at Restenneth priory in Forfarshire, his brother's resting place.[2] But the royal presence there also surely formed part of a concerted effort by David to further undermine the weakest link in the aristocratic chain recently ranged against him – namely Thomas Stewart, earl of Angus – by increasing royal control over that lord's sphere of influence.

Since 1357, David had favoured a number of laymen often to be found as followers of the earl of Angus: Alexander Montgomerie of Eaglesham, Alexander Scrymgeour of Dundee, Alexander Cockburn, the crusading esquire Richard Comyn and William Sinclair of Rosslyn (now Angus's brother-in-law). But the extant charter evidence certainly suggests that about 1358–60 David stepped up his network of lesser laymen in Tayside itself. Sometime during late 1359–early 1360, David seems to have granted For-farshire favour to local men John Balnehard, Robert Balbreny (of an un-specified shire office) and Sir Alexander Lindsay of Glenesk (a crusading associate of the Angus esquire, Norman Leslie, himself at that time fighting against the English in France). Then back at Edinburgh on 11 January 1360 David confirmed his father's grant of Old Montrose in Forfarshire to Sir David Graham (whose son had been a 1357 hostage), an act witnessed by the bishops of St Andrews and Brechin, John abbot of Dunfermline and the knights William Livingstone, Robert Erskine and Walter Haliburton. Nine days later at Perth, David granted the burgh of Dundee feu-ferm status for £20 per annum. By the last day of that month, though, the king had arrived at the shrival caput of Forfar itself where he reconfirmed the late Campbell earl of Atholl's grant of lands in the Mearns and at Inverbervie on the Mearns-Kincardineshire border to Sir Roger Mortimer, father of the royal mistress, Katherine. By 15 February David was back in Edinburgh where he granted Kincardineshire lands within Inverbervie to another royalist veteran of Neville's Cross, Sir Andrew Campbell: both of these last two acts had been witnessed by the Chancellor bishop of Brechin, Robert Steward, the earl of Douglas, Robert Erskine and the Lothian royalist knight, John Preston.[3]

But it was Erskine who enjoyed perhaps the most significant elevation by the crown in this region. David now seemed wholeheartedly prepared to pardon Erskine's ambivalent loyalty of 1350–4 and especially 1359 and to win the use of his undoubted talents in diplomacy and political networking: from early 1360, indeed, Erskine would be a paramount and indispensable

---

2 *RMS*, i, App. i, no. 138.
3 *RRS*, vi, nos. 229, 230, 231, 232; *RMS*, i, nos. 127, 189, 232 and App. ii, nos. 1226, 1232, 1311, 1313. See *Rot. Scot.*, i, 830 for a safe-conduct of October 1358 requested by a number of these men together just after Thomas, earl of Angus.

component of the king's daily council, fiscal and judicial administraion and diplomatic core. This was surely signalled on 23 March 1360 when at Stirling David granted Erskine a third of the Forfarshire lands of Pitkerro and a pension of a third of the royal Dundee rents: this act was witnessed, most significantly, not only by the usual suspects, the prelates of St Andrews and Brechin, the Steward, the earl of Douglas, Hugh Eglintoun and John Preston, but also by Thomas, earl of Angus, and Sir Roger Mortimer.[4]

Yet while Erskine was now receiving direct royal patronage for the first time, this was to be Angus's last recorded appearance at court. By then the earl must have been a mass of seething anxieties. Through his recent royal grants – and by his earlier favour in 1358–9 to the kin of his mistress, Katherine Mortimer, especially her father, Roger, her husband, William Ramsay, and his brother, Robert Ramsay, sheriff of Forfar – David had put in place a network of royal servants well able to exercise control over the country just north of Tay. Proof of this began to come in to the crown in April-May 1360. In an exchequer audit held at Perth – and perhaps partly overseen by David himself between 1 and 12 April – the royal revenues began to exhibit a relatively healthy increase. The customs brought in some £4,500, with Edinburgh alone (thanks to the trebling of the wool tariff) yielding over £1,300; the burgh fermes' return remained quite low but at least the fermes from Stirling, Perth and Crail had been recovered from the interference of the earl of Angus and the Steward.[5]

However, it is the first returns from the two contributions levied by parliament in 1358, intromitted at Perth in April-May 1360, which show that the crown increasingly had the upper hand in certain Lowland localities. Admittedly, the first contribution overall seems to have produced only £63 and, in general, collection of monies by royal agents from some shires and lordships was still gravely hampered by magnate resistance: from the first contribution only £13 came from war-torn Berwickshire; Clackmannanshire, where Sir John Menteith of Arran was sheriff, yielded only £14; Dumbartonshire, under the Steward's choice of sheriff in John Danielston, returned only 22/-! But the crown's men had managed to extract significant sums for the second tax from sensitive areas, amassing a total of £1,758. Some £189 had come from all the burghs; £73 from Stirlingshire; £38 from Peeblesshire; £150 from lands in Buchan, Aberdeenshire and Garioch; £68 from the earldom of Mar; £39 from Inverness-shire; £45 from Perthshire and £35 from the Steward's earldom of Atholl; £57 from Wigtownshire; £52 from Kyle Stewart and £40 from the lordship of Cunningham; and, perhaps most striking of all, £205 was collected in Fife and £280 from Forfarshire.[6]

4 *RRS*, vi, no. 233.
5 *Ibid*, no. 234; *ER*, ii, 7–33, 45–56.
6 *Ibid*, 34–44.

This last sum must have further enraged Thomas, earl of Angus, who had been removed by the king from the post of Chamberlain in 1358. But what made Angus feel especially vulnerable to royal encroachment on his interests was his continued role after the crisis of April-July 1359 as David's most valuable hostage to England, thus leaving behind his lands and regional following of lesser Scots to be poached openly by the crown. David had already had success in increasingly attracting the support of chivalric-minded knights and esquires, career-orientated clerics and Anglo-trading burgesses in Fife and the Lothians; at the same time, the absence of Thomas, earl of Mar, fighting for Edward III under contract in France in 1359, allowed David to increase his influence over Mar's lands to the north of Angus through such servants as Walter Moigne, a Neville's Cross veteran, whom the king rewarded with Kincardineshire forest lands on 27 May 1360.[7] Now the king's increased favour to men from Angus and the Mearns coincided with the earl of Angus's open breach of his parole from England by 15 March 1360: Thomas had seemingly forced his way home to Scotland to protect his own interests against a predatory monarch.[8] The state of affairs the earl found when he last appeared as a charter witness at David's court at Stirling on 23 March that year caused him to lash out in anger at the one person who so obviously encapsulated all of his fears, Katherine Mortimer.

According to Sir Thomas Gray, the contemporary Northumbrian chronicler and border knight released by the Scots in 1356, on the feast of St John the Baptist (24 June) 1360, when David and his party were returning north from Melrose Abbey along the Soutra road towards Edinburgh, 'a Scottish youth named Richard of Hull . . . pretended to speak with the said Katherine upon the king's affairs as they were riding . . . and struck her in the body with a dagger, killing her and throwing her from her horse to the ground'. But in Scottish annals, only Abbot Walter Bower – writing over eighty years later – commented upon this foul deed. It fell to Bower to assert that Hull (or Holly) and another man, 'Dewar', had killed Katherine on 'the consenting knowledge' of Thomas, earl of Angus, who was guilty of 'disturbances and damaging actions perpetrated by him against the community . . . abandoning the advice of older men of good sense . . . [joining] in the games of men of violence . . . [and] loose-living . . . '.[9]

David held Angus undeniably responsible, probably pursuing the earl in

7 *RRS*, vi, no. 236; Duncan, 'The 'Laws of Malcolm MacKenneth'', 246, 252, 262–70.

8 *Rot. Scot.*, i, 840 (safe-conduct south for Angus as hostage 8 August 1359), 847 (broken parole).

9 For what follows of Katherine and her murder, see *Chron. Scalacronica*, 162 and *Chron. Bower*, vii, 319–21.

person with an armed force after laying Katherine tenderly to rest in the Cistercian abbey of Newbattle in Mid-Lothian: Angus was seized and imprisoned in Dumbarton Castle where he would perish, apparently of natural causes, during a fresh outbreak of plague sometime in late 1362.[10] But it is highly unlikely that Angus had acted alone, for Katherine Mortimer – and what she and her royalist associates represented in terms of David's domestic and foreign policy – was a grave threat to several of Scotland's great nobles.

To Robert Steward and his adult sons the Bruce-Mortimer liaison was the central thrust of a threat on several landed fronts. Katherine Mortimer's husband, William Ramsay, had been seemingly expelled from Fife by the Stewarts and Isabella of Fife in late 1359: but Katherine's influence with the king might still see Ramsay restored to that title.[11] However, Katherine's father, Roger Mortimer, was in addition married to Margaret Menteith, a granddaughter of Alan, earl of Menteith, who had died in 1309 (and who had also had a tailzie claim to the earldom of Fife). Margaret Menteith's kinsmen, the Menteiths of Rusky and Sir John Menteith of Arran and Knapdale – with the support of the Stewarts – were then at feud over lands in the earldom of Menteith with the Drummonds, a murderous dispute which had raged since the 1340s at least, dragging in neighbouring families with associated land claims in the area, like the Murrays of Tullibardine (on the Drummond side) and the Campbells of Lochawe (on the Menteith side): Katherine Mortimer's parentage may have given her some peripheral claim in this feud but her relationship with the king put her in a position to influence its outcome.[12]

But in practice, it was probably the royalist cadre with which Katherine's father ran which posed the most direct threat to Stewart-Menteith interests in this valuable earldom, adjacent to Clydeside, Atholl and Strathearn, and which had been vacant since Sir John Graham's execution by Edward III in 1347. This must have become painfully apparent to the Stewart scions at Stirling on 17 May 1360 – just a month before Katherine's violent death – when the royal judiciary intervened in Menteith to pacify the feud which had most recently seen three Menteith of Rusky brothers slain by the Drummonds and their confederate, Walter Murray of Tullibardine. The new

10 *ER*, ii, 115, 168. David may first have taken Katherine's body to Soutra hospital (Prestwich, 'Katherine Mortimer's Death at Soutra', 110). Newbattle was perhaps a daughter house of Melrose.

11 For Roger Mortimer as a charter witness (to a grant of Angus lands) *c.* 1360 in the company of the Fife men, the bishop and prior of St Andrews, the abbot of Dunfermline, William Dischington, Ingelram Wyntoun and David Weymss, sheriff of Fife, see Fraser ed., *The Douglas Book*, iii, no. 24.

12 *RMS*, i, nos. 176, 177; *Scots Peerage*, iv, 272 and vi, 132–4; Boardman, *Early Stewart Kings*, 15–6.

sitting justiciars for north-of-Forth on that date (after David's dismissal of the earl of Ross in late 1358) were Sir Hugh Eglintoun and Sir Robert Erskine. It may have been the latter's new-found royalist faith which swung the decision of the assize decidedly in favour of the Drummonds.[13] On 22 July 1360 Erskine seems to have been rewarded by the king with a grant of the Perthshire barony of Kinnoul, quit of the dues of wardship, marriage or relief, but only after its resignation – whether under royal duress or not is unclear – by Isabella, Countess of Fife; about that time Erskine also seems to have become castle-keeper and sheriff of Stirling. His preference for the crown's side in this matter may have been determined not only by the patronage David could offer but by Erskine's partisan interest in the Menteith feud. For in March 1355 he had received a papal dispensation to wed a Christina Keith ('a kinswoman of the king') as his third wife to help pacify matters after Erskine had 'wounded and imprisoned Walter Menteith and his brother', Christina's kinsmen. Sir Robert Erskine thus had an undeniable vested interest in the 1360 Stirling assize.[14]

The assize outcome itself was certainly one-sided. As part of the pacification the revealing group of Sir John Menteith, Robert Steward and the earls of Douglas and Angus were all bound over to refrain from further pursuit of their quarrel with Sir John Drummond of Concraig, which suggests that a wider dispute had begun to spiral outwards from Menteith, embroiling many players with divisions ranged along national factional lines. John Drummond was most definitely in the crown's camp. He was the uncle of Margaret Logie, wife of Sir John Logie, a lord whom, as we have seen, David had tried to restore to the massive Perthshire lordship of Strathgartney in 1342 only to see Robert Steward as Lieutenant allow Sir John Menteith to reclaim it after 1346 and perhaps force the king to confirm Menteith's tenure there in April 1359: in much the same way, the king had tried to restore the Murrays of Tullibardine to their Perthshire lands about 1341. Although it is unlikely that David was already involved carnally with Logie's wife in addition to Katherine (though not unthinkable), the king had extended favour to John Drummond and his nephew, Margaret's brother Malcolm, before 1346, gifting them lands and the office of coroner in Perthshire, surely aggravating deliberately the tensions in Menteith as a result.[15]

But now, in spring 1360, in addition to protecting John Drummond from

---

13 *The Genealogy of the Most Noble and Ancient House of Drummond by William Drummond, Viscount Strathallan, 1681* (Edinburgh 1831), 65–8; Fraser ed., *Red Book of Menteith*, i, 109–15.
14 *RRS*, vi, no. 239; *ER*, ii, 78; *CPR*, iii, 564.
15 *RRS*, vi, nos. 14, 75, 281; *RMS*, i, App. ii, nos. 978, 1017, 1086; NAS GD 38 1/62/8; *Scots Peerage*, i, 453–5 and vii, 31–7.

the crown's greatest magnate opponents, the justiciars went so far as to insist that John should be allowed to have as his wife Margaret, Countess and heiress of Menteith (the daughter of Sir John Graham and his widow, Countess Mary of Menteith, who must have died about 1359). John Drummond had probably already begun a liaison and perhaps a family with Margaret, a fact which must have worsened the Menteith feud. For Margaret had originally been married to the Steward's ally, John Murray of Bothwell, who had died while a parole hostage for the king in England in 1351. Margaret had then been betrothed, as we have seen, to Thomas, earl of Mar, following intercession with the papacy between 1352 and 1354.[16] But by spring 1359 at the latest, the uneasy and childless Mar-Menteith marriage had been suspiciously annulled, hinting perhaps at some collusion between the king, Mar and Drummond.[17] Yet it is also likely that in securing John's marriage in 1360, David and Drummond thwarted the hopes of Robert Steward's third son, Robert: it may have been this ambitious young man – the future formidable earl of Fife/Menteith and Duke of Albany – whom David had in mind to send south as a hostage when England called for John Stewart of Kyle to be replaced by one of his brothers on 13 June 1360.[18]

John Drummond seems to have been allowed to adopt the style 'Lord' or perhaps 'Earl' of Menteith and sometime in 1360 received a grant from his wife of the lands of Aberfoyle which lay within the Strathgartney portion of western Menteith. This was a transfer which David would not confirm until 12 November 1361, but by then the Drummonds would have cemented their links to the crown both through a marriage to a daughter of Robert Erskine and Margaret Logie's elevation as the king's new mistress.[19] Thus for the moment David may have been forced to accept Stewart control of Fife at the expense of William Ramsay: indeed Isabella of Fife's grant of Kinnoul to

---

16 Fraser ed., *Red Book of Menteith*, i, 116–32 for Margaret's husbands; *CPR*, iii, 467, 522 for Mar dispensations.

17 According to *Chron. Fordun*, i, 317, Mar 'was betrothed to the heiress of Menteith; but afterwards, egged on by the devil, he, by trumping up colourable pretexts, and untrue pleas, got a divorce, without there being any offspring between them'. Perhaps just as suspect is the issue of a papal marriage dispensation for John Drummond and Margaret on 18 April 1360, a month before the Menteith assize at Stirling (*Vetera*, 315) and probably long after the couple had wed and had children.

18 *Rot. Scot.*, i, 849.

19 *RRS*, vi, no. 264; Fraser ed., *Red Book of Menteith*, ii, 245–7; *Scots Peerage*, vii, 32–7. Robert's daughter, Mariota Erskine, and her husband, Maurice Drummond, brother of Margaret Logie (née Drummond), were granted lands in the Perthshire barony of Megginch, near the baronies of Kinnoul (now held by Robert Erskine), Errol and Rait, by Thomas Bisset, in *c.* 1363–4: for Bisset as David's placeman in Fife, see below.

Erskine and the links of that knight and his fellow justiciar, Hugh Eglintoun, with the Steward (brothers-in-law by 1362) may have facilitated such a compromise. However, by redirecting control of the earldom of Menteith David had gained a considerable measure of territorial redress in central Scotland. The only other parties to gain from the May 1360 assize to calm the Menteith feud were the Campbells of Lochawe who were awarded Countess Mary's lands in Cowal which she had held of the Steward. This may have represented another face-saving compromise to pacify the Steward but it may also have been a further royalist attempt to detach the former Bruce in-laws, the Campbells, from their west-coast masters, the Stewarts: this was a ploy the Mortimers' connections with the other Campbell scions in Perthshire and Forfarshire may also have aided.[20]

These territorial disputes were the major concern of Robert Steward and his close kin and allies by 1360: the earls of Angus and Douglas were surely embroiled here through far more minor Perthshire land claims. However, there were two universal royal policy matters which may have united much magnate opposition to the king and his chivalric cadre and mistress at this time. First, there remained, of course, considerable ill-feeling and dread at the prospect of David seeking out a fresh succession-peace deal with Edward III, abortive terms for which only a year before had probably included the likely return of some of the Disinherited nobles to Scotland, disrupting existing magnate holdings, and a final end to the chance of alliance with France. Second, it was once again Sir Thomas Gray who, although surely mistaken in stating that Katherine Mortimer was a Londoner whom David had befriended during captivity, nonetheless asserted that the king 'could not dispense with her presence. He rode continually with her which display of favour was displeasing to some of the Scottish lord's. In this way, in the eyes of those magnates frozen out of royal favour, Katherine could have grown, all too easily, into a symbol of the Anglophile inner counsel of the king. Her husband and many of his associates had after all been fellow captives of the English with the king in 1346 or 1356 (after Poitiers) and had forsworn further war to secure their release, profiting heavily from their support of David since 1357 as a result.

Admittedly, David had not despatched any official embassy to England to resume such talks since the spring of 1359: the Stewarts, Douglas and others must have been content in part for the time being to see the ransom payment resumed during the following winter. But some Anglo-Scottish contact was maintained. In April 1360 Edward III issued a safe-conduct to a representative of Edward Balliol to travel to Scotland. In the same month passes were issued to the Scots royalists, John Herries of Terregles and John Lyle of

20 Fraser ed., *Red Book of Menteith*, i, 109–15.

Duchal (whom David had briefly made his new keeper of Edinburgh Castle), to visit Queen Joan in London as her 'familiars': both these men had been captured in battle alongside the king in 1346. In addition, David helped Archibald Douglas and William Towers of Dalry finalise their release from England after their capture in a border skirmish in 1358–9.[21]

These exchanges may themselves have helped facilitate an important formal meeting held at 'Rokelle' in Annandale on 1 May 1360. David himself, together with his Warden of the west march, John Stewart of Dalswinton, had agreed to meet the de Bohun earl of Hereford and consequently to share equally the administration and revenues of Annandale, excluding Lochmaben Castle and its lands: much of the lordship was still under English occupation but during the talks of the 1350s Scottish envoys had designated this a private concern which the Bruce king should negotiate in person.[22] However, moves towards full Anglo-Scottish talks may also have been resumed before Katherine Mortimer's murder in late June. A Scottish general council met at Perth about 12 April 1360, the very day upon which Edward III's army had threatened Paris. No record of proceedings survives but the council may have approved approaches which resulted in Edward III issuing a safe-conduct to a formal Scottish estates' embassy in late July.[23] Even if this were not the case, the political community *must* have generally expected some movement to be initiated by David on the diplomatic front soon, not least because France could no longer evade the conclusion of a full peace. Indeed, the treaty of Brétigny – agreed a week later on 8 May 1360 – marked the end for the foreseeable future of any hope of the kind of active Franco-Scottish alliance which the Steward had sought against the royal will in 1359. The new Anglo-French peace involved a promise to King Edward from John II and his son, Charles, that they would not use any of their alliances with Scotland; Edward in turn would ratify the treaty by August 1361.[24] David could now use his limited influence on the stability of this Anglo-French peace as a bargaining chip in talks with Edward and his war-weary council to try to reduce his ransom and improve his diplomatic circumstances.

By visiting Annandale at the beginning of May 1360, however, David also took advantage of an immediate opportunity to strengthen royal authority in southern and south-western Scotland and to reduce the influence of such

---

21 *Rot. Scot.*, i, 846–8; *ER*, ii, 50, 78.
22 *CDS*, iv, no. 47; Duncan, 'A Question about the Succession, 1364', 15–6.
23 *RRS*, vi, no. 234; *RPS*, 1360/4/1; *Rot. Scot.*, i, 851 (embassy of the bishop of Brechin, Patrick earl of March/Moray, Robert Erskine, Walter Wardlaw the archdeacon of Lothian and Sir John Preston).
24 Cuttino, *English Medieval Diplomacy*, 93–4; *Foedera*, ii, 487. On 24 October 1360, the French would, though, promise not to break their alliance with Scotland until the English ratified the treaty of Brétigny (PRO E30/66).

regional lords as William, earl of Douglas. Yet in doing so the king may have contributed to the backlash which cost his mistress her life. As we have seen, David may have intervened already in southern Scotland against Douglas in early 1360, perhaps in part to punish him for his complicity in the crisis of 1359. For at Edinburgh on 10 January 1360 the king may have obliged the earl to resign the church of Cavers in Roxburghshire, a key Douglas seat, to the Abbey of Melrose, as well as to pay for masses to be said by that house for the soul of William Douglas of Liddesdale, the earl's victim of 1353.[25] The Douglas earl, the Steward and a number of royal household knights also appear to have accompanied David to his summit with Hereford at 'Rokelle'. They were still with the king when he halted on his return journey at the Balliol foundation of Sweetheart Abbey on 5 May where he confirmed a thirteenth-century grant by Devorguilla (d. 1290), King John Balliol's mother. The rest of David's journey back to Edinburgh may have taken him through or past Douglas earldom territory in Buittle, Dumfriesshire, Liddesdale and Peeblesshire.[26]

Finally back in David's chosen capital of Edinburgh, the royal court would have resumed its seat in the castle which had until very recently been controlled by the Douglas earl. But, as we have seen, by May 1360 at the latest, perhaps many months earlier, the king had passed its keeping to Sir John Lyle of Duchal; there may also have been a growing role in that shire for Archibald Douglas, whom David would make Edinburgh's castle-keeper by 1362 and who was a close associate at Poitiers of Katherine Mortimer's husband, William Ramsay (the sheriff of Edinburgh for David before 1346): Archibald would receive an annual fee of £200 from the crown in his Edinburgh role. The Douglas earl cannot have been comfortable with the rising prominence of Archibald, his ambitious illegitimate cousin and a bastard of the Black Douglas icon, the 'Good' Sir James, and who had been left a close heir to the earl's family after the murder of the knight of Liddesdale. In the meantime, on 27 May 1360, while still in Edinburgh, David followed up his recent actions by issuing another letter warning the justiciar south-of-Forth – William, earl of Douglas – and other southern officials to desist from interfering in the regality of the Abbey of Melrose.[27]

Thus Douglas, like the Stewarts and Earl Thomas of Angus, may have felt his interests to have been increasingly under threat at the time of David's very

---

25 Brown, *Black Douglases*, 189; *RRS*, vi, no. 227. On the same day, David also inspected a Douglas earl charter to John Towers of lands in Lanarkshire (*ibid*, no. 228).

26 *Ibid*, no. 235.

27 *Ibid*, nos. 236–7; Fraser ed., *The Douglas Book*, i, 236 and iii, no. 23; *RRS*, vi, no. 51 (Douglas tailzie, 1342); *RMS*, i, App. i, no. 148; *ER*, ii, 50, 78, 92; *Chron. Fordun*, i, 377n; NAS RH 1/2/911 (Ramsay); Brown, *Black Douglases*, 55–6.

public association with Katherine Mortimer. He may also have been alarmed by the crown's mounting ability to raise cash from magnate localities. David had already apparently poached the services of William Gledstanes, Douglas's bailie at Melrose, as an official charged with overseeing sheep and wool movements in the marches. David's second journey into the marches in 1360 – and this time we know that Katherine was definitely with him – must have intensified these worries.[28] For not only did David's trip about 24 June come a month after the exchequer had received significant sums from Peeblesshire (where Douglas was sheriff), but it saw the royal party stop at the hotly contested Melrose Abbey only after handing over the third full instalment of the ransom to English representatives at the border.[29] It is surely highly suggestive that instead of once more entrusting this task to a lesser officer or, say, Patrick, earl of March, the king chose to accompany this 10,000-merk payment in person – the first instalment handed over in cash since the crisis of 1359. Indeed, it is surely not unreasonable to imagine that the armed security for this cash could have been best provided by the likes of Archibald Douglas, William Ramsay and the chivalry of Fife and the Lothians, perhaps even of Angus and Mar, and that some of the great magnates – the Steward, Douglas, Angus and March – may have been forced to come on, *or* been deliberately excluded from, this errand: each of these nobles had, as we have seen, withheld revenue or even deforced royal collectors within the last two years and/or colluded briefly in the forceful redirection of royal policy in 1359. No royal acts survive from the month of June 1360. But if these great nobles had been in attendance, they may have been obliged to watch their king take full advantage of the occasion by exchanging letters and messages with the English representatives and then celebrating the midsummer anniversary of Bannockburn (and St John the Baptist's feast) over the tomb of his father's heart at Melrose, all with Katherine by his side. The border meeting would most likely also have involved the exchange of the Steward's sons as hostages and, significantly, talk of the consequences of Angus's broken parole.

In short, whilst the fugitive Thomas, earl of Angus, had obviously been treated worst by David in recent months – and his landed interests were most directly threatened by the connections of the king's mistress – there were several other major magnates who must have felt by mid-1360 that Katherine Mortimer's death would be a useful gesture: a warning shot or vengeful blow to force the king to ease off in several areas. It is highly unlikely that Katherine had anywhere near the high level of political influence over David which the chroniclers Gray and later Bower suggest: her striking absence from any surviving contemporary Scottish government

28 *ER*, ii, 51, 68.
29 *Ibid*, 34–57; *Rot. Scot.*, i, 851.

or family record is surely proof of that. But by targeting this woman, these nobles could feasibly act by convention as loyal if disgruntled subjects and strike out at someone who could be made a scapegoat as the king's 'evil counsel' while the real focus of their enmity remained, in truth, the policies and person of the king himself. There is always the possibility, too, that Katherine was pregnant and Queen Joan known publicly to be ill or contemplating divorce before taking religious orders.[30]

Indeed, Sir Thomas Gray makes it plain that it was *'at the instigation of certain great men of Scotland'* (plural) that de Hull struck the fatal blow, although it is unclear whether or not this followed a plan laid well in advance or was a spontaneous act in the heat of the moment of the provocative June trip to the border and Melrose. The shady assassins can neither be positively identified nor tied directly to the earl of Angus: Hull might, though, just as easily have come from the following of the Steward or William, earl of Douglas, the latter being a close wartime associate of Angus in the 1350s. Sir Robert Dalziel (pronounced 'De-ell', hence 'de Hull'?), the earl of Douglas's 'sergeant' in the sheriffship of Lanarkshire, is a possible candidate: David would issue letters declaring this knight, then 'in England', forfeit while regranting his baronies of Dalziel and Motherwell in Lanarkshire in 1363 and 1366.[31] In this context, Bower's version of the killing, written in the 1440s, reads like a deliberate attempt to deflect guilt from the Stewarts and Douglas – the greatest houses of Bower's fifteenth-century world – to a single desperate party, the foolhardy and intemperate Angus who lashed out at the adulterous King David (who had thus sinned just like his biblical and saintly namesake, David of Israel).[32] The anonymous contemporary fourteenth-century sources of Fordun and Wyntoun make no mention of Katherine and her sorry fate at all, surely because these authors were even closer to the parties competing for power in Fife in the 1350s and '60s (many of whom lived until after 1400) and also close to the Bruce king, whose adultery could not be mentioned.

Death and Taxes, 1360–1

David must have been explosively angry at the slaughter of his mistress. For at least the third time in his troubled reign – just like Katherine's brother-in-

---

30 My thanks to Fay Oliver for this suggestion about Katherine; Prestwich, 'Katherine Mortimer's Death at Soutra', 116.

31 *Chron. Fordun*, i, 371–3; *RMS*, i, nos., 129, 227 and App. ii, no. 1341; Brown, *Black Douglases*, 45–7, 57. Robert Dalziel was English, having helped Malcolm Fleming, earl of Wigtown, escape after Neville's Cross (*Chron. Lanercost*, 337–9). 4 July 1364, at Perth, may also have seen David oversee hearings regarding the murder of his mistress: David inspected the resignation by a 'Robert Hull, lord of Ardorny' of the lands of Fyal in the former royal thanage of Alyth in Perthshire (*RRS*, vi, no. 324).

32 *Chron. Bower*, 321; 2 Kings 11:15 (Vulgate) or 2 Samuel 11:15 (NEB).

law, Alexander Ramsay, in 1342, and Ranald MacRuaridh in 1346 – a favoured royal subject had been slain while about royal business, at the orders of a noble who had felt his personal and political interests, forged in David's absence, threatened by the crown. This time it had been the most intimate and unarmed partner of the king to be 'wickedly killed' and the murder weapon had been drawn within sight of the monarch himself. On the morning of 25 June, David must surely have been resolved that on this occasion the guilty party would not escape punishment because of crown weakness, as in the previous cases.

Yet there is only limited, indirect evidence to suggest that David was able to enforce the weight of royal law. Angus was quickly arrested; David can be found apparently resuming his normal duties by issuing letters regarding the Abbey of Scone's forestry rights while at Perth on 5 July 1360. Angus was then imprisoned in the royal castle of Dumbarton where the expenses of his confinement would be paid until at least August 1362. Although all too typically no formal record of an assize (or indeed any proceedings) against Thomas has survived, it is also possible that in late October 1360, during a full parliament at Scone, Angus was tried for ordering the murder and forfeited of his lands and goods though not his life: the title 'earl of Angus' would not be used again until it was revived by the Red Douglas line in 1388.[33] In the intervening months in 1360, however, David certainly seems to have increased his input to affairs in Angus and the Mearns. There were further royal gifts of Forfarshire holdings made throughout the second half of the year to: Sir John Lindsay of Thorston, whom David had made sheriff of Ayr about 1358; to William, earl of Sutherland, at that time a hostage for the ransom in England, who had his lands in Angus, Kincardineshire and Aberdeenshire confirmed on 20 August 1360; to Sir William Chalmers, who may have had his grant of Forfar lands from a John St Michael confirmed when David visited Aberdeen about 14 September (and perhaps reviewed the homicide of another royal favourite, Sir David Barclay, who had been slain in 1350 in Aberdeen – according to Fordun's source – by a 'John St Michael' on the orders of the knight of Liddesdale); to Patrick, bishop of Brechin, the Chancellor; and to Alexander Strachan, whose father had been killed at Neville's Cross and who by 1362 at least would be made coroner of Forfarshire.[34]

---

33 *RRS*, vi, nos. 238, 243; *APS*, i, 19; *RPS*, 1360/10/1–2; Brown, *Black Douglases*, 83.
34 *RRS*, vi, nos. 241, 245, 248–9; *RMS*, i, App. i, nos. 145, 149 and App. ii, no. 1272; *Chron. Fordun*, i, 369; *ER*, ii, 113, 166. For this and later royal favour to the Strachans, see: Fraser ed., *Memorials of the Montgomeries*, ii, 1–9; *RRS*, vi, nos. 106, 351; *RMS*, i, no. 222 and App. ii, no. 1386; *ER*, ii, 76. A John Strachan was a collector of contribution monies in Angus at this time and a Thomas Strachan worked for the justiciar in Aberdeen (*ibid*, 40, 176).

But more significantly, David may also have taken a direct interest in the fate of the small earldom of Angus. He granted Angus's wife, Margaret Sinclair, a pension of £60 in her capacity as countess. Yet most tellingly of all, by October 1360 Thomas, earl of Mar, had returned from the continent to seek the hand of Angus's and Margaret's daughter, also Margaret, as his second wife, perhaps as much in pursuit of the neighbouring title and lands of Angus's earldom as for a woman of 'suitable rank' as his spouse: as the earl of Angus and Margaret Sinclair had only had a dispensation to wed in 1353, this heiress – the eldest of two girls – may have been very young (and Angus's forfeiture may have placed her marriage in the care of the crown).[35]

Elsewhere in Scotland, however, there is some evidence that David, just as in 1342, used the moral high ground ceded to the crown by the murder to extend royal authority against the interests of the other regional nobles behind Katherine's death. His aforementioned grant of the barony of Kinnoul to Robert Erskine in Perthshire west of Atholl, after its resignation by Isabella of Fife, occurred when David visited Perth on 22 July. Another visit to Perth about 20 October, just before that month's parliament, also saw the king confirm the knight of Liddesdale's grant of the Fife coastal barony of Aberdour to that lord's nephew and heir presumptive (after Archibald the Grim), James Douglas of Lothian.[36] This surely marks the beginning of the striking rise of James and his close family throughout the 1360s to prominence as a Douglas scion favoured by the crown alongside Archibald as a royal supporter in the Lothians and marches, an obvious challenge to the authority of the first Douglas earl who had occupied Liddesdale and his murdered godfather's Lothian lands centred on Dalkeith. It was surely about this time – perhaps at the October parliament – that the Douglas earl was finally removed as justiciar south-of-Forth. In late 1360 David also seems to have extended favour to another Black Douglas supporter, William Towers of Dalry, and perhaps to have rebuked earl William for his conduct as sheriff of Lanark.[37]

The Douglas earl and the Steward were thus present at what must have been another extremely tense parliament at Scone in October 1360. David seems to have taken considerable trouble to confirm many of the privileges of the burgh of Stirling, perhaps as a process of re-asserting royal control publicly over that seat after Angus's years of influence there. About this time David also seems to have granted out lands and river-crossing points to some lesser men bordering the Forth estuary and running away from Stirling towards Kinross and Fife: these men would have served the crown there

---

35 *ER*, ii, 78, 115; *RMS*, i, App. ii, no. 1301; *Vetera*, 300–4; *Scots Peerage*, i, 170.
36 *RRS*, vi, nos. 51, 239, 242.
37 *RMS*, i, App. i, no. 146 and App. ii, no. 1328; *ER*, ii, 82, 394.

under the guidance of both Robert Erskine as keeper of Stirling Castle and the king's half-nephew, Robert Bruce of Clackmannan.[38] Moreover, over the course of the next year or so, David embarked on a fairly substantial programme of royal castle repairs and modifications, including 'military engines', overseen by his new keepers at Stirling and Edinburgh, and by Danielston at Dumbarton. Whether or not these investments reflected David's fear of potential rebellion by his political opponents of 1359 is unclear. Castle-keepers Erskine and Archibald Douglas were among David's regular courtiers in the second half of the year along with the bishops of St Andrews and Brechin, Walter Haliburton, William Keith the Marischal, John Preston, William Livingston, Hugh Eglintoun and Walter Moigne, as well as the Steward, Douglas and March/Moray.[39]

Such patronage, and the existing crown officers in place, undoubtedly helped in the crown's still improving collection of royal revenues and ransom levies. The third contribution returns were intromitted between August 1360 and June 1361, yielding a total of £3,195 and including the predictably huge sum of £509 from Forfarshire; areas of Stewart, Douglas, March/Moray and Ross interest also contributed heavily both to this tax and to the clerical tenth granted by the Pope in 1359 which would yield £1,753 to the crown by December 1364. The Chamberlain's ordinary receipts also showed marked growth. For the year to May 1360, Walter of Biggar had intromitted £3,128; but for the year to June 1361 the exchequer took £4,895 from rents, customs and fermes. Clearly, David reaped the benefits of this income. Royal household expenditure between April 1359 and May 1360 had been a meagre £435, some 14 per cent of total income; but for the year to June 1361 – the twelve months after Katherine's death – David would spend at least £1,608 on his household, some 32 per cent of the Chamberlain's receipts not including rents, casualties and annuities which David had alienated to his chivalric cadre and kin.[40]

There was a fundamental reason, of course, why David could afford to switch so abruptly to a greater display of courtly outlay. In the wake of the Anglo-French treaty of Brétigny and his punctual deposit of the third ransom instalment, David had decided to cease further payments to England in the hope of negotiating a better deal with the peacetime Edward III. Katherine Mortimer's murder at the hands of his political opponents on the very day of a ransom payment may have stiffened the king's resolve in this direction. A safe-conduct issued to Scottish ambassadors on 26 July 1360

38 RRS, vi, nos. 243–6; RMS, i, App. ii, nos. 1356, 1365, 1375.
39 ER, ii, 25, 51, 79–80, 82 (watches and repairs at Dumbarton castle); 78–9, 83, 92 (a new well and well-tower, munitions and military engines for Edinburgh castle); 64, 75, 78, 113 (engines, repairs and munitions for Stirling Castle).
40 Ibid, 57–70 (fermes/contribution), 71–83 (Chamberlain).

seems to have been taken up: on 20 August Edward III appointed his own magnate and prelate envoys to discuss 'a perpetual league and peace with David de Brus' through that party's representatives, Patrick the Chancellor-bishop of Brechin, Walter Wardlaw, a papal collector and the new Arch-deacon of Lothian (replacing David's loyal cleric, Walter Moffat), the knights Robert Erskine and John Preston, and – suggesting perhaps that the Lancaster/Gaunt/Moray deal might again be tabled – the aged former Anglophile, Patrick, earl of March/Moray. No record of the outcome of these talks – if held – is extant. But either the October 1360 parliament or a council held at Edinburgh in November (for which, again, no proceedings survive) seems to have countenanced further negotiations.[41] On 12 January 1361 an embassy of two bishops, two earls and two barons with up to 150 retainers was issued with a safe-conduct to England: the bishops of St Andrews and Brechin, Archdeacon Wardlaw, the earls of Douglas and March/Moray and, again, Erskine and Preston.[42]

Yet even though David and his close supporters clearly wanted to press ahead diplomatically, the reality was that Katherine's murder had in no way given the crown a mandate to do so. Even though by the new year David had perhaps persuaded the earls of Douglas and March to once again at least consider sounding out the possible benefits to their houses in patronage and status of seeking an Anglo-Scottish peace, thus isolating the Steward and his sons, little or no headway seems to have been made in the talks of July 1360–spring 1361. In fact, Douglas and March/Moray may have proved a disruptive influence on these embassies, representative of the persistent opposition of much of the community to David's murky plans. Such understandable and active resistance to the dramatic changes proposed – like the return of the Disinherited, an alliance with England and the possible succession of a Plantagenet prince to the Scottish throne – may explain why David would refrain from calling another parliament or full council for almost two years after late 1360, until September 1362. The king's inability to persuade a majority of his subjects to back his succession plan reflected the dynastic and political limbo he still found himself in: separated from his queen, childless and heavily ransomed. This in turn prevented him from gaining the upper hand in domestic affairs.

There is surely more evidence to suggest that in the wake of Katherine's murder David continued to be badly compromised by political opposition. The imprisonment of Angus in Dumbarton in the care of the Steward retainer, John Danielston, may in itself have been forced upon the king, preventing him from executing and forfeiting Earl Thomas in full. By 16

41 *APS*, xii, 12; *RPS*, 1360/11/1.
42 *Rot. Scot.*, i, 851–2.

March 1361, David's talks with England had been reduced to smaller private approaches, with the king asking the English Chancellor, the bishop of Norwich, to admit William Landellis, bishop of St Andrews, and the royal secretary, John Carrick, 'on matters touching [David's] self and realm'.[43] The Steward and other magnates also continued to resist the crown's fiscalism and territorial intrusion. By June 1361 the Steward was even uplifting the ferms of the hotly contested royal lands of the *Abnethia* of Dull in northern Perthshire (formerly held by David's half-brother who died in 1333) in lieu of a debt owed to him by the king. A striking number of dioceses and, as we shall see, religious houses also began to withhold or fail to intromit their clerical tenth.[44]

Yet surely most frustrating of all for the crown was the rapid unravelling of the Menteith settlement. Sometime after July 1360 John Drummond of Concraig, the newly created earl of Menteith, died: by 9 or 16 September 1361 Robert Stewart, the Steward's third son, had requested a papal dispensation to allow him to wed Drummond's widow, Margaret, Countess of Menteith. This was a match which could have taken place as early as autumn 1360 and which was designed – as the Steward described it in writing to Avignon – 'for securing the common weal and safety of the whole realm of Scotland . . . [for] unless the treaty be carried out, it might be truly feared that all manner of dangers would threaten the earldoms of Strathearn and Menteith'.[45] This papal permit must have been accompanied in late 1360 or 1361 by the Stewarts' physical occupation of much of Menteith. Thus David, the only legitimate Bruce of his day, had lost that province to the Steward's brood just as the crown and its placeman had lost Fife to Walter Stewart in 1359. This was a reverse which at this juncture the connections of the king's cadre of Lowland knights and probable new mistress, Margaret Logie (née Drummond), could do little to counter: the crown was only able to make the token gesture of denying to Robert Stewart such full title as 'Earl' of Menteith as Sir John Graham (and, perhaps, Drummond) had enjoyed. As the Stewart plea to the Pope suggests, if David had tried to force any diplomatic or territorial issue to royal advantage at this time he would most likely have provoked a violent reaction from several of his entrenched regional magnates. No wonder, then, that on 26 January 1361 a surely pessimistic Bruce king secured a papal grant of a confessor's power to absolve him in death.[46]

---

43 *CDS*, iv, no. 59.
44 *ER*, ii, 72 – the Steward's access to Dull may have been given in lieu of the £40 pension which David had granted him in 1358–9 but which was not paid (*RMS*, i, App. ii no. 1226).
45 *Vetera*, 317; *CPR*, ii, 376; Fraser ed., *Red Book of Menteith*, i, 128–33; Boardman, *Early Stewart Kings*, 16.
46 *CPP*, i, 365.

The remainder of the king's thirty-eighth year, then, dragged on as one of relative inertia and stalemate. The limited evidence suggests that David's itinerary slowed in contrast to previous years, and his horizons seemed limited to a low-key policy of continuing to make small grants to crown men in sensitive localities while really waiting upon events to turn fortune his way. January 12 found him at Linlithgow where the peel was being repaired 'for the king's coming'. Here David issued the first of several grants in that month to James Douglas of Lothian, gifting him minor lands close to Edinburgh and in Dumfriesshire: the familiar daily council of the Steward, the Douglas earl, the bishop of Brechin, Erskine and Preston witnessed these transactions. Between mid-January and mid-April David remained in Edinburgh; only letters from the king allowing Melrose Abbey to negotiate independently with the English and ordering Arbroath Abbey in Angus to cease paying out 'profitless pensions' survive from this period.[47]

However, 17 April 1361 found the king at Perth – perhaps at the beginning of a northern justice ayre – with roughly the same daily council. There he remained until early May, inspecting a charter of Alexander III to the earls of Lennox, an act which William Ramsay of Colluthie witnessed. By 7 May David and his council were in Aberdeen, confirming the rights of the burgh's Carmelite friars and probably also appointing the Mar man, Walter Moigne, as sheriff of that shire. A number of royal acts survive in note form, imprecisely dated, for this period, too, in which the king granted minor lands and annuities to Lawrence Gilliebrand, William Keith the Marsichal and Moigne again.[48] By mid-June David, the Steward, Douglas and March (who in one royal act at least at this time was not given his full style as 'earl of Moray') were back in Edinburgh where the king inspected Robert I's grant of a tenth of all judicial income from Galloway to the Abbey of Holyrood. There then follows a gap of almost three months until David's extant acts resume at Dumbarton on 18 September 1361 where Sir John Kennedy of Dunure was granted Carrick lands and the king perhaps also granted out a number of minor Ayrshire and Dumfriesshire holdings. David may then have visited Thomas, ex-earl of Angus: the king's undatable acts about this time also include further Forfarshire grants, including the barony of Lundie (right on the edge of the Angus earldom) to the keeper of Edinburgh Castle, John Lyle of Duchal.[49] By 6 October the king was back in Edinburgh granting the 'cunzie [currency] house' in that burgh to the Florentine moneyer, John Mulekinn. This grant may have formed part of a

---

47 *RRS*, vi, nos. 250–6; *RMS*, i, App. ii, no. 1367.
48 *RRS*, vi, nos. 257–262; *RMS*, i, no. 264, and App. ii, nos. 1336, 1337, 1354, 1361–2, 1387, 1392, 1399, 1404–4.
49 *RRS*, vi, no. 263; *RMS*, i, no. 185 and App. ii, nos. 1366, 1370, 1385–6 (Alexander Strachan made coroner of Forfar and Kincardineshire).

wider crown fancy to consolidate Edinburgh as the royal capital and mint.
Undated acts survive from about 1361–2 in which David granted a number
of minor tenements and hinterland holdings, pastures, mills and pensions to
Edinburgh townspeople like the leading merchant, Roger Hogg, and lesser
Lothian nobles like William More of Abercorn and William Towers of
Dalry.[50]

On 12 November 1361, however, David moved north briefly to Scone,
most likely in the wake of John Drummond's death and the Stewarts' success
in Menteith. Royal damage-limitation included confirming the grant of
Margaret, Countess of Menteith, of Aberfoyle in Strathgartney to the
Drummonds; confirming Sir Alexander Menzies' possession of the lands
of Fothergill in Atholl, granted to him by *Clann Donnchaidh*, the Steward's
uneasy allies in northern Atholl; and finally, confirming in turn a grant of
Perthshire lands by Duncan, earl of Fife, to the *Clann Donnchaidh*. But
David's imprecisely noted lost acts for *c.* 1361 include no other siginificant
Perthshire grants beyond a few burgh tenements and minor ecclesiastical
transactions (including a 700/- pension for the Abbot of Inchmahome in
Menteith from the justice profits of the shires of Fife and Perth).[51] Yet it was
only in Fife – a region where David does not, however, seem to have resided
throughout 1361 – that the crown adopted a more aggressive approach.
During the second half of the year, David may have extended favour both to
Robert Erskine's brother, Alan (of Inchmartin in Perthshire), then keeper of
Loch Leven Castle, by appointing him as coroner of Fife; and to Sir Walter
Oliphant, who was given the former Stewart-controlled barony of Kelly and
who would become David's brother by marriage to a royal half-sister by
1365. Thereafter David seems to have been content to close out the year
back in Edinburgh: a few minor grants survive for early December, witnessed again by the likes of the bishops of Brechin and St Andrews, the
Steward, Douglas, Keith, Erskine, Moigne, Haliburton and Herries.[52]

Faith and Force: the Build-up to Civil War, 1362

David had, then, by no means set the country ablaze with royal retribution
or initiatives in the eighteen months after Katherine Mortimer's violent
death. In the end, it required two more probably totally unexpected deaths
to break some of the deadlock in Scotland. The first may have occurred
sometime in late 1361 – thus perhaps explaining David's recent grants

50 *Ibid*, no. 101 and App. ii, nos. 1352, 1357, 1363, 1384, 1388, 1393, 1402, 1409;
    RRS, vi, no. 266.
51 *Ibid*, no. 264; *RMS*, i, App. ii, nos. 1325, 1332, 1338, 1356, 1364, 1368, 1371,
    1390, 1395–6.
52 *RRS*, vi, nos. 265–6; *RMS*, i, no. 263 and App. ii, nos. 1353, 1365, 1372, 1373–4.
    For Oliphant, see below, ch. 10.

affecting Fife – or, as is more likely, shortly after August 1362. For by the end of that year at the latest the Steward's second son, Walter Stewart, 'lord of Fife', would be dead.[53] Yet in truth David may already have decided some time before this stroke of luck to break his acquiescence in Stewart dominance in central Scotland and to assert royal power over the Lowlands in general. The royal grant issued at Arbroath on 6 January 1362 seemed to signal as much. On that occasion the king *re*-confirmed to Bartholomew Leon (his envoy to the papacy in 1349) an original grant by John Graham, earl of Menteith, in early 1346 of the barony of Barnbougle near Linlithgow, this time with the explicit stipulation that if Graham's unnamed successors in Menteith – now the Stewarts and their cousin, Sir John Menteith – wished to recover these lands they would have to pay 2,000 merks in feudal casualties.[54]

But David's intervention in person in the most valuable of all the disputed lands, Fife, may have begun with a scare for the king. According to Bower, while crossing the Forth estuary by ship from North Berwick in Berwickshire north to Earlsferry in Fife in early 1362, David narrowly escaped shipwreck for the second time in his life. In thanks, he decided to expand an existing cult and build a chapel to St Monan close to where he had safely reached shore. This new shrine would be manned by at least four Dominican friars probably provided by the Priory of St Andrews. This is a much more credible foundation legend than that provided by Jean Froissart (who visited Scotland in 1365), that while praying to St Monan one of the arrow heads embedded in David's skull – and which allegedly gave him headaches at the full moon – dropped out of the king's nose.[55] David can, indeed, be found on 3 February 1362 at Ardross on the Fife coast, less than a mile west of St Monans and on land owned by one of his loyal knights, Sir William Dischington, who would be paid as royal master of works at St Monans and elsewhere throughout the decade; local tradition has also christened a 'Davy's rock', to be found a hundred yards or so offshore from the present-day church of St Monans.[56] But while David was undoubtedly capable of such acts of faith, the cruciform chapel he would pay over £613 to build at St

53 Boardman, *Early Stewart Kings*, 14–5.

54 *Ibid*, 16; *RRS*, vi, no. 267, an act witnessed by the bishops of St Andrews and Brechin, the Steward, the earl of March/Moray, Archibald Douglas and John Herries.

55 *Chron. Bower*, vii, 261, 464n (Froissart); Easson, *Medieval Religious Houses of Scotland*, 102.

56 *RRS*, vi, no. 268, when David ordered the Chamberlain to pay 1 merk a year from Dundee's fermes to the priory of St Andrews as granted by David, earl of Huntingdon (d. 1219); J. Turnbull, 'The Parish Church of St Monans', *Transactions of the Aberdeen Ecclesiological Society*, iii (1895), 180–92, 185; I.H. Forsyth & J.I. Chisholm, *The Geology of East Fife* (Edinburgh 1977), 178–9.

Monans over the next nine years – with timber shipped from as far as Inverness – gave the king a perfect foothold adjacent to both the lands of the contested earldom of Fife and the diocese of St Andrews as well as within a valuable stretch of arable land and coastal touns, ports and saltpans; it also allowed him to challenge the influence of the Douglas and March earls within the royal hinterland of the Forth estuary.[57]

That a royal foundation at St Monans gave David greater control over, and legitimate access to, Fife was partly due to the extent of the misty cult of that sixth-century Irish cleric whom David and his contemporaries, or Scots of the fifteenth century, seem to have turned into a Hungarian associated with St Adrian, the martyr of the isle of May in the Forth estuary. This spiritual zone certainly stretched from the Fife earls' ferry just west of Elie, on through Kilconquar parish and Inveray (now St Monans), resurfacing at the royal burgh and mills of Crail; it also ran further inland into mainland Fife. In addition, Inveray/St Monans also had a strong Bruce connection as a possession of Adam of Kilconquhar, a descendant of the ancient earls of Fife. Adam's widow, Marjorie, had been David II's grandmother and a daughter of Neil, the last Celtic earl of Carrick: Adam had died on crusade at Acre with Prince Edmund of England in 1272, perhaps having taken part in campaigns with the old pretender, Robert Bruce of Annandale, David's great-grandfather.[58] Royal possession of St Monans furthermore added an important link in a royalist chain which ran from St Andrews all the way along the northern Forth coast to Stirling: from the Augustinian priory at Pittenweem (with its out-house on the isle of May); past Newark castle, belonging to the royalist envoy of the 1350s, Sir James Sandilands, and a mere two hundred yards from St Monan's chapel; then past Dischington's lands at Ardross; through the Earlsferry; the royal manor at Kinghorn; James Douglas's lands at Aberdour; the Augustinian priory on the isle of Inchcolm; the royal manor at Inverkeithing; St David's (now Dalgety) bay and the Queens' ferry of St Margaret; then on to Culross and the shorter Forth crossings at Kincardine and Clackmannan where the king's cousin and Sir Robert Erskine held land.[59]

But as a part of the wider picture Earlsferry and St Monans also formed important points along the immensely popular pilgrims' way from Europe,

57 *ER*, ii, 114, 137, 169, 175, 221, 243, 289, 307, 333, 347, 357. For much of what follows, see Penman, 'Christian Days and Knights', 256–62.

58 A. Boyle, 'Notes on Scottish Saints', *IR*, xxxii (1981), 59–81, 66; J.M. McKinlay, *Ancient Scottish Church Dedications – vol. II Non-Scriptural Dedications* (Edinburgh 1914), 492–3; S. Fyall, *St Monans: History, Customs and Superstitions* (Durham 1999), 23–31; Macquarrie, *Scotland and the Crusades*, 57–9.

59 *RCAHMS: Counties of Fife, Kinross and Clackmannan* (Edinburgh 1933), 57–61 (Crail), 133–4 (Earlsferry and Ardross), 261–6 (St Monans and Newark), 310 (Kilconquhar) *et ad indecim*.

England and southern Scotland to St Andrews: as much is confirmed by the recent find near St Monans of a pilgrim's lead scallop badge from the shrine of St James of Compostella in Spain. This Scottish Lowland devotional route stretched south back over the Forth from Fife. The existing Inveray/St Monans shrine was originally in the patronage of the Cistercian nunnery in North Berwick, East Lothian, a barony-port which was itself, like its counterpart terminus at Earlsferry, an ancient possession of the earls of Fife. About 1358 David had installed his macer, Adam Cissour, as coroner of Berwickshire and keeper of the 'winter' port of North Berwick; by September 1365 David would also have appointed his St Andrews-trained chaplain, Walter Bell (an Oxford student in 1368), as vicar of North Berwick. In theory this gave David, through the St Monans cult and its associations, influence over the swelling pilgrimage traffic stopping at the chapel dedicated to St Mary at Whitekirk in East Lothian, just south of North Berwick, before taking the ferry across to Fife. Whitekirk is alleged to have been founded in 1309 on land held by the Augustinian monks of Holyrood (who provided David II's household chaplains after 1342) in memory of the defiance of Edward I's army by the Countess of March at nearby Dunbar Castle. This shrine to Our Lady the Virgin had been valuable enough for English pirates to strip it of its riches in Candlemas 1356 yet would have recovered to be celebrated by the Papacy in 1386 'for miracles brought by Jesus Christ'; by 1413 over 15,000 pilgrims to that shrine or passing through were said to offer some 1,422 merks annually. Thus by strengthening his associations with this devotional area about 1362 – as it surely flourished in the wake of a second bout of the Black Death that year – David may have secured a long-sought-after coping-stone to challenge the influence there of William, earl of Douglas, whose new cliff-top castle of Tantallon (begun *c.* 1350) overlooked Whitekirk, the Bass Rock and North Berwick. The latter was a barony which the Douglas earl himself would hold of Robert Stewart, earl of Fife and Menteith, after David's death in 1371, dominating the landscape which would form the stage of dramatic political conflict between Stewart crown and barons in 1406.[60]

In 1362, though, that the chapel of St Monans would be tangibly associated with the crown and the second Bruce king in person is made

60 P. Yeoman, *Pilgrimage in Medieval Scotland* (London 1999), 48, 50–1, 59–62, 116–8; C. Tabraham & D. Grove, *Tantallon Castle* (HMSO 1994); *RMS*, i, App. ii, no. 1184 (Cissour); Watt, *Scottish Graduates*, 34–5 (Bell); *APS*, i, 551, 565 (Douglas and North Berwick); *Chron. Bower*, vii, 291–3; *RCAHMS: County of East Lothian* (Edinburgh 1924), 17–21 (Dirleton), 57–67 (North Berwick and Tantallon), 71 (Bass), 125–8 (Whitekirk) *et ad indecim*; *Ibid: Country of Mid-Lothian and WestLothian* (Edinburgh 1929) and *ibid: City of Edinburgh* (Edinburgh 1951) *ad indecim*; Boardman, *Early Stewart Kings*, 292–7 for the events of 1406.

clear by the focal role the cult had to play at court. Most significantly, the feast day of St Monan was 1 March, the same as that of St David (of Wales), a feast upon which Edward III had sent the captive Scottish king wine to celebrate his namesake in 1357.[61] As such, St Monan's feast could in practice act as a quasi-personal cult for David, falling just four days short of his birthday and around which the chivalry, crusaders and clergy of the Lothians, Fife and the Lowlands in general could congregate at least once every year.[62] This would fit in well as the headline event of an annual itinerary which embraced other significant feast days which David seems to have marked with court ritual – a heady mixture, as might be expected, of the anniversaries of Bruce dynastic achievements, nationalist keystones and conventional religious observances.

These were dates which would have been commemorated by high mass and pilgrimages which on occasion saw the formal duties of government (e.g. the issuing of letters and charters) and household set aside.[63] These included the anniversaries of events like: the birth, inauguration and death of Robert I (11 July, 25/27 March, 7 June); the death of David's mother, Elizabeth de Burgh (7 November); David's own coronation and first marriage (24 November, 12 July); the deaths of the last 'MacMalcolm' kings from whom Robert I had claimed direct succession, Alexander II (8 July) and Alexander III (19 March); the battles of Stirling Bridge and Bannockburn (11 September and 23–4 June) but not those of Dupplin, Halidon Hill or Neville's Cross; and even perhaps the issue of the papal bull granting Scottish kings the rite of coronation and unction which David had been the first to use (13 June). Significantly, many of these dates – including the feast of St Monan – can be found commemorated in illuminated brieviaries known to be in Scotland about this time.[64]

Admittedly, David does not seem to have stopped all business to mark the feasts of Scottish national icons popularised by the crown and church in the thirteenth century, like St Andrew or St Margaret, in a similar way (although Bower insists that Margaret's feast and translation dates were 'always'

---

61 *CCR*, x (Edward III 1354–60), 347.
62 The available *RRS*, vi evidence shows that David at least can be found moving south to north of St Monans or vice-versa about every 1 March between 1362 and 1371.
63 The *ER* for the period reveal little of the likely numerous daily observances of the Scottish court, hinted at during David's captivity (above, ch. 6; Balfour-Melville, 'Papers relating to the Captivity of David II', 21–9). David's favoured dates after 1357 have been extrapolated by discounting the issue date (regardless of year) on all David's extant acts in *RRS*, vi, to reveal 'non-business days'.
64 E.g., C.R. Borland ed., *A Descriptive Catalogue of the Western Medieval Manuscripts in Edinburgh University Library* (Edinburgh 1916), 38–41. For psalters associated with the Ramsays of Colluthie and Queen Joan, see *Angels, Nobles and Unicorns: Art and Patronage in Medieval Scotland* (NMS 1982), 34–5, nos. C24, C27.

heeded). But the king could have marked their feast days and his own birthday by issuing grants as gifts as well as holding masses and distributing alms.[65] Yet David did seemingly stop government business to celebrate a number of regional Scottish cults favoured by his father, as well as many key Christian festivals: the feast of St Malachy (3 November), the Irish cult his great-grandfather had offended on pilgrimage; the highly popular feast of St Ninian of Whithorn (26 August); Candlemas (2 February); the Annuncia-tion, Assumption and Presentation of the Virgin (25 March, 15 August, 21 November), an extremely popular cult of the Middle Ages; All Souls (2 November) and Christmas, obvious regulars alongside other festivals of moveable date like Easter and Pentecost; St Benedict (21 March) and apostles Mark (25 April), Peter and Paul (29 June), and Thomas (21 December); the king also perhaps marked the feast of St Dénis (9 October), patron of the abbey near Paris which through its Scottish residents had helped David in exile as a child. Finally, predictably, David observed the feast of St Thomas à Beckett (29 December) as well as requesting several safe-conducts to his shrine in England as an 'in' with Edward III.[66]

These observances must have formed a vital and attractive component of the court life which David encouraged to draw the services of loyal, militarily experienced, ambitious and perhaps even wealthy men of chivalry, as well as men of trade and career-minded churchmen. In doing so, David would have been able to further personalise the St Monan cult by association with Edinburgh, the burgh closest to Holyrood Abbey. The mercat cross of the king's chosen chief residence was apparently dedicated to Monan: the existence of the cross and a 'St Monan's Wynd' are recorded in the late fifteenth century running alongside the burgh's tolbooth and St Giles' church where David had in 1358 dedicated an altar to that most fashionable of crusading saints, Katherine of Alexandria.[67]

---

65 *Chron. Bower*, vii, 99.
66 R.C. Reid, 'Caput of Annandale or the Curse of Malachy', *TDGNHAS* 3rd series (1965), 155–66 and D.E. Easson, *Charters of the Abbey of Coupar-Angus* (Edin-burgh 1947), 216 (Malachy); *ER*, ii, 226 (pilgrimage by Queen Margaret to St Ninians, Whithorn); *Rot. Scot.*, i, 828, 872, 881, 887, 900, 917, 928, 937 and *Foedera*, iii, 87 for David's safe-conducts to Canterbury; C.R. Cheney ed. (rev. M. Jones), *A Handbook of Dates* (Cambridge 1945–2000). For a far more detailed list of religious festivals marked by the English crown *c.* 1300–39, see Vale, *The Princely Court*, 308–10, 314–8. For comparison with Edward III's observances, see Ormrod, 'Personal Religion of Edward III' and Vale, *Edward III and Chivalry*. David may also have commissioned a monumental sculpture (now headless) in Durham marble of William I, founder of Arbroath, Abbey – dedicated to Beckett – and the second Bruce king's kindred spirit in his capture by England in 1174 (G. Henderson, 'A Royal Effigy at Arbroath', in W.M. Ormrod ed., *England in the Fourteenth Century* (Woodbridge 1986), 88–98; G.S. Gimson, 'Lion Hunt: a royal tomb-effigy at Arbroath Abbey', *PSAS*, cxxv (1995), 912–6).
67 P. Millar, 'The Mercat Cross of Edinburgh – its Site and Form', *PSAS*, xx (1886), 371–83; NAS GD 103/2/4/17; *RRS*, vi, no. 204.

Moreover, on a clear day the spire of the new chapel which David now planned in the east neuk of Fife would just have been visible from the L-shaped tower house upon the east-facing forework of Edinburgh Castle which David may already have decided to build but which would not be begun by the master of works, William Dischington, until 1367–8. David had already improved the stables, tilting ground and garden of the castle to embellish the park his father had created; the second Bruce king would also reconstruct the castle chapel to the Virgin Mary (turned into a granary by the English garrison of the 1330s) and oversee improvements to the crag-top complex's deep-well water supply with the aid of leading local burgess, Roger Hogg. The addition of a new royal lodging of three or more floors was thus clearly intended to elevate Edinburgh as *the* high-status residence of the realm for David's mature years, a desirable venue for receiving foreign guests and intimidating Scottish subjects, complete with underground vault – which may have been designed to hold royal revenues and papers – and chambers for king, queen and offspring.[68] Allied to this new structure, St Monan's chapel, when finished, would thus have marked the visible extent of royal power along and across the Forth estuary moving east from Edinburgh before the 'kingdom' of Fife vanished around the headland towards Crail and St Andrews; the new chapel would be an eastern beacon to match Dunfermline, Inverkeithing and Stirling on the northern and western horizons from Edinburgh. On the southern shore of the Forth, North Berwick and its distinctive 'Law' or hill to the east of Edinburgh formed a similar marker. Royal supporters had been confirmed, installed or built up by David since 1341 along this coast, in northern Peeblesshire and at Haddington, Dirleton Castle, Longniddry, Cramond, Abercorn, Linlithgow, Stirling and elsewhere in between, favouring such men as John Preston, William and Alexander Haliburton, the Maitlands, Alexander Cockburn and William Ramsay. Behind North Berwick Law, the earl of Douglas's awesome seat at Tantallon lay just out of the king's sight from Edinburgh, with the earl of March's castle further down the coast at Dunbar.[69]

68 *ER*, i, 238 and ii, cx, 79, 83, 113, 246, 308, 364, 393, 473, 551, 608; Malcolm, 'The Gardens of the Castle', 215–6; W.T. Oldrieve, 'Account of the recent Discovery of the Remains of David's Tower at Edinburgh Castle', *PSAS*, xii (1914), 230–70; MacIvor, *Edinburgh Castle*, 37–8; P. Yeoman, 'Edinburgh Castle', *Fortress*, no. 4 (1990), 22–6; N.A. Ruckley, 'Water Supply of Medieval castles in the United Kingdom', *Fortress*, no. 7 (1990), 14–26; G. Stell, 'The Scottish Medieval Castle: Form, Function and "Evolution"', in K.J. Stringer ed., *Essays on the Nobility of Medieval Scotland* (1985), 195–209.
69 *RRS*, vi, nos. 15, 18, 32, 41, 42, 89, 95, 97, 104, 107, 125, 127, 154, 171, 173–5, 189, 197, 250, 252, 266, 272, 274; *RMS*, i, App. i, nos. 147, 264 and App. ii, nos. 748, 901, 902, 911, 916, 922, 927, 962, 969, 981, 985, 1009, 1026, 1044, 1060, 1061, 1067, 1068, 1070, 1073, 1092, 1096, 1121, 1151, 1161, 1179, 1202, 1206, 1235, 1237, 1263, 1312, 1340, 1347, 1352, 1357, 1367, 1384, 1388, 1393, 1400, 1409.

In sum, the planting of the royal flag at St Monans in Fife in spring 1362 must have given David and his chivalric cadre of supporters a genuine boost in confidence. It must have heightened the sense of crown-led identity and community at that time and the hard-felt sense of exclusion from this cadre – despite their regular attendance at court – endured by the likes of the Stewarts, and the earls of Douglas, March and Ross: as one modern historian observes, 'the impression given by witness lists is of the great magnates doggedly maintaining their presence at court in the face of royal indifference to them'.[70]

David's new-found object of faith certainly heralded an intensification of the patronage of royal knights, esquires and clerics in that region and elsewhere throughout the rest of the year. Early April 1362 found David at Edinburgh issuing several grants which clearly underline the potency of his adherents' chivalric network. The king granted Fife and Edinburgh lands to John Bisset of Peebles; gifted the barony of Lenzie in Lanarkshire to Malcolm Fleming, nephew of the late earl of Wigtown; confirmed Robert Erskine's gift of Kinnoul church in Perthshire to Cambuskenneth Abbey (an act originally witnessed in 1361 by the bishop of St Andrews, David Graham, Roger Mortimer, David Fleming, Walter Greenlaw, the archdeacon of St Andrews, Alan Erskine, and clerk, Hugh Ross, whom David had recently given a 20-merk pension);[71] then the king confirmed the grant by David Graham (father of a hostage) of lands near Edinburgh to the ill-fated John Allincrum, deputy-sheriff of Peebles, who on 1 May in turn had the crown confirm his gift of these lands to the burgh church of St Giles in Edinburgh – Allincrum's Lothian and Peeblesshire following of lesser knights, esquires and clerics seems to have been substantial.[72]

February and March 1362 saw David's intervention at St Monans. It may have been at this juncture that he issued a number of acts of uncertain date concerning Fife and Lothian holdings. As well as making Alan Erskine keeper of Loch Leven, coroner of Fife and perhaps sheriff of Kinross, David had also appointed William Dischington of Ardoss as the sheriff of Fife sometime in or before 1362, replacing the traditional incumbent family of Weymss in this office (David Weymss had died c. 1359). In the same year, William Ramsay of Colluthie, former earl of Fife, re-emerged acting in the office of sheriff of Edinburgh: on 9 September at Aberdeen David would give this old knight a £20 pension 'for so long as he is in our retinue'.[73] But

---

70 Grant, *Independence and Nationhood*, 176.
71 *RRS*, vi, nos. 270–1; *RMS*, i, App. i, no. 151 and App. ii, nos. 1399, 1405.
72 *RRS*, vi, nos. 272, 274.
73 *ER*, ii, 74, 120; *RMS*, i, no. 109. About March 1362 Alan Erskine of Inchmartin also contracted to counsel and protect the abbot of Scone for 100 merks p.a. (NAS RH6/137).

it was surely in the wake of the death of Walter Stewart, Lord of Fife, that David was able to make his most substantial breakthrough in that region. For by the close of the year, perhaps much earlier, it must have become clear that David intended to elevate another of his crusading knights as his assignee earl of Fife, namely, Sir Thomas Bisset of Upsetlington in Berwickshire, a brother of John of Peebles and Thomas Bisset, prior of St Andrews.

As we have seen, Thomas had been on crusade to Prussia about 1356 with the Leslies, David Barclay, Walter Moigne and other Lowlanders now in crown service. He also had a record of affinity to the southern kingdom, his border lands obliging him to enter Edward III's allegiance in the late 1340s and presumably to forswear war against England. Thomas was therefore just the sort of Anglophile Scot tempted by cross-border landholding and chivalric service to any Christian king whom David liked to employ. Indeed, Bisset – whose heir had been offered as a hostage in 1354 and 1357 – may already have been closely involved in David's attempts to cut a deal with Edward III in 1359: on 24 July that year he had been admitted into the English king's special protection for his lands on the borders.[74] But more importantly, Thomas was unmarried in 1362 whilst William Ramsay, king's earl in 1358–9, appeared to have re-wed after Katherine Mortimer's murder. It was his marital status and military affinity which made Bisset the man of the moment because he could be matched with the freshly widowed Isabella of Fife and claim the earldom by right of this match.

Although it was probably public knowledge long in advance, that such a match was what David intended was signalled decisively on 10 January 1363 when Isabella appeared at St Andrews to grant to Bisset her northern Perthshire lands of Glasclune, adjacent to Clunie and Strathardle, east of Atholl; this was an act witnessed, ominously, by crown supporters, the bishops of St Andrews and Brechin, Robert Erskine and William Dischington, as well as Patrick, earl of March/Moray (whose interest may be explained by the fact that Isabella's first husband, William Felton, had been granted Dunbar lands in Berwickshire by Edward III about 1340). It is uncertain whether or not Isabella had transferred her allegiance willingly to the crown, walking out on Stewart abuse of her freedom since 1359 in search of stronger lordship from the king; or even if David had at some moment in the second half of 1362 forcibly taken possession of the heiress from the Steward's castle a few miles north-west of Fife at Methven. But at the caput of the earldom of Fife, Falkland Castle, on 28 December 1362, Isabella had already granted the reliefs of Weymss – on the Forth shore

---

74 *Rot. Scot.*, i, 757–8, 763, 797, 799, 837; *Foedera*, iii, 437; *CPP*, i, 345.

between Earlsferry and Kinghorn – to Alan Erskine of Inchmartin who was married to a Weymss heiress.[75]

This blow-for-blow exchange of power over Fife between the crown and Stewarts between 1358 and 1362 might alone have been enough to provoke a violent struggle between David and his heirs presumptive in 1362–3. Bisset's marriage to Isabella would, after all, snub bluntly the tailzie which Walter Stewart had agreed with Isabella *c*. 1361 that the earldom should be allowed to pass to his younger Stewart brothers in the event of his death. But, in fact, David's windfall success in Fife in 1362 and the fixed purpose and shrewd patronage with which he pressed home his advantage were to form just a single strand of a much wider range of royal advances made that year. These several simultaneous royal policy achievements were to present at least five of the great regional magnates of Scotland both with individual territorial worries and, crucially, would produce more general community-wide grievances against the crown: when these points of tension converged in late 1362, they would provoke an armed assault on David's person and authority.

By late 1362, indeed, the Stewarts had more than their exclusion from Fife to worry about. Their gravest worry resulted undeniably from the other unexpected death of that year when Queen Joan passed away about 7 September, aged forty-one. David's relief at this news must have been greater than his grief or regret. In terms of the king's concerns for his succession, the pain of losing his hostage nephew, John Sutherland, to the Black Death at Lincoln in September 1361 must also have been eased. David was now free to remarry in search of issue. By spring 1363, though again surely long before then, it was obvious he intended to take his Perthshire mistress, Margaret Logie, as his new wife: this news may indeed have encouraged Isabella of Fife to change allegiance.[76]

To wed anew, David may have had to arrange the annulment of Margaret's marriage to Sir John Logie, the rival of Sir John Menteith of Arran for the lordship of Strathgartney: it is possible that Margaret was already a widow but strategic divorce to affect landed succession was a ploy which David would use on several occasions during that decade. But whatever the method, David's goal was twofold. Of course, a marriage to Margaret might soon provide him with a Bruce son to offset the threat of

---

75 *RRS*, vi, no. 345; *RMS*, i, no. 221; W. Fraser ed., *Memorials of the Family of Weymss of Weymss* (3 vols., Edinburgh 1888), ii, no. 9; Boardman, *Early Stewart Kings*, 13–4, 33 n 72.

76 *RMS*, i, nos. 120, 124; C.L. Kingford, *The Grey Friars of London* (Aberdeen 1915), 74–5; Green, *Lives of the Princesses of England*, iii, 159; Prestwich, 'Katherine Mortimer's Death at Soutra', 116; *Chron. Bower*, vii, 323 for Sutherland. Sir Thomas Gray does assert that Margaret 'had lived with him [David] for a long time' (*Chron. Scalacronica*, 174).

the Stewart succession. But at the same time, Margaret's Drummond kindred and their Perthshire allies could aid the king's further undermining of Stewart interests in central Scotland, chiefly in Menteith, Strathearn and Atholl. That this was David's hope is suggested by his confirmation on 3 December 1362, while at the bishop of Moray's palace of Spynie in Moray, of the Steward's resignation of the barony of Tullibardine in Strathearn to Sir Walter Murray, the Drummonds' feud ally: the king would confirm this act for a second time at Elgin four days later. Back at Edinburgh on 17 February 1363, David would also confirm Maurice Drummond's sale of lands in Stormont – in lower Strathtay, adjacent to Dull and Atholl – to the leading Perth merchant and ransom financier, John Mercer.[77]

This royal intrusion into the Perthshire earldoms may have been all the more effective as it followed on the heels of an earlier royal achievement. On 26 July 1362, Archibald Douglas, keeper of Edinburgh Castle, had secured a papal dispensation to wed Joanna Murray, the daughter of David's favourite killed in 1346, Maurice Murray, earl of Strathearn, and the widow of Thomas Murray of Bothwell, the royal Pantler and the Steward's former lieutenant who had also died while a hostage in England in 1361. Joanna's mother, Maurice's wife, had been a grand-daughter of Sir John Menteith of Arran and Knapdale who had been the guardian of the Menteith earldom *c.* 1320 and the widow successively of Malise, seventh earl of Strathearn (d. 1329), and John Campbell, earl of Atholl (d. 1333).[78] It is clear that Archibald must have had considerable royal backing not only to get his woman but to ensure that he also secured the entire Murray landed inheritance. This included the formidable castle-barony of Bothwell in Lanarkshire as well as lands in Moray, Elgin, Mar (where Thomas Murray's mother had kept Kildrummy Castle as Countess), Kincardineshire and Angus. But it also involved Maurice Murray's barony lands at Drumsargard, Avondale, Strathaven and Stonehouse in Lanarkshire, Stewarton in Ayrshire, Hawick and Sprouston in Roxburghshire and lesser holdings in Annandale. This timely marriage may also have given Archibald access to Maurice's former network of military followers in Strathearn and Atholl.[79]

Thus, at a stroke, by once again interfering to stop the natural course of inheritance, David may have recovered access to a considerable part of the central Scotland network he had built up before 1346; he had also created almost instantly a major force to be reckoned with in Archibald the Grim, an ambitious warlord who could now act for the crown from his bases in various quarters of the realm. Archibald and David had once again thwarted

---

77 *RRS*, vi, nos. 212, 281, 287.
78 *Vetera*, 319–20; *Scots Peerage*, vi, 135–41. According to Wyntoun's source, Thomas Murray died in London of the plague (*Chron. Wyntoun*, vi, 249).
79 Brown, *Black Douglases*, 56–8, 96–7.

Stewart designs: Robert Stewart (junior) sought much of the Murray lands through his wife, the widow of Thomas's elder brother, John, a claim to terce which would see Robert in open feud with Archibald by 1368 at the latest, probably instantaneously.[80] But this Black Douglas bastard was now also strong enough to act as a strategic counter to the interests of the Douglas earl and March earl south of the Forth, as well as a crown agent in the south-west.

Archibald's marriage must have encouraged David's matchmaking in Fife and for himself later in 1362–3. The Northumbrian chronicler, Sir Thomas Gray, would assert that Margaret Logie was 'a lady who had been married already, and who had lived with him for some time. This marriage was made solely on account of love, which conquers all things.'[81] But Margaret Logie's locality connections were surely the main reason why David was prepared, remarkably, to become the first reigning Scottish king since the eleventh century to take a Scottish rather than an English or French wife. In many ways it was a measure of David's considerable weakness in the face of his domestic and diplomatic difficulties that he chose to do so. There were no obvious English princesses or aristocratic women available: marriage to an English noble house might not, besides, have been acceptable to Edward III. Yet Margaret Logie could even be looked upon as a further step-down for David in that she was not the heiress or widow of a Scottish earl or great provincial lord. She was, though, undoubtedly fertile if a little old for a royal bride (probably in her mid-to-late thirties), having already given Logie a son called John (that name again!): it will become apparent, too, that Margaret was possessed of a formidable personality and familial ambition and may have wielded tremendous influence over David.[82] She was also presumably younger than Isabella of Fife, although David surely felt himself prevented from simply marrying that widow because to do so would have breached the terms of the 1315 tailzie made between Robert I and Earl Duncan whereby the earldom of Fife (and its powers of enkinging) could not pass to the crown itself but only to its assignee.[83] At most, David may have planned a double wedding for early 1363, with Thomas and Isabella and Margaret and himself set to wed in Fife – at St Andrews or the bishop's manor of Inchmurdoch up the coast from Crail.

However, David's designs upon Margaret Logie must have heralded another eruption of the Menteith feud, a dispute which in 1360 had embroiled many nobles including the earls of Douglas and Angus and which must have been further aggravated by Archibald Douglas's rude

80 *APS*, i, 504–5.
81 *Chron. Scalacronica*, 174.
82 See below, ch. 10.
83 *RRS*, v, no. 72.

intervention in the Murray inheritance.[84] About the same time, the suspicions of the Stewarts and other lords may have been further aggravated by the death of Thomas Stewart, earl of Angus, in Dumbarton Castle sometime between August 1362 and March 1363, most likely during the fresh outbreak of plague which drove the king and the rest of the political community north during that winter.[85] The fate of Thomas's title and lands had not yet been decided but in the past three years or more David had very effectively poached the loyalties of more Forfarshire and Kincardineshire laymen. A growing paranoia that this was exactly what David continued to do, too, to their lands and affinities must also have afflicted Lowland magnates like Patrick Dunbar, earl of March/Moray, William, earl of Douglas, and, surprisingly, Thomas, Earl of Mar. The remaining known acts and itinerary of David during 1362 suggest their fears were entirely justified.

Since 1357, Earl Patrick Dunbar had been largely excluded from royal offices and patronage. David had also reached out to lesser Lothian men as his agents in the south-east, a group which included Walter Haliburton of Dirleton as sheriff of Berwickshire; the earl's half-brother, Sir Patrick (d. 1357), and his sons, George and John; the keeper of Dunbar Castle, Alexander Recklington (who would show an interest in crusades in the later 1360s); James Douglas of Lothian; the Sinclairs of Rosslyn; and John Edmonstone, whom David appointed as heritable coroner of Lothian while staying at Aberdeen on 5 November 1362. In addition, David had also excluded Earl Patrick's influence from the lordship of Annandale which he could claim through his Randolph wife. As we have seen, the king preferred to act as lord there himself and to employ traditional Bruce retainers like the Carruthers, Corrys and Johnstones; on 10 December 1362 David paid another visit to Mouswald in Annandale to reward the first of these families. Earl Patrick was also denied a post as a March warden.[86]

But by late 1362 David had also begun to intrude openly upon Patrick's second earldom of Moray, perhaps confirming the crown's intention to revive its use of this sensitive province, first mooted in 1359, as a bargaining chip in deals with Edward III and John of Gaunt. On 24 December 1362, while at Kinloss Priory, David confirmed the Moray lands of Andrew Urwell, a former Randolph retainer, in return for his rendering the same services to the crown (not to earl Patrick) as his father, John, had owed to the Randolph earls. January 5 1363 would find David at Spynie in Moray confirming Earl Patrick's grant of the offices of sheriff and constable of Elgin to William de Vaus, an east Lothian knight whose family had held Dirleton

84 Fraser ed., *The Red Book of Menteith*, i, 109–15.
85 *ER*, ii, 168; *Chron. Bower*, vii, 319–21.
86 *RRS*, vi, nos. 242, 251, 279, 282; *RMS*, i, App. ii, nos. 1624, 1685.

but who had already been captured at Neville's Cross and served David as a household steward in 1358-9. A fortnight later at Aberdeen, David confirmed Gilbert of Glencairnie's large barony in Moray.[87] David's grants to both Urwell and Gilbert were witnessed by a number of laymen including William Keith the Marischal (and sheriff of Aberdeen in 1359), a knight who by late 1367 at least would be acting as 'the king's lieutenant in Moray'. In such a role Keith may have forged a close working relationship with another royalist appointee, Alexander Bur, a cleric favoured by the king and Queen Joan in the 1350s and whom David had recommended as bishop of Moray by December 1362: this seat would see him act as the crown's buffer in the latter half of the decade against the aggressive lordship of the Steward's fourth son, Alexander, the future 'Wolf' of Badenoch.[88] Keith and Bur may both have been boosted in their roles by David's regular visits to Elgin, Kinloss and Spynie *c.* 1361-3.

To some extent, Earl Patrick could afford to be philosophical about David's encroachment on Dunbar interests: he was a very old man. But this was in no way true of William, first earl of Douglas, who was a few years younger than his sovereign. Of all the great magnates who had built up their own territory, following, reputation and influence in the king's absence after 1346, Douglas was surely the one who had the potential to become David's closest ally, an ideal relationship of royal lordship and Douglas service in the marches based upon patronage, their sympathetic interest in chivalric pursuits and their families' associations before 1329. In many ways this potential relationship had been realised in literature long before the archdeacon of Aberdeen, John Barbour, penned *The Bruce* of *c.* 1371-5. Barbour may have translated a French court romance of the mid-fourteenth century, *Les Trois Nobles Fils du Rois*, along with other works for David's court between his studies in Oxbridge and pilgrimages abroad before 1371. In this epic a Scottish prince, 'David', and 'an earl of Douglas' join forces on a quest in the company of their English and French counterparts and fight the Turks.[89] But by 1362 the personal rivalries between the energetic king and earl, Douglas's penchant for war against England and David's appreciation that some of his

---

87 *RRS*, vi, nos. 283, 285; *RMS*, i, nos. 103, 121; *ER*, i, 562.
88 *Registrum Episcopatus Moraviensis*, no. 287; Watt, *Scottish Graduates*, 67-70; R.D. Oram, 'Alexander Bur, Bishop of Moray (1362-1397)', in B.E. Crawford ed., *Church, Chronicle and Learning in Medieval and Early Renaissance Scotland* (Edinburgh 1999), 195-214.
89 Turnivall ed., *The Three King's Sons*; Graeme-Ritchie ed., *The Buik of Alexander*, i, xlii-xliii; R.J. Lyall, 'The Lost Literature of Medieval Scotland', in J.D. McClure and M.R.G. Spiller eds., *Bryght Lanternis: Essays on the Language and Literature of Medieval and Renaissance Scotland* (Aberdeen 1989), 33-47, 41. For Barbour's travels, see *Rot. Scot.*, i, 808, 897.

regional magnates exercised far too much autonomy, had pushed them irrevocably apart; this may have created more resentment on the earl's part towards the king than even the Gaelic-based Steward felt for his royal nephew, all the more so because David and Douglas were so alike in Lowland outlook.[90]

Indeed, Earl William disappears as a royal charter witness for over a year as early as 1 May 1362, perhaps removing himself from the king's court to his southern lands, emerging only to contemplate pilgrimage to Canterbury in the company of several other notable Scottish magnates later in the year.[91] This withdrawal coincided neatly with the rise of Archibald Douglas and his cousin, James of Lothian, as close royal adherents. Earl William could now only look on as the heirs by the tailzie of 1342 to William Douglas of Liddesdale's lands (which the earl had occupied since 1353) were heavily favoured by the king, Archibald in particular becoming Warden of the west march (replacing Stewart of Dalswinton) as well as keeper of Edinburgh Castle.[92] At some point in 1362 the earl may also have been frustrated to see David confirm Sir William Cunningham of Kilmaurs as 'lord' (really just bailie or guardian) of the Bruce earldom of Carrick. This was a grant which must have denied the rights of the Douglas retainer, John Towers of Dalry, by right of his father William's marriage to Eleanor Douglas, Countess of Carrick and the Douglas earl's sister: Towers was her third husband after the unfortunate Alexander Bruce (d. 1333, David's half-cousin by Edward Bruce and the Strathbogie earl of Atholl's sister) and James Sandilands of Newark, the Douglas knight who had worked for the crown before 1357.[93] Yet while David's grants to Lothian and south-eastern men in 1362 must also have reduced the Douglas earl's influence as much as they did that of Earl Patrick, it was another crown-magnate clash later that year which finally made a Bruce-Douglas confrontation unavoidable.

By 1362, Douglas's brother-in-law, Thomas, earl of Mar and lord of Garioch, was also increasingly at odds with the king. Always a maverick and heavily in debt by 1357, Mar had found himself at a loose end after the collapse of David's secret deal with Edward III in 1359 and the treaty of Brétigny of May 1360 brought an end to his employment in England's

90 S. Boardman, 'The Gaelic World and the Early Stewart Court' (forthcoming).
91 *RRS*, vi, no. 274; *Rot. Scot.*, i, 865 (safe-conducts south for Douglas and the bishop of St Andrews in October 1362; and for Douglas, the earl of March, the earl of Mar, Norman Leslie and others in November 1362).
92 *RRS*, vi, no. 51; *CDS*, iv, no. 100; Brown, *Black Douglases*, 40–2, 45–7.
93 *RMS*, i, App. ii, nos. 1243, 1330; *Scots Peerage*, ii, 436–7. By January 1364 Cunningham's daughter would have wed a former Balliol supporter in the south-west, either Fergus MacDowell or Fergus Maxwell of Caerlaverock. (NAS RH 2/6/6/4/26).

armies in France.[94] Late 1360 had seen Mar seek a solution to his problems by taking Margaret, the young daughter of Thomas, earl of Angus, as his second spouse. The tensions which were to erupt between David and his cousin, Mar, might suggest that this marriage had been the earl's own initiative in defiance of the wishes of the crown. However, it was Mar's aggressive lordship and search for money which really put him in David's black books. As early as August 1359 David had had cause to warn the former Chamberlain, Mar, to cease molesting the Tironensian abbey of Lindores in northern Fife (a foundation of David, earl of Huntingdon and lord of Garioch (d. 1219) but heavily favoured by the Fife earls). Mar had been seeking the homage and fealty of the monks there as freeholders of lands in Garioch: royal letters of December 1358 make it clear that David wanted these tenants to hold directly of the crown. David may have visited Kildrummy Castle in September 1359 and granted the liberties of the church of Garioch to Lindores to reinforce his point.[95] But by 1362 Mar was still at it. Under the events of that year, Sir Thomas Gray reported that David had cause to move against Thomas 'because of the extortions which the earl of Mar and his people had wrought upon the people of the district'.[96]

However, the actual occasion of David's clash with the earl spoke to tensions most of the other regional magnates of Scotland could relate to: the king's winning away of Mar's natural followers using patronage. David had indeed shown considerable favour to north-eastern men like the bishop of Aberdeen; William Keith the Marischal; Walter Moigne, a steward of the king's household by 1359; Lawrence Gilliebrand, a steward for Queen Joan in 1357 and envoy to Newcastle in 1360; David de Mar, treasurer of Moray (Mar's brother but Queen Joan's chamberlain by 1358); Thomas Hill (a valet to both David and Joan); and William Calebre and John Cromdale (Mar's clerks). Many of these men had visited David in captivity in England in the 1350s and were often to be found witnessing Mar's charters; after October 1357, however, they

---

94 *Rot. Scot.*, i, 842; NAS GD 124 (Mar and Kellie Muniments)/1/107; *HMC, x Mar & Kellie*, 6; Duncan, 'The 'Laws of Malcolm MacKenneth'', 262–3. For Mar back in Scotland by August-September 1359, see *HMC, x Mar & Kellie*, 3, 6; *Illustrations of the Topography and Antiquities of Aberdeen and Banff*, iv, 715–9, which also lists all Mar's trips abroad.

95 *RRS*, vi, nos. 205, 222, 223; *RMS*, i, App. ii, nos. 1284, 1297; J. Dowden ed., *Chartulary of Lindores Abbey, 1195–1479* (Scottish History Society, Edinburgh 1903), 196–200. The connection with earl David – from whom the Bruces claimed their royal descent – made Lindores a focus of Bruce interest: the Bruces had inherited a third of Garioch in 1237 and Edward Bruce (d. 1318) had even founded an altar there (*ibid*, 164; Stringer, *Earl David*, 31–4, 186–7, 240–52).

96 *Chron. Scalacronica*, 172–3 for what follows on Mar.

were also frequent crown charter witnesses.[97] By 1362, though, Mar finally felt that the king had pushed this too far. For the earl had fallen into dispute with Sir William Keith over lands or revenues in the north-east and the argument could not be settled by law. As was perfectly natural for a dispute involving two of his chivalric cadre, David oversaw a trial by combat between the two knights in the royal park at Edinburgh Castle, apparently requested by Keith the Marischal – suggesting Mar had been the aggressor – perhaps as early as May 1362 when David's extant acts last place him in the burgh that year and, significantly, the earl of Douglas was also last present as a witness for over a year.[98] According once more to Sir Thomas Gray:

> [Mar and William Keith] appeared armed in the lists at Edinburgh, the quarrel being settled there under the king's hand, who seemed more favourable to the said William than to the said earl, albeit he [the earl] was his near kinsman.

The fiery Mar felt slighted and broke openly with the king. As a result, David undertook a short siege of Kildrummy Castle, arriving there by 7 September with a small force which included Archibald Douglas, William Keith and Robert Erskine, as well as the Steward, but not, significantly, the earls of Douglas or March. According to Gray, the earl of Douglas – who was the heir by marriage to Mar's lands if he should die childless – was further angered by David's assault and subsequent forfeiture of Earl Thomas.[99]

However, David's solution of the Mar problem has all the hallmarks of a token show of force against a loyal but disgruntled subject seeking attention and reward: a useful locality man whom the king still wanted to befriend and employ. There is no evidence that the siege was a long or violent one. Indeed, the formidable round towers of Kildrummy seem to have surrendered quickly and, tellingly, were entrusted by the king to two Mar men he knew well, Walter Moigne and Ingelram de Wyntoun, both of whom would express an interest in crusading after 1363 along with other Mar adherents.

---

97 *RRS*, vi, nos. 234, 236, 264; *RMS*, i, App. ii, nos. 874, 903, 959, 1265, 1336, 1354, 1362, 1387; *ER*, i, 585–6, 618 and ii, 2, 49, 52; *Rot. Scot.*, i, 678, 736, 815; Duncan, 'The 'Laws of Malcolm MacKenneth'', 262–3. For Mar's charter witnesses, see: NAS GD 124 (Mar & Kellie Muniments); *Illustrations of the Topography and Antiquities and Aberdeen and Banff*, v, *passim*; *Scottish History Society Miscellany*, v, 12. David de Mar had also been a procurator for David's release talks (*CDS*, ii, no. 1642 *et ad indecim*); a John de Mar had also been a chaplain to Queen Joan (*CPR*, iv, 85, 104; *Rot. Scot.*, i, 815); John Cromdale was described as King David's kinsman (NAS GD 124 (Mar & Kellie Muniments)/110/113).

98 *RRS*, vi, no. 274.

99 *RMS*, i, no. 102.

Earl Thomas himself got a deal. The lands of Mar and Garioch reverted to the crown but David agreed to loan the earl 1,000 merks which he would pay back as £1,000 (33 per cent interest!) to recover his holdings over a period of five years. In the interim, Mar would return to serve Edward III in a self-imposed exile, a role for which he was given a pass to France on 20 February 1363.[100] This hints, above all, that as in 1359, Mar would have some role to play in David's negotiations for a full ransom-free peace with England. The king for his part was unlikely to demand the complete forfeiture of an heir to the throne after the Stewarts, no matter how lucrative his lands: the royal seizure of these holdings for a number of years should be viewed as judicial surety.[101]

David does not seem to have lingered over the siege, progressing on to Aberdeen apparently in a cautiously confident mood. He held a parliament or council there about 12 September 1362 – his first for almost two years.[102] Typically, no proceedings of this body survive but Mar's fate (as well as Angus's) may have been discussed. About this time, David issued the aforementioned pension to William Ramsay as well as further favour to the chapter of Aberdeen; those present at this limited session of the estates included the bishops of St Andrews and Brechin, the abbot of Dunfermline and abbot of Arbroath (in whose company David had spent his birthday that year), the Steward, William Keith, Robert Erskine, Archibald Douglas, John Herries of Terregles and Walter Moigne. Noticeably, the earls of Douglas and March were still absent or excluded from the king's inner circle of charter witnesses.[103] By 19 September David had returned to Kildrummy, an action which suggests the siege was over. There he may have remained until 13 October when he granted Dumbartonshire lands to Sir William Livingston, former sheriff of Lanarkshire. Thereafter, the resurgent plague forced David to remain in the north-east for another three months, mostly at Aberdeen but also in the forest of Kintore (23 November), at the new bishop of Moray's palace at Spynie (28 November to 3 December), Elgin (7 December) and Kinloss (Christmas Eve); his acts during this period included confirmations of Mar

---

100 *ER*, ii, 164, 166; *Rot. Scot.*, i, 870, 901; *Chron. Wyntoun*, vi, 249–50; *Chron. Bower*, vii, 319. Ingelram de Wyntoun witnessed a charter issued by William Keith at Kintore in May 1361 (*RMS*, i, no. 213). Mar's return to English service makes it likely that Andrew Wyntoun's chronicle source is wrong to attribute David's displeasure with Mar to the earl's work for Edward III.

101 Duncan, 'The 'Laws of Malcolm MacKenneth'', 264. Mar was included on a safe-conduct for a pilgrimage to Canterbury issued on 4 November 1362 in the company of the earl of March, the earl of Douglas and others (*Rot. Scot.*, i, 865), possibly requested before the siege, or perhaps as an act of contrition imposed in its wake.

102 *RRS*, vi, no. 276; *RPS*, 1362/1.

103 *RRS*, vi, nos. 277–9; *RMS*, i, nos. 104, 106–7, 109.

charters, Walter Murray's resignation of lands given to him by the Steward and the Randolph-Urwell grants.[104]

In short, David had ample cause to be pleased with his achievements of the last twelve months. In the new year, he must surely have anticipated decisive turning points in favour of the crown in several difficult areas, not least in his own dynastic situation. Fortune had brought luck his way at key moments in sensitive matters: he had clearly been energised in response to these opportunities and his sharp application had ensured significant footholds for the crown in Fife, Perthshire, Angus and Mar. However, it was also the case that by the beginning of 1363 the great magnates of Scotland would have increasingly common cause against their king in the rapidly accumulating territorial reverses he had inflicted upon them as individuals. In this context, conflict with the Stewarts and earls of Douglas and March, perhaps united in some uneasy alliance, might have been a distinct prospect and something the crown had made contingency against by investment in royal castle defences in 1360–1. But what made such confrontation unavoidable by late 1362 was that these lords could find even greater mutual ground against David and his supporters in the simultaneous progress the crown had made in two other controversial areas, Anglo-Scottish diplomacy and royal finance. Crucially, these grievances would allow the rebellious lords to represent their armed resistance in early 1363 as being in the interests of the wider political community.

The Scots' diplomatic approaches had, admittedly, progressed slowly since spring 1361 even though the death from plague of Henry de Grosmont, duke of Lancaster, in March that year had increased the likelihood of John of Gaunt – David's preferred royal nephew as his new heir presumptive – succeeding to all the Duke's northern English lands and, if the Bruce regime had its way, the earldom of Moray.[105] What surely slowed these talks down in 1361 was that what Edward III and his council really needed after the treaty of Bretigny was a sufficient regular income from their wartime ransoms to offset their painful deficit finance during the peace. David and his envoys would obviously find it difficult to persuade the English to bite once again at some form of peace deal which would involve the cancellation of the remaining 75,000 merks, no matter how small this sum in contrast to the figures demanded annually from continental nobles captured by forces under the Black Prince.[106]

However, by March 1362 at least, it was clear that a distrustful King Edward was wholly unwilling to relinquish his claim to the Valois' kingship.

104 *RRS*, vi, nos. 279–83; *RMS*, i, nos. 108, 110–1, 117, 122, 125.
105 Fowler, *The King's Lieutenant*, 217–8; Goodman, *John of Gaunt*, 37–42.
106 G.L. Harriss, *King, Parliament and Public Finance in Medieval England to 1369* (Oxford 1975), ch. xx.

The November 1361 deadline for both Edward and John II to issue their final binding renunciations under the peace treaty came and went. The French – with their shattered kingdom still prey to foreign mercenary companies now acting for themselves – fell rapidly behind with their ransom payments: by April 1362 some 600,000 écus were overdue.[107] The prospect of renewed Anglo-French conflict sometime in the near future must have seemed very real indeed to England's warrior generation and the Scots: the likelihood that the amicable but somewhat soft-touch and aging John II would soon be succeeded by the more aggressive Dauphin Charles must have heightened this feeling. That being so, David could now once again hope to trade on latent English fears of a renewed Franco-Scottish alliance: the spectre of disturbances on the border and the heavy costs of defence would have far outweighed the thus-far erratic return of 10,000 merks from the Scots per annum.

The French, of course, were in no position to help the Scots at that time and David would have pitched his approaches to Edward and his council in friendly tones. But the timing of the Scots' pursuit of a diplomatic breakthrough in 1362 is revealing. In April that year John of Gaunt finally fell heir to the entirety of the Lancaster inheritance with the death in suspicious circumstances of his elder sister-in-law. In the same month a sizeable Scottish embassy was granted passage to England 'on the business of David de Brus': it was manned by the usual crown loyalists although now Sir John Preston's place was taken by Norman Leslie, recently released by the English and home from devastated France, but – like his fellow ambassador from 1359, Robert Erskine – now firmly in David's pay after the removal of the earl of Angus. On 25 June 1362 English envoys were once more appointed to reach a final peace with the Scots.[108] If held, these talks may have demonstrated an even greater sense of urgency and personal sympathy between the two monarchs following the death of Queen Joan in September.

No details of these negotiations survive. Yet the events of the following year suggest strongly that by late 1362 David had gained an impetus towards a final agreement with England. Further momentum may have derived from the news that on 1 November Edward had reached a private indenture with his four French prince hostages, guaranteeing him some ransom and extra territory beyond Aquitaine.[109] It followed that on 14 March 1363 a safe-conduct to visit Edward III and his council was issued to the bishops of St Andrews and Brechin, the archdeacon of Lothian, Norman Leslie and David's secretary, John Carrick. This pass must have been

107 *Ibid*, 496–8; Sumption, *Hundred Years War*, ii, 473–91.
108 Goodman, *John of Gaunt*, 41–2; *Rot. Scot.*, i, 862, 864.
109 Sumption, *Hundred Years War*, ii, 498.

requested before the rebellion of the Stewarts and the earls of Douglas and March in spring that year. So too, perhaps, was a pass to England issued on 18 April 1363 to David himself together with forty retainers.[110] Thus the timing of what would be the rising of three earls – the Steward of Strathearn, Douglas and March/Moray – against the crown suggests that a large part of their motivation to joint action may have been the imminence of David's conclusion of a fresh treaty with Edward III along the lines of 1350–2 and 1359, involving a change in the succession and the possible return to Scottish lordship of some of the Disinherited. As we shall see, David would use his swift crushing of the earls' rebellion as a mandate for a large (and surely delayed) personal embassy to London in late 1363 where he did indeed draw up just such an indenture with Edward.[111]

These embassies to England were not cheap. Between April 1359 and August 1362 the crown spent some £892 at least on Anglo-Scottish diplomacy.[112] But by then David could well afford it. His decision not to pay the ransom in 1361 and 1362 allowed him to pocket the third contribution and the clerical tenth in addition to the crown's ordinary income from burgh fermes, justice and the inflated customs. The officers David had appointed in these years helped further boost the total royal revenue. At Perth in August 1362 the exchequer audit recorded receipt for the previous year of an impressive £7,380, almost double the returns of 1361, leaving the crown an amazing £4,544 in credit: this meant that although David spent only 15 per cent of this income on his royal household, this had amounted to a minimum of £1,105.[113]

But such royal fiscalism, while hostages like the Steward's heirs and Thomas Murray of Bothwell had been left to rot in England, was an irritant to some significant members of the Scottish estates: all the more so when another hostage, William, earl of Sutherland, David's former brother-in-law and who had replaced his dead son, John, in England, was given leave by Edward III to return to Scotland on 13 December 1362.[114] David would in no way be subject to the same level of criticism as James I for his neglect of Scottish hostages after 1424.[115] Yet many otherwise loyal crown subjects undoubtedly resented the pinch on their coffers when the ransom money

110 *Rot. Scot.*, i, 872.
111 As discussed below in ch. 9. *Chron. Bower*, vii, 323–5, written under a Stewart king, deliberately twists the evidence to date David's attempt to secure the passage of a succession-peace deal with England through parliament in 1363 to *before* the earls' rebellion and thus provoking their reaction.
112 *ER*, ii, 77, 80, 83.
113 *Ibid*, 107–18 – this was half the proportion spent in 1360 (32%) but two-thirds the sum (£1,608).
114 *Rot. Scot.*, i, 863, 867; *CDS*, v, no. 834.
115 Balfour-Melville, *James I*, 98–9, 102–3, 127–8, 143–9, 201–3, 293–5.

raised was not used by David for the purpose designated by the three estates. The Steward, Douglas and other earls were perfectly capable of withholding funds, although to do so openly might have encouraged David to order their entry as hostages as per the default clauses of the treaty of Berwick. Nonetheless, as we have seen, William, earl of Douglas, may even have been behind the death between May and August 1362 of John Allincrum, deputy-sheriff of Peebles, a man recently patronised by the king: the fermes of Peebles were 'unaccounted' as a result.[116] The clerical tenth certainly seems to have caused extra offence. Many church districts were late in intromitting their levies, and when they came in they included both strikingly large or suggestively low sums from areas of regional magnate dominance. For example, in July 1361, £87 had come from Peeblesshire, Lanarkshire and Eskdale, £64 from Carrick, Kyle, Cunningham and Lennox and £38 from Borthwick, but only 65/- from the Isles, 66/- from Galloway, £6 from Ross and just 3d from Angus and the Mearns. By August 1362 a further £121 had been taken from churches in Angus and the Mearns, £30 from Ross and £103 from Lanarkshire, Peeblesshire and Eskdale, but only £19 from Fife and Forfar and £20 from Stormont and Atholl.[117] According to Fordun's source – probably Thomas Bisset, prior of St Andrews, a clerical annalist usually favourable to David II – after the crown had extracted its permitted three years' worth of tenths from the church (1360, 1361 and 1362):

> nevertheless, when so much had been got, all the temporalities held from the king, or otherwise by churchmen, were, by that king's directions, made to contribute together with the barons and other freeholders of the kingdom – though the clergy of the kingdom made a strong stance against this.[118]

David's fiscal policies were, then, clearly in danger of alienating much of his natural support at a crucial time. Understandably, his gross revenues would have become further tainted by association with many of his other controversial policies in late 1362: his seizure of Angus, Fife, Mar and Garioch, his interference in the marriages of noble heiresses, and his diplomacy with England. David's new coinage, too, may have been linked notoriously with his talks with Edward III. The crown took 7d to 8d on every £ minted by his English-trained moneyer in Edinburgh; this would amount to a windfall of

---

116 *ER*, ii, 73, 108.
117 *Ibid*, 75, 109, 110, 163, 171.
118 *Chron. Fordun*, i, 378; Barrell, *The Papacy, Scotland and northern England*, 23–4, which also draws attention to an unnumbered manuscript of the earl of Haddington entitled 'Minute of the rollis of schireffis, Burrowes and Kirklandis anent king Davidis Ranson'.

almost £700 by September 1364. This might have been especially resented at a time of trebled customs in Scotland against a backdrop of a Europe-wide slump in wool prices, coinage devaluation and resurgent plague; the increased trade with England can only have offset these problems slightly and brought relative wealth to a small number of merchants, mostly in Edinburgh.[119] Accusations of greed could therefore have been levelled all too easily against the king, his chivalric cadre, Margaret Logie and the civil service, especially when it became known that David was, in a way, hoarding cash in a 'king's deposit' at Stirling Castle, which would contain at least £1,333 by December 1364. The absence of fully detailed surviving accounts from the clerk of the royal wardrobe from this period means it can never be known just how this swelling income translated into items and events of royal display. But it might reasonably be assumed that David began such royal consumer trends as the purchase of expensive Italian silks and jewellery from Flanders continued by his Stewart successors.[120]

It should come as no surprise, then, that when Robert Steward and his sons, and the earls of Douglas and March/Moray finally snapped in early 1363 and came out in force against their king's person and governance, the reasons they declared publicly were David's dismissal of their advice in favour of 'evil counsel' which had caused him to break his treaty with England, to stop paying the ransom and embezzle the money.[121] However, the earls' real motives derived from far deeper, more complex individual concerns to protect their patrimony from an aggressive, intrusive king and his supporters who really had the bit between their teeth in the second half of 1362 as the kingdom geared up for a royal wedding and decisive peace talks with England. All of these matters had come to a head at the turn of the new year. They were the catalyst of a potentially far greater challenge to royal authority in spring 1363 than the temporary browbeating of David's person and will in 1359. But the earls' rebellion was, nonetheless, a natural extension of these animosities.

119 *ER*, ii, 159–60; Gemmill & Mayhew, *Changing Values in Medieval Scotland*; Ditchburn, *Scotland and Europe*, 184, 193.
120 *Ibid*, 181; *ER*, ii, 180–2, incomplete account of Finlay of Kerys, clerk of the wardrobe, from 17 November 1361 to 13 December 1364, listing the purchase of coloured cloth, linen, canvas, ginger, pepper, galanga, crocus and other spices, but no total cost of disbursements: this officer had taken in, though, some £766 from the burghs and Chamberlain.
121 *Chron. Scalacronica*, 173–4.

NINE

The Defiant Ones: the Three Earls' Rebellion and the Succession, 1363–4

'At the same time the king of Scotland came to England to seek some reduction in the monies he owed to the king of England for his ransom, but went home without achieving his purpose.'

Chronicle of Henry Knighton, c. 1375–1400[1]

Men of Courage, Spring 1363

The first signs of trouble for David's regime, as all his plans seemed to converge towards a breakthrough in late 1362, may have come as early as the immediate aftermath of the siege of Kildrummy while the king remained in the colder north sheltering from the plague. David was at Elgin on 7 December. But just three days later his chancery rolls record his presence at Mouswald in Annandale, over 250 miles south as the crow flies – a hard, furious ride in so short a time. If David did have to brave the pestilence and make an emergency ayre to his south-western family lands, this may have been due to early disturbances caused by William, earl of Douglas, or Patrick, earl of March, or possibly the Steward's eldest son, John of Kyle-Stewart. Yet by 24 December the king's great seal was to be found being pledged back in the north-east at Kinloss. Such rapid movement, if necessary, may reflect what must have been the highly charged political atmosphere at that time.[2]

However, the major confrontation between the crown and its supporters, and the Stewarts, Douglas and March, seems to have erupted in the weeks after 9–10 March 1363: on those dates, in Edinburgh, the Steward and March were recorded as crown charter witnesses for the last time for over a month.[3] This Steward withdrawal from court thus perhaps came as little as eight days after a royal pilgrimage to St Monans in Fife and four days after the king's thirty-ninth birthday, a joyous week for the crown during which it might naturally have been made public just when David intended to wed Margaret Logie. Yet it was probably the Douglas earl, who had removed himself – or been excluded – from the inner royal circle of charter witnesses almost a year previously (May 1362), who kicked off the revolt with the greatest stir.

1 Chron. Knighton, 189.
2 RRS, vi, nos. 282–3; RMS, i, no. 125.
3 RRS, vi, no. 289; RMS, i, no. 221.

There are two contemporary and quite detailed chronicle accounts of the earls' rebellion. According to contemporary Northumbrian, Sir Thomas Gray, whose work ends in 1363:

> soon after that [the siege of Kildrummy], in the same season, there arose disagreement between the said David, king of Scotland, and William, Earl of Douglas, who had the sister of the Earl of Mar to wife, because of divers matters wherein it appeared to the said earl that the said king had not shown him such fair lordship as he would have liked. So he [Douglas] made a conspiracy, collected a large following, seized and garrisoned the castle of Dirleton, which castle was under ward of the king.[4]

Dirleton Castle would have been a logical point of attack for Douglas, sited just a few miles west along the road towards Haddington, Dalkeith and Edinburgh from his new castle at Tantallon on the East Lothian clifftops overlooking North Berwick and the Bass Rock. David had entrusted Dirleton's keeping to one of his Lothian cadre, Sir Walter Haliburton. That knight had been among the Neville's Cross captured, an ambassador for David to the Pope in 1349, and had received the barony of Bolton in East Lothian from the king in 1353 (some nine miles south of Dirleton), a grant confirmed in 1358; by June 1364 Walter would be serving as sheriff of Berwickshire and in 1369 would act as an envoy to England.[5] Moreover, as recently as 5 January 1363 – while still in the north at the bishop of Moray's palace at Spynie – David had confirmed a grant by Patrick, earl of March, of the 'sheriffship of Elgin' to Sir William de Vaus, a royal steward and a descendant of Dirleton's thirteenth-century baronial owners; by 1363, de Vaus would be part of David's Edinburgh household.[6] Clearly, Douglas's actions reflected his fears prompted by David's increasing encroachment upon his local lordship and affinity: in East Lothian and the south-east in general these overlapped with the interests of Patrick, earl of March, based just south of Tantallon at Dunbar.

However, it is clear from both Gray's *Scalacronica* and John of Fordun's anonymous pro-Bruce annals of that time that the Douglas earl soon moved to mask his private concerns behind confederacy with other great magnates: this group now selected what they could denounce publicly as crown policies damaging to the integrity of the community of the realm or the commonweal. As Gray continues:

4 *Chron. Scalacronica*, 173–4, for what follows.
5 *CDS*, iii, no. 1549; *Rot. Scot.*, i, 678; *CPL*, iv, 203; *RRS*, vi, nos. 126, 175, 319, 444; Tabraham and Grove, *Tantallon Castle*; Brown, *Black Douglases*, 57–8.
6 *RMS*, i, nos. 103, 121; J.S. Richardson, *Dirleton Castle* (Edinburgh 1982), 2–5.

The said earl, with the concurrence of the Steward of Scotland and the Earl of March, who affixed their seals to a petition laid before the said king, complained that the said king had forced them to break the conditions, to which they had sworn on the body of God before the king of England, about paying the ransom of the said king their lord, which had been levied by an impost on the commonalty and squandered by evil counsel, wherefore they demanded reparation and wiser government.

There was undoubtedly a large amount of political convention behind the fact that the rebels did not denounce the king but rather his 'evil counsel'. Yet Fordun's clerical source also stated that:

a great sedition and plot was set on foot and hatched in the kingdom of Scotland, by the greater and more powerful chiefs therof . . . indentures were drawn up, and sealed with their several seals . . .[7]

Some form of confrontation in daily council (or even in an unrecorded full council) between the king and earls – perhaps involving written statements of political stance – may indeed have occurred: an expression of grievances against the crown's fiscal policies and non-payment of the ransom would have been a legitimate basis for complaint to the estates. Yet, as in April-May 1359, in 1363 these magnates may have hoped that their collective resistance would force David to back down not only over the issue of the money and Scotland's relations with England, but over various locality matters. Fordun's source certainly hints that the precedent of their actions four years earlier may have guided the rebels' collusion in seeking to go one step further this time around:

The magnates met against their lord the king, and formed, among themselves, the design of bending him to their views upon a demand which, as every one could see, was an unrighteous one – of banishing him . . .

The Steward at least may have aimed at some form of comprehensive political settlement to his house's advantage, with David either confronted in a stage-managed council or parliament and forced to accept his own marginalisation during a new Stewart Lieutenancy – 'bending him' to Steward views as in spring 1359;[8] or with the king dethroned for treasonable contact with England; or even, if need be, with David destroyed in a swift

---

7 *Chron. Fordun*, i, 381–2 for what follows.
8 Penman & Tanner, 'An Unpublished act of David II, 1359'. That David had intended to hold a council or parliament at this time is at least suggested by the appearance of lesser nobles at court – men like David Annan and Walter Moigne about 9 March: the king may have hoped to secure the estates' approval for a royal mission to England for which a safe-conduct was issued by Edward III on 18 April 1363 (*RRS*, vi, no. 289; *Rot. Scot.*, i, 872).

civil war. In the end, though, the scattered fighting, brevity and complete failure of the rebellion which followed would seem to suggest that the other earls had far more limited objectives and would have been satisfed to secure their regional interests: Douglas and March perhaps sought only to force David to show them what they felt was 'fair lordship' – surely a measure of autonomy in their own spheres of influence as well as the fruits of royal favour in lands and offices. But even though the rebels clearly lacked political resolve as to their aims and the execution of their intent despite their common grievances against the king and his party, violent clashes became unavoidable at the outset. Both Gray and Fordun's source concur that the earls – even though they do not seem to have co-ordinated joint military action – directed their anger towards those Lowland men favoured by the crown at their expense. According to Fordun's cleric:

> they manfully rose up in great numbers, with arms in their hands, to gain their ends through force or fear. Accordingly, they took the king's adherents, wheresoever they could find them, and having taken them, threw them into prison. In hostile wise they fell upon towns and boroughs, and the whole country, and shared the spoils of the people, and wrought other damnable evils . . .

Gray's words echo this version and provide more factual detail:

> the king marched against the said earl [of Douglas], and when the king was in one district the earl rode into another against those who were of the king's party, imprisoning the king's people wheresoever he could take them. He marched to Inverkeithing by night and captured the Sheriff of Angus with a company of armed men on their way to join the king, and sent them to prison in various places.

This insistence that the violence of spring 1363 spread beyond Edinburgh and the Lothians is confirmed by the exchequer records of the period. Significantly, by 25 March 1363 David had moved to replace cleric Walter of Biggar as Chamberlain with Sir Robert Erskine, keeper of Stirling Castle and thus guardian there of the swelling 'king's deposit' of ready money: he had already been Chamberlain during the crisis years of *c.* 1346–51.[9] Not only does this switch help further pinpoint the timing of the revolt but it suggests that royal revenue and its collectors may have been a target of rebels enraged by David's misuse of the ransom.

But the account rolls also confirm the great part hard cash had to play in stabilising the situation for the crown. Large payments were made in 1363–4 for repairs and munitions at both Edinburgh and Dumbarton Castles. The

9 *ER*, ii, 161, 218.

earl of Angus's death as a prisoner sometime in 1362–3 may have made Dumbarton a focus for aggression from the Stewart lands in Clydesdale and Renfrew (and perhaps from Sir John Menteith of Arran). David seems to have taken cautious measures to secure that castle's loyalty. The keeper there was Sir John Danielston who, although a regular witness to Steward charters in this period, was paid for his services by the crown in 1363; but David also paid Sir Malcolm Fleming of Biggar (junior) to carry out repairs there, and by November 1364, at least, this knight had taken up the office once occupied by his uncle, thus apparently replacing Danielston.[10] In the same way, David's grant on 2 and 3 July 1363 of tenements in Edinburgh to Sir Alexander Recklington, keeper of Dunbar Castle, may have confirmed the crown's effective interference in the spring in Earl Patrick of March's chief castle and regional following: control of Dunbar would also have allowed the king's party to outflank the Douglas castle of Tantallon.[11]

But in 1363 extra munitions were also sent out to the castles of Stirling (under Erskine) and Kildrummy (which had been held since September 1362 for the crown by the Mar crusader, Walter Moigne). Clearly, the conflict threatened to spread north through Douglas's anger at his brother-in-law's *de facto* exile by the crown. The royal accounts also confirm the damages inflicted at the royal burgh of Inverkeithing in Fife, close to the Queen's ferry across the Forth to Edinburgh and the recently disputed Douglas lands of Aberdour. The exchequer rolls similarly record payment to compensate for corn trampled by the king's horses near Inverbervie in Angus – the lands of David's late mistress's father and other royalist knights. David also paid for the production of new royal banners in Aberdeen (although both this and the damaged crops may have been expenses incurred in besieging Kildrummy in 1362). That, as Gray suggests, the sheriff of 'Angus' or Forfar – then Sir Robert Ramsay – was captured at Inverkeithing by Douglas in the course of leading a force south to muster with the king is logical. Such a party of the chivalry of Angus might easily have been reassembled after the police action of the previous winter against the earl of Mar. Sir Robert could also proceed south through Fife to collect the affinity of his brother, William Ramsay of Colluthie, the widower of Katherine Mortimer of Inverbervie and the displaced earl of Fife. Significantly, both Ramsays were among the large body of men to whom David's regime would make timely individual payments in 1363.[12]

10 *Ibid*, 124, 168, 195, 344. The fact that crown payment for Angus's funeral was recorded *after* the expenses relating to the spring 1363 rebellion may point to the earl's death during the crisis. Danielston had witnessed the same charter as the Steward at Edinburgh on 9 March (*RRS*, vi, no. 289). The account for the 1362–4 fermes for Dumbarton was, suggestively, incomplete.
11 *RMS*, i, nos. 152, 160.
12 *ER*, ii, 154, 165, 166, 168, 176, 178; *RRS*, vi, no. 193 for David's gift of the barony of Longforgan in Perthshire to Robert Ramsay in 1358.

However, the fact that David actually paid for his troops rather than simply calling upon the traditional feudal host's free service of forty days a year was at once a measure of the strength of his financial position set against the speed with which he clearly needed armed men and his worries about the loyalty of royal support. On the only previous occasion (1346) when he had assembled a major host in anger, several magnates – two of them open rebels against the crown in 1363 – had deserted him. This time there would be no mistake. The safe-conduct issued on 18 April by Edward III for David and forty of his attendants to enter England may have been the king's way of leaving himself a back-door in case the rebels gained the upper hand.[13] But Fordun's source certainly made great play of how:

> . . . the king, acknowledging the vantage-ground of power, put forth his hand unto strength; and, wishing to check their rashness, and taking heed lest this insolence, if left unpunished, should in time to come, turn out an example unto others elsewhere . . . in order that he might break down the presumption of those men, and thwart their plans, mustered his lieges from the four corners of his land, offering them much money for their pay . . .

The exchequer rolls record a lump payment of some £618 to the royal force mustered at Edinburgh. At the equivalent rate of pay which English kings paid their troops at that time, David would thus have been able to field, say, some 8–900 men-at-arms for a fortnight. It is likely, though, that he paid his troops less and so could afford more infantry or a more select group of highly skilled and armed men for longer. For the period between 23 October 1362 and December 1364 David certainly also paid his clerks of the liverance – a John de Ros and John McKelly – well over £4,000, a figure which suggests an unusually large crown outlay on horses and supplies in the field.[14]

But it was the simultaneous payment of substantial sums to individual members of his chivalric cadre in key positions throughout Lowland Scotland, over and above the basic £618 of war-wages, which was the most telling

13 *Rot. Scot.*, i, 872 – see n 8 above.
14 *ER*, ii, 139, 148, 153, 164, 172, 176, amounting to over £2,100 to John de Ros for David's liverance. But John de Ros intromitted, unusually, a separate account for the period 23 October 1362 to 26 October 1363 in which he had received £1,929 but overspent by £8: thus some of this money must have been spent on the Kildrummy siege in 1362 (*ibid*, 180–6). Similarly, some of the £2,500 collected and disbursed by John McKelly between 25 March 1363 (the second day of the New Year but another date which may help pinpoint the rebellion) and 14 December 1364 must have been spent on David's trip to and from London in autumn 1363. Edward III paid his earls 8/- a day, banneret knights 4/-, knights 2/- and men-at-arms 1/- (Prestwich, *The Three Edwards*, 63–4). For de Ros as a Steward charter witness, see Fraser ed., *The Melvilles*, iii, no. 17.

feature of David's mobilisation. Admittedly, some of these sums included fees for office services, but along with gifts or remittances these monies were well-timed. Their recipients included: Robert Erskine (£418+)[15] and his esquire sons, Andrew, Thomas and Nicholas (£28), and brother Alan, keeper of Loch Leven Castle in Fife (£49); Sir John Lyle of Duchal, steward of the king's household (£690); John Gray of Broxmonth, the clerk of the rolls (£53), as well as John de Ros and John McKelly; William Cunningham, 'lord' of the earldom of Carrick (£13); John Logie, David's intended stepson (£3), his uncle Maurice Drummond (£20) and their ally in the Menteith feud, Walter Murray of Tullibardine (£13); John Danielston (£313) and Malcolm Fleming and his son, David, a clerk of the audit for the king (£82); the Abbot of Melrose, focus of recent tension between the king and the Douglas earl (£243, for wool); Sir Archibald Douglas, keeper of Edinburgh Castle (£412), Simon Reed, that castle's constable (£205) and his brother John (£132); the royal esquire, James Douglas of Lothian (£13) and the other south-eastern men, Walter Wardlaw, ambassador and archdeacon of Lothian (£56), Patrick Hepburn (£10, which may have been crown money to reimburse this man's 'liberacioun'), Walter Haliburton (£10), Alexander Cockburn (£8), William More of Abercorn (£13) and Simon Preston of Craigmillar (£10); Sir Robert Chisholm the keeper of Urquhart Castle (£18); the Mar men, Gilbert Armstrong, the ambassador and provost of St Andrews (£73), Walter Moigne (£8), Lawrence Gilliebrand (£10), Thomas Hill, the king's valet (£44) and Michael Logan (£5); William Keith, the all-important Marischal of the host (£10); Robert Ramsay, sheriff of Forfar (£20) and his neighbours Alexander Lindsay of Glenesk (£15), Alexander Scrymgeour, the constable of Dundee (£13), Andrew Campbell (£13) and the crusading brothers, Walter and Norman Leslie, who received the significant private sums of £80 and £30 respectively; and the Fife men William Ramsay, sheriff of Edinburgh (£86), and William Dischington, the royal master-of-works (£342).[16] As keeper of the 'king's deposit' and crisis-time Chamberlain, Robert Erskine must have played a key role in either disbursing these sums and the force's field wages on the spot, or at least in issuing promises for such payments.

Overall, then, perhaps more than at any other time, this was a moment when David felt it necessary – as Abbot Bower put it – to show:

> favour and affection to a great and exaggerated extent to his knights and men-at-arms who were very numerous at this time, who had been enlisted for undertakings of this kind . . .[17]

15 Erskine would also be paid some 600 merks for two years' work as Chamberlain in 1364 (*ER*, ii, 178; Duncan, 'The 'Laws of Malcolm MacKenneth'', 245).
16 *ER*, ii, 119 to 186 *passim*, or *ad indecim*.
17 *Chron. Bower*, vii, 361.

The day was undeniably won by the military expertise and bristling retinues of knights and men-at-arms such as Archibald Douglas – who according to Froissart 'everywhere had in his following a large company of knights and men of courage' – William Ramsay, Walter and Norman Leslie, Thomas Bisset, William Keith and Robert Erskine, as well as the men raised by the sheriffs of Edinburgh, Fife and Forfar.[18] David might have had some concerns over the fact that a number of these regionally influential laymen very often appeared in the household councils of rebel magnates like the Steward and earl of Douglas, witnessing charters, giving advice, receiving their patronage: these men could in theory have been turned against their king.[19] Yet even without these men in their camps, the rebel earls still commanded extensive resources and armed followings and – in the case of Douglas in particular – enjoyed considerable military repute. The Stewarts, moreover, could in theory call upon their *cateran* tenantry of warriors in northern Perthshire and Badenoch. But, in the end, aside from the obvious fact that few Scots would have had the stomach for another civil war, the resources at David's disposal and the shared chivalric ethos at court which he had established since 1357 ensured telling support for the crown; nor does the king seem to have been obliged to call upon his traditional family following from Carrick and Annandale. It is clear, too, that the Stewarts, Douglas and March were quickly separated and unable or unwilling to co-ordinate their efforts: their own affinities were perhaps sorely reduced by David's patronage. Finally, Fordun's source – while praising David's strong leadership – makes it clear that the 'king's people' played a decisive role in finally putting down the most persistent elements of the revolt:

> First . . . with his wonted forbearance, [the king] had a proclamation published, that they [the earls] and their abettors should leave off this foolishness, and be still. But as they were hardened in their stubborness, and defended their own doings, he went after them, with some men of courage, who listed to die sooner than see the woes of their nation and the desolation of the land . . .

Thomas Gray's arguably more neutral chronicle relates a similar story of

18 *Oeuvres de Froissart*, i, 334 and v, 446; *Chron. Bower*, viii, 35. The relative sizes of various nobles' peacetime entourages are suggested by the safe-conducts issued to these lords by Edward III: typically, the Leslies, like most of David's knights, would request passage for themselves plus 6 to 13 horsemen; the earl of Mar and Robert Erskine about 12 each; the earl of March 12 to 20; the earl of Douglas 12 to 30; Archibald the Grim 12 to 20 (*Rot. Scot.*, i, *ad indecim*).

19 E.g. Fraser ed., *The Melvilles*, iii, no. 17 and idem, *The Lennox*, ii, nos. 26–7 for Erskine and Lyle as Stewart charter witnesses *c*. 1362; idem, *The Douglas Book*, iii, nos. 20 and 23 for Archibald Douglas, William Ramsay, John Preston and John Herries as Douglas charter witnesses *c*. 1348–60.

success for the royalist party but one which gives a clear impression of the potency of David's personal leadership:

> The said king marched by night from Edinburgh, and very nearly surprised the said Earl of Douglas at Lanark, where he had lain at night, but [the earl] escaped with difficulty, some of his people being taken.

Again, the exchequer rolls hint at traces of this conflict in the west. For as well as the repairs to Dumbarton, £26 worth of damage was caused to sheep and wool at Dalry in Ayrshire belonging to Eleanor Douglas, Countess of Carrick, the earl of Douglas's sister. She was the widow successively of Alexander Bruce, James Sandilands of Calder and William Towers of Dalry, but by 1363 she had been re-married, to Sir William Cunningham of Kilmaurs in Ayrshire, the knight whom David had made 'lord' or guardian of the Bruce earldom of Carrick *c.* 1358–62 and a man among those paid for their services by the crown in 1363: there were also several other concerned parties with lands in this region including the Steward's son and heir, John Stewart of Kyle, William More of Abercorn, the Flemings, Patrick, earl of March, and Melrose Abbey. This being so, it is likely that the Douglas earl, who had been made hereditary sheriff of Lanarkshire in 1362, was able to use his castles of Lanark and Douglas as bases from which to hit crown resources and allies in that region.[20] When the royal force arrived unexpectedly to engage the earl, David would surely have called upon the local power of Archibald Douglas, now the owner of nearby Bothwell Castle and lordship as well as several Lanarkshire baronies. Once overrun, the Douglas earl most likely escaped south to somewhere like Cavers in Roxburghshire or Hermitage Castle in Liddesdale.[21]

All of these skirmishes would seem to have taken place in late March-early April 1363. No witness list is extant for the seven royal acts which survive for the period 9 March to 24 April.[22] On 20 April Edward III had revoked a safe-conduct issued to Earl Patrick of March and twelve of his men,

---

20 *ER*, ii, 165; *RMS*, i, App. i, no. 146.
21 Brown, *Black Douglases*, 57–8, 96–7. Amongst Douglas's men captured or pursued by the king may have been Sir Robert Dalziel whose lands of Dalziel (adjacent to Bothwell) and Motherwell in Lanarkshire David transferred to a Robert Stewart of Schenbothie (in Clackmannanshire) through a grant issued at Edinburgh on 23 March 1363: as we have seen, Dalziel was then described as 'residing in England' (*RMS*, i, no. 129).
22 *Ibid*, nos. 97–8, 100, 129, 137, 140; *RRS*, vi, nos. 290–1. These acts included a grant of the office of justice clerk north-of-Forth to Adam Forrester of Corstorphine; a grant of Edinburgh lands to John Graham; the office of coroner of Dumfriesshire to a Thomas Durrance; an annual for Alexander Cockburn from Haddington; and an inspection of a transfer of Fife lands.

suggesting either that the Bruce regime had informed the English king of the rebellion and sought his co-operation, or that Patrick had been taken into custody.[23] Yet according to Gray's account, he was not the first rebel earl to submit:

> The Steward of Scotland, without the knowledge or consent of his allies, made his peace with his lord the king; the Earl of Douglas did so by himself, and the Earl of March likewise.

Fordun's source suggests that the rebels had made the first approaches for a submission settlement and that the Steward may have come in to the king's peace before 31 March, just after the medieval new year. However, it was not until 24 April, in St Andrews, that the Steward reappeared as a royal charter witness, attaching his seal to a minor Fife grant alongside the bishop of Brechin, William Keith, Robert Erskine and Archibald Douglas.[24] That Robert Steward should have surrendered and plea-bargained with the king first is not surprising: his threatened place in the royal succession, his several sons and their interests in lands central to the king's plans – Fife, Menteith and northern Perthshire especially – and the personal antagonism between himself and his uncle, undoubtedly meant that Robert had much more to lose than Douglas in terms of his patrimony. The way in which David had dealt with both the earls of Angus and Mar may have served as a warning here. Nonetheless, the king was to exact a humiliating and potentially costly price from the Stewarts for their pardon.

Alarmed by the earls' violence, David probably did not even dare consider attempting to forfeit any of the rebel magnates of any of their provincial titles, not even a younger Stewart son or the aging earl of March (and still, technically, earl of Moray): to do so would have been to risk a major regional or even nationwide civil war in which his opponents would surely be far more committed and royal cash might not last the course of conflict. Better to take a quick clean put-down to the initial ill-organised rebellion, act the part of the magnanimous monarch in pardoning the guilty parties and then go on to exploit the moral high ground ceded by their treasonable actions and swift capitulation. Fordun's source, of course, put a far more public face on such political realism:

> So being a most meek man, who would rather forgive than avenge, [David] formed a wise resolution for the nonce, and decided to be indulgent towards them [the rebels], taking an oath of fealty from them, lest they should take upon them to do such things, and the community should go on and suffer greater woes . . .

23 *Rot. Scot.*, i, 872
24 *RRS*, vi, no. 291.

However, that David intended to exploit fully his victory as a mandate for his domestic and diplomatic agenda of 1362 was immediately signalled by the manner in which he took the Steward's submission. Both Fordun's source, and, following him, Abbot Bower, concur that the Steward swore his new oath of loyalty at the bishop of St Andrews' manor of Inchmurdoch in Fife, now Boarhills, a few miles up the coast from Crail and a peaceful spot in which David had resided as a child. Yet at the same time:

> the aforesaid lord David, king of Scotland, took to wife . . . a great lady, named Margaret of Logie, of high and noble birth, and born in his kingdom; and he endowed her with many lands and possessions, and raised her in honour with him, with the royal diadem.[25]

Thus the Stewarts' submission to royal authority was made to coincide very publicly with the king's new marriage and thus to legitimise his domestic and dynastic plans. Bower even reproduces the text of this oath, dating it to 14 May 1363: if genuine, it gives a remarkable snapshot of the endemic depth of factionalism within the Scottish political community at this time. Presumably requiring his going down on bended knee and offering his seal and sword to the king, the Steward's oath was given in the recorded presence of William Landellis the bishop of St Andrews, Patrick of Leuchars (in Fife), the bishop of Brechin and Chancellor, John, the abbot of Dunfermline (whose appointment Bower asserts David had recently approved), Walter Wardlaw, the archdeacon of Lothian (named as the king's secretary), Gilbert Armstrong, the provost of St Andrews, Erskine, the Chamberlain, Sir Archibald Douglas, Sir Robert Ramsay, Sir Thomas Fauside, Norman Leslie, Alexander Lindsay of Glenesk and 'many others': this was very much a strong core of the king's people. In addition to swearing his loyalty to 'my lord David' for the rest of his life, the Steward crucially promised that:

> I shall assist, defend and maintain and support in all proceedings begun or to be begun by my lord and his ministers and whomsoever my lord king wishes to call his faithful men, with all my strength against all men living whatever their condition or state may be. This is notwithstanding whatever contracts, bonds and oaths that I have made and maintained with Patrick earl of March and Moray, William earl of Douglas, John Steward of Kyle, Robert Stewart of Menteith my sons or anyone else . . . I oblige myself and promise by my forsaid oath that in future I shall make no contract, bond or oath with them, or any one of them, or with any one or any group whatever, without first letting my

25 *Chron. Fordun*, i, 382; *Chron. Bower*, vii, 323–9.

said lord king know, and requesting and obtaining his special licence . . .[26]

David's insistence upon the Steward's renunciation of his bonds with the other rebel earls underlined his fear of the potentially powerful faction thrown together by his policies of 1362. But the closing phrases of this dictated oath point to the far greater weight of retribution David sought to direct against his heirs presumptive. For if the Steward failed to support the crown in future against rebels, he would do so

> under pain of losing all right of succession to the kingdom of Scotland and to certain other lordships or lands which I acquire . . . [and of facing] perjury, dishonour, rejection and cancellation of my knighthood and defacing of my arms.

David had won but he was by no means in such a position of unassailable strength that he could move to destroy the Stewarts. Nevertheless, the consequences envisaged by any future breach of this oath ring like a hovering enabling act, a poised sword to allow David to inflict the fate of John Balliol – 'Toom Tabard', stripped of his title and honours – upon his leading opponent at the slightest sign of further transgressions. This was an emphatic display of royal authority. Given in Fife, the Steward's submission also lent itself to confirming the crown's upper hand in that provincial dispute. Sir Thomas Bissett and Isabella, heiress of Fife, were presumably married about the same time as David and Margaret: it is striking that many of the witnesses to the Steward's submission at Inchmurdoch were St Andrews-trained clerics and Fife men, several of whom can be associated with David's control of Countess Isabella from late 1362 onwards as well as including – in Landellis, Leuchars, Armstrong, Wardlaw and Erskine – David's leading ambassadors to England over the next seven years.[27]

The king, then, tightened the screws upon the Steward in April-May 1363. In contrast, David's treatment of the earls of Douglas and March was probably far more cautious. Earl Patrick did not reappear as a crown charter witness until 5 June according to the extant evidence. Earl William – who had resisted the king's party with the greatest violence – returned only on 16 July, also at Edinburgh.[28] Their treatment may have been proportional to their part in the rebellion. It is likely that Douglas at least – perhaps along with some of the Steward's sons – was warded for a time in Loch Leven Castle in Fife. Captained by the Chamberlain's brother, Alan Erskine, this substantial island fortress was visited by David about 25 April 1363. On

---

26 *Ibid*, 331–3
27 For Isabella's counsel, see: *RMS*, i, no. 221; NAS GD 148/4.
28 *RRS*, vi, nos. 296, 298.

that occasion the king granted Robert Erskine's son, Andrew, the lands of Raploch near Stirling; he also paid for a new boat for the castle about this time. Significantly, Loch Leven was where David would ward both Robert Steward and his fourth son, Alexander of Badenoch, in the autumn of 1368 for their later defiance of the crown.[29]

Thus David seems to have had a commanding grip of the situation. But he knew that if he was ever to persuade a majority of his significant subjects to accept some form of a succession-ransom peace deal with England – with all that this might involve in terms of the Disinherited and Scotland's military alignment – then he would have to have the two leading border magnates of his realm on board. Hence March and Douglas soon reappeared at court. Although Bower asserts that they had to submit individual written oaths of loyalty to the crown (and, presumably, renounce any bonds they had made with their confederates), there is no indication of their having been punished as ritualistically as the Steward. Instead, it followed that much of the remainder of that year was spent by David and his close circle in trying earnestly to win over the active support, or acquiescence for, his diplomatic agenda not only of these two earls, but of many other key members of the political community from all three estates.

The Road to London, April–November 1363

Between 9 March and 20 November 1363 – after which David departed on embassy to London – the crown issued between fifty and sixty acts, a considerable burst of activity and almost double the number of acts extant for each of the years 1362 and 1364. During that time, David's itinerary – while he still resided predominantly at Edinburgh – took him at least to St Andrews (24 April), Loch Leven (25 April), Dundee (12 May), on several occasions to Perth (24–6 May, 27 September, 20 November), Stirling (26 May, 6 October), Dunfermline (1 October) and Melrose Abbey (27–8 October). This surely represents a considerable canvassing effort by David and his chief councillors, one to which some of the normal activities of government may have been subordinated. It is clear that in 1363 there was no collection of royal burgh customs and fermes, or accounts rendered by the king's moneyer or wardrobe clerks: they were instead intromitted for two years in 1364. Such delay may of course reflect the damage and disruption caused by the rebel earls' attack on royal resources.[30]

But the fact that all traffic of Scottish merchants, church students and lay

---

29 *RMS*, i, no. 105; *ER*, ii, 80, 154, 167, 309, 347.
30 For the acts which follow, see: *RRS*, vi, nos. 289 to 311 and 293 from the *Addenda* section; *RMS*, i, nos. 97–8, 100, 105, 129, 136–8, 140, 142–6, 148–53, 155–6, 158–61, 162–9, 170–1, 173–5, 186; *APS*, vii, 159. For the clerks' accounts, see *ER*, ii, 119, 159, 161, 180, 183.

pilgrims to England (or at least Edward III's issue of safe-conducts to such Scots) seems to have ceased abruptly between April and November 1363 suggests that what David and his close counsel may also have been doing was keeping a tight lid on both government expenditure and just who was talking to the English.[31] Justice ayres may have been held in Banff, Kincardine and Inverness in late 1363 (and David was present at Stirling sheriff court in October) but in southern Scotland the king seems to have been anxious to take strict control of events and to ensure a majority of support for his planned talks with Edward.[32] In this context, David's grants of 1363 can almost all be shown to have been directed either to winning over wavering Scots, or to undermining the affinities of the crown's opponents, as well as to rewarding the king's loyal cadre. In conjunction with the money disbursed by the Bruce regime that year this would prove to be a highly effective policy.

A number of David's grants were directed towards sometime Steward retainers in crown service, for example to Alexander Cockburn, John Lyle of Duchal (who had all his Perthshire lands confirmed following the death of Joanna, Countess of Strathearn), Robert Stewart of Schenbothie, the Perth burgess-financier John Mercer (who oversaw the ransom finance in Bruges) and Robert Erskine.[33] Other grants were surely aimed at Stewart regional interests. David confirmed a grant by Mary, Countess of Menteith – the mother-in-law of Robert Stewart, Lord of Menteith – to Gillespic Campbell of Lochawe, of the lands which the Countess had held of the Steward in Cowal and Kilmun in Argyll: the fact that the king confirmed this transaction at least twice (25 May, 11 October) suggests that there was still some resistance to its passage from the Steward who had been obliged to resign these lands sometime in 1363. David's inspection in May 1363 of a grant to Gilbert of Glasserie (whose mother was a Campbell of Lochawe) may also have been designed to promote crown support in the north-west.[34] Similarly, David may have forced the Steward to reduce a rental he was owed by the Abbey of Holyrood for land in the Carse of Stirling from 128 merks per

31 *Rot. Scot.*, i, 872–80.
32 *HMC, lx Mar & Kelly*, ii, 8–9.
33 *ER*, ii, 134.
34 For Glasserie, see: *RRS*, vi, 103, 183–4; NAS GD 45 Dalhousie Muniments IV/27/102; *Highland Papers*, i, 134–46. David had granted the lands of John, son of Ewan of Argyll, to Glasserie in 1346 and again in 1358, ordering the sheriff of Argyll, Alexander MacNaughton (whom David had given forfeited lands in 1343 (*RRS*, vi, no. 488)) to give him sasine. In 1358, Glasserie had made bonds with his cousins, the Campbells of Lochawe (against all but the king, the Steward and the Campbells), and with David's nephew by marriage, John Macdougall of Lorn, as well as becoming the Campbells' bailie in Argyll. By 1363, Gillespic Campbell was sheriff of Argyll (*ER*, ii, 125).

annum to just 32 merks.[35] Robert Erskine was allowed to swap lands in Perthshire for those in Kyle, Ayrshire, of James Blair (a crusader who had received some patronage from David after 1357);[36] much of Kyle, of course, was held by the rebel John Stewart. David also confirmed a grant to the *Clann Donnchaidh*, the Steward's cateran tenants in Atholl: the king perhaps did so to pacify a troublesome element which would later be criticised for attacking the lands of Gilbert of Glencairnie in Moray and Atholl. Most notably, David's several trips to Perth in 1363 may have been necessiated by his need to monitor the Stewarts and their tenants.

At the same time, David made grants designed to increase his hold over Earl Patrick of March/Moray's affinity and lands. As well as his favour in Edinburgh to Alexander Recklington, keeper of Dunbar Castle, the king confirmed Patrick's grants to Sir John Hepburn and gave half of the barony of Tibbers and all of Morton in Dumfriesshire to March's nephew and heir, the young George Dunbar, who was already showing an interest in chivalric pursuits.[37] However, David also granted a pension of £40 to the March earl himself, an obvious indication that whilst keeping a tight leash on this past rebel, the king was also keen to ensure his ready acceptance of the fate of Moray and Scotland's foreign policy.

Earl William of Douglas was treated with the same softer touch. The king confirmed a Douglas grant to John Maitland, the earl's bailie in Lauderdale. Then in October David confirmed his father's grant of a £20 annuity to Robert Lauder of the Bass, a (deputy?) justicar of Lothian, whose father had been Robert I's justiciar and whose son, Alan, was keeper of the Douglas earl's castle at Tantallon. David also gave lands and a 19-merk pension from Forfar lands to Douglas's cousin, Alexander Lindsay of Glenesk, and gifted the forfeited lands of Adam Glendinning in Roxburghshire to a Henry Ashkirk, thus disenfranchising another member of the earl's Eskdale forest support. Yet earl William must have been compensated in part by David's remittance that year of £92 of his march lands' wool customs, hinting that, as with Earl Patrick, much of Douglas's disenchantment with the crown was financial or material, a matter of 'fair lordship'.[38]

Elsewhere, David seems to have been concerned to stabilise regions disrupted by the three earls' rebellion. He paid particular attention to Ayrshire, Dumfriesshire and his family earldom of Carrick: this included

---

35 For Robert I's initial reduction of this Abbey rental to the Stewarts from 160 to 128 merks in 1328, see *RRS*, v, no. 346.

36 For Blair, see: *RMS*, i, App. i, nos. 1172, 1217, 1236, 1467; Boardman & Penman, 'The Scottish Arms in the Armorial of Gèlre'.

37 *Rot. Scot.*, i, 884.

38 *Scots Peerage*, v, 280–7; *APS*, vii, 159; *RRS*, vi, no. 509; *ER*, ii, 51, 78, 132; Fraser ed., *Douglas Book*, i, 250–7; Brown, *Black Douglases*, 48, 82, 100–3, 171–5, 268–9.

Carrick lands for Sir John Kennedy of Dunure whom he had recently pardoned for slaying a priest who had falsely slandered that knight to the king. In Fife, David confirmed the trade monopoly against illegal traders of the royal burgh of Inverkeithing perhaps as a means of compensating for Douglas's attack. On 12 May a grant of land for a new tolbooth to the burgesses of Dundee (a burgh which David visited and where he may also have deployed William Dischington to build a new parish church spire) perhaps acted as a stopgap until Anglo-Scottish trade resumed.[39]

Throughout the year, however, David continued to extend substantial favour to established crown supporters. North of the Tay there were minor lands for John Crab of Aberdeen, the office of justice clerkship north-of-Forth for Adam Forrester, confirmations of grants by the earl of Mar to Lindsay of Glenesk (Ruthven in Forfarshire) and William Chalmers (son of Sir David, a knight well favoured by the crown before his death at Neville's Cross), and a handsome £40 annuity from the customs of Dundee for the bold Sir Walter Leslie. Moving south, there was royal favour for: John Graham of Torboulton; Alexander Fraser of Durris and Cowie; Adam Torrie, the royal moneyer in Edinburgh; John, abbot of Dunfermline (who was given four new pockets of Fife and Clackmannanshire land for his house); John Gray of Broxmonth, clerk of the Rolls, who received a handsome pension of 100 merks from the northern justice ayres; Roger Hogg, the leading Edinburgh merchant, parliamentarian and keen trader with England (with whom David had co-founded an altar to St Katherine in St Giles' church in the capital burgh);[40] William, earl of Sutherland – who received an extended safe-conduct to return from England in September 1363 – and his brother, Nicholas;[41] and David Fleming, who received a 20-merk pension from Kincardineshire. In addition, a number of magnates were rewarded explicitly for their service to the crown during the recent crisis. William, bishop of St Andrews saw his diocese confirmed in the customs of St Andrews burgh in thanks for his work 'for the benefit of us [David] and the commonwealth'. By the same token, Robert Erskine's large grant of Stirlingshire and Clackmannanshire (Alloa) lands from the crown in August 1364 would be rendered to 'our beloved confederate . . . for his thankful service and careful labour'.[42]

But even these gifts were outshone by the most significant of David's grants in summer 1363 – that given at Edinburgh on 8 June of 'all of the

39 Turnbull, 'The Parish Church of St Monans', 185 – local tradition holds that David gave Dischington a gold ring for his work at Dundee.
40 *RRS*, vi, no. 208; *CPL to Scotland of Benedict XIII of Avignon, 1394–1419*, 300. Hogg also received some cash from the crown at this time (*ER*, ii, 123).
41 *Rot. Scot.*, i, 874.
42 *RRS*, vi, no. 327.

earldom of Fife and its pertinences' to Sir Thomas Bisset of Upsetlington.[43] This was arguably the surest signal yet that the king would not be diverted from his goals by magnate recalcitrance. No witness list has survived for this act. But between April and November David's most regular counsellors seem to have been the bishops of St Andrews and Brechin, Robert Erskine, Walter Haliburton, John Lyle, Archibald Douglas, Thomas Bisset and John Herries of Terregles, occasionally joined by other royalists. Their presence must have helped the king keep a close check on his other regular daily companions, the Steward and the earls of Douglas and March.

Nonetheless, the political atmosphere of these months must have remained incredibly tense. That rivalry between competing interests was still a threat at this time is suggested by a remarkable surviving bond between Sir Robert Erskine and Sir William More of Abercorn, both ostensible royalists, sealed on 15 June 1363.[44] In this private agreement, Erskine – the royal Chamberlain, keeper of Stirling Castle and the 'king's deposit' and one of the crown's leading diplomats since 1360 – promised to arbitrate in the event of any future disputes involving William More and the Steward, William Keith the Marischal, Thomas, earl of Mar, Archibald Douglas and the Erskine kindred. This ambiguous and sweeping guarantee reflected a number of familial and factional conflicts, and was not simply a face-off between royal and Stewart parties. Clearly, there remained a sense that the feud between Keith and Mar – disrupted by David in 1362 – could re-ignite; in the 1350s David had also overseen an Erskine-Keith marriage to settle a land dispute. But more importantly, the Steward and his son, Robert, lord of Menteith (the widower and son of Elizabeth More respectively), may have been at odds with William More over the former lands of John Graham, earl of Menteith (d. 1347), who had resigned Abercorn in west Lothian (near the Queen's ferry across the Forth) for David to grant in turn to More; the crown had also helped attach huge fees to the recovery of all the Menteith lands. Worse, by 1363, it is also likely that Robert Stewart of Menteith and Archibald Douglas had squared up against each other after David's intervention to help the Grim Douglas secure the Bothwell-Murray inheritance through marriage.[45]

But that was not all. In June 1360 and November 1361 Edward III had paid William More large sums of money for his surrender to the English crown of the person of Maria Douglas, daughter and heiress of William

43 *RMS*, i, no. 158; Boardman, *Early Stewart Kings*, 22–5.
44 NAS GD 124 Mar & Kelly/516. This bond would be confirmed by David again in 1368 see below, ch. 10.
45 *RRS*, vi, nos. 104, 154, 208; *RMS*, i, App. i, nos. 815, 916; Fraser ed., *Red Book of Menteith*, i, 109–15; Boardman, *Early Stewart Kings*, 16–7; Brown, *Black Douglases*, 56–63.

Douglas of Liddesdale (who had agreed to hold his lands of the English king in 1352). For More, this must have led to tensions over that infamous knight's disputed inheritance not only with the Douglases – Earl William, Archibald and James of Lothian – but with Robert Erskine and his son, Thomas. The latter would wed Maria Douglas sometime between 1361 and 1367 and he and James Douglas would come to blows over her lands after her death in childbirth in 1368, a combat which would embroil their respective guardians Robert Erskine and Archibald Douglas and, eventually, the king. Still, in 1363, Maria's release from England and the restoration to her full title to Liddesdale, Eskdale, Dalkeith and elsewhere – thus denying Earl William of Douglas who had claimed these lands for himself since 1353 – may have been a windfall which Archibald and James Douglas and Robert Erskine hoped to procure by supporting David's diplomatic plans.[46] Robert Erskine may also have been keen to secure a good working relationship with William More as Erskine took a growing interest in the wealthy lands and resources (600 merks annually) of the Knights Hospitaller of St John in Scotland, mostly around Linlithgow, Torphichen and Edinburgh but with a house in each royal burgh and which More had only recently passed on to a new preceptor, David de Mar, that sharp lawyer trained in France and favoured by David and Queen Joan as the treasurer of Moray as well as being Earl Thomas of Mar's brother.[47]

David II could not help but be aware of the complex position in which Sir William thus found himself. More – a Neville's Cross veteran and the son of a former Chamberlain for Robert I and David before 1341 – appeared at court in Edinburgh on 16 July 1363 (when the Steward was forced to reduce his rental from the Abbey of Holyrood); on 28 October the king confirmed More's gift of lands to David Meldrum, son of Philip, a prominent royal household knight killed at Neville's Cross. But most telling of all, More – along with many of the men given lands, offices or cash by David since March 1363 – would take part in David's renewed embassies to London after November.[48]

The safe-conduct for David and forty retainers issued by Edward III in April 1363 could be used for passage south that winter. But David would still probably have sought fresh official approval for his embassy from the three estates in a council or parliament. One modern historian has suggested that a council may have been called in October 1363 in Edinburgh where the

---

46 CDS, iv, nos. 49, 63; *Rot. Scot.*, i, 748, 916; *Chron. Fordun*, i, 370n; *Registrum Honoris de Morton*, ii, no. 83; D. Sellar, 'Courtesy, Battle and the Brieve of Right, 1368 – A Story Continued', *Stair Society Miscellany*, ii (Edinburgh 1970–84), 1–12; Brown, *Black Douglases*, 37–8, 42–3, 72, 207.
47 *The Knights of St John of Jerusalem*, xxxii-xxxv.
48 *ER*, i, 178; *Rot. Scot.*, i, 168; *RRS*, vi, no. 298; *RMS*, i, no. 170.

issue of Anglo-Scottish relations was discussed with the 'chief nobles of the land'.[49] If so, then this could easily have been a very fraught assembly. But it is also possible that in the wake of the earls' submissions in late spring and the calculated dispersal of royal patronage since then, David felt confident enough simply to lead off an embassy on his own authority paid for with his 'deposit'. That confidence was reflected in the people he took south with him and the deal he sought from Edward III.

Third Time Lucky? Anglo-Scottish Talks, Winter 1363–4

David and his entourage must have left Scotland almost immediately after 20 November. Their journey to London must have been swift and their talks with Edward III remarkably brief. For by 27 November the two kings and their councils had concluded an 'indenture' for peace which David II was destined to present to a Scottish parliament at Scone in March 1364.[50] The rapidity of this accord suggests that, really, private letters and small, discreet embassies back and forth throughout the summer and autumn must have already progressed Anglo-Scottish talks – or built upon foundations laid in 1362 – to the point at which it merely required the two kings and their key subjects to meet in person to iron out details and formally close a deal. The Scottish esquire, John Herries, had certainly been given a lone safe-conduct to England in August 1363: he was among the Scots in David's retinue received by Edward III at Westminster some ten days after the November indenture was sealed. Sometime in 1363 David had also sent a gift of falcons to Edward III and received in turn the English king's macer, John de Ellirtoun, rewarding him with £10 for his expenses on 'negotiations in Scotland'.[51]

However, a far more important factor in determining David's confidence that he could safely leave his realm must have been the presence in his party of William, earl of Douglas. On 6 December the earl was given the gift of a

---

49 Webster, 'David II and the Government of Fourteenth century Scotland', 122. David did pay Sir John Lyle of Duchal, a steward of the royal household, some £108 out of the Perth customs for the expenses of a parliament at an unspecified location: no such assembly was held at Perth between August 1362 and December 1364, although this sum could have been used for the crucial Scone parliament of March 1364 (*ER*, ii, 178).

50 *RMS*, i, no. 186; *APS*, i, 492–5 (*RPS*, 1364/1–2); *CDS*, iv, nos. 91–2. The safe-conduct issued to the bishop of St Andrews on 5 December 1363 to travel to Rome may have been a pass to facilitate the Pope's ratification of this indenture (*Rot. Scot.*, i, 877).

51 NAS RH2/4/562; *ER*, ii, 129, 132, 183. Patrick Hepburn and David's valet, Thomas Hill, had also been south in summer 1363 (*ibid*, 121; *Rot. Scot.*, i, 678). Sir John Kennedy of Dunure was also granted passage to Canterbury and to France on 10 October and 16 November 1363 – this was in connection with his penance for killing a priest (*CPR*, *iv 1362–1404* 42; *Rot. Scot.*, i, 874).

gold cup and a purse of £13 by the English king. As we shall see, this meant
that sometime between 16 July and that autumn, Douglas had been won
over by his king's fresh offers of 'fair lordship': specifically, the inclusion in
the new indenture of clauses stipulating the return of the Douglas's family
lands in England and safeguards about the restoration of the Disinherited in
Scotland. Tempted (or threatened) back for now into the royal circle, the
Douglas earl thus appeared alongside David's other retainers at Westminster
who were also given money gifts by Edward III: Robert Erskine; Walter
Wardlaw; two unnamed household knights (probably two of John Lyle,
Walter Haliburton and William Dischington); an unnamed clerical steward
of the Bruce household (perhaps Gilbert Armstrong); John Logie, the king's
new stepson; the esquire 'Heryng' (John Herries?); a notary (perhaps
William Calebre, the Mar man and Chamberlain of Queen Margaret
who had facilitated Maria Douglas's 'sale' back to the Scots, aided in the
foundation at St Monans and was chaplain of the chapel to St Mary which
David had recently built in Edinburgh castle); and two further unnamed
squires, probably two of Thomas Hill, Nicholas Erskine or James Douglas
of Lothian (the last of whom would accompany David to London in
1369).[52] The available evidence also suggests that Thomas, earl of Mar,
may have been present to support his cousin, King David, and brother-in-
law, Douglas, in their negotiations. On 25 November Edward III paid Mar
£66 as part of his fee for services in France. Finally, Erskine's account as
Chamberlain for 1363–4 records disbursement of some £1,337 for the
'King's expenses in England' and an additional sum of £532 for the joint
expenses of the 'King and Queen' – it is thus possible that Margaret Logie
also accompanied her new husband and son south, perhaps with the
intention of visiting Canterbury while the men talked.[53]

   Leaving aside the actual terms of the indenture concluded for now, the
embassy clearly afforded David the opportunity to renew the 'rycht gret
specialtie' he had forged with Edward and his Queen, sons and court
through a shared interest in 'play' and Christian chivalry before 1357
and in 1359.[54] According to Froissart, it was on this occasion that the
king of Scots – whom he describes as being in England on pilgrimage to the
shrine of Our Lady at Walsingham in Norfolk – hastened to London when
he had word that Peter I of Cyprus was there on a recruiting drive across the
courts of Europe to raise a crusading army to recover Alexandria: 'the two
kings were much rejoiced to meet, and congratulated each other upon it'.
David and his men must have attended the two great 'celebrations' of

52 *CDS*, iv, no. 93; *ER*, ii, cx, 246; Watt, *Scottish Graduates*, 75.
53 *Rot. Scot.*, i, 880; *ER*, ii, 129–30, 164, 172, 178, 183.
54 *Chron. Wyntoun*, vi, 242.

feasting held by Edward in Peter's honour: the shifty King Waldemar of Denmark, who four years earlier had suggested a joint French, Scottish and Danish descent upon England, was also present.[55] But the Bruce king went even further. He must have promised in person the participation in Peter's bold venture of Scottish crusading knights and esquires. When Peter's force overran Alexandria briefly in October 1365, Walter and Norman Leslie would certainly be among their number, Norman in fact perishing at the city's gates: both men had safe-conducts to pass through England to the continent issued on 25 November 1363 and may thus have been among David's party in London at that time. But in 1365 David may also have encouraged a far larger body of Scottish knights to participate in Peter's noble cause. Edward III certainly issued safe-conducts for passage through England and 'across the sea' in autumn 1365 to a body of Scottish laymen and clerics and their retinues including: Archibald Douglas; Alexander Lindsay; David of Mar, the treasurer of Moray and the Scottish Knights Hospitaller; Walter Wardlaw; William Keith the Marischal; Thomas Bisset, lord of Fife (who had gone to Prussia with the Leslies in 1356); Richard Comyn; Lawrence Gilliebrand; Nicholas Erskine; John, the abbot of Dunfermline; and Alexander Recklington, keeper of Dunbar. This group would, though, have been just too late to join Peter I and the Leslies.[56]

But there is further evidence that Christian chivalry provided grounds for closer Anglo-Scottish relations in late 1363. On 6 December the earls of Douglas, Sutherland and March (a grouping which suggests Earl Patrick may also have been in London) were granted a safe-conduct to make a pilgrimage to Canterbury: on 6 and 13 December respectively, March and Douglas received further individual passes to the shrine of Beckett. This association with the kind of peacetime activity which David liked to cultivate (and which both earls had expressed an interest in before 1362) would have been all the stronger had David and Queen Margaret made use of the safe-conduct to Canterbury and Walsingham they too would receive on 20 February 1364.[57] But there were other instances of increased respect

55 T. Johnes ed., *Sir John Froissart's Chronicles* (2 vols., London 1868) i, 306; Contamine, 'Froissart and Scotland', 43–8. David's meeting with Peter was noted (mistakenly) by some English chroniclers as an Arthurian occasion upon which five kings in all – Edward III, David II, John II of France, Peter I and Waldemar of Denmark – gathered in London (*Chronica Johannis de Reading et Anonymi Cantuarensis, 1346–57*, ed. J. Tait (Manchester 1914), 158; F.S. Haydon ed., *Eulogium – Chronicon ab Orbe Ilsque ad annum domini M.CCC.LXVI* (3 vols., London 1863), iii, 233; E.M. Thompson, *Chronicon Angliae, 1328–88* (London 1874), 54).

56 *Rot. Scot.*, i, 875, 897; N. Housley, *Documents on the Later Crusades, 1274–1580* (London 1996), 5, 14, 55–7; Macquarrie, *Scotland and the Crusades*, 81–2; Penman, 'Christian Days and Knights', 267.

57 *Rot. Scot.*, i, 877, 881.

between the two kings during this visit. On 8 December Edward III paid £24 for the 'exsequies' of Queen Joan of Scotland: he and David may have held belated funerary rites for her after her death and burial in the London Greyfriars in September 1362. Also sometime in December 1363, 'at the instance of David de Bruys of Scotland, the king's brother [a non-title which does not seem to have bothered David and which surely existed only on English government papers], King Edward pardoned . . . one Peter Malore . . .' for an offence against an English justice official.[58] After this show of grace, it is also possible that the two royals and their parties spent Christmas together. In this company, such was the impression David and his subjects made upon Philippa, Edward's cultured Queen from Hainault, that she would later be moved in 1365 to write to the Scots king, Robert Erskine, and the earls of Douglas and Mar to recommend to their courts her countryman, Jean Froissart. The chronicler would spend time not only with David and these lords but also the Grim and Lothian Douglases, the earl of March and the 'earl' (*sic.* lord) of Fife – Thomas Bisset: all of these men may thus have been present with David in London in 1363.[59] This was just the kind of heady, cosmopolitan aristocratic coalition which David would have loved to make permanent. In all of this, the Steward and his sons and close allies were excluded completely and remained in Scotland.

Yet in December 1363 all these chivalric connections were arguably just the icing on the cake. David seems to have been far more concerned to use a revival of the general traffic between Scotland and England as a grand gesture to mark and legitimise his conclusion of a peace deal with Edward. For on 5–6 December, almost fifty significant Scots – together with individual retinues of between four and twenty men each – were granted passage to England. David perhaps intended that they should visit England throughout 1364 as a means of celebrating and cementing the treaty once it had been passed by a Scottish parliament: this could be done by holding a feast and, say, a tournament at Westminster, perhaps even to coincide with the festival of St Monan (1 March) or of St George (23 April) and the Garter lists.[60]

Among the Scots named on these joint travel documents were not only strong crown supporters and the core of David's chivalric cadre but many of the men whom the king had taken pains to favour with grants and money between April and November 1363. So once again we find included the familiars: John Lyle; John Maitland; John Herries and his son, Gilbert; Thomas Hill, David's valet; John, the abbot of Dunfermline; some canons of

58 *CDS*, iv, no. 4; *CCR*, *xi 1360–64*, 562.
59 J. Palmer ed., *Froissart – Historian* (London 1981), 26, which reproduces the Queen's letters of introduction. For Froissart in Scotland in 1365, see below, ch. 10.
60 *Rot. Scot.*, i, 876–7.

David's favourite abbey of Holyrood; Thomas Bisset and his son, William (named as a hostage for David in 1357); Robert and Nicholas Erskine; the new Queen's clerk, William Calebre; David de Mar, treasurer of Moray, who had also been a chamberlain for Queen Joan and procurator to England in 1357 to represent several bishops' stake in David's release;[61] William Gledstanes, David's wool-agent in the marches;[62] Hugh Eglintoun, the Steward's brother-in-law but also a chivalric poet, justiciar in 1360 and a past member of the Alexander Ramsay school of warfare;[63] James Douglas of Lothian and his brothers John and William;[64] John Edmonstone, the coroner of Lothian since November 1362 and a regular witness to James Douglas's charters;[65] William Ramsay, the ex-Fife earl; David Barclay of Brechin, the son of the former crusader who had served David against Douglas of Liddesdale;[66] the Lothian man, Andrew Valence (whose son was a hostage in 1357); William Newbigging, a Forfar man who can be associated with Sir Walter Oliphant, David's future half-brother-in-law and sheriff of Perth by 1365–7; Thomas Barry, a Glasgow canon who later achieved fame as a romantic poet celebrating the Scottish victory over England at Otterburn (1388) and provost of Archibald Douglas's collegiate church at Bothwell, but who served Walter Wardlaw when he became bishop of Glasgow in 1367 and to whom David paid a fee of £5 in 1363–4;[67] Alexander Fraser of Cowie, a ward of the crown in 1363;[68] John, son of Sir Robert Chisholm, keeper of Urquhart Castle and sheriff of Inverness;[69] and even Sir John le Grant, the Moray man and crusader who had fallen from favour when he joined the embassy to France of 1359. Finally, David added to this remarkable list by securing Edward's re-issue of the 1357 general safe-conduct to Scottish clerics travelling for study to Oxford and Cambridge. After December 1363, Scottish merchants also resumed trade with England in large numbers.[70]

---

61 Watt, *Scottish Graduates*, 382–4; *CPR*, iv, 3.
62 *Chron. Fordun*, i, 377n; *ER*, ii, 51, 78.
63 Fraser ed., *Memorials of the Montgomeries*, i, 16–9 and ii, 4–16. Eglintoun had also had a safe-conduct to England on pilgrimage in April 1363 in company with Thomas Somerville, John de Ros, Duncan Wallace, Patrick Hepburn, Alexander the bishop of Aberdeen and William Ruthven, the last such group that year until December (*Rot. Scot.*, i, 872).
64 *RRS*, vi, nos. 242, 251; *ER*, ii, 124; Brown, *Black Douglases*, 53–71.
65 *RRS*, vi, nos. 274, 376, 417, 430, 444.
66 *Rot. Scot.*, i, 869; *Chron. Fordun*, i, 369.
67 *ER*, ii, 131; Watt, *Scottish Graduates*, 31–2; Brown, *Black Douglases*, 94, 122, 130.
68 Fraser ed., *Frasers of Philorth*, 98–105.
69 *RRS*, vi, nos. 348, 374; *ER*, ii, 143, 187; A. Mackenzie, *A History of the Chisholms* (Inverness 1891), 20–1.
70 *Rot. Scot.*, i, 877–*passim*.

Incidentally, there is some (very) slight proof to suggest that these men may have been carefully vetted by David. Missing from their number are two knights from David's Edinburgh court who had already participated in cross-border travel: the east Lothian men, Sir John Preston and William de Vaus. Both had been captured at Neville's Cross and de Vaus at least had forsworn future war against England; both men had become regular charter witnesses for the crown after 1357. Preston had served as an ambassador to England in 1361 and overseen works at Edinburgh Castle; Vaus had become a steward of the royal household by 1361 and received confirmation of his sheriffship of 'Elgin' and royal forest land in Aboyne in Aberdeenshire in 1362–3.[71] However – although their surnames were common enough in northern England – it is possible that these two close servants of the Scottish king were the 'John de Prestesson' and 'William de Vaus' named amongst the band blamed for the murder of Sir John de Coupland in an ambush of 'premeditated assault' near Alnwick on 20 December 1363; the others named as the killers in a dubious assize dominated by Coupland's enemies and heard at Newcastle on 28 December 1363 by Lords Neville and Percy included the Northumbrian border lords 'John de Clifford, knight, Thomas his brother, Thomas Forrester, Robert Hutchinson [as well as] . . . Alan Fenwyk a Scot . . . and others with five pages . . . nine being armed and eleven being archers' who had 'at once fled to Scotland'. Significantly, David and his London entourage may have been passing through Northumberland on their return journey north just in time to become embroiled in this Northumbrian vendetta. The death of David II's unpleasant and ambitious captor at Neville's Cross may have been primarily a local feud but his demise was extremely timely in terms of smoothing the way for an Anglo-Scottish indenture.[72]

Coupland's position after 1346 as sheriff of occupied Roxburghshire and keeper of its castle had placed him in an excellent position to cry wolf about Scottish aggression or to harass the marches himself as a means of undermining the peace process. He was the only leading northern noble to be excluded from Anglo-Scottish talks after 1357, with his fellow captains Neville, Percy and de Lucy in particular participating in November 1363's negotiations. Coupland's infamous and ruthless pursuit of land, revenues

71 ER, i, 546, 562, 606 and ii, 76, 77, 83; RRS, vi, nos. 41, 158, 159, 171; RMS, i, nos. 103, 121, App. i, no. 111 and App. ii no. 1264; Rot. Scot., i, 678.

72 Calendar of Inquisitions Miscellaneous, iii, no. 531; Dixon, 'John de Coupland – Hero to Villain'; A. King, 'War, Politics and Landed Society in Northumberland, c.1296–1408' (unpublished Ph.D. thesis, University of Durham, 2001), 154–73. In March 1369, David would give lands north of Edinburgh to a Thomas Forrester, a burgess of that town (RMS, i, no. 242).

and power in northern England betrayed a character driven by self-interest, a hard-man whom the English crown had been forced to replace in office periodically in the face of complaints about his role as escheator. Coupland had already clashed with William, earl of Douglas, since 1353, being especially angered by the earl's seizure of Selkirk forest, Hermitage Castle and Liddesdale.[73] Thus by 1363, if David was to secure any sort of succession-peace deal involving the restoration of the Disinherited, Coupland – just like William Douglas, the knight of Liddesdale and murderous rival to Alexander Ramsay for the sheriffship of Roxburgh – would have to be pacified or otherwise neutralised if Earl William of Douglas was to be persuaded that a treaty would pose no threat to his interest in the marches. This being so, the outside chance that David had condoned Preston's and de Vaus's role in the destruction of his captor should not be dismissed. The king had already displayed a thirst for politic revenge in approving the deaths of William Bullock in 1342 and the knight of Liddesdale in 1353. Such a plot might also explain the absence of these two Edinburgh-based knights from the big safe-conduct to London of December 1363 – they were perhaps wanted men in England and thus the only obvious supporters of David left behind.

Even if not involved on the edges of Coupland's bloody end, David must have relished the news of his demise. But the king must have found even greater symbolic joy in the death of another former enemy about that time, that of the sad figure of Edward Balliol, aged eighty. Since 1356 Balliol had lived a reclusive existence in northern England, struggling to assert his lordship in his former lordship of Galloway in the face of opposition from his former followers and new men like Archibald the Grim; Balliol was dead by 27 January 1364 at the latest.[74] Such news may have given David and his council increased hope of being able to persuade a majority of the Scottish political community to accept peace with England after his party returned to Scotland by 1 January 1364.[75] However, it should now be made clear that the king and his council may well have had need of such a last-minute boost. For despite the convivial atmosphere at London, the promises of future

---

73 *Oeuvres de Froissart*, v, 131–7. For Coupland's interference in Selkirk forest *c.* 1357, see *Scottish History Society Miscellany*, v. no. 13; for the wasting of Roxburghshire, see Summerson, *Medieval Carlisle*, i, 310–1. *Chron. Bower*, vii, 271, 299–303 is noticeably anti-Coupland, emphasising the earl of Douglas's victories over him in the 1350s.

74 PRO E.199/49/47; Balfour-Melville, *Edward III and David II*, 17; Reid, 'Edward Balliol', 48. By 1363, David had even managed to install his former confessor, Adam de Lanark, as bishop of Whithorn or Galloway – he would have a safe-conduct to England on 20 February 1364 (Watt, *Scottish Graduates*, 325–6; *Rot. Scot.*, i, 881).

75 *RRS*, vi, no. 312.

contact with England and the large sums David had spent, the actual terms of the treaty offered by Edward III cannot have been exactly what David wanted. He was to have an extremely difficult time in presenting them to the Scottish parliament.

Debate at Scone, March 1364

The terms of the Anglo-Scottish indenture concluded in late November 1363 which David brought back to sell to his political community in early 1364 make it clear that although the king and his close counsel had done some hard talking with the English they had by no means had things all their own way. Most obviously, despite the two kings' amicable personal relations, Edward III and his council had no longer been willing to accept the elevation of a *younger* Plantagenet son as heir presumptive to Scotland. Now the English demanded that either Edward himself or his eldest son and heir replace David's favoured nephew, John of Gaunt, the English king's third son: full regnal union should be a real possibility.[76]

English insistence on this point was understandable. The political situation had changed markedly since 1350–2 and 1359. The peace of 1360 with the French was by this time badly undermined. John II's ransom payments were in massive arrears and the private deal Edward had concluded with his French hostage princes in late 1362 had collapsed by the following summer. In November 1363 John II had announced his intention to return to London to renegotiate the situation. But the continued activities of the foreign mercenary companies in France and Edward's stubborn refusal to relinquish his claim to the French title made the likelihood of the total abandonment of the treaty of Brétigny and renewed Anglo-French conflict a genuine fear. A cash-strapped Edward could not afford to give up cheaply his hold on a neutral and increasingly friendly Scotland and David's small but welcome ransom.[77] Yet at the same time Edward could not risk passing up completely another chance to profit from his closer relations with a king who had not paid his ransom anyway since 1360. In doing so in 1363, however, Edward had to be wary of giving too much to his former brother-in-law who had just remarried and presumably looked forward to sons of his own by Margaret Logie: a younger son deal was now too big a gamble

---

76 *APS*, i, 492–4 for the following terms of this indenture. A.A.M. Duncan has shown that a second indenture – based on a younger son of Edward III becoming David's heir – included in the Thompson/Innes *APS*, i, at 494–6, under the year 1364, really belongs to the talks of 1351–2 (BL Cott. Vesp. C. XVI; PRO E39/2/2; Duncan, 'Honi soit qui mal y pense', 127–8) – see above, ch. 5.

77 Sumption, *Hundred Years War*, ii, 496–502; Cuttino, *Medieval English Diplomacy*, 88–93.

for England to take only to see David cancel it out nine months later. Better for the English to up the ante and make demands which would either scare the Scots into remaining peaceful and paying off the ransom on time, or secure a unique opportunity to expand Edward's empire further without the need for war.

It was surely such reasoning which brought Edward and his council to make several very significant concessions to the Scottish embassy of 1363, striking changes from the treaty first offered in 1351–2 (although perhaps including terms first mooted in 1359). The first clause of the new indenture was the stipulation that Edward himself should become heir to a childless David II. But this was compensated for by the promise that the English would return possession of the towns and castles of Berwick and Roxburgh and the castles of Jedburgh and Lochmaben with all their hinterlands (including Annandale). This was a move which would restore Scotland to the full extent attained under Robert I by 1328 and give the Scots control of one of the leading wool ports of the isles.[78] But more importantly, whilst David's ransom would of course be cancelled, the English crown was to pay compensation to the Disinherited, naming the young Strathbogie earl of Atholl, Beaumont, Ferrers and the heirs of Talbot and 'all others' with a claim in this group.

Crucially, this meant that in contrast to 1352, Scottish lords now in possession of Disinherited lands north of the border would be left undisturbed. At the same time this was to be matched by a promise that the king of Scotland would 'be put in possession and in heritable estate of the greater part of the land and rents which his ancestors had in the kingdom of England, and should have satisfaction for the remainder in a suitable place', doing homage to the English king for these lands alone. Admittedly, this last clause was surely left deliberately vague and did not state whether this included the northern counties of England possessed by the kings of Scots until 1157 or simply the lordship of Tynedale and parts of Huntingdon allowed to some of the MacMalcolm royals before 1286. But, as we have seen, the chance at least of expanding territory back across the border must have been appealing to both David and some of his leading earls, barons and religious institutions. Most notably, the 1363 indenture also stipulated that the earl of Douglas should recover the heritable lands in England of his father (Archibald, the Guardian, d. 1333) and uncle (the 'Good' Sir James, d. 1330, who had recovered his English lands under the 1328 peace treaty): a full peace and return to cross-border landholding would further consolidate

78 A. Tuck, 'A Medieval Tax Haven: Berwick-upon-Tweed and the English Crown, 1333–1461', in R. Britnell and J. Hatcher eds., *Progress and Problems in Medieval England: Essays presented to Edward Miller* (Cambridge 1996), 148–67, 156–7.

Douglas's lordship in Liddesdale and the forest and *vis à vis* English Marcher lords like the Percies and Nevilles.[79]

The indenture then went on to outline a number of further promises to protect Scottish sovereignty, guarantees almost certainly emphasised by the Scots at Westminster in the light of the English insistence upon Edward III's or his heir's succession in Scotland. Inevitably, these stipulations were highly reminiscent of the treaty of Birgham of 1290 concluded between Edward I and the Scottish guardians as a marriage and regnal union contract: here, too, there was something for each estate.[80] Scotland was to remain a separate kingdom with its own coronation in the event of an English succession, for which purposes the stone of Scone should be returned north; Scottish church lands would also be restored. Scotland was to retain separate parliaments, a free church, its own laws and customs; there were to be no legal summons of Scottish cases to England and native Scots were to fill the benefices and government and shrival justice offices of the realm. The English monarch as king of Scots was to make no revocations of Scottish land. Scottish merchants were to be left to trade freely and not be obliged to go to Calais or pay more than half a merk per sack of wool in customs (a massive reduction from the sum then being levied by David's regime). The English monarch as king of Scots was furthermore not to alienate or divide up any of the Scottish realm to anyone who might do homage to him (as England's king). He was to receive the counsel of Scots on Scottish affairs and to introduce no new taxes or start any new wars in which to embroil the Scots. His Scottish subjects were to do no more than forty days' military service a year under the Anglo-Scottish alliance proposed by this treaty (and in the 1363 deal, unlike that of 1352, no specific Scottish troop numbers were named); longer service by individuals was to be paid for at the going English military rate and the Scots were not to fight in theatres of war where they had not previously served (a clause designed surely to spare their blushes in France). Finally, and generally, no laws were to be introduced by an English king of Scots which were contrary to the good of the Scottish realm.

There was a lot to consider. David was expected to sound out the opinion of his prelates and magnates on these terms and reply to Edward and his council by 7 April 1364. That these were not the ideal terms he had sought to extract from Edward can be inferred from the 'protestations' from both negotiating teams noted in the indenture's preamble (and from the comment of the English chronicler, Henry of Knighton, cited at the opening of this

---

79 *Foedera*, ii, 762; Stringer, *Earl David*, 200–68; *Atlas of Scottish History to 1707*, 418–21; Cameron & Ross, 'The Treaty of Edinburgh and the Disinherited (1328–32)', 250–1.
80 Stevenson, *Documents*, i, no. cviii; Barrow, *Bruce*, 27–37.

chapter). The documentation surrounding the resulting debate in Scotland's parliament also made it clear that David *had* re-tabled the idea of John of Gaunt – Edward's third eldest surviving son – as his heir, but that the English had said no.[81] That being so, it is possible that upon his return to Scotland, the attitude of David and his closest advisers to the November 1363 indenture package was in many ways ambivalent. There were many advantageous terms the king could work with, but the central concession to the English over the kingship was bound to be so controversial that David may have determined from the first to cut his losses and reject this treaty: he would, though, press for tacit parliamentary approval for further negotiations along preferred lines.

This may explain why so little royal activity can be identified between the Bruce party's return to Scotland by 1 January until the parliament at Scone on 8 March 1364. Only two crown acts survive from this period, both in favour of the diocese of Durham and its daughter priory within Scotland at Coldingham, gestures which were nonetheless bound to be designed to help sweeten Anglo-Scottish relations and land restoration. Between 2 and 6 January David also attended to a number of minor ecclesiastical provisions including a confirmation of Robert Erskine's grant to the abbey of Cambuskenneth outside Stirling and a dispensation of illegitimacy for royal cleric, William Calebre.[82] Yet these acts stand in stark contrast to the relative frenzies of royal patronage in advance of David's council in April 1359 and his trip south in autumn 1363. The king may have held a tournament at Edinburgh in January or February 1364 to commemorate his return from London – or more probably to mark his fortieth birthday on 5 March. He may also have ensured that William, earl of Sutherland, and Thomas, earl of Mar, were free to return home from England and support the crown in the forthcoming parliament.[83] But there is little sign of the energetic and material lobbying by the crown which might have been expected with such a difficult task ahead.

The political battle lines, though, were clearly being drawn. On 1 January David can be found at Edinburgh with the earl of Douglas, Erskine, Wardlaw, Armstrong and the household esquires, Herries and James Douglas of Lothian, all of whom had been in London. But the Steward seems to have avoided the royal court. He had issued a charter from

---

81 Duncan, 'A Question about the Succession, 1364', p. 10, clause 51 – the younger son plan 'quod iam oblatum' (now offered) which was rejected by Edward III.

82 *RRS*, vi, nos. 312–3 and pp. 47–8; *CPP*, i, 475–7.

83 *ER*, ii, 129, 177 (John Lyle and Simon Reed at the castle paid for the 'lists' at Edinburgh); *Rot. Scot.*, i, 878, 881. Edward III's revocation on 15 January of a safe-conduct to Sir Henry Kerr, sheriff of Roxburgh, may have been done to help David ensure full attendance at this parliament (*ibid*, 879).

Inchaffrey Abbey in Perthshire on 10 December 1363 in the company of the Abbot, the local men Thomas Fauside, Alexander Stewart (his fourth son) and Maurice Drummond, and the Perth burgess, John Mercer.[84] Then on 12 January 1364 the Steward was at Perth where he confirmed his £40 annuity from his lands in the Carse of Stirling to the church of the bishopric of Glasgow where he had been required to found an altar to the Virgin and St Kentigern as part of the cost of the legitimation of his first marriage and its offspring about 1347. It is a distinct possibility that in the wake of the failed rebellion or in the run-up to the 1364 parliament David and his counsel once more tried to cast doubt over the legitimacy of the Steward's sons by his first wife and their right of succession. Hence Robert renewed his penance in the company of his son and heir John Stewart of Kyle, his brother John, Sir Hugh Eglintoun, John Mercer and John de Ros.[85]

In short, Robert Steward must have been extremely apprehensive of the outcome of the March 1364 parliament. But the available evidence for the course of that assembly reveals ultimately that in fact the Stewarts and their supporters were able to make many convincing arguments in their defence and to counter some of the political lobbying David's party had managed. A.A.M. Duncan has identified and translated the remarkable *Quaestio,* or briefing 'booklet', prepared for this parliament by Walter Spyny, a cleric 'advanced in civil law' and secretary of William de Landellis, the bishop of St Andrews in the 1350s and 1360s (as well as a man patronised by the king): he would serve as bishop of Aberdeen between 1397 and his death in 1406. In his old age, Spyny recalled from memory his arguments both *for* and *against* the acceptance of Edward III as David II's heir presumptive. Cautious use should, of course, be made of this source and the official parliamentary record for 1364. The Aberdeen cleric of *c.* 1400–20 to whom Spyny related his recollections sought to present it as 'a warning for future generations'. This was at a time when anti-English sentiment in Scotland was in full swing in the wake of the Scots' victory at the battle of Otterburn (1388) and Henry IV's invasion of the northern kingdom (1400, discussed below in chapter 12) with a view to re-asserting overlordship. Scotland's political elite at that time was headed by magnates who had often been on the receiving end of David II's enmity, including John Stewart of Kyle (who

---

84 Fraser ed., *Memorials of the Montgomeries,* ii, 5.
85 NLS Adv. MSS. 22.2.18; *Registrum Episcopatus Glasguensis,* i, no. 302; Boardman, *Early Stewart Kings,* 18–20; see ch. 4 above. An assertion of the legitimacy of Robert Steward/Robert II's sons by his first wife can be found in the records of the Scots College in Paris – where they seem to have been assembled during the reign of James VI who hoped to be James I of England: this perhaps suggests that David II may have communicated doubts about the Stewarts' legitimacy to France and the Papacy. The 1347 papal dispensation secured by the Steward had of course gone through the French king (BN MSS. Clairambault no. 1226, fo. 45–61; *CPP,* i, 124).

became Robert III in 1390), Robert Stewart of Menteith (the earl of Fife/ Menteith and Duke of Albany by 1399) and the Black Douglases: these lords were committed to active alliance with France after 1377.[86]

Nevertheless, Spyny's booklet – drawing on the bible, papal decreetals and juristic tracts – lays out many of the arguments which must have been deployed by both camps not only in 1364 but throughout the preceding decade: from the ill-fated council of May 1351 and parliament of February 1352 – when, Spyny recalled, David received 'little or no courtesy from his own folk' – to the dramatic council at Dundee of April 1359. Moreover, the sequence of Spyny's fifty-seven points-of-order does suggest that what David and his close advisers intended in March 1364 was to persuade a majority of the political community to reject the idea of Edward III himself as the Bruces' successor but to embrace the advantages otherwise to be had from such a peace with England and try to close a similar deal involving the younger son, John of Gaunt, avoiding full regnal union. Spyny's task in 1364 had clearly been to 'spin' a lobbying manifesto to this end which the clerks of the leading magnates could use to persuade their patrons to back the crown: it was also a handsome academic exercise.[87]

However, reading between the lines, Spyny's paper in many ways succeeds too well in pulling down the case for Edward III's succession: it perhaps betrays quite consciously grave doubts amongst even David's close servants and supporters in 1363–4 about the practical repercussions and emotional fallout from the gamble of a deal with England. Beyond that, it surely proves once and for all that Scotland's parliament in the wake of the Bruce seizure of the throne and the Wars of Independence was no mere rubber stamp for royal wishes – the 'political community of the realm' could be riven by major differences for which a settlement could, nonetheless, be sought in a heated debate among the three estates. Spyny's repeated reference in his tract to the will of the 'populus' (people) in deciding the realm's fate underlines the consultative power of this body, closely involved in diplomatic decision-making since the king and Steward had begun to appeal to them on this matter in 1351–2. Throughout the second period of David's adult rule in Scotland, policy would be recorded after parliament and councils as having been variously 'agreed and assented by the three communities there present' (1357); decided by 'the king acting upon the

---

86 Duncan, 'A Question about the Succession, 1364', pp. 1–5 and clauses 1–6 (pp. 25–9); Watt, *Scottish Graduates*, 67–70, 503–6. Spyny had been abroad in the 1350s but was back in Scotland between 5 May and November 1363, at Elgin. He can thus be associated with Alexander de Bur, bishop of Moray by February 1363, and David de Mar, treasurer of Moray, two key royal agents in the north after 1363 – see below, chs. 10 and 11.

87 Duncan, 'A Question about the Succession', pp. 13–6.

counsel and consent of the communities' (1364); 'expressly granted and also publicly proclaimed by the king in the said parliament at the instance of the three communities' (1366); 'ordained and agreed by the deliverance of the three communities of the realm' (1367); given 'with the consent and confirmation of the assembled three communities' (1369); or 'ordained and decreed by the said assembled and chosen three communities' (1370). In contrast, the *acta* of Robert I's strictly controlled parliaments and councils had been recorded as the 'king decrees' or 'as the king wishes and commands'. Thus in 1364 David would have to work very hard to control the proceedings of the Scone assembly.[88]

The *Quaestio's* arguments for accepting the proposed indenture – which 'as is asserted by many, King David greatly favoured' – were outlined first (clauses 8 to 23).[89] Spyny opened with a universal constitutional argument. Traditionally, it was stated, kingdoms have been transferable like nobles' inheritance – 'since a people always has need to obey one prince, it matters little to change the person of the principate, and so long as he discharges his office in praiseworthy fashion, the concept of nation is not at all required'; besides, the treaty contained guarantees for a separate Scottish coronation and government. There then followed some defeatist realism from Spyny as devil's advocate: the Scots, it was argued, were too weak militarily to fight the English again – they were without 'a noble of the royal blood, or great lord, who is fit or able to lead the people' (a clear swipe at the Steward) nor could they expect any help from a neighbour (obviously meaning the French). Yet, worse still, the Scottish nobles were 'so senseless and almost lifeless as a result of the various battles, in which so many have fallen against the English, the enemy are so stout-hearted, our folk none or few, young and untrained . . .'. In any such war, moreover, the Scots could not hope to recover captured men from England because they were already paying the king's ransom and had 'behaved improperly concerning our hostages last given to them' (a clear dig at the resistance of Angus, the Stewarts and others in this role): the English, besides, would feel justly motivated to punish the Scots for their breach of the 1357 treaty.

Spyny's next clause, however, spoke once again to the underlying threat of civil war in Scotland after 1357 and the key role which the loyalty of castle-keepers had played between 1350 and 1363: David – who is 'presumed to agree' with the indenture and has many supporters – 'has all the strong places, and so there is not a safe place for *those who wish to resist*' (my italics). This practical but extremely negative political argument as to the

88 *Ibid*, p. 5; Tanner, 'Cowing the Community?'; Penman, 'Parliament Lost – Parliament Regained?'.
89 Duncan, 'A Question about the Succession', pp. 29–35.

virtues of peace and regnal union with England is then followed by a miscellany of further points: neither the French nor the Norwegians (angered by Scottish non-payment of the 1266 'annum' for the western isles) will be allies of Scotland; the English are strong fighters and lucky whilst still holding some of the Scots' border castles. If the Scots accept the indenture now, willingly, they would do so from a position of strength and good-feeling, thus securing a genuine ally in England and allowing for war-torn land to be re-worked, towns and trade to prosper and land values to increase: here additional reference might have been made in the debate to the English offer to slash the wool tariff which Edward III might impose on the Scots, a tax-cut which would have been a major boon to all three estates. But Spyny continues by arguing that the deal on offer was besides no different in its outcome than marrying a Scottish king's daughter to the English king (although Spyny does not say so, this is surely something which it might be thought David would have tried with an English prince had he had a Bruce daughter). Finally, the *Quaestio* argues that it would be better to have a Prince to rule over Scotland than to suffer 'a plunderer or tyrant': this vague jibe would seem to be a reference to Edward III's ruthlessness as an enemy of the Scots – as during the Burnt Candlemas of 1356 – or a sly dig at the Steward's lieutenancy of 1346–57.

These are all valid arguments to a greater or lesser degree with clauses designed to appeal to the estates of church and burghs as well as magnates. Much of the remainder of Spyny's booklet, however, is hereafter devoted to arguments against the proposed indenture (clauses 24 to 40). These points are grouped as a 'loyal opinion' faithful to the crown. But they hold back little in damning 'a proposal very damaging and dangerous to the kingdom of Scotland which would altogether betray, weaken and destroy the whole freedom of the kingdom, and would wipe out . . . all the magnates and the people'. Significantly, this heading may have been one of three clauses (or 'glosses') inserted into Spyny's booklet by a contemporary opponent of the treaty with England.[90] All told, these sections make a far more convincing case on paper than those in support of the indenture and surely reflect some of the diplomatic climate of *c.* 1390–1400 when Spyny recalled his text.

Tellingly for a churchman's work, this section opens (with another 'gloss') by citing the papal bull *Scimus Filii* of 1299 (in which Rome had called upon Edward I to show proof of his claims over Scotland) and asserts that Scotland was subject only to the Pope as a 'special daughter': if subjection occurred, the Scottish church would be swallowed by the English church just

---

90 *Ibid*, pp. 23–4, 35–47; description of opposition on p. 29, clause 6. The second 'gloss' was the point about the preference for an Anglo-Scottish royal marriage; the third about Scotland's special papal daughter status.

like the Welsh church of St David.[91] The English, it continues, cannot be trusted after their breach of the original peace in 1332. Like the Welsh and the Irish, the Scots will be wiped out: the Disinherited will dispossess those Scots now on their former lands despite Edward's promises. Without the right of taxes, revocations and higher customs the English king will furthermore have to live off Scotland 'by robbery' through the feudal casualties of ward, marriage and relief which the present Scottish king (David) does not exploit: thus all Scottish revenue will drain away to England. Traditionally, Spyny continued, there have always been independent Scottish kings – even under Arthur there was a separate Scottish monarch. But under Edward all the Scots magnates of royal blood would be destroyed and they would lose their (new) right of holy unction at their coronation. If the Scots gave up their realm willingly now, to rebel and fight for its recovery later would be treason against their superior (although Spyny does not point out that this had not stopped the Scots after 1296). Besides, why should they give in now when in 1351 they had been much weaker but still resisted? As to some of the lesser terms of the treaty, if Edward returned castles to the Scots now, when he succeeded David as king he would recover the same strongholds freshly repaired at Scottish expense. On a grander scale, the idea of a return to cross-border landholding had been opposed by Robert I, 'such a wise, vigorous and able man'. Overall, to accept English rule would be to betray the Scots' own memories and relinquish what their fathers and grandfathers (a generational fact especially true in the Steward's case) had fought for: it would at the same time be foolish, like falling for an English merchant's trick.

After this salvo, there follows a shorter section of arguments directly in riposte to those of the *Quaestio*'s points made in favour of Edward III's succession (clauses 41 to 52).[92] The English, Spyny opened, were also war-weary and their forces dispersed. Then – in a tone which suggests an attempt to turn the moral tables against David's honour – it is asserted that the king 'has caused to be put forward such difficult and hard proposals, so that he may prove whether the spirit of bravery or the spark of life is alight in anyone, in whom the spirit and mind of our lord king can find pleasure, since he sees that he wishes to stand for the freedom of the people . . .'. The *Quaestio* continues in this vein, insisting that David is not forgetful that his people 'have hitherto put up with much' for his person and kingship and will continue to do so: in that light, it would be better to pay the ransom and for Scotland to keep its own king. Moreover, it is asserted that 'we have many nobles ready to be made our leaders', an obvious reference to the unnamed

91 Stones ed., *Anglo-Scottish Relations*, 81–7 for this bull.
92 Duncan, 'A Question about the Succession, 1364', pp. 47–53.

Steward, his adult sons, the earl of Douglas and others. Then there is arguably an attempt (quoting the Bible's book of Daniel) to turn David's recent marriage against him: for the Scots can hope 'that God will bring them a child', dispensing with the need for such a peace with England. Besides, the ransom could be paid in full if David could live off his own royal resources and 'revokes inept grants made to the prejudice of the crown'. This was perhaps a barbed reference to his largesse to his chivalric cadre and in-laws like the Sutherlands in alienating former crown thanages and forest lands; or, more likely, to his controversial grant of Moray to the Duke of Lancaster of 1359. Continuing on this line, Spyny adds the vague argument that 'our disinherited' can also help pay the ransom when they recover their lands. This surely cannot have referred to all the Anglo-Balliol supporters (earlier described as the 'disinherited' in the booklet) but rather perhaps particular individuals such as the Strathbogie heir, recent exiles like the earl of Mar or bordermen whose lands remained occupied by the English. Overall, Spyny closes, it is surely better to resist the English than to simply let them have their way easily: they might, after all, run out of luck. Thus it would be better to fight and 'live at the common expense' than live under perpetual English cruelty, for English hatred will lead them inevitably to break the peace and try to destroy the Scots: proof of their intent, Spyny's paper insisted at its close, lay in the fact that an ungrateful King Edward had rejected David's offer in the recent talks of the chance to see his younger son, Gaunt, become David's heir presumptive.

It is very tempting to read these arguments as memories of actual Steward propaganda directed against David and his party in 1363–4, the view of a faction which would very definitely have trumpeted Spyny's suggested line that:

> anyone who is prepared to consider the future shrewdly and clearly, will manifestly and inevitably deduce that the king of England and his council who persuade and urge these proposals are seeking the destruction, eradication and total extermination of this people.[93]

These were fears surely given greater public expression after Robert Steward's accession as Robert II in 1371. Indeed, as we shall see, the invasion of Stewart Scotland in 1400 by John of Gaunt's son, Henry IV of England, to register a claim to the Scottish kingship may have brought the 1360s controversy boiling to the surface once more: Spyny's booklet could easily have been produced in this context.[94] But according to both contemporary

---

93 *Ibid*, pp. 51–3, clause 50.
94 A.L. Brown, 'The English Campaign in Scotland, 1400', in H. Hearder and H.R. Lyon eds., *British Government and Administration: studies presented to S.B. Chrimes* (Cardiff 1974), 40–54; see below, ch. 12.

English and Scottish chronicle accounts, both royalist and rebel parties had exchanged written propaganda during the earls' rebellion in 1363. Thus Spyny's booklet may be the only survival of what must have been a heated and potentially explosive debate and exchange of accusations in the Scone parliament of March 1364.[95] If so, the Steward and his sons and allies may have made a highly effective attack on David's court and policies in parliament. As well as criticising his partisan patronage and finances, the king's opponents may have used such briefing material to turn some of David's key chivalric court symbols against him through references to St David and King Arthur. They may also have set up a sword for the king to fall on by claiming the indenture was a test of Scots' patriotism and faithfulness to the sacrifices of the past seventy years. In doing so, Robert Steward surely took full advantage of the most crucial stand he was able to make consistently after Neville's Cross. That is, when it came to the question of regnal union, he was able to occupy Robert Bruce's political shoes as the defender of the independent community of the realm of Scotland and its institutions of parliament, nobility, church, burghs and law. This was an anti-English position which David had both chosen and been forced to deviate from after his capture in 1346. Thus in 1364, Robert I's name was easily invoked in Spyny's tract against the indenture that Bruce's son, David, favoured.

In doing so the Steward arguably fell heir to a powerful pedigree of Scottish community resistance to English overlordship. Between 1289 and 1295 the Scottish community had resisted what it feared as Edward I's attempts to undermine the integrity of its estates, in particular that his summons of Scots to fight in his wars in France would lead to the destruction of the nobility and 'middling sort' of the realm; this was an argument hijacked by Robert Bruce in his abortive rebellion against English rule in 1297. Thus in 1364 if the Steward and others had dwelt – as Spyny's booklet does – upon England's historical intention to destroy Scotland's landowners and independent church, such rhetoric would have tapped a long-held terror.[96] This argument may even indeed have caused powerful men like William, earl of Douglas, Patrick of March/Moray, Archibald Douglas, Robert Erskine, many other knights and, crucially, the prelates of Scotland to reconsider David's and Edward III's recent peace overtures and to worry anew about the Disinherited and their status under an English king of Scots: the prospect, really, of becoming smaller fish in the shallow, poorer end of a larger, richer pond. The earl of Douglas may also have felt distanced from

---

95 *Chron. Scalacronica*, 173–4; *Chron. Fordun*, i, 381–2; Boardman, 'Chronicle Propaganda in Fourteenth-Century Scotland'.
96 For Bruce in 1297 see 299; Barrow, *Bruce*, 83–4.

his king once more if arguments about the military weakness of Scotland and a lack of worthy noble leaders for war were made in parliament. Such statements may have confirmed to many David's blatant misunderstanding or denial of the Scots' national psyche as it had developed throughout the 1330s and 1350s: for all his show of chivalry the king was now grossly out of step with many Scots' inherent tradition of belligerence towards England.[97] The Steward might also have been able to tempt many to his side by pointing out that the aging and apparently ill John II of France had returned to London by 4 January 1364 because of the non-payment of his ransom. In theory, the Scots could once again suggest an alliance with John's far more bellicose son, the Dauphin Charles – who would soon be crowned – just as the Steward had done when Lieutenant about 1354–5, and again after placing David under duress in 1359: that the Steward may have been in contact with the French again can be inferred from John II's intercession with the papacy about 11 March 1363 on behalf of Sir Hugh Eglintoun to secure a dispensation for him to wed the Steward's sister.[98]

Finally, of course, the Steward could, if pressed, have argued something which Spyny surely did not dare write: that any king of Scots who brought in the English could be removed from the throne.[99] As one modern historian has pointed out, Robert Bruce had surely not intended (although his churchmen may have) that the passionate promise to the Pope of the Declaration of Arbroath of 1320 – that if Bruce brought in English dominion he would be 'driven out' as king by his subjects – could be applied as a statement of contractual kingship monitored by the first and second estates in parliament.[100] But in opposing the 1363 indenture, the three estates may indeed have invoked a large measure of the Declaration of Arbroath's spirit just as the Steward had done through parliament in 1352 when – according to the English chronicler, Knighton – the Scots had threatened to depose David and 'choose another king to rule them': this was resistance to which Spyny's booklet had alluded.[101] The parliamentary acts of succession of 1318 and 1326 – which had entailed the Stewart succession to the crown in law – contained, moreover, directions for the community of the realm to gather to choose a new king in the event of the

---

97 A. MacDonald, 'Profit, Politics and Personality: War and the Later Medieval Scottish Nobility', in Ditchburn & Brotherstone, *Freedom and Authority*, 118–30.

98 Sumption, *Hundred Years War*, ii, 499; *CPR*, iv, 87.

99 Duncan, 'A Question about the Succession, 1364' p. 3, argues that 'nowhere does Spyny say that his arguments are motivated by what he obviously feels, that the promises of the English are worthless'.

100 Grant, *Independence and Nationhood*, 35–6; Penman, 'Parliament Lost – Parliament Regained?'.

101 *Chron. Knighton*, 121–3; Duncan, 'A Question about the Succession, 1364', pp. 27–9 (clauses 4–5).

legitimate claimants' deaths. Finally, according to Abbot Bower, in 1371 Robert II would be 'voted' in as king after negotiations by the three estates.[102] Royal coronation oaths to protect the church and uphold the common law – probably repledged by David II in 1357–8 – might also have been generally invoked against the inbringing of the English by the crown. Thus as the leader of parliamentary opposition almost a decade before his own unexpected accession as king of Scots, Robert Steward – and his clerical advisers – may have had a strong sense of the limitations which might be placed upon royal power through parliament and general council.

Just what was said by whom at Scone in March 1364 – and who in the end took whichever side or sat on the fence – will never be known. But the most emphatic of the recorded *decisions* of that body, the first full proceedings to survive since 1357, would seem to suggest at the outset that the objections of the Steward and others had carried a majority. For in the end the parliament declared itself 'in no wise willing to accept, nor in any way assent to, those things which were sought by the king of England and his council'. Stipulations followed that parliament was, though, prepared to renew the Anglo-Scottish truce and continue paying the ransom.

However, what follows in the parliamentary record thereafter proves that this decision was not a complete defeat for David and his close supporters. For the estates concluded, in addition, to despatch Robert Erskine, Gilbert Armstrong and Walter Wardlaw as ambassadors to England and to call a council to consider the terms they secured. That such negotiated 'terms' referred not merely to a better truce and ransom deal is attested in Spyny's booklet. For the briefing document closes (clauses 53 to 57) with the recommendation that letters or envoys should be sent to England to say 'boldly and plainly' that 'this people, since it has chosen and adopted in a certain way a definite one of the sons of England, namely the lord John of Gaunt' as their prospective heir presumptive, thus refuses to accept the idea of Edward III or his eldest son, Edward the Black Prince, in this capacity: 'if [the English] reject this, since we shall know that this is not out of hatred of the son [Gaunt], it follows that they think that this will result in our annihilation . . .'.[103]

This insistence that the Scottish estates had already accepted the idea of John of Gaunt as their likely heir presumptive ahead of the Stewarts cannot be substantiated from the official government records of David's reign. It may simply be an error of memory or deliberate political lie by Spyny. But it is possible that it refers to a decision of one of the several Scottish councils or

---

102 *RRS*, v, no. 301; *APS*, i, 290, 465–6; *Chron. Bower*, viii, 365; Tanner, *Late Medieval Scottish Parliament*, 276–7.
103 Duncan, 'A Question about the Succession, 1364', pp. 55–7.

parliaments held since November 1357 for which proceedings are now lost: perhaps the Dundee council of April 1359 (when David granted the earldom of Moray to Lancaster); or the September 1362 session at Aberdeen (following Queen Joan's death); or an unnoticed council held before David left for London in 1363; or even the March 1364 parliament itself.[104] The arguments cited by Spyny in Gaunt's favour certainly suggest that David's camp had given Gaunt a great deal of thought. Indeed, the fact that Spyny could stress that Gaunt was married to a descendant of a niece of the (Comyn) earl of Buchan and thus his children would be half-Scots underlines the political value David had seen in Prince John's Lancastrian marriage and heritage in 1359. Moreover, Spyny's text pointed out that if Gaunt succeeded David as king, he would wield considerable influence for the Scots over the English council and that if his father or elder brother opposed his accession, there would be a breach between them and turmoil for the auld enemy.[105]

However, this final point hints only barely at the depth of dissimulation which David and his counsel may have deployed in presenting their case, not just in 1364 but in 1352 and 1359–63 as well. For, above all – although he would want to play the fact down in case English suspicions were confirmed – David could persuade the Scots that the acceptance of Gaunt was a mere feint designed to tempt the English into cancelling the ransom only for David to produce a son of his own, in turn annulling the projected change in the succession. This double-dealing may in part be reflected in the conflicting Scottish chronicle accounts of the 1364 parliament. After its coverage of the earls' rebellion Fordun's source (probably Thomas Bisset, prior of St Andrews) understandably makes no mention of the crown's defeat before the estates. In contrast, Andrew Wyntoun's anonymous source for the reign makes no mention of the earls' revolt of 1363 but does assert that parliament thereafter rejected a plan favoured by the king for a younger son of Edward III to be made his heir: as a result, David became 'wa and angry' with his subjects. Yet according to Abbot Bower some forty years later, not only was the three earls' rebellion actually *provoked* by David's plans and attempt to intrude an English succession but the Scone parliament had closed with a declaration:

> by all the three estates each together and all separately that they would never be willing to give consent to an Englishman to rule over them.

---

104 *APS*, i, 19–20 (*tabula*). It was surely expected that another parliamentary act of succession would be passed given that the 1326 act was out-of-date after Thomas Randolph's death in 1332.

105 Goodman, *John of Gaunt*, 70–87; M.E. Cumming-Bruce, *The Bruces and the Comyns* (Edinburgh 1870), 433–4.

They criticised the king's proposals as blinkered, since men of splendid character and standing were available as heir apparent. The three estates were bound to stick faithfully to those heirs by virtue of tailzies which had been agreed with the most solemn oaths. On this account the king, apparently convinced, turned to other matters.

However, Bower added, in the end the king had accepted parliament's rejection of an indenture favouring a younger son of Edward III because in offering it 'he had kept his promise to the English, and did not regret in his heart that his request had been refused'. This is a confusion of events which in part echoes Spyny's argument that David was merely testing his subjects' patriotic spirit: it may also be distorted by subsequent Stewart propaganda. Finally, it may also be Bower's attempt by analogy to criticise the foreign policy of his employer, James I (1424–37), whose proposal of peace with England instead of traditional alliance with France was opposed by Bower in a speech in parliament in 1433.[106]

More tangible proof, however, that what the royal party had really intended and secured at Scone in 1364 was the rejection of the tabled Edward III/*eldest* son indenture, and moves towards continuing talks concerning Gaunt, is the fact that David must have requested a safe-conduct for further envoys to visit England almost immediately after the November 1363 summit in London. Such a pass was indeed granted on 10 December 1363 to Erskine, Armstrong, Wardlaw and David Fleming with a retinue of thirty. This was surely not simply the body expected to notify Edward of the Scottish parliament's view on the indenture by 7 April 1364. If it was an embassy intended to press for a revival of the 1352/59 treaties, then the Scone parliament gave David what he wanted in part and had already planned for: a chance to try again.[107]

All of this can be inferred from the sketchy evidence. Nevertheless, it is certain that after this assembly David can only have looked back upon the past year with a sense of frustrating anti-climax: the parliamentary record does give off odours of a royal cover-up. True, negotiations with England would continue, allowing David to persist with stalling his ransom payments while enjoying the tax income. In the meantime, he could work upon denying Stewart ambition by fathering a son by his new queen. He could also look to Margaret Logie's connections to boost royal influence in Perthshire to match the hold on Fife of the king and his men. But David might also have had mounting fears that the arguments of opposition he

---

106 *Chron. Fordun*, i, 381–2; *Chron. Wyntoun*, vi, 251–3; *Chron. Bower*, vii, 321–3 and viii, 287–91. There is no mention of the indenture or the 1364 parliament in Froissart or other French chronicles.

107 *Rot. Scot.*, i, 878.

had heard raised once again so loudly in the March 1364 parliament – and which had contributed to the third public setback for a succession-ransom deal – would ultimately mean he could never hope to persuade a majority of his subjects to trust the path he favoured. As a sign of this, the Steward, from being at a nadir of abject submission to the royal will as a pardoned rebel in May 1363, had undoubtedly recovered much of his position by the end of the March 1364 parliament as a political force and the kingship's designated heir. David may also have been pained by cracks emerging in the aristocratic coalition he had forged in summer 1363: that is, not just the probable alienation once more of William, earl of Douglas, whose relations with David would deteriorate further between 1364 and 1371, but even amongst the king's close chivalric and clerical core. Doubts about the credibility and increasing irrelevance of David's Anglophile plans in a Scotland so attuned to hostility with its southern neighbour (and alliance with France) may already have begun to turn the heads of ambitious rising lords like Archibald and James Douglas and the Dunbar and Erskine heirs, men who also had local rivalries to distract them from the king's agenda (as Robert Erskine's bond with William More attested).

This drift and decline of some of David's natural and hard-won support is perhaps suggested by the material which Fordun collected for David's reign, written by an anonymous source now cautiously identified as Thomas Bisset, the prior of St Andrews, a brother of Thomas, earl of Fife, and a cleric who died in 1363: this is why Fordun's annals halt abruptly with the the earls' rebellion and David's marriage in Fife in 1363 and resume again under a new author only with David's death in 1371. Yet despite its obvious pro-David and anti-Steward bias, this section of Fordun's history (known now as *Gesta Annalia II*) may contain indirect criticism of David's relations with Edward III and England.[108] For in its coverage of the year 1298 not only does the *Gesta Annalia II* wholly damn the Comyns for their betrayal of William Wallace at the battle of Falkirk but it also asserts that Robert Bruce, soon to be king, fought there on the side of the English. Later Scottish writers, beginning with Bower, would allow Robert Bruce the redemption of being persuaded by the defeated Wallace – in a famous meeting at Carron Shore – to take up the patriotic cause. But that Fordun's source from the mid-fourteenth century should omit this saving tale may mark this work out as a reflection of mounting disgust at David II's diplomatic agenda which had accumulated since 1351 and which by the early 1360s had begun to alienate even

---

108 *Chron. Fordun*, i, 381–2; Broun, 'A New Look at *Gesta Annalia*'; Boardman, 'Chronicle Propaganda in Fourteenth-century Scotland'.

committed Bruce crown supporters.[109] Fordun's collected work may also
contain more overtly pro-Stewart comment. For under the year 1160 it is
recorded that when Malcolm IV, 'the Maiden' king of Scotland (1153–
65), returned from serving Henry II of England in war against Louis VII
in France, a rebellion was raised against him because:

> the Scottish lords seeing their king's too great intimacy and friendship
> with Henry, king of England, were sore troubled, and all Scotland with
> them. For they feared this intimacy had shame and disgrace in store for
> them.

This annal furthermore asserts that the six rebel earls who tried to seize
Malcolm at Perth were led by Ferchard, earl of Strathearn. In Malcolm's
day, it is arguable that aristocratic cross-border landholding was so widespread as to dilute such nationalistic feeling. But to Fordun's contemporary
audience in the late fourteenth century, the parallels between this incident
and the struggle of Robert Steward (also earl of Strathearn) against David II
would have been obvious.[110] In the same way, as we have seen, Andrew
Wyntoun's anonymous source, written c.1390 and collated c.1400–22
(shortly after Spyny's recollection of his *Quaestio*), may have deliberately
sympathised with the Steward against David by making no mention of the
earls' rebellion and by describing the rejected Anglo-Scottish indenture as a
younger-son plan. Yet even in 1364 such muttered criticism might have
received widespread sympathy. To add to that there must have been
considerable resentment of David's new wife, Margaret Logie. Indeed,
the 'many lands and possessions' she was given after her marriage and
coronation were extensive and she moved quickly to expand upon them: by
the end of 1363 Margaret was already in dispute with the bishop of Glasgow
over church provisions. The chroniclers' insistence that David had married
her for love alone 'which conquers all things' would later be undermined
with vitriolic hindsight by Abbot Bower who would spend several chapters
of his *Scotichronicon* condemning the 'serpentine' influence of women like
Margaret in politics and, by inference, David's poor choice of spouse. Later
Scottish writers – like the late fifteenth-century Pluscarden chronicler – were

109 *Chron. Fordun*, i, 101; *Chron. Bower*, vi, 95–7; *Blind Harry's Wallace by William
     Hamilton of Gilbertfield* (Edinburgh 1998), Book XI, 176–83. I offer a slightly
     different interpretation of this section of the *Gesta* to that offered in J.E. Fraser, "A
     Swan from a Raven": William Wallace, Brucean Propaganda, and *Gesta Annalia
     II*', *SHR*, lxxxi (2002), 1–22, at 17–9 which argues that the coverage of Falkirk
     contains both pro-Bruce and pro-Comyn propaganda: the Bissets *were*, though,
     pro-Balliol/Comyn *c.* 1296–1341.
110 *Chron. Fordun*, i, 256–7; G.W.S Barrow ed., *Regesta Regum Scottorum: The Acts
     of Malcolm IV, 1153–65* (Edinburgh 1960), 14–5; see also *The Chronicle of
     Melrose*, ed. J. Stevenson (Llanerch reprint 1991), 11–2.

more overt in their condemnation of David's fornicating ways and liaisons which denied the realm happiness, prosperity and a safe succession.[111]

In this climate, David – now well into middle age – would have to work quickly and much harder after March 1364 to control the concerns and influence of both individual magnates and the wider community in parliament if he was ever to realise his allied domestic and diplomatic obsessions; his new wife, too, can have had little time left in which to bear him a son. The sands were running out.

---

111 *Liber Sancte Marie de Melros* (Bannatyne Club, 2 vols., Edinburgh 1837), ii, nos. 466–7; *Registrum Episcopatus Glasguensis*, i, nos. 304–8; *Chron. Bower*, vii, 335–59; *Liber Pluscardensis*, ch. xlv. Margaret's interest in Glasgow diocese may have been allied to David's pressure on the bishop there, William de Rae, to question the legitimacy of the Steward's sons: in 1362–3 Rae had been in a dispute with his chapter in which John de Bothwell – a royal household clerk who had studied in England and for whom David secured two papal provisions in 1363 – acted as proctor (Watt, *Scottish Graduates*, 59; *CPP*, i, 465–6).

TEN

Dead End: the Margaret Logie Years, 1364–8

'A good master must fulfil three conditions: he must have power, ability, will to cure. One or two of these without the others . . . are of no avail.'

Henry, Duke of Lancaster, *Le Livre de Seyntz Medicines, c.* 1350[1]

'Ways' to Progress, March 1364 to June 1365

In March 1364 David II had been unable to capitalise upon the high ground he had won so decisively in the previous spring. Despite a new wife and a chided great nobility, not enough had fundamentally changed since 1359 in the king's domestic and international circumstances to allow him a breakthrough. As he entered his forty-first year, David undoubtedly harboured reasonable hope for such a shift in fortune in the near future. Yet Scottish chroniclers writing throughout the following century comment little on the events of the next four years. This was partly due to the lacunae left by the death in 1363 of Fordun's likely witness. But there is also a strong sense that the sources are silent because, with hindsight, these medieval historians – Wyntoun and Bower especially – felt nothing of note occurred in this period: these were indeed 'dark and drublie' days for Scotland devoid of patriotic, moral or chivalric glory, uninterrupted by a royal birth or a significant noble death, not even a really newsworthy plague, church council or tide-turning continental victory for France or England. Even Jean Froissart, who would be a guest in the households of David and a number of his nobles in 1365, would afterwards write nothing of the actual events of that time, instead simply naming his hosts and their castles and concentrating on the far more dramatic events of *c.* 1332–56 and the 1380s.[2]

This inertia leaves an overwhelming impression that after the Scone parliament of March 1364 David and his subjects, too, were waiting for some such watershed event: something to tip the balance of power in one direction. In many ways, the Scots held their breath with the rest of Europe's Christian kingdoms, watching to see if the as yet unfulfilled Anglo-French treaty of Brétigny would hold after the accession of Charles V following

---

1 Arnould ed., *Le Livre de Seyntz Medicines,* 157.
2 *Chron. Fordun,* i, 382–3; *Chron. Wyntoun,* vi, 251–3; *Chron. Bower,* vii, 331–59; *Oeuvres de Froissart,* ii, 137 and v, 133; Croft-Dickinson, *Scotland from the earliest times to 1603,* 176 (dark and drublie).

John II's death on 8 April 1364. The Scottish king, much like his Plantagenet and Valois counterparts over the next four years, had to play the long cautious game of stalling for time, gathering strength and resources until something turned in his favour – for David, say, an English collapse across the Channel and the arrival of a Bruce heir, ideally in that order.[3]

This waiting and repositioning was especially true of David's ongoing negotiations with England, for which evidence of several new and provocative proposals survives, though at times without clearly revealing the central enigma of who was really determining Scotland's changing aims in 1364–68. However, closer examination of the available papers suggests that there were moves which David and his close counsel initiated in those low-key years – both domestically and diplomatically – in an attempt to secure a more defendable or winning hand. These initiatives were accompanied by crown attempts (previously unappreciated by historians) to dampen his magnatial opponents' influence in council and, most especially, in full parliament: the latter had proved an unpredictable arena which David would choose tellingly – as in 1360–2 – to avoid for over two years after March 1364.

Yet, with time, control threatened to slip from David's grasp. By 1367, if not much sooner, his plans had to include a tactical admission by the crown that some of its key goals since 1357 might not be attainable, most notably the total exclusion of the Stewarts from the royal succession and the insertion of an English prince. Worse, by 1368, the king would have to make the far more honest and vulnerable admission that his marriage to Margaret Logie was an empty failure and that his waiting upon events had brought him once again to a potentially fatal point of isolation and weakness. This fresh danger David could only avoid through an unprecedented personal act for a Scottish royal – the divorce of his consort.

The weight of the surviving documentation from this period suggests that David made continued talks with Edward III a priority. The established ambassadorial team of Armstrong, Wardlaw and Erskine received further passes to England on 18 July 1364 and some hard bargaining must have taken place in the second half of that year in England.[4] Despite the 1364 Scone parliament's strongly expressed decision that these men should renegotiate the resumption of ransom payments and the truce, the ambassadors soon apparently had as their primary goal talks for a full 'bon pacis' with England. This was in keeping with David's private preparations in late 1363 to pursue the Gaunt plan in some form anyway, and it is likely that

3 Sumption, *Hundred Years War*, ii, 499–504, 512–8.
4 *Rot. Scot.*, i, 881.

many of the peace proposals which emerge in extant papers from 1365 onwards were the ideas of the Scottish king and his counsel.

The crown certainly resumed normal friendly contact with England. David and Margaret secured a safe-conduct to the shrine of St James at Walsingham (Norfolk) on 20 August 1364, although the king at least does not seem to have gone. But his chivalric cadre may have made such journeys. Passes to England and on to the continent were issued in the second half of 1364 to Archibald Douglas, Thomas Erskine (Sir Robert's eldest son), George Dunbar the heir to the earldom of March, Walter Biggar (the Chamberlain again by December 1364) and Simon Preston (constable of Edinburgh). Thomas, earl of Mar, continued to serve Edward III in arms reluctantly; William, earl of Sutherland, remained a lonely, childless hostage for the ransom in the south, his expenses paid by David.[5]

But while the crown awaited the results of talks in England, and surely kept a weather-eye on Europe, David could also resume his low-key policy of trespassing upon the territorial interests and affinities of his Scottish opponents. As a natural part of this process he continued to extend widespread patronage to men of chivalry, commerce and religion throughout Scotland. David also showed unsurprising favour to the family of his new queen. On 12 April 1364, just three weeks after the Scone parliament and while still at Perth, the king granted the former thanage of Tannadice in Angus to his stepson, John Logie. This was followed up a day later at St Andrews with a pension for the Sinclair widow of Thomas, earl of Angus. Then on 30 April, back at Edinburgh, the king gave his new brother-in-law, Malcolm Drummond (whose son had wed a daughter of Robert Erskine by 1363) the services and feudal casualties (ward, relief and marriage) of the free tenants of the Perthshire baronies of Cargill and Auchterarder as well as the Stirlingshire barony and Forth crossing of Kincardine.[6] Cargill had been held by the Muschet family from Robert I for half a knight's service while Auchterarder bounded the land of the Abbey of Scone and was just north of the former thanage of Kinclaven which had itself been a residence for Alexander III but was held by the Steward in 1361. Yet along with that other sometime Steward possession, the *Abnethia* of Dull in northern Atholl, Kinclaven had now been given to Queen Margaret as part of her dower lands.[7] With Sir Malcolm now enlisted to police these fiefs as well as holding

5 *Rot. Scot.*, i, 881–9; *ER*, ii, 113, 142, 166. On 30 October 1364 Edward III pardoned Thomas Balliol, the earl of Mar's 'brother', for the murder of one of Mar's servants (*CDS*, iv, no. 101).

6 *RRS*, vi, nos. 317–8; *RMS*, i, nos. 147, 172; *The Genealogie of the Noble and Ancient House of Drummond*, 40.

7 Grant, 'Thanes and Thanages', 80; *ER*, ii, 297–8; *Atlas of Scottish History to 1707*, 204. Margaret's brother, John Drummond, became bailie of Dull (*ER*, ii, lix).

other lands and offices around Strathearn, Menteith, Atholl, Dull, Strathtay, Strath Braan and Strathord, the Steward's fears that the Drummond kindred would forward crown influence at the heart of Stewart power were surely made real: Malcolm's new support at Kincardine-on-Forth also made him a close neighbour of Robert Erskine at Stirling and Alloa and the king's Bruce cousin at Clackmannan.

At the same time, David continued to sanction erosion of Steward influence in the west. As we have seen, by July 1364 at the latest, Malcolm Fleming (junior) was sheriff of Dumbartonshire and its castle-keeper. In December that year Malcolm had to be lightly reprimanded for interfering with the Abbey of Paisley, the Stewart family foundation, something David's past favourite, castle-keeper and 'foster-father', the late Malcolm Fleming, earl of Wigtown, had been warned off doing by the Steward in 1348. The king also used the Flemings to intrude Robert Erskine into Dumbartonshire and the Lennox by January 1365, surely in anticipation of his posting as keeper of Dumbarton's rock castle and port later in the decade: Erskine also received more Stirlingshire lands in August 1364. To all these Stewart fears could be added David's ominous and persistent appearances at Perth in April, June, July, September and November 1364 at least, a frequent presence sustained thereafter.[8]

The Steward's fellow rebels also continued to receive cool treatment from the crown. There was no patronage in 1364 for William, earl of Douglas, despite the largesse he had recently enjoyed in the king's company in London. Instead, the rewards went to the 'Good' and Liddesdale sides of that kindred. On 25 August 1364 Archibald Douglas was at the former Bruce castle of Lochmaben as Warden of the west march and 'Lieutenant of the king of Scotland' to conclude a deal with a representative of the earl of Hereford over their lords' joint administration of Annandale. Archibald had been assigned this office even though Earl William (and John Stewart of Kyle) had recovered much of this region from English occupation before 1357. Then in September and November 1364 David granted Sir James Douglas of Lothian an annual from several lands in Peeblesshire and royal park lands in Clackmannanshire: the latter had been forfeited by the crown from Sir Henry Kerr, a former sheriff of Roxburgh and adherent of the Douglas earl.[9]

8 *RRS*, vi, nos. 326, 327, 333, 335 (January 1365 – Thomas Fleming gives Erskine lands in the barony of Lenzie); NAS GD 45 (Dalhousie Muniments)/142 – a Fleming-Erskine land excambion, March 1369; *ER*, ii, 195, 221, 259, 295; *Atlas of Scottish History to 1707*, 172 ('Place-dates, David II, 1357–71') which shows that Perth was the king's most common venue for issuing charters after Edinburgh.
9 *CDS*, iv, no. 100; *RRS*, vi, no. 332; *RMS*, i, no. 181; *ER*, i, 568; *Chron. Bower*, vii, 297; Brown, *Black Douglases*, 167–8. Kerr had been captured with his brothers raiding northern England *c.* 1355 (PRO SC 56/27).

David also increased his stewardship of the territorial interests of the aging Patrick, earl of March and Moray, an octogenarian who now finally began to fade as a significant player. On 1 July 1364 David appointed Walter Haliburton, the sheriff of Berwick, to inquire as to whether or not the Berwickshire lands of Wester Lumsden belonged to the Priory of Durham. In doing so, David was arguably doing his part to reciprocate Edward III's investment in border tribunals and 'March day' justice to ensure the preservation of the Anglo-Scottish truce: this assize might also ease talks over the issue of restoring cross-border landholding. The thirteenth-century earls of March had given Lumsden to Durham Priory; but by August 1367 Earl Patrick would have been obliged to recognise that he had legally lost other Scottish border lands to that house.[10] Yet harsh as this might seem, in reality David had begun to soft-pedal his interference in Dunbar interests. Earl Patrick must have known that his heirs and nephews, George and John Dunbar, were already well placed within the chivalric cadre of the Bruce regime, a patronage link which also existed for James Douglas of Lothian's family.

The king must also have been looking forward to his recovery of the earldom of Moray upon Patrick's death. He already had officers in place in that region. His official control there would be added to his oversight of the earl of Mar's earldom and Garioch lands, a duty he continued through the royal chancery in 1364. Allied to this, David may also have been preparing to step up his erosion of the influence of William, earl of Ross, the Steward's brother-in-law. The king inspected three Ross charters in 1364 and may already have been considering the intrusion into the earldom of Ross of Sir Walter Leslie (whose family lands lay in the Garioch) which would be implemented after 1366. Altogether, this royal influence could surround and challenge Ross and Stewart power in northern Scotland from Inverness through Moray, Badenoch and the former earldom of Buchan to Kildrummy. Admittedly, though, David does not seem to have applied characteristic energy in backing up this policy with personal ayres to the north: no royal act was issued beyond Perth in 1364. The king seems only to have shadowed the southern justice circuit (taking him to Ayr and Dumfries) and, perhaps, spent Christmas in Linlithgow where he may even have begun hopefully to prepare the castle as a nursery.[11]

Nonetheless, in all of this there was really nothing new or unexpected. These royal acts may have stoked the general political tension but, really, the

---

10 *RRS*, vi, nos. 322, 379; Neville, *Violence, Custom and Law*, ch. 3.
11 *RRS*, vi, nos. 320, 321, 323, 330, 331; *RMS*, i, nos. 176–7. For Leslie and Ross, see below ch. 11. About 1361–2, David had asked a John Cairns 'to build the manor house there [Linlithgow] for the king's coming' (*RMS*, i, App. ii, no. 1367; J.A. Wilson, *A History of Cambuslang* (Glasgow 1929), 33).

remainder of this year gives a greater impression of a calming of the antagonisms which had erupted in 1363. As we shall see, parliamentary complaints of 1366–8 about noble feuds rumbling throughout the kingdom – and especially in the north – may point at mounting disturbances lost from the records of 1364 and further fuelled by this royal interference. But the Steward and Douglas certainly remained regular witnesses at court that year – as they had done between 1357 and 1362 – alongside the most prominent royalist witnesses, Archibald Douglas, William Keith, Walter Haliburton and John Herries of Terregles.

It was, instead, developments in talks with England which proved far more difficult to ignore. An indenture of provisional terms drawn up by Scottish and English envoys in the autumn or winter of 1364 has survived. In this document the English outlined a protocol whereby if the Scots agreed first to pay off the remaining ransom, then Edward III would consider one of three 'ways' of making progress towards a full peace: firstly, the restoration by the Scots of the lands of the Disinherited Anglo-Balliol lords and others to be named; secondly, the provision by the Scots of military assistance to England; and thirdly, payment by the Scots of a sum in addition to the ransom for the recovery of English-occupied Scottish lands. A vague fourth 'way', involving partial fulfilment of each of these terms, would also be considered.[12]

Clearly, as A.A.M. Duncan has shown, these were terms dictated by the English, based on past peace offers, but now reflecting their growing need for ready cash to police their European gains and in case of renewed war with France. Crucially, this late 1364 indenture no longer contained a succession-deal negating the ransom, a strong indication that Edward and his council no longer felt this a gamble worth taking: it had after all been rejected three times by the Scottish political community already and now David was re-married. Yet even the English retention of the unpopular clauses about the restoration of the Disinherited and a military alliance – points which had proved unpalatable to the Scottish estates in February 1352, April 1359 and March 1364 – may have in reality been designed to scare the Scots into remaining peaceful and paying the ransom, an opening bid to force the talks on to that end.

But if that was so, David's response may have been just as strategically minded, and his government's formulation of the Scottish reply brought him distinct political advantage at home. A council met in the Dominican Friary at Perth from 13 January 1365 to consider these 'ways' to peace. At least

---

12 PRO E39/2/17, printed by C. Johnson, 'Proposals for an Agreement with Scotland', *EHR*, xxx (1915), 476; reproduced, amended and discussed in Duncan, 'A Question about the Succession, 1364', 13–6.

thirty-nine individuals were named on the attendance sederunt for this body including Robert Steward, John Stewart of Kyle and 'Sir William, earl of Ross'. However, the earls of Douglas and March were conspicuously absent (just as in September 1362), and by far the majority of the significant men present could be described as royalists, headed by Keith the Marischal, Robert Erskine, Archibald Douglas, Walter Haliburton (and his brother, Alexander), Dischington, Mortimer, Annan, Fleming, Robert Ramsay and Alan Erskine. No record survives of the debate which must have taken place, only the decisions of this assembly.[13] But these statutes reveal that David was not prepared to give up his idea of a younger-son succession-deal and the cancellation of the ransom burden just yet, even if it only had value in buying time and prolonging these talks about talks. Moreover, this council's decisions also suggest that David and his close circle had been able to control and direct the three estates' representatives to toe the royal government's line.

The council agreed to send back ambassadors to try to negotiate a final peace with England based on three points or 'articles'. Firstly, an offer that the Disinherited noble families named in the 1351–2 and 1363–4 talks would be restored to their Scottish lands along with the descendants of other forfeited lords now named (including the Wakes of Liddesdale, although if this particular family proved problematic it was to be dropped in favour of finalising the other points first); secondly, a younger son of Edward III was to receive £1,000 worth of the former lands of Edward Balliol in Galloway in heredity, plus the isle of Man (valued at 1,000 merks), although Man might pass instead to the earl of Salisbury, in which case the younger prince was to receive an alternative 1,000 merks worth of land in England – both the prince and Salisbury were then to become liege men of the king of Scotland; thirdly, in order to ensure a firm peace, arrangements were to be sought whereby the Scottish king 'should cause war to be made for a time in some parts of Ireland which his men are able to approach easily' in the service of Edward III – however, this last was only to be pursued after Scottish and Irish border disputes had been settled with England.[14]

What this package did, on paper at least, was give the English some satisfaction on two of their three suggested 'ways to progress': the restoration of the Disinherited and military alliance. Promises of aid in Ireland avoided the thorny issue of fighting in France and were a timely carrot to England at a time when Prince Lionel, Duke of Clarence (Edward III's

---

13 *APS*, i, 495–6 (*RPS*, 1365/1/1–19) for what follows; this (*ibid*, 1365/1/6) is the first of five extant estates' sederunts for the reign.

14 *Ibid*, 1365/1/7–10. The value of the lands named by this parliament raises the possibility that in 1362 David hoped to use the lands of Mar – also valued at £1,000/1,000 merks – to deal with England.

second son, whom both Knighton and Bower would later insist David had wanted as his heir presumptive in 1363), was struggling to maintain order there as Lieutenant. In many ways, this proposed Scottish concession was a variation on Robert I's aid to his nephew, the de Burgh earl of Ulster, in 1328: it was also a useful ploy David had become aware of not only through Clarence's current difficulties but through abortive appeals in April 1344 directed to the Scottish and French crowns by Irish rebels and calling for a joint attack on England.[15] But, more importantly in 1365, the promise of up to 2,000 merks worth of Scottish land to an English prince might also have been designed to compensate the denial of extra cash sought by the English and to settle old tensions over the isle of Man in the Irish Sea. However, the gift of Galloway lands to this prince was surely just another way for David to introduce to Scotland John of Gaunt, now Duke of Lancaster, by the back door, after the manner of the abortive grant of the earldom of Moray in 1359 to Gaunt's father-in-law. Scottish crown influence in the south-west had improved of late with the new bishop of Whithorn, David's former confessor, Adam de Lanark, renouncing the allegiance of his See to York by 1363.[16] But by giving Gaunt the lordship of Galloway, not only might David deal with what was still a long-term problem zone for the Bruce regime but he would also secure a friendly neighbour for Carrick and an English enclave closer to the Duchy of Lancaster (he would also legitimise, ironically, succession for the incumbent of the old Balliol lands). At the same time, of course, through these proposals David again sought the outright cancellation of the ransom.

However, what is most striking of all is that, in contrast to the peace bids of 1352 and 1363, this time David was no longer being careful to soothe the fears of nobles like the Steward and Douglas about their likely loss of lands. Those Disinherited lords named laid claim to large holdings occupied by these Scottish magnates and others disfavoured by David, including the lands of Buchan (claimed by Beaumont – with half held by Ross since 1314), Liddesdale (Wake), Atholl and Badenoch/Lochaber (Strathbogie) and lands in Galloway and Lothian.[17] The self-imposed absence or deliberate exclusion of Douglas and March from the Perth proceedings must have helped push this item through. But David still took pains to bind all the potentially

15 Prestwich, *The Three Edwards*, 280–1; McNamee, *Wars of the Bruces*, 253; *Chron. Bower*, vii, 323; Nicholson, 'A sequel to Edward Bruce's invasion of Ireland'. For 1344, see G.O. Sayles, 'The Rebellious First Earl of Desmond', in J.A. Watt, J.B Marshall and F.X. Martin eds., *Medieval Studies presented to Aubrey Gwynn* (Dublin 1961), 203–30, at 219–22. My thanks to Michael Brown for this reference.
16 Watt, *Scottish Graduates*, 325–6; *Rot. Scot.*, i, 881.
17 Duncan, 'A Question about the Succession, 1364', 9–11; Nicholson, *Edward III and the Scots*, ch. 5.

troublesome earls to support this diplomacy: in doing so, the king may have
been obliged to exclude the Steward, too, from the final sessions of this
council. For, remarkably, the statutory record makes it clear that on 25
January 1365 this body's decisions were witnessed with:

> the seals of the said lord steward of Scotland, the earl of Strathearn,
> and the lord Patrick earl of March and Moray, and the lord William,
> earl of Douglas, who added their advice and consent to all and singular
> of the foregoing in the presence of our lord king at Edinburgh, after
> taking a bodily oath, although they were not personally present when
> the aforesaid [matters] were ordained at Perth; along with the seals of
> the lord earl of Ross, and of the other earls present . . .[18]

If this was so, then the Perth council had arguably produced exactly what
David and his close circle had wanted and then David had summoned to
Edinburgh Castle those former troublemakers (all named) he knew might
object to compel their co-operation. Moreover, the council had been bound
generally to 'approve, ratify and confirm', under pain of perjury, any deal
the ambassadors were able to conclude, and to swear a promise on the
Gospels to 'rise in concord, as if against a rebel to the king and the
subversion of the common weal, against anyone who breaks, impedes or
contradicts any of the foregoing in any way'. Such parties were to be obliged
by force to observe any resulting Anglo-Scottish agreement 'under pain of
being found guilty of breaking their fealty against the king's majesty'.[19]

At first glance, this would seem to be a bold move on the crown's part,
designed to bypass the near-fatal political opposition of 1363–4. However,
the king may not have had it all his own way as the council records suggest.
David was not so foolish as to believe that both the English and his Scottish
opponents could thus be brought to simply accept these unusual terms for
full peace. David and his counsel surely expected that pressure would come
from both these camps for payment of the ransom – from Edward as part of
a peace to help keep him solvent, and from the Scottish earls as part of a
limited truce to safeguard their lands and the Steward succession. The
Scottish political community in general seems also to have been inclined
to the more straightforward solution of ransom payment. Accordingly,
David and his regime may have had no option but to allow the estates in
council at Perth in 1365 to attach some conditions to the course the crown

---

18 *RPS*, 1365/1/19. In the *Black Book of Taymouth* transcription of the original
parliamentary record there appears to be a scribal error at this point which caused
the Thomson edition of the APS to read ' . . . although he was not personally
present . . . '. However, this cannot refer to David II as being absent from council
and only makes sense if it refers to the named earls collectively.
19 *RPS*, 1365/1/18.

sought to pursue in these talks: Robert Steward (until he was forced out of the council) and others may have been able to modify some of the articles. Besides, the king must also have known that the restoration of the Disinherited was still an unacceptable threat, too, to his own supporters, not least to Archibald Douglas, whose ambitions in Galloway would be thwarted by the January 1365 proposals if accepted. In this light, it makes sense to interpret these three new Scottish articles for peace, really, as bargaining chips (just like the three English 'ways' of late 1364) designed either to simply delay matters and keep the dialogue open or to secure favourable terms over the ransom which had now to be conceded and revived in some form. This was surely why the Perth council also made detailed provision for the repayment of the ransom during a truce.

For if the English would not accept a treaty on these terms, the 1365 council decided that:

> before a good and perpetual peace should be relinquished altogether, they [the envoys] shall concede the payment of the ransom to be made duly and tolerably, and also a perpetual mutual alliance of kingdoms, albeit not on terms of equal powers, which nevertheless by no means shall have the flavour of servitude . . .

Three ways were envisaged to reform and pay back the ransom. First, the 20,000 merks which the Scots had already paid would be negated and, 'beginning anew . . . six score thousand merks' would be paid in instalments of 5,000 merks a year over twenty-four years. If these terms were unacceptable to the English, then, with the 20,000 merks already paid again discounted, £100,000 (150,000 merks) was to be paid at 5,000 merks a year for thirty-four years. Lastly, if this package was rejected in turn, the Scots could start again and offer the original 100,000 merks of 1357 to be paid off in the same ten years at 10,000 merks a year.[20]

When scrutinised, none of these deals was perhaps as bad as it sounded for the Scots. True, their first two payments of 1357 and 1358 were being discounted and the English seemed to have refused to recognise the half-payment of 5,000 merks made in late 1359; the sums which the Scots now offered to owe also ranged alarmingly from £66,666 to £100,000 at a time when royal income reached only £8,000 per annum at best. But the terms for the two largest sums offered first of all gave the Scots two or three decades to pay, both at only 5,000 merks a year, a reduction of half from the terms of the original 1357 treaty of Berwick: at worst, under the third package, the Scots would only be obliged to resume the original payment scheme of 1357 after five years of evasion. It was surely some compromise along these lines

20 *Ibid*, 1365/1/12–13.

which David sought realistically at this juncture in his talks with England. Knowing that there was overwhelming pressure from both Edward III and many of his own subjects to resume payment, David looked to arrange matters so that his annual payments were either reduced and spread out – leaving him with enough income for his household and government and a much longer truce during which to continue talks for a full peace (and to sire an heir) – or, at worst, that the payments were reset at their original level.

Indeed, David and the council seem to have felt it most likely that the English would – if they accepted any of these terms – take up the highest annual return of 10,000 merks a year over ten years, the original 1357 deal. Accordingly, this was the only financial burden for which the January 1365 council also made further provision. If that plan was agreed, then the great customs were to be assigned to the ransom instalments to the sum of 8,000 merks a year; this was to be paid to the English at Bruges as before with the underwritten guarantee of the Scottish burgesses (and the seals of the burghs of Edinburgh, Aberdeen, Perth and Dundee were attached to these clauses).[21] But in addition, the council also agreed to levy a tax of 6d per £ (a fortieth) on lands and goods annually for the ten years needed to pay off the ransom in full with 2,000 merks from this levy being set aside each year for that purpose: any surplus from this levy, crucially, would go to cover the king's expenses. Among the oaths given in the council was a promise that no-one would 'impede or in any way contradict' this planned tax and no-one was to petition, either 'openly or in secret, for themselves or others', for gifts of lands and casualties from the royal demesne while this burden had to be met.[22]

In sum, rather than David and his government acting with a sound measure of 'circumspection . . . statesmanship and consent' from the estates after March 1364, as one modern historian has suggested, all these recorded decisions point to the direct exclusion from these crucial decisions of the rebel earls.[23] The king had acted to ensure that if the English accepted any of the Scots' new offers, the crown's interests would be protected. The three 'articles' represented the best-case scenario for David – the cancellation of his ransom and the deflation of Stewart power through the loss of the earldom of Atholl to the disinherited Strathbogie heir. But if, as seemed likely, Anglo-Scottish talks focused on the ransom and truce issues there was still room for manoeuvre. Even though some Scots at the Perth council may have managed through criticism and pressure to attach conditions to the crown's fiscal preparations – asserting that these monies were only to be

21 *Ibid*, 1365/1/14.
22 *Ibid*, 1365/1/15–6.
23 Webster, 'David II and the Government of Fourteenth-century Scotland', 126.

used for the ransom and to be collected by the Chamberlain – David still stood to gain something.

These contingencies quickly proved prudent. By 20 May 1365, Edward III and his council had predictably rejected the three Scottish articles for full peace. But even though they also resisted subsequent attempts by David's envoys to apparently secure a 25-year truce, they did agree to a short extension of the current truce (due to expire in 1367) until 2 February 1370 as well as a recalibration of the ransom figures. Here the Scottish ambassadors' hard bargaining and/or David's relationship with Edward's family yielded relief. For although the total due was reset at 100,000 merks, as anticipated in the Perth council's last clause, the annual payments were reset at a surely manageable 6,000 merks (£4,000), a drop of over a third from the 1357 rate. The first payment was due in January 1366, a shift away from the original instalment date of 24 June each year, midsummer, St John the Baptist's day and the anniversary of Bannockburn.[24]

Ranald Nicholson is thus surely wrong to insist that this was a wholly bad deal for David II.[25] The English ambassadors had not simply been allowed to dictate terms to the Scots and the resulting agreement was a compromise based on terms proposed by the January 1365 Perth council. David's government had struck the best deal possible in the circumstances, one that afforded relief on both the diplomatic and domestic fronts. They had been helped in this by the English need for cash following a year in which they had defeated France's ally in Burgundy (at the battle of Auray, September 1364) but looked set to lose their own ally in Brittany (May 1365) and to face French interference in Castile.[26] But better still for the Bruce regime, the English financial concessions to the Scots might now also bring David a windfall. For with the ransom reset at 100,000 merks the king could, in theory, not only claim up to 8,000 merks worth of customs a year but also levy the fortieth of tax contribution promised by the Perth council. However, now he would only have to give 6,000 merks away each year, leaving more for his own ends. He might also be able to take advantage of the anomaly that although the truce would only last to 1370, Scotland would have to pay the ransom for the next sixteen years. Overall, with the truce extended and the English placated with some cash, David could also look to keep pressing for full peace based on the terms mooted in 1363–4.[27]

---

24 *CDS*, iv, no. 108; NAS State Papers 6/3.
25 Nicholson, *Scotland – the Later Middle Ages*, 164–83, quote from 172.
26 Sumption, *Hundred Years War*, ii, 527–8; Cuttino, *English Medieval Diplomacy*, 94–6; Goodman, *John of Gaunt*, 43–5; Packe, *King Edward III*, 254–61.
27 Duncan, 'A Question about the Succession, 1364', 16–7, argues that the English limited the new truce extension to four years to ensure that the Scots did not try to avoid payment.

No wonder, then, that David acted quickly to ratify and bank this deal by issuing letters under his privy seal at Edinburgh on 12 June 1365: he sent word to the English of this confirmation by himself, significantly styled as having been given 'in council', by 15 July, along with a request for a safe-conduct to further talks for the usual team of the bishop of St Andrews, Erskine, Wardlaw and Armstrong. Yet all of this was actually done *before* David had called a formal assembly to scrutinise and approve this May indenture. He and his close counsel had been able to act alone because they had already secured the sealed promise of the January 1365 council – and separate recorded oaths from the three disgruntled earls – to agree to 'any' deal reached.[28] The ball was now even more firmly in the king's court.

A United Front, July 1365 to July 1366

David's mood by mid-1365 might, then, be said to have been confident but edgy. He had bought time and eased both English and Scottish impatience with his past actions. On the other hand there was no sign of a royal heir by Margaret and the king still avoided a full parliament. He refused even to call a general council to discuss the next diplomatic moves to be made. Instead what met from 24 July 1365 – again at Perth – is described remarkably by the Scottish parliamentary records as a 'congregation' of the king and just fifteen men – the leading magnates of the day, the ambassadorial clerics, Chamberlain and Chancellor, all apparently handpicked by the crown to ensure the royal agenda was forwarded. The fifteen were headed by the Steward, Patrick, earl of March/Moray and William, earl of Douglas, but also included the royal knights Erskine, Haliburton, Lyle, Roger Mortimer and David Fleming, and the bishops of St Andrews, Moray, Brechin and Whithorn. The surprising presence of men like Sir Hugh Eglintoun, Gillespie Campbell of Lochawe, John Luce the bishop of Dunkeld and John Mac-dougall of Lorn can have given the Steward little comfort.[29]

As well as presumably ratifying the May 1365 deal with England, this body – like that of January 1365 – discussed terms which might be offered to secure a full peace, rehashing the 'ways' and 'articles' of the first half of the year. Their recorded decisions again underline the extent to which David and his close advisers looked to dictate policy. The congregation concluded that if no better deal could be struck (than what, exactly, is not stated), then the Scottish envoys were to offer 400 armed men and 600 archers to assist the English when needed 'within England', at English expense on a perpetual basis. In return the English should be obliged to help the Scots in Scotland when necessary with just 200 armed men and

28 *RRS*, vi, nos. 346, 499; *CDS*, v, no. 838.
29 *APS*, i, 496 (*RPS*, 1365/7/1–3) for what follows.

300 archers at any time over the next 120 years, an interesting ratio of 2:1 revealing the Scots' collective view of a fair alliance 'albeit not on terms of equal powers', as they had admitted in January. However, if the English would not accept these terms, then the Scots envoys could concede that 'fighting men of those people of Scotland who are within the borders of Scotland and Ireland' – i.e. the western seaboard – would fight for Edward III in Ireland for three months a year for between five and fifteen years with the number of troops to be fixed by negotiation. All fifteen men of the congregation at Perth swore on the Gospels – as they had done in January's council – to observe any deal which might be struck based on these offers 'for the sake of peace'.

It is unclear if this assembly was prepared to countenance further concessions to the English over the matters of the Disinherited and the ransom, but the military alliance was still a live issue. As A.A.M. Duncan again points out, these troop figures are similar to those first mooted in Anglo-Scottish talks in 1351–2, plans which were strongly influenced by David's persuasive promises to Edward.[30] More importantly by 1365, however, the new suggestion that west-coast Scots would be drafted into English military service across the Irish Sea – expanding upon the Scots' peace 'article' of January – undeniably explains the summons and probable intimidation at Perth of Argyll men like Campbell and Macdougall. If this deal went through, David would have a means not only of defusing another troublesome outlying zone for the crown but of marginalising these lords through annual conscription abroad to Ireland, along with the Steward as lord of Bute, Cumbrae, Kintyre and Clydeside and perhaps also the earl of Ross and the MacDonalds. It is tempting to speculate, indeed, that John Barbour's later suggestion in *The Bruce* that Robert I had sent his ambitious brother and adult heir presumptive, Edward Bruce, to Ireland to be rid of him as a political threat in Scotland, was a conflation of a tactic aimed in 1365 by David at his Stewart nephew and heir.[31] But this plan may also have been born of complaints by the Scottish estates about lawlessness and tax evasion in the north and west, problems for which the crown would pursue Campbell, Macdougall, MacDonald, the Steward and others in parliament between 1366 and 1369.

These terms were presumably to be offered to the English by the Scottish ambassadors in talks scheduled for late summer-autumn 1365. David and his counsel had controlled matters tightly once more. The Perth 'congregation' of July does not appear to have discussed domestic matters

---

30 Duncan, 'A Question about the Succession, 1364', 17–9.
31 Duncan ed., *The Bruce*, 345, 593–5; *Chron. Fordun*, i, 348; R. Frame, 'The Bruces in Ireland, 1315–8', *Irish Historical Studies*, xix (1974), 3–37, 5–7.

and the crown would not call another assembly until January 1366. But David may have been encouraged to be even more authoritarian and rigorous in these proceedings by the presence in Scotland from spring 1365 of Jean Froissart, recommended to the Scottish king and nobility by his countrywoman, Queen Philippa of England. This chronicler of chivalry travelled around Scotland with David's court for 'quarter of a year'. The outward appearance of a well-ordered gathering of notables (just enough for a round table, as it were?) all agreeing to the royal will – rather than the unpredictable talking-shop of another full parliamentary debate like that of March 1364 – could thus be presented to this important, inquisitive guest, a man who could do so much to make or break the Bruce dynasty's image in Christendom.[32]

Never one to miss an opportunity, the second Bruce king, and his followers, clearly took pleasure in relating to Froissart a version of the heroics of Robert I's reign and the military events of the 1330s and 1340s (and especially of 1346) which painted David and his house in a worthy chivalric light but ignored utterly any part Robert Steward had played. Writing over twenty years later about the expedition of 1,500 French knights to Scotland in 1385, Froissart would describe the Steward – by then King Robert II – as having:

> red-bleared eyes, of the colour of sandalwood, which clearly showed that he was no valiant man, but one who would rather remain at home than march to the field . . .

Froissart also stressed how Robert II did not venture forth to greet his French guests in 1385 but remained safe in 'le sauvage Écosse', his lands in the Gaelic west.[33] But although the Steward was present at court throughout 1365, this was an image surely impressed upon the chronicler in that year, David's condemnation of a magnate who had deserted him at Neville's Cross and never crossed the border in anger again. At the same time, David and his chivalric cadre pointed out the royal building works at St Monans and Edinburgh, as well as the Arthurian associations of such royal castles as Dumbarton and Stirling, the latter hailed by Froissart as 'one of the castles known in the days of King Arthur and called Smandon [where] the knights of the round table used to return . . . as I was told when I stayed in the castle for three

---

32 *Oeuvres de Froissart*, xi, 254; Contamine, 'Froissart and Scotland', 51–2; Palmer ed., *Froissart – Historian*, 26. Froissart also states that Queen Philippa sent presents to the wives of Scottish nobles including the Countesses of 'March and Atholl'.

33 Brown, *Early Travellers in Scotland*, 8–15; Boardman, *Early Stewart Kings*, 123–4, 137–8.

days with King David'. A tournament was also held in the park at Edinburgh in 1365.[34]

Finally, at the king's behest, a large body of clerics, knights and esquires – headed by famous knights like Archibald Douglas and William Keith – prepared to follow their countrymen, the Leslies, to Alexandria, the crusading goal of the company of Peter I of Cyprus, who had been in London when David first met Froissart in 1363: these men of chivalry may also have intended to make a pilgrimage to the tombs of St John at Amiens or of St James at Compostella.[35] Such was the valour of the land, court and followers with which David presented his guest, that not only did Froissart give them an impressive write-up in his *Chroniques* but he also set his later romantic poem, *Méliador*, partly in Scotland. This epic of romantic chivalry features a young knight, Méliador, the son of the Duke of Cornwall, who wins the hand of 'Hermondine', heiress of 'Hermont', the king of Scotland and ally of King Arthur, after triumphing in a series of tournaments on the continent, in England, Ireland and in Scotland, at Stirling ('Signaudon') and Roxburgh Castles. That after 1337 Cornwall had become a palatinate possession of a prince of England (it was held by Edward III's eldest son and namesake, the Black Prince) might suggest that Froissart had been partly inspired to write of the duchy's heir becoming heir to Scotland by the abortive plans of the 1350s and 1360s whereby David II sought to admit the Plantagenets to his succession.[36] But more generally, Froissart may have helped disseminate the fame of David and his knights in their own day to such a degree that they more easily entered the mainstream of European chivalric tradition in the later fourteenth century. A contingent of pro-Bruce Scots certainly appear as an identifiable company in such works as the striking armorial of the

34 *Oeuvres de Froissart*, ii, 312–3; Fraser ed., *The Lennox*, i, 76; *ER*, ii, 25, 211, 222, 281. The Arthurian legends entered the Scottish chronicle tradition with the mid-fourteenth-century sources of Fordun and Wyntoun – see: F. Alexander, 'Scottish Attitudes to the Figure of King Arthur: a Reassessment', *Anglia*, 93 (1972), 17–34; R.S. Loomis, 'Scotland and the Arthurian legend', *PSAS*, lxxxix (1955–6), 1–21; G. Ashe ed., *The Quest for Arthur's Britain* (London 1971), 154. Edington, 'The Tournament in Medieval Scotland', 53–4, argues that David may also have established Stirling as a jousting centre.

35 *Rot. Scot.*, i, 893–7; A. Goodman, 'A Letter from an earl of Douglas to a King of Castile', *SHR*, lxiv (1985), 68–78.

36 A. Longnon ed., *Méliador* (SATF, 3 vols., Paris, 1895–99); P.F. Dembrowski, *Jean Froissart and his Méliador: Context, Craft and Sense* (Lexington 1983), 63–80; A.H. Diverres, 'The Geography of Britain in Froissart's *Méliador*', *Medieval Miscellany Presented to Eugene Vinaver* (New York 1965), 97–112; idem, 'Frois-sart's *Mélidaor* and Edward III's Policy towards Scotland', *Mélanges offerts à Rita Lejeune* (Gembloux 1969), 1399–1409; R. Barber, *Edward, Prince of Wales and Aquitaine* (London 1978), 107–8.

Count of Gueldres alongside the crusading and jousting cream of Europe.[37]

But Froissart's presence may also have obliged David to play the part of a confident lord – one who did not need to call parliaments – at peace with all his great subjects. The spring and summer of 1365 thus perhaps saw a further easing of tensions with some of the rebels of 1363. David certainly paid the earl of Douglas £80 for wine delivered to the royal household about August 1365: William was a regular crown charter witness between January and August that year. But much of David's desire to retain working relations with this earl must have sprung from Douglas's continued lordship draw for men of chivalry, especially in the Lothians and the south-east, regions favoured by the king. This was a reputation which the earl's connections with the French monarchy and his war record at Poitiers must have enhanced. It was natural that Froissart should also stay with the Douglas earl at Dalkeith Castle. Here, he reported seeing five esquire brothers, all of the name of Douglas of Dalkeith (James of Lothian and his brothers?) and employed in the royal household. But these men were also present in the Douglas affinity. Thus as much as Froissart's itinerary took him to strong crown men of the 1360s like the earls of Sutherland and Fife (Thomas Bisset), it also saw him meet men whose service together against England in the forest of Jedburgh in the 1350s – a group including Archibald Douglas, Mar, March, Sutherland, William Ramsay of Colluthie and Robert Erskine – reflected their achievements at times under the banner of the first Douglas earl. In the same way, Froissart's *Chroniques* would also do much to boost the fame of Robert I's champion, the 'Good' Sir James Douglas, and to restore the warrior name of William of Liddesdale. David had to be wary of trying to impose too selfish and aloof a royal monopoly on Scotland's martial reputation.[38]

Froissart's presence, though, brought no real lull in David's challenge to Stewart interests. On 28 February 1365 David had quite strikingly created an instant ally in Sir Walter Oliphant, the new husband of the king's

37 Boardman and Penman, 'The Scottish Arms in the Armorial of Gèlre'; P. Adam-Even ed., *L'armorial universal du herault Gèlre, 1370–95* (Switzerland 1971), 7–10, 52–55; C. Campbell, 'Scottish Arms in the Bellenville Roll', *The Scottish Genealogist*, xxv (1976), 33–52; C.J. Burnett, 'Early Officers of Arms in Scotland', *Review of Scottish Culture*, xii (1996), 3–13. The *ER*, ii, 29, 149 contains payments from the crown to one 'Nicholas of Flanders, physician', possibly the Gèlre armorialist, Nicholas de Hamyn, or a cleric whom Boece records David trying to intrude as bishop of Aberdeen *c.* 1342 (*Murthlacensium et Aberdonnensium Episcoporum Vitae*, 22–4). Froissart also wrote of 'hero knights' in Scotland at this time, naming 'Moray, Douglas, [Robert] Erskine, William Glendinning, Robert Bourme and Alexander de Ramsay'.
38 *ER*, ii, 200; *Oeuvres de Froissart*, iii, 207–9 and v, 119–20.

illegitimate sister, Elizabeth. On that day Oliphant received in free barony the lands of Gask on the eastern boundary of the earldom of Strathearn, lying between the Stewart lordship of Methven and Malcolm Drummond's new tenants at Auchterarder. Oliphant also received the lesser lands of Auchtertyre, Balcraig, Turin, Drimmie, Newtyle, Kinpurnie and Gallowhead in Forfarshire, Aberdalgie and Dupplin in Perthshire and Glensauch in Kincardineshire. This made this Perthshire knight, like his father for Robert I before him, an important crown agent in sensitive central Scotland: in 1368 he would be raised to temporary keeper (really constable) of Stirling Castle. Already, on 18 February 1365, David had given John Dundas the barony of Fingask in eastern Perthshire next to Queen Margaret's lands of Rait (for which the Steward had challenged David before 1346). David's grant of Gask lands to Oliphant and Dundas may have been resisted briefly by the Steward. For on 12 May 1365, at Perth, the Steward granted the lands of Foulis Gask to John Logie, the king's stepson, a surely punitive concession Robert can have little relished.[39]

David also targeted Stewart interests further north. On 25 September – significantly while again at Kildrummy Castle in Mar – David issued letters under his privy seal empowering Alexander Bur, bishop of Moray, to punish crimes committed by his tenants in Strathspey and Badenoch without the oversight of royal officers. As Stephen Boardman has pointed out, explicit in this regality was crown criticism of the Steward's control of this region while Lieutenant before 1357, citing specifically 'the defect of justice, the exercise of which failed at that time', as well as showing favour to a churchman who had risen in royal service to be installed as bishop in late 1362 and was now restored to ecclesiastical powers which deprived the Stewarts' terce rights over Badenoch (through Euphemia Ross, Countess of Moray, sister of the earl of Ross, widow of John Randolph, earl of Moray, and second wife of the Steward from 1355). Now the ambitious and wily Bur was set to be one of the king's secular fixers in the north and north-east.[40]

Elsewhere in the second half of 1365 David continued to favour relatives, knights and esquires. On 2 October he gave Alan Erskine, keeper of Loch Leven, the barony of Inchture, again in eastern Perthshire next to the Queen's lands; Erskine also received Fife lands that year. On 17 October Sir John Herries had his Dumfriesshire lands of Terregles confirmed in free

---

39 *RRS*, vi, nos. 336 to 343; *ER*, ii, 307; Fraser ed., *Red Book of Grandtully*, ii, 128–9. The Steward's charter was witnessed by John Stewart of Kyle, John Stewart (Robert's brother), Maurice Drummond, Walter Murray of Tullibardine (the Drummond's ally in their Menteith feud with the Stewarts), John and Hugh de Ros, John Mercer (the Perth merchant and ransom financier) and a 'John Karly'.

40 *RRS*, vi, no. 348; Boardman, 'Lordship in the North-East I', 2–3; Watt, *Scottish Graduates*, 67–70; Oram, 'Alexander Bur, Bishop of Moray', 195–214.

barony, a grant originally made in 1359 and which would be raised to a regality in 1367. David's favour to this Poitiers veteran, allied to several grants the king made at the end of the year to south-western men such as Sir William Cunningham and Sir John Kennedy, and in Peeblesshire to Sir William Geldstanes, might be viewed as further royal subversion of the Douglas earl's influence. Most of these grants were issued from Edinburgh. But David's itinerary took him through Lindores in Fife, Scone and Perth in August and Kildrummy and Dundee in September (when he confirmed some acts of the absent earl of Mar). In late October he gave Clackmannanshire lands to his cousin, Robert Bruce. Christmas that year may have been spent back in Perth.[41]

It was there on 14 January 1366 that another council gathered, but just what this body discussed is unknown. Its purpose may have been to further outline the process of raising and collecting revenues to help pay the reset ransom. The only recorded decision of this body which has survived is a statute ordaining the erection in each royal burgh of new trons (scales) for the weighing of wool to be overseen by newly appointed tronars and their clerks, charging one penny to the crown for each sack weighed. That this was a royal design for making money is at least suggested by David's gift in the previous December of land for a new tolbooth to the burgesses of the key wool-exporting burgh, Edinburgh, where the customs by now yielded at least 15 per cent of the crown's annual income; in April 1366 David would also grant the right to form a merchant guild to the burgesses of Perth whose leading merchant and moneylender, John Mercer, would again oversee some of the ransom finance at Bruges. If successful, this co-operation with the royal burghs would improve already healthy revenues.[42] On 22 January 1366 the king himself was able to ride south to oversee the exchange of the first 6,000-merk instalment of the renegotiated ransom at the border. This sum and more had been collected by the royal exchequer since mid-1365, combining customs returns with contribution loans from the burgesses, clergy and sheriffdoms. By May 1366 a further £3,518 had been received by the Chamberlain. David was able to use this to pay his own and (at £600) his ambassadors' expenses, as council had decreed. But by January 1366 David had also been able to revive the 'king's deposit', banking some £433 presumably in Stirling Castle with Robert Erskine.[43]

---

41 *RRS*, vi, nos. 344 to 350; *RMS*, i, nos. 187–8, 190–4, 196–200, 202–6, 208–14, 223.
42 *APS*, i, 497 (*RPS*, 1366/1/1); *RRS*, vi, nos. 350, 352; *Atlas of Scottish History to 1707*, 308; Grant, *Independence and Nationhood*, 236–7 (Table I: Wool and leather exports).
43 NAS SP6/2; *ER*, ii, 215–27. In the first part of this account the burgesses contributed some £666 while the sheriffdoms yielded £1,352.

However, although Edward III and his council were surely glad to have the money on time, the evidence of the next few months suggests that the English were losing patience with David. The Scottish king did little of note from late January through April 1366, spending time in Perth (26 January, 6 April, 10 April), Edinburgh, Montrose (31 March–2 April) and Arbroath (7–8 April): his acts included favour to Sir William Dischington (Fife lands), the Strachans (Kincardine lands), Sir John Innerpeffray (lands in Banff where he was sheriff) and William Keith: St Monans was presumably visited on 1 March just before the king's birthday.[44] But on 8 May 1366 another formal council was held at Holyrood, the king's favourite abbey. This gives the impression of a body quite hastily assembled (its personnel unknown) and its one surviving recorded decision a response to a harsh change in diplomatic relations with England. This council ordained that:

> upon the four points, namely homage, the succession, the dismember-
> ing of the kingdom and the perpetual aid of men of arms . . . after a
> lengthy discussion, the first three points were finally refuted as in-
> sufferable and unacceptable . . .[45]

It would thus seem that in talks for which no record is extant, held sometime in the spring of 1366, the English envoys had increased their demands from the Scots for peace. This would have been understandable, given Charles V of France's successful sponsorship of Bertrand of Guesclin's invasion of Castile, culminating in the usurpation of England's ally, Peter IV, by 29 March 1366. Edward III's recommendation in June 1366 to a London merchant that thirty-four casks of suspect wine were 'too thin' to sell in England but could be offloaded in Scotland instead certainly mirrors this sense that the two kings' friendship and political need for each other had suddenly lessened.[46]

However, A.A.M. Duncan has convincingly argued that the four points in fact rejected by the Scots council in May 1366 were not those here recorded: a scribe in error seems to have returned to the terms of 1363 instead of the four 'ways' (the Disinherited, mutual alliance, money over and above the ransom, and a combination of these points) put forward by the English in late 1364. Above all, Edward III and his sons would need cash and allies to recover their position in Europe: thus the ransom and military assistance were always likely to have been the main focus of any talks.[47] Yet the possibility should not be dismissed that at some point over the winter of

---

44 *RRS*, vi, no. 351; *RMS*, i, nos. 212–3, 215–20, 222, 233.
45 For what follows of this council, see *APS*, i, 497–9 (*RPS*, 1366/5/1–2); also *RMS*, i, no. 224 – letters of protection from the crown to Holyrood Abbey, 8 May 1366.
46 Sumption, *Hundred Years War*, ii, 528–43; *CDS*, iv, no. 122.
47 Duncan, 'A Question about the Succession, 1364', 17–9.

1365 and into spring 1366 the English had indeed upped the ante in their exchanges with Landellis, Wardlaw, Armstrong and Erskine. Besides, David and his close counsel must have retained some hope of such a final deal involving concessions on the succession and Disinherited. It is possible in this context that the recent negotiations had flirted with such matters.

But the remainder of the Holyrood council's resolutions make it clear that, as in 1365, the crown and its subjects knew that fulfilment of their ransom obligations remained the only realistic way to build towards a peace treaty. Although the May 1366 council agreed to send back ambassadors to try and once again negotiate for modification and peace based on the notion of a mutual military alliance, it also planned for fiscal contingencies:

> in case peace shall not finally prevail . . . it was determined there be a tax again, according to the true and old value of lands and rents, as much ecclesiastical as of others, through the whole kingdom, and these taxes shall be presented to parliament.

This fresh levy would help the crown pay the ransom. But it is very tempting to interpret what seems to be a first tentative call for a 'true' tax assessment, before an actual levy was set and raised, as the result of pressure placed upon the government by the three estates, headed by worried magnates like the Steward, Douglas and the bishops – those whose resources might be hit hardest. A call for such a comparative survey to see how the value of the Scottish kingdom's lands and rents had changed due to decades of war damage and the decimation of tenantry by plague since the 'old' value had been assessed in the late thirteenth century would certainly have met with much sympathy among already heavily taxed council members. They were surely aware that, under the May 1365 agreement with England, David could levy contribution and customs at a high rate but pay a lower sum than expected to Edward III. The May 1366 council's insistence that this new tax be set by a full parliament – called to meet at Scone two months later – again perhaps reflects some desire on the estates' part to see that the king live of his own resources as much as possible and that David should not be allowed to simply dictate to and manage the estates as in 1365. But the closing decisions of the Holyrood council still suggest that David retained the upper hand. For while the new assessment was being made by the Chamberlain and his clerks and the sheriffs, the council approved the far more ominous process – first toyed with in David's homecoming council of November 1357 – whereby:

> certain people are to be deputed by the king or chamberlain, and it shall be asked of each person individually, and set down in writing, how much each person is willing to give freely to the complete payment of the king's ransom within the next three years; and the same

donations shall be presented there in any case to the end that, the said negotiation of peace having failed, at the end of the four years for which the truce is now secured all the remainder of our lord king's ransom is available to be paid, so that disputes and penalties may be avoided, if the adverse side [the English] should be able to impose or claim any by the instruments which have been made upon the great truce and the release of the king.[48]

Paying off the ransom in full by February 1370 and the end of the truce, thus leaving Scotland free to resume her alliance with France against England – and without any further need of talk of changing the succession – was something the Steward, Douglas and others would have welcomed. Again it is tempting to read the voice of council opposition to the king at Holyrood into this clause (even though it might mean an uncertain drain on magnate income). The same could be said of the only other extant statute of this assembly, that henceforth new Scottish coinage should retain the same metal content as English specie (and, by implication, not be devalued by the crown) as well as be given distinguishing marks 'until it shall be possible to have mature advice in the next parliament on this'.[49] The estates were clearly increasingly distrustful of the crown's finances. But the seeming blank cheque of voluntary contribution demands which were now being placed upon the community cannot have been anything other than a crown initiative.

Such extraction of 'donations' from magnates at sums to be set in private talks with the king's officials would be an arbitrary policy which would later see James I (1424–37) condemned as a grasping tyrant.[50] In 1366, as in 1357, David II may have been able to justify it on the grounds of 'urgent necessity', this time with the added twist that the Scots had to counter the anomaly resulting from their ransom renegotiation with the English of May 1365 – a truce to 1370 but annual instalments of 6,000 merks until 1381. The estates also had some relief in prospect through the new 'true' assessment of land and rent values for general tax. However, the resentment of the king's ransom and tax fiscalism which had been shared by many significant Scots in 1362–3 might easily have been expected to reach new heights after May 1366. No dramatic change in the status quo in Scotland had been effected by the crown over the previous two years. But David's domestic antagonists must, nonetheless, have remained highly fearful of the intentions of a king still firmly in charge of the political initiative.

48 *RPS*, 1366/7/1 and 1357/11/4.
49 *Ibid*, 166/5/2; J. Davidson, 'Distinguishing Marks on the Later Issues of David II', *British Numismatic Journal*, xxi (1950), 155–63.
50 Brown, *James I*, 122–3, 139–40; *Chron. Bower*, viii, 251.

Perhaps, though, there is another way to make sense of changes in tone in the Holyrood council. One other surviving piece of significant evidence from 1366 might be viewed to suggest that David and his close circle were by now well aware that their diplomatic overtures to England of the last three years were getting nowhere fast and that influential magnates – not least Robert Steward – might once again be roused to direct reaction against the crown, as in 1363–4, if concessions were not forthcoming. In this context, the Holyrood council's rejection of the English demands for peace and preparations for the ransom – offset by promises of 'donations' of money to the crown – might be viewed as a series of working compromises worked out by all parties concerned. Such political give-and-take might certainly have been the case if the king himself had countenanced the request of 13 March 1366 to the Pope for a marriage dispensation for Robert Steward's eldest son and heir, John Stewart of Kyle, to wed Annabella Drummond, the niece of Queen Margaret, the daughter of the late John Drummond, lord of Menteith.[51]

It is surely correct to interpret this marriage – which must have taken place sometime between spring 1366 and April 1367 – together with the royal patronage extended to John Stewart in 1367–8 (discussed below) as a strong sign that David was by now prepared to recognise the Stewart succession in some form.[52] Not only did betrothal into the new royal line for Kyle – who had noticeably reached thirty without taking a wife – mean that David had for now at least given up all serious thought of securing a succession-deal involving an English prince, but it may also have been designed to ease local tensions in central Scotland.

It is likely, too, that this new familial connection was made through marriage without the approval of Robert Steward and by attempting to drive something of a wedge between father and son. After Robert's unexpected accession as king in 1371, tensions would arise between himself and Kyle, leading to the aging prince's seizure of power from his infirm father in 1384. After 1371 Kyle would rise at the head of an affinity packed with many of David II's Lothian and south-western knights: he would also name his own children after David and Queen Margaret. Even in March 1371 Robert II's swift recognition of John Stewart as his heir in an act of parliament may have been designed to ease internal tensions roused since 1366 as much as to stabilise the family's kingship.[53] Back in 1366, in the

---

51 NAS RH2/6/4/81. That David had intended to marry off Annabella to John Stewart for some time is perhaps suggested by his gift of £20 to her while she stayed at Stirling sometime in 1365–6 (*ER*, ii, 198). Annabella may have been a lady-in-waiting for Queen Joan in England *c*. 1358 (Green, *Lives of the Princesses of England*, iii, 154).

52 Boardman, *Early Stewart Kings*, 22.

53 *Ibid*, 49, 56–9, 123–5.

natural course of things, most of the political community would have expected Robert Steward to die before his younger uncle, King David: upon Robert's passing in turn Kyle would become monarch. With the prospect of having the ransom paid off by 1370 and his own son and heir admitted to Bruce favour, many of Robert Steward's local and dynastic grievances of 1363 would have been addressed and he might surely have been grateful to receive some respite from royal dislike by accepting this marriage. But subsequent events of 1366–7 suggest that Robert himself – and his position and lands – remained a focus of royal antipathy while his son's star rose or was sheltered. This way David, at least, could look to determine the handover to the Stewarts on his own terms, should it come to that. Meanwhile, of course, he may still have felt it possible that he would produce a child by his own Drummond wife even if many others must have come to utterly doubt the possibility.

Some sense, then, that the crown was backing down from its previously hard-headed pursuit of its domestic and diplomatic agenda – and seeking working co-operation through a Stewart-Drummond ally and others – may have marked the rest of 1366 and continued into 1367, yet left little trace in the historical record. It is not known just when the marriage of John Stewart and Annabella Drummond took place, but soon after the parliament held at Scone from 26 July 1366 seems likely. Certainly, the recorded decisions of that full body, the first since March 1364, would reveal a further dilution of David's control of events as well as ongoing clashes with his heir presumptive.

David's Policy Falters? July 1366 to June 1367

June and early July 1366 must have seen frantic activity on the part of the shrival and financial officers of the crown to begin the reassessment of the kingdom's lands and rents to report to parliament at Scone. It was testimony to the increasingly efficient and sophisticated bureaucracy which David's churchmen and lay officers had developed that some of this task may have been completed by 20 July and the rest reported by September that year (as parliament had asked).[54]

The results must have provided cold comfort for the estates. Their tax contributions would be much lower thereafter under the newly assessed *verus valour* (v.v.).[55] But generally lands had slumped in value by an average

---

54 For what follows on this parliament, see *APS*, i, 499–591 (*RPS*, 1366/7/1–21). Duncan notes that inclusion of the term 'freeholders' in the summons issued for this assembly may have been designed to ensure that only crown tenants attended and thus to limit the followings of magnates like the Steward and Douglas ('The Early Parliaments of Scotland', 54–5).

55 *RPS*, 1366/7/18.

of half (48%) since the *antiqua taxio* (a.t.) of pre-1286. The traditionally wealthy heartlands of the kingdom had been sorely hit. The massive diocese of St Andrews – stretching from Tayside through Fife and the Lothians to Berwickshire – had dropped from £5,414 (a.t.) to £3,507 (v.v.) and the Scottish bishoprics in total from £15,000 to £9,396. The hotly contested shires of Fife and Perth had slumped from £3,465 and £6,192 (a.t.) to £2,555 and £3,087 (v.v.) respectively, while Aberdeenshire – the focus of civil war and thus Bruce as well as Edwardian devastation between 1307 and 1337 – had declined from £4,448 (a.t.) to £2,588 (v.v.). Only Edinburgh's chief market and shire of three constabularies retained some buoyancy, dropping from £4,029 to £3,030. Further south, large areas of border territory and church jurisdiction remained under English control. For example, Roxburghshire slumped from £1,133 (a.t.) to just £523 (v.v.), while the Abbot of Melrose's lands could not even be accessed: Berwick-on-Tweed, of course, was lost. That the rest of western Europe suffered a similar decline in this period can have been of little comfort, if it was observed at all by the Scots.[56]

However, even before the full extent of this plunge in taxable resources was made graphically clear to king and estates, parliament had authorised another round of extraordinary taxation to meet the crown's domestic and diplomatic needs. Again, this was based on the assumption that even though envoys would be despatched south once again to seek peace, it was more likely that the truce ransom would still have to be paid. The usual ambassadors were apparently to offer all that had been tabled in the Scottish articles of 1365 as well as further improvements on mutual military alliance. But in the event of their failure on this front, the envoys were to seek an extension of the truce to twenty-five years and ransom payments at the current rate of £4,000 (6,000 merks). To meet these expected instalments parliament agreed that after final details of the *verus valour* had been reported to council at Edinburgh before the next feast of the Nativity of the Virgin (8 September) – and they would now include an assessment of the goods of burgesses and husbandmen – an immediate tax of 8,000 merks would be levied. The necessary £4,000 from this contribution was specifically assigned to the ransom (pending the return of the envoys) and a further 1,000 merks each was to be assigned to 'the king's debts and his expenses made in the meantime' and to 'the expenses of the ambassadors'. However, to have these last 2,000 merks in readiness they would be advanced as a refundable loan from the estates with 1,000

---

56 For discussion of this decline, see *Atlas of Scottish History to 1707*, 299, 302–5, 308; Gemmill & Mayhew, *Changing Values in Medieval Scotland*, 363–73; Nicholson, *Scotland – the Later Middle Ages*, 175–6.

merks given by the barons, 600 merks by the clergy and 400 merks by the burgesses.[57]

Behind these decisions there seems to have been what Abbot and tax-collector Bower would describe in the 1440s (with reference to James I's ransom 'expenses') as 'mature and healthy financial assistance' by subjects to the crown, a fruitful co-operation in parliament to their mutual benefit.[58] However, the other acts of the July 1366 parliament suggest strongly that although David and his government secured what was needed diplomatically and financially, they did not escape more explicit criticism and censure than had occurred in recent assemblies. This was directed at what might be seen as a neglect of domestic matters in favour of concerns with England since the last Scone parliament of 1364.

Much of the 1366 parliament's debate and grievances sought clearly to spread the realm's fiscal burdens evenly. It was enacted that none of the contribution should be used for purposes other than the ransom and envoys, not 'as a gift, remission or otherwise'. Churchmen were not to be further burdened or their teinds interfered with. The king's debts through requisitions for his household (prise) were to be paid promptly and no significant individual's retinue should be boarded upon churchmen or husbandmen – all hosts should be paid the going rate by travelling parties.[59] These were all fairly common entreaties from subjects to crown throughout medieval Europe. However, several acts of this Scottish parliament were also concerned with a breakdown in locality law and order with implicit criticism of the crown's partial justice. 'At the instance of the three estates', it was ordained that 'common justice be done to everyone without favour being shown to anyone . . . the letters written for the purpose of doing justice that should emanate from the king's chancery or otherwise from other ministers upon whom it is incumbent to make justice, shall not be revoked by any other letters under any seal whatsoever'. Moreover, it was also enacted that 'the king's remissions, granted or to be granted for whatever transgressions, should be null and void, and should not give satisfaction to the party within a year from the date of the same, unless . . . there has been a settlement openly made'. At face value, these acts suggest David's regime may have been guilty both of selling pardons for serious crimes and of leniency to crown supporters involved in disputes.[60]

Admittedly, some of this contemporary increase in lawlessness may have been due to the intransigence of some of David's magnate opponents as well as the beginnings of open expression of that most striking of cultural and

57 *RPS*, 1366/7/3–5.
58 *Chron. Bower*, viii, 305.
59 *RPS*, 1366/7/7–9.
60 *Ibid*, 1366/7/6 and/13

political prejudices in the Scottish kingdom, a Highland-Lowland divide. For the Scone parliament also specifically enacted that 'those rebels, namely of Atholl, Argyll, Badenoch, Lochaber and Ross, and others if there are any, in the northern regions or elsewhere, should be arrested by the king and his armed force to undergo common justice and particularly for paying off the contribution'. This was an act David could obviously use to his advantage in the localities, especially when combined with parliament's insistence that 'all king's officers, namely sheriffs and other lesser officials, whether within or outwith burghs, should obey the chamberlain and other higher officials under pain of the removal of them from their offices and without hope of restoration to the same henceforward': there was also a ban on the inclusion of 'lancers or archers' in the retinue of any nobleman, 'unless he maintains them for a reasonable cause, concerning which they are to be held to give their oath upon this question to the king's ministers, under pain of imprisonment of their bodies'.[61] David's intrusive lordship over the previous decade must have caused several magnates to bring large armed retinues to court and parliament. But some of the disturbances in the north and west may have been caused by long-term territorial disputes and the militarisation of the tenantry of rival neighbours stirred directly by David's interference in the previous two years. Certainly, the 1366 Scone parliament recorded the 'contumacious absence' (despite summons by the crown) of William, earl of Ross, and his brother and heir, Hugh, the Ross brothers' cousin John Hay of Tullibody, John MacDonald of the Isles and John Macdougall of Lorn.[62]

The Ross brothers – whose locality offices had already been revoked by the crown – must have been angered by David's sponsorship about that time of the marriage of the earl of Ross's daughter, Euphemia, to the royal crusading favourite, Sir Walter Leslie, now returned from northern Africa and an encounter with the English White Company in France. This match would certainly have taken place by 13 September 1366 when, at Perth, David granted the couple lands in the new forest of Dumfries. But a papal dispensation for the marriage was not secured until 8 December that year, and a complaint by Earl William and his lawyers lodged with the first parliament held after David's death in 1371 would claim that the king and Queen Margaret had taken a direct role in intimidating the Ross family into accepting this betrothal.[63] All in all, it seems as though Leslie's good

---

61 *Ibid*, 1366/7/10–11 and 15.
62 *Ibid*, 1366/7/1. For council's criticism of the crown in general at this time, see Penman, 'Parliament Lost – Parliament Regained?'.
63 *CPR*, iv, 59; *RMS*, i, no. 258; D. Forbes, *Ane Account of the Familie of Innes, 1698* (Aberdeen 1864), 70–3; Boardman, *Early Stewart Kings*, 45–8; Fowler, *Medieval Mercenaries*, 73, 324–6. For Leslie in Inverness in 1367, see Fraser ed., *Frasers of Philorth*, ii, 168–9.

marriage was, like Bisset's match to Isabella of Fife and, in a sense, John Stewart's to Annabella Drummond, an expression of royal territorial designs, this time backed up with physical, legal and financial threats.

As for MacDonald and Macdougall, these lords had always been violent towards each other.[64] But both they and the Ross brothers had been summoned to council in 1365 and may have been forced to contemplate service in Edward III's army in Ireland. They also seem to have been angered by the attempts of David's government to reassess them for taxation in summer 1366 (a ransom burden from which MacDonald, as an English ally, was exempt under the terms of the treaty of Berwick). Predictably, when the valuation returns were submitted in September 1366 it was reported that MacDonald (£1,320 a.t.), Macdougall (£420 a.t.) and Gillespie Campbell of Lochawe (£600 a.t.) had all refused royal officials' review of their Argyll-shire lands.[65] The same was true of Robert Steward, the father-in-law and brother-in-law of MacDonald and Ross respectively: his western lands of Cowal, Bute, Cumbrae, Arran and Knapdale (£1,000 a.t.) were closed to crown officers.[66]

Significantly, however, the Steward must have gone into the Scone parliament somewhat heartened by the death by at least April 1366 of Sir Thomas Bisset, David's second intruded lord of the earldom of Fife and husband of Countess Isabella. The king had certainly inspected a charter by 'Isabella *Stewart*, lady of Fife' in June 1365, a style which suggests that this heiress may in fact have been widowed in that year and that she certainly did not recognise her third marriage: she must soon have returned to the Stewart camp.[67] Nonetheless, the Steward would have been understandably worried by parliament's complaint in autumn 1366 about disturbances in Atholl and Badenoch, probably following pleas from Gilbert of Glencairnie in Moray about depredations by the *Clan Donnchaidh*, the leading cateran kindred of Badenoch who by 1368 at least would be in the service of the Steward's fourth son, Alexander Stewart. From Elgin on 20 April 1367 David would issue letters directly to Duncan of Atholl, the clan's chief, warning him to stop wasting the lands of Glencairnie's large hilly lordship with passes linking Mar to Strathspey, Badenoch and Moray. Such violence gave the king a genuine excuse to interfere in these lands. This had been an intent further signalled at the Scone parliament on 26 July 1366 by David's letters

---

64 *Acts of the Lords of the Isles*, 5–9; McDonald, *The Kingdom of the Isles*, ch. 6.

65 *RPS*, 1366/7/18; Crawford, 'The Earls of Orkney-Caithness', 31–2; Gemmill & Mayhew, *Changing Values in Medieval Scotland*, 267–73, argues that much of the decline in values in returns here was due to the 'erosion of royal authority'.

66 The royal heir presumptive's desire to protect these resources would have been understandable in the light of the decline from £4,057 (a.t.) to just £1,755 (v.v.) revealed in Lanarkshire where the Stewarts had large holdings.

67 *RRS*, vi, no. 345; *RMS*, i, no. 221.

to all royal officials in the north to enforce the secular penalties on wrongdoers requested by Alexander Bur, bishop of Moray, whom the king had empowered a year earlier to act in Badenoch and Strathspey.[68]

Moreover, this last act came on the same day as the Steward had to ratify further royal favour to the Logie-Drummond kindred. On 26 July, in full parliament, David granted his adolescent stepson, John Logie, the vast barony of Logie in free barony and regality, carving it out of the Stewart earldom of Strathearn in blench ferm after the Steward had 'surrendered' the barony to his king in the presence of the estates: the witnesses to this act included the earls of March, Mar and Douglas as well as a number of royalist knights.[69] As if this was not enough humiliation, on the same day the Steward then had to witness David's gift to Logie of the remaining royal lands in Annandale. David clearly intended to retain working control of these border lands for which his March Warden, Archibald Douglas, had to negotiate private administrative deals with the earl of Hereford: indeed, on 13 December 1366 David allowed his seals to be attached to a fresh agreement with the English earl which expanded the Scottish crown's judicial and revenue rights throughout the whole shire of Roxburgh and recognised John Logie's sasine (an indenture closed at London with the English treasurer, a cleric of Canterbury).[70] David surely envisaged an increased role in the future for young Logie as a crown agent in both central and southern Scotland: these provisions could have been made with the support of Logie's new cousin by marriage, John Stewart of neighbouring Kyle Stewart, who had recovered much of Annandale from England before 1357 (and would be granted the other Bruce provincial title of Carrick in 1368).

However, that this royal favour to Queen Margaret's son was still deeply controversial and unpopular in certain quarters is underlined by a bond of retinue ('de retenencia'), probably of November 1366, in which Sir John Kennedy of Dunure agreed to warn the queen and John Logie of all 'snares' or plots aganst them 'with all the power of his followers, without any deceit whatsoever, within the kingdom of Scotland, and chiefly within the lordship of Annandale'.[71] Admittedly, this arrangement also hints at the growing

---

68 *RRS*, vi, nos. 355, 370, 394–5; Boardman, 'Lordship in the North-East I', 3–4; Grant, 'The Wolf of Badenoch', 143. My thanks to Richard Oram for emphasising the extent and strategic importance of the Glencairnie lordship adjacent to the lordships of Abernethy and Moray's Strathdearn (*Atlas of Scottish History to 1707*, 202–3; A. Grant, 'The Higher Nobility in Scotland and their Estates, *c*.1371–1424' (unpublished D.Phil. thesis, University of Oxford, 1975), 379).

69 *RRS*, vi, no. 353; *RPS*, 1366/7/19–20; Grant, 'Service and Tenure in Late Medieval Scotland', 159–60.

70 *RRS*, vi, nos. 354, 363; *CDS*, iv, nos. 127–8; *Rot. Scot.*, i, 899.

71 *A Historical Account of the Noble Family of Kennedy, Marquess of Ailsa and Earl of Cassilis* (Edinburgh 1849), 12n; Grant, 'Service and Tenure in Late Medieval Scotland', 162–6.

capacity for independent action, tinged with aggressive paranoia about her political position, which would betray Margaret to be a liability whom David could not afford to keep after 1368. In 1366, though, despite three years of childless marriage, the Logies remained central to royal plans.

As the 1366 Scone parliament closed, therefore, David must have had mixed feelings about his position. The Steward and the earl of Ross appeared to be under the royal cosh, primed for a royal assault on their northern influence. The other rebel earls of 1363 were quiet and compliant and the estates had signed off on more taxation and talks with England. Nonetheless, parliament had also given an indication that the political community would only tolerate these policies for so much longer unless there was a corresponding return in royal justice, peace, and tax-easing. The early signs were that fiscal resistance and territorial disputes were only further provoked by crown interference in the north, and that Anglo-Scottish talks were stagnating.

David's actions in the second half of 1366 may have seen him attempt to deal with some of these domestic issues. He moved from Scone to Dundee and on to Aberdeen between mid-August and early September, returning south to Edinburgh by October via Arbroath (6 September) and Perth (13 September). No evidence of justice ayres survives from this period but these may have been held in the king's presence. Among royal grants issued in this period were a gift of half of the thanage of Formartine between Aberdeen and Buchan to William, earl of Sutherland; the (ultimately unsuccessful) settlement of a marriage dispute which saw the territory of the Aird, the sizeable province nestling between the barony of Urquhart, Ross and the Beauly Firth, partitioned between Sir William Fenton, the Chisholms and the Frasers of Lovat; another grant of Fife lands at Ardross along the coast from St Monans to William Dischington; and the aforementioned grant to Walter Leslie and his new wife. The Steward and the earls of March/Moray and Douglas accompanied the royal household north at this time. By 14 December David was to be found on a southern ayre at the border peel of Drumelzier in Peeblesshire, issuing a confirmation of a grant of Lanark-shire lands by the daughter and heiress of the late Sir William Douglas of Liddesdale, Marie, to her cousin and heir, Sir James Douglas of Lothian – again the Steward and Douglas earl were witnesses. Back at Edinburgh for Christmas, the king also inspected the late John Randolph, earl of Moray's grant of Aberdour in Fife to the Liddesdale Douglas line, lands he had already confirmed to James Douglas of Lothian while at Drumelzier (perhaps suggesting that William, earl of Douglas, had challenged this grant).[72]

---

72 *RRS*, vi, nos. 357–65; *RMS*, i, nos. 230, 252, 254, 257–8, 260–1.

The new year continued in the same vein. Another council seems to have been held at Perth about 13 to 20 January 1367, although no record of decisions regarding diplomacy and crown finance has survived. However, the extant royal acts issued there included a charter of entail of the Lothian lands of the Byres to William Lindsay, resigned by the crusading knight, Alexander Lindsay (to whom the king had granted Kincardine lands in May); a transfer of the Perthshire barony of Kinnoul (a former Fife possession next to Queen Margaret's lands) to Nicholas Erskine, Robert's son; and, most remarkably, a restoration of Thomas Fleming, the grandson of David's late favourite, to the earldom of Wigtown – although the king's denial of a full regality to Thomas surely reflected his doubt that this Dumbarton-based kindred could ever do as good a job for him in the south-west as Archibald Douglas, and might besides upset John Stewart of Kyle or Kennedy of Dunure. At Dumbarton on 21 February 1367 David also confirmed John Drummond junior (bailie of Dull for the Queen) in Stirlingshire and Perthshire lands. The Steward, March/Moray and Douglas earl were again among the witnesses to these acts along with knights like Archibald Douglas, Haliburton, Dischington, Moigne and Erskine.[73]

However, at this juncture the Scottish envoys in England suffered a rebuke which seems to have caused David to further rethink his domestic tack, if he had not already begun to do so. Even though the second instalment of the newly settled ransom was handed over on time in January 1367, on 8 February Edward III abandoned the talks and ordered defensive measures to be taken on the borders 'as any hope of peace [is gone], as is clear from the response of their [the Scots'] messengers recently made to us'. Not only were the English unwilling to accept any Scottish offers based upon the 'articles' and 'ways' mooted in the previous eighteen months, but behind David's persistence with these clauses they now perceived duplicity and hostile intent. According to the near-contemporary English chronicler, John of Reading, Edward even berated the Scottish envoys, demanding that they send a delegation to an English parliament at York and place men-at-arms at English diposal instead of preparing to attack England while her troops were in Castile under the Black Prince Edward of Aquitaine and John of Gaunt.[74] The spectre of Edward I in 1294–6 lived on.

Edward III may have been right to suspect David. There is ample evidence that from mid-1368 onward – despite the truce – ambitious border lords like Archibald Douglas and George Dunbar, by then tenth earl of March, used

---

73 *RPS*, 1367/1/1; *RRS*, vi, nos. 366–8, 500; *RMS*, i, nos. 231, 246–7, 251. *ER*, ii, 172 for John Drummond as a collector of clerical tax in Brechin diocese.
74 NAS SP6/5; *Chron. John de Reading*, 180, 347–8. The usual Scottish envoys had received a pass to England on 18 August 1366 valid until 2 February 1367 (*Rot. Scot.*, i, 909–10).

force to recover Scottish march lands under English occupation: it will be shown that by then both these lords were very close to David II. But their aggression towards England may have started much earlier, taking up where the earl of Douglas had left off in 1358 in recapturing Hermitage castle. Certainly in 1366 the Priory of Durham could complain that their hospital at Tweedmouth had been burned by Scots: the following year, the Bishop of Carlisle wrote to David to complain about the growing frequency of breaches of the truce. This in turn provoked unofficial English raids into Annandale.[75] But in 1367 English fears may also have been roused by Scottish aggression elsewhere in opposition to the plans of the Plantagenet crown. According again to John of Reading, Scots were not only present in the French forces of Henry of Trastamera when he was defeated by the English at the battle of Najera on 3 April 1367, but, after the Anglo-Scottish talks broke down, Reading alleges that Scots left their realm to ally with the Danes and Norwegians in plundering Ulster. Both these unsubstantiated assertions may be echoes of Scottish incursions encouraged by Robert Steward, especially the aggression in Ireland, where in 1365 the Scottish crown had envisaged west-coast Scots serving Edward III.[76]

Revived anger against Stewart armed followers may in part explain why on 31 May 1367 David was to be found at Perth – close to the Steward lordship and castle of Methven – to issue a charter of the earldom of Atholl to John Stewart and his Drummond wife. This was an act witnessed by the usual royal inner circle, the bishops of St Andrews and Brechin, the earls of March and Douglas, Robert Erskine, Walter Haliburton, David Annan and John Edmonstone. But it must first have required the Steward's resignation of Atholl to the king in court. The charter itself makes it clear that John was to provide for the 'deficiencies' of his father, presumably in dealing with the lawlessness in Atholl and beyond into Badenoch which parliament had had cause to cite in 1366 and on which David had given notice in April 1367. But in doing so, David in part wrested away official control, at last, of the earldom which his nephew had forced the king to concede to him in 1342; still, John Stewart, like his father, was also denied full title to this ancient land. A fortnight later, on 15 June, David again issued letters reaffirming the bishop of Moray's powers over Badenoch and Strathspey *vis à vis* royal justiciars of the earldom of Moray (headed by William Keith the Marsichal).[77]

75 *CPR*, iii, 534; *RRS*, vi, no. 379; CRO, DRC1/1 fo. 155; A.J. MacDonald, 'Crossing the Border: a study of the Scottish military offensives against England, *c.*1369–*c.*1403' (unpublished Ph.D. thesis, University of Aberdeen, 1995), 1–17, and *idem*, *Border Bloodshed*, 21–2.
76 *Chron. John de Reading*, 184; Goodman, 'A Letter from an Earl of Douglas to a King of Castile', 68–78, 69; Sumption, *Hundred Years War*, ii, 546–8.
77 *RRS*, vi, nos. 372, 374; *Registrum Episcopatus Moraviensis*, no. 287.

However, while the Atholl grant was an olive-branch to John Stewart, it was also further proof that David had given up the idea of persuading a majority of his subjects and Edward III to accept the Anglo-Scottish peace terms mooted in 1365–6: for Atholl had been one of the titles claimed by the Disinherited. It could be said that the transfer of the main Stewart earldom was in fact a punitive measure made from a position of increasing crown weakness. With the failure of the talks – and active English fears of war – David lashed out at the Steward over an old score. The result, besides, may have been effective only on paper: there is little evidence that John Stewart possessed effective control of Atholl before 1371, and the northern law-lessness continued. Far from being a major body blow to the Steward, this act may in fact reflect a mounting sense of vulnerability for the still childless king – a weakness which he worked even harder to remedy throughout the rest of 1367.

Royal Policy Unravels, June 1367 to May 1368

The surviving royal acts from June to late September 1367 give an im-pression of relative calm in royal Scotland. These included grants to such royalist knights as Sir Alexander Ramsay, grand-nephew of the famous knight; Alexander Stewart of Cambusnethan; esquire John Herries (the Poitiers veteran now given a regality of Terregles in Dumfriesshire); and John Craigie and John Crichton (each given a Roxburghshire barony resigned by the bishop of St Andrews).[78] However, such low-key items of business may hide fraught efforts on David's behalf to avoid a full breakdown in relations and possible conflict with England as well as trouble ahead at home.

The king was at first successful. In early September 1367, at Morislaw in Roxburghshire, fresh arrangements were concluded for 'great days of march' to settle border disputes at designated meeting places in the east and west marches: there is evidence that these arbitrations were working again by the end of that month with the restoration of Dunbar family lands to the Priory of Durham.[79] However, in doing so David had had to take careful precautions, as with parliament and council, to ensure that matters progressed as he – and not his magnate detractors – saw fit. Thus the Scottish representatives at Morislaw were headed by Archibald Douglas as Warden of the west march. But the posts of Wardens of the middle and east marches were shared on this sensitive occasion by the usual incumbents, the earls of Douglas and March, joined by the predominantly royalist crew of the bishops of St Andrews and Glasgow (Walter Wardlaw, the former

---

78 *RRS*, vi, nos. 373, 375, 376; *RMS*, i, no. 267.
79 *CDS*, iv, no. 134; *RRS*, vi, no. 386; Neville, *Violence, Custom and Law*, 51–9.

ambassador archdeacon of Lothian, secured in this see by the king by 14 April 1367), Robert Erskine, Walter Leslie, Walter Haliburton, Hugh Eglintoun and Duncan Wallace (the sheriff of Ayr). That the two former rebel earls were upset by these chaperones and the independence of royal action in general is made plain not only by March's apparent refusal to hand over his seal to append to this border agreement, but by the two earls' 'contumacious absence' at a long parliament held at Scone from 28 September until 20 October 1367: in 1368–9, the Douglas earl would continue to be 'indisposed' to co-operate on border matters.[80]

The recorded statutes of this parliament of autumn 1367 make it clear that all negotiations for peace with England had come to a standstill for now.[81] All David could salvage from this stalemate was the estates' permission that should the opportunity for fresh talks arise, then the king could appoint envoys to send south without first seeking the approval of council or parliament – something he had done on occasion anyway since 1363. However, David was surely able to extract this concession from his subjects with apparent ease because he and his close advisers had once again moved to control the personnel and agenda of what might be a difficult assembly. The absence of Douglas and March must have helped, but the king was also placed at an advantage by the first instance of a bureaucratic development celebrated as enlightened administrative 'progress' by nineteenth- and twentieth-century constitutional historians of Scotland, the 'election' of committees of representatives from each estate to attend to business while the remaining members were spared time and expense and gladly went home to deal with the harvest. The men named to stay on this occasion were dominated by crown supporters with Robert Steward and his third surviving son, Robert, lord of Menteith, surrounded, at least, by Bruce-friendly churchmen and burgesses as well as John Stewart of Kyle, Keith the Marischal, Robert Erskine, Archibald Douglas, Walter Leslie, Haliburton and Eglintoun.[82]

Yet by this stage David badly needed such potential support. The third 6,000-merk instalment of the ransom would be handed over to England on time in January 1368. But it was surely the case that despite the contributions and customs granted by recent estates' assemblies, the Scots were again beginning to struggle to raise sufficient funds for the king's remaining debts

80 *CDS*, iv, nos. 47, 100; *RPS*, 1367/9/11; *Foedera*, ii, 841; *CCR 1369–74*, 338. For Wardlaw as bishop, see Watt, *Scottish Graduates*, 569–75.
81 *APS*, i, 501–3 (*RPS*, 1367/9/1–14) for what follows of this assembly.
82 *Ibid*, 1367/9/1 and /8; Rait, *The Parliaments of Scotland*, 21–5, 240–5; *Acta Dominorum Concilii: Acts of the Lords of Council in Civil Causes, ii 1496–1501*, ed. G. Neilson and H. Paton (Edinburgh 1918), vii-xliii; Tanner, *Late Medieval Scottish Parliament*, introduction; Penman, 'Parliament Lost – Parliament Regained?'.

to England and his everyday domestic expenses. Between January 1366 and January 1367 some £4,526 had been collected as contribution alongside the Chamberlain's total receipts of just £5,714. But by the end of the fiscal year to January 1368 this contribution yield would remain constant only at the cost of leaving the Chamberlain just £1,731: non-payment of taxes, loans and donations from certain quarters clearly made inroads into the royal resources.[83] Any resulting default on David's obligations due to a drop in income – possibly leading to the king's re-imprisonment in England under the treaty of Berwick, if the Steward and other earls could evade this fate in his stead – might soon be added to the collapse of peace talks.

This was surely why an early recorded decision of the September 1367 parliament at Scone was to grant David a remarkable second Revocation, by the following Michaelmas (29 September), of all royal lands dating back to the 'time of king Robert or king Alexander [III]' (a suspiciously vague term perhaps designed to aid crown control of Fife), and all casualties of relief, ward and marriage as well as pensions therefrom: this was in addition to the Revocation David had secured but scarcely used in 1357. Admittedly, the parliamentary representatives did insist that this should be applied evenly, even to regalities, and that no revoked lands or casualties were to be re-alienated by the king without the estates' 'mature' advice; similarly, anyone caught defrauding the exchequer (to which all items for revocation were to be reported at Perth in January 1368) or petitioning for relief or a pension was to be prosecuted. However, events would soon make it clear that this was another legalistic windfall which David could and would exploit. It would certainly become normal practice for Scottish kings to make only one such recovery of royal resources on their twenty-fifth birthday or as close to the start of their active majority as possible. But before parliament closed in 1367, the middle-aged David had already issued orders for the second Revocation to be proclaimed by sheriffs and bailies (beginning in Fife) and for individual letters to be issued to safeguard the resources of wealthy institutions like the abbeys of Scone and Arbroath.[84]

These steps promised some improvement in royal income but the parliament went further. Not only was there a further customs hike on all items except white wool – raising tariffs to four times the levels of 1357 – but David at last relented on a matter he had worked hard to resist in 1357–8. The parliament of July 1366, too, had insisted that Scottish coinage retain parity of precious metal content with England's specie. But now David

---

83 NAS SP6/6; *ER*, ii, 254–64, 286–91.

84 *RPS*, 1367/9/2–6 and /12–14; *RRS*, vi, nos. 382, 384. For discussion of David's use of feudal casualties, see: Duncan, 'The 'Laws of Malcolm MacKenneth'', 242–3; C.A. Madden, 'The royal demesne in northern Scotland during the later middle ages', *Northern Scotland*, 3 (1977–8), 1–24, at 2–3.

secured permission to devalue the Scottish mint and thus produce more ready money for the ransom.[85] On 7 October 1367, following a parliamentary ordinance of 27 September, the king authorised his Warden of the Mint and royal moneyer to debase the Scottish coinage by between 5 and 10 per cent. Thereafter, the mint at Edinburgh would produce twenty-three-and-a-half pennies per pound of silver as opposed to the English rate of twenty-two-and-a-half (although David's later issues consisted mostly of groats and half-groats of silver worth 4d and 2d): the king was to have 7d in every £ of new specie for his own ends. It must also have been about this time that David ordered an issue of the first Scottish gold coins. This was apparently a small run (of which only four examples survive today) of large 'nobles', worth eighty silver pennies, modelled closely on the issue of Edward III of 1351 and bearing the bold image of a king with armorial shield aboard a ship (representative of Mother Church) beneath a God-like hand stretching down from the clouds. David might well have wished for more such pennies from heaven. Both issues undoubtedly started Scotland's specie off on the steady downward spiral of devaluation which took it to the point where twelve Scots pound would be worth a single English pound by the early sixteenth century.[86]

Just what else this 1367 parliament discussed is unknown. Nor is there any evidence that the king moved to punish Douglas and March for their absence. Indeed, for the remainder of the year the king seems to have stayed in Edinburgh, his only act of note the confirmation of Simon Reed as constable of the castle (a grant which reflected Archibald Douglas's distractions on the borders).[87] Once again, David was presumably waiting upon developments in Anglo-Scottish relations and the completion of his clerks' surveys of what land could be revoked to the crown. By January 1368 some dialogue with London seems to have been re-opened: in that month Sir Walter Leslie was added to the usual embassy of three clerics and Esrkine to visit King Edward. In that month, too, the third 6,000-merk ransom instalment was paid.[88]

However, 1368 – the thirty-ninth year of David's reign – soon began to shape up to be more eventful than the year before. January 19 found the

85 *RPS*, 1367/9/9–10; *RRS*, vi, no. 385.
86 Nicholson, 'Scottish Monetary Problems in the 14th and 15th Centuries', 106; D. Bateson, *Scottish Coins* (Aylesbury 1987), 6; Grant, *Independence and Nationhood*, 240 (Table III: Currency Changes).
87 BL, MSS Harley 4693, fo. 6r; *RRS*, vi, no. 501; *RMS*, i, no. 279.
88 *Rot. Scot.*, i, 916–7. Leslie also received a separate safe-conduct to go to England on 26 January 1368 in company with the royalists William More of Abercorn, Alexander Lindsay of Glenesk, William Ramsay of Colluthie (junior), Richard Comyn, John Craigie and Roger Corry of Annandale, possibly to attend a tournament.

Scots king and his court (including the Steward, March and Douglas) at Strathord, the former Perthshire barony of the earl of Fife; from there David granted another charter of lands in Moray. A day later, the royal party was at Perth where the exchequer was receiving reports on revocation properties.[89] By 17 February the work of this body was sufficiently advanced to be presented to a general council scheduled at Edinburgh (for which the attendance list does not survive). But the brief records of this body make it clear that there were still deep divisions between the king and his chivalric circle on the one hand and several great magnates on the other. Although men like Walter Leslie, Alexander Lindsay, the Drummonds, Walter Haliburton, Robert Erskine, William, earl of Sutherland, Robert Bruce (the king's cousin), William Dischington, John Logie and William Keith were to be affected by the Revocation, the highest sum they were expected to pay to retain royal demesne gifted to them since 1329 was £100 (from the highly favoured Keith for the thanage of Aboyne) and most demands were for between just £10 and £30. A number of these men and other crown supporters would besides have their lands and casualties confirmed by the king 'notwithstanding' this parliamentary Revocation, a process David began on 25 February by confirming a pension to Cambuskenneth Abbey from crown demesne for the sake of his own soul and that of his queen.[90]

In contrast, Robert Steward was asked to pay £120 for his Badenoch lands which he had held by right of his wife since only 1355: the bishop of Moray, to whom the crown had given jurisdictional rights over the Badenoch tenants, was charged only £4. Elsewhere John MacDonald of the Isles was asked for £200 for Lewis and Lochaber and a further £200 for Garmoran. Finally, David seems simply to have forfeited the casualties of the sheriffdom of Aberdeen from William, earl of Ross, without any possibility of restoration, whilst at the same time confirming William Keith's control of a £10 rental and the person of Ross's pawn in Caithness, William Sinclair. Clearly, David's regime had used the Revocation to aim at nobles beyond the pale who had resisted contribution assessment in 1366. This must have heightened political tensions. Certainly, for Steward and Ross, these fines would be a preamble to open if intermittent confrontation with the king.

That it was the crown which actively sought these reckonings is evident from the events of the next few months. In early March the royal court moved north, first to Stirling then Perth between 4 and 8 March (astride David's birthday and presumably via St Monans), confirming three grants to

---

89 *RRS*, vi, nos. 387–8.
90 *APS*, i, 528–30 (*RPS*, 1368/2/1–2) for this assembly's records; *RRS*, vi, nos. 389–90. See also *ibid*, nos. 401, 504–5 ('notwithstanding').

Robert Stewart of Schenbothie (from Clackmannanshire). By early May, David had advanced into Moray (via Aberdeen) to Elgin and Forres, ordering the judicial officers of Inverness-shire to give the justice teinds of the bishopric of Moray to its prelate: the Steward and March – with concerns at Badenoch and Moray – were among the witnesses to these acts, but not the earl of Douglas.[91]

Yet according to William, earl of Ross, the real purpose of this trip was to enforce not merely the revocation of some of the crown demesne in the north and north-east held by the Rosses, but the transfer of *all* of his holdings, as well as those of his brother and heir, Hugh Ross of Philorth, to Sir Walter Leslie, his son-in-law by 1367. In his written complaint lodged with Robert II's first parliament in June 1371, the earl of Ross would insist that, faced with this prospect, he had written to Robert Steward, Thomas earl of Mar, William Keith (then 'lieutenant of the earldom of Moray'), Patrick, bishop of Brechin the Chancellor, and Euphemia Ross, his sister (John Randolph, earl of Moray's widow and the Steward's second wife), asking them all to help his attorneys recover his lands from the king.[92] If this fear of disinheritance by David can thus be dated to late 1367–early 1368, it may explain why the Ross earl, too, was cited for 'contumacious absence' from the Scone parliament of autumn 1367 alongside Douglas and March.

However, Ross's complaint continued, his letters to the key magnates of the north had been entrusted to a clerk, John de Gamery from Caithness, who:

> was waylaid on his journey by John de Aberchirder, calling himself the esquire of the said Walter Leslie, who arrested him, abused his servant because he would not tie his master to the tail of his horse, despoiled him of his letters, and took him into woods and waste places, compelling him to deliver up the box containing the letters to the said Sir Walter, and pay a ransom.[93]

As a measure of the kind of intimidation some of the great magnates of the realm would receive at the hands of the king's chivalric cadre in the last few years of David's reign, this was nasty, if fairly petty, stuff. As a result, when Ross 'came to the king at Aberdeen to complain and sue for his lands'

---

91 *Ibid*, nos. 391–6.
92 Forbes, *Ane Account of the Familie of Innes*, 70–3; Fraser ed., *Frasers of Philorth*, ii, 312–3; Boardman, *Early Stewart Kings*, 170; *Registrum Episcopatus Moraviensis*, no. 287 (Keith).
93 David would grant Leslie the thanage of Aberchirder in Banff in 1370 for one knight's service and with the added proviso that should the heirs to this land (the Lindsays of Crawford) recover its reversion, then Leslie would retain the superiority. Interestingly, the church of Aberchirder was dedicated to St Monan (*RMS*, i, no. 316, 339; Forbes, *Ane Account of the Familie of Innes*, 73–4).

sometime *c.* 1367–9, he was without support and found he could not do so without granting to David, 'for the use of John Logy', the Plater forest lands in Forfarshire. Yet even after he had made this grant the king tried to bamboozle Earl William over dinner with 'a great schedule of questions . . . [and] with many authorities of civil law'. In panic, Ross then fled back to his earldom and his brother Hugh went into hiding as a fugitive. But when the earl had to meet the king again at Inverness:

> the Lady Margaret of Logie, then Queen, with her council, hearing that I had thus returned without agreeing with Sir Walter [Leslie] nor with her, gave precept and command that I should be arrested and im-prisoned, and all my lands seized and recognozed in the king's hands.

Admittedly, some of these events would perhaps take place when David visited Inverness in late 1369: the transfer of Ross to Leslie would be completed in parliament in October 1370. But the initial encounters of this process may indeed have occurred in spring 1368 – as a sequel to Leslie's marriage to Ross's daughter, Euphemia, and perhaps in revenge for the demand of William and Hugh that an entail of their lands be the price for trying to help David get out of gaol in England in 1351–2.[94] If so, this clash may have been one of the last occasions when Queen Margaret acted in consort with her husband.

The Ross confrontation is stark proof that Margaret had become a liability after five years of fruitless marriage. She was clearly a formidable dynast and forceful character. She must have used considerable personal influence over David to build a significant territorial bloc for the Logie-Drummond kindred in central and southern Scotland: Ross's testimony raises the possibility that the king's favour to John Logie in Strathearn and Annandale in 1366 was the direct result of pressure from the woman who might give him a child (as does Kennedy's promise to report plots in the borders to the queen). In addition to her Perthshire dower lands, by 1368 Margaret was also drawing a substantial income from the customs and fermes of the burghs of Aberdeen and both Kinghorn and Inverkeithing on the Fife coast: she would later claim to the Pope that she had amassed a personal fortune of 8,000 gold nobles and 60,000 florins (about £14,400 sterling) as well as jewelry. These were acquisitions we have seen she was quick to protect.[95] There is evidence, too, of a dispute between Margaret and the bishopric of Glasgow before 1367; her direction of the king's power against Ross, with the advice of her own 'council', would also, as we shall

94 See above, ch. 5.
95 *ER*, ii, 131, 138, 154, 157, 259, 287, 297–8, 343, 344; NAS RH2/6 – Vatican Transcripts 1273–1395 (a papal letter of June 1374 to Robert II which lists all the possessions and lands claimed by Margaret).

see, be turned on Robert Steward and his fourth son, Alexander. But while Margaret's work for her own son may have been designed to protect him after David's death and the Stewarts' accession – thus admitting the couple's infertility – her grasping ambition even stretched beyond this life: sometime in 1368 she ordered a marble tomb from London for herself and David to be prepared in Dunfermline Abbey alongside those of St Margaret, the other MacMalcolm royals and Robert I, Randolph and Andrew Murray.[96]

All of this must have been highly provocative to great nobles expected to sanction and pay heavy taxes, revocation compositions and 'donations', as well as to do without royal patronage and an effective say in government between 1364 and 1368. At the time of the confrontation over Ross in spring 1368, Earl William certainly knew he could appeal to several enemies of both the king and queen. Patrick, earl of March/Moray was on his way out, making his last appearance in the written record in July 1368 before his death.[97] But the Steward was obviously a disgruntled royal target for money and labels of lawlessness in the north and shared an interest with Ross, his brother-in-law, in the earldom of Strathearn: John Logie was being intruded on both their family lands.

But at the same time Thomas, earl of Mar, too, had fallen out, seemingly for good, with his royal cousin over their five-year arrangement for the Mar earldom agreed in September 1362. By late 1367 Thomas was no longer in the pay of Edward III, effectively unemployed, and he returned to Scotland to find the crown's knights still in place on his lands. Under the second Revocation, moreover, by July 1368 David would have claimed back the valuable and strategically vital lordship of Garioch given to Thomas for his domestic and diplomatic support in 1358–9 (perhaps with the intention of granting it to Walter Leslie?). Mar must also have been angered by David's continuing favour in Moray to his former feud enemy, William Keith. Mar's presence in late May 1368, not with David in Inverness, but with his own brother-in-law and heir presumptive, William, earl of Douglas (who had been so enraged by David's attack on Mar in 1362), at Cavers in Roxburgh-shire, along with his knights John le Grant (the rebel envoy to France of 1359) and Thomas Balliol, seems a very ominous sign.[98] This heightened sense of shared magnate grievances against an aggressive crown inevitably infiltrated parliament once again.

96 *Registrum Episcopatus Glasguensis*, ii, nos. 304–8; *ER*, ii, 300, 348.
97 *RRS*, vi, no. 406.
98 *Ibid*, no. 404; *RMS*, i, no. 285; *Illustrations of the Topography and Antiquities of Aberdeen and Banff*, v, 160; *Liber Sancte Marie de Melros*, ii, no. 468. Other witnesses to these acts included Duncan Wallace, William Lindsay of the Byres and William Maitland. See Stringer, *Earl David*, 31–4 for Garioch.

Turning Point, June 1368

Indeed, some of the recorded decisions of the assembly held at Scone after 12 June 1368 paint an image of a realm by now on the verge of both serious internal and external conflict.[99] No record of those in attendance has survived, only a note of the 'prelates, nobles and burgesses having been summoned who there were willing and able to be present, some compearing by commissioners, however others being absent contumaciously'. This impression of poor and reluctant attendance is compounded by the tone of this parliament's recorded acts. Magnate disputes seem to have been dealt with first, clearing a backlog of appeals out of recent justiciar ayres which David may have accompanied north and south. The king's interest in some of these cases must have been less than impartial.

Tellingly, Sir David Annan, one of the king's chivalric cadre (a fellow prisoner in 1346 and a household chamberlain for Queen Margaret), along with 'the barons of the earldom of Angus', had been involved in a dispute with the earl of Ross's attorneys since July 1366 over a confrontation which had taken place at the justice ayres of Sir Robert Erskine held at Forfar and Dundee. Parliament's decision was that the earl's men were to be fined £10 for their part in what may have been Ross's refusal to give up the privileges and revenues afforded by his former office as justiciar: but appeals were to be held at a later date.[100]

A jurisdictional judgement was also given in a dispute between Robert Stewart, lord of Menteith, and Sir Archibald Douglas, the former insisting that the latter should have compeared in parliament to hear Stewart's claim by right of his wife – the widow of Sir Thomas Murray of Bothwell (d. 1361) – to the third of lands which Douglas held by right of his wife, Joanna, daughter of Sir Maurice Murray, earl of Strathearn (d. 1346): in this matter, the king was obliged to order both men to compear in a lesser court. But in yet another case the king fined William Borthwick and Alan Lauder the huge sum of £1,000 each, penalties which were to be guaranteed by Robert Steward, Duncan Wallace (sheriff of Ayr) and Sir William Lindsay of the Byres. The Steward must have looked upon both this decision against Lauder, a bailie for the Stewart lands in Berwickshire (as well as keeper of the Douglas earl's castle at Tantallon), and to some extent the Menteith ruling, as further slights to his family interests. A similar bias may also have been perceived by Thomas, earl of Mar, who was named as a guarantor for

99 *APS*, i, 504–6 (*RPS*, 1368/81–19) for what follows of this assembly.
100 *Ibid*, 1368/6/1; *ER*, ii, 225, 229. This dispute between Ross and the men of Angus may also have involved Walter Leslie who in March 1366 can be found dealing with England to settle debts of the late Thomas Stewart, earl of Angus (*Rot. Scot.*, i, 901). In 1371, Ross's complaint would assert that David had denied him suit at the justiciary court at Inverness (Forbes, *Ane Account of the Familie of Innes*, 72–3).

peace in a dispute between the Angus men, John Brown and Robert de Umfraville, on pain of the loss of £500: that William Keith was named as a guarantor on the other side indicates that this feud was part of these lords' long-running antipathy.[101]

However, such local disputes aside, this parliament linked the more general threat to the peace of the realm from unchecked violence in the north directly to the current poor state of relations with England. More so than in any previous meeting of the estates, it was now felt – as a result of the report of the ambassadors just returned from England – that it was 'not profitable to enter into nor to attempt negotiation with the king and council of England upon having peace' based upon the articles and ways of 1364–7. This was clearly no longer a matter upon which David and his close counsel could simply dictate to managed meetings of the estates. In fact the record states that after 'mature deliberation and assiduous counsel *for four days and more . . .*' in parliament, it was ordained that since the truce was to last anyway until February 1370 – and thereafter the king of England had to give at least six months' warning of a return to war – 'it was still not proper nor expedient to enter nor attempt negotiation concerning the granting of any of the said points'. But the parliamentary record also asserted that these points for peace had already been rejected as 'unsuitable, intolerable and incapable of being observed, and expressly leading to servitude' by a recent full parliament (surely that of July 1366) 'at which more numerous and more important people were present than now are here present'.[102] This underlines the growing lack of co-operation which David faced from key members of the political community by mid-1368.

These stumbling blocks also reveal the high degree to which many Scots now expected – and, with no hostages to worry about, perhaps welcomed – a likely return to war and the end of controversial peace talks. It was with a view to preparing for fresh Anglo-Scottish conflict and the defence of the kingdom that it was enacted that 'all disagreements moved between magnates and nobles other than by the course of common law ought to be settled and laid to rest quickly by the king'.[103] To this end, it was further recorded that David had:

---

101 *RPS*, 1368/6/2–5 and /7; NAS GD45 Dalhousie Muniments II/16/31 and GD 86 Fraser Charters/7; Fraser ed., *Douglas Book*, i, 250–7. Lauder also served as a clerk of the justiciary south-of-Forth in the 1360s (MacQueen, *Common Law and Feudal Society in Medieval Scotland*, 81) and had received a charter from the earl of Douglas in 1366 (*HMC, xi Duke of Hamilton Papers*, 208). The June 1369 parliament also brought to peace the feuds between John Lindsay and Thomas Scott and between Patrick Gray and William Fenton of the Aird under pain of 1,000-merk fines (*RPS*, 1368/6/6).
102 *Ibid*, 1368/6/9–10.
103 *Ibid*, 1368/6/10.

by his own voice expressly warned and commanded the steward of
Scotland, the earl of Mar, John Stewart, lord of Kyle, and Robert
Stewart, lord of Menteith . . . that they shall preserve the communities
of the realm unharmed from all those living within the bounds of their
lordships.

In addition, parliament called for the king and Steward to constrain John
MacDonald, lord of the Isles, John Macdougall of Lorn and Gillespie
Campbell of Lochawe – all troublemakers cited by the estates in 1366–7
– to cease harm to others, pacifying the north and Isles in the event that the
political community might have to shelter there during war with England.[104]
To further prepare for that end, parliamentary discussion had resulted in a
decision that the king was to write 'immediately and with urgency' to the
king of England concerning 'days of repair' on the marches to ease tensions.
Significantly, it was also recorded that the former Wardens of the march in
the east, the earls of March and Douglas, were to have counsel with the king
about this post 'although they may not be now well disposed to the work'.
Archibald Douglas could be trusted as keeper of the west march but the
royal castles of Loch Leven, Edinburgh, Stirling and Dumbarton were to be
inspected by the knights Walter Leslie, Walter Haliburton, Hugh Eglintoun
and Walter Moigne and the current keepers (Alan Erskine, Archibald
Douglas, Robert Erskine and Malcolm Fleming respectively) who would
then report any repairs required. Useful baronial castles were also to be
inspected at the king's discretion and arrangements made for contracts of
manning and victualling with the noble owners of those found 'capable of
defence and impregnable': poorly maintained castles were to be cast
down.[105]

Such days of heated argument and raised voices, followed by all of these
preparations, would seem to suggest that David now recognised that his
policy of the last five years and more had run out of steam: his efforts had
brought him no decisive gains at home or abroad (except, perhaps, time).
Peace with England was not possible based on either the succession-ransom
deal of 1352/1359/1363 or the really more disruptive 'ways' and 'articles' of
territorial and fiscal compensation and military alliance suggested since
1364. The will of the majority of the Scottish political community – surely
egged on by Robert Steward as in 1364 – was now to pay the ransom until
war broke out. The estates would only have been confirmed in such a
prognosis by developments on the continent in 1368 where Charles V of
France seemed poised to both intervene again against England in Castile and
to reclaim authority over Gascony, exploiting the unpopularity there of

104 *Ibid*, 1368/6/11–12.
105 *Ibid*, 1368/6/13–15.

English taxes and mercenary companies throughout war-torn France: Anglo-French war and the possibility of Franco-Scottish alliance would result from this breach of the stillborn treaty of Brétigny.[106]

Admittedly, hidden within the 1368 parliament's decisions were powers the king could once again use to reduce and control the influence of those great magnates who had fallen foul of and resisted his policies since his liberation from England. But David's time for dictating policy, stringing talks along and reaping the benefits of unavoidable taxes and magnate acquiescence had arguably run out. Remarkably, the June 1368 parliament was the first since 1357 which did not grant additional tax contributions to help pay the ransom. All that was done was to raise the wool custom again (to meet the hike on other goods imposed in 1367) until the ransom was paid, the truce ended or this revenue was otherwise directed to the king's expenses.[107] The taxes granted in 1366–7 were still in place and the royal revenue for the fiscal year to January 1369 would be a solid £8,383 (leaving David £331 in the black after the ransom had been paid and able again to redeem his jewelry, pawned at Bruges).[108] But if the truce was broken, David would lose future levies.

With the advantage of hindsight, then, it is clear that this parliament must have signalled to the king that to meet this new state of affairs – the very real likelihood of war with England at some point in the future – he would soon have to realign his political influence in Scotland. Over the next few months he would do exactly that, seeking the closer support of lords and knights capable of both fighting the old enemy and containing the Bruce regime's magnate opponents at home. But for David this watershed also meant reaching another momentous decision: the abandonment of his issueless and increasingly unpopular marriage to Margaret Logie. He would have to do this if he was to avoid in late 1368 the same kind of vulnerability he had suffered in 1359 when, separated from his first wife, some of his great magnates had forced him to ditch talks with England and seek alliance with the then Dauphin Charles of France.

Later events again suggest that the first sign that Margaret was on her way out was another royal act issued at the end of the difficult Scone parliament of 1368. On 22 June the king granted the Bruce family earldom of Carrick to 'our beloved kinsman', John Stewart of Kyle and his wife, Annabella Drummond, and their heirs.[109] Parliament's demand that Kyle be ordered to pacify his lands was surely not a direct criticism of his lordship, rather a

106 Sumption, *Hundred Years War*, ii, 569–74.
107 *RPS*, 1368/6/16.
108 *ER*, ii, 80, 263, 291; Stevenson, 'Medieval Associations with Bruges', 99.
109 *RRS*, vi, no. 400; *APS*, i, 531 (*RPS*, 1368/6/18); Boardman, *Early Stewart Kings*, 22–5

mandate for him to act in his new earldom of Atholl, resigned by his father the year before. But now the addition of Carrick was surely not merely a further sign that David recognised that Kyle would most likely succeed him on the throne as things stood. It was also perhaps given as a form of compensation to John Stewart in advance of the imminent devaluation of his marriage to a Drummond when David annulled his own marriage with Annabella's aunt. That this drastic royal attempt to salvage something from the stagnation of the royal marriage and crown policy between 1364 and 1368 was also deeply unpopular with David's opponents is suggested by the witness list of 'the three estates' appended to this crucial grant to John Stewart: the bishops of St Andrews, Brechin and Dunblane, Thomas, earl of Mar, Robert Erskine, William Keith, Archibald Douglas, Hugh Eglnitoun and William Dischington all attached their seals – but those of the Steward and earls of Douglas, March and Ross were all missing.

ELEVEN

All the King's Men: 1368–70

'And his men that were with him did David bring up, every man with his household . . . these be the names of the mighty men whom David had . . .'

II Kings 2:3 and 23:8[1]

The New Bruce Party, July 1368 to January 1369

Five years of further repetitive effort in diplomacy and domestic politics (and, presumably, in the royal bedchamber) had come to nought for David II. By midsummer of 1368 the crown and its close supporters were sorely aware of the dangers of further forcing on parliament moribund negotiations and unpopular finance. The king could no longer afford to remain locked into increasingly unworkable plans for peace with England. Nor could he depend so heavily at home upon support from a group of men of chivalry interested primarily in European or African adventure, many of whom had forsworn war with England: in the likely event of such conflict, David would instead need to be able to call upon nobles and knights effective in aggression on the border. But most urgently of all, he had to be rid of his unhelpful second wife.

According to Abbot Bower, David's divorce from the 'evil' influence of Margaret Logie was completed about Lent 1369, *c.* 14 February. However, while that may be true, as we have seen, these proceedings were begun months earlier. Margaret's last official appearance as queen in the extant government record dates from 4 January 1368, when the king requested another safe-conduct for both of them to go on pilgrimage to Canterbury. They never made the trip. In late March that year, David alone sought a safe-conduct for William Calebre, Margaret's chamberlain, to pass to England on official business.[2] The queen may have been with David in the north-east of Scotland in May when the earl of Ross fell foul of royal intimidation. But as we have seen, the June parliamentary grant of the earldom of Carrick to John Stewart surely signalled the beginning of her end.

Again according to Bower in the 1440s, the reason cited for the annulment was Margaret's failure to bear David an heir. But one of the abbot's

---

1 Vulgate reference; or 2 Samuel 2:3 and 23:8 (NEB).
2 *Chron. Bower*, vii, 359; *Rot. Scot.*, i, 917, 921; *ER*, ii, 345 (payment in process of divorce 1368–9).

later continuators, the chronicler of the priory of Pluscarden in Moray, would further insist that Margaret 'had pretended to be with child but was not'.[3] This was surely closer to the justification which David would have preferred to present to the Papacy through a Scottish churchman-lawyer like David de Mar, past treasurer of Moray and by 1367 the new archdeacon of Lothian.[4] Remarkably, though, even the faint possibility of an heir may have bought Margaret a little more time. Bower asserts that just before her divorce the queen persuaded David to arrest Robert Steward and his fourth son, Alexander Stewart of Badenoch, only to release them in time for a parliament at Scone (which Bower does not date).[5] An anonymous Scottish chronicle fragment following John of Fordun's work dates this arrest precisely to Edinburgh on 13 October 1368: an exchequer entry does record payment for the ward of the Steward and his son at Loch Leven Castle in Fife sometime between January 1368 and January 1369.[6] Thus this antipathy between queen and royal heir presumptive in autumn 1368 could just as easily have flared over the threat of an eleventh-hour Bruce succession as over territorial disputes in Strathearn, Atholl and lands further north.

Yet in reality Margaret – with the annulment set – may only have been acting in the autumn to protect the interests of her son, John Logie. An act issued by David at Edinburgh on 26 July 1368, again granting the regality of Logie in Strathearn to John after its resignation by the Steward (an act first issued to Logie in July 1366), clearly underlines the crown's desire to maintain the presence and support of the Drummond-Logie menfolk in Perthshire.[7] By January 1369 David would also have overseen the transfer to John Logie of Margaret's *fermes* in the *Abnethia* of Dull – which had been worth £54 to the Steward in 1361. Margaret's Perthshire lands of Stobhall, Cargill and Kyndeloch would similarly be passed to Maurice Drummond. In addition, by January 1369 David would have reclaimed for the crown Margaret's other Perthshire and Fife dower lands as well as the *fermes* of Aberdeen (worth £962 in March 1368). The discarded queen was left with only a pension of £100, of which David had paid just £92 by 1370.[8]

---

3 *Liber Pluscardensis*, 233. Adam Abell asserted similarly that 'because sche wes barret he put hir fra him' (S.M. Thorson, 'Adam Abell's "The Roit and Quheill of Tyme": An edition' (unpublished Ph.D. thesis, University of St Andrews, 1998), 207).

4 Watt, *Scottish Graduates*, 382–4.

5 *Chron. Bower*, vii, 333.

6 Bodleian Library, Oxford, MS. Fairfax 23, folios 110r-116v; *ER*, ii, 309 (Stewarts' ward), 349 (repairs to castle). Many thanks to Steve Boardman for this chronicle reference which provided evidence to correct my original suggestion that the Steward and his son were arrested in spring 1368 with the Steward absent as a royal charter witness from 10 May to 14 June (Penman, 'The Kingship of David II', 463–4, *RRS*, vi, nos. 394–7).

7 Ibid, nos. 353, 406.

8 *ER*, ii, 298; *RRS*, vi, nos. 421, 428.

However, there were two allied strands to this new royal marital policy, the second of which may do more to explain the timing of the Steward's arrest in October 1368. For David initiated his divorce with the clear intention of wedding another younger, better-connected woman. The fact that she was also Scottish – rather than, say, an English bride – is proof that the stabilisation of his position at home was still David's primary concern. But it is possible, too, that this woman had already become the king's mistress long before mid-1368.

This new comely focus of royal hope was to be Agnes Dunbar, the sister of George and John Dunbar, half-nephews and heirs to Patrick, earl of March/ Moray (and all children of a Randolph mother). These two were vigorous, clearly ambitious esquires in their twenties who had already shown a desire to follow their father, Sir Patrick Dunbar (d. 1357), as warriors against England and as crusaders: they had already received some patronage from the crown since 1357. That Agnes's elevation to royal mistress heralded her brothers' rapid ascent in royal favour is confirmed by David's two grants to George on 25 July 1368, at the end of a month's stay at Stirling. Most significant of all, one of these acts confirmed to George the resignation of the earldom of March itself. The octogenarian Earl Patrick was last present as a royal charter witness the next day (to David's charter to John Logie): Patrick must have died shortly thereafter, thus cementing the reversion of the earldom of Moray to the control of the crown.[9]

But as well as looking more directly to Agnes's relatives as vital royal supporters in the south-east and border marches, David's marriage plans also drew him closer to the Dunbars' neighbour, Sir James Douglas of Lothian. In December 1372 Agnes would be contracted by her brother, George, tenth earl of March, to wed this James Douglas, by then styled of Dalkeith in East Lothian. Yet it is possible that this had been a match intended originally to take place in 1368, until David II himself had stepped in to take advantage of Agnes's connections. For either match to take place, though, Agnes would have had to be separated from her first husband – to whom she had already borne two sons – Sir Robert Maitland of Thirlestane, the head of a Lauderdale and Peeblesshire family in the service of the Douglas and March earls.[10] This expedient divorce and rearrangement of intended spouses must have raised some adverse comment from contemporaries. Abbot Bower may later have alluded to David's regard for 'other men's wives as superior to his own wife . . . Royal morals will be lacking, he will lose respect'. Georgian and Victorian historians followed this lead in

9 *Ibid*, no. 405; *RMS*, i, nos. 291–2.
10 *Scots Peerage*, v, 280–7; *APS*, vii, 159; *RRS*, vi, no. 509; Fraser ed., *Douglas Book*, i, 250–7; Brown, *Black Douglases*, 48, 100–3; Boardman, *Early Stewart Kings*, 23, 37 n120.

condemning David's adulterous ways.[11] But David had interfered in magnate marriages before (Fife, Mar, Angus, Menteith) and that this was his intent in 1368 is betrayed by the shower of patronage directed upon James Douglas (and the Maitlands) in the months following the June 1368 parliament at Scone.

The educated and well-read James Douglas's rise was indeed impressive.[12] At Dundee on 28 November, David confirmed a grant of Fife lands by the late Earl Duncan to James's late uncle, William Douglas of Liddesdale; the king also confirmed a grant by the Steward to William of lands in the West Lothian barony of Bathgate (lands originally given to the Stewarts as a wedding gift by Robert I in 1315–6). Both these acts seem to represent royal recognition of James as Liddesdale's heir by right of the controversial tailzie forced on the king in 1342. Then at Edinburgh on 2 December David gave James the royal annual rents pertaining to the lands of Eshiels in Peeblesshire for life: he also seems to have overseen an exchange of some of Queen Margaret's lands between James and Walter Moigne and Thomas Bisset (junior, son of the late lord of Fife).[13]

This was followed at Perth by a council between 8 and 10 December for which no recorded proceedings survive.[14] Three royal charters do remain for 9–10 December, one of which saw David order his justiciars south-of-Forth (Sir George Abernethy, Sir John Edmonstone and Thomas Irvine) to make an inquest of mortancestor into the right of James Douglas to succeed his uncle, Liddesdale, in the lands of the baronies of Kilbucho and Newlands in Peeblesshire. But most striking of all, David added to this on 5 January 1369, while still at Perth, by granting James the right to construct a new castle in the East Lothian barony of Dalkeith.[15] Clearly, the king had granted this valuable estate to James sometime in the previous six months following a resignation by Earl William of Douglas: Froissart would later record that in 1365 he had visited Dalkeith then in the earl's possession.

---

11 *Chron. Bower*, viii, 41. Bower cites this prophecy by the 'seer of Bridlington' with reference to David Stewart, Duke of Rothesay (d. 1402), but this may be propaganda spread by Albany and Douglas to play up 'the rioutous living and convivial acts' of their political opponent, borrowed from talk of David II's reign (S. Boardman, 'The Man who would be King: The Lieutenancy and Death of David, Duke of Rothesay, 1399–1402', in N.A.T. Macdougall and R.A. Mason eds., *People and Power in Scotland: Essays in Honour of T.C. Smout* (Edinburgh 1992), 1–27).

12 *Registrum Honoris de Morton*, ii, no. 193; Grant, 'Service and Tenure in Late Medieval Scotland', 147–8.

13 *RRS*, vi, nos. 409–13; *ER*, ii, 297. For 1316, see *RRS*, v, nos. 378, 391.

14 *APS*, i, 297, App. 34, p. 172 (*RPS*, 1368/12/1). At least the bishops of St Andrews and Brechin, the Steward, the earl of Douglas, Keith, Erskine, Archibald Douglas, Walter Haliburton and John Herries were in attendance (*RRS*, vi, no. 415).

15 *Ibid*, nos. 415–7, 419.

That David would later have cause to issue a second grant of Dalkeith to James suggests strongly that Earl William would attempt to resist what he must have seen as the crown's design to restore James to the knight of Liddesdale's full lands and offices in southern Scotland (including the sheriffship of Roxburghshire).[16] A new fortress at Dalkeith could, if need be, give the crown in Edinburgh extra protection against the Douglas earl at Tantallon. But other lords must have felt hard done by with David's favour to James. On 3 February 1369, back at Edinburgh, the king gave James lands in the royal constabulary of Kinghorn in Fife (from where Queen Margaret had drawn cash) free of obligations of duties and pensions; then, while at Methven in early 1369, Robert Steward also seems to have been obliged to resign the lands of Kellor in Strathearn to James, an act later confirmed on 1 February 1370 by Euphemia, Countess of Strathearn and Moray, the Steward's independent-minded second wife.[17]

For David, closer relations with James Douglas were well worth such a price, for they strengthened connections with his cousin, Sir Archibald Douglas. The 'Grim' knight and leader of a considerable armed following was already keeper of Edinburgh Castle – proving invaluable in the crisis of 1363 – as well as Warden of the west march and lieutenant in the crown-Logie lordship of Annandale: by late 1369, Archibald's position would be recognised officially with his elevation to the former Bruce (once Balliol) lordship of Galloway. But Archibald was also Douglas of Liddesdale's heir alongside James by dint of the tailzie of 1342 and an illegitimate claimant to the Douglas earldom.[18] David had been especially careful in mid-1368 to keep both these alternative scions to the Douglas earl happy in crown service by safeguarding their inheritance. This had involved David's careful intervention in a magnate dispute which threatenened to shatter his new royal coalition before it had even had a chance to function.

A justiciar's assize of 1 June 1367 at Dumfries had declared James Douglas of Lothian's right to the Dumfriesshire and Galloway lands of Marie, late daughter of Douglas of Liddesdale. However, as we have seen, Marie had returned to Scotland from England about 1363 after cleric William Calebre (originally from Mar but by 1362 a crown man) had negotiated the reversion of her initial 'sale' across the border by Sir William More of Abercorn in 1360–1. Sometime before 1367, though, Marie had wed Thomas Erskine, Sir Robert's son, only to die with a stillborn child.

---

16 *Oeuvres de Froissart*, iii, 207–9 and v, 119–20; Contamine, 'Froissart and Scotland', 53. For the 1342 tailzie of Liddesdale lands, see *RRS*, vi, nos. 42, 45, 51.

17 *Ibid*, no. 425; *Registrum Honoris de Morton*, ii, no. 110. The Steward's grant was witnessed by Robert Erskine, John Stewart (the Steward's brother), Thomas Erskine, John Herries, David Annan, Patrick Hepburn and Alexander Stewart.

18 Brown, *Black Douglases*, 53–75.

Thomas claimed the child had lived long enough for him to be heir to the Liddesdale inheritance: James Douglas challenged him. By mid-1368 the two esquires were irreconcilable and the king had to give permission for them to fight a trial by combat in the royal park at Edinburgh. Armour was bought for the pair in England and they were knighted in turn by their elders, Sir Robert Erskine and Sir Archibald Douglas. But according to the annals of Fordun's chronicle, after the first few blows:

> the king mediated very carefully between them, and after the said Thomas had been given a certain sum of money which had already been offered by the said James in previous negotiations, and a further sum by the king himself out of his own magnificence for the sake of concord and because of his affection for both parties, Thomas yielded his claim. Both parties were led simultaneously from the park and the whole lands of that lord William remained with the said James by hereditary right.[19]

David's anxious personal intervention makes it clear that he had learned a bitter lesson resulting from the fallout from the Mar-Keith combat, also fought in Edinburgh, in 1362. In contrast to that occasion, in 1368 damage to the royal affinity was carefully avoided. The bond made by Robert Erskine and William More in 1363 (with vague promises to arbitrate in any dispute involving the Steward, Archibald Douglas, the earl of Mar, William Keith and Erskine with More) had underlined the capacity for such a dispute to disrupt wider factional lines as well as for the king to lay down contingencies to resolve conflict.[20] In parliament at Perth on 6 March 1369, David would significantly confirm a grant of Stirlingshire lands from More to Erskine: sometime in that year George Dunbar, too, would confirm a grant to More – an act witnessed by Archibald and James Douglas as well as the Dunbar men, William Dischington and Alexander Recklington. By late 1368 George also seems to have granted to James Douglas the useful castle-barony of Morton on the border not far from Dischington's peel at Liddale, an act confirmed by David the following year. But by then David had done much to smooth over the cracks and placate and reward all those integral to his new noble party.[21]

During the month he spent enjoying Sir Robert Erskine's hospitality at

---

19 *Chron. Fordun*, i, 370n; *Registrum Honoris de Morton*, ii, no. 83; *Rot. Scot.*, i, 916; *CDS*, iv, nos. 49, 63; Sellar, 'Courtesy, Battle and the Brieve of Right, 1368 – A Story Continued', 1–12.

20 NAS GD 124 (Mar & Kelly)/516.

21 *RRS*, vi, no. 427; NAS GD 28 Yester Writs/28. William More may also have been in dispute about 1369 with the Stewarts: on 17 April 1371 Robert II would order the archdeacon of Dunkeld to hear a suit between More and the Abbey of Paisley (NAS RH2/6 Vatican Transcripts I/19).

Stirling in July 1368, some of David's first acts had been to confirm Erskine possessions in Clackmannanshire ('notwithstanding' the 1367 revocation), in Forfarshire and in the former earl of Mar's possession of Garioch.[22] Furthermore, the Erskines would be closely tied in to the new Bruce-Dunbar marriage. By 1370 Sir Thomas Erskine would have taken over from Archibald the Grim as sheriff and keeper of Edinburgh Castle while his father, Robert, kept Dumbarton and Stirling: it was in the royal apartments in the latter castle that Agnes Dunbar would be installed in finery as the king's consort-in-waiting in 1370–71.[23] And, of course, it was into Sir Alan Erskine's care in Loch Leven Castle that father and son, Robert and Alexander Stewart, would be warded in October-November 1368. Finally, John Dunbar, too, joined Nicholas Erskine and James Douglas's brothers as esquires in the royal household.[24]

Understandably, magnates like the Steward and the earl of Douglas may have had even more cause to be alarmed by the prospect of this new crown coalition. Margaret Logie's removal and increased royal favour to particular kindreds threatened to give David even more direct power in central Scotland. For example, on 3 January 1369 Isabella, countess of Fife, probably in the face of royal duress (as with other acts she would issue before 1371), gave James Douglas a grant of a £20 pension from Fife lands. Then on 17 January 1369, while at Restenneth (where his infant brother's body was interred), David granted the Perthshire barony of Rait (gifted to Queen Margaret) to his cousin, Sir Robert Bruce of Clackmannan, settling a dispute over Stewart influence there which had first flared before 1346.[25] Robert Bruce was now added to a growing list of royal associates in this region, including the Erskines, Drummonds and David's half-brother-in-law, Walter Oliphant: by 15 March 1369 Margaret's former Perthshire lands of Ferdell would also have been alienated to the royal standard bearer, Alexander Scrymgeour of Dundee.[26] Coupled with David's confirmations to John Logie, and the possibility of a Bruce-Dunbar heir in the near future, such royal activity may have been enough to provoke Robert Steward into the beginnings of a pre-emptive reaction, one forestalled by his arrest at Edinburgh on 13 October 1368 and his imprisonment presumably until a fortnight or so before the council at Perth in early December. Stewart failure to deal with lawlessness in Badenoch – as cited by the June 1368 parliament – may have given the king a legitimate reason to detain the heir presumptive

22 *RRS*, vi, nos. 399, 402–3.
23 *ER*, ii, 357, 364.
24 *ER*, ii, 174, 176, 309, 347; Thomas Erskine and George Dunbar had already had a joint safe-conduct to go abroad in September 1364 (*Rot. Scot.*, i, 884).
25 *Registrum Honoris de Morton*, i, 78–80; *RRS*, vi, no. 421; see above, ch. 3.
26 *RRS*, vi, no. 428.

and his fourth son: it is possible that Alexander Stewart went back into ward a short time later, pointing to ongoing aggression in the north against Alexander de Bur, bishop of Moray. But there is a suggestive gap in the run of extant royal charters issued between 24 August and 12 November 1368, enough time for a near crisis to have flared and for the Stewarts to be gaoled.[27]

In sum, in the six months after the Scone parliament of June 1368, David had apparently successfully initiated the process of realigning his political interest and support in Scotland and breaking some of the deadlock of the last five years: in many ways he had recreated the radical new position he had secured through defeat of the three earls' rebellion and marriage to Margaret in 1363. Nevertheless, the king still had much work to do. The fact that the Steward was quite quickly released in late 1368 and that Margaret Logie was free to attempt to block David's finalisation of their annulment suggests he still had to tread warily. There might, after all, be a hefty price to pay for his unresolved relations with England and in return for revitalised Scottish support.

Re-invested Bruce Kingship, February to October 1369

Since the Scottish parliament's rejection of further peace talks with England in June 1368, Anglo-French relations had only worsened. On 19 November 1368, Charles V formally renounced the treaty of Brétigny: his troops were preparing to help Henry of Trastamera in Castile once again as well as to interfere in Gascony. The English could do little of significance to respond. Edward, the Black Prince and lord of Aquitaine, was chronically ill and bankrupt; Edward III himself was now in his sixties, and was beginning to show a decline in leadership qualities. English problems in Ireland had been compounded in October 1368 by the death of Edward's second son, Lionel, Duke of Clarence.[28]

All this surely meant that, more so than ever since 1357, there was a growing will in Scotland to either pay off in full or to simply scrap the king's ransom but above all to then resume war against England and alliance with France. David II must have been well aware that these were sentiments which could easily be shared not simply by the Stewarts and the earl of Douglas but by the crown's now closest chosen allies and future in-laws, Archibald and James Douglas and the Dunbars. Such anti-English aggression was an inherent part of these southern lords' outlook, their inheritance from the generation of Robert I and the 'good' Sir James Douglas, a natural force of lordship and identity which David could not totally resist. Scottish

27 *APS*, i, 297, 532; *RRS*, vi, nos. 407–8
28 Sumption, *Hundred Years War*, ii, 543–70.

raiding on the borders really had not ceased after 1346, the earls of Douglas and March certainly sanctioning stealthy recovery and expansion of their holdings between 1357 and 1368: Archibald Douglas, too, had been captured raiding northern England in the company of Douglas border followers in 1358–9. After David helped secure his release in 1362, Archibald looked to assert his own independent military lordship in the western borders. So it was that throughout 1369 and 1370 David would apparently condone – or at least not prevent – the increased harrying and recovery of English-occupied territory in the borders by the lesser Douglas scions, the Dunbars and their followings. As a recent study has shown, these raids in 1369–71 and beyond targeted lands in Annandale, Roxburghshire and Berwickshire, extensions of the west and east marches guarded by Archibald Douglas and earl George respectively.[29]

However, it should not be forgotten that for David this was not all bad news of uncontrollable magnate self-interest redirecting royal policy toward England. True, these raids ran the risk of provoking English attack. But in the meantime they also increased royal revenues from these regions through the recovery of land (including former Bruce family possessions). Moreover, they gave employment to knights and esquires within a Lothian and borders affinity shared by the Douglases, Dunbars and the crown. Yet far more importantly, if well-timed, this military pressure might also force Edward III and his council to make concessions to secure Scotland as a neutral ally in the event of full Anglo-French war: the death in battle of England's ally, Peter IV of Castile, on 14 March 1369 and Edward III's defiant resumption of the title of 'King of France' on 11 June 1369 seemed to make this inevitable.[30] Thus England might have been all the more inclined to concede to the Scots either an extension of the truce (beyond February 1370), a reduction of the ransom or, even better, a full peace and the return of border lands.

David certainly worked in pursuit of these goals throughout 1369 while his magnate partners asserted and expanded their lordship in the south. The first few months of this year give the impression of a much more confident king. At Dundee on 6 January 1369 David made crusader Sir Richard Comyn the keeper of the forest of Darnaway in Moray, replacing the rebel envoy of 1359, Sir John le Grant. This was the beginning of an itinerary which took the king through Montrose, Restenneth and Perth before returning to Edinburgh, and saw him extend favour to a number of knights,

29 *Rot. Scot.*, i, 848; MacDonald, *Border Bloodshed*, 12–20. A Scottish Church Council *c*. 1368–9 also sought a papal declaration of excommunication against English clerics imposed on the border benefices of the see of Glasgow (D.E.R. Watt, *Medieval Church Councils in Scotland* (Edinburgh 2000), 124–5).

30 Sumption, *Hundred Years War*, ii, 570–4.

including Robert Bruce of Clackmannan, James Douglas, James Blair (of
Ayrshire lands), Sir John Abernethy (Fife lands and an Aberdeenshire
pension), Sir Alexander Lindsay of Glenesk and Sir Alexander Cockburn;
the witnesses to these acts included the Steward and Douglas earl accompanied typically by the knights Robert Erskine, Walter Leslie, Walter
Haliburton, David Annan, John Edmonstone, Archibald Douglas and
William Dischington. All of this was in part by way of preparation for a
parliament at Perth held from 6 to 17 March 1369.[31]

Most of the recorded decisions of this assembly survive and make it clear
that David and his close counsel were determined to be even more bullish in
their control of events. The crown seems once more to have been selective in
just who it summoned to attend. Significantly, although William, earl of
Douglas (or at least his seal), is listed as a witness to several of the king's grants
issued during the parliament, he sent in a procurator to the chamber floor:
whether or not this was his own or the king's choice remains uncertain.[32] But
others (unnamed) were cited once more as being 'contumaciously absent' –
perhaps the earl of Ross and the MacDonald lord of the Isles. However, once
assembled, like the parliament of 1367, this body was reduced to committees
and the remaining members of the estates were sent home. A small group of
clerical lawyers – the bishops of Moray, Dunblane and Brechin, the abbot of
Dunfermline, David de Mar archdeacon of Lothian and several clerks (all very
much crown men) – were chosen to deal with falsed legal judgements,
although in the end these hearings were postponed due to Lent. But a larger
'general business' committee was also named: this included the Steward,
Douglas's proxy and Thomas, earl of Mar, but also George, the new earl of
March, Archibald Douglas, Robert Erksine, William Keith, Walter Leslie,
James Douglas, David Graham, Walter Haliburton, Alexander Lindsay,
William Dischington, David Fitzwalter,[33] Roger Mortimer, John Strachan,
Robert Dalziel (all listed as knights) as well as John Macdougall of Lorn,
Gillespie Campbell, John Kennedy, Alan Erskine, William Newbigging,
Alexander Cockburn, William Meldrum and Thomas Irvine.[34] This in itself
is a telling ranking of the realm's important men at this time.

The main concern of the business committee seems to have been with the
suppression of breaches of the peace and tax-evasion in the Highlands and
Islands first noted by the estates in 1366. But parliament in 1369 was still to
be directed in this vein against crown antagonists, decreeing that:

---

31 *RRS*, vi, nos. 419 to 426; *RMS*, i, nos. 239, 280, 281, 285, 287, 289.
32 For this detail and the rest of this parliament, see: *APS*, i, 173–5 (*RPS*, 1369/3/1–
    12).
33 Fitzwalter had been granted the Lanarkshire barony of Cadzow by the king while at
    Lindores on 27 December 1368 (*RRS*, vi, no. 418).
34 *RPS*, 1369/3/1–4.

the lord steward and his sons should answer in this way for the earldoms of Strathearn, Atholl and Menteith, and for all their other lands and lordships within the highland regions . . . to do full justice without delay and prevarication to transgressors . . . so also that amends should be made to the complaining parties . . . and that they should answer for, submit to and apply themselves to our lord the king and his ministers in the matter of collections and contributions . . .

Once again, oaths were extracted from Robert, John and Robert Stewart (junior) to this effect 'under certain penalties imposed upon them in the same place by the king': the absence of a mention of Alexander Stewart and Badenoch may indicate that the fourth son had returned to gaol as an incentive to overall Stewart co-operation. Elsewhere, similar obligations were to be placed upon the Highland lands of the earls of Mar and Ross, Macdougall of Lorn and Gillespie Campbell. All these men had been indicted by parliament before. But now separate attention was also given to empowering the crown or its agents to 'compel and force with a firm hand in diverse and convenient places John [MacDonald] of the Isles and his sons . . . to come to the king's obedience and stand to law, and undergo services and charges [taxes] with mainlanders'.[35]

These statutes were perhaps predictable. However, the insistence that the MacDonalds were now to be forced to contribute taxes hinted at a crown intention to continue paying the ransom. It was, then, in the parliamentary clause dealing with Anglo-Scottish relations that David was surely concerned above all to get his way: the implicit criticism in the Highland acts of his regime's failure to put down lawlessness could be tolerated if it was in part deflected onto his domestic and diplomatic opponents. In this, David seems in part to have prevailed, for parliament declared that Wardlaw and Erskine should be sent 'forthwith to negotiate with the English concerning the prorogation of the truce [beyond February 1370] if it can be had, or about beginning any other good negotiation'. Admittedly, only a 3d in the £ levy (an eightieth – half again of the 1367 tax) was to be raised to cover the envoys' expenses.[36] No other diplomatic contingencies were made: the estates would wait and hear what the ambassadors encountered. Nonetheless, that this was what David himself was really committed to – the pursuit of talks underpinned with unofficial border aggression to procure a ransom reduction, truce extension or peace – is made clear by Edward III's grant on 10 March 1369 of a safe-conduct to the Scottish king and forty men

35 *Ibid*, 1369/3/5–7. This parliament also recorded that the disturbances in the north and Isles were still preventing payment of the annum owed since 1266 (and repledged in 1312) to Norway for the Western Isles (*ibid*, 1369/3/10).
36 *Ibid*, 1369/3/8.

to come to England: as in 1364, David must have requested this pass long before parliament met at Perth that month.[37]

With plans thus laid for Anglo-Scottish talks in April 1369, David used the next few weeks to further exploit the powers granted by parliament against troublemakers in the north as well as to dispense rewards to his Lowland supporters. The king had begun this process during the Perth parliament with several grants, headed by a gift of the vast upland lordship of Glen Lyon, between Strathearn and Atholl, to John Macdougall of Lorn and his wife, David's niece. As Stephen Boardman has suggested, this may have been quite an effective attempt by the crown to win back the active support of an Argyll neighbour of the Steward recently accused of tax evasion: by 1370 Macdougall would be working for the crown as bailie in the disputed *Abnethia* of Dull, Queen Margaret's former lands.[38] In theory this would give the crown an ally against the Steward, MacDonald and Ross, with authority over a swathe of territory and passages ranging from Macdougall's west-coast castles at Glencoe and Duror, through Glen Lyon across the bounds of the Steward's Perthshire lands to the former Fife earls' lordships of Strathord and Strathtay. In much the same way, David may also have sought to sway the local loyalty of Gillespie Campbell of Lochawe by granting him on 15 March 1369 a confirmation and exemption of relief for some of the Argyll coastal lands denied to him by the crown in 1358. David would continue to build upon this speculative interference over the next two years.[39]

However, David also granted favour at Perth to solid royalists like Sir John Lyle of Duchal (Stirlingshire lands), Alexander Scrymgeour, Sir John Abernethy (Kinghorn lands in Fife), John Edmonstone (the thanage of Boyne in Banff), Thomas Forrester and William Dischington, who was then styled as keeper of Liddale Castle in Roxburghshire (Fife and Edinburgh lands).[40] Then, back in Edinburgh on 10 April, David issued letters granting his secretary, John Lyon (who would rise to be Chamberlain under Robert II until his murder by his disgruntled former patron, Sir James Lindsay of Crawford), a pension from the northern justice ayre.[41] Four days later the king confirmed the foundation by 'Sir James Douglas of Dalkeith' of a

37 *Rot. Scot.*, i, 928. That the last act of this parliament ordained that Lanark and Linlithgow should replace Berwick and Roxburgh ('which are and ought to be') on the Court of Four Burghs' hearings at Haddington, underlines David's intention to recover these towns and their lands by treaty (*RPS*, 1369/3/11).

38 *RMS*, i, no. 237; Boardman, 'The Tale of Leper John and the Campbell Acquisition of Lorn', 231–2.

39 *RRS*, vi, no. 429.

40 *Ibid*, nos. 427, 428, 430; *RMS*, i, nos. 235, 236, 238, 241, 242, 293.

41 *ER*, ii, 358; *RRS*, vi, no. 431; *Chron. Bower*, vii, 389; Boardman, *Early Stewart Kings*, 79–81.

chantry in Dalkeith chapel. This grant's original witness list confirms the potent coalition of southern magnate followings which David had helped forge since June 1368: the bishop of St Andrews, Archibald Douglas, John Herries, William Dischington, John Edmonstone, John Abernethy, James, Henry and William Douglas (Dalkeith's brothers) and John and Walter Livingston.[42] Still at Edinburgh on 18 April, David confirmed to Sir William Cunningham (the former keeper of Carrick) Lanarkshire lands 'notwithstanding the recent revocation': to this the king added lands in Queen Margaret's former possession of Kinclaven in Perthshire in return for the service of one knight (as well as lands for Cunningham's son, Andrew). The main witnesses to these and other minor acts and letters issued at this time (to the Friars preachers of Elgin and Inverness and to Arbroath Abbey) were typically the bishops of St Andrews and Brechin, Archibald Douglas, Erskine, Dischington, Walter Leslie, Alexander Lindsay and Edmonstone, alongside the surely politically battered-and-bruised Steward and earl of Douglas.[43]

A number of these close royal councillors, though, would have been expected to hold the fort when, sometime after 22 April, David used his safe-conduct and left once more for London. The king took with him a group reflecting the recast magnate party around the crown, including Robert and Thomas Erskine, James Douglas of Dalkeith, John Edmonstone, William Dischington and cleric John de Carrick (the king's secretary and Chancellor by May 1370). Significantly, these men would not only receive gifts from the English monarch but borrow 1,000 merks as well which they would repay by February 1370 (the end of the truce as set in 1365).[44] Overall, their mission seems to have gone well. They arrived at Westminster by 16 May at the latest when, at David's request, Edward III pardoned some English townsmen who had plundered a wrecked Scottish ship. Edward had shown his 'brother' a similar courtesy of mercy in late 1363. It is thus likely that David was able to some small extent to trade upon what was left of their 'rycht gret specialtie' in personal terms to bridge the diplomatic drift and breaches of the truce of the past five years.[45]

Yet, by this juncture, it must have been the greater danger of imminent Anglo-French war which obliged Edward and his council to assure themselves of Scottish neutrality. Edward may not yet have been aware that

42 *RRS*, vi, no. 435.
43 *Ibid*, nos. 432–40; *RMS*, i, nos. 243–5, 290.
44 *CDS*, iv, no. 165; PRO E403 (Issue Rolls) /403 membranes 24 (£20 to Dischington), 25 (£4 to Robert Erskine and John Carrick), 26 (£266 to James Douglas, Erskine, Edmonstone and Carrick).
45 *CPR, xiv, 1367–70*, 235; *Chron. Wyntoun*, vi, 242.

French envoys had been despatched to Scotland and would be waiting for David upon his return.[46] Nonetheless, the English were sufficiently motivated to agree to extend the truce with Scotland for fourteen years (to 1384, when David would be sixty) as well as to discount the 1365 resetting of the full ransom and reduce the figure remaining to 56,000 merks: this would mean annual payments from the Scots of just 4,000 merks (or £2,667), a further reduction of 2,000 merks a year from the recalibrated rate of 1365, a full two-thirds less per year than the original 1357 treaty had demanded and taking account once more of 20,000 merks paid by the Scots before 1360 (but still ignoring the 5,000 merks paid late in 1359). In addition, the Scots were to receive half the rents and justice profits of the lands in Roxburghshire still occupied by the English. Moreover, David, too, was extended a personal loan of 1,000 merks by Edward III.[47]

This was the deal which David concluded at Westminster on 18 June 1369, after which he returned promptly to Scotland by 14 July to have a formal gathering of the political community ratify it at Edinburgh on 20 July.[48] In thus prolonging the truce the second Bruce king might indeed have been 'slightly out of touch with the [anti-English] attitudes of his subjects, the results of which were potentially or actually divisive'.[49] But in the difficult international circumstances of the late 1360s, this deal at least in part vindicated David's grasp of the wider context and his play of the long diplomatic game.

However, it was highly unlikely that David would simply have left Anglo-Scottish relations there, and there were real problems lurking in the background. Further Anglo-Scottish peace talks would take place throughout the rest of 1369 and 1370. David, as ever, clearly hoped to build on his first approach to negotiate a fuller peace, probably involving a total mitigation of the ransom and perhaps also some of the clauses tabled in talks between 1357 and 1368 – an English place in the succession, the restoration of the Disinherited, a mutual military alliance etc. Indeed, the 1,000 merks loaned to the various knights who had accompanied David south in May is

46 *Issue Roll of Thomas de Brantingham*, ed. F. Devon (London 1835), 396 – orders from Edward III to northern sea-captains to 'intercept the messengers of the King of France, being in Scotland' (cited in MacDonald, *Border Bloodshed*, 21).

47 PRO E39/37; *Rot. Scot.*, i, 933, 938; *RRS*, vi, no. 441; *ER*, ii, 345. 24,000 merks had been paid 1365–9.

48 PRO C71/49, m.3; *RPS*, 1369/7/1; *RRS*, vi, no. 444; *Rot. Scot.*, i, 934, 938; *CDS*, iv, no. 154. The Scottish seals included those of the bishops of St Andrews, Glasgow, Dunkeld, Brechin and Dunblane; the Steward, the earl of Mar, George earl of March, William earl of Douglas and John Stewart earl of Carrick; William Keith, Archibald Douglas, Robert Erskine, James Douglas, Walter Leslie, Walter Haliburton, Alexander Lindsay and John Carrick.

49 MacDonald, *Border Bloodshed*, 22.

reminiscent of the 600 merks which Edward III had paid Thomas, earl of Mar, to serve in his continental forces after 1359.[50] Some confidential (or unrecorded) plan to activate a mutual Anglo-Scottish alliance and present it to parliament for consideration may explain why safe-conducts to enter England and France (royal title to which Edward III claimed two weeks before closing his deal with David) were issued to key Scots in June 1369: this group was headed by Archibald and James Douglas, Robert and Thomas Erskine, William, earl of Douglas, John Stewart, earl of Carrick, Edmonstone, Sir William Cunningham, Hugh Eglintoun and John Herries of Terregles, although the inclusion of the bishops of St Andrews, Glasgow and Dunkeld and John de Carrick may simply indicate a more cordial reason for these passes, perhaps further talks or pilgrimage.[51] Military service for English pay in continental theatres, if pursued, was besides not going to be popular with everyone in Scotland. This idea had already been rejected on several occasions by the estates. The Steward and Douglas earl, moreover, could still play the French alliance counter-card: crucially, as in 1351 and 1354, these magnates had had at least a few weeks to entertain French envoys in Scotland while David was in London in May-June 1369.[52]

As to the money loaned to David by Edward III, this may have been used both as a general sweetener and – not in fact to kick-start David's rumoured idea of a pilgrimage or crusade – to aid his legal counsel tackling the spirited obstruction of Margaret Logie. Abbot Bower would later assert that, enraged by the planned annulment:

> Margaret secretly boarded a ship in the Firth of Forth (well supplied with money) and made for the papal court. She arrived at Avignon where the pope was then to be found. By making an appeal she transferred her legal case there, and disturbed the whole kingdom by her legal action.[53]

Although Margaret probably did not leave Scotland until after David's death in February 1371, her lawyers stopped the king's planned marriage to Agnes Dunbar dead in its tracks. If this legal suit was what David needed English gold for,[54] then it should come as little surprise that the English – confronted with continuing Scottish harassment on the borders despite the

---

50 *Rot. Scot.*, i, 836. In 1369, Edward was still paying Thomas of Mar and his brother, Thomas Balliol – PRO E403/438 membranes 9 (£10 to Balliol) and 29 (£20 to Mar).

51 *Rot. Scot.*, i, 931–3.

52 *ER*, ii, 328, 348.

53 *Chron. Bower*, vii, 359.

54 As per Guy de Dampierre's famous jibe of 1299 that 'the pope and cardinals are very greedy, and you can gain little or nothing . . . without doing them big favours and giving big presents' (Vale, *Princely Court*, 21).

new truce – would also (at least in 1371–2) help Margaret with her legal and travel costs: this might increase the possibility of an English succession to the issueless Bruce line. Disinclined though Pope Urban V was to help the English, his lack of sympathy for the Scottish king would extend both Edward III and Robert Steward a favour: separated but not divorced, David could not remarry and sire heirs. It may also have been as a means of winning back papal approval that David professed mounting interest in his later years in crusade to recover the Holy Land, a project close to Urban's heart.[55]

We should look upon events in Scotland throughout the rest of 1369 and into 1370 as taking place against a background of ongoing Anglo-Scottish talks – probably once more along the lines of 1365–8 – as well as a period of crown anticipation of breaking free of Margaret Logie and finally tying the knot with the new Dunbar-Douglas-Erskine coalition. Between July and September 1369, in which month a council was due to meet, David remained in Edinburgh to reward support for his domestic and diplomatic plans. Besides confirming the privileges of the abbeys of Melrose (then still under English jurisdiction), Holyrood and Arbroath, David granted the lands of Clerkington in Lanarkshire to Archibald Douglas on 1 August. On 20 August the king confirmed a charter by Patrick Ramsay of Colluthie, a son(?) of the former earl of Fife (d. c. 1364–6): on 9 November, the same Patrick Ramsay, described as David's esquire, would receive a gift of £30 from Edward III for his expenses to London and back. Before that, on 4 September, David gave Sir Alexander Fraser, sheriff of Aberdeen, all the lands of the former royal thanage of Durris in Kincardineshire for the service of a knight.[56]

The short general council which then met at Edinburgh after 16 September 1369 seems to have been dominated once more by David's knights and prelates. This assembly had been called to discuss the results of Anglo-Scottish talks held since March. The news that same month, that John of Gaunt would leave for Aquitaine with an army to help his elder brother, the Black Prince, fight off the French, may have inclined the Scots to await events on the continent once more. But no record of the estates' diplomatic

55 *CDS*, iv, nos. 193, 197 (safe conducts and a loan for Margaret from England in February and June 1372); *Chron. Bower*, vii, 361; Barrell, *The Papacy, Scotland and northern England*, 161–2; G. Mollat, *The Popes at Avignon, 1305–78* (New York 1963), 160–2, 265; Housley, *The Later Crusades*, 40–3, 67–9. A threatening letter of 1366 sent by the Turks to the Pope – proclaiming the sack of Alexandria and the repulse of David's friend, Peter I of Cyprus – seems to have been circulated around the European kingdoms at this time, probably to whip up support for a crusade: it is reproduced in *Chron. Bower*, vii, 449–51.
56 *RRS*, vi, nos. 445–48; *RMS*, i, nos. 303, 326, 347; *RPS*, 1369/7/2; *CDS*, iv, no. 165.

decisions has survived. Just what was proposed for peace – or whether or not there was further reaction against such talks and a condemnation of violence in the north of Scotland – is not known.[57] Nonetheless, the extant charters which David issued during this council give some hint of his intent and suggest that the crown was still largely in control.

On the first day of the council David inspected a grant of Robert I to the border abbey of Melrose of all the wardships, reliefs, marriages and justice profits from Roxburghshire up to a sum of £2,000 a year.[58] The revival of this grant must be taken to indicate that the English had complied with the terms of the truce renegotiated in June returning to the Scots half of the profits from English-occupied lands in that shire. But at the same time David also appointed Archibald Douglas to collect these revenues for the Abbey, a responsibility which had first been given to the Grim's natural father, the 'Good' Sir James.[59] Thus Archibald – described at this time as 'our dear and special knight' – was to some extent to be tied in by vested interest to David's peace policies. The knight seems to have been happy to contemplate the benefits of peace. As well as participating in border march days and collecting revenue, Archibald can be found sending his own men of business and merchants to trade in England: sometime in 1369 he concluded a private deal with the Percies – his English march counterparts – in which both parties agreed to present truce-breakers to each other.[60] Similarly, Walter Wardlaw, bishop of Glasgow and ambassador, had had his diocesan powers in the marches (which embraced Melrose Abbey) and his private mercantile rights in England recognised by Edward III as part of the June 1369 agreement: Edward thus dropped his support at Avignon for an English clerical claimant to the Glasgow See.[61] Many other Scottish magnates and clerics continued to take part in pilgrimages to England: between June and December 1369 passes to shrines were issued to Wardlaw, Richard Comyn, Walter Leslie, John Gray the clerk of the Rolls, Robert Erskine, the bishop of St Andrews, John Barbour the archdeacon of Aberdeen, John Carrick the king's secretary (and 'gardien de prive seal'), John Herries, Sir Hugh Eglintoun, John Stewart, earl of Carrick, and the Douglases – James, Archibald and Earl William and his wife, Margaret of Mar.[62]

Archibald's new influence over Melrose could undoubtedly be used to erode that of his cousin, the earl of Douglas: David, too, would visit the abbey (and his

---

57 *APS*, i, App. 36, p. 173 (*RPS*, 1369/9/1–); Sumption, *Hundred Years War*, ii, 585; C. Allmand, *The Hundred Years War: England and France at War c.1300–c.1450* (Cambridge 1989), 22–3.
58 *RRS*, vi, no. 450.
59 *RRS*, v, no. 269; *APS*, i, 483; *Liber Sancte Marie de Melros*, no. 361.
60 *CCR 1369–74*, 338; *Rot. Scot.*, i, 932; Neville, *Violence, Custom and Law*, 54.
61 *Rot. Scot.*, i, 92; Watt, *Scottish Graduates*, 569–75.
62 *Rot. Scot.*, i, 933–6; *RRS*, vi, no. 444 and p. 12.

father's shrine) sometime in 1369–70 when he confirmed the grant by George, earl of March, of the nearby castle-barony of Morton in Dumfriesshire to James Douglas of Dalkeith.[63] But this grant makes it clear that enhanced royal control in the east and middle marches was to be allied to Archibald's grip on the west. On 18 September this was made plain when David granted Archibald – 'for his diligent labour and gracious service done efficaciously and effectively' – all the royal lands in Galloway between the rivers Cree and Nith: this was given with the same bounds granted by Robert I to his brother, Edward Bruce, as Lord of Galloway about 1309 (and presumably for the same return of ten knights' service).[64] Abbot Bower would later state that 'when Galloway rebelled he [Archibald] subdued it for the King, whereupon the King conferred it on him'.[65] There is no evidence of particular unrest in the south-west at this time. Nonetheless, as Michael Brown has shown, Bower's comment reflects David's dependence upon the Grim's ability after 1364 to use strong military leadership to contain the native kindreds in what had been a Balliol-Comyn enclave, far bettter than anyone in crown service. This grant of the lordship of Galloway was also a final admission that the Fleming earls of Wigtown were not up to the job of countering native intransigence and acting as a royal buffer against the neighbouring earldom of Carrick and lordship of Kyle Stewart, now both in the possession of John Stewart, as well as the Douglas earl's lands east of Annandale: significantly, Earl William was at the September council but did not witness the Galloway grant.[66]

However, this intervention in the south-west was also a further part of royal plans to wed Agnes Dunbar and knit her kindred and allies into a crown network of lordship south of the Forth. Sometime after 23 August 1369, during a visit to Dunbar Castle, David inspected a grant (which had pre-dated his moves for divorce) of George, earl of March, to Sir John Maitland of Thirlestane and his son, Robert, and daughter-in-law, Agnes Dunbar, of the barony of Tibbers in Dumfriesshire.[67] Thus the Maitlands were to be compensated in part for their loss of Agnes with a place in the Dunbar-Douglas network stretching from the south-west to the Merse and Lothians. Archibald and James Douglas had already secured Dumfriesshire lands with the support of the crown: James had been given Morton by the earl of March and, probably about the same time as George Dunbar had received a resignation of his aged uncle's earldom in parliament in July 1368, the king had given George the Dumfriesshire baronies of Glenken and

---

63 *Ibid*, no. 508; *Registrum Honoris de Morton*, ii, no. 101.
64 *RRS*, v, no. 451; Barrow, *Bruce*, 276–7.
65 *Chron. Bower*, viii, 35.
66 Brown, *Black Douglases*, 62–4.
67 *RRS*, vi, no. 509; *APS*, vii, 159. Is it possible Margaret Logie had also blocked Agnes's annulment?

Mochrum: these were lands which David had taken from Earl Patrick of March before 1346 and given to the Fleming earls of Wigtown.[68] Moreover, the Maitlands' grant of Tibbers had probably been confirmed about the same time as David's revival of the Galloway lordship and further grants to the Maitlands and Douglas of Dalkeith: on 4 September 1369 David had inspected a grant by William, earl of Douglas, of Thirlestane in Lauderdale to Sir John Maitland; in the following weeks the king would grant Peebles-shire lands to James Douglas, and lands in Edinburgh to his brother, Henry Douglas; on 18 September David also gave former Bisset lands in Fife to Sir William Dischington, his master of works.[69]

In retrospect, it might have been expected that David should really have rewarded such a vital figure as Archibald Douglas with the lordship of Galloway much sooner. After all, the crown certainly needed a trusted man in this sphere. However, Galloway had been touted as a possible title for alienation to an English prince as part of peace talks in 1365.[70] Thus David's formal gift of this province in 1369 to the man who had long held sway there anyway may have marked some admission that this idea had been irrevocably dropped from Anglo-Scottish talks (along with the notion of restoring the earldom of Atholl which had been transferred to John Stewart in 1366). Yet this in no way meant that negotiations had foundered. On the contrary, the available evidence suggests that throughout the summer of 1369 some little progress had been made and the September Scottish council countenanced further approaches. Between October 1369 and April 1370 there was a distinct increase in the number of Scots crossing the Channel to serve Edward III in France: this included a number of Annandale men as well as the out-of-favour Thomas, earl of Mar, and his 'brother', Thomas Balliol.[71] Moreover, in the weeks since his return from England in July, David had given the waiting French ambassadors the royal run-around. Indeed, the exchequer rolls record that the unnamed envoys of Charles V were kept waiting some sixteen weeks. There is no evidence, either, that David actually received them or agreed to further exchanges with the French king.[72]

To keep Scotland's options as wide as possible, such contact with France

---

68 *RRS*, vi, nos. 52, 506; *Registrum Honoris de Morton*, ii, nos. 99, 100; R.C. Reid ed., *Wigtownshire Charters* (Scottish History Society, 3rd series, Edinburgh 1960), xxx.

69 *RRS*, vi, nos. 449, 452; *RMS*, i, no. 327

70 See above, ch. 10.

71 *CDS*, iv, nos. 165, 173 (John Somerville and his men-at-arms and archers; 'William Westone, William Strachy, John Young, Robert Johnson, John Lemyngtone, John Hogg, Thomas Fistleighe, Thomas Galsagathe, Piton Hogg' and Thomas Balliol).

72 *ER*, ii, 328 (£3 12/- for the French ambassadors' journey from Perth to Aberdeen which David himself undertook between 19 and 27 October), 348 (£66 13/- 4d for the French envoys' sixteen-week wait).

would have been wise after the failure of the English campaign in Gascony and Charles's confiscation of Aquitaine in November 1369.[73] But David's persistence with Anglophile diplomacy may have provoked further intransigence from Robert Steward. The latter must already have been angered by David's plans to wed Agnes Dunbar and his partial favour to her menfolk, the Douglases, Erskines and the likes of John Stewart, John Logie and John Macdougall of Lorn. But on 18 September – the very same day as David's grant of the lordship of Galloway – the Steward witnessed an act at court yet was *not* recorded with his usual style as 'earl of Strathearn'. He would remain without this title until a single act on 15 December 1369, then seemingly lose it again until 7 April 1370.[74] Of course, this may have been a punishment prompted by continuing Stewart failure to pacify their tenants in the north; or, as has recently been argued, Robert may have got wind of the king's plans both to arrange the marriage of his esquire, Agnes's brother, John Dunbar, to the Steward's daughter, Marjorie, and to intrude John as another royalist lord of the hotly disputed earldom of Fife.[75] But these harsh constraints on the throne's heir presumptive – together with the bullying of the earl of Douglas at council and, as we shall see, the crown's actions in the north in late 1369 – would arguably mark the high water line of royal authority in David's reign.

North and South, *c.* October 1369 to Spring 1370

About mid-October David and an apparently well-attended court undertook a northern circuit. A justice ayre was probably overseen and David would spend some time with Agnes Dunbar at Aberdeen.[76] But there may also have been a large military presence on this trip to bring to heel miscreants in Moray and beyond. From Edinburgh the royal party had moved to Perth, then Montrose, and, by 27 October, as far as Aberdeen. The king's passage was marked by several grants to supporters and the enforcement of local interests. David's grants to James Douglas of Peeblesshire lands and tax-exemption in Fife have been noted. Elsewhere, Sir William Ramsay of Dalhousie, a grand-nephew of David's chivalric favourite – and

73 Allmand, *Hundred Years War*, 22.
74 *RMS*, i, nos. 295, 336; *RRS*, vi, nos. 452–5.
75 Boardman, *Early Stewart Kings*, 24, 37 n125, where it is noted that this royal threat of the forfeiture of Strathearn may also have extended to the barony of Methven but did not stop the Steward from continuing to seal his own charters with the style of earl (NAS GD86 Inventory of Fraser Charters /7, dated 19 October 1369). Similarly, at Renfrew (while the king was in Edinburgh) on 30 May 1370, the Steward would be obliged to grant his brother-in-law, Sir Hugh Eglintoun, the right to re-enter the post of bailie of Cunningham notwithstanding the fact that someone had been ministering in this office 'through Hugh's sufferance' – perhaps David's man, Sir William Cunningham, or his son, Andrew (Fraser ed., *Memorials of the Montgomeries*, ii, 7; *RRS*, vi, no. 470).
76 *ER*, ii, 328, 345 (including spices sent to Agnes at Aberdeen).

the steward of the household which had cared for Agnes Dunbar in Aberdeen in recent weeks – was given the lands of Nether Libberton near Edinburgh. While in Aberdeen, the king also made William Chalmers justice-clerk north-of-Forth. The witnesses to these acts included the Steward, the Douglas earl, Robert Erskine, Archibald Douglas, Walter Leslie and William Dischington (now a justiciar north-of-Forth).[77]

However, the primary objective of this northern itinerary was to receive the submission to royal authority of John MacDonald of the Isles, which David did at Inverness on 15 November.[78] There does not appear to have been any armed clash: MacDonald simply acquiesced. Even if more 'friendly ways' (as the March 1369 parliament had put it) had brought pressure to bear on John after at least three years of parliamentary calls for such royal action in the north, the threat of force must still have lain behind David's persuasiveness. MacDonald must have been especially impressed by the presence of warriors like the Grim Douglas and Leslie and their armed followings by the king's side. Pressure might also have been applied in recent months through letters from John's former ally, Edward III. Yet MacDonald's submission had most likely been brokered by his father-in-law, Robert the Steward, under duress from the Scottish crown. MacDonald's submission was not, though, to be followed by David's systematic deconstruction of his territorial influence over the Isles, the west coast and Lochaber (a former part of the defunct regality of Moray which might have been reclaimed under the terms of the 1367 revocation). Instead, MacDonald acknowledged unspecified 'negligences' which had angered the king and undertook in future to obey royal officers and, most significantly, to pay tax contributions, thus undoing his exemption under the treaty of Berwick.

To ensure that John and his tenants fulfilled these promises, David initiated a policy which fifteenth-century Stewart kings would also use against the *Ri Innse Gall*. MacDonald had to enter two hostages into royal custody through his father-in-law, Robert Steward, who also gave assurances for his behaviour: MacDonald's grandson, Angus, and bastard son, Donald, were thus warded in Dumbarton Castle which by January 1369 was under the care of Sir Robert Erskine.[79] Thus, rather like Edward I in his

---

77 *RRS*, vi, nos. 453, 454, 455 (Douglas); *RMS*, i, nos. 295, 332, 333, 334, 336.
78 *Acts of the Lords of the Isles*, no. 6; *APS*, xii, no. 30; Grant, 'Scotland's 'Celtic Fringe'', 124–5; Nicholson, *Scotland – the Later Middle Ages*, 178–9.
79 *ER*, ii, 344. At Perth on 29 October 1369 David granted Lanarkshire lands to Robert Danielston, son of John, the former keeper of Dumbarton, perhaps signalling this kindred's continuing role as everyday constables at that castle despite Erskine's intrusion (*RRS*, vi, no. 453). This may have been granted in part-compensation for David's confirmation of the Lanarkshire barony of Cadzow to David Fitzwalter in December 1368, lands John Danielston had enjoyed an income from before 1359 (*ibid*, no. 418; *ER*, i, 582).

policing of Scotland as a whole in 1296, David seemed content at most with hostages, the chance of income from the Isles and their tacit recognition of his writ. Even in the short time that remained of David's reign, there is evidence that MacDonald broke his vows, not least in refusing taxes. Nevertheless, this summit at Inverness in late 1369 was an emphatic display of royal power. David could also have used this trip north to inflict upon William, earl of Ross, more of the pressure to resign lands which would later form the basis of Ross's parliamentary complaint in 1371.[80] At the same time David and his close counsel may also have been responsible for the elevation of cleric Alexander of Kilwhiss (near Collessie in Fife), the dean of Moray under Bishop Bur since 1368, to be the new bishop of Ross following the death of prelate Alexander Steward by February-May 1371.[81] The crown's continued custody of Robert Steward's son, Alexander Stewart, may also have been exploited to impose order on the Stewarts in Atholl and their tenants in Badenoch.[82]

David certainly used his return trip south to add further to the interest of his supporters in the north, north-east and elsewhere. While still at Inverness on 16 November, David made Sir John of Innerpeffray his sheriff of Banffshire. At Aberdeen on 4 December – with Agnes Dunbar in attendance – the king ordered all royal officials not to exact services from the lands of the bishopric of Moray, presumably to leave the hardnosed bishop, Alexander de Bur, better-resourced to police this region himself. Then at Montrose on 8 December David inspected a charter by Sir Walter Leslie to John Urquhart of lands in Buchan and Forfarshire. He also inspected a charter by Hugh Ross, the outlaw brother of William, earl of

80 Forbes, *Ane Account of the Familie of Innes*, 70–3; Fraser ed., *The Frasers of Philorth*, ii, 312–3; Boardman, *Early Stewart Kings*, 170. For example, on 28 November 1369 John Hay of Tullibody, sheriff of Inverness, and the Ross earl's cousin (cited for contumacious absence in parliament in 1366), may have been obliged by the crown to resign lands near Leuchars in Fife to John Lyon, the king's secretary (NAS Henderson of Fordell GD 172/121): the witnesses to this act included James Douglas of Dalkeith, Walter Leslie, William Dischington, Walter Bisset of Lossyndrum and others. Sometime in 1369 Bur, the bishop of Moray, petitioned against Hay's collection of multures at 'Qaurelwode' in Moray, a process witnessed by the bishop's allies, Nicholas Sutherland, Walter Bisset, John Sinclair of Forres, Robert Innes and others (*Registrum Episcopatus Moraviensis*, no. 153). At Aberdeen in April 1368, Hay may also have been obliged to buy the marriage of his own wife from John Logie (NAS RH1/6/37).

81 Watt, *Scottish Graduates*, 315–6, although Kilwhiss's earlier appointment as dean of Ross by 1350 may have been due to the favour of Bishop Roger of Ballinbreth who had resigned his see to Alexander Steward by November 1350. For the latter as a charter witness for the earl of Ross and his brother, Hugh, see: *ibid*, 509–10; NAS RH 6/140; MacInnes ed., *Calendar of Writs of Munro of Fowlis*, 2–4; Fraser ed., *The Chiefs of Grant*, iii, 9–11. My thanks to Richard Oram for this point about Kilwhiss's Fife links.

82 *ER*, ii, 349.

Ross, 'then in hiding in woods and inaccessible places': this grant had also given Sir Adam Urquhart, the sheriff of Cromarty (an office he had received in 1359 after David had confiscated it from Earl William of Ross) lands in Buchan which the crown was at that time trying to revoke from the Ross family.[83]

As David moved further south, so his acts dealt with more Lowland matters. On 9 December at Montrose he gave Sir James Douglas yet another charter of entail of the barony and castle of Dalkeith, surely an act designed to reject any lingering challenge from the earl of Douglas to a sasine first given in 1368. Yet more significantly, while still at Aberdeen, David had granted James the leadership of all the men on his lands throughout the kingdom as well as the right to 'riding in the marches' where he had lands in Dumfriesshire and Galloway.[84] Crucially this would have enhanced James's freedom on lands held in Strathearn (Kellor) and from the earl of Douglas and Countess of Fife. This may have signalled a final assertion of independence for the Lothian knight away from the Douglas earl into the service of his king.[85]

Finally back in Edinburgh by 11 December, David must have issued summons for a parliament to be held at Perth the following February. The acts he issued in the weeks leading up to this assembly reflected the king's relative confidence in the achievements of the last eighteen months and rewarded some of his closest supporters. On 15 January 1370 he granted the barony of Inverarity in Forfarshire to Walter Leslie's associate, Alexander Lindsay of Glenesk, after its resignation by Margaret Sinclair, the widowed countess of Angus. Then on 7 February David ordered Sir William Dischington, as a justiciar north-of-Forth, to inquire into the complaint of the bishop of St Andrews against the burgesses of Cupar: Dischington was to report to parliament after deploying 'the worthies and more faithful men of the sheriffdom' of Fife, a group the crown had worked hard to shape since 1357. Then, on 8 February, David elevated George, earl of March's castle-burgh of Dunbar on the Lothian coast to the status of a free burgh of barony.[86] As one historian has noted, this included the right for the port of

83 *RRS*, vi, nos. 456, 458; *RMS*, i, nos. 296, 300.
84 *RRS*, vi, nos. 457, 459; Brown, *Black Douglases*, 60–1. A grant of the leadership of all their tenants may have been something David offered, too, to men like Walter Leslie, Robert Erskine and Archibald Douglas.
85 On 2 January 1370, this new status may have been recognised – perhaps through crown pressure – by John Stewart earl of Carrick's confirmation of a gift of the Lothian lands of Bondington to James Douglas, an act witnessed at Edinburgh by the Abbot of Holyrood, Hugh Eglintoun, David and Andrew Fitzwalter, John Herries, John Kennedy and Andrew Cunningham – William More and William Dischington may also have been present (*Registrum Honoris de Morton*, ii, nos. 105–6).
86 *RRS*, vi, nos. 460, 462; *RMS*, i, nos. 297, 302, 337, 340, 342; NAS B.65 (Calendar of St Andrews charters)/10.

Dunbar (which David himself visited in 1369) to use the cocket seal of a royal burgh both at home and abroad: this must have been intended by the crown to encourage Scottish abbeys, freeholders and merchants in the borders to export goods – especially wool – via Dunbar rather than Berwick where lower customs set by Edward III bit hard into Edinburgh's trade. David also allowed the monks of Melrose Abbey – with its vast sheep flocks – to export wool via Edinburgh at a reduced customs rate of 13/4d per sack (as opposed to 15/- or 20/-) and he let Scottish merchants in Edinburgh, Haddington, Linlithgow and North Berwick export English wool they had purchased at a grossly reduced 6/8d or 13/4d per sack. This competition would cost Edward III some £2,930 in 1371–2 as at least 1,172 sacks of English wool went out via Dunbar and Haddington.[87]

However, David's favour to George Dunbar in February 1370 may also have reflected the resurfacing of growing disquiet amongst the trading classes and a complaint against the crown. This and other grievances were soon voiced more clearly by the estates. Once again in David's 'second reign', parliament proved a periodically difficult forum in which to deflect censure by the three 'communities'. Like a number of its predecessors in the last decade, the body which met at Perth from Monday 18 February 1370 passed several acts which, if enforced, could be used to the advantage of the crown as well as the benefit of the realm. But within these acts there was again implicit – and sometimes overt – criticism of the king, his ministers, officers and royal policy. Clearly, David had not been able to solve all his problems since June 1368. Many of the matters touched upon at Perth were, indeed, all too familiar themes.

According to the two (often very) different extant versions of this assembly's decisions, parliament had been called and charged to discuss 'many [or several] points touching the standing of the kingdom and the king, and his means of living, and also things which concern common justice'.[88] If this suggests that it had not been solely the royal government's desire to hold a parliament, the first few acts of the meeting seem to make that plain.

Admittedly, recent precedent was followed. A separate committee for falsed judgements and other matters of common justice was elected to meet separately at the Friars Preachers of Perth and to report back on cases on the penultimate day of parliament. This was a body again dominated by royalist clerics and justiciar-knights: the bishops of Brechin and Dunblane, the abbot of Dunfermline and a number of clerks, William Keith the Marischal, Archibald Douglas,

---

87 Tuck, 'A Medieval Tax Haven', 157–8; Ditchburn, *Scotland and Europe*, 164–69; J. Donnelly, 'An Open Port: The Berwick Export Trade, 1311–1373', *SHR*, lxxviii (1999), 145–69.
88 For the recorded acts of this parliament, see: *APS*, i, 507–9 and 533–6 (*RPS*, 1370/2/1–41, including the *Black Book* version).

James Douglas, Robert Erskine, William Dischington, David Fitzwalter, David Graham, Roger Mortimer, Duncan Wallace, David Fleming, William Meldrum, Alexander Cockburn, Thomas Irvine and several burgesses.[89] Little wonder, then, that this group found in favour of some of its own friends and members, including the bishop of St Andrews, James Douglas, David Fleming and David Graham.[90] Moreover, even though the second committee appointed to deal with 'general business' included Robert Steward and John Stewart, earl of Carrick, they were by far outnumbered by additional crown men including George, earl of March, and Walter Leslie. Furthermore, the olive branch of a grant of the lands of Balmonth in Fife to William, earl of Douglas, given on 14 January seems to have failed: the earl again sent in a procurator (Duncan Wallace, sheriff of Ayrshire) whilst his brother-in-law the earl of Mar, John MacDonald of the Isles and Gillespie Campbell were all cited for 'contumacious absence'.[91] Clearly, some potential troublemakers had again been excluded or had chosen to absent themselves and David's success in Inverness in November 1369 was already crumbling. Finally, it does not seem as if this assembly was to be limited to just what the king wanted it to discuss and sanction. Although it was ordained that no-one on either committee was to bring in 'any other person' as counsellor or retainer to the hall, the general business committee's remit was also 'to negotiate certain and secret business of the king and realm', probably in matters of diplomacy.[92]

Finance seems to have been this parliament's greatest concern, and its opening act was another first for Scotland and a trick David may have learned from Edward III. Remarkably, all unpaid expenses for hospitality and prise for the royal household amassed since the king's release in 1357 until the fiscal year 1368 were to be cancelled.[93] This has all the traits of a windfall any authoritarian monarch would dearly love to extract from his subjects. But this parliamentary committee attached conditional clauses which reveal this to have been a concession granted for the price of reform of current royal practices. In the future 'everything to be taken for the king's work and expenses' was only to be extracted from lands customarily

---

89 The burgesses included Adam Forrester, John Mercer, John Gill, Adam Pingle and John Rollock: that these were mostly crown men is suggested by the grant of a £10 pension and the office of clerk of the cocket of Edinburgh which David gave Rollock in 1369 (*ER*, ii, 359).

90 It should be noted, though, that some of these disputes only involved notable crown men, for example, that between William Keith and Nicholas Sutherland, for which the former was fined £10.

91 *RMS*, i, no. 341.

92 *RPS*, 1370/2/1–6 and /25–30.

93 *Ibid*, 1370/2/7 and /31; Harriss, *King, Parliament and Public Finance in Medieval England to 1369*, 376–83. A short while before this moratorium was declared David had been prepared to pay off royal debts with a reduction of a third (*ER*, ii, 346–7).

designated to meet this burden, and those affected should have certification of what was owed from the exchequer. Above all, it was declared that 'the king should live and arrange for his household according to the extent of his means': this should start with a ministerial promise that future assessments for prise would be based not on the amount of land held by an individual, but on the true value of the livestock, crops or other goods thereon.

These safeguards seem to have been sought from the crown in the same way that the 1366 parliament had demanded a 'true' assessment of land values before taxation. That royal income and tax burden should still have been such a sore point with many in the political community in 1370 is understandable. The exchequer audit that year was also held at Perth in the weeks before the parliament, remitting a total income of £10,217, the highest yet in David's kingship. Even with the payment of 4,000 merks (£2,667) in ransom to England, and the return of the £666 which David had borrowed from Edward, the king was still left with a profit of over £1,300 after all his outgoings were accounted: this was the largest surplus of the reign (barring the year 1361–2 when with the ransom stopped David banked over £4,000, an invaluable sum come the rebellion of 1363).[94] However, parliament's complaint in 1370 about prise and the cancellation of royal debts accumulated *c*. 1357–68 makes it clear that the exchequer had not disbursed all of David's obligations – the community was surely right to seek redress for a decade of annual tax, hiked customs, (unrecorded) private 'donations' and prise. Some substantial Scots, of course, had responded again by non-payment and deforcement of collectors. Despite the high income of 1369–70, many individuals and lands continued to refuse the crown's exactions. Only £480 had been collected from the 3d in the £ granted by the estates in March 1369. Territories in central and northern Scotland under the control of the Stewarts and their allies continued to yield little. Starthearn and Garioch in particular were cited by the auditors for failing to remit the small sums they owed: there was no evidence that MacDonald of the Isles, the Campbells or the earl of Ross had contributed.

No wonder, then, that parliament took its chance to impose further conditions on the kingdom's finance. Most strikingly there was an insistence that in order to spread the cost of supporting the crown and ransom more evenly throughout the realm – easing the burden of the wool-producing lands of the south – David was to dispose 'himself to undertake a stay, at certain and opportune times, in the highland regions, in which he ought and will be able to have more useful prises and a better market price, and similarly to pacify the country and to punish malefactors'.[95] The king may

94 *ER*, ii, 339–49 for what follows of this audit.
95 *RPS*, 1370/2/8 and /32.

have played a telling role in parliament in ensuring that the Highland regions actually named for such royal occupation were those of his domestic opponents in the west: Kintyre, Knapdale and Arran held by the Steward and Sir John Menteith, as well as the lordships of MacDonald of the Isles, Macdougall of Lorn and Campbell of Lochawe. But here again was strong evidence of a step the wider political community required. This reflected a growing Lowland-Highland cultural, political and economic gulf in four-teenth-century Scotland, although it was surely not yet so divisive as that expounded famously by Fordun's annals over a decade later wherein:

> the [English/Teutonic speaking] people of the low coast are home-loving, civilised, trustworthy, tolerant and polite, decently attired, affable and pacific, devout in their worship of God, yet always ready to resist an injury at the hands of their enemy. The highlanders and people of the islands, on the other hand, are a wild and untamed race, primitive and proud, given to plunder and the easy life, clever and quick to learn, handsome in appearance though slovenly in dress, consistently hostile and cruel to the people of the English, and, when the speech is different, even to their own nation. They are, however, loyal and obedient to their king and country, and provided they be well governed they are obedient and ready enough to respect the law.[96]

However, in the parliamentary calling to royal attention in 1370 of the need for an equitable presence as well as to justice in the west and north there was again criticism of a king who, although personally intimidating, preferred increasingly to reside in Edinburgh or to visit periodically other eastern castles, burghs and religious houses, and to leave justice beyond the Mounth to his officers. Fifteenth-century Stewart kings of Scots like James II and III would suffer similar parliamentary rebukes, not always worded so softly.[97] In the same way, in February 1370, David became the first king of Scots to be openly corrected by parliament for granting (and probably selling) pardons for homicide: it was ordained that 'our lord king henceforth should grant remissions for murder to no party, unless it was previously discussed and unanimously delivered by the three com-munities in parliament'. Nor did David's officers escape censure. 'Because almost each community complains grievously about the sheriffs and other ministers of the king in the country', the Chamberlain and justiciars were ordered to investigate all officers serving since 1357 and if need be to imprison them at the king's will until their punishment could be decided in council or parliament. In addition, no officer was to act upon any royal

96 *Chron. Fordun*, i, 24.
97 Tanner, *Late Medieval Scottish Parliament*, 39–55, 159–61.

act – be it given under the great, privy or David's personal signet seal – which contravened the common law.[98]

All in all, this might be construed as a fairly damning indictment of the judicial record and practices of the king and his government pressed into statute by the three estates.[99] What lay behind it was surely a festering sense that over the past decade the justice (as well as the finance) of David and his supporters had become partial, designed to favour the king and his predominantly Lowland, south- and east-facing policies and court: as a result, order in some quarters had been neglected or become unenforceable. To some extent, these parliamentary acts, as recorded, smacked of convention: they were, of course, couched in respectful terms. But they still contained a mounting level of expectancy which David would surely have had to deliver upon after 1370–71. The Stewart kings and lieutenants over the next thirty years would certainly suffer further estates' censure and even a sudden loss of power justified on the grounds of their failure to do justice in the north: they also did their best to avoid taxes and to 'live of their own'.[100] It is likely, then, that David got more of a shock than usual from the proceedings of the February 1370 parliament. He can have been only slightly cheered by the concession of some new customs, including a 40d in the £ tariff on the exportation of gold and silver bullion, the same on the export of horses and 12d in the £ on oxen and cattle; probably to help collect these levies, it was enacted that burgesses and merchants were not to go abroad without the permission of the king or Chamberlain.[101]

By the same token, David may also have been somewhat disappointed by the parliamentary committee's decision on Anglo-Scottish relations. The committee may have discussed the matter for days but their recorded decision was brief, familiar and to the point: 'the three communities deliver that it does not seem expedient to them to send ambassadors in England now to have negotiation, matters standing as they are . . .'. This may not have come as a surprise to the crown, given that little of note had altered in Anglo-French relations since summer 1369: war still threatened but had not yet broken out. It is likely therefore that the Anglo-Scottish talks which had taken place since the previous June had generated no new avenues to a fuller peace: an 'indenture' mentioned in passing by the parliamentary record of

---

98 *RPS*, 1370/2/11–13, /35–6 and /38.
99 Parliament also concerned itself with the finer details of law on this occasion, for example passing a final act ordering sheriff's sergeants (or 'mairs') to keep a register of their summonses and actions for reference in court – failure to do so would count against them ibid, 1370/2/39).
100 Boardman, *Early Stewart Kings*, 131–2, 148–53, 195–7, 214–5.
101 *RPS*, 1370/2/9–10, /15 and /33–4.

1370 probably refers to English offers made since June 1369 based on terms of the past five years. Parliament did at least agree that David should send letters to the English welcoming the chance of further talks at Durham in the coming Easter 'upon the renewal of a good peace by all ways and means'. David's new secretary, layman John Lyon, did take missives to Edward III. However, parliament's addition of the proviso that such negotiations would only proceed 'always excepting those points which were formerly refused' strongly suggests that neither the Scots nor their king expected the English to offer anything fresh.[102]

It was in this context that David seems to have had no choice over the next twelve months but to countenance further border raids by the Douglases, Dunbars and their followings; as a symptom of the same trend, the level of Anglo-Scottish antagonism at sea also rose markedly in these months.[103] As we shall see, the king may even have come to the decision by the end of the year that it was time to consider abandoning the talks with England altogether. But in the first half of 1370, at least, David and his closest household officers persisted with some contact with England despite the characteristically lukewarm backing this diplomacy had been given by the estates at Perth.

As in previous years, before parliament had gathered, the king had clearly requested another safe-conduct for himself and forty retainers to go to England: this was issued by Edward III's government on 28 February. On 12 April 1370 another safe-conduct to England (requested by David's letters from Edinburgh on 16 March) would be issued to the familiar embassy of the bishop of St Andrews, Erskine and John Carrick who had now replaced the venerable Patrick of Leuchars as Chancellor. Then on 28 May David would present Edward III with a black courser, a prize horse possibly bought in France and taken south by the Scottish royal court's herald and harper, Thomas Roter. One of David's valet esquires, a John Cochrane, would be paid in June for services as an archer to Edward at Calais. Secretary Lyon would also go south again in June 1370 when he paid off the remaining money owed to King Edward by the Erskines, Douglas of Dalkeith and Edmonstone: Lyon would be accompanied by John McKelly, the Scots king's clerk of the Liverance, and Duncan Petyt, a clerk of the audit. In all, David would spend over £533 on contact with England between January 1370 and January 1371, a sum comparable with previous

---

102 *Ibid*, 1370/2/14 (this decision is not reproduced in the *Black Book* version); CDS, iv, no. 173 (Lyon); Duncan, 'A Question about the Succession, 1364', 14–20.
103 MacDonald, *Border Bloodshed*, 14–22; for incidents at sea involving English and French attacks on Scottish shipping, see CDS, iv, nos. 163–4; Devon, *Issue Roll of Thomas de Brantingham*, 396; Stevenson, 'The Flemish Dimension of the Auld Alliance', 40.

years.[104] However, the fact that these visits south included none of the royalist knights who had been so prominent in such traffic in 1368–9 – the Douglases, Dunbars, Erskines and their followers – may mean that these men were now inclined increasingly to border violence and alliance with France. If so, they – like parliament – would bring pressure to bear upon the king.

In fact, it was surely only through several royal charters issued at Perth that David was able to act with full independence during the parliament of February 1370. Crucially, these grants included a flurry of acts stepping up direct royal intervention against the influence of the earls of Ross and Mar from Inverness to Garioch. On 26 February David did grant lands in Banffshire to Hugh Ross, brother and heir to Earl William. But a day later the king gave Sir Walter Leslie a reversion of the thanages of Kincardine (near Kildrummy Castle in Mar) as well as Fettercairn and Aberluthnot a few miles further south. These were lands given originally by David to his brother-in-law, William, earl of Sutherland (who was possibly now dead), before 1346, and which Leslie was now to hold as one barony for two knights' service; on the same day Leslie was also given the thanage of Aberchirder in Banff (close to earl William of Ross's lands carved by Robert I from the former Comyn earldom of Buchan). Then, on 3 March, David granted the burgesses of Inverness a feu of their annual fermes owed to the crown at £80, probably in response to a lobby by the townsmen.[105] The king surely did not yet know that over the next few months his moves against Ross and Mar would be among the final firm successes of his reign. But he could not have avoided the sense that yet again some new initiative at home and abroad was required. According to the exchequer accounts, the king intended to celebrate his birthday on 5 March at Scone: that this festivity did not take place may reflect his subdued mood.[106]

A Change of Tack, Spring to October 1370

David had missed the window of opportunity in domestic and diplomatic affairs which he had forced open in late 1368–early 1369. After eighteen months of effort he was still not married to Agnes Dunbar, the English had conceded little at the bargaining table, and the potency of the crown's new magnate coalition was at risk of ebbing away, denied a suitable platform for its strengths. So it was that whilst contact with England was maintained in the summer of 1370, David moved to steal the thunder of his opponents of c.1351–9 and to approach France.

104 *Rot. Scot.*, i, 937–8; *CDS*, iv, no. 173; *ER*, ii, 356–8. Carrick witnessed as Chancellor on 4 April 1370 (*RRS*, vi, no. 464; Watt, *Scottish Graduates*, 89–91).
105 *RMS*, i, nos. 298, 338–9, 344–5; *RRS*, vi, no. 463; Grant, 'Thanes and Thanages', 73, 75–6.
106 *ER*, ii, 358.

In retrospect, the first clear signal that this might be the king's intent came on 4 June 1370 when John Lyon secured from Edward III a six-month delay in the payment of the next ransom instalment until 24 June 1371: solemn personal promises were given by David that the remaining 52,000 merks would be paid on time.[107] Unlike 1359, though, this time there could be no claim of poverty to justify such a delay: as Scottish Chamberlain, Walter Biggar's income by February 1371, indeed, would have reached the massive total of £15,359 – the crown had more resources then than in January 1370 when Biggar had delivered the last ransom instalment to Berwick.[108] Instead, this delay requested from London must have reflected David's feeling that he could now afford to take the risk of stopping payment and seeing if France had something better to offer, or if that approach and the halt in cash would frighten the English into peace concessions. It was a logical extension of the long diplomatic game which David had played since 1357 and not something forced upon him as in 1359. He could only have been encouraged in this view by the obvious deterioration in England's position in Europe and its royal family's leadership. English weakness is betrayed by Westminster's consent to the ransom delay. After the death of Queen Philippa in August 1369, Edward III had rapidly become distanced from power: indeed, the last seven years of his life would see his dependence upon his mistress, Alice Perrers, and his household favourites widely criticised at home. John of Gaunt became the real power at Westminster.[109] But the increased chance that Gaunt himself might even succeed as king of England (as his son, Henry IV, would do in 1399) must also have further diluted any hopes David had of concluding his original peace deal based on the concession of a place in the Scottish succession to a Plantagenet prince.

However, although the need for a firmer peace with England may indeed have become of 'leisurely importance' by 1370,[110] there was surely also considerable pressure in Scotland upon David to consider an active alliance with France. This would have come not simply from old antagonists like the Steward and earl of Douglas but from the crown's closest allies headed by the other Douglas scions, the Dunbars and Erskines. By 1371 William, earl of Douglas, Archibald Douglas and George Dunbar in particular would have recovered a clutch of further Roxburghshire holdings, so reducing the English presence north of the River Tweed to a thin pale south of the border

107 PRO E.39/5/7; *RRS*, vi, no. 471; *Rot. Scot.*, i, 938.
108 *ER*, ii, 355.
109 Duncan, 'A Question about the Succession, 1364', 20; Campbell, 'England, Scotland and the Hundred Years War in the Fourteenth-century', 206–8; Cuttino, *English Medieval Diplomacy*, 93–5; Goodman, *John of Gaunt*, 44–8; Ormrod, *The Reign of Edward III*, 32–5.
110 Nicholson, *Scotland – the Later Middle Ages*, 172–4.

forests and abbeys. In 1370, small-scale Scottish raids would even be mounted against Berwick and beyond into Northumberland: by the close of the year the English crown would again be readying border defences against the Scots.[111]

It makes perfect sense, then, that David entrusted an embassy to France sometime before January 1371 to Archibald Douglas, Lord of Galloway. The Grim knight was the obvious magnate, with an established reputation in France as a child at Gaillard and as a Poitiers veteran, but one whom David felt he could actually trust to serve the Bruce regime's interests. Archibald may have visited Charles V between 4 April and 24 July 1370 when he was notably absent as a crown charter witness. That his embassy was one fully sanctioned by his king is made clear by royal payment of some £1,500 in expenses for the trip, with Archibald himself receiving £223. The rogue embassy of 1359, in stark contrast, had been paid only £280 in total well after the fact even though that party had actually concluded an indenture (and gone on to secure Papal help), whereas no treaty appears to have resulted from Archibald's contact. In the same way the other key Scottish envoy to France in 1370 was John Gray of Broxmonth in Roxburghshire, a borders man but also David's royal clerk of the Rolls. The king gave Gray a grant of burgh mills in Peebles in May 1370; then Charles V gave him £100 in July for his services as 'the secretary of our beloved cousin, king of Scots . . . and against England and our other enemies'.[112]

That David may now have been prepared to consider a return to open aggression against England through Scottish lords he liked is also suggested by the grantees he favoured in late spring and summer 1370. At Edinburgh on 6 and 7 April he again issued his confirmation of William, earl of Douglas's resignation of Dalkeith barony to Marie Douglas and thus in turn to Sir James Douglas: that this knight had requested this act points to ongoing opposition to his sasine by the earl. On 6 May David also gave Sir James the lands of Leaths in the former Balliol barony of Buittle in Dumfriesshire because it had been forfeited by the Douglas earl for 'un-licensed alienation' to Sweetheart Abbey.[113] There was also favour for the Agnes Dunbar coalition kindred of the Erskines: at Stirling on 16 April David gave Sir Thomas Erskine lands in Stirlingshire and issued fresh letters appointing Sir Robert as keeper of Stirling Castle for life with an added pension of a hefty 200 merks from the lands of nearby Bothkennar. That the Erskines were a kindred who would be interested in war against Edward III can be inferred not only from Sir Robert's past role in the 1359 embassy to

111 CRO D/Mus/2 Box 21/69; MacDonald, *Border Bloodshed*, 21–3.
112 *ER*, ii, 4, 50 (1359), 355, 356, 363 (1370); *RMS*, i, no. 294; AN JJ102/220. Also sent to France in 1370 was a William Dalgarno, a clerk of the audit (*ER*, ii, 363).
113 *RMS*, i, no. 310; *RRS*, vi, nos. 465, 469.

France but from the pension of £500 which would be given by Charles V to Robert's second son, Sir Nicholas Erskine, in 1372.[114] Elsewhere, on 14 March 1370, David gave Stirlingshire lands and a 20-merk pension to another Poitiers veteran and former Douglas man, John Herries of Terregles, who was also paid as a seemingly occasional constable of Stirling Castle. There were lands and pensions, too, for the royal chapel of St Monans (20 merks per annum); Sir James Lindsay of the Byres; Sir John Inchmartin (money from holdings in Atholl); the former Chancellor bishop of Brechin, the aged Patrick Leuchars, and his burgh of Montrose; and Sir Alexander Lindsay of Glenesk (of lands resigned by the widowed Countess of Angus). The mainstay witnesses to these acts again included the Steward and Douglas earl alongside the royalist bishops of St Andrews and Glasgow, the earl of March, Archibald Douglas, Robert Erskine, Walter Haliburton, William Dischington, Walter Leslie and Chancellor John Carrick.[115]

However, David's inclusion on 6 May 1370 of clauses guaranteeing land rights contingent upon a peace with England in charters issued to Sir Walter Leslie does suggest that all this activity in France was geared ultimately as a scare tactic, designed to force the English to make further concessions.[116] Moreover, the fact that these talks with France produced no treaty of military alliance as yet may point to another motive for David's approach. Charles V would also have been a useful ally in the Bruce regime's legal fight to finally divorce Queen Margaret. By now, as Bower reports, an impasse must have been reached such that:

> [after] the king's proctors had travelled to the apostolic see, the case was bitterly disputed, and the pleading between the advocates of the contending parties was so prolonged that a book compiled from that source . . . is longer [in] wordage than the contents of the Four Psalters.[117]

The legal papers of this scandalous dispute (which Bower claimed to have seen) are now lost. But sometime before January 1370 David had certainly had to pay John de Peebles, a Glasgow cleric in the service of Walter Wardlaw, the bishop of Glasgow and crown envoy to England, to travel to 'Rome' (sic). Sometime in 1370–1 the king would also send John de Carrick, royal secretary, Chancellor and – by the end of that year – bishop-elect of

114 *RMS*, i, nos. 305, 318; AN J621 no. 77.
115 *RRS*, vi, nos. 463–69; *RMS*, i, nos. 304, 306, 309, 312, 315, 319 (confirmation of a grant by Thomas Bisset), 320, 321, 322, 346, 348; *ER*, ii, 333, 357 (Herries) and vii, 38 and viii, 127, 626 (St Monans).
116 *RMS*, i, no. 316; *Historical Records of the Family of Leslie, 1067–1869*, i, 68–9. Similar terms had been included in a grant to Robert Erskine in 1369 (Grant ed., *Charter Chest of the Earldom of Wigtown*, 33–4).
117 *Chron. Bower*, vii, 359, 502–4.

Dunkeld (a See usually influenced by leading Perthshire lords) to 'Rome' with John de Peebles again in tow. By 17 November these men had been joined on their runs to the Curia by the lawyerly Sir Duncan Wallace, sheriff of Ayr and procurator of the earl of Douglas at recent parliaments.[118] At Perth on 22 October David would issue three charters to Wallace, of lands in Ayrshire and Stirlingshire and a pension from Kincardineshire: the likelihood that David had been able to effectively poach Duncan from Earl William's service surely stemmed from the knight's marriage about that time to Eleanor Douglas, Countess of Carrick, Douglas's sister but also the successive widow of former crown men, Alexander Bruce and James Sandilands. Finally, late in the same year, David also made a second large payment of £1,840 to ambassadors going to both 'France and Rome'. Thus David's despatch of Archibald and various clerks to Charles V may have been just as much about avoiding papal censure for his questionable request for a marriage annulment by seeking French assistance to influence Pope Urban V against Edward III and his potential fifth column, Margaret Logie.[119]

Worse still, if Margaret was successful in her appeal, David's territorial plans might also be badly upset. While at Edinburgh on 6 May David had received the resignation by William, earl of Ross, of the forest lands of Plater in Forfar and then returned an immediate fresh infeftment of these holdings to the earl. This may have been a sign that the king now intended all Ross lands to be given to Sir Walter Leslie, the husband of William's only daughter: as much is also suggested by David's reissue of his grant – on the very same day – of the thanages of Aberchirder (Banffshire) and Kincardine (Mar) to Leslie.[120] If so, then Margaret's son, John Logie, was no longer to be intruded to these Forfar forest lands (as Ross would later claim had been the royal couple's original aim); some compensation, though, may have been extended to Logie on 6 May with a royal confirmation of his gift of peat to the Friars Preachers of Perth.[121] Moreover, Logie seemed destined to remain a key ally for David in Strathearn and Annandale no matter how much his mother meddled.

However, Margaret's sabotage of the crown's marriage plans may also have disrupted David's intentions for the premier earldom of Fife. As we have seen with this long-running theme, by the terms of the 1315 tailzie

118 *ER*, ii, 344, 356; Watt, *Scottish Graduates*, 89–91, although Carrick would fail to secure the see of Dunkeld as by November 1370 it had been given to Michael of Monymusk, dean of Glasgow, who was in Avignon when news of the death of Bishop John Luce arrived there (*ibid*, 403–4).
119 *ER*, ii, 358; *RRS*, vi, no. 474, *RMS*, i, nos. 356, 358.
120 *Ibid*, nos. 311, 316.
121 *RRS*, vi, no. 470; Forbes, *Ane Account of the Familie of Innes*, 70–3.

between Robert I and Earl Duncan, the crown had the right to name its own assignee to this title so as to ensure that it was held by a lord closely related to the throne but not subsumed within it. This had been the source of heated dispute between David and the Stewarts since 1341. Thomas Bisset, lord of Fife, whom the crown had forced upon Duncan's daughter, Countess Isabella, in 1363, had died about 1366. After 1368 David clearly hoped to follow his marriage to Agnes Dunbar with the intrusion of another member of his chivalric household to this land – the esquire, John Dunbar, who would be the king's brother-in-law. But Margaret Logie's resistance may have forced the king, in part, to compromise over this affair. Countess Isabella would complain in March 1371 – just a month after David's death, at the same time as Ross's protest – that the king had forced her to resign her earldom (probably sometime in late 1369) and then granted it about April-May 1370 to John Dunbar who compensated her with a pension of £145; the presence of a strong royalist group around Isabella at Falkland castle in Fife in December 1369 – when she resigned Kinnoul in Perthshire to James Douglas of Dalkeith – underlines the king's ability to have her coerced.[122] Isabella's loss of Fife was followed on 11 July 1370 by a papal dispensation for the marriage of John Dunbar to Robert Steward's eldest daughter, Marjorie. This was a match which may already have taken place: according to sixteenth-century chroniclers, it did so without the 'avise of hir fader' and through Marjorie's 'treasonable seduction'.[123]

It is possible, though, that the marriage of Dunbar to Marjorie Stewart was the only way David could get his heir presumptive to accept the transfer of Fife for a third time, a concession he had to make in the face of Stewart anger. There is a sense also that John Dunbar was himself anxious to wed a woman who would be a sister (or, as it turned out, a daughter) of a future Stewart king. Nonetheless, this and other royal grants in spring-summer

122 *RMS*, i, App. ii, no. 1624; NAS RH6/176; Boardman *Early Stewart Kings*, 37 n 127. For Isabella's 1371 complaint, see: NLS Charter no. 698; Fraser ed., *Red Book of Menteith*, ii, 251–6. For December 1369 see: NAS GD150 (Register of Morton)/ 20; *Registrum Honoris de Morton*, ii, no. 102. The witnesses to this grant were William Dischington, Alexander Lindsay, Andrew Valence and Andrew Erskine. Similarly, sometime in 1370, Isabella conceded the lands of Layne in Edinburgh to John Logie, David's stepson, an act witnessed by the bishops of St Andrews and Dunblane, Dischington, Andrew Ramsay of Lethy and Isabella's 'steward', Valence: in 1377, the bishop of St Andrews had to swear before an inquest that this last grant had been made with the stricture that the crown could not undo it (Fraser ed., *Red Book of Grandtully*, ii, nos. 77–8). Valence had been captured at Neville's Cross and gone to London with David in 1363 (*Rot. Scot.*, i, 678, 876). For another grant by Isabella to a crown Edinburgh man, the son of the merchant Roger Hogg, see NLS MSS. Adv. A. 10.
123 *CPR*, iv, 85; Stewart, *Genealogical History of the Stewarts*, 439; *Chron. Boece*, ii, 337 – both chronicles cited by Boardman, *Early Stewart Kings*, 24.

1370 must still have been highly provocative. Countess Isabella, significantly styling herself the 'widow of Walter Stewart, lord of Fife' (and not Bissett) would immediately throw off Bruce control after David's death and retailzie her earldom to Robert Stewart, lord of Menteith: John Dunbar would be left with no choice but to swap the Fife title for that of the reduced earldom of Moray in the north.[124] But back in mid-1370, Dunbar's elevation may have provoked dangerous rumblings of discontent. It is tempting to speculate, indeed, that some growing crisis lay behind the long gap in royal acts between 24 July and 9 September 1370. The latter day would find David at Melrose Abbey perhaps on a mission to defuse the resurgent anger of William, earl of Douglas. The late summer of 1370 may also have been the time of David's arrest and ward on the Bass Rock in the Firth of Forth of Thomas, earl of Mar, the Douglas earl's brother-in-law and a man still apparently excluded from his own lands.[125]

If this was so, then David and his close advisers would appear to have ridden out and contained the objections of the Stewarts, Ross, the Douglas earl and Mar once more, at a time when the unwed and still childless second Bruce king was, again, highly vulnerable. The impression is given that these great magnates were easily subdued and fearful of their king and his supporters, if not completetly 'cowed' into submission as Ranald Nicholson asserts.[126] However, the cold fact was that by then both the king's determination to prevail and the earls' anger may have been tempered, respectively, by the resignation of mortality and the expectancy of relief. Time had suddenly run out – David was dying.

124 Fraser ed., *Red Book of Menteith*, ii, 251–6; Boardman, *Early Stewart Kings*, 51–3.
125 *RRS*, vi, no. 473; *RMS*, i, no. 365; *ER*, ii, 357. Mar was at Kildrummy castle on 20 August 1369 but on 23 October 1370 David would confirm a grant by Sir John Bonville to Walter Moigne, the Mar man the crown had paid since 1362 to keep Kildrummy (*Illustrations of the Topography and Antiquities of Aberdeen and Banff*, v, 720–1; *RMS*, i, no. 368). However, like David's imprisonment of the earl of Angus in Dumbarton in 1360–2, the ward of Mar on the Bass, close by the Douglas earl's castle of Tantallon, may have been a compromise forced upon a king who would have preferred full forfeiture of this miscreant.
126 Nicholson, *Scotland – the Later Middle Ages*, 181–2.

TWELVE

The Wrong Man: After David, 1371–c. 1400

'Scotland now complains because the breeze that brought her fertility is being chased away, And fear is being let loose, and plots laid for revolt'.

Anonymous, *c.* 1371[1]

The Debt of Nature, 1370–1

The arrow wounds to the head which David had sustained at Neville's Cross in 1346 seem to have troubled the king on and off over the twenty-five years following that fateful battle. He was still being treated by English physicians and his own men of the 'leche' in 1357. A doctor, John the Englishman, had been paid by the royal household in 1359, probably for services rendered during the king's visit to London. January 1361 had seen David ask the papacy for the right to appoint a confessor solely for the royal person. And, of course, Froissart would record that the royal motive for building St Monans in 1362 was to give thanks for that saint's relief of the headaches which each full moon brought on, but which were surely due to the last barb lodged in the king's skull. It was thus possibly the gradual movement of this arrowhead – and any infection its deterioration caused – which would cut David's life short six weeks before his forty-eighth birthday, seven years younger than his father (who still fathered twins at fifty), even two years younger than the unlucky Alexander III. That, or some other disease – perhaps inherited – which medieval doctors and chroniclers were unable to describe as anything other than a fever. The same malady could conceivably have been behind David's inability to reproduce.[2]

David's visit to Melrose Abbey in September 1370 might equally, then, have been a last conscious payment of respects to his father's heart. The acts issued by the king over the next few months also give the impression of a man trying to settle some of his affairs, in particular to secure the position of several of his chivalric cadre beyond the inevitable Stewart succession to the throne which would soon follow.

1 Cited in *Chron. Bower*, vii, 361–5 at 365.
2 NAS RH 2/4/562 Transcripts of English ER Issue Rolls, 1310–65/15/3/1357; *Rot. Scot.*, i, 799; *Chron. Bower*, vii, 464n; *ER*, i, 616 (John); *CPP*, i, 365 (confessor); Bannerman, *The Beatons*, 59–62; M.H. Kaufman & W.J. MacLennnan, 'Robert the Bruce and Leprosy', *Proceedings of the Royal College of Physicians of Edinburgh*, 30 (2000), 75–80.

Thus, while at Melrose, David confirmed a charter by the Douglas earl to one of his Lanarkshire tenants. A week later he was back at Edinburgh where he granted a pension to crusader Sir Richard Comyn. But two days later David granted to Robert Steward, earl of Strathearn, the valuable Perthshire barony of Methven with the notable addition of some 100 cows and 300 sheep from royal lands at Balmonth in Fife: this was the only direct grant of lands which the Steward ever received from his royal nephew. In the light of what was to come this must be interpreted as a peace offering to the man who would soon become king, perhaps involving the regrant of lands revoked by the crown in 1367 or the formal confirmation of a title suppressed in conjunction with Strathearn in 1368–9. This was followed on 18 September 1370 by a grant to John 'Heryng' (who may have accompanied David south in 1363) of Glasclune in north-eastern Perthshire, lands which the late Sir Thomas Bisset had originally given to Countess Isabella of Fife following their marriage.[3]

Thereafter, late October 1370 saw what would be the last parliament of the reign at Perth and firm signs that the king anticipated his end. No record of the statutory decisions of this body has survived. It is likely that the estates simply did not discuss the state of Anglo-Scottish and Franco-Scottish relations or taxation: those matters would soon be reviewed by the new Stewart regime. But as well as David's aforementioned grants to Sir Duncan Wallace and 'Eleanor Bruce' (née Douglas) a number of significant acts witnessed in this parliament have survived.[4]

Issued on 24 October (following a resignation the day before), one of these acts was the culmination of David's intervention in the north since 1368: a regrant of the earldom of Ross, the lordship of Skye and other lands (with some exceptions in the shires of Aberdeen, Dumfries and Wigtown) to their current owner, Earl William of Ross, but with a tailzie in the event of his death to Sir Walter Leslie, his son-in-law. The Steward, the earls of Douglas, March and Carrick, Archibald Douglas, Robert Erskine, Alexander Lindsay of Glenesk, William Dischington 'and many other barons' were the witnesses to what was thus effectively the casting of a tailzie similar to that imposed upon Duncan, earl of Fife, in 1315 but with the pragmatic difference that the crown was now prepared to accept a female succession. In doing so, David disinherited the man who had at one time sought to succeed to his brother's lands in return for helping the king secure his release from England in 1351–2: Hugh Ross of Philorth. Hugh died, apparently still a fugitive from the crown, sometime before 14 February 1371. But that Earl

---

3 *RMS*, i, nos. 350, 351, 353, 365.
4 *APS*, i, 298, Appendix p. 177 (*RPS*, 1370/10/1–2); *RMS*, i, nos. 356, 358; *RRS*, vi, no. 474.

William of Ross had complied only to avoid the royal circle's wrath was made clear in his complaint to parliament in March 1371 that he had acted under extreme duress, 'owing to King David's rigour and in fear of his indignation'. Ross and many of the witnessing magnates may, of course, have complied in the belief that David's imminent death would allow this wilful act to be undone.[5]

Nevertheless, Leslie was for now confirmed as the leading light of a royalist network in the north. William, earl of Sutherland, had been killed in a local dispute sometime in 1369–70 but the 'bold' crusader Walter was surely well able to fill his shoes, compensating for his lack of a natural following in the north with his wealth and military following from Angus and Mar.[6] In this, Leslie was ably supported by William Keith the Marischal and 'lieutenant of Moray', Alexander de Bur, bishop of Moray, Sir Richard Comyn, the Mar men Moigne and Meldrum, and the officers of Aberdeen-shire, Banffshire and Inverness-shire (the Fentons, Chisholms, Frasers, Bissets, Chalmers and others); there was a grant for Moigne of Aberdeen lands on 23 October 1370, perhaps in recognition of his services as justice-clerk and in recently codifying a treatise of some of the finance and administration pertaining to the royal household.[7] Tellingly, Robert Steward may now have been content to go along with this royal intrusion into Ross because in the end it relieved some of his own lordship concerns. By helping to disinherit Earl William, the Steward need no longer worry about the familial claim of his second wife, Euphemia Ross (the Ross earl's sister and widow of John Randolph, earl of Moray) to the earldom of Strathearn or about territorial clashes over Badenoch (part of Moray's regality until 1346). It may have been to further deal with this issue that on 24 October 1370 King David granted the lands of Kinloch in Perthshire to the Steward's fifth son (his first son by Euphemia Ross), David Stewart – named after the Bruce king: this youth would become earl of Strathearn in March 1371 (but die by c. 1389–90). On the same day in October 1370, David also made a

5 *RMS*, i, no. 354; *APS*, i, 537; Fraser ed., *Frasers of Philorth*, ii, 206–7; Forbes, *Ane Account of the Familie of Innes*, 70–3. See NAS RH2/64/40 and *RMS*, i, no. 298 for Hugh.

6 Fraser ed., *The Sutherland Book*, i, 45–7. Tradition has it that earl William of Sutherland was killed at Dingwall in 1370 in retaliation for the murder by his brother, Nicholas, of a Mackay at an assize (MacKay, *Book of MacKay*, 44–5).

7 *RMS*, i, no. 368; Duncan, 'The 'Laws of Malcolm MacKenneth'', 262–4. For the homage and fealty of many of these lay men at the bishop of Moray's court in the late 1360s, see: *Registrum Episcopatus Moraviensis*, nos. 286, 287, 288; Fraser ed., *Frasers of Philorth*, i, 168–9; E.C. Batton ed., *The Charters of the Priory of Beauly with Notices of the Priories of Ardchatten and Pluscardine and of the family of the Founder, John Byset* (London, Grampian Club 1877), 87–91. For the association of some of these men with Leslie in the north, see *Illustrations of the Topography and Antiquities of Aberdeen and Banff*, ii, 217–8, 383 and iii, 43, 133 and v, 715, 720.

grant of lands in the hotly disputed *Abnethia* of Dull to a Donald Mac-Nayre.[8]

However, the most striking indication of David's preparation for death was his issue at Perth under the great seal, following parliament's 'consent and assent', of letters granting all the prelates of Scotland the right to leave and distribute personal property by will at their deaths. Prior to this, the goods and church revenues of any dead bishop had fallen to the king during the resulting vacancy.[9] David's act might be viewed as a parting act of piety in response to 'prelates [who had] petitioned urgently concerning this' and a reward for clerical consent to (unpopular) direct ransom taxation of the ecclesiastical estate in 1359–63 and 1365–6: David's letters were certainly important enough to be recorded in full seventy years later by a grateful Abbot Bower. Moreover, in return, all bishops were to establish 'continually in cathedral churches one perpetual chaplain specifically to celebrate one mass . . . for us [David] in our life and after our death for the salvation of our soul and the soul of our lord father of honourable memory, also for the healthy estate of each of our heirs and successors while they shall live and for the souls of the same when they shall pass away from this life'.

Significantly, however, the internal form of these letters also suggests that Robert Steward, king-in-waiting, had already begun to take over the reins of power. Remarkably, some of the more unusual wording of this act indicates that it was penned by the same scribe who had worked for the Steward as Lieutenant in 1356–7 and who had then written the commission to the three rogue ambassadors to Paris in May 1359: in the latter year David may have been under duress from the future rebel earls of 1363 with the Steward looking to act again as *de facto* Lieutenant. It is likely, then, that Robert Steward's servants had already been intruded into some of the royal chancery by late 1370. Indeed, the unprecedented emphasis given within David's grant to the prelates of the 'consent and assent of Robert Stewart, steward of Scotland, our nephew, and his children . . .', who appended their seals before the rest of the community, surely confirms anticipation by all present of a Stewart succession to the throne. Likewise, the witnesses listed at the act's close were the Steward and John Stewart, earl of Carrick, 'his first born son and heir', Thomas, earl of Mar (heir to the kingship after the Stewarts and who had presumably been released from the Bass by his royal cousin), George, earl of March, and William, earl of Douglas: these were the big men who would now decide Scotland's future. Nonetheless, that this parting gift to the churchmen of Scotland was very much David's brainchild

---

8 *RMS*, i, nos. 355, 360; Boardman, *Early Stewart Kings*, 56, 75–9, 88–9, 95.
9 *RMS*, i, no. 372; G. Donaldson, 'The rights of the Scottish Crown in episcopal vacancies', *SHR*, xlv (1966), 27–35; Watt, *Medieval Church Councils in Scotland*, 124.

– perhaps even designed to deprive the Steward of future windfall income as king – is suggested by the Stewart crown's breach of its terms by as early as 1374–5 when the Pope had to upbraid Robert II for withholding the goods of the late Walter Wardlaw, bishop of Glasgow, who had been very much a Bruce man before 1371.[10]

With parliament closed in October 1370, it may have been at this time of his life that David, like his father, really wished he could go on crusade or pilgrimage to the Holy Land. One version of Abbot Bower's work (following Wyntoun's anonymous but contemporary late fourteenth-century source) would later assert that:

> the king himself, when he was about to set out for the Holy Land to tame the ferocity of the pagans with all his might, appointed guardians for the kingdom, and determined to go over there with a military force . . . But in the end, forestalled by a visitation of the Most High, bitter death did not spare the kingly fate, but extinguished and brought to an end under its fatal law a king who was scarcely approaching mature manhood.[11]

David would probably have been able to raise the funds for such a personal voyage. But really, the overwelming sense of the king's last few weeks is one of anticlimax, giving the impression of a man resigned to his fate without even the energy for a last ceremonial pilgrimage within Scotland. At Dundee on 1 November, David confirmed charters by the absent Hugh Ross and William, earl of Ross, to Alexander Sinclair, the son of the Rosses' former place-man in Orkney; present with the king were the bishops of St Andrews and Brechin, the Steward, the earl of Douglas, Erskine, Archibald Douglas, Dischington, Alexander Lindsay and Walter Leslie, as they probably were throughout the remaining few weeks of the king's life. Yet David does not seem to have travelled home to Edinburgh via St Monans. A week later, 9 November, found him at Perth when he issued a charter of Kinross lands to Sir John Barclay.[12]

The end of December found David back among the building works of his

10 *Chron. Bower*, vii, 455–7; *CPL*, iv, 145, 206; Barrell, *The Papacy, Scotland and northern England*, 162. Many thanks to Roland Tanner not only for pointing out to me the scribal similarities between the 1357, 1359 and 1370 acts but for providing a convincing redating of the prelates' act from the speculative July 1368 x January 1369 offered by Bower's editors – a date based upon their mistaken substitution of 'Thomas earl of Fife' for Thomas of Mar. See Penman & Tanner, 'An Unpublished act of David II, 1359'; *RRS*, vi, no. 141. All twelve bishops of Scotland would seek papal confirmation of their testamentary rights on 1 January 1372 (*Vetera*, 346 no. 694; *Registrum Episcopatus Aberdonensis*, ii, 122–4).
11 *Chron. Wyntoun*, vi, 244; *Chron. Bower*, vii, 361.
12 *RRS*, vi, nos. 475–6; *RMS*, i, nos. 361–2.

projected tower-house at Edinburgh Castle from where he does not seem to have moved until death. He issued only a handful of more minor acts. Tellingly, the most significant of these was a massive pension of 1,000 merks a year from the fermes and customs of the burghs of Aberdeen and Haddington (which Queen Margaret had held) to the focus of all his unrealised hopes of the last three years, his mistress Agnes Dunbar. This was surely a completely sentimental grant, an unreasonable and unsustainable imposition to place on a realm heavily taxed for ransom. A final extant charter dates from 29 January.[13] If a medical crisis followed, no record of treatment has survived in the royal accounts. The end itself may have come suddenly. By the morning of Saturday 22 February 1371, David II was dead.[14]

The Stewart Kingdom of Scotland

Upon David's death, the fifty-five-year-old Robert Steward took the throne as Robert II. The new king must have exhaled an immense sigh of relief with the premature passing of his uncle. With what might in some eyes have seemed hasty disrespect, David's remains were interred not – as he had planned as early as 1366 – at Dunfermline Abbey in Fife beside his father, mother and aunt and Alexander III's royal kin, but before the high altar at Holyrood. Although this was a suitable spiritual home given David's connections with the abbey which had supplied his Augustinian household chaplains since 1342, it was more likely chosen because it was closest to hand, only a mile distant from Edinburgh's castle rock. No record survives of substantial monies disbursed by the Stewart crown for David's funeral arrangements, a stark contrast to the £1,000 or more laid aside by the Bruce minority government for Robert I's marble tomb or even the £682 which would be spent on the resting place of the unimpressive Robert II at Scone Abbey in 1390: it is possible that payment for David's marble coffin was made instead by his former noble and clerical supporters, men like Archibald the Grim who re-endowed a hospital at Holyrood in 1379 dedicated to the memory of Robert I, David II, Edward Bruce and the 'Good' Sir James Douglas.[15] In

---

13 *RMS*, i, nos. 362 (the Dumfriesshire barony of Glencarne to Robert Danielston), 363 (to John Wallace of Forfar lands), 364 (to a Brice Wyche of Kinross lands); *RRS*, vi, nos. 477 (Agnes Dunbar), 478 (inspection of a charter by Donald earl of Lennox).

14 *Chron. Fordun*, i, 382; *Chron. Bower*, vii, 361.

15 *Liber Cartarum Sancte Crucis* (Edinburgh 1840), 90–95; *ER*, i, 150, 167, 175, 213–5, 221 and ii, 242, 279–80, 300, 348, 585, 592, 608, 622; *CPL to Scotland of Clement VII of Avignon, 1378–94*, ed. C. Burns (SHS, Edinburgh 1976), 34. In July 1371 and May 1372, however, safe-conducts were issued to William Cuppil and Andrew Painter (of Edinburgh) to go abroad and for William Patryngton, John Wulseleye and Galfrado Mason to enter Scotland, all to 'make the tomb of David Bruce' (*Rot. Scot.*, i, 945, 949; *Registrum Cartarum Ecclesie Sancti Egidii de Edinburgh* (Bannatyne Club, Edinburgh 1859), 28, 275, 281; M.R. Apted and S. Hannabuss eds, *Painters in Scotland 1301–1700: A Biographical Dictionary* (Edinburgh 1978), 24).

1371, though, David's quick, expedient burial was symptomatic not only of the Stewarts' understandable desire to smother and sweep away the memory and legacy of the second Bruce king but of their preoccupation with the new crises and opportunities which David's passing brought to the first months of their regime. Indeed, the events of the first few years of the Stewart dynasty betray much of the impact of both the strengths and weaknesses of David's rule.

After enduring more than a decade of frustration and humiliation in the royal presence, Robert Steward was not allowed a fresh start. Even before he could be crowned, Robert found his succession challenged by his former ally in rebellion, William, earl of Douglas, who moved quickly to seize his chance to throw off the crown's strangulation of his influence since 1357. 'Surrounded by an armed force', the earl opposed the Steward's elevation at what is asserted by at least one Scottish chronicler to have been the first council or parliament of the reign held, bizarrely, at Linlithgow. Incredibly, Abbot Bower also speculated that Douglas actually demanded the throne by 'claiming to be a candidate for elevation . . . in the Comyn or Balliol interest'.[16]

In truth, the earl's only reasonable claim to the kingship rested upon his marriage to Thomas, earl of Mar's sister, a cousin of David II (because Thomas had a Bruce grandmother and great aunt). But what Douglas was surely doing was threatening Robert Steward with the spectre of David's indentures with Edward III of 1351–2, 1359 and 1363 (the latter of which Douglas had helped negotiate) and the prospect of the alternative succession of Prince John of Gaunt, a Comyn of Buchan descendant and an heir of the English king who had held the Balliol claim to Scotland since November 1356. Earl William's son, James Douglas, would welcome Gaunt into a brief and comfortable exile in Scotland in 1381. Yet in reality what Earl William craved in 1371 and had to be given for the sake of domestic peace was the restoration of his house's political dominance south-of-Forth denied to him by David since 1357. Robert II thus 'tretyt' and bought the earl of Douglas's allegiance with the justiciarship, the Wardenship of the middle march, a hefty pension and a marriage for his son and heir, James, to a Stewart princess.[17]

Crucially, however, this was a timely compromise brokered by the central figures of David II's close counsel and chivlaric cadre of 1368–71, Sir Robert Erskine and George and John Dunbar. These men had collectively faced

---

16 *Chron. Bower*, vii, 365–7.
17 Boardman, *Early Stewart Kings*, 40–6; *Chron. Wyntoun*, vi, 264–5. For what follows on Douglas's gains and much of the dismantling of David II's affinity after 1371, I am heavily indebted to Stephen Boardman's chs. 2 and 3. See Mackenzie, *Rise of the Stewarts*, 79, for a possible genealogy of the Douglas claim.

Douglas down with what Wyntoun's source describes as a sizeable army and 'the Stewartis rycht to be [king]'.[18] The Erskines' possession of three key royal castles gave them the balance of power in the kingdom: Thomas Erskine's keepership of Edinburgh in David's name might even have resulted in a temporary state of siege – thus the need for an *ad hoc* meeting of the estates or select peace talks at Linlithgow twenty miles to the west (along the roads to Stirling and Scone or Lanarkshire and Clydeside). Nevertheless, in reconciling the Douglas earl and Robert II – who was then crowned king at Scone on 26 March 1371 – David's former party also sought to ensure their own survival and prosperity under Stewart rule. Most of David's hard-working bureaucratic clerics – including John of Carrick, the Chancellor, and William of Biggar, the Chamberlain – were easily able to make the transition into Stewart service, serving the state as an institution allied to the sovereign national church rather than a family line.[19] But for those ambitious territorial and political laymen who had prospered at the expense of others since 1357 by backing David, the future at the hands of hungry regional nobles at last unleashed on the status quo of territorial lordship was highly uncertain.

The Stewarts – like the Douglas earl – proved extremely capable of seizing the moment. Within two months of David's demise private deals had been struck by Robert II's sons over the long-disputed provinces of Menteith (23 March 1371), Fife (29–30 March 1371) and Badenoch which confirmed these lands as full Stewart titles.[20] Other titles and offices would be chosen for 'Stewartisation' by force. This was an expansion of the Stewart 'family firm' which in many ways the new king had no choice but to countenance and exploit. It was also a cold reality which had to be recognised by the Erskines, Dunbars, lesser Douglases and other David II men.

Predictably, the most substantial men of the Bruce circle were able to work with the new regime, though often at a high price. Arguably, Sir Archibald Douglas, lord of Galloway, fared best. Robert II confirmed Archibald's control of the Murray-Bothwell inheritance in 1371, and his feud with Robert Stewart, now earl (not just lord) of Menteith and Fife, was settled.[21] Archibald was also employed to return to France to renew the Franco-Scottish alliance by June 1371 in terms of mutual military support

18 *Chron. Wyntoun*, vi, 264.
19 *ER*, ii, cxxv; Watt, *Scottish Graduates*, 89–91.
20 NLS Charter no. 698; NAS RH 1/1/2/1; Fraser ed., *Red Book of Menteith*, ii, 251–4; *Registrum Episcopatus Moraviensis*, 472–3; *RMS*, i, nos. 382, 530, 558; Boardman, *Early Stewart Kings*, 50–52, 71–4. The Fife indenture revived the 1309 agreement whereby that earldom would revert to the Menteith heirs of the Fife earldom, a tailzie overridden by Robert I in 1315 (*RRS*, v, no. 72).
21 *RMS*, i, no. 401; Boardman, *Early Stewart Kings*, 66 n42.

similar to those struck in 1351, 1355 and 1359.[22] But in 1372 Archibald was also in a position to buy out the Fleming earls of Wigtown, embellishing his aggressive lordship in Galloway, Nithsdale, Annandale and the marches.[23] The Grim Douglas would go on not only to play a prominent part in border warfare but, through an alliance with Robert Stewart of Menteith and Fife (made Duke of Albany by 1399), succeed after 1388 to the Black Douglas earldom itself and snub the Dunbars in pursuit of a marriage for their daughters to the Stewart heir to the throne. It would be Archibald's offspring who preyed upon the Dunbars' earldom in the east march after 1400, bringing to a climax the erosion of that family's power which had really begun with David II's death.[24]

George Dunbar, earl of March, did receive a royal Stewart marriage and the lordships of Annandale and Man from Robert II in 1371. But as western march Warden, Archibald the Grim would intrude on Annandale and George's brother, John, would be deprived of Fife through Countess Isabella's immediate collusion in spring 1371 with Robert Stewart to whom she tailzied that title: over the next fifteen years John Dunbar was sytematically undermined in his compensatory possession of parts of the earldom of Moray by Alexander Stewart, the new king's fourth son.[25] The longer-term fate of George and John Dunbar, as we shall see, would involve exile to England and forfeiture in the wake of Stewart and Douglas power games by 1400. Although the Dunbars would for a while recover their lands after 1409, their lordship was fatally weakened and in the end succumbed to James I's acquisitiveness in 1434.[26]

Agnes Dunbar, David's intended queen, saw better times only briefly. There is no evidence that she ever received her 1,000-merk pension granted by her loving king. But by 1372 she was wed to James Douglas of Dalkeith and would give him two sons and two daughters before her death about 1378.[27] Her new husband had quickly slipped back into Black Douglas service, tempted by a huge retainer from Earl William of 600 merks in 1371: Dalkeith was also named as understudy for Archibald the Grim's embassies to France by the new Stewart King and was confirmed in 1372 in his

22 *APS*, i, 559–60; *ER*, ii, 356, 363 and iii, xcviii–civ.
23 Fraser ed., *Douglas Book*, i, 321–35 and iii, no. 327; Brown, *Black Douglases*, 63–7, 74 n41.
24 Boardman, *Early Stewart Kings*, 147–68, 227; Brown, *Black Douglases*, chs. 3 and 4 *passim*; MacDonald, *Border Bloodshed, ad indecim*.
25 *RMS*, i, nos. 405, 473, 521, 553; *Rot. Scot.*, i, 957; NAS GD1/202/1; *Registrum Honoris de Morton*, ii, 101–2; Boardman, *Early Stewart Kings*, 50–2, 72–6, 132–5, 175–6 – the Wolf's advance began with a grant of Lochindorb Castle in 1371.
26 Brown, *James I*, 155–6.
27 *Scots Peerage*, vi, 344–50; Fraser ed., *Douglas Book*, i, 256–8 and iii, no 374; *ER*, ii, 364 shows Agnes in receipt of a single payment from Robert II of £69.

disputed lands of Kellor in Strathearn by David Stewart, the new young earl of Strathearn. In many ways, it was Dalkeith's middling rank which enabled him to escape the wrath of Stewart and Douglas earl frustrations: James played a similar role to his cousin in the intermittent wars against England between 1377 and his death in 1420. In 1388 his support for the Grim and Robert Stewart, earl of Menteith and Fife, would secure him the lordship of Liddesdale by right of the controversial tailzie of 1342 (imposed on David).[28]

However, other crown men from the 1360s were much less fortunate. Sir Robert Erskine remained prominent at court but found his control of castles and offices wrested away by the Stewarts and Douglases: Dumbarton again passed to Stewart control (under Sir John Danielston); Stirling was gifted by Robert II to Robert Stewart of Fife and Menteith in February 1373; custody of Edinburgh Castle was quickly ceded to John Stewart, earl of Carrick, and his adherents, the Flemings; the justiciarship north-of-Forth was filled by Alexander Lindsay of Glenesk (who wed a niece of Robert II while his son wed a princess) and his kin.[29] The Erskines were surely tainted by their close association with David since *c.* 1360 and as past feud rivals of Douglas of Dalkeith. Although compensated with handsome pensions, by the time of his death in 1385 Robert Erskine, and his sons, had been pushed to the fringes of actual power and obliged to find service abroad or in the retinues of Stewart and Douglas earls.[30] The Erskines thus never fulfilled the promise for which Sir Robert seemed destined. His descendants were also to be thwarted over their hopeful claims to the earldom of Mar – vacated by the death of the unpredictable Earl Thomas in 1374 – by the first Douglas earl (d. 1377), the Drummonds, successive Badenoch Stewarts and the Stewart crown in turn over the next eighty years.[31]

A much swifter eclipse befell Walter Leslie. This 'bold' knight had undeniably been David's most controversial and alien intrusion into established regional interests; without the protection of the Bruce monarch Walter suffered badly. William, earl of Ross, lodged his vitriolic *querimonia* or complaint against David and the crusader at the Scone coronation parliament of March 1371 and began to recover full control of his lands only to die in his late sixties in February 1372.[32] Although thereafter Leslie

28 *Registrum Honoris de Morton*, ii, 94–5, 111–3; NAS GD 150/26; Boardman, *Early Stewart Kings*, 151–3, 162–4; Brown, *Black Douglases*, 59–60, 82–90, 107–9; MacDonald, *Border Bloodshed*, 25, 33, 52, 83, 85, 173.

29 *RMS*, i, no. 554; *ER*, ii, 344, 357, 364–5, 393, 396, 458; NAS RH2/6/4, 103; Boardman, *Early Stewart Kings*, 44, 47–8, 53, 72.

30 *ER*, ii, 415, 433, 460, 472; Boardman, *Early Stewart Kings*, 52–5, 68 n55–6, 119–21; AN J621 no. 77.

31 Boardman, *Early Stewart Kings*, 261–4; Brown, *James I*, 156–60, 200.

32 *Ane Account of the Familie of Innes*, 70–3; *Scots Peerage*, vii, 237–9.

gave much of the land he had received from David II to his Lindsay associates, his designs on the earldom of Ross and what had been granted to that house in Buchan since 1308 fell prey by the end of the 1370s to Alexander Stewart's empire-building along with the adjacent Dunbar earldom of Moray.[33] Long before then, Walter – like a number of David's chivalric cadre – had found things so hot that he preferred periodically to resume his crusading and mercenary career abroad: in fact, in the weeks immediately following David's death safe-conducts to the continent were issued by Edward III's government to Walter Leslie and others, including Sir John Abernethy, Alexander Ramsay of Dalhousie (junior), Simon Reed (David's constable of Edinburgh Castle) and Bartholomew Leon (David's ambassador to the Papacy in 1350 and his man in Barnbougle, a detached Menteith holding). It was during a pilgrimage to the Holy Land that Leslie's half-brother, Alexander Lindsay of Glenesk, died about March 1382, a month after Walter's own demise from unspecified causes at Perth: Leslie's widow (the earl of Ross's daughter) was in turn forced to marry prince Alexander Stewart of Badenoch who was set to write his name into infamy in the north.[34]

David II's former stepson, John Logie, might soon have wished that he could join Leslie abroad. Without David's lordship, Logie also fell foul of Robert Stewart of Menteith who displaced him from his regality of Logie and Strathgartney: the Dunbars and Douglases deprived Logie of power in Annandale. Queen Margaret's appeals to the papacy against her divorce by King David may initially have stalled the stripping of her son's assets. But favour from Pope Gregory XI for the Logie cause ended with Margaret's death and burial in Marseilles in 1375. Thereafter the Logie-Drummond kindred enjoyed only an intermittent recovery of favour when John Stewart, earl of Carrick, seized power between 1384 and 1388 and became king as Robert III in 1390, and when this monarch's son in turn, David Stewart, Duke of Rothesay, acted as King's Lieutenant between 1399 and his death in 1402.[35] Gilbert of Glencairnie suffered a similar isolation in northern Perthshire and Moray, abandoning his lands there by the late 1370s to *Clann Donnchaidh* raids. At the same time John Macdougall of Lorn found the writ granted him by David II over Glen Lyon and neighbouring Dull enveloped by Alexander Stewart's violent protectionism: the land of Lorn

33 *RMS*, i, nos. 446, 621; Boardman, *Early Stewart Kings*, 48–9, 73–82.
34 *Rot. Scot.*, i, 943, 944, 955; Macquarrie, *Scotland and the Crusades*, 85, 88, 127; Boardman, *Early Stewart Kings*, 77–9.
35 *Ibid*, 71, 135, 141, 185; Barrell, *Papacy, Scotland and northern England*, 161–2. Malcolm Drummond, brother of Annabella, wife of John Stewart of Kyle/Robert III, did wed Isabella, daughter of William, earl of Douglas, sometime before 1388 (*Scots Peerage*, iii, 153–4).

itself was soon claimed by the Stewarts through marriage.[36] But no-one suffered worse at the future 'Wolf' of Badenoch's hands than David's policeman-bishop in the north-east, Alexander de Bur, bishop of Moray, who despite numerous bonds of protection sealed with this son of Robert II after 1371 came to blows on many occasions, culminating in the notorious destruction of Elgin Cathedral by the 'Wolf' and his sons in 1390.[37] Leslie, Logie, Glencairnie, Macdougall and the bishop thus suffered long and lingering assaults from rival Stewart lordships – although Bur was able to work with the paternal Stewart crown. Other lesser followers of David II were more mildly if crudely deprived after his death: for example, William Dischington lost his sheriffship of Fife and northern justiciarship (to Alan Erskine and the adaptable Sir Alexander Lindsay of Glenesk) and crusader Richard Comyn was ousted in 1371 as keeper of Darnaway forest as Robert II restored the le Grants.[38]

However, between 1371 and 1390 and beyond, the legacy of David II's reign and the Bruce dynasty as a whole had not merely had a generally negative impact upon that regime's close supporters from the 1360s. Most significantly, doubts about the Stewart succession had not ended with Douglas's pay-off in 1371. Indeed, the question soon deepened to reveal internal divisions in Scotland as well as potentially grave external threats.

Beyond Douglas's possible tactical ploy, there is little or no evidence that any major player in Scotland in 1371 dwelt seriously upon David's ideas for an English, or a realigned Scottish, succession: the majority of the political community accepted that there was no realistic regal alternative to the Stewarts. Abbot Bower would later make the remarkable assertion that in March 1371:

> the three estates of the realm met in the royal town of Linlithgow, and began to negotiate over the choice of their future king. They amicably voted in favour of the illustrious prince Sir Robert Stewart, King David's nephew, in accordance with his hereditary position and with the implications of the tailzies originally drawn up on this matter.[39]

However, this mid-fifteenth century chronicle emphasis upon the consultative powers of the estates surely reflects the growth between 1371 and *c.* 1445 of parliament's supervisory ability to influence royal policy and not any genuine debate over the legality of a Stewart succession after David

36 Boardman, *Early Stewart Kings*, 76, 169, 180; *idem*, 'The Tale of Leper John and the Campbell Acquisition of Lorn', 188–9.
37 Grant, 'The Wolf of Badenoch'; Boardman, 'Lordship in the North-East I'; *idem*, *Early Stewart Kings*, 175–6; Oram, 'Alexander Bur', 202–4.
38 *RMS*, i, no. 825; Boardman, *Early Stewart Kings*, 48.
39 *Chron. Bower*, vii, 365.

Bruce's death. By contrast, John of Fordun's contemporary annals –
resuming after an eight-year gap – recorded merely that David died (of
what is not stated) and Robert 'succeeded by right of inheritance': this is
arguably reflected in the level of unanimity behind Steward's accession
expressed by Bower.[40]

Nonetheless, Bower's version of events does point to estate powers of
bestowing the security of community consensus upon royal acts which
Robert II and others must have been anxious to use in 1371. The act of
succession passed swiftly by the coronation parliament at Scone in late
March that year and which recognised John Stewart, earl of Carrick and
Atholl, as heir to the throne was surely designed to settle tensions between
king and prince resulting from David II's favour after 1365 to John and his
Drummond wife. This was a far more tangible legacy of David's attempts to
recast the royal succession. Doubts raised, too, since 1341 about the
legitimacy of Robert II's children by his first (retrospective) marriage also
seem to have caused problems which the Stewart regime looked to solve in
parliament. In 1373, the estates ratified another act of succession, this time
detailing a tailzie of the kingship through Carrick, his male issue or, failing
that line, through his brothers and their sons in turn. The preamble of this
act asserts that its purpose was to:

> avoid the uncertainty of the succession and the evils and misfortunes
> which, in very many kingdoms and places, arise and in times past have
> arisen from the succession of female heirs.[41]

With the consequences of Alexander III's death in 1286 ingrained in the
political memories of the leading Scottish families of the late fourteenth
century this provision made sense, especially as John Stewart of Carrick
– by then in his mid-thirties – would have only two daughters, Margaret
(who wed Archibald the Grim's son in 1390) and Elizabeth, but no son
until the birth of David Stewart (the future Duke of Rothesay) in
1378.[42]

Yet in 1373 denial of the right of female succession – the very
inheritance path which had brought the Bruces and the Stewarts the
throne – also allowed Robert II to perhaps calm tensions between the
offspring of his first and second marriages. The fresh Franco-Scottish
treaty of alliance of June 1371 included the agreement that if Robert II's
succession was disputed, then the French king would not intervene to

40 *Chron. Fordun*, i, 382; Tanner, *Late Medieval Scottish Parliament*, 276–8.
41 *APS*, i, 196–7, 549; S. Boardman, 'Coronations, Kings and Guardians, Politics,
    Parliaments and General Councils, 1371–1406', in Tanner and Brown eds.,
    Parliament and Politics in Scotland: 1286–1567 (forthcoming).
42 *Scots Peerage*, i, 14–7.

help any individual heir of his Scottish counterpart but would leave the issue to be settled by the prelates and magnates of Scotland under that realm's laws: significantly, this treaty also recognised the possibility of English interference in the Scottish succession.[43] But through these tailzies and treaty of 1371–3, the legitimacy of Robert II's three eldest living sons (by his first wife) thus became enshrined in parliamentary principles first established in the succession acts of 1318 and 1326 which had helped guarantee Stewart political survival in the face of David's challenges between 1341 and 1371. Robert II's second wife and queen, Euphemia Ross – who seems to have been sufficiently at odds with her husband in 1371 over the standing of their two young sons, David and Walter, to be excluded from a Scone coronation until the following year – now had to accept the status quo.[44]

All told, this was an extremely nervous beginning for the new royal dynasty. Robert II – like John Balliol/I (1292–6) – had been for the first five decades of his life a leading regional magnate. He had neither the personal charisma nor the natural authority to attempt to rule as king over his former peers and equals with the same authoritarian hand of leadership and active (and, when necessary, violent) intervention as a Robert I or, to a lesser extent, a David II. This was the case not least because for the past forty years as Lieutenant or royal heir presumptive, the Steward had often led and directed sections of the political community in parliament – and at least once in arms – in opposition to independent and increasingly centralised Bruce monarchy. Besides, the myriad of young, energetic and competing noble scions of the Stewart and other regional houses who now looked to dominate the political landscape after 1371 allowed Robert II no scope simply to dictate policy and patronage as king. Abbot Bower's later description of Robert as a tall, willowy man, 'humble and gentle, friendly in appearance, a cheerful man, an honourable king, witty in his responses', if unwise in fathering so many legitimate children and bastards, presented really no more convincing a figure of royal authority than Froissart's depiction *c.* 1385 of a pale, cowardly and aged king, skulking on his west-coast family lands while his sons and nobles ran the kingdom's domestic and military affairs.[45]

But these severe limitations and the Stewart need for caution extended, too, into foreign relations while Robert II still remained influential in the 1370s. Although Robert renewed the Franco-Scottish alliance in June 1371,

43 Robertson ed., *The Parliamentary Records of Scotland*, 120–4.
44 My thanks to Stephen Boardman for emphasising this point *re* Euphemia's coronation; *Early Stewart Kings*, 72, 75; *Chron. Bower*, vii, 365.
45 *Chron. Bower*, vii, 367; *Oeuvres de Froissart*, ii, 312–3; Boardman, *Early Stewart Kings*, 123–4, 136–9.

the new king and his government chose to continue paying David II's ransom until the death of Edward III in 1377, leaving only 24,000 merks unpaid: in fact, under Robert II the Scottish estates paid more of the ransom than under David himself.[46] Scottish concerns that Charles V of France was not actually in a position to aid them in renewed all-out war against England may have been compounded by the threat posed until 1374–5 by Queen Margaret Logie's lobbying in Avignon where she had arrived by July 1372. The danger of full papal interdict upon Scotland passed not with Robert II's appeals for the intercession of the French King in January 1374 but with Margaret's death a year later.[47]

Unwilling as yet to give full military vent to his Anglophobia, Robert II instead countenanced continued unofficial border raiding by those magnates active on the marches before 1371 – the Douglases and Dunbars – joined now by the Stewart king's own sons. The early 1370s saw much of Berwickshire recovered by the Scots as a result.[48] But the king also paid for an impressive courtly antidote to David II's Anglophile leanings by commissioning Archdeacon John Barbour's epic romance, *The Bruce* (*c.* 1371–5). As well as further legitimising the Stewart succession through closer association with Robert Bruce's reign of 1306–29, by giving prominent heroic roles to Sir James Douglas and Walter Steward, Barbour's poem also allowed the generation of Robert Steward and his sons, William, earl of Douglas, and Archibald of Galloway, to recast and lay claim to what they saw as the Bruce dynasty's true legacy and their part in its patriotic maintenance against England. This was a role which David II (and the unlucky Randolphs) had only been able to champion briefly before 1346. Such heroic patriotism thus became a Scottish mantle worn even more closely by the succeeding generation of Scots who after 1377 fought in alliance with France (with their treaty further renewed in 1383) in campaigns against England. This fresh aggression culminated in a famous victory at Otterburn in 1388: most of David II's Lowlands chivalric cadre participated with relish in these wars in the affinities of

---

46 *Rot. Scot.*, i, 945, 953, 982–3; NAS SP6 (Treaties with England)/9; BL MSS 24,511 folios 83–5. In all, 75% of David's ransom was paid off in contrast to just 14% paid by Charles of Blois, *c.* 57% of John II's and just 16% of James I of Scotland (Given-Wilson and Bériac, 'Edward III's Prisoners of War', 829–30).

47 On 21 May 1371 and 16 June 1374 Papal letters were sent to Scotland demanding that Robert II restore Margaret and her son, John Logie, to their lands and goods (NAS RH2/6 (Vatican Transcripts)/21, 25; *CPL*, iv, 94, 99, 120). Like David II, Robert II had to send various clerics and knights to the papacy to plead the case against Margaret (*ER*, ii, 435; *Chron. Bower*, vii, 503). For papal gifts to Margaret and her funeral expenses, see Barrell, *The Papacy, Scotland and northern England*, 161–2.

48 MacDonald, *Border Bloodshed*, 26–38.

Stewart, Black and Red Douglas, Dunbar and Lindsay (of Crawford) earls.[49]

By the 1380s, however, time and the interaction of the political legacy of the Bruce dynasty period with the rivalries of his own kin had overtaken Robert II. The Stewart princes of the blood and other regional nobles and their followings were ambitious men schooled and blooded politically in David II's time. They had been prepared in that reign to act both within and then outwith the law to defend and expand their own interests *vis-à-vis* an aggressive king. After 1380, these lords proved willing to escalate their autonomy beyond the control of much weaker Stewart personal monarchy. Hence in November 1384 Carrick and the second Douglas earl affected a coup in royal council, marginalising the aging Robert II and setting up a Lieutenancy which pursued open war with England, according to Froissart failing even to consult the old king – whom they 'ignored . . . entirely' – and even arresting him in 1388. At the end of that same year the now lame Carrick – with Douglas killed at Otterburn – was supplanted as Lieutenant in turn through a stage-managed council coup by Robert Stewart, earl of Fife and Menteith, and his ally, Archibald the Grim, now third earl of Douglas, a situation mitigated only slightly by Carrick's accession as Robert III in 1390.[50] These seizures of power were, as we have seen, a logical extension of the attempts to limit and redirect David II's personal kingship in

---

49 Barbour also penned a now lost Stewart genealogy asserting the legitimate Trojan origins of the new Stewart dynasty. Duncan ed., *The Bruce*, introduction; McDiarmid and Stevenson eds., *Barbour's Bruce*, introduction; *Foedera*, (0), vii, 391; L.A. Ebin, 'John Barbour's Bruce: Poetry, History and Propaganda', *Scottish Literary Journal*, lx (1972); R.J. Goldstein, *The Matter of Scotland: Historical Narrative in Medieval Scotland* (Lincoln 1993), chs. 6 and 7; C. Edington, 'Paragons and Patriots: National Identity and the Chivalric Ideal in Late Medieval Scotland', in D. Broun, R.J. Finlay and M. Lynch eds, *Image and Identity: The Making and Remaking of Scotland Through the Ages* (Edinburgh 1998), 69–81; A. Grant, 'The Otterburn War from the Scottish point of view, in A. Goodman and A. Tuck eds, *War and Border Societies in the Middle Ages* (Oxford 1992), 30–64; M. Brown, "Rejoice to hear of Douglas': The House of Douglas and the Presentation of Magnate Power in Late Medieval Scotland', *SHR*, lxxxvi (1997), 161–84; MacDonald, 'Profit, Politics and Personality' and *idem*, *Border Bloodshed*.

50 *Oeuvres de Froissart*, x, 289–93, 333–9, 376–95; Bodleian Library, Oxford, MS. Fairfax 23, f. 116; Boardman, *Early Stewart Kings*, chs. 5 and 6; Brown, 'Scotland Tamed?', 129, 134. As Stephen Boardman and Dauvit Broun have pointed out, the events of 1388–90 may also have seen the rewriting of historical chronicles with a view to justifying changes in the royal succession, just as with David II's reign (see above, ch. 9, n 108–9): one manuscript version of the *Gesta Annalia* II section of Fordun – dated to St Andrews *c*. 1388–1405 – includes the assertion that William I of Scotland had become king despite being a *younger* brother of Earl David of Huntingdon, paralleling Fife's challenge to Carrick in 1390 (D. Broun, 'Review of *Chron. Bower*, v and vi', in *SHR*, lxxiii (1994), 132–5; Boardman, 'Coronations, Kings and Guardians, Politics, Parliaments and General Councils, 1371–1406').

the 1350s and 1363. By 1402, these methods would have been taken a step further with the political murder (really regicide) of Robert III's son, heir and Lieutenant of the realm, David Stewart, Duke of Rothesay, at the hands of Fife/Menteith/Albany and the fourth Douglas earl: yet even Rothesay's starvation to death in Falkland Castle had been a method deployed by King David in response to similar provocation from his noble antagonists as early as 1342.[51]

Here again we might perceive at once the strengths and weakness of David II's kingship. The seeds of the dramatic events and bitter rivalries of the reigns of the first two Stewart kings of 1371–1406 – and perhaps, indeed, the later conflict between James I and James II and the Stewart and Douglas earls[52] – can be said to lie in the dominant political circumstances forged *before* 1371. Moreover, men like Carrick, Robert Stewart of Fife/Menteith/ Albany and the Douglas earls might be said to have looked to David as a potent and adaptable model of lordship, drawing lesser territorial lords and knights from the Lowlands into their service through a well-patronised cult of chivalry and using this support to attempt to control royal government, local offices, crown finance, meetings of the estates and foreign policy. However, in the actions of such magnate houses in the 1360s in resisting much of David's agenda, and then in the 1380s and 1390s in challenging and sidelining infirm Stewart kings, there lies overwhelming evidence to suggest that had David II lived longer, his reign might easily have erupted into a civil war which he could not have been sure to win.

For even if he had secured a third marriage and fathered a child in the early 1370s, the second Bruce king would have been increasingly isolated and surrounded by the scions of a growing number of greater and lesser territorial dynasties. The natural desire of such men for greater status, autonomy and influence on domestic and foreign policy would almost assuredly have left David vulnerable to the same challenges and margin- alisation that would befall his Stewart successors, not least from Robert Steward's several sons anxious to secure their birthright of central power, provincial control and glory in war. The 'covyne' of David's close noble supporters related to his mistress might easily have attracted mounting criticism, just as would happen in the final years of Edward III's reign.[53] Continued ransom taxation, too, could only prove unpopular in the long run, with the three estates conditioned to fiscal consultation. Furthermore, unchecked noble violence in the north might easily have been David's undoing. The Stewart earls of Carrick and Fife/Menteith would certainly

51 Boardman, 'The Man who would be King', 16. For 1342, see above, ch. 3. At the same time, the Stewart earl of Buchan neutralised the Drummond earl of Mar.

52 Brown, 'Scotland Tamed?'.

53 Given-Wilson, *The Royal Household and the King's Affinity*, 142–60.

use the pretext of lawlessness in the Gael to seize power in general council in 1384 and 1388, a grievance allied to the then king's alleged inability to defend the border with England.[54]

Indeed, together with the Douglases and Dunbars and their followings, these lords would have been all too willing to either forcibly redirect David's pursuit of a peace with England had that king not died in 1371; or, if David had lived on and chosen to ally with France, these nobles would have moved to deprive him of personal control of renewed war against the 'auld enemy'. The shifting and violent noble factions of the 1380s also make it clear that the new daily council and regional alliances which David worked so hard to forge between 1368 and 1371 might have rapidly fragmented. The ability of the younger Stewarts to attract lesser knights and esquires to their affinities and French service would have been an all too tempting alternative to the far more passive Christian chivalry favoured by an issueless Bruce king who had really done nothing of note in battle since 1346 and even then lost heavily.

Aged just forty-seven, then, David had been all too close to being dangerously out of date, isolated and out of his depth. The sad fact that his long reign would determine much of the political agenda of the late fourteenth century but leave no real personal legacy from his kingship is all too clearly reflected in the speed with which he was forgotten. Indeed the last real tangible effect of David's impact came in August 1400 when a singular – but eerily familiar – confrontation transpired at Edinburgh.

During the previous winter, Henry IV (1399–1413), the new Lancastrian king of England, following the murder of his cousin, Richard II, had resolved to avenge in person Scottish border transgressions by leading an army north. But the English host's passage through the eastern border marches of Scotland that summer was not the usual trail of unchallenged destruction.[55] After his host crossed the River Tweed, Henry spared the lands of George Dunbar, earl of March, brother of David II's intended third queen. Not only was Dunbar the English king's distant cousin but he had just become Henry's willing vassal and ally against the Scottish crown after his daughter had been thrown over for marriage by Prince David Stewart, Duke of Rothesay, the heir to the Scottish throne and – from late 1399 – the Lieutenant of the realm on behalf of his enfeebled father, Robert III (John Stewart of Kyle). Rothesay preferred the far more valuable match with a daughter of Archibald the 'Grim', third earl of Douglas, now the Dunbars' main rival for power in the Scottish borders. Thus the Dunbars were denied a glittering royal marriage for a second time in thirty years and seemed

54 Boardman, *Early Stewart Kings*, 119–25, 131–5, 201–15.
55 Brown, 'The English Campaign in Scotland, 1400', 40–54; MacDonald, *Border Bloodshed*, 138–42.

doomed to remain also-ran magnates in Stewart Scotland, a sore fact hammered home in early 1400 when Rothesay forfeited them for their contact with England and allowed the Douglases to move in on their lands.[56]

At the beginning of the new century, then, the Dunbars and a number of their Scottish tenants were only too glad of the opportunity to guide and aid Henry IV with the hope of devastating the lands and strongholds of East Lothian to the north and west of Dunbar Castle. Yet when the English army reached Holyrood Abbey, a mile east of Edinburgh Castle, Henry reined in his forces. He spared that Augustinian house – where the modest marble tomb of David II lay before the high altar – in thanks for the refuge it had given Henry's father, John of Gaunt, Duke of Lancaster, when in exile from political turmoil in England in 1381: Henry may also have met many of the Scots who had then visited his father, particularly those of David II's former retinue who had an active interest – like Henry c.1388–90 – in the crusade to Prussia.[57] Yet instead of then burning the royal burgh of Edinburgh and digging in to besiege Rothesay and the Douglas earl's son and heir in its crag-top castle, Henry began to issue a series of demands. Not only did the irate English king seek personal satisfaction for slanders in Scottish letters captured aboard a ship bound for France, but he renewed the seemingly traditional call for royal Scottish homage to the monarchs of England and laid claim to the Scottish crown itself by right of his father. Such a remarkable bid may have been based, optimistically, upon Gaunt's descent by marriage from the former Comyn earls of Buchan;[58] but this imperialistic claim is much more likely to have been founded with greater certainty upon the several proposed treaties of c. 1350 to 1371 between David II and Edward III whereby Gaunt was to have become heir presumptive to the Scottish throne in the event of David's failure to produce a son. A novel hint that this was so in 1400 lies in Henry IV's use of the same wooden chest which had held the English crown's papers relating to 'the ransom of David de Brus' to hold material to back up the Lancastrian claim to the Scottish throne: this box survives even today (see plate 10).[59]

For the young Rothesay, this must have been unnerving in the extreme. There were many significant Scottish nobles and churchmen who remem-

---

56 For what follows in 1400, see: *Chron. Bower*, vii, 31–7; Brown, *Black Douglases*, 99–113.

57 Goodman, *John of Gaunt*, 82–4; Paravicini, *Die Preussenreisen*, ii, 115–35; L. Toulmin-Smith ed., *Expeditions to Prussia and the Holy Land Made by Henry Earl of Derby* (Camden Society, 2nd series, London 1894), lii; Boardman and Penman, 'The Scottish arms in the Armorial of Gèlre'.

58 Young, *The Comyns*.

59 PRO E27/9; described in C. Jenning, *Early Chests in Wood and Iron* (PRO pamphlets no. 7, 1974), 2–3, plates I and II.

bered these mooted deals with England from the days of David II which would have displaced the Stewarts in the royal succession. Rothesay had even been named for the second Bruce king, his grandfather's uncle. Now in 1400 the prince must have looked down from the windows of the recently completed 'David's Tower', only too well aware that there was little he could do to repel Henry IV and his army. In particular, Rothesay could expect no assistance from his uncle, Robert Stewart, Duke of Albany and earl of Fife and Menteith, the most powerful magnate of the day, whom he had begun to fatally alienate. Uncertain what to do, the headstrong Rothesay even sent word to the English king at Leith challenging him to a setpiece combat – presumably to take place in the Bruce-built royal park below the north wall of the castle – to decide who would carry the day.[60]

This was a chivalric gesture which David II might well have appreciated. But as it turned out, Rothesay need not have bothered. Time, supplies, money and domestic troubles brought Henry up short like many of his predecessors in Scotland and the English army withdrew at the end of August having inflicted, according to Abbot Bower, 'only a little damage to the country'. The Stewart dynasty and other key players in the Scottish political community resumed their internal rivalries, culminating in the political murder of Rothesay by Albany in collusion with the new fourth Douglas earl in 1402. In truth – even though Robert III, Albany and the Grim Douglas earl had learned their trade in David II's reign – these men can have given little or no lasting thought to what had really been the final echo of that dead king's rule. To Stewart- and Douglas-dominated Scotland, at thirty years' remove, David Bruce's kingship had been a difficult if not embarrassing period to forget or re-write. Hence the possibility of an English succession in Scotland had proved, by 1400, to be an irritating and anachronistic irrelevance.

These Scottish nobles must have been aware that their present disputes and affinities were in large part a direct outcome of the crown-magnate relations forged under the Bruce dynasty and most especially during David's forty-one-year reign. Moreover, had he lived, Rothesay might have realised that in David II – who had also taken up power when young – he had a model of kingship which he in turn might have applied to help him assert his own authority over a number of ambitious noble houses. Yet only Henry IV (and George Dunbar, who must have reminded the English king of his father's pacts with the Bruce regime) seemed to take the history of David's reign seriously, as more than a mere bargaining chip in relations with Scotland. However, in staking his claim in 1400, Henry was attempting in vain to rekindle the concerns of a Scottish regime which after 17 October

60 Boardman, *Early Stewart Kings*, 223–54; MacDonald, *Border Bloodshed*, 191.

1346 had, in Stewart eyes, fatally lost its way and should never again be mentioned. That it had been the conflict of Neville's Cross which had been the crucial turning point of David II's reign and committed that king to a bitter quest for unobtainable goals was also echoed dimly twenty-nine years after his death: for the 'Bruce ransom chest' was decorated with the arms of the English victors of that battle, Neville, Percy and David's infamous captor, John de Coupland.

'A ruler of middling excellence'?

'Thus David, prince of fools, wished to catch fish in front of the net, and thereby lost many and caught but few . . .'

Chronicle of Lanercost, c. 1346[1]

In speculating about David II's fate beyond 1371, it is not hard to imagine that, despite his many problems, had he lived this monarch would have given the next generation of Scottish lords anxious for central and local power a good run for their money. He would surely have been able to craft and maintain a sizeable royalist party, not least by exploiting internal Stewart rivalries. Putting aside David's fatal inability to produce an heir (if that is ever possible in assessing any monarch), his impressive personal qualities and political abilities cannot be denied. Indeed, his strengths as king of Scots were recognised and noted even by Scottish chroniclers living and writing under Stewart kings over the century after David's death. Whatever the failings of this king lamented by modern historians (typically when comparing David to his father), late fourteenth- and fifteenth-century writers felt they knew their man. The closing comments about David's rule of Prior Wyntoun's *Orygynale Cronikil* are particularly revealing.[2] Written by an anonymous cleric *c.* 1390–1400 (then collated by Wyntoun *c.* 1420), who sought to rehabilitate Robert Steward's career before 1371 after the attacks on this lord by Fordun's earlier source, this work nonetheless regarded David as having become a fearfully masterful king:

> Lo, how raddour gert him dred be,
> And bot a boy with him brocht he;
> Yet than for his stout governyng
> He gert his folk haif sic dreding
> Off him, that nane durst nyth him here,
> Bot gif he specially callit were.
> He led with raddour sa his land,
> In all the tyme he wes regnand
> That nane durst weill withstand his will;
> All worth obeyand him till.

1 *Chron. Lanercost,* 337.
2 *Chron. Wyntoun,* vi, 234–5, 251 for what follows.

For Wyntoun's source, it was this 'raddour' – his stern personal authority – which had made David such an effective ruler. Above all:

> Raddour in prince is worthy thing;
> For but raddour all governyng
> Sall wyle worth and displisit be;
> And quhare that men may raddour se,
> Men will dreid to trespas, and sa
> A king pecable his land may ma.

But Wyntoun's anonymous source also saved particular praise for David's attendance to justice not only through personal ayres to the borders and days of march with English lords but, by establishing:

> Schirrawe cowrtis throw al the lande
> He gert be coursse halde, and folowande
> Ilka yhere a justry
> He gert haulde fellounly;
> And syne his parlyment at Scoyne
> Quwhar al walde be delyverit sone.
> He was al manly, war and wysse.
> Thus in al furme of justrice
> He left his lands at his endynge.

This strong approval of David's rule was echoed in the 1440s by Abbot Bower. The *Scotichronicon* in fact contains a veritable outpouring of lament for the second Bruce king despite being written as a continuation of Fordun's work which had simply drawn a veil over the reign after 1363.[3] Bower adds not only his own thoughts but reproduces an epithetical poem for the king, possibly by a contemporary of that reign. Thus, according to the chronicler himself, although the reign nearly ended in battle in 1346 thanks to the king's youth, impatience and poor counsel, by 1371 David could be said to have:

> reformed his kingdom with excellent laws, he punished rebels, he calmed his subjects with undisturbed peace, and he united to their fatherland by means of one legal contract Scots speaking different tongues, both the wild caterans and the domesticated men with skills. And this was not achieved without a great deal of enthusiasm and hard work.

The funerary poem for the king was inevitably much more florid. David, it insisted, would be missed because:

---

3 *Chron. Bower*, vii, 359–65 for what follows.

He is highly regarded by the English, and revered for his strength,
He is regarded as truthful, and blessed for his goodness . . .
What grief! What lamentation! What a dear prince is afflicted!
What raging! What roaring! What a masterful leader has departed!
What numbness! What a noise! What a dear knight . . .
A generous knight, he was kindly as a ruler, cheerful,
Handsome, a peace-maker, courteous in his gentle goodness;
A worthy leader, given to unobtrusive acts of charity . . .
His unremitting exercise of authority well pacified the kingdom
And he increased the places of note in the region . . .
Savagery has disappeared, imperial law has triumphed,
Honesty has increased, there is general quiet in the country . . .
And he made it his business to keep the people visibly in obedience to
  the law . . .

The preceding chapters have presented much evidence which could be said to justify these chronicle claims for David as a strong lawgiver firmly in command of his subjects. During both periods of David's active majority sheriff courts and justice ayres were held regularly in Scotland, both north and south of Forth, a fact underlined by rising returns in shrival and justiciar income. More importantly, by far the majority of locality officers were quickly established after the king's returns in 1341 and again in 1357 as knights appointed by the crown as opposed to regional nobles and their followers. Admittedly, there is little hard evidence that David regularly oversaw justice ayres in person, even though council in November 1357 had asked him to do so 'to inspire terror in delinquents'.[4] But David can be shown to have undertaken a number of timely northern and southern circuits, to have participated in border days of peace and truce indentures, and to have taken a personal interest in pacifying disputes involving individual magnates. Wyntoun's source certainly cites David's summary justice at Dumfries against Sir James Lindsay about 1359 for his murder of Sir Roger Kirkpatrick, sheriff of Ayr, as proof of the king's judicial presence south of Forth.[5] As we have seen, David had also used chivalry to help settle feuds between Keith and Mar and the Erskines and Lothian Douglases: in the first instance the king had also made a firm display of royal force in taking Kildrummy Castle in Mar in 1362 and then reached a negotiated settlement with the earl. The intervention of the crown and justiciars had also helped defuse tensions in Menteith in 1360. Clearly, there was much truth in the assertion of Bower's poet that David 'has brought together men at variance with each other by means of trustworthy utterances'.[6]

4 *APS*, i, 491; *RPS*, 1357/11/7.
5 *Chron. Wyntoun*, vi, 241.
6 *Chron. Bower*, vii, 363.

As Wyntoun's source suggests, parliament can also be shown to have fulfilled its growing role as a supreme court and legislator during David's reign. As early as 1344 we find David overseeing a parliamentary assize to adjudicate over the fate of the earldom of Strathearn and to bring the Douglas-Ramsay feud in Lothian to an end.[7] In the 1360s, however, parliament's judicial role intensified with the election of committees of the estates to hear territorial and jurisdictional disputes. David was, at least on paper, responsive to parliament's call for checks on the actions and 'sufficiency' of crown officers.[8] More generally, as A.A.M. Duncan has shown, the 1360s were a period in which the crown and its clerical bureaucracy revitalised the organisation of government and the codification and application of the law.[9] David's regime also seems to have been able eventually to respond to the estates' repeated calls for the assertion of the law in northern Scotland. Indeed, David's defeat, exile and brief (1370) imprisonment of the earl of Mar, his receipt of the submission of John MacDonald, Lord of the Isles at Inverness in 1369, the bringing to parliament of Gael magnates like Macdougall of Lorn and Campbell of Lochawe, and the brief imprisonment of Robert Steward and his son, Alexander of Badenoch, in 1368–9, were the achievements which probably lay, if unstated, at the heart of the later chroniclers' praise for David's kingship. For when combined with David's punishment of the intemperate earl of Angus in 1360 and the crown's swift and – according to Bower – 'merciful' suppression of the three earls' rebellion in 1363, these actions point to a king well able to control his great landed subjects when they threatened to overreach their station and disturb the peace of the realm. Crucially, both Wyntoun's source and Bower focus on this ability of the second Bruce king to ensure 'al worth [nobility] thar obeyand him till'. Indeed, that so many of these royal policing achievements lay in the last few years of the reign – really after the king's divorce from what Bower saw as the malevolent influence of Queen Margaret – was enough to cause the abbot to conclude that David had died tragically young, 'before scarcely approaching mature manhood . . . *while he was ruling his kingdom as a king should*'.[10]

However, this last assertion betrays Bower's contemporary agenda in his treatment of the recent history of the Scottish kingdom. As a tax collector for James I (1424–37), Bower looked upon that hard-headed aggressive Stewart monarch as a stabilising force, a shepherd (to use the Abbot's metaphor) well able to protect the flock from the predation of what the writer perceived as the nobility-in-wolves'-clothing who were naturally inclined to feud

7 See ch. 3.
8 Penman, 'Parliament Lost – Parliament Regained?'.
9 Duncan, 'The 'Laws of Malcolm MacKenneth''.
10 *Chron. Wyntoun*, vi, 234–5; *Chron. Bower*, vii, 261.

amongst themselves, plunder from common subjects and flout the law of the crown. For Bower, James had been the great 'lawgiver king' who, despite an acknowledged brutal streak in his treatment of his greater nobles and an unpopular tax regime, had been martyred in the cause of keeping regional magnate self-interest in check when he was murdered by the followers of Walter Stewart, earl of Atholl, at Perth in February 1437. The factional noble violence which followed in the wake of James's death only served to intensify Bower's conviction – as a victim of this conflict *c.* 1440–3 – that an intimidating, no-nonsense king was the best way to ensure 'peace and tranquillity'. Bower's history of James I's reign was written with a clear view to advising the young James II on what he needed to do to reassert law and order over his nobles both at the centre and in the localities: in the 'vile times' of Bower's 1440s it was the 'very absence of fear' of a forceful king which allowed the nobles to abuse their power.[11]

In turn, Bower's assessment of David II's reign is also influenced by this desire to advocate strong monarchy and loyal subjects in the mid-fifteenth century. Indeed, Bower's unusual focus on David's dealings with the Highlands seems more relevant to James I's troubled efforts to overawe the MacDonald lordship of the Isles and neighbouring clans. James I began this campaign well by trapping the Lord of the Isles and many other chiefs into custody, a coup reinforced by initial royal military victories in the north up to 1429. However, two defeats by lordship forces by 1431 and mounting estates' distrust of crown taxation for such campaigns led to the collapse of James's northern policy.[12] In this context, Bower's praise of David's northern tactics make sense:

> [David] was cautious in the following way, namely by persuading and inducing one chieftain to kill or capture [another one], or bring before the king someone else like him [in his place], after promising the movable and immovable goods of the dead man to him at a price. When these goods of the man selected had been promised and given, each of the rebel caterans deceived and destroyed another in turn, until the kingdom became peaceful, the threat of wicked men was removed and the common folk could obtain the peace and security that they wanted.[13]

11 M. Brown, ' "Vile Times": Walter Bower's last Book and the Minority of James II', *SHR*, lxxix (2000), 165–88; S. Mapstone, 'Bower and kingship' in *Chron. Bower*, ix, 321–38 at 324–5. Dr Mapstone points out that Bower applied favourable epitaphs to only a few Scottish kings to give examples of the kind of strong monarch he hoped James II would become – David I, Alexander II, Robert I, David II and, of course, James I: David II is surely the least convincing of this group. For a biography of Bower, see *ibid*, 204–9.

12 Brown, *James I,* 93–108.

13 *Chron. Bower*, vii, 359–61.

These tactics could be said to begin to reflect what David had attempted to do by elevating first William, earl of Sutherland, and then Walter Leslie and John Macdougall in the north and north-west. But although David did secure a seemingly bloodless submission from John MacDonald of the Isles in 1369, and he did divide and rule elsewhere, there is no real evidence that he had been especially effective in person in ending lawlessness in the north in the manner Bower describes. In reality, this was surely Bower's prescription for strong royal action against the Gael in the 1440s and beyond. It is likely, then, that this and other sections of Bower's history of David II's reign contain exaggeration and distortion of that king's nonetheless considerable abilities.

The same can be said for the assessment of Wyntoun's anonymous source. Writing at a time of similarly intense magnate factionalism, political murder, coups in parliament, the eclipse of the crown and infamous violence in the north in the 1390s, this cleric, too, was surely in search of an adaptable model of strong kingship for dealing with unruly nobles: a charismatic monarch to look back upon while observing caution in avoiding offence to the Stewart family and other nobles dominant after 1371 but who had previously suffered at the hands of David and his supporters.[14]

Nevertheless, that David II was not in fact as powerful or unchallenged in his authority as these chroniclers assert is borne out by closer examination of the political stalemate which emerged by the 1360s. Born into tremendously difficult circumstances, David assumed the responsibilities of kingship and of reasserting Bruce monarchical authority as early as possible: even then it could be argued that he was unavoidably a decade late. In his 'first kingship' after June 1341 he could more readily call upon the potent model of his father and seemed well able, at a very young age, to deploy crown patronage and leadership in war against England as a means of restoring the central position of the king and court as the political focus of the realm for the majority of significant subjects. However, in doing so David had to clash with the entrenched regional interests of several of the key baronial families elevated by the first Bruce regime, not least the Stewarts, Douglases and other kindreds who had led the fight against England in the 1330s. This was a cold, low-key conflict which, at first, David was less than convincing in waging, as made clear by his climbdown in the face of the self-interest of the Steward and Douglas of Liddesdale in 1342. Within four years the king and his support had set these magnates on the back foot. But the real battle outside Durham in October 1346 provided David's domestic opponents

14 Boardman, 'Chronicle Propaganda in Late Medieval Scotland', 40–3; Nicholson, 'David II, the historians and the chroniclers', 75–6.

with their first and really their greatest opportunity to react against his 'lack of fair lordship' in undermining their autonomy and lands.

After the desertion of Steward, Ross, March and others, David was incredibly lucky to survive Neville's Cross. But the next eleven years in English captivity were both a major setback to David's domestic agenda and the period in which the factional lines in Scotland were firmly drawn. David displayed remarkable energy in making friends, lobbying and compromising in an attempt to cut the deal for his release which he felt would put him back on the road to domestic dominance. But in the end he returned to his kingdom only after a blunt personal rejection by a Scottish parliament of his proposed succession-peace deal with England and the unpredictable calamity of the defeat and capture of the French king. David re-entered Scotland having picked up in England a number of new considerations to add to his chief policy of chivalric lordship as a means of winning support. But he was confronted once again by firmly entrenched regional magnate interests, an heir presumptive with a spreading familial empire and three political estates increasingly expectant of having a direct say in the affairs of the realm. The king was also strikingly out of step with the mounting Anglophobia of many of his subjects.

Despite these obstacles, however, David soon seemed to regain the upper hand. Cautious enough at first to satisfy some of the local ambitions of the houses of Stewart, Douglas, Dunbar and others, by 1359–60 there were real signs that the crown had recovered control of most of the key locality offices and foreign policy from these magnates. As before 1346, patronage was the key. David's both genuine and calculated use of the ethos of Christian chivalry and his distribution of lands, offices and, very often, money to aspiring lesser nobles, knights, esquires, career clerics and merchants soon brought results, particularly in parliament and council where new laws and ransom taxes were initially approved with little trouble. Nevertheless, within eighteen months of his return David's commitment to two policy areas proved dangerously provocative.

Firstly, what can only be described as his personal obsession with the gamble of outsmarting both Edward III and the Steward by concluding a succession-peace deal to mitigate his 100,000-merks ransom by admitting an English prince as his heir-in-waiting – and then going on to father a son of his own – was never something of which he could convince a majority of his subjects, even some of his closest or would-be supporters. The threat this diplomatic ploy posed to the aristocratic status quo which had emerged since 1306 – and particularly during David's incapacity between 1329 and 1341 and then 1346 and 1357 – was just too great. Robert I himself had been all too aware of this dilemma and had found no lasting solution to the Disinherited. David's policy was arguably a non-starter even before further historical, jurisdictional, ecclesiastical and emotional (Anglophobic) opposition might be raised among Scotland's political community after 1346. Nonetheless, David's deadly serious revisiting of this diplomatic idea in 1359, 1363–4 and beyond only served to give Robert Steward and other detractors of this Bruce regime more power to obstruct the king.

For the Stewarts, the earls of Douglas, Angus, March, Ross and others could use this genuine general grievance about David's ambiguous dealings with England after 1350 to mask their equally pressing individual concerns about the crown's second aim: the undermining of select regional magnate interests in lands and offices to redraw the map of political power in Scotland. David's patronage of his expanding chivalric affinity and his mistresses' relatives had proved profitable in this regard, bringing the crown *de facto* control of the earldoms of Fife and Menteith as well as the key royal castles, justiciarships and swelling coffers by 1359. But when these domestic contests threatened to coalesce in the king's favour in conjunction with his talks with England, the backlash against the crown was surprisingly sharp. By 1360 David had only narrowly escaped being forced to conclude a secret alliance with France by the Steward, the Douglas earl and others: but he had lost control of Fife and Menteith. Parliament and council, too, were becoming increasingly difficult arenas to control and steer in the direction the king desired. The crown's elaborate scheme for introducing the English prince, John of Gaunt, to Scotland through a Lancaster-Moray grant had been blown apart by Scottish opposition. David chose to avoid the pitfalls of days-long debate and statutory rebuke in parliament for over two years between April 1360 and September 1362 and for a similar period after March 1364. The king's well-connected mistress, Katherine Mortimer, wife of William Ramsay, earl of Fife (1358–60), was also a casualty of this intensifying cold war.

However, David's reaction to Katherine's slaughter in June 1360 again exposes his limitations. Although the king was able to arrest one of the guilty party, Thomas Stewart, earl of Angus, and imprison him until his death in 1362, this magnate was only the weakest link in the shifting aristocratic group aligned against the crown: there is no evidence that Angus was forfeited by the crown in parliament. In the same way, David's siege and temporary forfeiture/exile of Thomas, earl of Mar, in 1362 – and his imprisonment in 1370 – as well as the crown's bullying of William, earl of Ross, in the late 1360s were marginal victories for the king and his close supporters. David and his chivalric cadre were never collectively strong enough to attempt to break Stewart or Black Douglas power decisively through more direct confrontation. Royal attempts to undermine these great magnates by stealth – and to police Mar with military force – provoked an attempted military coup. Yet even in the wake of the crown's comprehensive defeat of the three earls' rebellion of spring 1363, with David newly wed and hopeful of an heir, the crown did not feel in a position to immediately forfeit the Stewarts of land or their place in the succession. Instead, the king sought to revolutionise his situation by reviving his ransom-succession deal with England, this time with the involvement and vested interest of William, earl of Douglas, and Patrick, earl of March, the Stewarts' co-conspirators. However, all David's patronage of inclusion, and his hard diplomatic bargaining in London and lobbying at Scone came to nought. In parliament in March 1364 the Steward – again, it is likely, with the worried support of nobles like the Douglas and March earls – roused sufficient hatred of the Plantagenets, allied to opposition to the restoration of the Disinherited and the possibility of an English royal succession: David's planned panacea for the Bruce regime's problems was again bluntly vetoed. The only real headway David made in the twelve months after the rebellion was in re-establishing with force royal control in Fife (at least until the death of Sir Thomas Bisset in 1366). That parliament allowed Anglo-Scottish talks to continue can have been of little comfort to the king.

This was the high-stakes political stand-off which characterised the remainder of David's reign. The king and his close noble and ecclesiastical supporters continued to seek a breakthrough in negotiations with Edward III and his sons and council, talks for which Scotland's parliament/council was usually willing to pay. As with that other bellicose king of Scots who had been captured by the English, William I (1165–1214), David's offers to London to ease the burdens of his release became less and less convincing with the passage of time. In the late 1360s, when it became apparent that the terms on the table still included the threat of the 'dismemberment of the realm' under an English heir to the throne, the Stewarts and others were able to harness the insecurity of a majority of the Scottish political community to reject the talks decisively in 1368. As in 1352, 1359 and 1364, the Stewarts and others could rouse deeply-felt opposition to the crown through arguments about the familial sacrifice of the last seventy years in war against England, the alternative of the French alliance, the untrustworthiness of the descendants of Edward I, the patriotism of Robert I and the binding legitimacy of the parliamentary acts of succession of 1318 and 1326. Directed criticism among the three estates also grew and spread to David's financial policy. After 1364 there were statutory demands not only that royal taxation be based on a fresh assessment of Scottish land values greatly reduced by decades of war but that the king spend the revenues raised on designated purposes only and share the burden of supporting his household more evenly across the realm, including the Highlands and lordship of the Isles: non-payment of tax continued in such outlying zones. By 1369–70, parliament was also more vocal in its criticism of royal officers and justice, especially in the north.

In the face of such legitimate concerns, David gradually came around to a superficial compromise. His talks with England after 1364 also sought the coping stone of a renegotiation of the remaining ransom, and favourable terms were concluded on two occasions, May 1365 and May 1369, the latter indenture greatly reducing the annual burden to just 4,000 merks. However, David also sought domestic compromise and respite. By 1366, he had reached some accommodation with the next generation of Stewarts in the form of the man most likely to succeed him as monarch if he died childless, John Stewart of Kyle, who by late 1368 had been made earl of Carrick and Atholl with the approval of the Steward and the king. This was a realistic royal admission of the need for some level of Bruce-Stewart co-operation which seems to have initially survived the irrevocable breakdown of David's second marriage.

But this would not prevent him from attempting to seize a further opportunity to dislodge the Stewarts from the succession. David's plans to divorce Margaret Logie by mid-to-late 1368 and wed Agnes Dunbar signalled a second revitalisation of the royal circle. It was with the support of Archibald Douglas, Lord of Galloway by 1369, his cousin, James Douglas of Dalkeith, George Dunbar, the new earl of March, his brother John Dunbar (made lord of Fife in 1370), the Erskine kindred and Sir Walter Leslie and his extended north-eastern crusading cadre, to add to the crown following in the Lothians, Fife and Angus, that David entered upon arguably the most impressive years of his rule. The period 1369–71, however brief, saw David not only force John MacDonald of the Isles to submit and William, earl of Ross, to sign away his family lands; but the Douglas earl and Stewarts found themselves excluded from parliament or their titles threatened and their persons briefly gaoled respectively. They could do little as David again made significant inroads into redressing the balance of lordship in favour of the crown and its supporters in Ross-shire, Moray and the north-east, Perthshire and Lochaber, Mar and Angus, Fife and the Lothians, the south-west and the southern marches. By 1370, David may also have been contemplating a *volte face* in foreign policy with approaches to France and aggression on the Anglo-Scottish border: this may further explain why Abbot Bower later considered David – as he apparently shied away from peace with England – to have died 'while he was ruling his kingdom as a king should'.[15] With an unprecedented income of almost £15,000 – despite non-payment of tax in some predictable quarters – a year before his death David might indeed seem to have arrived, as Ranald Nicholson believed, at a position of formidable power and 'intensive' royal government, dominant over the entirety of his realm

15 *Chron. Bower*, vii, 261.

with the backing of a 'nobility of service . . . [whilst] almost all who held
the rank of earl were cowed into submission'.[16]

But in the last two years of his reign David was a still masterful king who
nevertheless could not follow through and do what he really wanted in his
own kingdom: break and harness the Stewarts, Douglas and other lords and
earls, father a son, and conclude a treaty with England which ended his debt
and allowed him independence both at home and abroad. Many of Scotland's great regional nobles were forced into abeyance, kept in check by
David's unquestionable personal 'raddour' and the collective intimidation of
his chivalric daily council and locality support: the aura of power around the
king and his court was certainly intimidating. Neither Wyntoun's source nor
Bower exaggerated when they emphasised the style of lordship and patronage which had won David such a position of authority and support.
Wyntoun's anonymous contemporary of the reign highlighted how:

> Agayne the stout richt stout was he;
> Til sympyl he schewit gret debonarte.
> He gaf to gud men largely
> And walde mak sa prewaly . . .
> His mennys hartis til hym wan he.[17]

Bower, too, as we have seen, stressed David's 'favour and affection to a great
and exaggerated extent to his knights and men-at-arms who were very
numerous at this time . . .'. In addition, the epithetical poem of 1371 which
Bower recorded more generally praised how the king's:

sweet company of followers enhanced his popularity
He has cultivated the prelates of the clergy by treating them with
respect,
and has desired the magnates to come to his side with their power;
he made a statute that burgesses could exchange their goods with his
permission,
and he made it his business to keep the people visibly in obedience to the
law . . .[18]

David was careful not only to favour laymen of crusading stock or with the
ambition to serve the crown but he intervened personally to secure such
privileges as Oxbridge study and testamentary rights for clerics, or free trade
and monetary equality (at least until 1367) with England for the burghs.
Such widespread patronage brought David considerable backing from all

16 Nicholson, *Scotland – the Later Middle Ages*, 182.
17 *Chron. Wyntoun*, vi, 241.
18 *Chron. Bower*, vii, 363.

three estates. Yet whilst this ensured that he was able to place several earls in ward for a short time or to raise regular taxation to pay for ambassadors, he could never persuade a majority of his subjects to countenance the crown's complete forfeiture and destruction of a regional noble – be it Angus, Mar, Ross or the Steward and his sons; nor could the king pack and control parliament in order to conclude a succession treaty with England and legally outmanoeuvre his opponents. Moreover, by 1368, if not much earlier, there must have been a mounting sense amongst David's antagonists that they and their kin simply had to outlast the sorely isolated Bruce king. In the meantime, David and his circle might erode their influence or slap them down for a while, but the crown could not afford to strike a telling blow for fear of provoking a wide-ranging civil war and a far more concerted effort than in 1352, 1359 or 1363 by a sizeable section of the community to 'bend him to their will' or 'banish him' or much worse, with the option of adult Stewart alternatives, recognised by acts of parliament, waiting in the wings.

This sense of time running out for David and the Bruce dynasty only heightened with David's failure to make a clean break with Margaret Logie and to cement his revamped coalition with a new queen and child. Even amongst David's closest followers of 1369–71 – Archibald and James Douglas, George and John Dunbar, and the Erskines – there is the impression that they knew that they had to exploit their position of the moment quickly to gain sufficient influence to survive the expected change of regime. Unlike the king and some of his knights, these were noble kindreds which were not fixed single-mindedly upon a two-party conflict in Scottish politics. All three families certainly maintained working relations with the Stewarts and Douglas earl and looked primarily to advance their local interests: the love of the Grim, Dalkeith and the Dunbars for raiding northern England was also more in tune with the Stewarts' and Douglas earl's agenda of the 1350s and, as it turned out, the 1380s.

Ironically, then, it was the outcome of David's relative impotence – his inability or unwillingness to risk initiating a decisive clash or reckoning with his greatest domestic opponents – which so attracted the praise of Wyntoun's source and Bower. For Bower, in particular, had lived through the disturbed reign of a king, James I, who did not shirk tackling what he saw as over-mighty magnates head-on, a policy which had spectacularly violent results.[19] By contrast, David was a king who seemed able to contain some of his great magnates without messy fall-out and to reward others. As one historian has argued, because of this factional stalemate David's reign was thus relatively quiet.[20] But whilst there was frequent compromise, there was

19 Brown, *James I.*
20 Grant, 'Fourteenth-Century Scotland', 362.

also unrelenting political tension when David was in his realm and a blow-
for-blow exchange of manoeuvres over key titles, offices and the succession.
Bower either did not know – or chose to ignore the fact – that this *relative*
domestic peace *c.* 1363–71 was due as much to David's reluctant acceptance
of his weaknesses as to his strengths.

David's shift to abandon France in favour of England after 1346 was as
much a personal as a political decision. Edward III and his sons, the kin of
David's first queen, were undeniably charismatic and civilised hosts, seduc-
tive 'winners' at the forefront of the European chivalry of the day. By
contrast, fighting for Scotland's traditional ally, France, had proved personally disastrous for the Bruce king. His own capture and the massacre of
his loyal followers outside Durham gave him a score of further reasons to
plainly hate and distrust the Steward and his large brood and adherents.
David's feelings can only have been hardened by the decade he was forced to
spend in England while the Steward as Lieutenant, William, lord of Douglas,
and other opportunist Scottish nobles became committed agents of French
aggression against England. It was David's natural personal distaste for this
policy and understandable fear of these men which drove him to persist with
his schemes for an Anglo-Scottish peace after 1357 despite three resounding
rejections of such plans by the Scottish estates. With the advantage of
hindsight, it might be argued that any other Scottish king – certainly most of
the Stewart monarchs of the fifteenth century – would have quickly
abandoned the ransom, what few Scottish hostages remained and the truce
with England and sought once more to play French fears off the ailing
Edward III and the overstretched English war effort, at the same time
forcefully regaining command of the Scottish nobility's contact with the
continent.[21] But David would not even consider this change of tack until
1370, nine years after the death of, for him, the last significant hostage, John
Sutherland. In the same vein, fifteenth-century Stewart kings would not
baulk at striking the crown's magnatial opponents first and dealing with
legal and political niceties in parliament after the fact.

Later medieval and modern Scotland might have been very different if
David had produced a child in the early 1360s; or destoyed the Steward –
perhaps with legal cause in 1363 – and smoothed over his subjects' alarm at
such ruthless action with patronage all-round, especially to the Douglases
and Dunbars; or forced a deal with England through parliament and further
cultivated the national interest in trade and cultural exchange with the
south; or simply more actively developed his professed royal interest in the
crusades. But all of this speculation underlines the reality that in David's

21 James I, released from England in 1423–4, had done this by 1428 (Balfour-Melville,
    James I, 103, 159, 293–5).

inability to achieve these goals, in the unfulfilled and unfinished business of his kingship by his childless late middle age, lies the open verdict which might so easily be returned upon his personal rule. The epithetical poem which Bower later recorded certainly contained some passages which were somewhat more ambivalent about David's lasting achievements as king:

> David preserved his energies with the firmness of an outstanding king,
> While he sustained the pressures put upon him by the neighbouring kingdom
> He increased the wealth and glory of his poor kingdom . . .
> The fertility of the land obeyed his wishes . . .
> So too the useful element of the sea . . .
> He wanted to enter into a truce agreement for his kingdom,
> He managed to smear his fellow king with sweetness;
> He held on to what he settled, he refused to go back on agreements . . .
> He is highly regarded by the English . . .[22]

This was a far cry from the 'revels in English gardens' expected of the second Bruce ruler and expressed in the funerary laments for Robert I. David had undoubtedly grown to be a man of commanding presence, a tough, skilled politician, a shrewd champion of knight errantry and a forceful manager of men. But his rule – both in the period 1341–6 and at the height of his mature power in the late 1360s – was never absolutely convincing, perpetually compromised by both the circumstances he had inherited and returned to in 1341 and, more crucially, those he had created for himself in and after the fateful year of 1346: these were severe constraints which David felt so acutely after 1357 that he only sought out Scottish wives and which the birth of a Bruce heir would not necessarily have dissolved. It was left to fifteenth-century kings of Scots to really develop the model of hard-headed, pre-emptive kingship first provided by David's father, Robert I, rulers who initiated direct confrontation with what they perceived as over-mighty magnate and dynastic opponents. It was James I (1424–37) and James II (1437–60), indeed, who employed violence and aggressive patronage to destroy the magnatial houses which had really benefited and survived to emerge dominant from the minority, captivity and two majorities of David II – the Fife/Albany and Badenoch Stewarts and the Black/Lothian Douglases. These later monarchs also took European brides and sought to exploit Anglo-French conflict.[23]

In sum, David's eighteen years of personal rule were a period rather of

---

22 *Chron. Bower*, vii, 363–5.
23 Brown, 'Scotland Tamed?'; McGladdery, *James II*; N.A.T., Macdougall, *An Antidote to the English: the Auld Alliance, 1295–1560* (East Linton 2001), chs. 3 and 4.

dogged effort than tangible success for the crown. In dealing with and complicating the consequences of his father's usurpation and control of the throne, David oversaw the most crucially formative era of late-medieval Scottish politics. But the Bruce dynasty's isolation and extinction and the posthumous reversal of David's key policies by the Stewarts and Douglases meant that by the early sixteenth century Scottish commentators had already cooled in their views of this monarch's personality and rule. Even John Mair (1467–1550), the Cambridge- and Paris-educated professor of theology at St Andrews and author of *History of Greater Britain* (1521) – a work in favour of Anglo-Scottish amity and union – could find no achievement of this king to celebrate. For Mair, James I was instead the greatest of late-medieval Scotland's kings, a monarch who had learned from English government and imposed justice on over-mighty magnates. But of Robert I's son, Mair could only write that:

> I can even David with rulers of middling excellence only: in matters of war he had but small experience; in the affairs of the world he did not prosper; but the temper of his mind was not otherwise than one of constant endurance, and fear he knew not.[24]

This seems a realistic assessment of a cunning, gutsy, energetic but ultimately unfulfilled king. David had surely done enough to justify the positive epitaphs he would receive from Wyntoun's source and Bower. But in truth, any medieval monarch who dies leaving neither an heir of his own blood nor an enduring and praiseworthy personal legacy of military, political and cultural achievement and expansion must be regarded as a failure. David II can only have gone to his early grave regretting bitterly the political legacy and events which had led him to 17 October 1346 and the three wasted decades of deep personal frustration which had followed in its wake.

24 Mair, *A History of Greater Britain*, 306–8.

Bibliography

MANUSCRIPT SOURCES
NAS – National Archives of Scotland, Edinburgh
B65 St Andrews Burgh Charters
GD1 Miscellaneous Writs
GD28 Yester Writs
GD38 Dalguise Muniments
GD42 Dunecht Writs
GD45 Dalhousie Muniments
GD50 John MacGregor Collection
GD79 King James VI Hospital, Perth
GD86 Fraser Charters
GD121 Murthly Castle Muniments
GD122 Little Gilmour of Liberton and Craigmillar
GD124 Mar and Kellie Muniments
GD148 Craigans Writs
GD150 Morton Papers
GD172 Henderson of Fordell Collection
GD297 J. and F. Anderson Collection
RH1 Register House Royal Charter Transcripts
RH2/4 Register House English Issue Roll Transcripts
RH2/6 Register House Vatican Transcripts
RH6 Register House Charters
SP6 State Papers – Treaties with England

NLS – National Library of Scotland, Edinburgh
Adv. MSS A.10
Adv. MSS 22.2.28
Ch. no. 698

AN – Archives Nationales, Paris
JJ36 nos. 620, 621
JJ76 no. 76/6,217
JJ74 nos. 4,757; 4,892
JJ102 no. 220
J621 no. 77
J677 nos. 7–13
P.14 nos. 73–4, 473–4

BN – Bibliothèque Nationale, Paris
Nouv. Acq. fr. nos. 6,214; 9,236–9
MSS Clairambault 43 nos. 141, 143
             109 no. 141
             212 nos. 64–7
             1,226 nos. 45–61
MSS Fr. 2,643, f. 13v., 97v; Fr. 2,675, f. 45v; Fr. 7,413 f. 556–560v.
Add Ch. 4,162

BL – British Library, London
Add. MSS nos. 19,797; 24,511–2; 30,666; 33,245
Cotton Vesp. C. XVI; F. VIII
Harley MSS nos. 115; 4,693
Stowe MSS. 1083

PRO – Public Record Office, Kew
C. 47 Chancery Miscellanea
C. 49/6/29
C. 71/49
E. 27/9 – 'the Bruce ransom chest'
E. 30
E. 39 Exchequer Scots documents
E. 101/101/29/26 and /482
E. 199/49/47
E. 403 Issue Rolls
SC 1 /39/32; /42/19, 94–5
SC 37/137
SC 41/19

Cumbrian Record Office, Carlisle
CRO, DRC1/1
CRO D/Mus/2 Box 21

Northumbrian Record Office, Newcastle
NRO 76 ZSW Swinburne Mss (Part 1)
NRO 358/1–46 Riddell Mss

Bodleian Library, Oxford
MS. Fairfax 23

PRINTED RECORD SOURCES

Ane Account of the Familie of Innes (Spalding Club, Aberdeen 1864)
Acta Dominorum Concillii: Acts of the Lords of Council in Civil Causes, ii, 1486–1501, ed. G. Neilson and H. Paton (Edinburgh 1918)
The Acts of the Lords of the Isles, 1336–1493, eds J. and R.W. Munro (Scottish History Society, Edinburgh 1986)
The Acts of the Parliaments of Scotland, eds T. Thomson and C. Innes (12 vols, Edinburgh 1814–75)
Anglo-Scottish Relations, 1174–1328: Some Selected Documents, ed. E.L.G. Stones (Oxford 1965)
L'Armorial universal du herault Gèlre, ed. P. Adam-Even (Berne 1971)
Calendar of Close Rolls, 1354–60 (London 1908)
Calendar of Documents Relating to Scotland, ed. J. Bain (5 vols, Edinburgh 1881–8)
Calendar of Entries in the Papal Registers relating to Great Britain and Ireland: Papal Letters, eds W.H. Bliss et al. (16 vols, London 1893)
Calendar of Entries in the Papal Registers relating to Great Britain and Ireland: Petitions to the Pope, vol. i, ed. W.H. Bliss (London 1986)
Calendar of Inquisitions Miscellaneous, vols ii and iii (London 1937)
Calendar of the Laing Charters, 854–1837, ed. J. Anderson (Edinburgh 1899)
Calendar of Papal Letters to Scotland of Benedict XIII of Avignon, 1394–1419, ed. F. McGurk (Scottish History Society, Edinburgh 1976)
Calendar of Papal Letters to Scotland of Clement VII of Avignon, 1378–94, ed. C. Burns (Scottish History Society, Edinburgh 1976)

Calendar of Patent Rolls, 1367–70 (London 1913)

Calendar of the Register of Simon de Montacute, Bishop of Worcester, 1334–37 (Worcester 1996)

Calendar of Writs of Munro of Foulis, 1299–1823, ed. C.T. McInnes (Scottish Record Society, Edinburgh 1930)

Catalogue des Comptes Royaux de Phillippe VI et de Jean II, 1318–1364, ed. R. Cazelles (Paris 1984)

Charters of the Abbey of Coupar Angus (Scottish History Society, 2 vols, Edinburgh 1947)

Charter Chest of the Earldom of Wigtown (Scottish Record Society, Edinburgh 1910)

The Charters of the Priory of Beauly with Notices of the Priories of Ardchatten and Pluscardine and of the family of the Founder, John Byset, ed. E.C. Batton (Grampian Club, London 1877)

Chartulary of Lindores Abbey, 1195–1479 (Scottish History Society, Edinburgh 1903)

'David II's Appeal to the Pope', ed. E.W.M. Balfour-Melville, *SHR*, xli (1962), 86.

'Debate in General Council', ed. E.W.M. Balfour-Melville, *Scottish History Society Miscellany*, ix (Edinburgh 1958), 36–56.

A Descriptive Catalogue of the Western Manuscripts in Edinburgh University Library, ed., C.R. Borland (Edinburgh 1916)

Documents on the Later Crusades, 1274–1580, ed. N. Housley (London 1996)

The Exchequer Rolls of Scotland, eds J. Stuart *et. al.* (23 vols, Edinburgh 1878–1908)

Foedera, Conventiones, Litterae et Cuiuscunque Generis Acta Publica, ed. T. Rymer (20 vols, London 1704–35)

Fraser, W., ed., *The Book of Caerlaverock* (2 vols, Edinburgh 1873)

Fraser, W., ed., *The Chiefs of Colquhoun and their Country* (2 vols, Edinburgh 1869)

Fraser, W., ed., *The Chiefs of Grant* (3 vols, Edinburgh 1883)

Fraser, W., ed., *The Douglas Book* (4 vols, Edinburgh 1885)

Fraser, W., ed., *The History of the Carnegies of Southesk* (2 vols, Edinburgh 1867)

Fraser, W., ed., *The Lennox* (2 vols, Edinburgh 1874)

Fraser, W., ed., *The Melvilles, Earls of Melville and Leslies, Earls of Leven* (3 vols, Edinburgh 1890)

Fraser, W., ed., *Memorials of the Family of Weymss of Weymss* (3 vols, Edinburgh 1888)

Fraser, W., ed., *Memorials of the Montgomeries* (2 vols, Edinburgh 1859)

Fraser, W., ed., *The Red Book of Grandtully* (2 vols, Edinburgh 1868)

Fraser, W., ed., *The Red Book of Menteith* (2 vols, Edinburgh 1880)

Fraser, W., ed., *The Sutherland Book* (3 vols, Edinburgh 1892)

The Frasers of Philorth, ed. A. Fraser (3 vols, Edinburgh 1879)

Highland Papers, ed. J.R.N. MacPhail (Scottish History Society, 4 vols, Edinburgh 1914–34)

A Historical Account of the Noble Family of Kennedy, Marquess of Ailsa and Earl of Cassillis (Edinburgh 1849)

Historical Papers and Letters from the Northern Registers, ed. J. Raine (Rolls Series, London 1855)

A History of the Family of Seton during Eight Centuries, ed. G. Seton (Edinburgh 1896)

Illustrations of the Topography and Antiquities of the Shires of Aberdeen and Banff, eds J. Roberston and G. Grut (Spalding Club, 5 vols, Aberdeen 1847–69)

An Inventory of the Lamont Papers, 1231–1897 (Scottish Record Society, Edinburgh 1914)

Issue Rolls of Thomas de Brantingham, ed. F. Devon (London 1835)

Itinéraire de Phillippe VI de Valois, ed. J. Viard (Paris 1913)

The Knights of St John of Jerusalem in Scotland, eds I.B. Cowan, P.H.R. Mackay and A. Macquarrie (Scottish History Society, Edinburgh 1983)

Journaux de Trésor de Phillippe VI de Valois, ed. J. Viard (Paris 1899)

Leslie of Balquhain, Col. K.H., *Historical Records of the Family of Leslie* (3 vols, Edinburgh 1869)

Liber Carta Prioratus Sanctii Andree in Scotia (Bannatyne Club, Edinburgh 1841)

Liber Cartarum Sancte Crucis (Bannatyne Club, Edinburgh 1840)

Liber Sancte Marie de Melros (Bannatyne Club, 2 vols, Edinburgh 1837)

Memorials of the Order of the Garter, ed. G.F. Beltz (London 1841)

The Red and White Book of Menzies, ed. D.P. Menzies (Glasgow 1894)

The Miscellany of the Scottish History Society (12 vols, Edinburgh 1893–1994)

National Manuscripts of Scotland, Facsimiles, 1029–1649 (2 vols, Southampton 1867–71)

'Negotiations for the Ransom of David Bruce in 1349', ed. C. Johnson, *EHR*, xxxvi (1921), 57–8.

The Parliamentary Records of Scotland, ed. W. Robertson (London 1804)

'Proposals for an Agreement with Scotland', ed. C. Johnson, *EHR*, xxx (1915), 476.

Die Preussenreisen des Europaischen Adels, ed. W. Paravicini (3 vols, Simaringen, 1989–)

'A Question about the Succession, 1364', ed. A.A.M. Duncan, *Scottish History Society Miscellany*, xii (Edinburgh 1994), 1–57.

The Records of Elgin, ed. W. Cramond (New Spalding Club, 2 vols, Aberdeen 1903–8)

The Records of the Parliaments of Scotland (CD-ROM, Scottish Parliament Project, St Andrews, forthcoming)

Regesta Regum Scottorum I: The Acts of Malcolm IV, 1153–65, ed. G.W.S. Barrow (Edinburgh 1960)

Regesta Regum Scottorum V: The Acts of Robert I, 1306–29, ed. A.A.M. Duncan (Edinburgh 1986)

Regesta Regum Scottorum VI: The Acts of David II, 1329–71, ed. B. Webster (Edinburgh 1982)

The Register and Records of Holm Cultram (Cumberland and Westmorland Antiquarian and Archaeological Society, Kendal 1929)

Registrum Cartarum Ecclesie Sancti Egidii de Edinburgh (Bannatyne Club, Edinburgh 1859)

Registrum de Dunfermlyn (Bannatyne Club, Edinburgh 1842)

Registrum de Panmure, ed. H. Maule of Kelly (2 vols, Edinburgh 1874)

Registrum Episcopatus Aberdonensis (Spalding and Maitland Clubs, 2 vols, Edinburgh 1845)

Registrum Episcopatus Glasguensis (Bannatyne Club, 2 vols, Edinburgh 1843)

Registrum Episcopatus Moraviensis (Bannatyne Club, 2 vols, Edinburgh 1837)

Registrum Honoris de Morton (Bannatyne Club, 2 vols, Edinburgh 1853)

Registrum Magni Sigilli Regum Scotorum, eds J.M. Thomson and J.B. Paul (11 vols, Edinburgh 1882–1914)

Registrum Monasterii de Passelet (Maitland Club, Glasgow 1832)

Reports of the Royal Commission on Historical Manuscripts (London 1870–)

'A Roll of the Scottish Parliament, 1344', ed. J.M. Thomson, *SHR*, ix (1912), 235–40.

Rotuli Parliamentorum, ed. J. Strachy *et al.* (6 vols, London 1767–7)

Rotuli Scotiae in Turri Londinensi et in Domo Capitulari Westmonasteriensi Asservati, ed. D. Macpherson (2 vols, London 1814–9)

Vetera Monumenta Hibernorum et Scotorum Historiam Illustrantia, ed. A. Theiner (Rome 1864)

The Book of Wallace, ed. C. Rogers (2 vols, Grampian Club 1889)

Wigtownshire Charters, ed., R.C. Reid (Scottish History Society, 3rd series, Edinburgh 1960)

NARRATIVE AND LITERARY SOURCES

The Anonimalle Chronicle, 1333–81, ed. V.H. Galbraith (Manchester 1927)

Barbour's Bruce, eds M.P. McDiarmid and J.A.C. Stevenson (Scottish Text Society, 3 vols, Edinburgh 1986)

The Bruce-John Barbour, ed. A.A.M. Duncan (Edinburgh 1997)

The Chronicles of Scotland compiled by Hector Boece, translated into Scots by John Bellenden, 1531, eds R.W. Chambers and E.C. Batho (Scottish Text Society, Edinburgh 1938–41)

Hectoris Boetii Murthlacensium et Aberdonensium Episcoporum Vitae (New Spalding Club, Aberdeen 1894)

Bower, Walter, *Scotichronicon*, ed. D.E.R. Watt *et al.* (9 vols, Aberdeen 1987–99)

Brown, Hume, *Early Travellers in Scotland* (Edinburgh 1891, reprint 1973)

The Brut or Chronicles of England, ed. F.W.D. Brie (Early English Text Society, 2 vols, London 1906–8)

The Buik of Alexander, ed. R.L. Graeme-Ritchie (Scottish Text Society, 3 vols, Edinburgh 1925)

Child, F.J., ed., *The English and Scottish Popular Ballads* (5 vols, London 1888)

Chronica Johannis de Reading et Anonymi Cantuarensis, 1346–57, ed. J. Tait (Manchester 1914)

Chronica Monasterii de Melsa, ed. E.A. Bond (3 vols, London 1868)

Chronicle of Melrose, trans. J. Stevenson (Llanerch reprint 1991)

Chronicon Angliae, 1328–88, ed. E.M. Thompson (London 1874)

Chronicon Domini Walter de Hemingburgh, ed. H.C. Hamilton (2 vols, London 1848)

Chronicon Galfridi le Baker de Swynebroke, ed. E.M. Thompson (Oxford 1889)

Chronicon de Lanercost (Maitland Club, Glasgow 1839)

Chronique de Jean le Bel, ed. J. Viard and E. Déprez (2 vols, Paris 1904)

Chronique de Normandie du XIV Siècle, ed. A. and E. Molinier (Paris 1882)

Chronique des Quatre Premiers Valois, 1327–93, ed. S. Lucé (Paris 1862)

Chronique Parisiene Anonyme de 1316 à 1339, ed. A. Hellot (11 vols, Paris 1885)

Chronique de Richard Lescot, Religieux de Saint Dénis, 1328–44, avec continuation à 1349, ed. J. Lemoine (Paris 1896)

Chronographia Regum Francorum, ed. J. Mornavillé (3 vols, Paris 1897)

Continuato Chronicum Robertus de Avesbury de Gestis Mirabilibus Edwardii Tertii, ed. E.M. Thompson (London 1899)

Drummond, W., Viscount Strathallan, *The Genealogie of the Noble and Ancient House of Drummond* (Edinburgh 1831)

King Edward III by William Shakespeare, ed. G. Melchiori (Cambridge 1998)

Eulogium – Chronicon ab Orbe Ilsque ad annum domini M.CCC.LXVI, ed. F.S. Haydon (3 vols, London 1863)

Expeditions to Prussia and the Holy Land Made by Henry Earl of Derby, ed. L. Toulmin-Smith (Camden Society, 2nd series, London 1894)

Fordun, Johannis de, *Chronica Gentis Scotorum* ed., W.F. Skene (Edinburgh 1871–2)

Sir John Froissart's Chronicles, ed. T. Johnes (2 vols, London 1868)

Giovanni Boccaccio – The Decameron, ed. G.H. McWilliam (London 1972)

Les Grandes Chroniques de France, ed. J. Viard (10 vols, Paris 1953)

Gray, Sir Thomas, *Scalacronica: the Reigns of Edward I, Edward II and Edward III*, trans. H. Maxwell (Glasgow 1907)

Gray, Sir Thomas of Heton, *Scalacronica*, ed. J. Stevenson (with transcript by John Leland) (Maitland Club, Edinburgh 1836)

Historical Poems of the Fourteenth and Fifteenth Centuries, ed. R.H. Robbins (New York 1959)

Hume, David, of Godscroft, *The History of the Houses of Douglas and Angus* (3 vols, Edinburgh 1644)

L'Istoire et Croniques de Flandres, ed. K. de Lettenhove (2 vols, Brussels 1879)

Kervyn de Lettenhove, H. Baron, *Oeuvres de Froissart publiées avec les variantes des divers manuscrits* (24 vols, Paris 1870–7)

Knighton's Chronicle, 1337–96, ed. G.H. Martin (Oxford 1995)

Le Livre de Seyntz Médicines: the unpublished devotional treatise of Henry of Lancaster, ed. E.J. Arnould (Oxford, Anglo-Norman Texts II, 1940)

Leslie, Bishop John, *The Historie of Scotland*, eds, E.G. Cody and W. Murison (2 vols, Edinburgh 1895)

Liber Pluscardensis, ed. F.J.H. Skene (Edinburgh 1877–80)

Maior, John, *A History of Greater Britain, 1521*, ed. A. Constable (Scottish History Society, Edinburgh 1892)

Méliador, ed. A. Longnon (SATF, 3 vols, Paris 1895–99)

Memorials of London and London Life in the XIIIth, XIVth and XVth Centuries, ed. H.T. Riley (London 1868)

Récits d'un Bourgeois de Valenciennes, ed. K. de Lettenhove (Louvain 1877)

Rerum Britannicarum Medii Aevi Scriptores: Political Poems and Songs (2 vols, London 1857)

The Three Kings' Sons, ed. F.J. Turnivall (2 vols, London 1895)

Blind Harry's Wallace by William Hamilton of Gilbertfield (Edinburgh 1998)

Wyntoun, Andrew of, *The Original Chronicle of Andrew of Wyntoun*, ed. A. Amours (Scottish Text Society, 6 vols, Edinburgh 1903–14)

SECONDARY SOURCES
1. Books

Abercromby, P., *The Martial Achievements of the Scottish Nation* (2 vols, Edinburgh 1711–5)

Aitchison, N., *Scotland's Stone of Destiny* (Stroud 2000)

Allmand, C., *The Hundred Years War: England and France at War, c.1300–c.1450* (Cambridge 1989)

Angels, Nobles and Unicorns: Art and Patronage in Medieval Scotland (NMS 1982)

Ashe, G. ed., *The Quest for Arthur's Britain* (London 1971)

Balfour-Melville, E.W.M., *Edward III and David II* (Historical Association Pamphlet G. 27, 1954)

Balfour-Melville, E.W.M., *James I, King of Scots, 1406–37* (London 1936)

Bannerman, J., *The Beatons: a Medical Kindred in the Classical Gaelic Tradition* (2nd edition, Edinburgh 1998)

Barber, R., *Edward, Prince of Wales and Aquitaine* (London 1978)

Barker, J., *The Tournament in England, 1100–1400* (Woodbridge 1986)

Barnie, J., *War in Medieval Society: Social Values and the Hundred Years War, 1337–99* (London 1974)

Barrell, A.D.M., *The Papacy, Scotland and northern England, 1342–1378* (Cambridge 1995)

Barrow, G.W.S., *Robert the Bruce and the Community of the Realm of Scotland* (3rd edition, Edinburgh 1988)

Bateson, D., *Scottish Coins* (Aylesbury 1987)

Belleval, R. de, *Jean de Bailleul roi d'Écosse et sire de Vimeu* (Paris 1886)

Boardman, *The Early Stewart Kings: Robert II and Robert III, 1371–1406* (East Linton 1996)

Bothwell, J.S. ed., *The Age of Edward III* (Woodbridge 2001)

Boulton, D., *The Knights of the Crown: the Monarchical Orders of Knighthood in the Middle Ages* (London 1987)

Brooke, D., *Wild Men and Holy Places: St Ninian, Whithorn and the Medieval Realm of Galloway* (Edinburgh 1994)

Brown, M., *James I* (Edinburgh 1994)

Brown, M., *The Black Douglases: War and Lordship in Late Medieval Scotland, 1300–1455* (East Linton 1998)

Burton, J.H., *The History of Scotland* (8 vols, Edinburgh 1897)

Cazelles, R., *Société Politique, Noblesse et Couronne sous Jean le Bon et Charles V* (Paris 1982)

Cohn, S.K., *The Black Death Transformed: Disease and Culture in Early Renaissance Europe* (London 2002)

Cumming-Bruce, M.E., *The Bruces and the Comyns* (Edinburgh 1870)

Cuttino, G.P., *English Medieval Diplomacy* (Indiana 1985)

Dalrymple, Sir David, Lord Hailes, *Annals of Scotland from the Accession of Malcolm III to the Accession of the House of Stewart* (3 vols, 3rd edition, Edinburgh 1819)

Délachenal, R., *Histoire de Charles V* (5 vols, Paris 1909)

Dembrowski, P.F., *Jean Froissart and his Méliador: Context, Craft and Sense* (Lexington 1983)

De Vries, K., *Infantry Warfare in the Early Fourteenth-Century: Discipline, Tactics and Technology* (Woodbridge 1996)

Dickenson, J.W., *The Battle of Neville's Cross* (Durham 1991)

Dickinson, W.C., *Scotland from the Earliest Times to 1603*, revised by A.A.M. Duncan (Oxford 1977)

Ditchburn, D., *Scotland and Europe: The Medieval Kingdom and its Contacts with Christendom, 1214–1560 – Vol. 1: Religion, Culture and Commerce* (East Linton 2000)

Donaldson, G., *Scottish Kings* (London 1967)

Duffy, S. ed., *Robert the Bruce's Irish Wars: the Invasions of Ireland 1306–1329* (Stroud 2002)

Duncan, A.A.M., *The Nation of Scots and the Declaration of Arbroath, 1320* (Historical Association Pamphlet G. 75, 1970)

Duncan, A.A.M., *Scotland – the Making of the Kingdom* (Edinburgh 1974)

Duncan, A.A.M., *The Kingship of the Scots, 842–1292: Succession and Independence* (Edinburgh 2002)

Ewan, E., *Townlife in Fourteenth-Century Scotland* (Edinburgh 1990)

Forsyth, I.H. and Chisholm, J.I., *The Geology of East Fife* (Edinburgh 1977)

Fowler, K., *The King's Lieutenant: Henry of Grosmont, First Duke of Lancaster, 1310–1361* (London 1969)

Fowler, K., *Medieval Mercenaries: Vol. I – the Great Companies* (Oxford 2001)

Fyall, S., *St Monans: History, Customs and Superstitions* (Durham 1999)

Gemmill, E., and Mayhew, N., *Changing Values in Medieval Scotland: a Study of Prices, Money and Weights and Measures, c. 1260–1542* (Cambridge 1995)

Gillingham, J., *Richard I* (Norfolk 1999)

Given-Wilson, C., *The Royal Household and the King's Affinity: Service, Politics and Finance in England, 1360–1413* (London 1986)

Goldstein, R.J., *The Matter of Scotland: Historical Narrative in Medieval Scotland* (Lincoln 1993)

Goodman, A., *John of Gaunt: the Exercise of Princely Power in Fourteenth-Century Europe* (London 1992)

Graham, F., *Famous Northern Battles* (Newcastle 1977)

Grant, A., *Independence and Nationhood: Scotland, 1306–1469* (Edinburgh 1984)

Grant, A. and K.J. Stringer eds, *Medieval Scotland: Crown, Lordship and Community – Essays presented to G.W.S. Barrow* (Edinburgh 1993), 274–96.

Green, M.A.E., *Lives of the Princesses of England* (6 vols, London 1849–55)

Harriss, G.L., *King, Parliament and Public Finance in Medieval England to 1369* (Oxford 1975)

Hodgson, J.C., *A History of Northumberland* (15 vols, Newcastle 1893–1940)

Housley, N., *The Later Crusades: from Lyons to Alcazar, 1274–1580* (Oxford 1992)

Jenning, C., *Early Chests in Wood and Iron* (PRO pamphlets no. 7, 1974)

Johnson, P., *The Life and Times of Edward III* (London 1973)

Kingford, C.L., *The Grey Friars of London* (Aberdeen 1915)

Loray, T. de, *Jean de Vienne, Amiral de France, 1341–1396* (Paris 1877)

Loxton, H., *Pilgrimage to Canterbury* (Newton Abbot 1978)

Lynch, M., *Scotland – A New History* (Edinburgh 1991)

MacDonald, A.J., *Border Bloodshed: Scotland, England and France at War, 1369–1403* (East Linton 2000)

Macdougall, N.A.T., *James III – a Political Study* (Edinburgh 1982)

Macdougall, N.A.T., *James IV* (2nd edition, East Linton, 1997)

Macdougall, N.A.T., *An Antidote to the English: the Auld Alliance, 1295–1560* (East Linton 2001)

MacGregor, P., *Odiham Castle, 1200–1500: Castle and Community* (London 1983)

MacIvor, I., *Edinburgh Castle* (Edinburgh 1993)

Mackay, A., *The Book of Mackay* (Edinburgh 1906)

Mackenzie, A., *A History of the Camerons* (Inverness 1884)

Mackenzie, A., *A History of the Chisholms* (Inverness 1891)

Mackenzie, A., *A History of the MacLeods* (Inverness 1889)

Mackenzie, A., *A History of the Mackenzies* (Inverness 1894)

Mackenzie, A., *A History of the Munros of Fowlis* (Inverness 1898)

Mackenzie, A.M., *The Rise of the Stewarts* (London 1935)

Mackinnon, J., *The Constitutional History of Scotland* (London 1924)

Mackintosh, A.M., *The Mackintoshes and the Clan Chattan* (Edinburgh 1903)

Mackintosh, J., *The History of Civilisation in Scotland* (4 vols, Edinburgh 1878)

MacNaughton, D., *The Clan MacNaughton* (Edinburgh 1977)

McDonald, R.A., *The Kingdom of the Isles: Scotland's Western Seaboard, c.1100–c.1336* (East Linton 1997)

McGladdery, C., *James II* (Edinburgh 1987)

McKinlay, J.M., *Ancient Church Dedications – vol. II Non-Scriptural Dedications* (Edinburgh 1914)

McNamee, C., *The Wars of the Bruces: Scotland, England and Ireland, 1306–28* (East Linton 1997)

Macquarrie, A., *Scotland and the Crusades, 1095–1560* (Edinburgh 1985)

MacQueen, H.L., *Common Law and Feudal Society in Medieval Scotland* (Edinburgh 1993)

Neville, C.J., *Violence, Custom and Law: the Anglo-Scottish Border Lands in the Later Middle Ages* (Edinburgh 1998)

Nicholson, R., *Edward III and the Scots: the Formative Years of a Military Career, 1327–35* (Oxford 1965)

Nicholson, R., *Scotland – the Later Middle Ages* (Edinburgh 1974)

Ormrod, W.M., *The Reign of Edward III: Crown and Political Society in England, 1327–77* (London 1990)

Ormrod, W.M. and P. Lindley eds, *The Black Death in England* (Stamford 1996)

Packe, M., *King Edward III* (London 1983)

Palmer, J. ed., *Froissart: Historian* (London 1981)

Penman, M., *The Scottish Civil War* (Stroud 2002)

Prestwich, M., *The Three Edwards: War and State in England, 1272–1377* (London 1980)

Prestwich, M., *Edward I* (London 1988)

Pyne, W.H., *The History of the Royal Residences* (3 vols, London 1819)

Rait, R.S., *The Parliaments of Scotland* (Glasgow 1924)

Richardson, J.S. and Tabraham, C., *Dirleton Castle* (Historic Scotland 1992)

Rogers, C.J. ed., *The Wars of Edward III: Sources and Interpretations* (Woodbridge 1999)

Rogers, C.J., *War Cruel and Sharp: English Strategy Under Edward III, 1327–1377* (Woodbridge 2000)

Rollason, D. and Prestwich, M. eds, *The Battle of Neville's Cross, 1346* (Stamford 1998)

Roncière, C. de la, *Histoire de la Marine Française* (2 vols, Paris 1899–1900)

Ross, J.R., *The Great Clan of Ross* (Toronto 1972)

Saint-Clair, R.W., *The Saint Clairs of the Isles* (New Zealand 1898)

Sochon, S., *Château Gaillard* (Condé sur Noire 1985)

Stringer, K.J., *Earl David of Huntingdon: A Study in Anglo-Scottish History* (Edinburgh 1985)

Summerson, M., *Medieval Carlisle: the City and the Borders from the Late Eleventh to the Mid-Sixteenth century* (2 vols, London 1993)

Sumption, J., *The Hundred Years War: Vol. I – Trial by Battle* (London 1990)

Sumption, J., *The Hundred Years War: Vol. II – Trial by Fire* (London 1999)

Tabraham, C. and Grove, D., *Tantallon Castle* (Historic Scotland 1994)

Tanner, R., *The Late Medieval Scottish Parliament: Politics and the Three Estates, 1424–1488* (East Linton 2001)

Thomson, T., *A History of the Scottish People* (6 vols, Edinburgh 1893)

Tuck, A., *Crown and Nobility, 1272–1461: Political Conflict in Late Medieval England* (Oxford 1985)

Tytler, P.F., *History of Scotland* (8 vols, Edinburgh 1829)

Vale, J., *Edward III and Chivalry: Chivalric Society and its Context, 1270–1350* (London 1982)

Vale, M., *The Princely Court: Medieval Courts and Culture in North-West Europe, 1270–1380* (Oxford 2001)

Watt, D.E.R., *Medieval Church Councils in Scotland* (Edinburgh 2000)

Whyte, I.D., *Scotland Before the Industrial Revolution: An Economic and Social History c.1050–c.1750* (London 1995)

Wilson, J.A., *A History of Cambuslang* (Glasgow 1929)

Yeoman, P., *Medieval Scotland* (London 1995)

Yeoman, P., *Pilgrimage in Medieval Scotland* (London 1999)

Young, A., *Robert the Bruce's Rivals: The Comyns, 1212–1314* (East Linton 1997)

Ziegler, P., *The Black Death* (London 1969)

2. Articles in Edited Books and Journals

Alexander, F., 'Late Medieval Scottish Attitudes to the Figure of King Arthur: A Re-assessment', *Anglia*, xciii (1975), 17–34

Ayton, A., 'English Armies in the Fourteenth-Century', in A. Curry and M. Hughes eds, *Arms, Armies and Fortifications in the Hundred Years War* (Woodbridge 1994), 21–36

Bannerman, J.W.M., 'The Lordship of the Isles – Historical Background', in K.A. Steer and J.W.M. Bannerman, *Late Medieval Monumental Sculpture in the West Highlands* (Edinburgh 1977), 201–13

Bannerman, J.W.M., 'The King's Poet and the Inauguration of Alexander III', *SHR*, lxviii (1989), 120–49

Barrow, G.W.S., 'The Wood at Stronkalter: a Note on the Relief of Lochindorb Castle by Edward III in 1336', *SHR*, xlvi (1967), 77–9

Barrow, G.W.S., 'The ferry at Inverennok', *IR*, 52 (Spring 2001), 101–4

Beam, A., 'One Funeral and a Wedding: The Neglected History of Scotland's Forgotten Kings', *History Scotland*, Vol. 3 no. 1 Jan/Feb 2003, 16–23

Bliese, J.R.E., 'Saint Cuthbert and War', *Journal of Medieval History*, xxiv (1998), 215–41

Boardman, S., 'The Man who would be King: the Lieutenancy and Death of David, Duke of Rothesay, 1399–1402', in R.A. Mason and N.A.T. Macdougall eds, *People and Power in Scotland: Essays presented to T.C. Smout* (Edinburgh 1992), 1–27

Boardman, S., 'David II: Scotland's Crusader King?', Dept. of Scottish History, University of Edinburgh, Occasional Paper (1993), 1–13

Boardman, S., 'Lordship in the North-East: the Badenoch Stewarts I. Alexander Stewart, Earl of Buchan, Lord of Badenoch', *Northern Scotland*, xv (1996), 1–30

Boardman, S., 'Chronicle Propaganda in Fourteenth-Century Scotland: Robert the Steward, Fordun and the 'Anonymous Chronicle'', *SHR*, lxxvi (1997), 23–43

Boardman, S., 'The Tale of Leper John and the Campbell Acquisition of Lorn', in E.J. Cowan and R.A. MacDonald eds, *Alba: Celtic Scotland in the Medieval Era* (East Linton 2000), 219–47

Boardman, S., 'Coronations, Kings and Guardians, Politics, Parliaments and General Councils, 1371–1406', in K. Brown and R. Tanner eds, *Parliament and Politics in Scotland: 1286–1567* (Edinburgh, forthcoming)

Boardman, S., 'The Gaelic World and the Early Stewart Court' (forthcoming)

Boardman, S., and M. Penman, 'The Scottish Arms in the Armorial of Gèlre' (forthcoming)

Boyle, A., 'Notes on Scottish Saints', *IR*, xxxii (1981), 59–82

Broun, D., 'Review of *Chron. Bower*, v and vi', *SHR*, lxxiii (1994), 132–5

Broun, D., 'A New Look at *Gesta Annalia* attributed to John of Fordun', in B.E. Crawford ed., *Church, Chronicle and Learning in Medieval and Early Renaissance Scotland* (Edinburgh 1999), 9–30

Brown, A.L., 'The English Campaign in Scotland, 1400', in H. Hearder and H.R. Lyon eds, *British Government and Administration: Studies presented to S.B. Chrimes* (Cardiff 1974), 40–54

Brown, M.H., 'Scotland Tamed? Kings and Magnates in Late Medieval Scotland: a Review of Recent Work', *IR*, xlv (1994), 120–46

Brown, M.H., 'The Development of Scottish Border Lordship, 1332–58', *Historical Research*, lxx (1997), 1–22

Brown, M.H., ''Rejoice to hear of Douglas': The House of Douglas and the Presentation of Magnate Power in Late Medieval Scotland', *SHR*, lxxvi (1997), 161–84

Brown, M.H., ''Vile Times': Walter Bower's last Book and the Minority of James II', *SHR*, lxxix (2000), 165–88

Burne, A.H., 'The Battle of Neville's Cross', *Durham University Journal*, xli (1949), 100–6

Burnett, C.J., 'Early Officers of Arms in Scotland', *Review of Scottish Culture*, xii (1996), 3–13

Cameron, S., 'Sir James Douglas, Spain, and the Holy Land', in T. Brotherstone and D. Ditchburn eds, *Freedom and Authority: Scotland c.1050–c.1650 – Historical and Historiographical Essays presented to Grant G. Simpson* (East Linton 2000), 108–17

Cameron, S. and A. Ross, 'The Treaty of Edinburgh and the Disinherited (1328–1332), *History*, lxxxiv (1999), 237–56.

Campbell, 'Scottish Arms in the Bellenville Roll', *The Scottish Genealogist*, xxv, ii (1978), 33–52

Campbell, J., 'England, Scotland and the Hundred Years War in the Fourteenth Century', in J.R. Hale, J. Highfield and B. Smalley eds, *Europe in the Late Middle Ages* (London 1965), 184–216

Contamine, P., 'Froissart and Scotland', in G.G. Simpson ed., *Scotland and the Low Countries, 1124–1994* (East Linton, 1996), 43–58

Dakers, H.J., 'The First Issue of David II', *British Numismatic Journal*, xxiii (1938–41), 51–8

Davidson, J., 'Distinguishing Marks on the Later Issues of David II', *British Numismatic Journal*, xxi (1950), 155–63

Diverres, A.H., 'The Geography of Britain in Froissart's *Méliador*', in *Medieval Miscellany Presented to Eugene Vinaver* (New York 1965), 97–112

Diverres, A.H., 'Froissart's *Méliador* and Edward III's Policy towards Scotland', *Mélanges offerts à Rita Lejeune* (Gembloux 1969), 1399–1409

Dixon, M.C., 'John de Coupland – Hero to Villain', in D. Rollason and M. Prestwich eds, *The Battle of Neville's Cross, 1346* (Stamford 1998), 36–49

Donaldson, G., 'The Rights of the Crown in Episcopal Vacancies', in *idem*, *Scottish Church History* (Edinburgh 1985), 31–9

Donnelly, J., 'An Open Port: The Berwick Export Trade, 1311–1373', *SHR*, lxxviii (1999), 145–69

Drury, J.L., 'The Monument at Neville's Cross', in D. Rollason and M. Prestwich eds, *The Battle of Neville's Cross, 1346* (Stamford 1998), 78–96

Duncan, A.A.M., 'A Siege of Lochmaben Castle in 1343', *TDGNHAS*, xxxi (1954), 74–7

Duncan, A.A.M., 'The Early Parliaments of Scotland', *SHR*, xlv (1966), 36–58

Duncan, A.A.M., '"Honi soit qui mal y pense": David II and Edward III, 1346–52', *SHR*, lxvii (1988), 113–41

Duncan, A.A.M., 'The Regnal Year of David II', *SHR*, lxviii (1989), 105–19

Duncan, A.A.M., 'The War of the Scots, 1306–23', *TRHS*, 6th series, ii (1992), 125–51

Duncan, A.A.M., 'The Laws of Malcolm MacKenneth', in A. Grant and K.J. Stringer eds, *Medieval Scotland: Crown, Lordship and Community – Essays Presented to G.W.S. Barrow* (Edinburgh 1993), 239–73

Duffy, S., 'The Bruce Brothers and the Irish Sea World, 1306–29', *Cambridge Medieval Celtic Studies*, xxi (1991), 55–86

Edington, C., 'Paragons and Patriots: National Identity and the Chivalric Ideal in Late Medieval Scotland', in D. Broun, R.J. Finlay and M. Lynch eds., *Image and Identity: the Making and Re-making of Scotland Through the Ages* (Edinburgh 1998), 69–81

Edington, C., 'The Tournament in Medieval Scotland', in M. Strickland ed., *Armies, Chivalry and Warfare in Medieval Britain and France* (Stamford 1998), 46–52

Fraser, J., '"A Swan from a Raven': William Wallace, Brucean Propaganda, and *Gesta Annalia II*', *SHR*, lxxxi (2002), 1–22

Germain, A., 'Projet de déscente en Angleterre concerte entre le gouvernement français et le roi de Danemark Valdemar III pour la délivrance de Jean roi', *Mémoriales Société Archéologique Montpellier*, iv (1955), 409–34

Gimson, G.S., 'Lion Hunt: a royal tomb-effigy at Arbroath Abbey', *PSAS*, cxxv (1995), 901–16

Given-Wilson, C., and F. Bériac, 'Edward III's Prisoners of War: the Battle of Poitiers and its Context', *EHR*, Sept. 2001, 802–33

Goldstein, R.J., 'The Scottish Mission to Boniface VIII in 1301', *SHR*, lxx (1991), 1–15

Goodman, A., 'A Letter from an Earl of Douglas to a King of Castile', *SHR*, lxiv (1985), 68–78

Grant, A., 'Earls and Earldoms in Late Medieval Scotland, 1310–1460', in J. Bossy and P. Jupp eds, *Essays presented to Michael Roberts* (Belfast 1976), 24–41

Grant, A., 'The Development of the Scottish Peerage', *SHR*, lvii (1978), 1–27

Grant, A., 'Crown and Nobility in Late Medieval Britain', in R. Mason ed., *Scotland and England 1286–1815* (Edinburgh 1987), 34–59

Grant, A., 'Scotland's 'Celtic Fringe' in the Late Middle Ages: the MacDonald Lords of the Isles and the Kingdom of Scotland', in R.R. Davies ed., *The British Isles, 1100–1500* (Edinburgh 1988), 118–41

Grant, A., 'The Otterburn War from the Scottish Point of View', in A. Goodman and A. Tuck eds, *War and Border Society in the Middle Ages* (Oxford 1992), 30–64

Grant, A., 'The Wolf of Badenoch', in W.D.H. Sellar ed., *Moray: Province and People* (Scottish Society for Northern Studies, 1992), 143–61

Grant, A., 'Thanes and Thanages, from the Eleventh to the Fourteenth Centuries', in A. Grant and K.J Stringer eds, *Medieval Scotland: Crown, Lordship and Community – Essays presented to G.W.S. Barrow* (Edinburgh 1993), 39–81

Grant, A., 'Disaster at Neville's Cross: The Scottish Point of View', in D. Rollason and M. Prestwich eds, *The Battle of Neville's Cross, 1346* (Stamford 1998), 15–35

Grant, A., 'Service and Tenure in Late Medieval Scotland, 1314–1475', in A. Curry and E. Matthew eds, *Concepts and Patterns of Service in the Later Middle Ages* (Bristol 2000), 145–79

Grant, A., 'Fourteenth-Century Scotland', in M. Jones ed., *New Cambridge Medieval History IV, c.1300–c.1415* (Cambridge 2000), 345–74

Harari, Y.N., 'Inter-frontal Cooperation in the Fourteenth Century and Edward III's 1346 Campaign', *War in History*, 1999, 9 (4), 379–95

Henderson, G., 'A Royal Effigy at Arbroath', in W.M. Ormrod ed., *England in the Fourteenth Century* (Woodbridge 1996), 88–98

Kaufman, M.H. and W.J. MacLennan, 'Robert the Bruce and Leprosy', *Proceedings of the Royal College of Physicians of Edinburgh*, 30 (2000), 75–80

Kermack, W.R., 'Kindred of the Bear', *The Scottish Genealogist*, xix, i (1972), 14–5

King, A., 'Englishmen, Scots and Marchers: National and Local Identities in Thomas Gray's *Scalacronica*', *Northern History*, xxxvi, 2 (2000), 217–31

King, A., "According to the custom used in French and Scottish wars': Prisoners and casualties on the Scottish Marches in the Fourteenth century', *Journal of Medieval History*, 28 (2002), 263–90

Leve, M., 'Thomas Beckett à Gisors et son culte l'Eure', *Connaissance d'Eure*, 89 (1993), 24–5

Lomas, R.A., 'The Durham Landscape and the Battle of Neville's Cross', in D. Rollason and M. Prestwich eds, *The Battle of Neville's Cross, 1346* (Stamford 1998), 66–77

Loomis, R.S., 'Scotland and the Arthurian Legend', *PSAS*, lxxxix (1955–6), 1–21

Lyall, R.S., 'The Lost Literature of Medieval Scotland', in J.D. McClure and M.R.G. Spiller eds, *Bryght Lanternis: Essays on the Language and Literature of Medieval and Renaissance Scotland* (Aberdeen 1989), 33–47

MacDonald, A., 'Profit, Politics and Personality: War and the Later Medieval Scottish Nobility', in T. Brotherstone and D. Ditchburn eds, *Freedom and Authority: Scotland c.1050–c.1650 – Historical and Historiographical Essays presented to Grant G. Simpson* (East Linton 2000), 118–30

MacQueen, H.L., 'The Kin of Kennedy, 'Kenkynnol' and the Common Law', in A. Grant and K.J. Stringer eds, *Medieval Scotland: Crown, Lordship and Community – Essays presented to G.W.S. Barrow* (Edinburgh 1993), 274–96

Madden, C., 'The royal demesne in northern Scotland during the later middle ages', *Northern Scotland*, 3 (1977–8), 1–24

Malcolm, C.A., 'The Gardens of the Castle', *BOEC*, xiv (1925), 101–20

Mapstone, S., 'Bower on Kingship', in D.E.R. Watt *et al.*, eds, *Walter Bower's Scotichronicon* – vol. ix (Aberdeen 1998), 321–8

McHardy, A.K., 'Some Reflections on Edward III's Use of Propaganda', in J.S. Bothwell ed., *The Age of Edward III* (Woodbridge 2001), 171–92

Millar, P., 'The Mercat Cross of Edinburgh – its Site and Form', *PSAS*, xx (1886), 371–83

Moir-Bryce, W., 'The Black Friars of Edinburgh', *BOEC*, iii (1910), 13–104

Neville, C.J., 'The Political Allegiance of the Earls of Strathearn during the War of Independence', *SHR*, lxv (1986), 133–53

Neville, C.J., 'Keeping the Peace on the Northern Marches in the Later Middle Ages', *EHR*, cix (1994), 1–25

Nicholson, R., 'The Siege of Berwick', *SHR*, xl (1961), 19–42

Nicholson, R., 'A sequel to Edward Bruce's invasion of Ireland', *SHR*, xliii (1963), 30–40

Nicholson, R., 'David II, the historians and the chroniclers', *SHR*, lxv (1966), 59–78

Nicholson, R., 'Scottish Monetary problems in the Fourteenth and Fifteenth Centuries', in D.M. Metcalf ed., *Coinage in Medieval Scotland, 1100–1600* (2nd Oxford Symposium on Coinage and Monetary History, British Archaeological Reports #45, 1977), 102–15

Oldrieve, W.T., 'Account of the Recent Discovery of the Remains of David's Tower at Edinburgh Castle', *PSAS*, xlviii (1914), 230–70

Oram, R.D., 'Bruce-Balliol and the Lordship of Galloway: the South-West of Scotland and the Wars of Independence', *TDGNHAS*, lxvii (1992), 29–47

Oram, R.D., 'Dervorgilla, the Balliols and Buittle', *TDGNHAS*, lxxiii (1999), 165–81

Oram, R.D., 'Alexander Bur, Bishop of Moray (1362–1397)', in B.E. Crawford ed., *Church, Chronicle and Learning in Medieval and Early Renaissance Scotland* (Edinburgh 1999), 195–214

Ormrod, W.M., 'The English Government and the Black Death of 1348–49', in *idem* ed., *England in the Fourteenth Century* (Woodbridge 1986), 175–88

Ormrod, W.M., 'Edward III and his Family', *Journal of British Studies*, xxvi (1987), 398–424

Ormrod, W.M., 'Edward III and the Recovery of Royal Authority in England, 1340–60', *History*, lxxii (1987), 4–19

Ormrod, W.M., 'The Personal Religion of Edward III', *Speculum*, lxiv (1989), 849–77

Penman, M.A., 'A fell conuiracioun agayn Robert ye douchty king: the Soules conspiracy of 1318–20', *IR*, 50 (1999), 25–57

Penman, M.A., 'The Scots at the Battle of Neville's Cross, 17 October 1346', *SHR*, lxxx (2001), 157–80

Penman, M.A., 'Christian Days and Knights: the religious devotions and court of David II of Scotland, 1329–71', *Historical Research*, lxxv (2002), 249–72

Penman, M.A., 'The Earl, The King, His Lover and The Ransom: Passion, Power and Politics in Bruce Scotland', *History Scotland*, Vol. 2 no. 1 Jan/Feb (2002), 26–31

Penman, M.A., 'Parliament Lost – Parliament Regained? The Three Estates in the Reign of David II, 1329–71', in K. Brown and R. Tanner eds, *Parliament and Politics in Scotland: 1286–1567* (Edinburgh, forthcoming)

Penman, M.A., and R. Tanner, 'An Unpublished act of David II, 1359', *SHR* (forthcoming)

Prestwich, M., 'Katherine Mortimer's Murder at Soutra', in B. Moffat ed., *SHARP: The Fourth Report on Researches into the Medieval Hospital at Soutra, Lothian Region, Scotland* (1992), 110–8.

Prestwich, M., 'The English at the Battle of Neville's Cross', in D. Rollason and M. Prestwich eds, *The Battle of Neville's Cross, 1346* (Stamford 1998), 1–14

Reid, N.H., 'Crown and Community under Robert I', in A. Grant and K.J Stringer eds, *Medieval Scotland: Crown, Lordship and Community – Essays presented to G.W.S. Barrow* (Edinburgh 1993), 203–22

Reid, R.C., 'Caput of Annandale or the Curse of Malachy', *TDGNHAS*, xliv (1955), 155–66

Reid, R.C., 'Edward Balliol', *TDGNHAS*, xxxv (1956–7), 38–64

Rogers, C.J., 'The Scottish Invasion of 1346: with an appendix by C.J. Rogers and M.C. Buck', *Northern History*, xxxiv (1998), 51–82

Rogers, C.J., 'The Anglo-French Peace Negotiations of 1354–1360 Reconsidered', in J.S. Bothwell ed., *The Age of Edward III* (Woodbridge 2001), 193–213

Rollason, L., 'Spoils of War? Durham Cathedral and the Black Rood of Scotland', in D. Rollason and M. Prestwich eds, *The Battle of Neville's Cross, 1346* (Stamford 1998), 57–65

Ross, A., 'Men for All Seasons? The Strathbogie Earls of Atholl and the War of Independence, Part 1 – Earl John (1266x1270–1306) and Earl David III (c. 1290–1326)', *Northern Scotland*, 20 (2000), 1–30

Ross, A., 'Men for All Seasons? The Strathbogie Earls of Atholl and the War of Independence, Part 2 – Earl David IV (1307–35)', *Northern Scotland*, 21 (2001), 1–15

Ruckley, N.A., 'Water Supply of Medieval Castles in the United Kingdom', *Fortress*, no. 7 (1990), 14–26

Sayles, G.O., 'The Guardians of Scotland and a Parliament at Rutherglen in 1300', *SHR*, xxiv (1927), 245–50

Sayles, G.O., 'The Rebellious First Earl of Desmond', in J.A. Watt, J.B. Marshall and F.X. Martin eds, *Medieval Studies presented to Aubrey Gwynn* (Dublin 1961), 203–30

Sellar, D., 'Courtesy, Battle and the Brieve of Right, 1368 – A Story Continued', *Stair Society Miscellany*, ii (Edinburgh 1970–84), 1–12

Simpson, G.G., 'The Declaration of Arbroath Revitalised', *SHR*, lvi (1977), 11–33.

Simpson, G.G., 'The Heart of Robert I: Pious Crusade or Marketing Gambit?', in B.E. Crawford ed., *Church, Chronicle and Learning in Medieval and Early Renaissance Scotland* (Edinburgh 1999), 173–86

Stell, G., 'The Scottish Medieval Castle: Form, Function and 'Evolution'', in K.J. Stringer ed., *Essays on the Nobility of Medieval Scotland* (Edinburgh 1985), 195–209

Stevenson, A., 'The Flemish Dimension of the Auld Alliance', in G.G. Simpson ed., *Scotland and the Low Countries, 1124–1994* (East Linton 1996), 28–42

Stevenson, A., 'Medieval Scottish Associations with Bruges', in T. Brotherstone and D. Ditchburn eds, *Freedom and Authority: Scotland c.1050–c.1650 – Historical and Historiographical Essays presented to Grant G. Simpson* (East Linton 2000), 93–107

Stewart, I., 'Scottish Mints', in R.A.G. Carson ed., *Mints, Dies and Currency: Essays to Albert Baldwin* (London 1971)

Stones, E.L.G., 'The Submission of Robert Bruce to Edward I *c.* 1301–2', *SHR*, xxxiv (1955), 122–34

Tanner, R., 'Cowing the Community? Coercion and Fabrication in Robert Bruce's Parliaments, 1309–18', in K. Brown and R. Tanner eds, *Parliament and Politics in Scotland: 1286–1567* (Edinburgh, forthcoming)

Thurley, S., 'Royal Lodgings at The Tower of London, 1216–1327', *Architectural History*, xxxviii (1995), 36–57

Tuck, A., 'A Medieval Tax Haven: Berwick-upon-Tweed and the English Crown, 1333–1461', in R. Britnell and J. Hatcher eds, *Progress and Problems in Medieval England: Essays presented to Edward Miller* (Cambridge 1996), 148–67

Turnbull, J., 'The Parish Church of St Monans', *Transactions of the Aberdeen Ecclesiological Society*, iii (1895), 180–98

Tyerman, C.J., 'Philip VI and the Recovery of the Holy Land', *EHR*, c (1985), 25–52

Watson, G., 'The Black Rood of Scotland', *Transactions of the Scottish Ecclesiological Society*, ii (1909), 27–46

Webster, B., 'The English Occupation of Dumfriesshire in the Fourteenth Century', *TDGNHAS*, xxxv (1956–7), 64–80

Webster, B., 'David II and the Government of Fourteenth Century Scotland', *TRHS*, xvi (1966), 115–30

Webster, B., 'Scotland without a King, 1329–41', in A. Grant and K.J. Stringer eds, *Medieval Scotland: Crown, Lordship and Community – Essays presented to G.W.S. Barrow* (Edinburgh 1993), 223–38

Yeoman, P., 'Edinburgh Castle', *Fortress*, no. 4 (1990), 22–6

Young, A., 'Noble Families and Political Factions in the Reign of Alexander III', in N. Reid ed., *Scotland in the Age of Alexander III, 1249–1286* (Edinburgh 1988), 1–30

3. Works of Reference

Apted, M.R. and S. Hannabuss, *Painters in Scotland, 1301–1700 – a Biographical Dictionary* (Edinburgh 1978)

Chambers, R., *A biographical dictionary of eminent Scotsmen* (5 vols, Glasgow 1855)

Cheney, C.R. (revised M. Jones) ed., *A Handbook of Dates* (Cambridge 1945–2000)

Donaldson, G. ed., *Scottish Historical Documents* (Edinburgh 1970)

Easson, D.E., *Medieval Religious Houses: Scotland* (London 1969)

Emden, A.B. ed., *A Biographical Register of the University of Oxford to A.D. 1500* (3 vols, Oxford 1957)

Houston, R.A., and W.W.J. Knox eds, *The New Penguin History of Scotland* (London 2001)

Lynch, M. ed., *The New Oxford History of Scotland* (Oxford 2002)

MacGibbon, D. and T. Ross, *The Castellated and Domestic Architecture of Scotland* (4 vols, Edinburgh 1887)

McNeill, P.G.B. and H.L. MacQueen eds, *Atlas of Scottish History to 1707* (Edinburgh 1996)

McNeill, P.G.B. and R. Nicholson eds, *An Historical Atlas of Scotland, c.400–1600* (Edinburgh 1975)

Paul, J.B., *The Scots Peerage* (9 vols, Edinburgh 1904–14)

RCAHMS: *City of Edinburgh* (Edinburgh 1951)

RCAHMS: *County of East Lothian* (Edinburgh 1924)

RCAHMS: *Counties of Fife, Kinross and Clackmannan* (Edinburgh 1933)

RCAHMS: *Counties of Mid Lothian and West Lothian* (Edinburgh 1929)

Roskell, J.S., L. Clark and C. Rawcliffe eds, *The History of Parliament: the House of Commons, 1386–1421* (4 vols, Stroud 1993)

Talbot, C.H., and E.A. Hammond, *The Medical Practitioners of Medieval England: A Biographical Register* (London 1965)

Watt, D.E.R., *A Biographical Dictionary of Scottish Graduates to A.D. 1410* (Oxford 1977)

4. Theses

Beam, A., 'The life and career of John Balliol *c.*1210–68' (unpublished M.Phil. dissertation, University of Stirling, 2003)

Crawford, B.E., 'The Earls of Orkney-Caithness and their relations with Norway and Scotland: 1158–1470' (unpublished Ph.D. thesis, University of St Andrews, 1971)

Grant, A., 'The Higher Nobility of Scotland and their Estates, 1371–1424' (unpublished D.Phil. thesis, University of Oxford, 1975)

King, A., 'War, Politics and Landed Society in Northumberland, *c.* 1296–1408' (unpublished Ph.D. thesis, University of Durham, 2001)

MacDonald, A.J., 'Crossing the Border: a study of the Scottish military offensives against England, *c.*1369–*c.*1403' (unpublished Ph.D. thesis, University of Aberdeen, 1995)

Macquarrie, A.D., 'The Impact of the Crusading Movement in Scotland, 1095–1560' (unpublished Ph.D. thesis, University of Edinburgh, 1982)

MacQueen, H.L., 'Pleadable Brieves and Jurisdiction in Heritage in Later Medieval Scotland' (unpublished Ph.D. thesis, University of Edinburgh, 1985)

Penman, M.A., 'The Kingship of David II of Scotland, 1329–71' (unpublished Ph.D. thesis, University of St Andrews, 1999)

Reid, N.H., 'The Political Role of the Monarchy in Scotland, 1249–1329' (unpublished Ph.D. thesis, University of Edinburgh, 1984)

Sinclair, J., 'The Life and Times of Edward Bruce' (unpublished BA dissertation, University of Stirling, 2002)

Thorson, S.M., 'Adam Abell's "The Roit and Quheill of Tyme": An Edition' (unpublished Ph.D. thesis, University of St Andrews, 1998)

Index

Abell, Adam, sixteenth-century chronicler 372n3

Aberchirder, thanage of 400, 404; John de 363

Abercorn 94, 266, 299

Aberdalgie (Perthshire) 343

Aberdeen: burgh 58–9, 65, 73, 77–8, 81, 86, 98–100, 112, 120, 149, 168, 183, 190n52, 208, 210, 254, 259, 267, 272–3, 287, 298, 321, 336, 355, 363–4, 372, 389n72, 390–3, 412; shire 59, 65, 96, 120–1, 125, 158, 208, 216, 218, 244, 254, 306, 350, 355, 362, 380, 408; sheriff 23, 59, 65, 96, 110, 142n9, 208, 218, 222, 259, 273, 277, 386, 409; bishop(ric) 51, 81, 88, 109n45, 142, 190n52, 209, 210, 312, 342n37 – see Deyn, Kinnimound

Aberdour (Fife) 88n38, 255, 262, 287, 355

Aberfoyle (Perthshire) 248, 260

Aberluthnot (Kincardineshire) 115, 216n66, 400

Abernethy, George 137, 374

Abernethy, John 380, 382–3, 417

Abernethy, Margaret, Countess of Angus 96n70, 105, 121

Abernethy (Moray) 354n68

Abernethy, William 111n116, 120

Aboyne (Aberdeenshire), thanage 59, 306, 362

Adam de Argento, royal moneyer 121

Adamton (Ayrshire) 170

Aird (Ross-shire) 355, 367n101

Alexander II, King of Scotland (1214–49) 15, 264, 432n11

Alexander III, King of Scotland (1249–86) 15, 19, 28, 37, 59, 81n13, 112, 259, 264, 328, 360, 407, 413, 419

Alexandria 220, 302–3, 341, 386n55

Allincrum, John of, clerk, deputy-sheriff of Peebles 202, 217n69, 220, 267, 281

Alloa (Clackmannanshire) 298, 329

ambassador(s): to England 93, 137, 147, 152, 163, 166, 168, 178, 180n17, 184, 186–7, 215, 221, 225, 240, 249–50, 256–8, 279, 284, 294–5, 301, 306, 320, 322, 327, 332, 337–9, 344, 346, 350–1, 356, 359, 361, 379, 381, 383–7, 398–400, 439; to France 229–32, 365, 402–4, 410; to papacy 93, 176, 229–32, 284, 403–4, 417; from France to Scotland 384–6, 389

Angus, earl of – see Stewart, Thomas

Angus, earldom of 24, 30, 32–4, 66, 77, 121, 125, 132, 135–6, 168, 205, 239, 252,

254–5, 259, 270, 277–8, 281, 287, 366, 374, 437

Annan, Battle of (1332) 49–50

Annandale 15–6, 22, 27, 55, 59, 83, 86, 93–4, 106, 112, 118–20, 122, 124–5, 127, 144, 167, 170, 174, 176, 237, 250, 270, 272, 283, 290, 309, 329, 354, 357, 364, 375, 379, 388–9, 404, 415, 417

Annan, David 101, 136, 146, 152, 163, 175, 202–3, 220, 235, 239, 285n8, 332, 357, 366, 375n17, 380

Annan, Henry, sheriff of Clackmannan 25

annulment 219, 225, 227, 229, 248, 252, 269, 327, 369–78, 385–6, 388, 403–4, 417, 431, 437, 439

Aquitaine 54, 279, 356, 386, 390

Arbroath: abbey 28, 56, 71, 73, 78–9, 96, 142, 169, 180, 202, 209, 239, 259, 265n66, 277, 360, 383, 386; burgh 56, 261, 345, 355; Declaration of (1320) 23, 81, 171, 319

Ardross (Fife) 261–2, 355

Argyll 22, 23, 84, 99–100, 121n11, 206, 339, 352–3, 382; bishopric of 119n6; sheriff of 296n34

Armstrong, Gilbert, provost of St Andrews 170n82, 230n97, 289, 293–4, 302, 311, 320, 322, 327, 338, 346, 361

Arran, lordship of isle of 25, 28, 35, 68, 83, 353, 397

Arthur, King 28, 303n55, 316, 318, 340–1

Ashkirk, Henry 297

assessment, for taxation 196–9, 208, 219–21, 346–50 (verus valour, 1366), 353, 356n73, 362, 396, 436

assize 107–8, 246–7, 254, 431

Assynt (Sutherland) 100

Atholl, Duncan of 353

Atholl, earldom of 24, 30, 32, 34, 55, 57, 60–1, 68–9, 80, 82, 87, 91, 100, 101n83, 103, 107, 114, 125, 143, 145, 167, 177, 200, 212, 217, 239–40, 243, 246, 255, 260, 268, 270, 281, 297, 309, 328–9, 333, 336, 352–3, 357–8, 370, 372, 381, 389, 392, 403, 437

Auchterarder (Perthshire) 39, 48, 328, 343

Auchtertyre (Forfarshire) 343

Audrehen, Arnoul de, d'Aubigny 62, 71, 75, 185

Auray, Battle of (1365) 337

Avondale (Lanarkshire) 270

Avignon 38, 54, 64n65, 145, 192, 239, 258, 385–7, 404n118, 421

Aylth (Kincardineshire) 101n83